THE THREE-DIMENSIONAL NATURE OF RESEARCH APPROACHES

NINTH EDITION

METHODS TOWARD A SCIENCE OF BEHAVIOR AND EXPERIENCE

WILLIAM J. RAY
Pennsylvania State University

WADSWORTH
CENGAGE Learning

Australia • Brazil • Japan • Korea • Mexico • Singapore • Spain • United Kingdom • United States

**Methods: Toward a Science of Behavior
and Experience, Ninth Edition**
William J. Ray

Psychology Editor: Erik Evans

Assistant Editor: Gina Kessler

Editorial Assistant: Rebecca Rosenberg

Technology Project Manager:
Lauren Keyes

Marketing Manager: Michelle Williams

Marketing Assistant: Melanie Cregger

Marketing Communications Manager:
Linda Yip

Project Manager, Editorial Production:
Tanya Nigh

Creative Director: Rob Hugel

Art Director: Maria Epes

Print Buyer: Paula Vang

Permissions Editor: Mardell Schultz

Production Service: Buuji

Text Designer: Laurie Albrecht

Copy Editor: Linda Ireland

Cover Designer: William Stanton

Compositor: ICC Macmillan Inc.

For product information and technology assistance, contact us at
Cengage Learning Customer & Sales Support, 1-800-354-9706.

For permission to use material from this text or product,
submit all requests online at **cengage.com/permissions.**
Further permissions questions can be e-mailed to
permissionrequest@cengage.com.

Library of Congress Control Number: 2007939790

ISBN-13: 978-0-495-59491-8

ISBN-10: 0-495-59491-1

Wadsworth
10 Davis Drive
Belmont, CA 94002-3098
USA

Cengage Learning is a leading provider of customized learning solutions with office locations around the globe, including Singapore, the United Kingdom, Australia, Mexico, Brazil, and Japan. Locate your local office at **international. cengage.com/region.**

Cengage Learning products are represented in Canada by Nelson Education, Ltd.

For your course and learning solutions, visit **academic.cengage.com.**

Purchase any of our products at your local college store or at our preferred online store **www.ichapters.com.**

Printed in the United States of America
1 2 3 4 5 6 7 12 11 10 09 08

To Ronan, as he begins his new life of exploration and discovery

One thing I have learned in a long life:
that all our science, measured against reality,
is primitive and childlike—and yet it is the
most precious thing we have.

ALBERT EINSTEIN

Brief Contents

1 WHAT IS SCIENCE? 1

2 INTRODUCTION TO THE METHODS OF SCIENCE 26

3 DEVELOPING THE HYPOTHESIS 54

4 ETHICS 84

5 DESCRIPTION OF BEHAVIOR THROUGH NUMERICAL REPRESENTATION 112

6 INFERENTIAL STATISTICS: MAKING STATISTICAL DECISIONS 141

7 TESTING THE HYPOTHESIS: A CONCEPTUAL INTRODUCTION 161

8 CONTROL: THE KEYSTONE OF THE EXPERIMENTAL METHOD 181

9 APPLYING THE LOGIC OF EXPERIMENTATION: BETWEEN-SUBJECTS DESIGNS 199

10 EXTENDING THE LOGIC OF EXPERIMENTATION: WITHIN-SUBJECTS AND MATCHED-SUBJECTS APPROACHES 228

11 THE ECOLOGY OF THE EXPERIMENT: THE SCIENTIST AND RESEARCH PARTICIPANT IN RELATION TO THEIR ENVIRONMENTS 246

12 QUASI-EXPERIMENTAL, CORRELATIONAL, AND NATURALISTIC OBSERVATIONAL DESIGNS 269

13 SINGLE-SUBJECT DESIGNS 301

14 QUESTIONNAIRES, SURVEY RESEARCH, AND SAMPLING 321

15 SHARING THE RESULTS 348

16 BEYOND METHOD 374

APPENDIX A GUIDELINES FOR NONBIASED LANGUAGE IN APA JOURNALS 393

APPENDIX B PRINTED ARTICLE 405

APPENDIX C ARTICLE MANUSCRIPT 419

APPENDIX D TABLES 429

CONTENTS

PREFACE   xv

INTRODUCTION   xxi

1 WHAT IS SCIENCE?   1

SCIENCE AS A WAY OF KNOWING   3
   Tenacity   4
   Authority   4
   Reason   6
   Common Sense   6
   Science   7
   Pseudoscience and Superstition   9
THE SCIENTIFIC APPROACH   10
EARLY APPROACHES   11
OVERVIEW   15
STUDYING BEHAVIOR AND EXPERIENCE   16
BEHAVIOR: A ROAD INTO THE SUBJECTIVE EXPERIENCE OF
   RESEARCH PARTICIPANTS   18
THE PEOPLE WHO PERFORM SCIENCE   22
KEY TERMS AND CONCEPTS   23
SUMMARY   23
REVIEW QUESTIONS   24
DISCUSSION QUESTIONS AND PROJECTS   24
INFOTRAC COLLEGE EDITION: EXERCISES   25

2 INTRODUCTION TO THE METHODS OF SCIENCE   26

NATURALISTIC OBSERVATION   31
THE CORRELATIONAL APPROACH   33
THE EXPERIMENTAL METHOD   34
   Definitions in the Experimental Method   35
   Causation   38
   Exploratory Research   38
LOGIC AND INFERENCE: THE DETECTIVE WORK OF SCIENCE   39
   Validity   40
   Propositional Logic   41
SCIENTIFIC OBSERVATION: THE RAW DATA OF SCIENCE   47
EVALUATING SCIENTIFIC RESEARCH   49

COMMUNICATION IN SCIENCE   49
KEY TERMS AND CONCEPTS   50
SUMMARY   51
REVIEW QUESTIONS   52
DISCUSSION QUESTIONS AND PROJECTS   52
INFOTRAC COLLEGE EDITION: EXERCISES   52

3 DEVELOPING THE HYPOTHESIS   54

MAKING OUR HYPOTHESES CONCRETE   55
MAKING OUR HYPOTHESES LOGICAL   58
    The "I Wonder What Will Happen If" Hypothesis and Inductive Reasoning   58
    The "I Expect This Would Happen If" Hypothesis and Deductive Reasoning   59
    Strong Inference   60
CREATING TESTABLE RESEARCH HYPOTHESES AND THE PROBLEM
    OF MEASUREMENT   60
OVERVIEW   63
IDEAS COME FROM EVERYWHERE   63
INTUITION AND REVELATION   72
THE SCIENTIST'S GUIDE TO HAVING AN IDEA   73
TOOLS FOR LIBRARY RESEARCH   74
    Journals and Books   75
    Computer Databases   76
    The Internet   78
CONCLUSION   80
KEY TERMS AND CONCEPTS   81
SUMMARY   81
REVIEW QUESTIONS   82
DISCUSSION QUESTIONS AND PROJECTS   82
INFOTRAC COLLEGE EDITION: EXERCISES   82

4 ETHICS   84

ETHICAL CONSIDERATIONS OF PSYCHOLOGICAL EXPERIMENTATION   86
THE RIGHTS OF THE SCIENTIST AND THE RESEARCH PARTICIPANT   87
THE EXPERIMENT AS AN ETHICAL PROBLEM   88
INGREDIENTS OF THE INITIAL SCIENTIST–PARTICIPANT DIALOGUE   89
    Voluntary Participation   89
    Informed Consent   89
THE RIGHTS OF THE RESEARCH PARTICIPANT AND THE RESPONSIBILITIES
    OF THE EXPERIMENTER   90
WHAT IS HARMFUL TO A RESEARCH PARTICIPANT?   91
ETHICAL GUIDELINES OF THE AMERICAN PSYCHOLOGICAL ASSOCIATION   91
INSTITUTIONAL REVIEW BOARD   94
DECEPTION STUDIES   97
    Obedience-to-Authority Research   98

It's Not a Crime the Way I See It   99
Bypassing the Bypass   101
DEBRIEFING: WHEN IS ENOUGH ENOUGH?   102
THE PARTICIPANT AS COLLEAGUE   103
ANIMALS AS SUBJECTS   104
KEY TERMS AND CONCEPTS   109
SUMMARY   110
REVIEW QUESTIONS   110
DISCUSSION QUESTIONS AND PROJECTS   110
INFOTRAC COLLEGE EDITION: EXERCISES   111

5 DESCRIPTION OF BEHAVIOR THROUGH NUMERICAL REPRESENTATION   112

MEASUREMENT   113
SCALES OF MEASUREMENT   114
Nominal Measurement   114
Ordinal Measurement   115
Interval Measurement   116
Ratio Measurement   116
Identifying Scales of Measurement   116
MEASUREMENT AND STATISTICS   117
PICTORIAL DESCRIPTION OF FREQUENCY INFORMATION   118
DESCRIPTIVE STATISTICS   121
Measures of Central Tendency   121
Measures of Variability   123
PICTORIAL PRESENTATIONS OF NUMERICAL DATA   128
TRANSFORMING DATA   130
STANDARD SCORES   131
MEASURE OF ASSOCIATION   132
KEY TERMS AND CONCEPTS   138
SUMMARY   139
REVIEW QUESTIONS   139
DISCUSSION QUESTIONS AND PROJECTS   139
INFOTRAC COLLEGE EDITION: EXERCISES   140

6 INFERENTIAL STATISTICS: MAKING STATISTICAL DECISIONS   141

PROBABILITY   143
THE NORMAL DISTRIBUTION   147
HYPOTHESIS TESTING   152
EXAMPLE OF INFERENTIAL STATISTICS: THE t TEST   153
ANALYSIS OF VARIANCE   157
KEY TERMS AND CONCEPTS   159

SUMMARY   159
REVIEW QUESTIONS   159
DISCUSSION QUESTIONS AND PROJECTS   159
INFOTRAC COLLEGE EDITION: EXERCISES   160

7   TESTING THE HYPOTHESIS: A CONCEPTUAL INTRODUCTION   161

THE CONTEXT OF EXPERIMENTATION: AN EXAMPLE   164
TYPES OF VARIATION   165
    Chance Variation   165
    Systematic Variation Due to the Independent
        Variable   166
    Systematic Variation Due to Confounds   167
STATISTICAL HYPOTHESIS TESTING   168
THREATS TO INTERNAL VALIDITY   172
    History   172
    Maturation   173
    Testing   174
    Instrumentation   174
    Statistical Regression   174
    Selection   175
    Mortality   175
    Selection–Maturation Interaction   176
    Diffusion or Imitation of Treatments   176
CONCLUSION   177
KEY TERMS AND CONCEPTS   178
SUMMARY   178
REVIEW QUESTIONS   179
DISCUSSION QUESTIONS AND PROJECTS   179
INFOTRAC COLLEGE EDITION: EXERCISES   179

8   CONTROL: THE KEYSTONE OF THE EXPERIMENTAL METHOD   181

CONTROL ACHIEVED THROUGH PARTICIPANT ASSIGNMENT AND
    SELECTION   182
RANDOMIZATION   188
    Random Sampling   189
    Random Assignment   189
CONTROL ACHIEVED THROUGH EXPERIMENTAL DESIGN   190
CONTROL AS RELATED TO THE LOGIC OF EXPERIMENTATION   193
KEY TERMS AND CONCEPTS   196
SUMMARY   196
REVIEW QUESTIONS   196
DISCUSSION QUESTIONS AND PROJECTS   197
INFOTRAC COLLEGE EDITION: EXERCISES   197

9 APPLYING THE LOGIC OF EXPERIMENTATION: BETWEEN-SUBJECTS DESIGNS 199

BETWEEN-SUBJECTS DESIGN TERMINOLOGY 200
COMPLETELY RANDOMIZED DESIGN 201
MULTILEVEL COMPLETELY RANDOMIZED DESIGNS 201
FACTORIAL DESIGN 206
FACTORIAL DESIGNS: THE LOGIC OF EXPERIMENTATION AND
   THE INTERACTION EFFECT 210
EIGHT POSSIBLE OUTCOMES OF 2 × 2 FACTORIAL EXPERIMENTS 216
INTERPRETATION OF SUBJECT VARIABLES WITH FACTORIAL DESIGNS 222
ADVANTAGES OF FACTORIAL DESIGNS 224
KEY TERMS AND CONCEPTS 225
SUMMARY 225
REVIEW QUESTIONS 225
DISCUSSION QUESTIONS AND PROJECTS 226
INFOTRAC COLLEGE EDITION: EXERCISES 226

10 EXTENDING THE LOGIC OF EXPERIMENTATION: WITHIN-SUBJECTS AND MATCHED-SUBJECTS APPROACHES 228

WITHIN-SUBJECTS DESIGNS 229
   An Illustration of Within-Subjects Research 232
   Advantages and Disadvantages of Within-Subjects Designs 233
   Counterbalancing 235
   Repeated Measures 236
MIXED DESIGNS 237
MATCHED-SUBJECTS DESIGNS 239
   Matching as a Control Procedure 240
   Matching as an Experimental Procedure 241
   Terminology 243
KEY TERMS AND CONCEPTS 243
SUMMARY 244
REVIEW QUESTIONS 244
DISCUSSION QUESTIONS AND PROJECTS 244
INFOTRAC COLLEGE EDITION: EXERCISES 245

11 THE ECOLOGY OF THE EXPERIMENT: THE SCIENTIST AND RESEARCH PARTICIPANT IN RELATION TO THEIR ENVIRONMENTS 246

ECOLOGY 249
EXPERIMENTER FACTORS 250
   Biased Data Collection 251

Biased Interactions with Research Participants   255
Some Ways to Avoid Experimenter Bias   256
SUBJECT FACTORS   258
Placebo Factors   260
Demand Characteristics   262
CULTURAL AND SOCIAL BIAS   265
KEY TERMS AND CONCEPTS   266
SUMMARY   266
REVIEW QUESTIONS   267
DISCUSSION QUESTIONS AND PROJECTS   267
INFOTRAC COLLEGE EDITION: EXERCISES   267

12 QUASI-EXPERIMENTAL, CORRELATIONAL, AND NATURALISTIC OBSERVATIONAL DESIGNS   269

CLOSED AND OPEN SYSTEMS   270
QUASI-EXPERIMENTAL DESIGNS   281
Time Series Design   281
Interrupted Time Series Design   282
Multiple Time Series Design   284
Nonequivalent Before–After Design   286
Retrospective and Ex Post Facto Designs   289
CORRELATIONAL PROCEDURES   290
NATURALISTIC OBSERVATIONS   292
Concerns While Making Naturalistic Observations   294
To Conceal or Not to Conceal; To Participate or Not to Participate   296
Strengths and Weaknesses of Naturalistic Observation   297
KEY TERMS AND CONCEPTS   298
SUMMARY   298
REVIEW QUESTIONS   299
DISCUSSION QUESTIONS AND PROJECTS   299
INFOTRAC COLLEGE EDITION: EXERCISES   299

13 SINGLE-SUBJECT DESIGNS   301

TYPES OF SINGLE-SUBJECT DESIGNS   305
CASE STUDY DESIGNS   306
Naturalistic Case Studies   306
One-Shot Case Studies   307
EXPERIMENTAL SINGLE-SUBJECT DESIGNS   309
Reversal Design   310
Multiple-Baseline Design   314
Multielement Design   316
Making Sense of Single-Subject Experimental Results   317
ALTERNATIVE TYPES OF SINGLE-SUBJECT RESEARCH   317

KEY TERMS AND CONCEPTS   318
SUMMARY   318
REVIEW QUESTIONS   319
DISCUSSION QUESTIONS AND PROJECTS   319
INFOTRAC COLLEGE EDITION: EXERCISES   319

14 QUESTIONNAIRES, SURVEY RESEARCH, AND SAMPLING   321

QUESTION CONSTRUCTION AND FORMATS   325
    Types of Questions   325
    General Considerations   328
    Special Techniques for Reactive Questions   331
METHODS OF ADMINISTERING A SURVEY   332
    Face-to-Face Interviews   332
    Telephone Interviews   335
    Mail Questionnaires   336
    Computer Questionnaires   337
    Internet Research   337
    Surveys: Conclusion   338
SAMPLING   338
    Probability Sampling   340
    Nonprobability Sampling   342
SAMPLE SIZE   343
RELIABILITY AND VALIDITY   344
KEY TERMS AND CONCEPTS   345
SUMMARY   345
REVIEW QUESTIONS   346
DISCUSSION QUESTIONS AND PROJECTS   346
INFOTRAC COLLEGE EDITION: EXERCISES   346

15 SHARING THE RESULTS   348

COMMUNICATION WITH OTHER SCIENTISTS: THE SCIENTIFIC ARTICLE   349
PREPARING YOUR ARTICLE   350
    Abstract   351
    Introduction   353
    Method   357
    Results   361
    Discussion   362
    References   365
PUBLISHING YOUR ARTICLE   368
WHAT MAKES A GOOD ARTICLE?   369
KEY TERMS AND CONCEPTS   371
SUMMARY   372

REVIEW QUESTIONS   372
DISCUSSION QUESTIONS AND PROJECTS   372
INFOTRAC COLLEGE EDITION: EXERCISES   373

16 BEYOND METHOD   374

DIMENSIONS OF RESEARCH   375
BEGINNING WITH A QUESTION   377
LIMITATIONS TO FINDING ANSWERS   378
   Our Tools   378
   Our Shared View of the World   379
   Our Psychological Limitations   382
SCIENCE AS A COMPLEX HUMAN PROCESS   383
VALUE IN SCIENCE   384
RELEVANCE   386
SCIENCE AS A MEANS OF TRANSCENDENCE   387
KEY TERMS AND CONCEPTS   390
SUMMARY   390
REVIEW QUESTIONS   390
DISCUSSION QUESTIONS AND PROJECTS   391
INFOTRAC COLLEGE EDITION: EXERCISES   391

APPENDIX A
GUIDELINES FOR NONBIASED LANGUAGE IN APA
JOURNALS   393

APPENDIX B
PRINTED ARTICLE   405

APPENDIX C
ARTICLE MANUSCRIPT   419

APPENDIX D
TABLES   429

GLOSSARY   437

BIBLIOGRAPHY   440

INDEX   451

PREFACE

Science is an important way of knowing about the world. Some years ago I noticed that our students not only did not look forward to our course on research methods, but also actually dreaded taking the course. That concerned me on a number of levels. First, my colleagues find research exciting and are always willing to ask questions about how the world works and especially how psychology can help to explain these processes. Clearly something was not being conveyed to students about the fun of doing science. Second, given the variety of information sources confronting us every day in terms of the web, newspapers, political statements, and infomercials on television, it seemed important to me that all of us think about the information we receive and how we evaluate it. Even if students never perform research beyond what they read about in textbooks, it is critical that they are informed consumers of information and know how to evaluate what they read. Third, science plays a pervasive role in our society and often is the touchstone for making large-scale governmental and corporate decisions about which programs to implement. Thus, it is imperative that citizens in our society understand the language that is being used. Finally, psychological science has a meaning both for our society and for us. It is one of the few areas where we study not only the behavior of others and ourselves but also our own internal experiences. Unlike most areas of scientific inquiry, the study of ourselves presents a variety of both opportunities and problems for performing science. Studying ourselves makes it more difficult to know how we know what we know, as well as how we know what we don't know. For these reasons I have continued to think and write about science throughout my career, including this textbook.

In this book we come to see that science is a process that has influenced Western civilization for at least the last 500 years. The hallmark of science is a method for helping us to know when we are wrong. Anyone can claim that something is true. We watch politicians and advertisers do this every day as they claim to have the answers to all our questions. Throughout history leaders have asked us to rely on authority rather than test what is being said. "What do you mean the earth is not the center of the universe?" or "The earth is not flat" was once stated by the authorities of the day. Today, science is the best method that we have for testing our assumptions about the world and ourselves. With this in mind, one of the major goals in writing this book was to introduce students to the basics of doing science and to the spirit that motivates many scientists. A second goal was to help students to make the transition from viewing themselves as outside observers of science to those who participate in the process of science.

The responses of students and colleagues to the first eight editions of this book have been persuasive in suggesting that these initial goals are being accomplished. That is, it is possible to produce a highly readable book that students can learn from, and when they are done, they will carry with them a greater understanding of the techniques of science as well as the experience of doing science. As I have moved through the various editions of this book, I have seen psychology change in its approach and subject matter. This edition reflects many of these changes. This book began with Dick Ravizza as a coauthor, and that first edition reflected, as have the later ones, important discussions between the two of us concerning the nature of science, the nature of psychology, and, at times, the nature of life. Since that time these discussions have been continued with colleagues, students, reviewers, and almost anyone else who would listen and discuss these issues. For this reason the plural "we" has been retained. As I have moved throughout other editions of this book, the "we" has been ever changing. Some of the people who have helped me to think about science are acknowledged at the conclusion of this preface. Others, including students who have taken this course, continue to offer suggestions, clarifications, new information, and additional changes that contribute to the overall quality of this book, and I appreciate this input.

The Ninth Edition

Based on feedback from numerous faculty, a major structural change has been untaken in this edition. The ethics chapter has been moved from the end of the course to Chapter 4. This allows readers to understand that ethical considerations take place early in the process of designing research. In terms of content, every chapter in this edition has been revised. Because many individuals are concerned about information that is being passed off as scientific when it is not, I have added new information on pseudoscience. Throughout, I also help readers understand differences between a scientific approach and opinion, including that presented on the web. I have also added new research examples from the psychological literature, as well as how we evaluate numerical changes. As in previous editions, information on analysis of variance (ANOVA) and an understanding of power and effect size is included. I also continue to include an increasingly important information resource, that of the World Wide Web, and to offer links to relevant research sites. For example, links to issues of research integrity from the Public Health Service, the American Association for the Advancement of Science, and the National Institutes of Health have been included. Also included is access to InfoTrac® College Edition, which is a wide-ranging source of information including encyclopedias, reference books, magazines, and scientific journals accessed through the web. Although exercises with InfoTrac College Edition are included at the end of each chapter, faculty can also supplement specific topic areas of their own interest through these resources including the use of online research articles. The variety of important and valid sources available to students on the web has also been detailed. As with every edition of this book, examples and research studies have been updated, and clarifications have been added to help students in their learning. Over the past decade, I have seen a shift in the teaching of this course, with a growing number of colleges and universities presenting the methods course in a large lecture format. In response to this, I have followed the suggestions of faculty and students to clarify the presentation of some of the more important or difficult concepts through illustration and extended discussion. Let me briefly describe the goals and directions, which I have continued in this ninth edition.

Philosophy of Science

One idea that I try to convey from the very beginning is the relationship of science and philosophy. I do this not only through the introduction of propositional logic in Chapter 2 but also through a discussion of individuals who have shaped our ideas about science. For example, in the first two chapters, students are introduced to Newton's rules of reasoning and the views of Karl Popper and Thomas Kuhn on how science works. I also show students how some approaches to science, such as the use of strong inference and the development of a research program, have allowed certain fields to move at an accelerated rate. Likewise, I show that science cannot be performed without reference to values. I do this in the discussion of the ecology of the experimental situation in Chapter 11 and the discussion of ethics in Chapter 4, as well as throughout the text. In the overall discussion of the philosophy of science, I note the manner in which science itself is evolving and point to Donald Campbell's ideas concerning the evolution of scientific techniques.

However useful, abstractions alone do not teach students about science as it is practiced, much less how to practice science themselves; thus, I also emphasize the concrete. I attempt to involve the student earlier in the process of experimentation in this edition. For example, in Chapter 3 I include detailed information on how to use major library reference works such as PsycINFO, *Science Citation Index, Social Science Citation Index,* and the information available from the National Library of Medicine (for example, MedLINE). Because most researchers access this information from the web, a discussion of Internet resources is also included. However, we still need basics. In the discussion of descriptive statistics in Chapter 5, I teach students how to read and plot graphs. In Chapter 15 I teach students how to write up an experiment and include a valuable checklist that can be used for writing an article and presenting a research proposal. Numerous examples from published articles also are included. Because of our desire to make science concrete, I have included interviews with active psychologists on how they first obtained the ideas for their studies. These interviews are followed by a discussion of how to turn an idea into a testable hypothesis.

The Logic of Making Testable Hypotheses

Although most students grasp the idea of asking testable questions, they often have an uncertainty of what exactly it is they are testing in research. To help clarify this point, I have presented the process of hypothesis testing both conceptually and practically. In Chapter 6 I present a conceptual understanding of inferential statistics and probability. I likewise stress the process of making decisions and the importance of logically ruling out alternative hypotheses. Although this process begins in the first chapter and continues throughout the book, Chapter 2 emphasizes the use of logic and drawing conclusions. This information is important for those who seek a career in research and for anyone who wishes to understand the daily headlines involving scientific research.

Discussion of Various Designs, Including Correlational Designs

An understanding of the logic of experimental design, including the concept of control and the process of making inferences, remains the heart of this edition. However, I have also expanded the discussion of procedures to employ when the experimental situation does not allow for traditional experimental designs. For example, I have expanded the coverage of correlational designs to reflect the ways in which such areas as behavioral medicine and developmental and social psychology rely on such approaches. I have likewise expanded the discussion of single-subject designs in Chapter 13. As in the previous edition, information on quasi-experimental approaches and naturalistic observation is also included. Chapter 14 is devoted to questionnaires, survey research, and sampling, which provides students with a basic understanding of how to construct questionnaires and the logic involved in sampling procedures.

■ Clarification of Important Concepts

To help faculty to teach this course and students to understand the material better, I have made a special effort to define and illustrate what I know to be general problem areas for students. Also, I have included material at the end of each chapter that not only summarizes the main points but also includes questions to test comprehension and discussion questions and projects for better integration of the material. Included in this section are designs for the students to criticize and conclusions to evaluate. My talks with faculty across the country have led me to pay special attention to certain topics. For example, the concept of interaction effects is illustrated with not only research examples but also numerous possible outcomes that are graphically represented. Given that an understanding of interaction effects continues to be a major problem for students, I have added even more actual examples from the literature in this edition. I also carefully walk students through the interpretation of interaction effects. These discussions are facilitated by the explanation of the concept behind the F ratio. Beginning in Chapter 7 and continuing throughout the rest of the text, the logic of the F ratio is used in the discussions of experimental control and variation. By emphasizing the factors that influence either the numerator or the denominator of the F ratio, students can grasp conceptually what factors will influence their acceptance or rejection of the null hypothesis. I give special attention to two other problem areas for students: the meaning of causation in science and the use of the terms *error* and *chance* in relation to experimentation.

■ New Directions

In using the title *Methods Toward a Science of Behavior and Experience,* I wanted to convey a sense not only of where experimental psychology has been but also of where it might be going. I expand on this idea in Chapter 16, in which I discuss the potential for a scientific psychology. I point out that psychology was once almost a battleground for those who were interested in behavior and those interested in experience. But today, with scientific studies of such topics as attention, emotion, awareness, animal cognition, and especially consciousness, I see a new group of scientists who are interested in both behavior and experience, not only in others but also in themselves.

■ Acknowledgments

This book grew out of discussions concerning our experience of science and the role it currently plays in psychology. I would like to acknowledge the many individuals who joined me in these discussions. In relation to the first edition, Dale Harris spent his time discussing his perspective on the history of the experimental movement in psychology. I appreciate the willingness of Jude Cassidy, Jeff Parker, Nora Newcombe, Carolyn Sherif, Lance Shotland, and Andreas Keil to discuss how their ideas came about and how they began their important research programs. I appreciate the help of our colleague Mel Mark for his careful reading of and critical suggestions on the chapters related to inferential statistics and survey research. I also appreciate Judith Kroll's willingness to share with me her notes and ideas for helping women to find more of a home in science and Gordon Hall's perspective on multicultural research. Theresa Vescio was also very helpful in sharing with me ways to increase students' understanding of difficult concepts. Many colleagues at Penn State and other institutions in this country, Canada, Europe, and Asia have shared with me knowledge and experiences in doing science. Others told me ways that they use to teach experimental methods and the values they wish to impart. For their time and thoughtful consideration, I am extremely appreciative.

Many colleagues around the country shared their experience of teaching with us and made this book richer in many ways. I appreciate their careful reading of the earlier editions and their invaluable suggestions based on their experience with the book. In particular, I would like to acknowledge the reviewers of the first edition: Robert T. Brown, University of North Carolina, Wilmington; Dennis Cogan, Texas Tech University; Paul Eskildsen, San Francisco State University; Henry Gorman, Austin College; Les Herold, California State University, San Bernardino; Alan C. Kamil, University of Massachusetts; Nancy Kirkland, Trinity College; Elizabeth Lynn, San Diego State University; Henry Morlock, State University of New York, Plattsburgh; Howard B. Orenstein, Western Maryland College; Ronald Rossi, Lyndon State College; Mark S. Sanders, California State University, Northridge; Kathryn Schwarz, Scottsdale Community College; Keith Stanovich, Oakland University; Barbara Tabachnick, California State University, Northridge; W. Scott Terry, University of North Carolina, Charlotte; and Sheila Zipf, San Francisco State University.

I would also like to thank the reviewers of the second edition: Earl Babble, Chapman College; Elizabeth Capaldi, Purdue University; Elvis C. Jones, Frostburg State College; John M. Knight, Central State University; Judith E. Larkin, Canisius College; John J. Meryman, San Jose State University; Thomas O. Nelson, University of Washington; and Mark A. Sabol, Creighton University.

And I express our gratitude to the reviewers of the third edition: Philip G. Benson, New Mexico State University; Alexis Collier, Ohio State University; Eric S. Knowles, University of Arkansas; Mark D. Pagel, Oxford University; Kirk H. Smith, Bowling Green State University; and Marty Wall, University of Toronto.

The comments of reviewers for the fourth edition resulted in a number of major changes. Reviewers for that edition include Jonathon D. Brown, University of Washington; Clarke A. Burnham, University of Texas at Austin; Henry A. Cross, Colorado State University; Raymond T. Garza, University of California, Riverside; Mary Gauvain, Scripps College; Elizabeth L. Glisky, University of Arizona; Joellen T. Hartley, California State University, Long Beach; Alan C. Kamil, University of Nebraska, Lincoln; Philipp J. Kraemer, University of Kentucky; W. Trammell Neill, Adelphi University; Howard A. Rollins Jr., Emory University; and Barry S. Stein, Tennessee Technological University.

Reviewers for the fifth edition include Deane Aikins, Pennsylvania State University; Steve Buck, University of Washington; Nancy Eldred, San Jose State University; Philip Freedman, University of Illinois; Michael Gaynor, Bloomsburg University; Elizabeth Glisky, University of Arizona; Judith Kroll, Pennsylvania State University; Mark Pitt, Ohio State University; Joseph F. Sturr, Syracuse University; and Jenny Wiley, Virginia Commonwealth University.

For the seventh edition, reviewers include Kevin Apple, James Madison University; Jill Booker, University of Indianapolis; Martin Bourgeois, University of Wyoming; Cynthia L. Crown, Xavier University; Lisa Fournier, Washington State University; Elizabeth Yost Hammer, Belmont University; Kurt A. Hoffman, University of California, Davis; Richard F. Martell, Montana State University; Debra L. Valencia-Laver, California Polytechnic University, San Luis Obispo; Heidi A. Wayment, Northern Arizona University; and Doug Wedell, University of South Carolina, Columbia.

Reviewers for the eighth edition include Gordon Pitz, University of North Carolina, Chapel Hill; Gwen Lupfer, Indiana University, South Bend; William Kelemen, California State University, Long Beach; Paul Fedorchak, Plymouth State University; Jonathan Pettibone, Southern Illinois University, Edwardsville; Kirsten Rewey, University of Minnesota; William Langston, Middle Tennessee State University; Nancy Darling, Bard College; John Sparrow, University of New Hampshire, Manchester; and Steve Seidel, Texas A&M University, Corpus Christi.

Reviewing is somewhat of a lost art, and I appreciate the consideration given this ninth edition as demonstrated by the constructive comments and suggestions provided by Molly Lynch, Northern Virginia Community College; John L. Wallace, Ball State University; Maria L. Dittrich, George Washington University; Cindy Silitsky, St. Thomas University; Doug Wedell, University of South Carolina; Lisa Fournier, Washington State University; Peter J. Marshall, Temple University; Frederick Bonato, Saint Peter's College; Jonathan Thomas, Roosevelt University, Chicago; Yun Chu, University of Hawaii at Manoa; Mark D. Graham, CSU Northridge; Jonathan Lytle, Temple University; Corrine Lim-Kessler, Monmouth College; Chehalis Strapp, Western Oregon University; David Bridgett, Yale University; Sheryl Leytham, Grand View College. I hope that the book has not suffered from my inability to implement all of their suggestions.

I found the production staff at Wadsworth to be excellent and wish to thank them for their efforts. It is never an easy task to turn a manuscript into a finished product, and such efforts often go unnoticed. I also appreciate my association with Erik Evans, the psychology editor at Wadsworth, for his consistent concern with quality publishing. Finally, I would like to invite both students and faculty to write me with their comments concerning the book or examples from their courses or the literature that have helped to clarify the material. You may write me at the Department of Psychology, Penn State University, University Park, PA 16802 or send an e-mail to wjr@psu.edu. I will do my best to include your suggestions in the next edition.

William J. Ray

INTRODUCTION

Y ou are about to begin a voyage of wonder and curiosity, of questionings and doubts. Historically, it is a voyage that human beings began many generations ago and that scientists like you embark on every day. It is a voyage into the nature of ourselves and the world in which we live. It is a voyage with a particular focus: science. For some of you, science offers a new way to view the world. Learning about science, like learning about anything new, offers added perspective, which can in turn lead to a very real expansion of your own consciousness. For those of you already familiar with science, this book offers a deeper exploration of the science of behavior and experience. It is important to emphasize from the outset that learning about science is an expansion of what you already are. It is an option, an alternative that you are free to use or not to use as you explore and interact with our world. You choose how and when to use it. In fact, after taking this course, you may decide it is not a way that you wish to view the world at all, and you may never use it again.

Some students are hesitant to explore science because they believe it is cold, antihumanistic, and even antireligious. They believe it separates us from our beliefs, our faiths, our feelings, and ourselves. This is a serious and limiting misconception. Many of our colleagues in all fields of science are as open to humanistic and spiritual traditions as they are to science. We believe that science—a science of behavior and experience—will someday assist us in a profound exploration of all our great humanistic and spiritual traditions. This task of helping all of us more fully explore and understand our own potential may be the major function of science in the future evolution of human consciousness.

Our voyage into the science of behavior and experience begins by stressing that there are many childlike qualities that we hope will always remain part of us. Genuine laughter, spontaneous play, intimacy, curiosity, and creativity are some childlike qualities that form the very foundation of mature human experience. In a similar way, the scientific method that we are about to explore has firm roots in the simple way that children go about exploring their world. With this in mind, we begin our exploration of science by viewing ourselves as children who wish to explore. The world awaiting the child includes not only the outside world but also the child's own psychological experience. Through this child, who is one aspect of ourselves, we approach the question of how we go about performing a science of behavior and experience. We will watch the child search for knowledge and mature into three distinct aspects, which we can define as actors in our drama of psychological inquiry.

The first aspect, or role, is that of the scientist. It is the active role in our drama. The task before you is to learn how the scientist goes about doing science. In this book we will watch the child learn the role of the scientist. We will come to see that many activities of present-day, mature scientists are simply extensions of the way that we approached the world as children. As you learn about this role, you will learn about the types of questions that scientists ask, the types of answers that they accept, and the way in which knowledge is approached and verified.

The second aspect, or role, is that of the research participant. This is the passive role in our drama. The research participant is the particular organism that the scientist chooses to study. In fact, it is the various experiences and behaviors of the participant that form the content of psychology. The paradox for scientists interested in the study of human behavior and experience is that, although the subject matter is "out there" in the individuals who we study, because we are also human, it is at the same time "in here" in us. In a very real sense, as we study other people and animals, we also study ourselves.

The third role is that of the witness. This role is not always recognized, yet in many ways it is the most important because it maintains a balance between the scientist and the research participant, the active and passive aspects of this process. The witness, who is also us, stands back and watches the scientist do science and the research participant behave and experience the world. One task of the witness is to teach that both the scientist and the research participant are limited because each sees the world only from his or her own perspective.

As the witness teaches us that there is a broader perspective from which we can appreciate both viewpoints simultaneously, we begin to mature and realize the richness of the scientific process and the wonder of approaching knowledge of reality. In this vein it is the role of the witness to remind us that the experience and understanding of life require more than just a description of miles of blood vessels, reinforcement schedules, and chemicals interacting with each other. It is the witness who asks whether the science of the scientist is relevant, ethical, and generally worth doing. But most important, it is the witness who brings together the procedures of the scientist and the experience of the research participant and allows them to have a relationship in the first place.

Once we have developed these aspects of ourselves—the scientist, the research participant, and the witness—we will be in a better position to understand the strengths and weaknesses of using science to study ourselves. Until that time we would like to suggest that you neither accept nor reject the scientific approach but rather that you allow that it may have something to offer you. That is, you can allow yourself to become actively involved in trying to solve problems and answer questions using this method while remaining free to remember the problems and limitations of the scientific approach. As in anything else, it is only through active involvement that you will come to understand fully what the method has to offer. Let's now begin the drama of science with a problem—how did we as children come to know the world?—and from this develop methods for a science of behavior and experience.

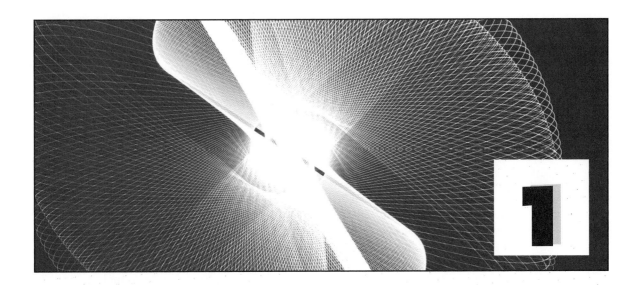

WHAT IS SCIENCE?

SCIENCE AS A WAY OF KNOWING
Tenacity
Authority
Reason
Common Sense
Science
Pseudoscience and Superstition

THE SCIENTIFIC APPROACH

EARLY APPROACHES

OVERVIEW

STUDYING BEHAVIOR AND EXPERIENCE

BEHAVIOR: A ROAD INTO THE SUBJECTIVE EXPERIENCE OF RESEARCH PARTICIPANTS

THE PEOPLE WHO PERFORM SCIENCE

Science is above all a human activity. One obvious meaning of this is that people perform science. Another equally accurate meaning is that all people perform science in some form. After all, the methods of science are simple extensions of the ways all people learn about their world. Science in many ways is similar to the way we have been learning about the world since we were infants. We learn through interacting with our world. Consequently, each of you knows this aspect of science well because you have been using it in one form or another since you first began toddling about and discovering the world. You probably know much more about the scientific method than you think you do.

Watch a young child. When something catches his or her eye, the child must examine it, study it, observe it, have fun with it. Next, the child wants to interact with it, touch it, feel it. From passive observations and active interactions, the child slowly learns about the world. Some interactions are fun: "If I tip the glass, I get to see the milk form pretty pictures on the floor." Others are not so much fun: "If I touch the red circles on the stove, my fingers hurt!" From each interaction, the child learns a little more about the world.

Like the child, scientists are exploring the unknown—and sometimes the known—features of the world. All basic research strategies are based on one simple notion: *To discover what the world is like, we must experience it.* To have an idea about the nature of the world is not enough. Instead, like the child, scientists experience the world to determine whether their ideas accurately reflect reality. Direct experience is an essential tool because it alone allows us to bridge the gap between our ideas and reality.

However, there is another aspect to science that many people do not think about. This is the aspect of *doubt*. One way in which we doubt is to question the common wisdom—whether it holds that the world is flat or that all our behavior is learned—and to seek different models of the world. In science we use doubt to question our research and ask whether factors other than the ones that we originally considered might have influenced our results. By doing this we come to see that science is a combination of interaction with the world and logic. Thus, as we will discuss throughout this book, science is more than just watching; it is rare that data actually speak for themselves.

In general, there is no single scientific method, any more than there is one art or one education or one religion, yet there is a general process called *science*. This process consists of experiencing the world and then drawing general conclusions (called *facts*) from observations. Sometimes these conclusions or facts are descriptive and can be represented by numbers. For example, we say that the moon is 238,000 miles from the earth or that the average human heart rate is 72 beats per minute. Other times these facts are more general and can describe a relationship or a process. For example, we say that it is more difficult to learn a second language after puberty than before or that as we age we hear fewer high-frequency sounds. Whatever the topic, the known facts about a particular subject are called *scientific knowledge*.

Much of our scientific knowledge is based on a history of research in a particular area. How we perform research is what this book is all about. Many conceptions of scientific research picture a man or a woman in a white lab coat, laboriously writing down numbers, and later milling about in a cluttered office trying to make theoretical sense out of these findings. This conception may be partly accurate, but it is not a total picture of science. A scientist, like all of us, is human and as we shall see this fact contributes to both the promises and problems of doing science.

In this book, we stress this aspect of science, which becomes apparent when the available facts are viewed in light of human value. It is this aspect of value that allows us to see one set of numbers as more relevant or potentially more useful than another. This combining of fact and value results in a humanistic approach to scientific understanding. Scientific understanding helps us to see the *how* and *why* of the world and thereby to understand nature in a fuller perspective. In many cases, this understanding raises new questions, which in turn can be answered by using science to examine the world. In other cases, these new facts can be applied in real-life settings (technology) and make life easier for everyone. Thus, at its best, science begins and ends in human experience.

In the introduction to this book, we described three actors in the drama of science: the scientist, the research participant, and the witness. In our study of behavior and experience, it is the scientist who experiences the world and then formulates general facts or conclusions that describe it. The participant is the one who is studied in an experiment. In some cases, these roles are simple; in others, such as the study of human consciousness, the situation is more complex because we must use our own consciousness to study consciousness. Finally, the witness provides the perspective, the concerns for value, and the relationship of science and its facts to other aspects of human life.

SCIENCE AS A WAY OF KNOWING

All of us at times fall into the trap of viewing science as the best way, or even the only way, to study behavior and experience. If you find this happening to you, beware! Although our culture emphasizes science as an important way of knowing, it is not the only way, and like all ways of knowing, it has certain limitations in its methods. To emphasize this, we offer science as merely one way of examining human processes. There are others; art, philosophy, religion, and literature are all fruitful ways or channels through which we can gain new ideas about human behavior and experience. Psychology has drawn on many of these traditions and will surely continue to do so.

Having a fruitful source of ideas, whether it is our literary, spiritual, scientific, or artistic traditions, is an important part of understanding behavior and experience. However, a second and perhaps even more important aspect of learning about psychology is the process of determining whether a new idea is accurate. In contrast to other ways of knowing, science offers not only a fertile source of new ideas but also a powerful method for evaluating the ideas we have about reality. That is to say, science helps us to know if our ideas about the world are wrong.

For example, suppose someone tells you to buy a new exercise machine, or a well-known spiritual leader says that if you meditate twice a day you will be happier, or someone tells you that if you eat only a low-carbohydrate diet you will be healthier and live longer. These are instances in which you are confronted with new ideas that may have an important impact on your life. Because some time and effort are involved in these examples, and given the track record of some exercise specialists, spiritual teachers, and fad diets, you may be hesitant to change your habits unless you know it will be worthwhile. So you are faced with the task of evaluating the suggestions and deciding whether these ideas are right for you. How do you decide? In the remainder of this section, we examine several ways people decide whether to accept new ideas about the world. For a more detailed discussion of these ways of accepting belief, see the work of American philosopher Charles Peirce (Cohen & Nagel, 1934; Kerlinger, 1973, 1986). We are obviously biased and believe that the best way to respond to new ideas, especially for society at large, is to use science to evaluate these new ideas and then use the results of this research to help make a decision.

■ Tenacity

Peirce uses the term *tenacity* to refer to the acceptance of a belief based on the idea that "we have always known it to be this way." People at various times have said, "Women make bad soldiers," or "You can't teach an old dog new tricks," or "Science is always beneficial." These statements are presented over and over again and accepted as true, yet they are rarely examined and evaluated. This is an all-too-common method of accepting information. Television advertising and political campaigns use this technique when they present a single phrase or slogan repeatedly. Even an empty phrase repeated often enough becomes accepted as true. As has been said, if you tell people something often enough, they will believe it.

As a way of learning about the world, there are two problems with this method. First, the statement may be just an empty phrase, and its accuracy may never have been evaluated. The statement may gain wide acceptance through its familiarity alone. Second, tenacity offers no means for correcting erroneous ideas. That is, once a belief is widely accepted solely on the basis of tenacity, it is difficult to change. Social psychologists have shown that once a person accepts a belief without data to support it, the person often will make up a reason for accepting the belief as true. In fact, the person may even refuse to accept new information that contradicts this belief. In the case of the diet example, a decision to begin a certain diet simply because it is said to be beneficial would be acceptance based on tenacity. Accepting ideas about experience and behavior simply because they are familiar to us or widely believed by others is an extension of the childish behavior of the 3-year-old who copies the words and behaviors of others. For the child this is an efficient beginning for learning about the world, but for the rest of us it is limiting.

■ Authority

A second way we may accept a new idea is when an authority figure tells us it is so. Acceptance based on authority is simple because we only have to repeat and live by what we are told. In many cases, referring to an authority, especially in areas about which we know nothing, is useful and beneficial. When we were young, our parents often used the method of authority for directing our behavior. In the past, health care and education were based almost exclusively on authority. If a famous physician or educator said something was true, almost everyone believed it to be true. Even today, we often rely on the judgment of an authority when we consult physicians, psychologists, scientists, or consultants. Likewise, religious training often relies on the authority of religious leaders and elders for establishing correct religious procedures.

Although authority brings with it a stability that allows for consistency, it is not without problems. The major problem of accepting authority as having sole access to truth is that authority can be incorrect and thus send people in the wrong directions. For example, as long as everyone accepted the view that the earth was the center of the universe, no one thought to study the orbit of the earth. Consequently, it is important to examine the basis

Box 1.1

Galileo: The Transition from Authority to Empiricism

For many scientists Galileo is a symbol of change in the rules of evidence. Of course, many people influenced the beginning of scientific thought during the Renaissance, beginning with Copernicus, Kepler, and the philosopher Bacon. However, Galileo and Newton (see Box 1.2) often are called the greatest founders of modern science (compare Holton, 1952; Russell, 1984). Before their time, intellectual questions were answered by referring to authority, usually the authority of the Church. The Church of this period in turn looked to the Greek philosopher Aristotle for answers to "material" questions—what today we call natural science.

Suppose a person wanted to know which of two balls would hit the ground first if they were dropped from a tall building. Until the time of Galileo, the method of answering this question would be to refer to Aristotle's theory, which stated that the world is made up of four elements: earth, air, water, and fire. According to Aristotle, each element acts according to its own nature. To answer the question of which of two bodies would hit the ground first, one would reason that the two objects, composed of the element earth, would seek to return to earth and thus fall down. If one object weighed more than the other, it would be reasoned that this heavier object contained more of the element earth than the lighter one and would naturally fall faster. Thus, it would be concluded that the heavier body would hit the ground before the lighter one. No one would have thought to actually drop two objects from a tower and observe which hit the ground first. Answers were always given in terms of authority.

Galileo successfully replaced the method of authority with that of experimentation. This movement toward experimentation was greatly aided by Galileo's own inventions, such as the telescope, the thermometer, an improved microscope, and a pendulum-type timing device. Each of these instruments allowed people to experiment and answer for themselves the questions of nature. After establishing that balls rolling down an inclined plane act similarly to falling objects, Galileo successfully challenged the authority of Aristotle concerning two falling weights. With Galileo's work, a new science based on observation and experimentation was beginning. Galileo was part of a revolution that was to challenge authority. In fact, Einstein, in a later preface to Galileo's *Dialogues*, said that Galileo's main theme in his work was the "passionate fight against any kind of dogma based on authority." Although initially Galileo was well received in some quarters and even given life tenure in his professorship at the University of Padua, he later found himself at odds with the Church in Rome and spent the last 9 years of his life under house arrest near Florence.

of the authority's claims. Are these claims based on opinion, tradition, revelation, or direct experience? How valid are the sources of this information? In the meditation example, if you decided to meditate simply because a well-known spiritual leader advised it, you would be basing your decision solely on the authority of this person. Box 1.1 discusses the transition from authority to experimentation in the beginning of modern science.

■ Reason

Reason and logic are the basic methods of philosophy. Reason often takes the form of a logical syllogism such as "All men can't count; Dick is a man; therefore, Dick can't count." We all use reason every day as we try to solve problems and understand relationships. As useful as it is to be reasonable, however, reason alone will not always produce the appropriate answer. Why? One potential problem in the reasoned approach is that our original assumption must be correct. If the original assumption is incorrect or at odds with the world in which we live, then logic cannot help us. For example, the syllogism that concluded that Dick can't count is logically valid even though it is based on the absurd premise that all men can't count. Much of traditional economic theory was based on the assumption that a given person would always put his or her own interests first, the so called "rational man." However, recent research in social psychology and economics presents a more complicated picture in which humans do not behave rationally when dealing with money or helping others. The good news is that we will often help others when there is no apparent gain for ourselves. Thus, the weakness of using reason alone is that we have no way to determine the accuracy of our assumptions. We can have situations in which our logic is impeccable, but because our original assumption is inaccurate, the conclusion is silly.

■ Common Sense

Common sense may offer an improvement over acceptance based on tenacity, authority, or reason because it appeals to direct experience. Common sense is based on our own past experiences and our perceptions of the world. However, our experiences and perceptions of the world may be quite limited. The optical illusions that you probably studied in introductory psychology gave you a clear example of how our perceptions can lead us to incorrect conclusions. There can also be a bias in the way we think.

Piattelli-Palmarini (1994) suggests that just as there are optical illusions, there are also cognitive illusions that lead us to be certain but wrong in our answers. Furthermore, research in social psychology has shown that we make different psychological attributions depending on whether we observe or participate in a given situation. If we are asked to explain why someone made a bad grade, we tend to make internal attributions, such as "She's not a good student" or "He isn't smart." However, if we received a bad grade on a test, we would tend to make external attributions, such as "I had three tests that day" or "The test was unfair."

Whereas common sense may help us deal with the routine aspects of daily life, it may also form a wall and prevent us from understanding new areas. This can be a problem, particularly when we enter realms outside our everyday experience. For example, people considered Albert Einstein's suggestion that time was relative and could be different for different people to be contrary to common sense.

Likewise, it was considered contrary to common sense when Sigmund Freud suggested that we did not always know our own motivations or when B. F. Skinner suggested that the concept of free will was inapplicable to the behavior of most individuals. We might also assume that the stable process is the healthier one. However, research using nonlinear (chaos) analysis has suggested, for example, that the patterns of a healthy heart are erratic and those of a pathological heart can be regular (Goldberger & Rigney, 1991).

■ Science

We end our discussion of the ways people accept new ideas by discussing science. Philosopher of science Alfred North Whitehead (1925) suggested that there are two methods for what he called the "purification of ideas" and that these methods are combined in the scientific method. An idea is evaluated or corrected through (1) dispassionately observing by means of our bodily senses (for example, vision, hearing, and touch) and (2) using reason to compare various theoretical conceptualizations based on experience.

The first method is a direct extension of the commonsense approach just described. Unlike a given person's common sense, however, science is open to *anyone's* direct experience. Presumably, any person with normal sensory capacities could verify any observation made by a scientist. To aid people in repeating the observations of others, some scientists (see Bridgman, 1927) have emphasized the importance of *operational definitions* in research. As you will see in Chapter 2, operational definitions direct *how* observations are to be made and what is to be observed and measured.

The second method is a direct application of the principles of logic. In this case, however, logic is combined with experience to rule out any assumptions that do not accurately reflect the scientific experiment. This blend of direct sensory experience and reason gives science a self-corrective nature that is not found in other ways of accepting ideas about the world. One important technique is replication, in which a procedure is repeated under similar conditions. For example, if an experiment is found to give similar results in different labs and even in different parts of the world, this lends support to the conclusions. This means that scientific conclusions are never taken as final but are always open to reinterpretation as new evidence becomes available. In other words, the method of science includes a feedback component by which conclusions about the world can be refined over time. It is the refining of ideas through both experimentation and reason that allows science to be a fruitful method for knowing about the world.

Historically, the methods of modern science can be traced to the 17th century. The work of Sir Isaac Newton generally is credited as representing the beginning of modern science. Box 1.2 describes Newton's rules of reasoning in science. These rules form the basis of the modern scientific approach: the law of parsimony, the assumption that there exists a unity to the physical universe in which we live, the possibility of generalizing from experiments, and the acceptance of empirical data over opinion. In many ways, these rules are as applicable today as they were when they were written more than 300 years ago. Alan Kazdin (2003b) begins his discussion of the key characteristics of psychological science with parsimony or the idea that we should consider simpler explanations over complicated ones. A second key characteristic is that we consider rival alternative explanations of our findings. Throughout this book, we consider a variety of ways in which environmental or other factors may have influenced research findings. Third, replication is central to doing good science. If a scientific finding reflects the world in which we live, we would expect, as Newton suggested, that the results from similar experiments performed in different labs around the world would be similar. A fourth characteristic of science is that we consider our results with great care and apply appropriate logic to the situation. Overall, the scientific approach helps us to draw valid inferences from our research in describing the world.

Box 1.2

Newton's Rules of Reasoning

Born the year after Galileo's death, Newton produced a body of work that represents the beginning of modern science as we know it. Whereas Galileo fought with philosophers of his day and was persecuted by the Church for his beliefs, Newton lived in a new age in which science through experimentation and reason began to bear fruit.

In the 1680s, Newton's classic work *Principia* was published (Newton, 1969 reprint). Designated by science historian Gerald Holton (1952) as "probably the greatest single book in the history of science," this work describes Newton's theories of time, space, and motion as well as his rules of reasoning for science. Science, called *natural philosophy* by Newton, is based on four rules of reasoning.

Rule 1

We are to admit no more causes of natural things than such as are both true and sufficient to explain their appearances.

To this purpose the philosophers say that Nature does nothing in vain, and more is in vain when less will serve; for Nature is pleased with simplicity, and affects not the pomp of superfluous causes.

Today we call this rule the law of parsimony. The rule simply states that natural events should be explained in the simplest way possible.

Rule 2

Therefore to the same natural effects we must, as far as possible, assign the same causes.

As to respiration in a man and in a beast; the descent of stones in Europe and in America; the

light of our culinary fire and of the sun; the reflection of light in the earth, and in the planets.

This rule reflects Newton's belief in a natural order, which requires that the same gravity causes stones to fall in Europe and in America.

Rule 3

The qualities of bodies, which admit neither intensification nor remission of degrees, and which are found to belong to all bodies within the reach of our experiments, are to be esteemed the universal qualities of all bodies whatsoever.

For since the qualities of bodies are only known to us by experiments, we are to hold for universal all such as universally agree with experiments; and such as are not liable to diminution can never be quite taken away. We are certainly not to relinquish the evidence of experiments for the sake of dreams and vain fictions of our own devising; nor are we to recede from the analogy of Nature, which is wont to be simple, and always consonant to itself. We in no other way know the extension of bodies than by our senses, nor do these reach it in all bodies; but because we perceive extension in all that are sensible, therefore we ascribe it universally to all others also.

Newton continues with a long discussion of this principle. Briefly, it states that what we learn from our experiments can be applied to similar structures outside the reach of our experiments. For example, the properties of gravity and inertia should apply to the moon and other planets as they apply to stones and other objects with which we experiment.

(continued)

(continued)

Rule 4

In experimental philosophy we are to look upon propositions inferred by general induction from phenomena as accurately or very nearly true, notwithstanding any contrary hypotheses that may be imagined, till such time as other phenomena occur, by which they may either be made more accurate, or liable to exceptions.

This rule we must follow, that the argument of induction may not be evaded by hypotheses.

This rule simply states that theories obtained from experiments should be considered true or approximately true until new experimental evidence shows the old to be incorrect. Ideas developed from experiments should not be changed just because we like another hypothesis better.

These four simple rules have directed the physical sciences for the past 300 years. Since the 20th century, they have been applied to the social and behavioral sciences as well.

■ Pseudoscience and Superstition

One of our goals in this book is to help you think critically. We do this in the context of science. We emphasize ways to evaluate information and come to valid conclusions. However, as human beings, we have a long history of relying on magic and superstition as ways to guide our decisions. In fact, in the next section we will tell you about a king some 2,500 years ago who based his war plans on what an oracle told him would happen in the future. Even today some hotels do not have a 13th floor, since this is seen by some to be unlucky. Many individuals and sports teams have rituals that they think will help them to win. Some people carry lucky charms or wear certain clothes to important meetings because they think this will help them to succeed. We are told to blow out all the candles on our birthday cakes and to not walk under ladders. Even our newspapers have daily horoscopes to tell us what types of activities to engage in that day. Why we give extra emotionality to a common event like seeing a black cat is an interesting question. Most likely it is part of our long evolutionary history. We may emotionally believe that something is true and hate the thought of giving up that particular idea or belief. This is made even more complicated by the way that, as research shows, when we believe something to be true, we tend to look only for supporting evidence and to dismiss any contradiction to our belief as an exception. Without a method to test our ideas, we will never know the validity of our conclusions.

We also want to warn you that a variety of individuals make claims in the name of science that are not actually based on rigorous scientific procedures. Often these are individuals who want to sell you something. You see this every day in terms of certain video commercials as well as claims on the Internet. Some of these claims have made their way into popular books and even have been reported as true in the mass media. For example, the idea that you can learn while you sleep was a popular one during parts of the 20th century. This idea found its way into a variety of movies and novels and was even spoofed on an episode of the Simpsons. The Simpsons had it correct, since various scientific research studies have not been able to find evidence supporting the claim of learning during sleep. However, even today you can go on the web and buy materials that claim to help you learn languages, study for exams, and improve a variety of abilities while you sleep. All of these items are supposed to be based on scientific research, or at least that is what the websites say. This phenomenon of presenting information as if it is based on science when it is not is referred to as *pseudoscience.* In this sense, *pseudo* means false. Thus, pseudoscience is false science. Often claims of pseudoscience are based on testimonials that present only one side and have not been evaluated by others studying similar phenomena using valid scientific methods. For this reason, scientists pay particular attention to research that has been evaluated by other scientists before it is published. This process is called *peer review,* and journals that follow this procedure are called *peer-reviewed journals.* One characteristic of pseudoscience is that it is not found in peer-reviewed journals. As we continue throughout the book, we will help you to identify pseudoscience and to develop some of the skills of critical thinking to evaluate its claims.

Just because something is not based on science does not mean that we should not consider it. Many of us love to read science fiction and other types of fantasy literature. Such writing makes us consider possibilities and other ways of thinking about our world. As we will see in this book, scientists are always considering alternative explanations and sometimes ideas that are crazy. However, considering that something could be true does not mean that it has scientific support. Thus, we need a means for testing our ideas. We particularly need ways of knowing if we are wrong, which is one of the important aspects of science we will present in this book.

THE SCIENTIFIC APPROACH

In this chapter we examine the scientific approach through various informal illustrations, examples, and stories. In Chapter 2 we discuss more formally the methods of natural observation and experimentation. Among other things, we emphasize that a major characteristic of science is a reliance on information that is *verifiable through experience.* That is, it must be possible for different people in different places and at different times using a similar method to produce the same results.

Once you know the methods of science and have used them in a variety of situations, you will be in a position to evaluate science as a method of knowing about the world that includes the behavior and experience of yourself and others. More important, you will be in a position to decide whether science is the way you choose to understand the world. First, however, let's begin to understand what science is by looking at three early efforts to understand the world. Although these efforts attempted to be systematic, today we would call them pre-experimental or quasi-experimental. That is, in none of these procedures was an actual experiment conducted. Our purpose is to focus on the manner in which the problem was solved—particularly the efforts to be systematic—and what errors were made. You might also recall instances from your own life when you attempted to solve problems in similar ways.

EARLY APPROACHES

The first example concerns extrasensory perception (ESP). According to the historian Herodotus (trans. 1942), Croesus, who was king of Lydia from 560 to 546 BC, became concerned with the increasing power of the Persian army because Lydia was located between Persia and Greece. King Croesus knew the Persian armies to be strong and therefore did not want to attack them unless it was certain he would win. He needed someone who could foretell the future. As an enlightened consumer, Croesus wanted to know that the information he received was true. To determine this, he constructed a test of the oracles who were said to foretell the future best. Croesus's assistants were to go out into Greece and Libya where famous oracles lived. The assistants were to visit each oracle on a specific day and at a specific time and ask, "What is the king doing at this moment?" Because the king told no one what he was actually doing at that moment, he reasoned that only a true oracle, one capable of extrasensory perception, could answer correctly. The assistants all returned to the king and reported their answers. Only one oracle, the oracle at Delphi, gave the correct answer. In fact, according to Herodotus, this oracle answered the question before it was even asked. (The king had been making lamb stew.)

Although the king had the beginnings of a scientific approach to experience, he had not learned the role of chance in science or the nature of the language of science. Trusting his research, the king honored the oracle and asked the important political question of whether he should go to battle against the Persian armies. The oracle replied that in such a contest a mighty empire would be destroyed. This was all the king needed to assemble his armies and attack. When the battle was over, a mighty empire had been destroyed as the oracle had predicted; the problem for the king was that the empire destroyed was his own, and he was taken prisoner.

| CONCEPT CHECK 1.1 | As you read your morning newspaper, you see that a famous scientist has said that cancer will be cured in the next year. If you believe this statement, is your belief based on scientific reasoning? |

The king, like many others after him, failed to realize that a single correct answer may not be sufficient to allow us to draw valid conclusions. Likewise, the king did not realize that the language of prediction must be precise in directing our attention toward possible outcomes. Let's look at another attempt to understand the world, this one dating back almost 2,000 years.

In the second century AD, Galen, a well-known physician, described a woman who complained of insomnia (Mesulam & Perry, 1972). The problem was to determine the factors that led to the insomnia. Galen first decided that the problem was not mainly physical. Following this determination, he began to notice the woman's condition during his examinations. It happened that during one examination, a person returning from the theater mentioned the name of a certain dancer, Pylades. At this point Galen observed an increase in the woman's pulse rate, along with a change in her facial color and expression. What did Galen do next? To answer his questions about what was affecting the woman, he began to experiment. In his own words,

> The next day, I told one of my following that when I went to visit the woman he was to arrive a little later and mention that Morphus was dancing that day. When this was done the patient's pulse was in no way changed. And likewise, on the following day, while I was attending her, the name of the third dancer was mentioned, and in like fashion the pulse was hardly affected at all. I investigated the matter for a fourth time in the evening. Studying the pulse and seeing that it was excited and irregular when mention was made that Pylades was dancing, I concluded that the lady was in love with Pylades, and in the days following, this conclusion was confirmed exactly. (Galen, trans. 1827)

Galen went past observation and began to ask, "I wonder what will happen if I do this?" He performed what we now would call a *single-case experiment* (see Chapter 13). Notice that Galen checked to determine that it was not the name of just any dancer that produced a change in pulse rate or even just a man's name. He sought to discover what factors brought on an irregular pulse by examining a number of alternatives. From this investigation, he concluded that only the name of one particular man, repeated on different occasions, produced the effect.

Consider a story that took place in Europe about 150 years ago. A physician named Ignaz Semmelweis faced a serious problem when he noticed that previously healthy women who had just given birth to healthy children were dying. The women died of a condition that included fever, chills, and seizures. Although numerous theories were offered—which attributed the deaths to such causes as bad diet, unhealthy water, and even the smell of certain flowers—Semmelweis knew that other women in the same hospital who ate the same food, drank the same water, and smelled the same flowers did not die. Consequently, he reasoned, it was not the food, water, or flowers that caused the deaths. Yet the fact remained that women who had just given birth died of the mysterious condition.

Semmelweis became aware of a crucial clue when he learned that an assistant who had accidentally cut his hand during an autopsy later died after displaying the same symptoms as the mothers. What was the connection between the death of the assistant and the deaths of the mothers? Was there any connection at all? Semmelweis reasoned that the autopsy laboratory where the assistant had worked might be the cause of the mysterious deaths. To evaluate this notion, he traveled to other hospitals and recorded what physicians did just before delivering babies. From these observations, he learned that when the physicians who delivered the babies came directly from a pathology lecture in which diseased tissues were handled or from performing an autopsy, the death rate was highest. Semmelweis suggested that it was the physicians who were transferring the diseases from the pathological tissue to the healthy mothers, just as the assistant had accidentally infected himself with the knife cut.

The physicians of the day were outraged at the suggestion that they were the cause of the women's deaths. But Semmelweis found further evidence by demonstrating that in hospitals where some births were assisted by midwives rather than physicians, the mothers assisted by midwives survived at a much higher rate. In a rather striking, though not totally controlled, experiment, Semmelweis is said to have placed himself at the door to the delivery ward and forced all physicians who entered to wash their hands first. The number of deaths decreased dramatically. Although not everyone accepted Semmelweis's findings, these data spoke for themselves, and modern medical practice has been shaped by this event (Glasser, 1976).

These three stories—of Croesus, Galen, and Semmelweis—show the beginnings of a scientific approach to human problems. Croesus faced the problem of how to evaluate information offered by various oracles. To do this, he devised a test: an evaluation of the sources to decide which one he would use to direct his behavior. But we do not consult oracles today, you might argue. True, but we do develop far-reaching social programs and treatments. For example, is *Sesame Street* a useful means for teaching disadvantaged children? In psychotherapy, would you gain more by just talking with your favorite professor than by going to a clinical psychologist? If you want to avoid heart attacks, should you change your diet, run 4 miles a day, meditate, or just do nothing? To answer these questions, we, like Croesus, need to perform evaluation research, and the methods of science offer us one approach.

Croesus's experience also reminds us of two potential pitfalls to knowing about the world. These are the roles of chance in the events we observe and the need for unambiguous statements. Croesus's single question to the oracle might have been answered correctly by a lucky guess. To decrease the chance of a lucky guess, Croesus might have asked the oracles several questions. In essence, such a safeguard would have constituted a replication (repeating a procedure under similar conditions) of his experiment. Today, simple replication of a new finding is a powerful way to decrease the likelihood that it is a fluke. Croesus also surely recognized, in retrospect, that he had misinterpreted the oracle's ambiguous answer about the battle. To minimize the chances of ambiguities, scientists carefully and systematically define their words as precisely as possible.

Galen wanted to learn why a particular woman did not sleep. To do this, he first observed the woman; that is, he just spent some time with her and noticed what happened. Once he realized that the woman's heart reacted to a dancer's name, he began to test his observations. At this point, Galen moved to a more sophisticated process than Croesus's simple consultation with the oracle. Galen sought evidence of a causal relationship by examining the woman directly. In doing this, he anticipated a major shift in how we seek to know about the world.

Croesus, by contrast, sought his answers from authority. The authorities of his time were the gods, who spoke through the oracles. A more empirical approach would have been for Croesus to develop a system of spies and scouts to provide information about the Persians' strength based on direct experience. Galen went beyond the ungrounded opinions or guesses of available authorities and relied on his direct experience. Galen's appeal to direct experience reflects an alternative approach to knowing and in a real way reflects an alternative level of consciousness, toward which modern science continues to evolve. Indeed, for several generations now, science has been rebuilding our knowledge and understanding of the world on the basis of direct experience.

The choice of basing our actions on evidence from experience or on unfounded opinion probably has been with us in some form for thousands of years and currently confronts each of us countless times every day. Yet basing one's actions on direct experience of the world sometimes appears time-consuming and more difficult than simply consulting some expert or acting on a hunch. In the long run, because our actions invariably take place in the world, the wiser alternative is to base actions on experiential knowledge of the real situation. Mere opinions of others provide a convenient answer, but in the long run, as Croesus found out, reality prevails.

In the third story, Semmelweis had a different problem to solve. To determine why some previously healthy women were dying after giving birth, he examined a number of factors. *He observed the patients with a definite purpose in mind.* He asked, "How are these women being treated that is different from the way other patients are treated?" That is, he sought to determine what was unique to these patients. Was it diet? Flowers? Doctors? Then an unexpected event occurred; an autopsy assistant died of the same symptoms. This gave him the clue that led to the solution of the problem. This example shows that science is not only a method that scientists engage in to solve problems and learn about the world but also a procedure that allows for unexpected events to play a part, whether in the form of accident or human error. One of the rich aspects of science includes unpredictability, serendipity, and what is often called luck. However, luck can work either way, as Croesus found out.

Notice how Semmelweis used logic and simple common sense to design his tests so that his observations would lead to a better understanding of the problem. Semmelweis was trying to understand what was related to the mothers' deaths. For example, because the laboratory assistant died with similar symptoms, Semmelweis reasoned that perhaps he died from the same cause. Semmelweis's observation that more deaths occurred when doctors delivered babies after handling diseased tissue led him to reason that perhaps the cause was somehow related to the diseased tissue. In other cases he tried to rule out *factors that were not responsible* for the deaths. For instance, because patients who did not die ate the same food and drank the same water as those who died, Semmelweis reasoned that the food and water were not possible causes and could be eliminated from further consideration.

There was nothing particularly extraordinary about any of these conclusions. In fact, they reflect the simple common sense that we all possess. What was exceptional was that Semmelweis saw relationships that others overlooked. When simple common sense and reason are combined with direct sensory experience, a desire to understand reality, and the courage to accept new facts, science emerges as a powerful means of asking and answering questions about reality.

Our final comment on Semmelweis's work is that his desire to know and understand led to the development of a series of investigations that approached the problem from several directions. Once he had gained the clue from the death of the assistant, he set out to answer his question through a series of observations. First, he observed that the new mothers in his hospital were not treated differently from other women; that is, he observed that they were not given different food or flowers or treated by different doctors. Second, he allowed himself to consider a possible connection between the death of an assistant and the deaths of the mothers. Third, he went to other hospitals to determine whether his ideas or hypotheses were limited to his hospital or whether they were true for other hospitals as well. Fourth, he concluded that the problem was that the physicians handled diseased tissue and then delivered babies without washing their hands, even though this conclusion was unpopular. Fifth, he performed an indirect test of his theory by comparing the difference in death rates of women assisted by physicians who had handled diseased tissue and those assisted by midwives who had not. Sixth, he began a direct test of his theory by insisting that physicians wash their hands as they came into the delivery ward. The power of Semmelweis's procedure was not in any one test of his ideas because it is almost impossible for any single procedure to answer all questions. Semmelweis was successful because he began with a problem and followed it through to the end by means of a series of observations.

Before you think that what Semmelweis did was a historical event and has nothing to do with our time, you might want to read an article published in the *New England Journal of Medicine* in 1998. The story began in an intensive care unit (ICU) in New England in which newborn babies were getting sick from an unusual form of yeast infection. When experts were called in to investigate, they began to suspect that the yeast infection came from dogs. Of course, there are no dogs in a newborn ICU, so how did the yeast infection get to the unit and, once there, how did it spread from child to child? The experts' best guess was that it got to the unit from one or more pet owners. Now how do you think it spread? You got it! The nurses and doctors on the unit spread the infection when they did not wash their hands thoroughly. There is one additional piece of information you may want to know, especially if you are planning to do research in this type of situation. When asked, two thirds of the professionals said that they scrubbed between patients 100% of the time. However, when the experts watched the staff at work, they discovered that these professionals washed their hands between handling newborns only about one third of the time. As we will see later in this book, verbal reports and observed behaviors may not always go together. Thus, scientific approaches often use multiple measures for gaining more complete information concerning a topic.

 # OVERVIEW

Let's pause for a moment and review what we have covered so far. In the preceding sections, we described the scientific approach to problem solving. We began with children learning about the world by interacting with it. In particular, we suggested that such interaction leads to a notion of science as a way of knowing through experience. We characterized science as a process for drawing conclusions that describe the world. We discussed science not as a sacred entity to be worshipped but as a simple extension of the way all of us—not just children—learn about the world.

We then gave an overview of science by relating the stories of Croesus, Galen, and Semmelweis. We pointed out the manner in which aspects of these stories anticipated important issues in present-day science. These correspondences included the need for unambiguous statements, the need for discovering what does not affect the behavior as well as what does affect the behavior, and the importance of a series of tests or research studies for developing a solution to the problem. Science combines experience, reason, and the desire to answer questions about our conceptions of reality. To accomplish this goal, scientists create theories to help explain their experiences. As we will see later, evaluating ideas and theories is also a large part of what science is all about. Furthermore, the approach to solving problems that we call science is not new but represents a way of solving problems that we all use to some extent every day.

 CONCEPT CHECK 1.2   "The major reason why Semmelweis's approach was superior to that of Croesus is that we know ESP not to be real—no one can foretell the future." Do you agree?

STUDYING BEHAVIOR AND EXPERIENCE

In the preceding discussion, we emphasized that scientists view themselves as using sensory experience to evaluate their ideas concerning the world. This appeal to experience and experimentation as opposed to authority is crucial for two reasons. First, it represents a genuine attempt to pause and observe the external world. Second, reliance on sensory experience means that not only scientists but also any other person with normal sensory capacities and training can observe the particular behavior under study. The ability of anyone to use his or her own senses to verify the raw data of any scientist provides a strong and essential safeguard that our observations of the world remain as free as possible of the unintended or intended biases of any particular scientist. The process of relying on sensory experience to verify our ideas about reality is called **empiricism.** Empiricism has been an important approach in the history of psychology. Of course, pure empiricism can lead us to erroneous conclusions, but combined with the scientific method, it has been a productive approach for psychology.

It also should be pointed out that in our study of behavior and experience, we study our topics on a variety of levels. At times, we discuss at a cognitive level, as when we consider how people think or solve certain problems. At other times, we may move to the physiological level and consider how a particular neurotransmitter is involved in memory, emotion, or schizophrenia. At still other times, we may examine behavior from an extremely broad perspective as we ask how a group of people behaves and experiences a particular event, such as an earthquake or a nuclear reactor accident. As we point out throughout the book, answering a particular research question may lead to one type of research approach rather than another. It is part of your job to ask which type of research approach will give you the most useful information for the question you are asking. Helping you understand how to choose an appropriate research approach is part of the goal of this book.

Throughout the book we also want to help you understand what science will not do for you. For example, it will not give you the final answers to all questions of importance to humans. Science will give you a method for understanding the reality in which we live. It is also important to understand that the answers we receive from science depend on the perspective from which they are asked; there exist various levels of analysis. Although we assume and have assumed for at least the past 100 years that the fundamental processes on each level—cognitive, emotional, physiological, molecular—can be explained scientifically, it is a mistake to assume that information from one level can explain completely the worlds of behavior and experience on another level.

As the title of this book implies, we are dealing with two worlds in our study of behavior and experience. One is the objective, physical world in which anyone can observe appearance and *behavior.* The other is the subjective world of personal psychological *experience,* which is completely private. Science—whether it is biology, physics, chemistry, psychology, sociology, or zoology—focuses on the objective world of appearances and behavior. In the behavior of people, molecules, internal organs, or electrons, what scientists observe and measure are observable objects in the real world. Psychology has continued this tradition, and many studies that you perform and read about consist of the observation and measurement of behavior. However, because the subject matter of psychology focuses in part

Table 1.1

Four Ways of Studying Psychological Processes			
		Process Under Study	
		Inner Experience	Outer Appearance (Behavior)
Focus of Study	"I" (self)	1	3
	"You" (others)	2	4

on humans, psychology is faced with a greater challenge. Not only can we observe humans behaving, but we also can ask them about their inner experiences: their thoughts, feelings, and sensations. Furthermore, because we share the same array of psychological processes, we also can observe our own behavior and experiences.

This diversity offers us a challenge. The challenge is to explore and understand scientifically the behaviors as well as the experiences of ourselves and others. E. F. Schumacher (1977) emphasized this diversity when he pointed out that using experience and behavior to study psychological processes in ourselves and others leads to four possible fields of knowledge. For our purposes, we consider these as four possible ways of studying psychological processes. They are summarized in Table 1.1.

In Table 1.1 cell 1 represents that with which we are all immediately acquainted. This is our private experience of being who we are and living in our world. It is a largely unshared, subjective experience open to no one but ourselves. However, as we suggest later, it may be possible to explore this space scientifically and systematically. For example, Irwin and Whitehead (1991) asked whether the methods of psychophysics could be applied to the experience of pain to give us a more objective measurement of an individual's subjective experience.

Cell 2 represents the inner world of all beings other than ourselves. Of course, we have no direct experience of the subjective world of others. But we can ask such intriguing yet unanswerable questions as, "What does it feel like to be you?" "Do my cats experience the world as I do?" "Do you and I both see a red apple as the same color?" Some researchers in psychology try to understand how other people perceive the world and how those people might represent their perceptions internally (compare Shepard, 1983; Simon, 1978). Such a researcher is interested in the experience of other people as they deal with their world cognitively.

For example, Simon and others have sought to describe how expert and novice chess players decide on making a particular move. They found that a chess expert does not plan ahead any further than a novice does. This is only one of the many observations cognitive scientists have made as they try to understand how we experience and process the world around us. In seeking to understand how someone experiences the world, clinical and personality researchers have studied the types of associations that one has to different categories of knowledge, as well as the manner in which certain groups (for example, schizophrenics) experience the world. Physiological psychologists also consider questions from cell 2 when they ask whether the nervous system of a cat produces a view of reality different from that produced by the nervous system of a human.

Cell 3 represents our outward behavior: "How do I appear in the eyes of others?" Some aspects of psychology, such as psychotherapy, may focus on helping people learn about how

"ALTHOUGH HUMANS MAKE SOUNDS WITH THEIR MOUTHS AND OCCASIONALLY LOOK AT EACH OTHER, THERE IS NO SOLID EVIDENCE THAT THEY ACTUALLY COMMUNICATE WITH EACH OTHER."

others perceive them. We could also ask, "How am I represented in the sensory system of nonhuman organisms?"

Cell 4 represents the behaviors of other people or animals that anyone can directly observe, measure, or objectify. Included are physiological responses such as heart rate or electroencephalogram (EEG) measures, as well as self-report responses, as in a memory experiment. This cell has been the traditional domain of psychological research throughout the 20th century.

We can use the four ways of studying psychological processes presented in Table 1.1 to ask how we might conduct a science of behavior and experience. In cell 1 we ask, "How do I study my own inner experience?" In cell 2 we ask, "How do I study your inner experience?" In cell 3 we ask, "How do I study my own behavior in terms of how others see me?" In cell 4, the one we focus on most in this book, we ask, "How do I study your behavior?"

But what about the subjective experience of participants in psychological experiments? We cannot study these subjective experiences directly using the methods we know today. However, we can use a research participant's behavior, which includes self-report, as a means of learning about his or her internal world. That we use behavior to study subjective experience indirectly is an important idea. Consequently, it will be helpful to step back and discuss the idea in some depth.

BEHAVIOR: A ROAD INTO THE SUBJECTIVE EXPERIENCE OF RESEARCH PARTICIPANTS

Sometimes we want to ask questions that are difficult for participants in scientific experiments to answer directly. For example, we cannot just ask an animal (other than humans) directly whether it is color-blind or what particular color it sees. However, we can create situations in which an animal would display different behavior in the presence or absence of a particular color. We discuss this and other approaches later in this section. There are also cognitive, emotional, and out-of-awareness processes that are difficult to identify even in humans. For example, how can you explain an image you have in your head? How do we know when someone is dreaming?

At times, we are able to answer such questions through the use of **marker variables.** A marker variable is an event that occurs along with the process we are studying. For example, Aserinsky and Kleitman (1953) discovered that dreaming was accompanied by rapid movements of the eyes; hence, the state in which dreaming occurs is called rapid eye movement (REM) sleep. In neuropsychology research we may want to know whether people can perceive certain forms or patterns after damage to a particular part of the brain that leaves them without personal awareness of what they have seen. For example, such people may be able to recognize that they have seen a face but not that the face was of a person they had known. It is possible to use psychophysiological markers in such cases, particularly electrodermal activity, to demonstrate that a person with brain damage is physiologically able in the absence of conscious recognition to differentiate between faces from his or her past and unknown faces.

There is even a phenomenon called *blindsight,* in which people who are normally blind and say they see nothing can correctly identify the locations of particular patterns in experimental situations. Surprising as it may seem, Kolb and Braum (1995) used a similar blindsight procedure with normal-sighted people to suggest that information can guide behavior without entering subjective awareness. If this is true, then this suggests that we can be influenced by experiences but not be aware of them, as well as be aware of how experiences influence our decisions. But how can we study this? At Oxford University in England, Navindra Persaud, Peter McLeod, and Alan Cowey (2007) had been studying an individual with blindsight. They asked him to make a bet on whether he had seen a stimulus or not. Thus, he had to perform two tasks. The first was to say whether a pattern on the computer screen was present or not. The second was to bet on how certain he was. What these researchers discovered was even though he was correct about the presence of a stimulus 70% of the time, he was correct in his bet only 50% of the time. This suggested that although he could process the stimuli, he was not aware of them or otherwise he would have been more correct in his bets.

To follow up on this, these researchers asked college students to play a card game called the Iowa gambling task. The goal of the game is to win as much money as possible. At the beginning of the game, the students were given $400. Then the participants picked a card from one of four stacks of cards. When they turned the card over, the card told them whether they had won or lost money. They did this 100 times. Before the participants turned a card over, they could place a bet of either $10 or $20. The participants could choose from any of the four stacks. Unknown to them, two of the stacks of cards were set up to result in the participants winning on average, and the other two stacks to result in greater losses. A variety of studies showed that after about 40 cards, participants began to choose mainly from the two stacks that resulted in positive outcomes. However, it was only after about 70 trials that the participants begin to optimize their betting. This suggested to these researchers that unconscious learning comes before conscious awareness, and that betting can be a way to measure the beginning of awareness in a task (Persaud, McLeod, & Cowey, 2007).

What if we want to study what appear to be nontraditional claims? For example, Cytowic (1989) was interested in studying the process of *synesthesia:* perceiving with a different sense than would usually be the case. He studied people who said they saw colors when music was played or perceived weight when tasting an intense flavor. How you go about researching difficult processes may be different in each case, but it will still rely on inference, or drawing conclusions based on theoretical and experimental situations.

Assume that you want to know whether an animal sees colors. You cannot directly experience what the animal experiences in the presence of color; you must find a method for asking the animal. You must accept that you can never scientifically answer the question directly, but you can answer it indirectly. That is, you begin by reasoning how the animal's behavior would be different in the presence and in the absence of color. You can create a situation in which being able to experience color is necessary for the animal to solve a certain problem.

One way this problem has been approached is through the use of a conditioning paradigm using a Skinner box or similar apparatus. The Skinner box was designed for use with small animals such as rats or pigeons. It contains a lever on one wall near a food dish. Most Skinner boxes are electronically automated so that a single press or a certain number of presses on the lever causes food to be dropped into the dish. For example, you could program the food-delivery system in such a manner that the animal would receive food each time the lever was pressed when a light of a particular color (for example, green) was on. When either a light of another color (for example, blue) or no light was on, the animal would not receive food for pressing the lever. How do you think the animal would respond if it could see colors? How would it respond if it could not see colors?

Imagine yourself as this animal, and you will see how we could use the animal's behavior to tell us whether it can distinguish green from blue. If, as an animal, you could see colors, then you would soon learn to press the lever only when the green light was on and not to press the lever when either the blue light or no light was on. What if you could not see colors? When would you press the lever? You would probably learn quickly not to press the lever when no light was on. But what about when there was a green or blue light on? If you could not see colors, you would never distinguish between the blue and the green light. Thus, you would probably guess whenever either light was on.

If we made systematic recordings of your lever pressing over a period of time, we would be able to infer whether you could distinguish a blue light from a green one. We might then set up other discrimination problems (red versus blue, yellow versus green, and so forth). From this information, we could infer whether you could see colors. In our approach to solving this problem, we could use two techniques for inferring the experience of our research participants.

The first would be to create a situation in which different experiences give rise to different behaviors. The second would be to imagine oneself as the research participant and role-play the responses to gain an experimental perspective. Of course, this second technique is difficult to use when the organism (for example, a bat or a dolphin) has a nervous system sensitive to entirely different stimuli. Also, we must avoid the mistake of assuming that other organisms (or even other humans) think, feel, and act in the same manner as we do.

The scientific study of experience rests on the assumption that a person's behavior is a manifestation of what he or she is experiencing. This assumption is made whether we are studying how animals see colors or how a baby distinguishes his or her parents from other adults. (How might you conduct this experiment?) If we are studying human emotions, we may assume that aggressive, attacking behaviors are related in some way to an experience of anger in our research participants.

In a similar way, if we are studying factors that facilitate the experience of joy in preschool children, we might take increased laughter as evidence that joyful experiences have taken place. In these cases we use the behavior of our research participants (aggressive attacks and laughter) to study their subjective experiences (anger and joy). Seen in this light, *behavior and experience are two sides of the same coin.* In the case of anger, for example, the research participant's feeling of anger is the internal and unseen experiential aspect, and the research participant's aggressive attacks are the external and observable behavioral aspects. In a preceding section, we saw how Galen inferred his patient's love for Pylades when he observed her behavioral—in this case, physiological—reactions to hearing Pylades's name.

The use of objective behavior to study subjective experience is by no means new. We are all good at reading the psychological states of people from their behavior. If your professor walks into class with a scowl, you immediately assume that he or she is experiencing some sort of negative emotion. In science, however, we would go a step further and test our assumption.

For example, MacLeod, Mathews, and Tata (1986) were interested in whether anxious people tended to pick out either socially or physically threatening words (such as *failure* or *cancer*) when presented with both threatening and nonthreatening words. In more technical terms, was there a processing bias for encoding emotionally threatening information?

In an intriguing study, these researchers asked research participants to watch a computer screen on which both threatening and nonthreatening words were presented quickly. During the study, a dot would appear on the screen, and the research participants were instructed to press a button as fast as possible when they saw the dot. At times, the dot appeared at the location just occupied by a threatening word, and at other times in the location occupied by a nonthreatening word. It was reasoned that if the research participants' reaction times were shorter in the case of the threatening words than the nonthreatening words, then it could be inferred that the research participants were directing their gaze to the threatening words. That is, by measuring the reaction time from the appearance of the dot to the time the individual pressed the button, these researchers were able to infer the manner in which emotionally threatening words are processed. From the results of the study, the authors concluded that in comparison to nonanxious people, anxious people shift their attention toward emotionally threatening words.

It should be stressed that the use of objective behavior and appearances to study phenomena that cannot be observed directly, such as subjective experience, is not unique to psychology; it is a common feature of all sciences. For example, in physics we discuss the construct *gravity,* yet we never see gravity. Instead, we observe the movement of objects toward the earth and make inferences about gravity. Nor do we study magnetism directly, but we do observe the movements of iron filings, iron bars, charged particles, and various types of gauges, and we make inferences about magnetism.

In the same way, Semmelweis never saw a physician carrying germs into the delivery room; indeed, at that time germs could not even be seen. Yet using indirect evidence, Semmelweis was able to pinpoint the unobservable but very real cause of the mothers' deaths. A construct is a concept used in a particular theoretical manner that ties together a number of observations. In a nutshell, many major constructs of science—such as gravity, time, evolution, electricity, genetic transmission, learning, and even life itself—are discussed and examined indirectly through their manifestations in the physical world. Thus, in science we use the observation of physical events to make inferences about not only the physical world but also the unseen processes that underlie it.

✓	CONCEPT CHECK 1.3	You read in a newspaper that dogs can hear tones that humans cannot hear. How might you design an experiment to test this?

THE PEOPLE WHO PERFORM SCIENCE

As we said at the beginning of the chapter, science is a human activity; only people perform it, and all people perform it in one form or another. It is important to remember that all people means *all* people. This reality is not portrayed accurately in the movies and on television. Typically a white man in a white lab coat is shown, and often not a very interesting one at that. However, this is only part of the truth. Men and women of all races are scientists. Not only is it true today, but it also has always been the case.

Every great culture has an important history of scientific achievements, whether it is in mathematics, physics, chemistry, or the social sciences. It is clear that all people of the world are represented in the history of science. However, some people are more visible than others, and sometimes we do not even see the people who are there. For example, you may have heard of the Ladd-Franklin theory of color vision and assumed it to be the work of Mr. Ladd and Mr. Franklin when in fact it was the work of Ms. Christine Ladd-Franklin in the early 1900s (Furumoto, 1992; Scarborough & Furumoto, 1987).

It is important to remember that women have been an integral part of psychology since its beginning as a science more than 100 years ago. In fact, even from the beginning, psychology has had a larger percentage of women than any other scientific discipline (Furumoto & Scarborough, 1986). Although we say this, we know that some students in our classes still do not believe that they can become scientists because of their race or gender. We hope that those who believe this way will reconsider this assumption or at least gather data to test their hypothesis. To this end, there are websites directed at sharing information for minor-ity students interested in a career in science (for example, http://sciencecareers.sciencemag .org/career_development/miscinet). There are also websites directed at women in science (for example, http://www.sciencecareersweb.net/PSU2DE/WomenInScience.htm).

Another meaning of the statement that science is a human activity is that we perform science with the support of and in communication with other scientists. Because a group of people shares our search and values, it is possible for scientists to work together as a larger body of searchers after truth. Sometimes scientists communicate with each other harmoniously, and new discoveries and formulations are the result of the work of many different people. At other times, the opposite is the case. As if in a race, the individual scientist, hoping to be the first to make a discovery, competes against other scientists and even against scientists as a group.

Remember, performing science is just one role or activity of scientists. Scientists are people, and as people they do what people everywhere do. They love and hate. They have good ideas, and they have bad ideas. They have thoughts and feelings. Some may want attention and fame, and others may want to be left alone. Scientists feel lonely and sad as well as happy and gregarious. Science is not a means for avoiding what is human within us, although some scientists try to use science in this way. Science is merely a systematic way of using experience to test our ideas about the world.

At times in our history, we have forgotten that scientists are human. We have thought of scientists as *objective,* without feeling, and oblivious to the human condition in general and to what is going on around them in particular. To be sure, there have been such instances, but in these cases it is the failure of the witness and not of the scientist or the research participant that is the basis of the problem. When we discuss ethics, we develop this idea further.

In the final analysis, the human sensitivity of scientists adds life and spirit to the scientific enterprise. Thus, what is unique about science is not the people who are scientists but their methods and the relationships between the people who practice science with these methods.

KEY TERMS AND CONCEPTS

1. **Nature of science**
   A. Roles of scientist, research participant, and witness
2. **Ways of accepting knowledge**
   A. Tenacity
   B. Authority
   C. Reason
   D. Common sense
   E. Science
3. **The scientific approach**
   A. Verifiable through experience
   B. Newton's rules of reasoning
4. **Examples of early approaches to science**
   A. Croesus and the establishment of criteria for evaluation

B. Galen and the examination of alternative factors
C. Semmelweis and the development of a series of studies

5. **Studying behavior and experience**
   A. Empiricism
   B. Studying experience through behavior
   C. Use of constructs
6. **The nature of scientists**
   A. Science is performed by people.
   B. All people perform some type of science.
   C. Science requires the support of and communication with others.

SUMMARY

1. The purpose of this chapter is to introduce you to science as an approach to learning about ourselves and our world. As a problem-solving approach, science offers an important means of evaluating ideas.
2. People have used a variety of ways of accepting or rejecting ideas throughout history. Basing our approach on the work of Charles Peirce, we discussed the strengths and weaknesses of five of these (tenacity,

authority, reason, common sense, and science). We also discussed pseudoscience and superstition.
3. Science is useful for evaluating ideas because it is self-corrective; that is, results from experiments offer a feedback mechanism to help clarify ideas.
4. For thousands of years, people have tried to understand their world better. We looked at three historical events to help clarify the scientific approach. The

(continued)

SUMMARY (*continued*)

stories of Croesus, Galen, and Semmelweis pointed to the need for unambiguous statements, the need for testing factors that do and do not affect behavior, and the importance of a carefully designed series of observations. In sum, science combines experience, reason, and a desire to answer questions about reality.

5. Psychology is interested in the study of outer appearances (behavior) as well as inner experiences. Using a schema presented by Schumacher, we asked how we might study the behavior and experience of ourselves and others.

6. There are times when researchers want to know about the internal processing of an organism but either cannot or, as we discuss in later chapters, do not want to ask directly. Because we can assume that an organism's behavior is related to its experience, we can ask such questions as, "Does a cat see colors?" or "Can babies tell the difference between their parents and other adults?" In this manner, we use behavior to make inferences concerning the inner worlds of various organisms.

REVIEW QUESTIONS

1. What are the ways of accepting or rejecting ideas, as suggested by Peirce?
2. What is pseudoscience?
3. Discuss the changes in science before and after the time of Galileo.
4. How is science self-corrective?
5. In simple language, what are Newton's four rules of reasoning?
6. What was progressive about Croesus's approach to the oracles?
7. How was Galen's approach scientific?
8. How did Semmelweis approach the problem of mothers dying soon after childbirth?
9. Give some examples of what would be included in a discussion of behavior and experience and how modern psychology approaches these areas.
10. Describe an experiment that would show whether an animal is color-blind.

DISCUSSION QUESTIONS AND PROJECTS

Questions in this section are based on ideas presented in the text and require you to use what you have learned or to draw from your own experience. Some of the questions are designed to stimulate discussion; they have no single right answer.

1. While watching television, pick out five commercials and notice the way in which they try to convince you that their products are good. Which of Peirce's ways of knowing do they suggest? (*Hint:* Some of the suggestions may be nonverbal; for instance, the use of a famous person suggests knowledge through authority.)
2. Discuss the statement "Science is above all a human activity."
3. Discuss how the roles of scientist, research participant, and witness are exemplified and portrayed in our society. What different disciplines in a college or university are devoted to each of these roles?
4. It was suggested that science is a self-corrective process. What are the advantages and disadvantages of a self-corrective system?

5. Develop an experiment that would determine whether someone who was unable to speak could experience emotions.
6. Name some constructs that cannot be seen but are important in our everyday lives.
7. Discuss how you might study your own behavior. For example, how would you determine whether you practiced your guitar better in the morning or at night? How could you determine the effects of extra sleep on your school work and on your feelings in general? What could you do to get your professor to tell better jokes?
8. A researcher was looking for the reasons people fail in college. To help answer this question, the researcher took a group of students who flunked out of college and a group of students who got good grades. Both groups were given a test of self-esteem. It was found that the group that flunked out had lower self-esteem than the group that did not. From this the researcher concluded that low self-esteem is one of the causes of failure in college. Comment on this conclusion.

INFOTRAC COLLEGE EDITION: EXERCISES

Throughout this book, we will give you sources of information that are found on the Internet. We begin this most intensively in Chapter 3. However, for now we want to acquaint you with a source of information available with this book, InfoTrac College Edition. This is a wide-ranging source of information including encyclopedias, reference books, magazines, and scientific journals. To learn about InfoTrac College Edition, you should go to its website at http://infotrac.thomsonlearning.com. Enter the site and then the password included with this book. Once you are into the system, enter the name Semmelweis, whom you learned about in this chapter, and read about his life in one of the reference books available. You can also enter particular terms, such as *empiricism*, and learn more about those subjects. Throughout the book, if you encounter a specific scientific phenomenon in a chapter, such as REM sleep or blindsight, that you wish to know about, you can enter those terms.

As an exercise, use InfoTrac College Edition to find an article entitled "The gestural origins of language," by Michael C. Corballis. (*Hint:* Enter the author's name and you will also see other articles this author has written.) The article was published in the March–April 1999 issue of *American Scientist*. In reading this article, think about how scientists use logic and reason to understand processes that are difficult to study in a laboratory. In this case, scientists were studying the role that gestures have played in the evolution of human language.

You may also be interested in articles on career development in women, which can be found by entering "Women and career development." You will see a variety of articles discussing this topic in a variety of journals. You will also see a review of this area by Susan Phillips and Anne Imhoff. This article was published in the 1997 volume of the *Annual Review of Psychology*.

As you will learn, you can use InfoTrac College Edition to find articles on a variety of topics. For example, if you are interested in posttraumatic stress disorder, you can enter that term. You will see a variety of articles including one published in August of 2004 in the *British Journal of Psychology* titled "Post-traumatic stress disorder and anxiety symptoms in children exposed to the 1999 Greek earthquake" by David Groome and Anastasia Soureti. You can also see how researchers have studied superstition in an article by Marjaana Linderman and Marieke Saher in the *British Journal of Psychology* in 2007. A newspaper report in the January 23, 2007, *New York Times* article entitled "Do you believe in magic?" by Benedict Carey describes studies of magical thinking across the world. Finally, if you check the box to limit the search "to refereed publications," you will obtain only references from peer-reviewed journals.

If you go to the Wadsworth Psychology Resource Center at http://www.wadsworth.com/psychology_d/templates/student_resources/workshops/workshops.html, you will find workshops related to research methods and statistics. The first workshop asks the question, "What Is Science?" As you go through this workshop, you will see many of the concepts that you just read about in this chapter.

☑ Answers to Concept Checks

1.1 Although it is possible that cancer could be cured in the next year, the basis of your acceptance was authority, not science. Accepting what a famous person says, whether he or she is a scientist, the president, or a 6-year-old child, is a reliance on authority, not science. Science requires that the information be evaluated through observation and reason according to an established procedure. As you will see, we could accept the statement that a particular type of cancer would be affected by a particular treatment as a hypothesis to be tested. After the test, we could make a scientific statement about the hypothesis.

1.2 One major reason Semmelweis's approach was superior was that he sought to determine not only what *did* influence an event but also what *did not*.

That is, he sought to determine which factors were not related to the deaths of the mothers as well as the one that was. Another important reason was that he used a series of observations to test his question. Whether ESP is real is in no way related to why Semmelweis's approach was more productive than that of Croesus.

1.3 An easy way to test this hypothesis is to observe the dog's reaction to the tones. If you want to determine which tones the dog can or cannot hear, then you can pair each tone with a cue for receiving food. You will need to make sure that the dog does not use any of its other senses to obtain the food. For example, you will not want the dog to be able to see you producing the tones.

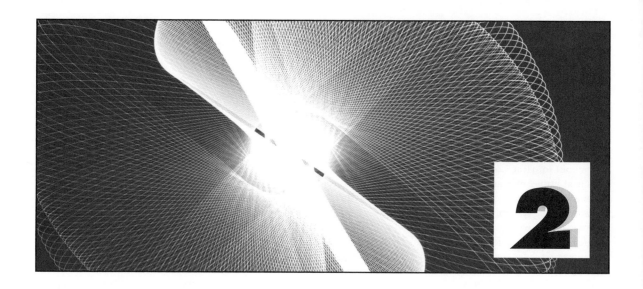

INTRODUCTION TO THE METHODS OF SCIENCE

NATURALISTIC OBSERVATION

THE CORRELATIONAL APPROACH

THE EXPERIMENTAL METHOD
Definitions in the Experimental Method
Causation
Exploratory Research

LOGIC AND INFERENCE: THE DETECTIVE
WORK OF SCIENCE
Validity
Propositional Logic

SCIENTIFIC OBSERVATION: THE RAW
DATA OF SCIENCE

EVALUATING SCIENTIFIC RESEARCH

COMMUNICATION IN SCIENCE

Most of us remember how different our first few weeks of college were from anything we had known before. Remember how you expected your roommate or your professor to act, and how you reacted when they did not act that way? If you stop and think about your first reactions to college, you can see that there were three aspects of these experiences. First, there was an idea or expectation concerning what was about to happen in college. Second, there was the actual experience of what did happen during those first few weeks—and it was probably quite different, at least in some respects, from what you had expected. Third, there was the resulting reorganization of your ideas about college and the potential impact of this experience on your life.

The methods of science closely parallel these three aspects of your experience. First, scientists begin with an idea or expectation. As we will discuss, a formally stated expectation is called a *hypothesis*. The scientist says, "I expect this to happen under these conditions," and thus states the hypothesis. Second, scientists look to experience to evaluate the accuracy of their ideas or expectations about the world. That is, they try to find or create the situation that will allow them to observe what they are interested in studying. Through observation and experimentation, scientists can begin to evaluate their ideas and expectations about the world. As mentioned in Chapter 1, learning about the world through observation and experimentation is an example of *empiricism,* which means nothing more than the acceptance of sensory information as valid. Third, on the basis of their observations and experiments, scientists seek to draw conclusions or inferences about their ideas and expectations. They reorganize their ideas and consider the impact of the new information on their theoretical conceptualizations.

As mentioned earlier, science is a way of determining what we can infer about the world. In its simplest form, the scientific method consists of asking a question about the world and then experiencing the world to determine the answer. When we begin an inquiry, what we already know about our topic leaves us in one of a number of positions. In some cases, we know little about our topic, or our topic may be very complex. Consequently, our ideas and questions are general. For example, how does our memory work? What causes mental illness? What factors make a fruitful marriage? How can we model the brain?

If little is known about a particular phenomenon, it often is useful simply to watch the phenomenon occur naturally and get a general idea of what is involved in the process. Initially, this is accomplished by observing and describing what occurs. This scientific technique is called **naturalistic observation.**

A classic example of this approach is Charles Darwin's observation of animals in the Galápagos Islands, which formed the basis of his theory of evolution. More recently, the study of animals in the wild has led to new insights into animal cognition and social systems. Scientists have continued to return to the Galápagos Islands with more advanced methods (such as observing molecular DNA changes) and still continue to update and confirm Darwin's original ideas. (See Weiner, 1994, for a review of this work.)

Another example of this method has come from observing female dwarf mongooses in Tanzania's Serengeti National Park over several years (Morell, 1996). Before this research was conducted, it was assumed that the dominant female in a pack of animals would be under the least stress and the subordinate females under the most. However, by examining some 14 packs of animals, scientists have found that dominant female mongooses show the highest level of cortisol, a stress hormone, when compared with all other females in the pack. Other researchers (for example, De Waal, 2000) seek to understand how animals and humans use peacemaking to resolve aggressive episodes. Did you know that chimpanzees, like humans, often kiss their partner on the mouth after a fight?

At other times, we may want to understand certain aspects of a complex system with the goal of better describing how one aspect of the system may be associated with another aspect. For example, we may want to know whether people who have friends have fewer health-related problems than people who do not or whether eating certain foods is associated with not having cancer. How would you go about answering such questions? One way is to examine and note the relationship between a person's health and the number of friends that person has. But how are you to understand these data? Look at an example of a similar question of the relationship between smoking tobacco and having lung cancer. The first step is to ask whether two events go together. In this example, researchers sought to determine whether, when one event occurred (a person smoked tobacco), the other event also occurred (the person had cancer). Such a scientific approach is called by various names, including the **correlational approach.**

As we will see later in this book, just finding that a relationship exists between two events does not allow us to determine exactly what that relationship is, much less to determine that one event actually caused the other event to happen. If we want to state that one event produced another event, we need to develop a much stronger case for our position. For example, we could see how some single event over which we have control affects the phenomenon we are studying. To do this, we begin to interact with the phenomenon. We structure our question in this form: "If I do this, what will happen?" Numerous questions can be asked in this way, such as, "Will you learn words better if each word is of the same class (for example, food words) than if they are from different classes (foods, cars, and toys)?"

As our knowledge grows, we may even get to the point of formulating specific predictions. In this case, our questions are structured in the form, "If I do this, I expect this will happen." Sometimes our predictions are more global, and we predict that one factor will be stronger than another. We might predict that more people are likely to help a stranger if they perceive the environment to be safe than if they think it is dangerous. Sometimes, however, we may know enough about an area to make a more precise prediction, or *point prediction.* For example, we might predict that 3 months of exercise will lead to a 10-mm Hg decrease in blood pressure. These approaches, in which we interact directly with the phenomenon we are studying, are examples of the **experimental method.**

During the 1980s a different type of scientific approach was developed within psychology, especially in response to cognitive questions. The approach was based less on observation or direct manipulation than on attempting to establish a model (either conceptual or mathematical) capable of performing operations similar to the topic being studied. This approach is called **modeling.** For example, Freeman and his colleagues asked whether they could develop a model based on calculus that would mimic the brain's electrical patterns of an animal sensing odors (Freeman, 1991, 1999, 2004).

Rumelhart and McClelland (1986) instituted a broad program of modeling in which they sought to model human cognitive processes by assuming that the architecture of the brain is that of a massive parallel processing machine. Testing such models requires that one compare the output of the model with that obtained in actual experimentation. For example, Cohen, Dunbar, and McClelland (1990) compared simulated data based on their model and actual data from an experiment in the performance of a Stroop color-word task. Other models have been developed to describe how individuals choose among a variety of choices such as which automobile to buy (Usher & McClelland, 2004) or how English text as you are reading now is encoded (Martin, 2004). Although these techniques are beyond the scope of this text, we want you to know about their existence.

Before we continue, we want to emphasize that there is no set number of methods for practicing science. Methods are developed in response to specific questions. Often our area of study determines which methods we use. For example, in sciences such as astronomy and zoology, scientists often use **retrospective,** or **post hoc** (after the fact), **methods;** like Darwin, a zoologist might ask how a certain species developed. Clinical psychologists use similar methods when they speculate on the development of personality or the origin of mental illness. Other areas of psychology may rely on *single-case approaches* when the problem they are studying is rare, such as a specific brain disorder.

For example, Antoine Bechara and his colleagues studied three patients with particular lesions or injuries to areas deep within their brains (Bechara et al., 1995). The first patient had damage to the hippocampus, the second had damage to the amygdala, and the third had damage to both areas. Using a classic conditioning procedure in which a loud sound (unconditioned stimulus) is paired with a color or sound (conditioned stimulus), these researchers were able to show different effects depending on the type of damage to the brain. In particular, damage to the amygdala resulted in a lack of conditioning, but the person was able to describe the color or tone paired with the unconditioned stimulus of a loud sound. However, damage to the hippocampus resulted in the opposite effect: The person did show conditioning but could not describe the conditioned stimuli. The person with damage to both areas of the brain neither knew about the stimuli nor showed the effects of conditioning. We discuss single-case experiments as well as case study and other approaches to research later in this book.

We also want you to know about another approach, called **qualitative methods** (Camic, Rhodes, & Yardley, 2003; Leong & Austin, 1996; Taylor & Bogdan, 1998). Actually you already know about qualitative methods, since you often ask your friends what they think about a certain movie or how they like particular pieces of music. Qualitative methods emphasize the subjective state of the person under study and are particularly useful when we wish to describe the experience of a particular person or group. For example, there are times when it is important to understand how clients experience various forms of psychotherapy, what the experience of depression is for a particular person, or even how parents experience their children or their parenting roles. The focus group, in which individuals talk about a particular topic, consumer product, or political candidate, is one type of qualitative research.

Qualitative research is useful when you initially study ongoing processes or seek to understand little-researched processes. For example, Martin, Sadlo, and Stew (2006) asked individuals to describe their experience of boredom, which helped these authors suggest how future research in this area should be conducted. In another qualitative study, Deutsch and Saxon (1998) interviewed mothers and fathers concerning how much praise or criticism each participant received from others concerning the amount of time spent in parenting and at work. Thus, one aspect of the qualitative tradition is a reliance on the phenomenological or subjective aspect of experience. There can be a real richness and depth in the description of subjective experiences. This approach has a long history in philosophy and sociology and has recently gained recognition in psychology. For example, qualitative approaches reveal that some parents of young children with conduct disorders often feel that they are being held hostage by the situation and lose contact with their partners. This work by Webster-Stratton and Spitzer (1996) describes the progression from coping efforts, to intense feelings of inadequacy, to feelings of helplessness in such parents. Such insight into the subjective feelings of parents of oppositional and aggressive children may help therapists develop better approaches for both the parents and the children in such situations.

An interesting and important approach in qualitative research is called the *action-project method* (Young, Valach, & Domene, 2005). In this approach, individuals are videotaped discussing a particular topic. The individuals then watch the video separately, and the video is stopped at natural points approximately every minute. Each person comments on how he or she thought or felt during specific segments. These reactions form the data for the qualitative analysis. By repeating the process over a period of time, this procedure could be used to study various relationships, for example, between adolescents and their parents. An intriguing use of this technique is with suicide attempters (Valach, Michel, Dey, & Young, 2002). Often studies of people who have attempted suicide rely on interviews with mental health workers (for example, Valach, Michel, Young, & Dey, 2006). For a variety of reasons, people who have recently attempted suicide often hold back or withdraw in these interviews. However, having these people watch the interviews on videotape and comment on their thoughts and feelings supplies the qualitative researcher with additional, and sometimes more informative, data than the original interview itself.

A variety of sources are available for understanding qualitative research, including the journal *Qualitative Research in Psychology* and various books (for example, Camic, Rhodes, & Yardley, 2003) and chapters in books (for example, Babbie, 2008, which discusses qualitative methods in relation to field research). For an overview in relation to clinical psychology, the interested reader should consult Kazdin (2003b). As with any approach, the question arises of how to view the trustworthiness of the information presented, which is a topic of debate within the field of qualitative methods (Leong & Austin, 1996).

In contrast to qualitative methods, the methods we emphasize in this book often are called **quantitative methods.** Using quantitative methods, there is generally an emphasis on behavior as opposed to experience as well as an attempt to describe constructs in terms of numbers and find laws or patterns that describe behavioral processes. In this chapter, we focus on three main approaches: *naturalistic observation, correlational approaches,* and *experimental manipulation.*

Let's consider the relationship between the scientist and the research participant in each method. With the naturalistic method, the scientist is passive and observes carefully the activity of the research participant. In this method, the scientist does not try to change the environment of the research participant. The research participant simply goes about normal activity and the scientist watches, preferably without influencing the participant's behavior. In this way, the scientist can make a detailed description of some aspect of the research participant's natural behavior.

In contrast, when using the experimental method, the scientist is more active, and the research participant's activities are restricted. The scientist intentionally structures the situation so that he or she can study the effect of a particular factor on the research participant's behavior. In between these two approaches are correlational methods, which may range from simple observation and correlation of factors to a more active manipulation, although without the same degree of manipulation and control characteristic of the experimental method.

As an analogy, we can view each method as an extension of the way a child explores his or her world, although the scientist and the child have very different goals in mind. A common way children and scientists begin to explore a new phenomenon is simply to watch it occur naturally. In the process of watching, the child and the scientist may describe what they see. However, the scientist usually goes further and uses mathematical terms to specify what is being seen. As a further step, both children and scientists extend their observations by means of limited interaction with the phenomenon.

Once we as scientists begin to see the relationship involved in a particular phenomenon, we can study it more precisely with more controlled manipulations. From this understanding, we may even move from science to technology and use our understanding profitably in our everyday lives. This general approach works for a child, and it works for scientists, too, although on a more complex level.

To provide you with a more accurate conception of how the scientific method is an extension of our everyday activities, we examine the three fundamental scientific strategies mentioned previously: the naturalistic observation technique, which is akin to a child observing a phenomenon; the experimental method, which is akin to a child interacting with the phenomenon to learn more about it; and the correlational approach, which, depending on the situation, may be more or less like either of the other two methods. Let us now turn to a more detailed discussion of each method.

NATURALISTIC OBSERVATION

Imagine that it is 20,000 years in the future and you have been sent to a strange part of the galaxy to study members of a particular species that have been described by astronauts as "cultural apes." Assume that you could arrive at the appointed place and remain undetected. Because you know virtually nothing about these cultural apes, the method of naturalistic observation would be an efficient way to get a general idea of these beings.

Like many scientists who have studied animals in the wild on 19th- and 20th-century earth, you might set up a blind so that you would not be detected and observe the behavior of these apes. Often with animals in the wild, scientists try to find a place where the animals come together, such as a watering hole, and set up an observation post near this place. After some preliminary observations, you find that these cultural apes meet every morning in large structures. Consequently, you set up your observation post within one of these structures. Assuming that you remain undetected, what would you do next?

The answer is deceptively simple yet difficult to accomplish. *You just watch.* "Just watching" might be compared to seeing a movie in a foreign language that you do not understand. It is easy to see the interactions between the actors in the movie, yet you can only guess what they mean. In the beginning, the most difficult part of just watching is not to guess. Until you have observed a given interaction repeatedly, you can easily distort what you are seeing by your expectation that it occurs in a certain way. After much observation, you may begin to notice certain patterns of behavior by the apes. For example, they may say "Hello" each time they meet and "Good-bye" each time they leave each other. One hallmark of naturalistic observation is the discovery of patterns in the behaviors of different organisms.

An important part of the naturalistic technique is to record what you observe. At one time, the only method of recording was to reduce the observations to written notes or drawn pictures, much as Darwin did when he went to the Galápagos Islands. Today, however, we can record the observed behavior digitally so that we can listen or watch the behavior at a later time. Of course, scientists are still an important part of the process because they select what will be recorded and thus determine the observations for later analysis. So once we have observed many instances of the typical behavior of this species, we can withdraw from our observation post and begin to analyze our recorded observations. We now can begin to make summary statements about the natural ongoing behavior of these species.

Coming down to earth, let's consider the work of one scientist who has used the naturalistic method. Nikolaas Tinbergen (who received the Nobel Prize for his research) became interested in autistic children. Because little was known about the overall behavior of autistic children, Tinbergen began his work by using the naturalistic observation method and simply observed autistic children (Tinbergen & Tinbergen, 1972). Autistic children do not communicate with others. Often they just walk around making sounds to themselves or hitting their heads against a wall. As Tinbergen watched these children, he observed that there was a pattern to their abnormal behavior in that this behavior appeared most often when they were in an unfamiliar social situation. Even a smile from a stranger might be followed by an attempt by the autistic child to withdraw from the situation.

Tinbergen also was interested in how autistic children were different from "normal" children. To understand these differences, Tinbergen observed normal children and also children with varying degrees of autism. He found that some facial expressions displayed by the autistic children differed from those of the normal children. Thus, the naturalistic method offered a starting point for describing differences between autistic and normal children.

Another scientist who used the naturalistic method of observation is Konrad Lorenz. (Lorenz also received the Nobel Prize for his behavior research.) Lorenz (1952) described the behavioral interactions in a colony of jackdaws:

> A jackdaw sits feeding at the communal dish, a second bird approaches ponderously, in an attitude of self-display, with head proudly erected, whereupon the first visitor moves slightly to one side, but otherwise does not allow himself to be disturbed. Now comes a third bird, in a much more modest attitude which, surprisingly enough, puts the first bird to flight; the second, on the other hand, assumes a threatening pose, with his back feathers ruffled, attacks the latest comer and drives him from the spot. (p. 149)

At times, field observations may bring to light unknown patterns of behavior that in turn lead to new theories concerning these behaviors. For example, Nelson, Badura, and Goldman (1990) reviewed field studies showing a seasonal shift in the activity patterns of rodents. These animals tend to show the greatest amount of activity at night during the summer; in the winter, they show more activity during the daylight hours. Once a scientist knows an animal's patterns in the wild, ideas can be developed concerning the function such patterns serve as well as the mechanism that controls these patterns.

Rowsemitt (1986), for example, suggested that the winter/summer pattern of activity level in the rodents allows for better use of energy because being active during the winter day allows the animals to avoid extreme cold, and being active during the summer night allows them to avoid the extreme heat of day. To understand the mechanism that mediates the seasonal shift in activity patterns, a scientist may want to use the experimental method, which we discuss later in this chapter. Rowsemitt thought the change in the activity level of the rodent to be controlled by one particular hormone, testosterone, and centered his research in this area. However, one could also study a variety of other factors.

In summary, the naturalistic observation method has four characteristics:

1. Noninterference is of prime importance. Scientists using this method must not disrupt the process or flow of events. In this way we can see things as they really are, without influencing the ongoing phenomenon.

2. This method emphasizes the invariants or patterns that exist in the world. For example, if you could observe yourself in a noninterfering manner, you might conclude that your moods vary with the time of day, particular weather patterns, or even particular thoughts.

3. This method is most useful when we know little about the subject of our investigation. It is most useful for understanding the "big picture" by observing a series of events rather than isolated happenings.

4. The naturalistic method may not shed light on the factors that directly influence the behavior observed. The method provides a description of a phenomenon; it does not answer the question of why it happened.

To better understand how one variable is related to another, we use the correlational method. This method emphasizes scientists' ability to describe whether and to what degree two variables are associated with each other. Through this approach, scientists are better able to understand and describe our world.

THE CORRELATIONAL APPROACH

At times you may want to know whether a relationship exists between two events that cannot be manipulated easily. For example, you may want to know whether playing sports or drinking alcohol in high school is more associated with developing heart problems later in life. Barefoot, Dahlstrom, and Williams (1983) sought to determine whether one's emotionality (especially hostility) during medical school was associated with coronary heart disease later in life. In many studies of this type, it would be unethical or impractical to manipulate the events actively (for example, drinking alcohol in high school or provoking emotionality in graduate school). What you can do instead is collect information on the particular events under study without attempting to manipulate these events. Formally, we ask whether the frequency or magnitude of one event is related to the frequency or magnitude of the other event, but we do not attempt to establish how one event influences the other. This type of research is called correlational research or natural association research (Ray, 1989).

Correlation is a measure of association that we present statistically in Chapter 5. For now, we can introduce some of the basic ideas. In correlational studies, the researcher is interested in asking whether there is an association between two variables, but he or she does not attempt to establish how one variable influences the other. Establishing that such an association exists may be the first step in dealing with a complex problem.

For example, a physiological psychologist might ask whether a person's pulse rate is related to the age of the person. To answer this question, she could simply measure various people's heart rates and correlate these measures with their ages. What would this tell us? First, it would tell us how heart rate and age are related. If they were to increase together—that is, if low heart rates were associated with young ages, medium heart rates with middle ages, and high heart rates with older ages—then this relationship would be called a *positive correlation*. However, if low heart rates were associated with older ages and high heart rates with younger ages, then this relationship would be called a *negative correlation*. Of course, as you will see in Chapter 5, few relationships are perfectly related to one another. Thus, we use a mathematical technique, the correlation statistic, to reflect the *degree* of an association between two variables.

What we cannot know from correlational research is whether either variable influences the other. That is, if two variables are related, what might the reason be for the relationship? As you begin to suggest factors that might have produced a high degree of relationship, you realize that a third, unspecified variable actually may have influenced the two variables in the correlational study. Thus, the nature of a correlational study is to suggest relationships but not to suggest which variable influences which other variable.

It is often said that correlation does not imply causality. For example, a researcher might want to know whether a relationship exists between the type of food one eats and the likelihood of one having a heart attack. An approach would be to examine the diets of people who have had heart attacks and of those who have not. What if there were a high association between eating steak, for example, and heart attacks? You could conclude little other than that there was an association or correlation between the two variables. The association of two factors does not in itself imply that one influences the other. However, if there is a *low* correlation between the events, you can infer that one event does *not* cause the other. A high degree of association is always necessary for establishing that one variable influences another; a correlational study is often the first step for providing the needed support for later experimental research, especially in complex areas.

 CONCEPT CHECK 2.1   A physician reports data from a study that compares the amount of television a person watches with his or her health. The point is made that people who watch more television are sicker; therefore, watching TV is bad for your health. Someone in the audience says, "No! That is not the case. Sick people have nothing to do, so they watch TV." Whom do you believe?

THE EXPERIMENTAL METHOD

As we suggested, you already know a great deal about the experimental method. Indeed, all of us have used it in one form or another to explore our world since we were small children. Like the child, the scientist begins to interact with the phenomenon that he or she is studying and asks the question, "If I do this, what will happen?" From these interactions, the scientist gains increased understanding of the phenomenon under study. To test this understanding further, the scientist asks, "Was what happened really a result of what I did?"

To give you a more accurate understanding of how scientists learn from interacting with the environment, let's consider the following line of fictitious research. Before we actually describe the study, we want to suggest that you, both as a scientist and as an informed consumer, consider many of the "scientific" claims that you hear on television or read in magazines and look for alternative explanations to the claims being made. Thinking scientifically is not something you do only when you design experiments; rather, it is a way of approaching all information.

Assume that the makers of a brand of children's cereal, Roasty-Toasties, claim that their breakfast cereal helps children to grow. In their enthusiasm to demonstrate the claim and add "scientific evidence" to their television commercials, the company designed the following experiment. A group of children were given daily a bowl of Roasty-Toasties with cream, bananas, and sugar. After several months, each child was weighed. It was found that they gained an average of 8 pounds each. The company concluded that the weight increase was due to the nourishing breakfast, and consequently the company recommended this breakfast for all children. When a thoughtful scientist heard the results, he admitted to their appeal but added that several things bothered him. One thing was that the children also ate lunch and dinner. Consequently, the weight gain might be due to the food eaten at these other meals.

Dismayed that they had not thought of that, the company designed a new experiment. This time it used two groups of children. The average age and average weight were the same for each group. For breakfast, one group received the recommended cereal with cream, bananas, and sugar; the other was given scrambled eggs. The two groups ate approximately the same foods for lunch and dinner. After several months, each child was weighed. It was found that there was an average gain of 5 pounds in the group that received the recommended breakfast cereal and an average gain of only 1 pound in the group that was given eggs for breakfast.

The company was excited and assailed our thoughtful scientist with the new findings, which seemed to confirm the earlier results. The scientist pointed out that he was even more impressed than before. However, he grew silent again, looked up, and asked, "Could the weight gain be caused by the cream, sugar, and bananas and not by the cereal?" Although the company was confident that the results were due to the cereal, logically the scientist was right. The entire effect could have been due to the cream, sugar, and bananas, and not the cereal.

Crushed by the scientist's keen insight, the company's researchers returned to the laboratory. After much debate, they decided to do the following experiment. As before, one group received the cereal with cream, sugar, and bananas for breakfast, but now another group received equal amounts of cream, sugar, and bananas (but no cereal) each morning. Once again, lunch and dinner were approximately the same for both groups, and the children's weights at the onset of the study were about the same. The company researchers were confident of replicating the earlier findings. After several months, they weighed each child. Much to their dismay, they found that children in both groups gained an average of 5 pounds. The group that received cereal did not gain more weight than the other group.

■ Definitions in the Experimental Method

The goal of the fictitious study just described was to determine whether eating cereal affected the growth of a child. The **hypothesis,** or idea being tested, was that eating the new cereal influenced growth. To test its hypothesis, in the final study the company gave its cereal to one group of children and not to a second group. The group that received the cereal is called the **experimental group.** The group that did not receive the cereal is called the **control group.** A control group is a group that is treated exactly like the experimental group except for the factor being studied. In this case, the factor being studied was the

Table 2.1

Design of the Final Roasty-Toasties Study			
	Pretreatment Weight	Treatment	Posttreatment Weight
Group 1 (experimental)	50 lb.	Cereal with cream, bananas, and sugar	55 lb.
Group 2 (control)	50 lb.	Cream, bananas, and sugar without cereal	55 lb.

breakfast cereal. The control group was subject to the effects of all the same factors as the first group except for the cereal. The study is characterized in Table 2.1.

In any experiment we must define the terms in the hypothesis so that the hypothesis can be tested. To minimize possible confusion, the crucial terms in the hypothesis are defined clearly in reference to concrete operations. This definition is called an **operational definition,** and it forms a crucial link between our ideas and the world. Kerlinger (1973, 1986) suggests that there are two types of operational definitions: *measured* and *experimental.* The first type relates to measurement and may specify both *how* observations are to be made and *what* is to be observed and measured. For example, in a study that measures anxiety during certain types of tasks, it would be necessary to define operationally how anxiety was measured. That is, were the anxiety scores derived from self-report measures, physiological measures such as heart rate, or observation of a specific behavior? The second type of operational definition refers to experimentation. This type of operational definition describes how experimental procedures are to be followed.

For example, in a study that examines the effects of praise on improvement in psychotherapy, it would be necessary to define operationally both what praise is and under what conditions it is to be given and withheld. In one sense, operational definitions function like a recipe for a cook. In the same way that it would be difficult to follow a recipe that said only "Heat eggs, milk, and flour" (without specifying the amounts of the ingredients, the temperature at which the mixture is to be heated, and so on), it would be impossible to test a hypothesis that said only "Anxiety hurts performance." For a complete understanding, it would be necessary to specify (that is, operationally define) how anxiety is to be measured and how performance is to be assessed. Thus, one of the first tasks in developing a research study is to specify the operational definitions related to measurement and experimentation.

It should be pointed out that we are using the term *operational definition* in the more popular and less technical sense. We are not speaking of the total definition of a construct, a point we discuss in more detail in Chapter 3. (For a more complete discussion of operational definitions and the related concept *reduction sentences,* see Suppe, 1977.)

In the imaginary cereal experiment, the researchers had to define operationally both what was meant by the construct *growth* and how the eating of the cereal was to be manipulated experimentally. The variable that an experimenter manipulates in an experiment is called an **independent variable.** A variable is said to be independent when its levels are established by the experimenter before the experiment begins and are thus independent of anything that happens during the experiment. In this manner the independent variable precedes and potentially influences the measurements that we take in an experiment.

The aspect of the world that the experimenter expects will be affected by the independent variable is the **dependent variable.** The dependent variable is so called because if a relationship does exist, its value *depends* on the independent variable. Our experience suggests that some people confuse the concept of independent and dependent variables. Thus, it is important to remember that (1) it is the independent variable that you as experimenter control and (2) it is the dependent variable that you as experimenter measure. Because the independent variable is the variable you manipulate, some people remember this by saying "**I** manipulate the **I**ndependent variable."

In the cereal experiment, the researchers hoped that growth would be enhanced through ingestion of the new cereal. However, because there are many aspects of growth (physical maturation, height, weight, intellectual ability, emotional maturation), the task of deciding which aspect to measure is difficult. Notice that their final decision to define growth operationally in terms of weight is quite arbitrary and ignores other aspects of growth that might be evaluated.

The difference in the magnitude of the dependent variable for the control and experimental groups is called the **treatment effect.** Ideally, the only difference between the experimental and control groups should be the independent variable. If we are certain that this is the case, then we can infer that any difference in the magnitude of the dependent variable is due to the independent variable. If there were more than one difference between the two groups, then we would not know which of these differences was responsible for any treatment effects that we might observe. (Note, however, that more complex experimental designs, called *factorial designs,* allow us to investigate the effects of two or more independent variables in the same experiment. This class of designs is discussed in Chapter 9.)

If we suspect that some unintended factor may also be operating, then the truth or validity of the experiment is seriously threatened, and the entire experiment must be questioned. In the second cereal experiment, the fact that the control group did not receive cream, bananas, and sugar constitutes an alternative explanation for that group's lower weight gain. Whenever two or more independent variables are operating, the unintended independent variables (those not chosen by the experimenter) are called **confounding variables.** In the second experiment, the cream, sugar, and bananas represent this type of confounding variable.

Other confounding variables may covary with the independent variable and be more difficult to notice. For example, assume that a researcher compared a new medication against a problem-solving approach for the treatment of anxiety. If she found the problem-solving approach to show a greater reduction in anxiety, could she conclude that problem solving produced the reduction? Although that is one possibility, it also may have been the case that spending time with a professional produced the reduction in anxiety. That is, because giving medications requires less time with a patient than discussing problem-solving techniques, the results found may not have been due to the independent variable as planned in the study but rather to a confounding variable: time with the patient. We discuss confounds and their influence in more detail in Chapters 7 and 8.

CONCEPT
CHECK 2.2
A study was conducted to determine whether using videotapes rather than audiotapes to learn German during the semester influenced the grade received on a final exam in German. Name the independent and the dependent variables in this study.

■ Causation

Before we continue, we would like to clear up some confusion experienced by a number of people when the word *caused* is used. In psychology, when we speak about an independent variable causing a change in a dependent variable, we mean that these two variables reflect a consistent association. That is, with every change in the independent variable, there comes a related and predictable change in the dependent variable. The idea of causality in science is generally a conclusion concerning the relationship between the independent and dependent variables. If research shows that each time we change one aspect of a situation, a predictable change follows in another aspect, we usually say that the first aspect caused a change in the second. As we repeat an experiment in varying situations and under different conditions, if the same relationship between the independent variable and the dependent variable continues to hold true, then we have more confidence in our conclusion. Many philosophers of science see causation as something we ascribe to the situation, and they remind us that what we are really doing is making inferences about the world (that is, epistemology) rather than making statements about what really exists (that is, ontology). As we discuss later in this chapter, modern physics is now regarded as the study of *observations of reality* rather than the study of *reality* itself.

Another way to discuss causation is to consider what conditions are required for an event to occur. In particular, we discuss *necessary* and *sufficient* conditions (compare Copi, 1986). A necessary condition is the condition that *must* exist in order for the particular event to occur. For example, it is necessary for a human being to be a woman in order to become pregnant. Although it is a necessary condition, just being a woman in itself will not make one pregnant. For this to occur, there must also exist a sufficient condition. A sufficient condition for the occurrence of an event is a situation that, when it happens, produces the event. For example, we say that fertilization is a sufficient condition for producing an embryo.

To consider another example, we can say that the presence of oxygen alone is a necessary but not a sufficient condition for combustion to occur. However, the presence of oxygen at a certain critical range of temperatures is a sufficient condition for combustion. Likewise, we would not say that feeding milk to a child is a necessary condition for producing growth because a variety of substances fed to a child will produce growth. In the scientific literature, the word *cause* sometimes has been used in the sense of a necessary condition and at other times in the sense of a sufficient condition. This has led many researchers to suggest that we avoid the word altogether. Although we find it difficult to avoid the word completely, we have sympathy with the search for exact definitions. In this book, when we do use the word *cause,* we do not mean the one and only cause but rather the case in which two events (the independent variable and the dependent variable) are systematically connected in a variety of situations.

■ Exploratory Research

Psychologists often use the experimental method either more or less rigidly, depending on how much they already know about the phenomena that they are studying and the types of questions that they want to ask. In some cases, following an extensive library search for relevant information, a scientist may realize that almost nothing is known about a particular phenomenon and simply wonder what effect a given treatment will have on a person's experience. Given this situation, the scientist can use the experimental method in either of two ways.

First, when we have no idea what the effect of the independent variables will be, we are sometimes content to give the experimental treatment to a single group of research participants and then informally observe the research participants to get some idea of what aspects of behavior are affected by the independent variable. This initial exploratory use of the experimental method often is used in the initial stages of various experiments, including psychotherapy research and drug evaluation studies. Strictly speaking, this way of gaining information is not an experiment because it does not involve a control group or test specific hypotheses. It is no more than a simple demonstration that may provide either clues to fruitful independent variables for more refined analysis or potential attributes of behavior that should be reflected in the future selection of dependent variables.

The second way we use the experimental method as an exploratory tool occurs when we have some idea about which aspects of behavior will be affected by the independent variable and, consequently, have a reasonable idea about what types of dependent variables and control groups we should use, yet we do not understand the phenomenon well enough to make a specific prediction. In this way, our understanding of the phenomenon is refined progressively by a more detailed search for influential factors (independent variables that produce treatment effects) and by a more accurate estimate of their influence (measured by the dependent variables) on the phenomenon under study.

At other times, when we know a great deal about a particular topic, we can move beyond the exploratory uses of the experimental method. In these cases we are able to formulate specific predictions that reflect a more detailed theoretical understanding of the phenomenon. Because we have a clearer understanding, we can refine our independent and dependent variables and our use of control groups so that we can isolate more precisely the important relationships involved in the phenomenon being studied.

Whether we use the method of naturalistic observation, the correlational approach, or the experimental method, the task before us is to make inferences about the research participants' experience from the behaviors we observe. These inferences generally are related to our hypothesis or some larger theory that we want to evaluate. Thus, after we look at the world through these methods, we are faced with the task of deciding how to evaluate new information that we receive in light of both the methods used and our theoretical perspective. To accomplish this task, we use reason and logic. In particular, we ask whether the results of our methods as well as our conclusions are valid. To aid you in evaluating your own research and that of others, we focus on the question of validity and differentiate among some common types of validity in the next section. We also take a brief look at propositional logic.

LOGIC AND INFERENCE: THE DETECTIVE WORK OF SCIENCE

Perhaps you have heard the story of our friend from Boston who got up every morning, went outside his house, walked around in a circle three times, and yelled at the top of his voice. His neighbor, being somewhat curious after days of this ritual, asked for the purpose behind his strange behavior. The man answered that the purpose was to keep away tigers. "But," the neighbor replied, "there are no tigers within thousands of miles of here." To which our friend replied, "Works quite well, doesn't it?"

How could we demonstrate to our friend that his yelling is not causally related to the absence of tigers? One strategy might be to point out that the absence of tigers might have come about for other reasons, including the fact that there are no tigers roaming in the greater Boston area. In technical terms, we would say that yelling could be a *necessary* condition but not a *sufficient* condition for the absence of tigers. Our friend's reasoning was incorrect because it overlooked many other plausible explanations for the obvious absence of tigers. Although our friend sought to infer a relationship between his yelling and the absence of tigers, his inference was weak.

Logic is particularly important in science as an aid to answering the question "What question should my experimental study answer to test my ideas about the world?" That is, logic can help us to answer questions of *inference.* Inference is the process by which we look at the evidence available to us and then use our powers of reasoning to reach a conclusion. Like Sherlock Holmes engaged in solving a mystery, we attempt to solve a problem based on the available evidence. Did the butler do it? No, the butler could not have done it because there was blond hair on the knife and the butler had black hair. But perhaps the butler left the blond hair there to fool us. Like a detective, scientists try to determine other factors that may be responsible for the outcome of their experiments or to piece together available information and draw general conclusions about the world. Also like the detective, the scientist is constantly asking, "Given these clues, what inference can I make, and is the inference valid?" Logic is one method for answering these questions.

Validity

Logical procedures are also important for helping us to understand the accuracy or validity of our ideas and research. *Valid* means true and capable of being supported. Historically, we have discussed various types of validity in psychology, which arise from differing contexts. These contexts range from developing types of tests to running experiments. The overall question is "Does a certain procedure, whether it is an intelligence test or an experiment, do what it was intended to do?" In the next chapter, we will emphasize validity associated with issues of measurement including the ability of our instruments and experimental apparatus to give us true results. In this chapter we look at psychological research and focus on two general types of validity and the logic of our conclusions (Campbell & Stanley, 1963). The first is **internal validity.** The word *internal* refers to the experiment itself. Internal validity asks the question "Is there another reason that might explain the outcome of our experimental procedures?" Students are particularly sensitive to questions of internal validity, for example, when it is time for final exams; they can make a number of alternative suggestions about what the exam actually measures and why it does not measure their knowledge of a particular subject. Like students, scientists look for reasons (threats to internal validity) that a particular piece of research may not measure what it claims to measure. In the case of our friend from Boston, the absence of tigers near his house could have reflected a long-standing absence of tigers in his part of the world rather than the effectiveness of his yelling. We discuss specific threats to internal validity in Chapter 7.

The second type of validity is **external validity.** The word *external* refers to the world outside the setting in which the experiment was performed. External validity often is called **generalizability.** Remember the story of Semmelweis from Chapter 1. His finding that the deaths of the mothers who had just given birth were the result of physicians touching them after handling diseased tissue was true not only for his hospital but also for all other hospitals. Thus, in addressing the question of external validity of Semmelweis's work, we would infer that his answers could be generalized to other hospitals with other women and not just to his own original setting. Now consider the story of Galen. We would not fault his research concerning why the woman did not sleep, but we would say that it lacked external validity, or generalizability. Although the insomnia of one particular woman was attributed to her love of a particular dancer, it is not true that all women who suffer from insomnia are in love with dancers. In summary, internal validity refers to the internal consistency or logic of the experiment that allows the results to be meaningful. External validity, however, refers to the possibility of applying the results from an internally valid experiment to other situations and other research participants.

We logically design our research to rule out as many alternative interpretations of our findings as possible and to have any new facts be applicable to as wide a variety of other situations as possible. In many real-life situations in which external validity is high, however, it is impossible to rule out alternative interpretations of our findings. In a similar way, in laboratory settings in which internal validity is high, the setting is often artificial, and in many cases our findings cannot be generalized beyond the laboratory. Consequently, designing and conducting research is always a trade-off between internal and external validity. Which one we emphasize depends on the particular research questions being asked.

Before we continue we would like to clear up one misconception that some students have. It is the idea of designing "the one perfect study." Although we strive to design good research, there are always alternative explanations and conditions not studied in any single study. It is for this reason that Donald Campbell, who introduced scientists to the idea of internal and external validity, also emphasized the importance of replicating studies. If the same study is performed a number of times with similar results, then we can have more assurance that the results were valid. Even better, if the study is performed in a variety of settings around the world, we have even more confidence in our results.

In the next section, we examine propositional logic. However, before you begin that section, we suggest that you try to solve the problem presented in Box 2.1. (*Hint:* In problem solving, as well as in science, it is often more important to show what is not true rather than just focus on what is true. The solution to the problem relies on one type of logical argument, called modus tollens, that you will learn about in the next section.)

 CONCEPT CHECK 2.3   A tabloid newspaper recently described a diet in which sleep caused a person to lose weight. All the person needed to do was to exercise directly before going to bed and not eat for 6 hours before this time. The diet worked not only with the original group of research participants but also with a variety of other groups. Discuss the internal and external validity of this study.

■ Propositional Logic

In the previous section, we introduced the terms *internal validity* and *external validity* and emphasized the scientist's attempt to rule out alternative explanations. In this section, we emphasize the way in which a scientist relies on the rules of formal logic to both *deduce* and *induce* valid conclusions. As a starting point, keep in mind that **deduction** (to deduce) is

Box 2.1

"Think" Squares

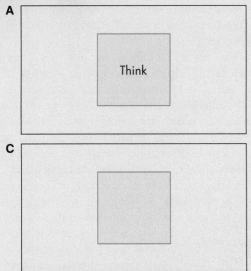

The illustration in this box represents four cards: A, B, C, and D. Assume that each card has a square with or without the word "Think" on one side, and a triangle with or without "Think" on the other side. Which of the cards would you have to turn over to determine whether every card that has a "Think" square on one side has a triangle without "Think" on the other?

We will make a prediction, based on previous experience, that you chose cards A and D. You may be in good company—many people choose these cards—but you were wrong. However, you were right when you chose card A. As you correctly reasoned, card A must have a triangle without "Think" on the other side for the statement to be true. However, if you turned over card D, which we did when we first tried the problem, you missed the point of the statement. The statement talks about what is opposite a "Think" square and says nothing about what is opposite a triangle. The other card that we need to turn-over to solve the problem is card B. We need to

demonstrate that the negative of the statement is not true; that is, we need to demonstrate that there is no card that has a "Think" square on one side and a "Think" triangle on the other side.

We begin with the hypothesis that all cards with a "Think" square on one side have an empty triangle on the other side, which we want to test. We then move to the real situation in which there are four cards. One of these four cards, A, has a "Think" square, and we can test the truth of the statement just by turning over card A. Now comes the problem. We have tested all the visible "Think" squares (card A), so what do we do next? If it is true that all "Think" squares have empty triangles on the other side, then it must also be true that no card with a "Think" triangle has a "Think" square on the other side. Once we realize this, we know that we must look at card B to test this assumption. Thus the correct answer is cards A and B.

Source: After Wason (1977).

the process by which one moves from a general theory to particular statements concerning data, whereas **induction** (to induce) is the process by which one moves from a particular set of data to a general theory or concept.

When we begin with a statement and arrive at its logical consequences, this is called *deductive* reasoning. For example, we use deductive reasoning when saying, "If it is true that schizophrenia is genetically determined, then we should find greater similarity in the presence or absence of the disorder between twins than between strangers." On the other hand, when we begin with an observation and figure out a general rule that covers it, this is called *inductive* reasoning. For example, inductive reasoning might be of the form, "I just saw a monkey use sign language to ask me for food; therefore, it is true that monkeys can communicate with humans." In summary, deductive reasoning goes from theory (the premise) to data (the conclusion), whereas inductive reasoning goes from data to theory.

Suppose a friend said to you, "You know, all experimental textbooks are really dull." You might respond, "That's not true; I am reading one right now that is really interesting." (Well, what did you expect that we would have you say?) This is a logical way to disprove the statement "All experimental textbooks are really dull." By finding an exception to a statement, you can show it to be false.

To begin an introduction to deductive logic, let's consider this procedure in a formal way. You begin with the statement "If this is an experimental textbook, then it will be really dull." This statement is presented in a certain "If . . . then" form. Each part has a particular name. The first part, "If this is an experimental textbook," is called the **antecedent.** The second part of the statement, "then it will be really dull," is called the **consequent.** The antecedent is referred to by the letter p and the consequent by the letter q. We now will discuss four types of propositions of the form "If p, then q." These four types are presented in Table 2.2. We should point out that other forms besides "If p, then q" are studied in propositional logic (compare Copi, 1986; Kourany, 1987).

Let's return to our original statement. Several logical consequences may follow from that statement. Suppose this is indeed an experimental textbook; then it follows that it will be really dull. In propositional logic, the reasoning is written out as follows:

> If this is an experimental textbook, then it will be really dull.
> It is an experimental textbook.
> Therefore, it will be really dull.

Technically, this is an argument of the form "If p, then q; given p (it is an experimental textbook), then we can conclude q (it will be really dull)." This form of argument is called confirmatory reasoning or **modus ponens.** Confirmatory reasoning is logically valid. We use it often in both our everyday lives and science.

However, not all forms of argument are logically valid. Suppose we have an instance in which q is true; what does this say about p? That is, if I can find a book that is dull, does that demonstrate that it is an experimental textbook? Of course not. There may be other kinds of books that are dull. Yet people make the following type of argument:

> If anxiety is increased, then heart rate will be increased.
> Heart rate is increased.
> Therefore, anxiety is increased.

In such a situation, we can think of many reasons why heart rate could be increased (for example, running up the stairs, doing mental arithmetic) without anxiety being increased.

Table 2.2	Forms of Propositional Logic	
	Modus Ponens (confirmatory) If p, then q. p. Therefore, q.	*Modus Tollens (disconfirmatory)* If p, then q. Not q. Therefore, not p.
Valid Arguments	If anxiety is increased, then heart rate will be increased. Anxiety is increased. Therefore, heart rate will be increased.	If anxiety is increased, then heart rate will be increased. Heart rate is not increased. Therefore, anxiety is not increased.
	Affirming the Consequent If p, then q. q. Therefore, p.	*Denying the Antecedent* If p, then q. Not p. Therefore, not q.
Invalid Arguments	If anxiety is increased, then heart rate will be increased. Heart rate is increased. Therefore, anxiety is increased.	If anxiety is increased, then heart rate will be increased. Anxiety is not increased. Therefore, heart rate will not be increased.

This form of argument is called **affirming the consequent.** Although it is a logically invalid form of argument, one sees it used almost daily. The cartoon on the next page offers one example of this form of reasoning. Technically, the argument could be stated as follows:

> If I were a cat, I would have four legs.
> I do have four legs.
> Therefore, I am a cat.

Let's now take the situation in which p is shown not to be true. What can we logically conclude? Again, we begin with a statement of the form "If p, then q."

> If I were a cat, I would have four legs.
> I am not a cat.
> Therefore, I do not have four legs.

Of course, this is not a valid argument. We know that other animals besides cats have four legs. The dog in the cartoon is not a cat but has four legs. Thus, if p is not true, it does not follow that q is also not true. This invalid form of argument is called **denying the antecedent.** Consider the following:

> If Freud's theories are correct, then his therapy will be effective.
> Freud's theories are not correct.
> Therefore, his therapy will not be effective.

© Sidney Harris, ScienceCartoonsPlus.com

This is logically invalid. However, we still hear people using this form of invalid reasoning by suggesting that because Sigmund Freud's (or Fritz Perls's or B. F. Skinner's or Carl Rogers's) theories have been shown to be incorrect, his therapy cannot be effective. The effectiveness of a particular therapy is determined empirically; such a determination has little to do with theoretical formulations.

This brings us to the fourth situation. If the consequent is not true, then what does this tell us about the antecedent? (If q is not true, then p is . . . ?) If q is not true, then p is also not true. Returning to a previous example and modifying it appropriately, we have the following argument:

> If I were a cat, I would have four legs.
> I do not have four legs.
> Therefore, I am not a cat.

This is a valid form of reasoning. It is called *disconfirmatory reasoning*, or **modus tollens.** In the Freud example, we could make the following valid argument using modus tollens:

> If Freud's theories are valid, then his therapy will be effective.
> His therapy is not effective.
> Therefore, Freud's theories are not valid.

Karl Popper (see Box 2.2) suggests that modus tollens arguments are at the heart of the scientific testing of theories. He points out that our theories should lead to some prediction.

Box 2.2

Philosophy of Science: Sir Karl Popper (Falsification Approach)

Sir Karl Popper has devoted much of his career to answering the questions "What is science?" and "How is science performed?" Although these questions may at first seem easy to you, consider such areas as astrology and Marxism. Could these approaches be considered scientific? Why not?

Falsificationism is the name given to Popper's description of how science is performed. Falsificationism suggests that science should be concerned with disproving or falsifying theories through logic based on observation. How is this accomplished? First, a scientist must create a consistent falsifiable hypothesis. A falsifiable hypothesis is one that can be shown to be false. For example, the hypothesis "It will rain in Tuscaloosa, Alabama, on Tuesday, December 23, 2017" is falsifiable: If it does not rain on that day, the hypothesis will be shown to be false. Likewise, the hypothesis "All objects regardless of weight will fall to earth at approximately the same speed" is falsifiable; it can be tested by experiment. However, a hypothesis such as "ESP (extrasensory perception) exists" is not falsifiable. Even the hypothesis "Gravity exists" is untestable. It may be true that both ESP and gravity exist, yet until the hypothesis is stated in a form that can be falsified, the hypothesis is not testable. Second, once a scientist has a falsifiable hypothesis, the task is to develop a test of the hypothesis. Third, the hypothesis is tested. Fourth, if the hypothesis is shown to be false, a new hypothesis is developed.

Using this model, Popper emphasizes science as a process for the elimination of false theories. Further, Popper suggests that the elimination of false theories is aided by placing one theory in competition with other theories. In this sense science is a form of natural selection with a more fit theory being the result (Popper, 1959). If you accept the suggestion that all psychological research is inductive in nature, you must then conclude with Popper that the major role of science is the falsification of incorrect theories. This line of reasoning also leads one to conclude that science, particularly psychology, never *proves* a hypothesis. Science, according to Popper, only shows that the hypothesis has not been proved false.

Note: Although Popper usually is discussed in terms of the falsification position, his recent writings emphasize research programs rather than single theories. Even for Popper, science is more than just eliminating false theories.

If the prediction is found to be untrue, then we conclude that our theory is incorrect. This is valid reasoning. However, the opposite is not the case. Finding that a prediction is true does not logically lead one to conclude that the theory is true, any more than having four legs made the dog in the cartoon into a cat. Research results may fail to refute a theory, but they cannot prove the theory to be correct. Thus, Popper suggests that our efforts in science should be concentrated on attempting to disprove hypotheses; he calls this procedure *falsification*.

We want to emphasize that deductive logic is one of many tools of the scientist. Like the experimental method, logic is an approach to knowledge designed to help us to evaluate and direct our research questions. Because of the complexity of the world in which we live and the limits of our own minds in perceiving this complexity precisely, we find ourselves as scientists using a combination of both inductive and deductive approaches to knowledge in our science as well as in our lives. We often use deductive and inductive approaches as a means of gaining information, which becomes a clue as we attempt to interact with and understand the world in which we live. Logic offers us a means of evaluating the inferences we draw from these clues. Logic helps us to understand the limits on our claims to certitude. Quite often logic helps us to see that we do not know enough to make any claim at all. In this manner, logic tends to make the scientific process conservative in its claims. However, it does not follow that our research topics, our ideas, or our theories also must be conservative.

 # SCIENTIFIC OBSERVATION: THE RAW DATA OF SCIENCE

Have you ever heard the question "If a tree fell in the middle of the forest without anyone around, would there be any sound?" This question reflects a philosophical problem in science that was solved in physics at the beginning of the 20th century. Until that time, the notion of physicists was that they study *events* in the world. In this earlier worldview, the job of the scientist was to be a passive observer and accurately watch events that take place either in the real world or in experiments. There was no thought that the process of observing might influence the perception of the very events being observed. From the earlier perspective, it was meaningful to ask whether the sound existed. However, this has changed.

According to modern physics, scientists do not record events. Instead, scientists record their *observations of events*. They record their experience of the world and base their science on these perceptions. This development amounts to a simple acceptance of the fact that in science we can get no closer to the world than our observations of it.

Let's return for a moment to the child who is discovering the world for the first time. Imagine that you are a small child who is still crawling and cannot yet stand. As you move around your world, what do you see? What do you know about events that take place and objects that are more than 3 feet above the ground? Some events you may know by their sound, such as a passing car or your father's electric razor. Other events you may recognize only by smell, such as the cooking of bacon or bleach being added to the wash. Other events you could know only from the sensation involved, such as your father or mother picking you up and throwing you in the air and catching you. Suppose someone could talk with you at this age and ask you to describe what the world was like. What would you say? How would the adult you were talking to react to your description? Would he or she say it was a true, accurate, and acceptable view of the world?

As you begin to answer these questions, you see that your description as a child was from your own perspective. You also may realize that it is difficult to say whether this description was true or false. From your viewpoint as an adult, it was incomplete. In the same way that the view of a child's world is relative to where and when the child lives and observes the world, the view of the scientist and, consequently, the *facts of science* are *relative* to the current notions of working scientists and the instruments that they use to make observations.

Box 2.3

Philosophy of Science: Thomas Kuhn

When Newton said, "I stand on the shoulders of giants," he was referring to the people who came before him and on whose work he was able to build his scientific system. Many of us have similar ideas when it comes to the progression of science. We think that each new discovery is simply added to old discoveries, with the results being a gradual accumulation of knowledge.

Thomas Kuhn (1970) suggests that this view is wrong. Kuhn proposes that science actually goes through a series of revolutions. Following each revolution, a new system or method for performing science is instituted. The new system or worldview is called a paradigm, or set of assumptions, which guides scientific activity until a new revolution and paradigm shift take place. The stable period between revolutions is called normal science. Normal science is the process of problem solving, which most of us think of when someone uses the term *science*. Normal

science for Kuhn is always science performed in relation to a particular paradigm.

As an example of the role of paradigms, assume that you were a mapmaker in a culture that believed the world was flat. You would draw your maps as if the world were flat because that was the accepted belief. As a mapmaker, you would never think to question this belief; it was a given in your task of drawing maps. Then there came a mapmaker's version of a scientific revolution. The paradigm shifted to that of a world that was round. As a mapmaker, you would now draw the world as if it were round and you would continue with this system until a new revolution came along. This, of course, was the replacing of the earth as the center of the solar system with the sun as the center. In the same way that mapmakers work in relation to present-day assumptions and beliefs about the world, Kuhn suggests that scientists also work in relation to a set of beliefs or paradigms until these are replaced by a revolution.

The current notion concerning science and accepted methods, which encompasses a philosophical way of seeing the world, is called a **paradigm.** Philosopher of science Thomas Kuhn has elaborated a particular view of how science progresses, based on the concept of paradigm (see Box 2.3). Although there is much debate about the exact meaning of the word *paradigm,* most scientists understand it to mean shared beliefs, which include topics to be studied and the types of answers that will be given. For example, the current scientific paradigm in psychology emphasizes the importance of quantitative measurement. Thus, scientific psychology, as you will learn it, directs you toward topics that can be measured quantitatively.

Not only are the results and conclusions of our research relative to our current notions of science, but they also may relate to our own psychology. Consider the role of the experimenter in the psychological experiment. Do you think your own state (hungry, sad, tired, excited, and so on) could influence the data of an experiment? That is just one of the factors that we consider later in this book. The important point now is to realize that the state of the experimenter is important. Because the scientist is not *passive* but is *actively* searching for answers, he or she can actually influence the event being recorded by the very manner in which the observation is being made. The scientist can change the world and our understanding of it. Thus, the scientist is more than a passive observer; he or she is a real actor in the drama of science.

EVALUATING SCIENTIFIC RESEARCH

Regardless of the amount of work involved in scientific research, an extremely important aspect of *any* research endeavor is whether the final product is worthy of being reported to the scientific community. We must ask whether our conclusions are *accurate,* capable of being *replicated,* and *relevant* to others. In this book we emphasize four ways to ensure the high quality of our research.

The first is through impartial, systematic observation using logically sound experimental design. The experimental method based on random sampling and assignment (as we describe later) is the most powerful class of research design currently available. We emphasize this technique in the initial chapters of this book and later discuss some other scientific approaches.

The second way to ensure meaningful research is through statistical description and inference. We show how statistics can help us to decide whether our results are due to some causal agent or merely to chance.

The third method of quality control is through reason and logic. In discussing logic we emphasize types of validity as well as types of propositional logic and how they help us to evaluate research.

The fourth and final way is by emphasizing perspective and context. In particular, we suggest that conclusions be viewed from the perspectives of the scientist, the research participant, and the witness.

Although this book emphasizes the perspective of the scientist, it is important to remember the experiences of the research participant and the perspective of the witness if our conclusions are to have meaning. We believe that through these four ways of evaluating research a person can use science and maintain the high level of excellence that a science of behavior and experience requires.

COMMUNICATION IN SCIENCE

Unlike the child who is busy learning about the world, scientists must share what they learn about the world with other people, especially other scientists. More than 2,000 years ago, Aristotle emphasized this when he taught that science has two parts: inquiry and argument. In modern terms, inquiry is represented by the research that answers our questions about the world, and argument refers in part to the scientist's responsibility to inform others of the findings. Consequently, we design our research, record our observations, and summarize our findings in a manner that others can understand. For scientists to answer a question in terms that only he or she can understand would not be complete science because it is not shared knowledge. The final product of mature science is a communication that summarizes a conclusion about the world and is directed to both scientists and nonscientists.

Learning to communicate in science may be compared to learning a foreign language. One of your first tasks is to learn the vocabulary of science. You need to understand what a scientist means by certain words. You initially may say that is easy because many scientists speak English anyway. That may be true, but it can also be a problem because English words can have slightly different or even totally different meanings when used in the context of a scientific statement.

For example, suppose you were reading a newspaper article concerning a new discovery in subatomic physics. The article is about particles with "color and charm." If you were to talk to a physicist, you would find that in this context *color* and *charm* have nothing to do with colors or with the particles being appealing. These words have special meaning for the physicist.

Likewise in psychology, common words may be used in a special or technical way. For example, B. F. Skinner discussed *negative reinforcements* as applied to people, yet negative reinforcements have nothing to do with punishment, as many people think. Likewise, Carl Jung invented the words *extravert* and *introvert,* which have a technical meaning different from their uses in newspapers and magazines. Even as common a word as *sex* was given a scientific meaning (by Freud) as distinctive as the physicists' terms *color* and *charm.*

At first, the language of science may seem strange. Yet, as with any language, once you learn some words and phrases, you can begin to understand what is going on. This understanding will be useful not only to those of you who pursue careers as scientists, but also to all of us in our daily interactions with the world as we try to understand what we read about science and strive to become more educated consumers. You have a twofold task. First, you must seek to understand how words are used in research in a technical way. You cannot just assume that because you have heard a word, you already know its meaning. Second, in writing your own reports, you must seek to define your words and ideas as precisely as possible so that others can understand and follow what you are saying.

KEY TERMS AND CONCEPTS

1. **Overview of science**
   A. Hypothesis
   B. Observation, correlation, and experimentation
   C. Inference and conclusion
   D. Modeling
   E. Qualitative methods
   F. Quantitative methods
2. **Types of questions**
   A. "If I do this, what will happen?"
   B. "If I do this, I expect this will happen."
3. **Role of scientist**
   A. In naturalistic observation
   B. In experimental method

4. **Naturalistic observation**
   A. Four characteristics
      • Noninterference
      • Determining patterns
      • Useful for "big picture"
      • Descriptive
5. **Correlational approach**
   A. Positive and negative correlations
   B. Association versus causality
6. **Experimental method**
   A. Key question
      • "Was what happened really a result of what I did?"

(continued)

KEY TERMS AND CONCEPTS (*continued*)

B. Definitions
- Hypothesis
- Experimental group
- Control group
- Operational definition, two types
- Independent variable (also called treatment variable)
- Dependent variable
- Treatment effect
- Confounding variables

7. Causation in science
  A. Necessary conditions
  B. Sufficient conditions
  C. Correlation

8. Validity
  A. Internal validity
  B. External validity and generalizability

9. Forms of propositional logic
  A. Deduction and induction
  B. Correct reasoning
    - Confirmatory (modus ponens)
    - Disconfirmatory (modus tollens)
  C. Incorrect reasoning
    - Denying the antecedent
    - Affirming the consequent

10. Falsificationism
  A. Karl Popper

11. Paradigm
  A. Thomas Kuhn

12. The language of science

SUMMARY

1. Science is one way of learning about the world that involves articulating an idea or hypothesis, using experience developed in research to evaluate the idea, and drawing conclusions or inferences from experimentation and observation about the idea or hypothesis.

2. Observation is an important part of science. The naturalistic observation procedure emphasizes observation and has four characteristics: (a) noninterference, (b) observations of patterns and invariants, (c) development of the "big picture" or learning about an unknown process, and (d) provision of descriptions rather than pinpointing specific factors that influence one another.

3. Experimentation is also an important part of science. It offers a means of creating control and determining the manner in which one factor influences another. This determination is aided by the use of a control group, which allows the researcher to evaluate the effects of the independent variable on the dependent variable.

4. Another type of research is called correlational study. The purpose of this research is to determine the association between two variables but not the manner in which one variable affects another.

5. A very important part of science is the use of logic and inference. The particular task is to draw conclusions and rule out alternative hypotheses. The study of propositional logic points to both the logical and the illogical conclusions that may be drawn from general statements.

6. A researcher must question the validity of conclusions drawn from research. Two major types of validity are discussed. Internal validity refers to the experiment itself and asks whether there are alternative explanations (such as confounding variables) that would invalidate the reported relationship between the independent and dependent variables. External validity poses the question of generalizability and asks to what other groups or situations a particular set of findings might be applicable.

7. Science reflects a history of observations of events. As a recorder of observations, it is important for researchers to be sensitive to factors that can influence the records they make and to understand that any record is always presented from a certain perspective, recently called a *paradigm*. It is likewise important that communications in science be clear and be stated in such a manner that they can be evaluated.

REVIEW QUESTIONS

1. What is one difference between *qualitative* and *quantitative* methods?
2. What are four characteristics of naturalistic observation?
3. What is an *experimental group,* and what is a *control group*?
4. What is an *operational definition,* and is there more than one type?
5. In the final cereal experiment, identify the independent variable and the dependent variable.
6. Distinguish between a *sufficient* and a *necessary* cause.

7. What is meant by the terms *internal validity* and *external validity*?
8. What does the term *falsificationism* mean in science?
9. How would modern physics answer the question, "If a tree fell in the forest without anyone to hear it, would there be any sound?"
10. What are the two invalid forms of propositional logic discussed in this chapter? Give an example of each.
11. What are the two valid forms of propositional logic discussed in this chapter? Give an example of each.

DISCUSSION QUESTIONS AND PROJECTS

1. Use the library as the site for a naturalistic observation study. Go to the library, find a place from which you can observe, and record what you see. One focus might be the pattern of interactions among people in the library. If you were an outsider looking at these data, what might you conclude about the function of the library for students?
2. Give the "Think" squares problem in Box 2.1 to some of your friends. Using naturalistic observation, record what they do as they go about solving the problem. You might time them, record what they say (if anything), notice facial expressions, and so on.
3. Have another group verbalize what they are thinking as they try to solve the "Think" squares problem. You might decide whether there are similarities in the verbalizations of the different people. If you record the verbalizations, it will make the task easier. How do you go about deciding whether the verbalizations of two different people are similar? What categories do you look for?
4. Put people who are knowledgeable about a particular sport in one group and people who know little about it in another group. A knowledgeable person should describe in detail some particular play or move from the sport; you then ask both groups to recall what was said. Notice whether there is any difference between the two groups in the amount of recall. What other differences are there between the two groups?

5. Discuss how you might turn the observations in Questions 3 and 4 into experiments. What would be the independent and the dependent variables?
6. Assume that you followed the directions in Question 4 and found that people who knew about the sport remembered more. Discuss the following conclusion: "This experiment demonstrates that playing sports helps to increase your ability to remember, so sports should be required in all schools."
7. Discuss the statement, "Scientists do not record events but only their observations of events."
8. An experimenter was interested in creativity. In particular, she wanted to know whether a person is more creative at one time of day than another. At the time, she was teaching two sections of an introductory psychology course. One class met from 8:00 to 9:00 A.M. and the other from 4:30 to 5:30 P.M. She used a well-known creativity test and gave the test to each of her classes. When she scored the test, she found that those who took the test in the morning did better than those who took it in the afternoon. The experimenter concluded that, in general, college students are more creative in the morning than in the afternoon. Discuss this conclusion. Are there other ways in which these data might be interpreted?

INFOTRAC COLLEGE EDITION: EXERCISES

Using InfoTrac College Edition, you can learn more about two philosophers of science who were introduced in this chapter, Sir Karl Popper and Thomas Kuhn, by entering their names. Another topic introduced in this chapter was logic. Using InfoTrac College Edition, look up the article called "Deductive reasoning," by Johnson-Laird, which

(continued)

INFOTRAC COLLEGE EDITION: EXERCISES (*continued*)

was published in the 1999 *Annual Review of Psychology.* (*Hint:* You can either enter *Johnson-Laird* or the term *deductive reasoning.*) As you read this article, think about how we may use logic differently in everyday life as compared with science. You may also think about how our tendencies to think in a certain way in everyday life (for example, to always look for proof and not refutation) may bias our scientific world. You can also look at the article on "thinking" by Arthur B. Markman and Debre Gentnre

in the 2001 *Annual Review of Psychology.* This article also discusses deductive reasoning.

To help you better understand the material in this chapter, you can go to the Wadsworth Psychology Resource Center at http://www.wadsworth.com/ psychology_d/templates/student_resources/workshops/ resch_wrk.html. There you will find a workshop on "Experimental Methods" that highlights some of the concepts presented in this chapter.

☑ Answers to Concept Checks

2.1 Neither, we hope. Although either or both could be correct, a correlation will not give you that information. A correlation will only describe a relationship but not the direction of the relationship. That is, you cannot state whether one variable influenced another or even whether there was a third variable that influenced both.

2.2 The independent variable is the variable that the experimenter manipulates. The type of tape, video versus audio, is the independent variable. The dependent variable is the score or measurement influenced by

the independent variable. In this case, the final exam grade is the dependent variable.

2.3 Because the results were obtained in a variety of settings, we may assume there are few problems with the external validity of the study. However, there may be a problem with the internal validity because the experiment does not actually show that sleep is a necessary condition for weight loss to take place. It may be that the exercise and not eating for 6 hours will result in a weight loss even without sleep.

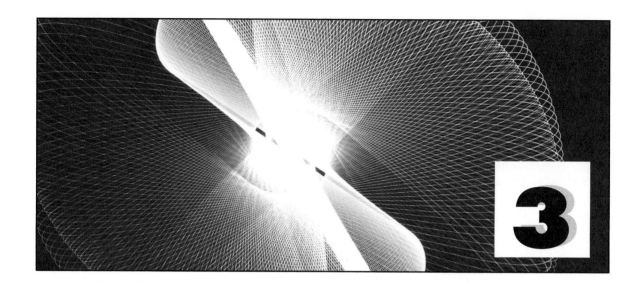

DEVELOPING THE HYPOTHESIS

MAKING OUR HYPOTHESES CONCRETE

MAKING OUR HYPOTHESES LOGICAL
The "I Wonder What Will Happen If" Hypothesis
and Inductive Reasoning
The "I Expect This Would Happen If" Hypothesis
and Deductive Reasoning
Strong Inference

**CREATING TESTABLE RESEARCH
HYPOTHESES AND THE PROBLEM
OF MEASUREMENT**

OVERVIEW

IDEAS COME FROM EVERYWHERE

INTUITION AND REVELATION

**THE SCIENTIST'S GUIDE TO
HAVING AN IDEA**

TOOLS FOR LIBRARY RESEARCH
Journals and Books
Computer Databases
The Internet

CONCLUSION

Imagine that your instructor in this course has just announced that you are to begin an *experiment* of your own and that you are to start right now. What do you do? Where do you begin? This chapter answers these questions and helps you to begin your first experiment. As Lewis Carroll once said, the best place to begin is at the beginning.

As with any other human activity, excellence and enjoyment in research begin with genuine interest in the topic. When confronted with their first experiments, students may overlook the fact that research begins with interest. Consequently, your first task is simply to sit back and let your interests emerge. Some of you have already done this and are aware of your interests in various areas of psychology. For most of you, however, strong interests have not yet begun to emerge. One way of discovering your interests is to begin exploring various areas of psychology and observing your reactions to each area.

For example, you might look through your introductory psychology book and see which areas engage you. Once you realize what areas interest you, you might go to the library and look through some textbooks or other books specifically devoted to these areas. You might also talk with psychologists who live in your community and learn more about what they do and what types of questions they ask in their daily work. As your interests unfold, keep in mind that the interests of even the most dedicated person are not constant. They fluctuate from day to day; sometimes they are strong, and sometimes they are forgotten. Over a period of years, a scientist may change interests many times. Regardless of the constancy of interests, they can be valuable guides that enable us to enjoy our interactions with the world.

When researchers are interested in a given topic, they learn all they can about it. They go to the library and read about the topic. They go to conferences and talk to other researchers about it. They actively think about the topic. After a time, many researchers find their topic spontaneously arising in their thoughts as they take showers, as they fall asleep, as they eat breakfast. Like a child playing with a new toy, scientists consider their topics from ever-changing perspectives. Some researchers even amuse themselves by trying to describe their topics as if all their ideas about it were backward. The main idea is that they *play* with their thoughts to gain new perspectives.

MAKING OUR HYPOTHESES CONCRETE

The essence of a scientific experiment is to see whether our ideas about the world are accurate. In its simplest form, it is an interface, a meeting point, between our ideas and reality, between our psychological world and the physical world. This distinction is one aspect of the differentiation we made in Chapter 1 between experience (psychological world) and behavior (physical world). To bridge this gap successfully, we first must realize that our intellectual ideas or hypotheses about the world, like our emotions or sensory experiences, are personal experiences. They cannot be shared directly with other people, no matter how hard we try. They are private knowledge. Yet science is objective in that its conclusions can be seen and checked by anyone.

This points to a dilemma: How can we scientifically evaluate our completely private ideas about the world? One answer is to define or represent our private ideas in terms of specific behaviors or concrete activities that anyone can witness or repeat. These representations of psychological events in the physical world are called operational definitions. An *operational definition* defines events in terms of the operations required to measure them and thus gives our idea a concrete meaning. For example, the idea that watching violence on television increases aggression is certainly a reasonable and potentially important notion. Yet before we can test it, we must define exactly what is meant by violence on television. Is a program with an unseen murder more violent than an exciting boxing match? Should violence be rated by how many minutes it appears on the screen, by the particular type of act, by how much blood is shown, or by a combination of all three? Likewise, to perform this research we need to devise some measure of aggression. Let's take another example. Suppose we wanted to test the idea that psychotherapy is effective. Before we could do that, we have to define what psychotherapy is and what can be considered a measure of effectiveness. We would have to adopt operational definitions.

An operational definition takes a general concept, such as aggression or effectiveness, and places it within a given context; that is, *it redefines the concept in terms of clearly observable operations that anyone can see and repeat.* For example, we might define *aggression* as the number of times a child hits a toy after watching a violent television show. Likewise, we might define *effectiveness in psychotherapy* as measured by a score on a personality test or how well a person functions in personal relationships or at work. We could also use the number of days that a person stays out of a mental hospital as an operational definition of the effectiveness of therapy.

In each case we have redefined an idea in terms of specified operations. We define an idea (psychological world) in terms of operations (physical world) that are required to produce the phenomenon (physical world) that the idea (psychological world) represents. The cyclic nature represents what science is all about: movement back and forth between our ideas and physical reality. Operational definitions make it possible to tie our ideas and hypotheses to objects and operations in physical reality.

One problem we face with operational definitions is that a given concept may be defined in several ways. Conversely, a given operational definition defines only a limited aspect of the original concept. Although we all realize that the grade you receive on a multiple-choice final exam is a narrow facet of all you may have learned in a college course, it is, strictly speaking, an adequate operational definition of your performance. However, from a larger perspective we would want to use multiple operational definitions to help us to understand the meaning of our **construct** that would inform our theory concerning this construct.

Suppose we were interested in studying the effectiveness of a new form of psychotherapy on severely depressed people. Regardless of the research design we use, one task we would face is operationally defining the dependent variable: depression. We know that depression can manifest itself in a variety of ways (Figure 3.1). Each of these ways can become the focus of an operational definition of depression. For example, we know that the biochemistry of depressed patients undergoes certain changes, so these characteristics would constitute an adequate operational definition of depression. We also know that therapists generally agree on which patients are depressed, so we might operationally define the degree of depression in our research participants by the estimates of various therapists.

Figure 3.1

From any one global construct, there are several possible operational definitions, depending on the questions asked and the type of population studied

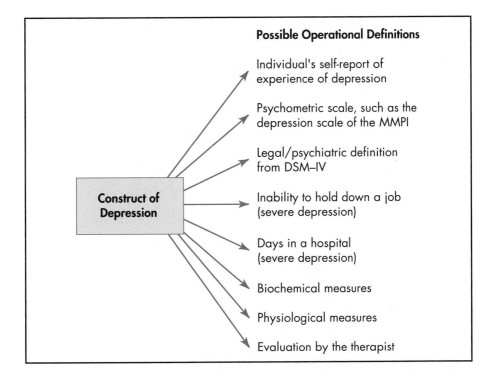

Possible Operational Definitions

Individual's self-report of experience of depression

Psychometric scale, such as the depression scale of the MMPI

Legal/psychiatric definition from DSM–IV

Inability to hold down a job (severe depression)

Days in a hospital (severe depression)

Biochemical measures

Physiological measures

Evaluation by the therapist

Construct of Depression

However, the question of which operational definition is best is tricky. Ideally, it is safest to use several operational definitions. In this case, we might define depression as a certain score on some depression test plus a "depressed" rating by a therapist and the participant's subjective report of feeling depressed. If this battery of operational definitions is not possible, then at least we should select one that is known to be correlated with others. In selecting operational definitions, remember that they are arbitrary but are often guided by previous research in the area.

When we specify the operational definition, we are helping others to understand the manner in which our measurements took place. As Cronbach and Meehl (1955) point out, however, it is rare for a researcher to accept an operational definition as the sole definition of the construct being studied. Although we may define *hunger* operationally in an animal experiment as "amount of time since last feeding," Cronbach and Meehl suggest that we also have other ideas in mind when we use the construct *hunger*. For example, the construct of hunger might also be related to the amount of energy an animal would expend to seek food. This multiplicity of meaning represents such an important point that Cronbach and Meehl suggest that we need to be concerned about a particular type of validity they call *construct validity.*

Construct validity asks whether the procedure that we are using is actually an adequate definition of the construct that we are measuring. This is an important concept. If we have a test for intelligence, we would want to know what factors or constructs determine the score of this particular test. In terms of an experiment, we want to know how valid is our inference about the construct that we are measuring, based on the specific manipulations and measurements used. Thus, one must ask whether dropping an apple gives us an adequate basis for making inferences about the construct of gravity. Likewise, in our depression example, one must ask whether a particular measure of depression allows us to make valid inferences about the construct of depression.

CONCEPT CHECK 3.1   Which of the following is an operational definition of verbal ability: (a) the ability to read a book, (b) the ability to watch television, (c) the score on the verbal part of the SAT, or (d) the ability to have a conversation?

MAKING OUR HYPOTHESES LOGICAL

As mentioned in Chapter 2, when we begin our experiment we are in either of two positions concerning what we already know about a research area. In some cases we already know a great deal and can use the experimental method to test specific predictions and hypotheses. Hypotheses of this type take the form "I expect this will happen if. . . ." In other cases we know little and use the experimental method as an exploratory tool. Hypotheses of this type take the form "I wonder what will happen if. . . ." As it turns out, the types of logic underlying these two types of hypotheses are fundamentally different.

■ The "I Wonder What Will Happen If" Hypothesis and Inductive Reasoning

If we are working in a new area (for example, the early days of AIDS research) and know little about the phenomenon that we are studying, we have no clear ideas from which to make specific predictions. In this case we use naturalistic observation, correlational studies, and the experimental method to generate new data from which we can begin to formulate a preliminary idea about how the phenomenon is organized. This process of generalizing from a specific instance or even several new facts to a more general idea is called *inductive reasoning* (Figure 3.2). We use inductive reasoning to increase our knowledge by generalizing new facts to a new understanding.

For example, we use inductive reasoning when, observing a chimpanzee using sign language with a person, we conclude that chimpanzees can communicate with humans. We are generalizing from a specific event to a general idea about how the world is. The danger with this form of logic is overlooking unobserved factors that may be responsible for the effects that we observe. For example, you may know someone who is 106 years old and eats yogurt. From this observation, you may conclude that yogurt makes people live longer.

Figure 3.2

Inductive and deductive relationships between observation and theory

Observations → **Induction** → Idea or theory about relationships that exist in the world

In the early stages of studying a phenomenon, scientists move from observations to theory. Some philosophers of science, such as Karl Popper, believe that psychology is at this stage, and thus induction remains the main experimental method of psychological research.

Observations ← **Deduction** ← A well-established theory that predicts observations

Once a comprehensive theory is developed, predictions can be made from the theory and tested through experimentation. Classic physics is a clear example of a science that uses this procedure.

This is an invalid use of inductive reasoning because any number of other factors may contribute to this person's longevity. As mentioned in Chapter 2, the internal validity supporting this conclusion is questionable.

■ The "I Expect This Would Happen If" Hypothesis and Deductive Reasoning

If we already knew a great deal about a particular phenomenon and had formulated a clear-cut idea or theory, then we might deduce a specific hypothesis to predict how unexamined but related phenomena operate. In its simplest form, *deductive reasoning* takes the form of an if-then statement: If my idea about the world is correct, then this cause should produce the following effect. For example, we use deductive reasoning when we say, "If it is true that schizophrenia is determined genetically (general idea about world), then we should find a greater incidence of the disorder between twins than between strangers (specific consequence of heredity)." The terms of the hypothesis could be defined operationally, an experiment conducted, and a decision made about the accuracy of this particular hypothesis. If the hypothesis is supported, then this new fact strengthens the confidence we have that schizophrenia is genetically determined. If it is not supported, then we have reason to question our idea that schizophrenia is determined genetically. Thus, the outcome of the experiment helps us to infer logically the relationship between events. As we observe throughout the book, the stronger our research design, the better we can infer a given relationship between events.

■ Strong Inference

An important procedure for examining hypotheses is that of *strong inference* (Platt, 1964). Platt proposes that certain fields of science have progressed quickly because of the adoption of the method of strong inference. The following four steps characterize strong inference:

1. Devise alternative hypotheses.
2. Devise a crucial experiment (or several experiments) with alternative possible outcomes, each of which would exclude one or more of the hypotheses.
3. Carry out the experiment to get clear results.
4. Return to step 1 with further refinements of the supported hypothesis.

Let's see how we could apply this technique. Suppose that you lived during the time of Galileo and wanted to apply this procedure to the study of falling weights. Aristotle assumed that if you dropped two weights, the heavier would land first, whereas Galileo suggested that both weights would hit the earth at the same time. Applying the method of strong inference, we could drop two weights and hypothesize that if the heavier weight hit first, then Aristotle's hypothesis would be supported, whereas if they hit at the same time, Galileo's hypothesis would be supported. Once it was determined that Galileo's hypothesis was supported, then a scientist could begin further refinements of the theory. Moving to current times, a variety of psychological studies have taken a strong inference approach. For example, one study asked whether in newly married couples, opposites attracted or whether the individuals selected romantic partners who were more like them (Luo & Klohnen, 2005). According to the results of this study, there was little data to suggest that opposites attract; rather, the data suggested that people tend to marry others who are highly similar in attitudes and values to themselves.

Platt likens the procedure of strong inference to climbing a tree: Each choice is dependent on the previous one taken. Platt sees strong inference not only as a method for rapid progress in science but also as a procedure at the heart of every scientist's thinking:

> Obviously it should be applied as much to one's own thinking as to others'. It consists of asking in your own mind, on hearing any scientific explanation or theory put forward, "But sir, what experiment could disprove your hypothesis?"; or on hearing a scientific experiment described, "But sir, what hypothesis does your experiment disprove?" (Platt, 1964, p. 352)

This quote includes an extremely important point. We need to consider not only what results would support our hypothesis but also what results would disprove our hypothesis. In this manner, Platt's procedure of strong inference emphasizes the problem-solving aspects of science and the search for adequate theoretical conceptualizations, as well as serving as a heuristic to help you to determine whether your ideas about the world are stated in the form of a testable hypothesis.

CREATING TESTABLE RESEARCH HYPOTHESES AND THE PROBLEM OF MEASUREMENT

Making the transition from a general idea to a testable research hypothesis is not always a simple task. Most students present their ideas in the form of a general statement and tend to ask global questions. It is not that their questions are unimportant or uninteresting; it is just

"IT MAY VERY WELL BRING ABOUT IMMORTALITY, BUT IT WILL TAKE FOREVER TO TEST IT."

that they are untestable in the form in which they are presented. It is only with considerable work and practice that an interesting idea can be rephrased into a testable hypothesis that clearly spells out a specific relationship among variables.

Many areas of psychology are rarely researched because of the difficulty in making the transition to adequate research hypotheses. Areas such as romantic love, creativity, extrasensory perception, sanity, and mental illness are some examples. Because of the nature of the questions, some areas may even be outside the realm of testability, as illustrated by the cartoon. Even for the experienced scientist, the transition from a general idea to a specific research hypothesis requires careful thought and consideration. Often, as Cohen (1990) suggests in his discussion of methodology, "less is more." By this he means that in designing a study it is important to keep it simple and not to study too many different aspects of a particular phenomenon at one time. It is not always easy to ask a question that can be answered scientifically.

One aspect of the transition to a testable research hypothesis is **measurement.** Measurement considerations help determine the way that we develop our operational definitions. We want to make certain that our variables are measured accurately and consistently. In technical terms we speak of **reliability** and **validity.** For a method of measurement to pass the test of reliability, the measurements must be consistent.

For example, a bathroom scale is reliable if it gives you the same weight no matter how many times you stand on it (assuming your weight does not change between weighings). Most of our measures such as intelligence or treatment effectiveness show more variation than a physical measure such as weight. For this reason when researchers are first designing a measure for a particular construct (for example, depression), it is common for the researchers to give the same measure over a number of occasions under similar conditions. They then examine the consistency of the research participants' responses to determine **test–retest reliability,** which is the correlation between the scores on each of the testing occasions.

In any study you want to use instruments that show a high positive **correlation** between these occasions. In addition, we also need the people who make the observations in a research study to be reliable in their ratings of particular behaviors. Like test–retest reliability, we can correlate the ratings of different observers when examining the same behavioral pattern. This is referred to as interrater reliability and will be discussed in greater detail in Chapter 11.

For a method of measurement to pass the test of validity, it must be accurate. In the example of the bathroom scale, the reading must accurately reflect your weight in some unit of measurement such as pounds. Now suppose that a well-meaning friend wanted you to lose weight, so he or she set your scale at 5 pounds overweight. At 5 pounds overweight, your scale would still be *reliable;* that is, it would continue to give you a *consistent* weight each time you weighed yourself. However, at 5 pounds overweight, the measurement would not be *valid;* that is, the scale would not reflect your *true* weight.

To be valid, a measurement must reflect the *true* score within certain limits. These limits are determined by what we know scientifically about a given construct. Unlike a physical measure such as temperature, which is based on the kinetic theory of heat, most of our measures—such as anxiety or intelligence or reaction time—are based on less well-articulated theory. For this reason questions of reliability and validity must be considered in some detail, and we will address them throughout this book. Our goal is to use methods of measurement that as much as possible are both accurate (valid) and consistent (reliable) in our experiments.

To return to your psychological experiment, it is your task to choose methods of measurement that are both accurate (valid) and consistent (reliable) in relation to the question that you are asking. Yet how do you select methods of measurement that are both reliable and valid for your purposes? You can either begin from scratch and demonstrate that your methods of measurement are indeed reliable and valid or review the literature to determine which methods of measurement have been used by others and adopt those methods.

Because the first option for many areas of study often is a difficult and lengthy process requiring highly technical expertise, we recommend that you choose the second option and pattern your measurement devices on those that have been established in the literature. We do not recommend that you do this blindly but that you continue to remember the problems of reliability and validity. Even if you are merely having a person press a button that measures reaction time, you still must determine what construct this device validly measures. In other words, if you were interested in the construct of information processing, you would first ask what would be a good measure of information processing. You would look for a measure with numerous empirical studies to support it, and you might conclude that reaction time was one such measure. In the final analysis, the task of choosing good measures is yours, although you may be greatly aided by previously published studies as well as by your own experience in experimentation.

	CONCEPT	The clock in the animal behavior lab is always 5 minutes fast. Would it be a
	CHECK 3.2	reliable instrument to use to time 30 minutes of free play for animals?

OVERVIEW

It may seem as if you have many decisions to make—and in a sense you do—but you also must remember that much of the process of performing science is learned through experience. Although there are guidelines for how to perform experiments and answer questions through science, many of the procedures that must be devised are learned through performing experiments. As you become more familiar with the process of experimentation, you will come to see which considerations of good experimental design are most appropriate in which situations. For now, you must rely mainly on understanding the logic of experimentation.

As we discuss in the next section, all experiments begin with an idea or consideration of the world in which we live. This consideration or idea is then formulated in terms of a general statement or question. For example, you may think that schizophrenia is related to diet or that anxiety is related to too much homework, or you might be interested in the factors that produce helping behavior. Whatever your idea, you must then translate it into a scientific research question or hypothesis; that is, you must develop a testable statement that points out what specific variables are to be examined and the hypothesized relationship between them.

At this point you rely on operational definitions, as we discussed previously. If you have clearly stated (1) your independent and dependent variables, (2) how each is measured, taking into account reliability and validity, (3) the hypothesized relationship between the independent and dependent variables, and (4) how this hypothesized relationship is to be tested, then you have passed one of the major hurdles of performing a scientific experiment (Figure 3.3).

Once you have overcome this hurdle, you are ready to move on and consider the process of experimentation itself, which we return to in Chapter 7. As you consider this process, we also want you to think about how your research participants may be influenced by your procedures (which we describe in great detail in Chapter 4 when we discuss ethical considerations). Before that, we want to supply you with some tools that can help you with your research. Let's first look at how some psychologists came up with ideas for research.

IDEAS COME FROM EVERYWHERE

Every experiment begins with an idea. These ideas can come from anywhere. As we will see, we may get our ideas from other people, newspapers, television, other scientists, students, our own experiences, or just out of thin air. One of our colleagues, Jude Cassidy, is a developmental psychologist who began her career as a dancer. Although most of us do not make

Figure 3.3

Steps required before
experimentation

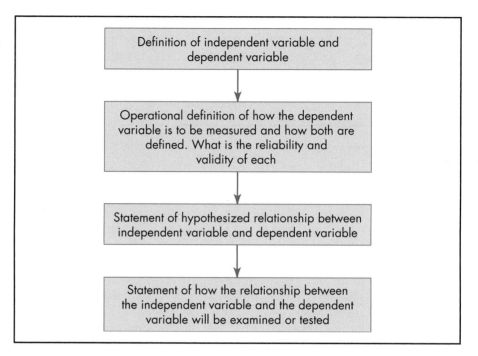

a connection between dance and psychological research, she was able to use her previous experience to inform her award-winning research in the area of mother–infant attachment. Here, she describes her work in her own words:

> I never had a psychology course in college. I was an English major, and after college I went to New York and I was a dancer. At that time I had some friends who were doing infancy research, looking at mother–child interactions. Because it was New York, there were lots of conventions and meetings and conferences in the city. When various friends would go to one of these mother–baby conferences, sometimes I went along as a friend. At these conferences they would show a lot of videotapes of mother–infant interaction, and I found these tapes aesthetically pleasing—beautiful to watch—very, very powerful. Babies obviously don't talk in that first year, yet this is really an incredibly rich relationship and a lot happens in that first year between the mother and her infant.

> By the time the baby is a year old it is not hard at all to see which babies are really depressed. I spent a lot of time looking at videotapes and looking at movements; it was like a dance. When I watched these videotapes I felt that I was watching a dance between this mother and this baby. As a dancer I was very tuned in to the power of the nonverbal communication—the power of physical movements to communicate meaning. So when I would see mothers and babies doing things together, it was very clear to me and very easy for me to believe and understand that these were powerful ways of communicating with each other. These physical movements had messages and meanings for the babies in relation to the babies' developing a sense of their relationship with their mother and their own self-worth. I really liked watching them.

> I hurt myself dancing and after a while realized that I might have to stop dancing. During that same time, I decided to take a graduate course in New York about parent–child interaction. I

took this course just for fun while I was still dancing. I read lots of all the basic mother–infant interaction literature and found it interesting, and liked it. I quickly discovered that the best way to learn what I wanted to know was to study developmental psychology. I just kept reading and reading, one book led to another, and I quickly found out about Mary Ainsworth and went to study with her.

My first research project actually grew out of being a dancer. Ainsworth's main procedure for looking at attachment quality in infants is called the "strange situation." It is a 20-minute laboratory procedure with the mother and baby in which the mother leaves the room and then returns. I was learning how to code videotapes of this situation—how to qualify the infant–mother attachment. Basically, the main thing that you look at is the baby's responses to the mother on her return. But you also see a lot of other things happening during that 20 minutes of time which previously had not been coded. The session takes place in a toy-filled playroom. So you see the baby playing. There are also a couple of chairs in the room where the mother sits. I was coding 18-month-olds—toddlers—who can walk, but a lot of them are still uneasy on their feet and still sort of precarious sometimes. Here is this room full of toys and very quickly the toys get spread out all over the floor, and the mother leaves and returns. Most babies would be interested in getting to her, or getting to the door to look for her. So they would have to negotiate around these toys.

When I was watching the tapes, because I had been a dancer, I was really tuned in to movement and people's use of their body. There is a wide variation in the way babies use their bodies in this space. Some babies would plough through the toys instead of carefully stepping over them. They would pick up a toy and misjudge its weight. They'd get tangled in things. They would trip, fall, bang their heads. They'd walk into the wall. They would try to get on a chair and keep falling off.

Even though naturally all babies would fall and look like Charlie Chaplin in some way, some babies seem to be more careful of their own body boundaries and to have a beginning sense of negotiating the environment with their bodies. There seemed to be a wide range in this. Both Ainsworth's research and Bowlby's attachment theory suggest that secure babies, because they are secure in their mother's availability if needed, can attend better to the environment. Secure babies can explore and can attend to the rest of the environment whereas insecure babies are less free to explore the environment. So, here was something that I noticed by watching. We label this "the ability to negotiate the environment." We made a very simple checklist and we watched and coded the first 6 minutes in the laboratory playroom before the mother leaves. In this study we found individual differences associated with attachment categories, as the theory predicted. (Used with permission of Jude Cassidy)

Because of her experience with dance, Dr. Cassidy started noticing the patterns of behavior between mothers and their infants. She then asked whether a relationship existed between the patterns of these interactions and some psychological factors such as activity level or depression. This in turn brought her into contact with the literature in the field and sent her to graduate school. In graduate school she learned to research mother–child interactions, and she began a series of correlational studies to find out whether the types of mother–child interactions described by attachment theory were related to developmental processes, such as the ability of young children to move about in their world. As we think about this research, we realize that questions such as the ones Dr. Cassidy asked can be approached using a variety of designs, including naturalistic observation, correlational studies, and more experimental lab situations, such as the "strange situation."

Another of our colleagues, Lance Shotland, is a social psychologist who was discussing bystander behavior with his class. Their discussion turned to the factors that influence whether one person will help another in times of trouble. This discussion raised questions that led him to conduct a series of studies. Here is how his idea developed:

> While teaching social psychology I got interested in why people don't seem to act when men attack women. For a long time I gave the standard explanation of why people don't help. What happened was that students in the class began to give me other explanations to account for why people don't help. The questions from students gave me the idea that the standard explanation may not be the total answer. What I did was go back to an actual situation in which a woman named Kitty Genovese was killed in front of over 30 people in the streets of New York without anyone calling the police or giving aid.
>
> The story is that at 3 a.m. a woman named Kitty Genovese arrived home and parked her car in a parking lot across from her home. She walked across the street from the parking lot and started to walk toward her home. She became uneasy as she was walking since someone was walking toward her and she didn't like the way he looked. She became extremely uneasy and turned around and started to walk toward a police telephone. She never reached the police call box. He overtook her and stabbed her. She screamed, "OH MY GOD, I HAVE BEEN STABBED!" With that scream, windows were opened, people's heads came out, and lights came on. The people shouted. With that, the man got scared and ran off. He then jumped into his car and drove away. A bus then came by and people got out of the bus. People in the houses then closed their windows and went back to sleep. She apparently was not helped by anybody. She managed to crawl to another building and the man came back and overtook her and stabbed again. Again she screamed. Again, windows opened and lights came on. Again the people shouted and the man again ran off. The third time, he came back again, and this time he killed her. The entire event took over a half an hour.
>
> This is a true event that happened in New York City in 1964. No one who looked out of the apartment windows had done anything that was effective except to scare him off. To have been really effective, the people would have to have helped her, but no one bothered to do that. At that time, the New York papers said "what's going on in New York?" and talked about apathy. A couple of psychologists named Latané and Darley decided to research the question of bystander intervention. In their research, Latané and Darley concluded that numbers in themselves may not be important and in fact people in large crowds may leave it to others. These psychologists called this "diffusion of responsibility." Also, the fact that other people are not intervening gives others the feeling that they are not really seeing the situation correctly.
>
> Well, this is what I always told my class, and my class felt there were other things going on. So I returned to a book that was composed of interviews with the people who watched the Kitty Genovese murder. In this book, *Thirty-Eight Witnesses,* I read the bystanders' own accounts of what was going on. One of the things they said was that they were scared. I really don't know why, because they were safe in their homes. But also what they seemed to say was that they thought it was a lovers' quarrel. I became interested in that, and what I did was to go to *The New York Times* and started to search through several years, looking for cases where men were attacking women, and what I found is that it does occur with fair frequency since *The New York Times* generally does not report crime news.
>
> Another case happened in the middle 1970s. There was a situation where a man raped a woman in full view of some 30 people. They watched the whole thing. They didn't do anything, and it was only a half block away from a police station. Again, what you find from interviews was that the people thought it was her boyfriend. I began to wonder if this was the

Figure 3.4

Steps involved in forming a research hypothesis

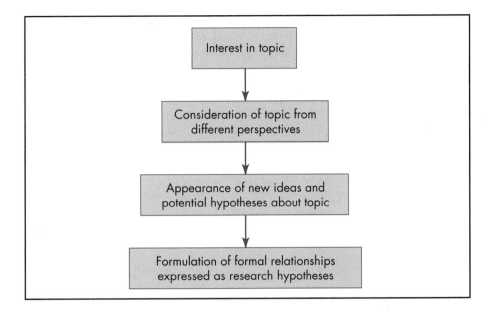

controlling factor in the behavior of bystanders. What I did was to test this. I also went further and wondered what bystanders assume if they don't know the relationship between people. The first thing I wanted to test was: If bystanders perceive a relationship between a woman and her attacker, will they intervene less frequently than if it is a situation where a strange man is attacking a strange woman? (Used with permission of Lance Shotland)

At this point, Dr. Shotland had an idea, an educated guess, that stemmed partly from his students' dissatisfaction with the standard explanation and partly from his reading of first-person accounts of crimes. His idea was that one important factor that determines whether a woman would be helped is whether the man and woman are perceived to have a relationship. As a social scientist, Dr. Shotland wanted to test his idea in an experiment. Before he could design the experiment, however, he had to restate the idea in a statement or hypothesis that could be tested in a scientific manner. Figure 3.4 outlines the steps that Dr. Shotland needed to go through before he could begin an experiment.

We have already discussed the first two steps: (1) being interested in a topic and having an idea and (2) considering and thinking about the topic from different perspectives. The third step is formulating the initial question: whether a bystander's perception of the relationship was important for a woman to be helped. The fourth step is reformulating the question into a research hypothesis.

The specific research hypothesis that Dr. Shotland sought to test was this: If bystanders perceive a relationship between a woman and her attacker, they will be less likely to intervene than if the victim and the attacker are perceived to be strangers. To test this hypothesis, Dr. Shotland designed an experiment in which a fight was staged between a man and a woman. Suppose you were a research participant in the experiment. What would you do if you walked out of a classroom and saw a man and a woman fighting and yelling at each other? Do you think you would be more likely to intervene if the woman yelled, "I don't know why I ever married you," or if she yelled, "I don't know you"?

To determine the dependent and independent variables, let us reexamine the structure of a research hypothesis. When a researcher sets up a hypothesis, it is of the general form "If I do this (independent variable), then this will happen (dependent variable)." In his study, Dr. Shotland manipulated the bystanders' perceptions of the relationship between the man and the woman. In one condition the man and woman were portrayed as married ("I don't know why I ever married you") and in the other as strangers ("I don't know you"). Thus, the independent variable (the variable under Dr. Shotland's control) was the relationship between the man and the woman. The dependent variable—that is, what was measured—was whether the research participants, who were genuine bystanders in the experiment, intervened.

A good question at this point is, "What do you mean by *intervene*?" Dr. Shotland operationally defined *intervening* as any one of four activities: (1) calling the police on a nearby phone, (2) asking a person working nearby to help, (3) shouting at the man attacking the woman, or (4) trying to stop the fight. Now that you know what was measured, an extremely important question arises: How was the dependent variable measured? In this study, Dr. Shotland used a simple procedure; he just counted the number of people who did or did not intervene in the staged fight.

The results were consistent with Dr. Shotland's hypothesis. Under the condition in which there was an apparent marriage relationship, 20% of the bystanders intervened, whereas in the stranger condition, 80% of the bystanders intervened. Dr. Shotland did not stop at this point but performed additional studies that controlled for alternative explanations of the data (Shotland & Straw, 1976). The article describing the study illustrates well how scientists perform research, control for alternative explanations, and modify their studies as new information comes to light.

Following these studies, the research was extended to examine what type of cry for help brought the most help (Shotland & Stebbins, 1980), as well as what behaviors and attributions would be necessary in a perceived dating situation for bystanders to decide that rape was involved (Shotland & Goodstein, 1983). Further research has examined which social norms and behaviors lead to compliant sexual behavior, to "token" resistance to sexual advances, and to various forms of rape (Shotland, 1992).

Let's now turn to another researcher and see how she obtained her ideas. The researcher is a developmental psychologist, Nora Newcombe.

It all began in graduate school when I shared an office with another woman. One day she asked me what I thought about studying how children go about saying what they want. That is, how they express imperative intent (for example, saying, "Bring me some orange juice"). I thought that was a very interesting idea. It is interesting to me because there is a theoretical position presented by Robin Lakoff that adult men and women differ in how they express imperatives. She stated that women are more tentative and unsure. According to Lakoff, women say things like "Would you please open the door" rather than "Open the door," or even hint by saying "It's hot in here" rather than "Open the window."

Assuming Lakoff was right, I thought it would be interesting to see if children already showed this type of sex-role differentiation. But first I wanted to test Lakoff's theory with adults. You see, Lakoff is a linguist and had presented her ideas in the form of a theory but had never tested them in a scientific manner. That is, she never collected data from men and women to see if their speech styles indeed did differ.

Another woman, Diane Arnkoff, and I began our research at this point. We did what seemed most straightforward, which was to bring people in and ask them to talk with each other. We brought people in two at a time—either two men, or two women, or a man and a woman.

We did this because we thought it was probably important to determine not only if men and women differed in their speech styles but also whether they differed according to whether they were talking to a member of the same sex or opposite sex. In our first study the people didn't know each other. We gave them a set of topics to talk about, but also told them they could talk about anything else they liked. We then turned a tape recorder on and left them for 15 minutes. (Used with permission of Nora Newcombe)

In performing this study, Dr. Newcombe sought to test the general idea that men speak differently from women, especially when asking for something or giving commands. If we look at the general pattern of "If I do this, what will happen?" we can see that Dr. Newcombe paired men with men, women with women, and men with women and then observed the outcomes. The next question we ask is, "What was measured?" The dependent variable was speech style, which was operationally defined in relation to Lakoff's theory. Specifically, the number of qualifiers (such as "you know," "kinda," "I guess," and "maybe") and the number of indirect statements (such as "It is really cold in here, isn't it?") were noticed. The next question is, "How were these measured?" Dr. Newcombe used two measures. The first was to count the number of qualifiers and indirect statements each person uttered during the 15 minutes of recording. Then she measured the total amount of time each person spoke. (If one person in the pair spoke almost all the time and the other one said little, then it would be difficult to draw conclusions from the frequency numbers alone.) Thus, Dr. Newcombe used a second measure, which was the number of qualifiers each person used, divided by the total time that person spoke. Likewise, she calculated the number of indirect statements divided by the time the person spoke. She found that there were no differences between the speech styles of men and women as operationally defined.

Let's continue this section with an interview with Jeffrey Parker, who is a developmental psychologist. Dr. Parker studies the nature of children's friendships. You will notice that he became interested in the nature of children's friendship based on his own personal experience. However, he needed to go beyond his own experience and examine some of the universals in children's relationships. For those of you interested in research careers, he offers an excellent model of finding research opportunities at your university as well as finding a graduate school that offers the type of research to which you are attracted. As you read his description of his work, notice the manner in which he attempts to develop a rich understanding of the phenomena under study through interviews with children and how he in turn uses this information to design experimental studies to better define the variables at play. Finally, he defines friendship scientifically in terms of five critical dimensions, which are used for future research.

I study kids' friendships and I study them as basic relationships. I didn't set out to be a psychologist. In college, I set out to be a journalist. I liked doing journalism. But in retrospect, I realized that it wasn't the events that I was attracted to. What I really liked about journalism was meeting the people and interviewing the people. It was the interesting people that I liked talking to. I was really drawn to that. However, I took a child psychology course outside my major and really loved it. I realized I was mostly interested in the social dynamics, especially in children. Some of that came from my own history. We moved several times and they were at critical ages. I found those moves very tough. It was tough to relocate and to make new friends. However, my best friends had also been my real source of support during those moves. In looking at developmental psychology, I thought that friendships had been underrated resources in people's lives. Thus, I wanted to study friendships from a scientific standpoint—to ask the question what are these friendships that kids have? How do they work?

As an undergraduate I volunteered in a research lab which was looking at social support. The goal of the lab was to quantify the amount of social support that kids had and see what difference social support made. My task was to go interview kids. Actually, what I did was to walk through a kid's neighborhood and to let them tell me about all the kids they knew in the neighborhood and all the adults and all the sources of support they had. By walking with them, they would remember when they got to the park where they played and they would tell me all these very rich stories about their lives and their friends. I remember one girl who lived in a very upscale neighborhood who could have everything she wanted. But there were no kids in the neighborhood. We sat on the steps and it was very touching that she had lots of people in her life who loved her but no kids nearby to play with. It became clear how important it is for kids to have people close by who are your peers. So in undergraduate school I learned how to interview kids and read everything I could about friendship. When it was time to go to graduate school, I knew this was what I wanted to study. Fortunately for me I found a graduate school that had a number of faculty who studied children and their interaction patterns. One of the people I worked with taught me how to carefully observe interactions which we coded from videotapes. I spent endless hours as a graduate student watching two best friends talk to each other. This really taught me to notice how kids manage their interactions. The other faculty member taught me how to do survey research and to constantly ask, "what does it all mean?" And "how can we help kids who have problems with relationships?"

Since graduate school my students and I have been doing a lot of work on children's friendships beginning with naturalistic observation and following that up with more experimental methods. We've been looking at the variety and evolution of friendships. Sometimes, we will do a naturalistic observation study and see how kids interact when adults are not around. We think a lot about interpersonal processes such as self-disclosure and gossip and how individuals show intimacy. We then think about how to quantify that and relate it to kids' lives. For example, our work has shown that popularity and friendship are different processes. Even if you are not popular, just having a best friend makes a big difference in quality of life for kids.

Another type of study we did was to go to a summer camp and live there. We had a cabin of our own and the kids knew we were researchers from the university. It was basically a naturalistic observation study. We were able to ask kids about their relationships every week or so. We could actually follow the relationships over time so we could see how their friendships begin to develop. We got to see the friendships forming and breaking up and reforming again. In the literature no one had looked at the evolution of friendships over time. One of the things we discovered was that there were differences between the friendships of boys and girls. With boys, for example, if two boys and their friends came to summer camp and if these two boys became friends at summer camp, then their friends also tended to become friends. With girls we found that although two girls might become friends at camp their friends would not necessarily become friends. When I mentioned this study to someone they suggested that perhaps girls were more jealous and therefore did not encourage their friends to become friends with each other. In this way they were able to manage their relationships. This made us ask the question of how the kids manage their relationships in a broader social context and also got us interested in the question of jealousy.

We went to the literature concerning jealousy and essentially nothing was known concerning kids. We did find information on jealousy in adults. However, that research was basically about romantic relationships. Thus, in terms of kids and jealousy we found ourselves in completely new territory. However, we were able to adopt some of the core concepts from the adults' jealousy literature to that of kids. The students in the lab and I had a lot of discussions about what it meant to be jealous and what jealousy is. We especially discussed how to measure it. We knew that jealousy was something that could not just be observed so we had to think what could we do to get into the minds of these kids. We set out then to think about all the standard ways of doing this. What we decided to do was to create realistic scenarios that would describe specific interactions. In order to do this we asked everyone we knew to tell us stories about kids and jealousy. Some of our friends told us about times they had been jealous when they were kids. We also talked with our neighbors' kids and we asked them to tell us about being jealous. From this huge collection of events we were able to create scenarios. For example, one scenario might talk about you and your friend planning on going to a new CD store when it opened. You read in the paper that the store has opened. You call your friend only to learn that your friend has already gone with someone else. How would you feel? It turns out that some kids would feel jealous at their friend going with someone else and other kids would not. Anyway, we were able to put together about 40 or so of these stories. We first gave these stories to some pilot kids to make sure there was a range of reactions to the stories, that is, not everyone reacted the same way. We were also able to remove the stories that were confusing and difficult to understand. At this point we had about 25 stories of which some 15 related to jealousy which we could have kids react to.

Overall, in studying the critical aspects of friendship, we came up with five critical dimensions which helped us to measure friendship. First, there is the amount of time and enjoyment that two kids derive from each other. Second, there is intimacy and the disclosure of personal secrets. Third, there is the dimension of advice in terms of do you go to this person for information about living life. Fourth, there is the dimension of validation. Simply stated, this dimension just asks if the other person makes you feel good about yourself. And finally on the negative side, there is the dimension of conflict. Using these dimensions we were able to develop and validate a questionnaire that measured friendship. Using this measure, we are examining in our research what aspects predict which kids have high quality friendships and which don't. (Used with permission of Jeffrey Parker)

Let's conclude this section with an interview with Andreas Keil, a psychologist who performs neuroscience research. In his case, events from his life helped to shape the types of research questions that he was interested in answering. For example, Dr. Keil's interest in jazz led him to think about timing patterns and rhythms and how these are seen in the brain. Although his initial work studied these brain patterns using electroencephalography (EEG), his research program has used a variety of brain-imaging techniques including functional magnetic resonance imaging (fMRI) and magnetoencephalography (MEG). (As a student he was fortunate to be at a university that had these facilities.) He also illustrates how scientists seek information from a variety of areas when current research in psychology cannot answer questions. In his case it was the new area of nonlinear dynamics, or chaos theory. Notice, too, that he was able to perform his initial research using a very simple stimulus, the figure on a pizza box from Paris.

I have always been interested in music especially jazz. Throughout my life I have thought about rhythms and patterns and how things are expressed in the world. When I started graduate school my own patterns changed quickly on a number of levels. On a personal level, my son was born and I got to watch the rapid and often unpredictable changes in his mental and behavioral states. I also was asked to play in a local jazz group. Intellectually, I ran into the Mandelbrot book on chaos theory and his ideas concerning how patterns could exist in what appeared to be random behavior. Unfortunately, what I was initially learning in psychology graduate school did not seem to give me any understanding of either my son or my music. No one seemed interested in this type of change. Thus, I read everything I could in chaos theory. I read about the applications of coupled oscillations in laser physics, ocean waves, social behavior as well as other areas of application. I became fascinated by the possibility of modeling the seemingly erratic changes that were present in my environment. Given that I needed to come up with a project for my master's degree, I thought how can I apply these ideas to the brain. Fortunately, in my department there were experts in using EEG activity to reflect brain states. Thus, it was straightforward to use EEG to study the relationship between temporal dimensions of the brain and behavioral activity. I was immediately grasped by the fact that the brain appears to use oscillations on all of its levels to accomplish the credible task of experience and behavior. Even more interesting, it seemed that whether I was looking at the single cell level or the level of groups of cells, brain cells oscillate in a complex but clearly nonrandom manner. Now the tough part was integrating this information with what we know about cognition and emotion. This started a program of research which has attempted to describe the underlying brain states associated with cognitive and emotional processes. Let me give you an example of one such study. Using the logo of a French pizza service (Pizza Bruno's) we tried to follow the brain and behavioral changes that were associated with perception of various different "gestalts" across time. The pizza figure was special in that it showed a happy or a sad face depending on how the figure was turned. The figure was printed on the cardboard pizza container. Although the actual box showed the phrase "I ate at Bruno's" under the happy face, we just used the face alone. In our experiment, the figure of the face was turned in a circle such that the participant saw the sad face become happy and then the happy face become sad. This shift of perspective happened in a sudden jump. One moment you saw a happy face and in the next a sad face. At the point of this shift of perspective, EEG activity in the brain also changed. We found that the brain's rapid oscillations increased when a new percept was formed. (Used with permission of Andreas Keil)

The focus of this chapter is on obtaining ideas. We hope that the five interviews in this chapter have increased your understanding of several important ideas related to the science of behavior and experience. One of these ideas is that scientists are people, and as people they differ in the manner in which they discover and develop ideas. Some people learn from their previous experience, some from their classes, some from talking to other people, some from reading the work (scientific or not) of others, and for some the ideas just seem to come out of thin air.

INTUITION AND REVELATION

Depending on the particular era in which people have lived, ideas that seem to pop into one's mind have been considered the voice of God, meaningless chatter, an activation of the right hemisphere of the brain, nonscientific, mystical as well as meaningful, or an example of psychological intuition. We really do not know much about the workings of our brains, especially when it comes to our own thought processes. At this point in our understanding of the process of science and how we obtain our ideas, we are much like the baby in Chapter 1, who watches and tries to see the world. Although we do not know where spontaneous ideas come from, we can examine some cases in which spontaneous or intuitive ideas have influenced the course of science and the work of individual scientists.

One of the most famous examples of a scientist whose ideas just popped into his consciousness is Albert Einstein. When asked how he came upon ideas and solved problems, Einstein replied,

The words or the language, as they are written or spoken, do not seem to play any role in my mechanism of thought. . . . The above mentioned elements are, in any case, of visual and some of muscular type. Conventional words or other signs have to be sought for laboriously only in a secondary stage. (Koestler, 1964, p. 171)

In other places, Einstein speaks of having a bodily sensation concerning the answer to a problem or says that ideas just came to him while sailing. However, he goes on to state that often the translation from the body state to scientific notation required years. Einstein's image of a man riding on a beam of light proved to be one intuitive vision that changed science. Although this vision came in a single instant, Einstein spent considerable time working out his theory of relativity and communicating it to other scientists.

Another interesting example of ideas coming from unexpected places is the case of the German chemist Friedrich Kekulé. In 1865 Kekulé was sitting in a chair watching the fire when he fell asleep. He later reported the following dream:

Again the atoms were gamboling before my eyes. This time the small groups kept modestly in the background. My mental eye, rendered more acute by repeated visions of this kind, could now distinguish larger structures, of manifold conformation; long rows, sometimes more closely fitted together; all twining and twisting in a snakelike motion. But look! What was that? One of the snakes had seized hold of its own tail, and the form whirled mockingly before my eyes. As if by a flash of lightning I awoke. (Koestler, 1964, p. 118)

This simple dream of a snake biting its own tail led to the idea of a ring of carbon atoms, which led to research that changed the field of organic chemistry. Through this dream, Kekulé came to suggest the idea that the molecules of certain chemical compounds are best described as consisting of closed rings.

Despite the spontaneity of these insights, they were preceded by years of intensive work by these scientists in their respective areas of interest. Furthermore, their insights had to be translated into the language and workings of science, which requires not only effort on the part of the scientist but also adequate preparation for understanding the insight in the first place.

THE SCIENTIST'S GUIDE TO HAVING AN IDEA

In the 1920s Graham Wallas became interested in how scientists solve problems. Because little was known about this process, Wallas began by reading the works of famous scientists, particularly Hermann von Helmholtz and Henri Poincaré. Wallas (1926) concluded that the scientific process could be described in four stages.

The first stage is *preparation*. This is the stage in which a person becomes interested in a problem, learns all he or she can about it, and examines it from various perspectives. Although we do not know why we become interested in the topics that we do, at some point one topic or idea becomes more interesting to us than others. It was at this stage that Dr. Shotland became interested in the alternative reasons that his class gave for people's failure to help a woman who is being attacked. This initial stage begins with the scientist's interest and then involves assembling available information on the topic. Assembling information to get an accurate picture of a research area may take many trips to the library and may involve reading and rereading many crucial articles. Dr. Shotland not only talked with his class but also read all he could about bystander behavior, finally examining eye-witness accounts of an event that concerned his topic.

The second stage described by Wallas is called *incubation*. This is the stage in which Einstein goes sailing or Kekulé takes a nap. This stage is close to meditating on a topic but not thinking about it. One common report is that these new ideas often appear spontaneously and catch us by surprise while we are thinking about something else. Keep in mind also that the incubation stage may take years, as it did with Einstein.

The third stage of the process described by Wallas is called *illumination*. At this point, the idea or solution begins to emerge into consciousness. The emerging idea could take the form of the dream of Kekulé or the bodily sensations of Einstein, or it could be simply an idea that comes out of nowhere. In this stage one sees an answer that was not seen before or even a totally new method of viewing the world.

For a scientist, seeing the picture is not enough, and this brings us to the fourth stage: *verification*. This occurs when you test your idea or hypothesis to see whether it fits the real world. The verification stage is what the remainder of this book is all about.

Yet it is important to realize that there are some human aspects to performing science, which involve learning everything you can about a topic that interests you, then mulling over this information, and finally permitting yourself to find your answers in strange places. In trying to understand how scientists obtain the ideas for their experiments, keep in mind that they are already familiar with much of the published work in their areas of interest. Consequently, an essential first step is to spend time in the library becoming familiar with various content areas in which you might be interested. To assist you in this process, the next section describes several resource tools that psychologists commonly use to explore new areas of interest.

 CONCEPT CHECK 3.3   Professor Fraud said that all research ideas should come from your dreams. His archrival, Professor Limited, said no idea that comes from a dream has a place in science. How would you react to their statements?

 ## TOOLS FOR LIBRARY RESEARCH

Sometimes people are interested in a general area and would like to learn more about it before they attempt to perform an experiment. For example, beginning psychology students may say they want to study memory or health and emotion or why people help others in emergency situations or what the important factors in understanding date rape are or what makes one person a leader. Where can they go for more information? Of course, they can go directly to experience and attempt to learn more about the topic from the world itself. Yet this may not be an efficient method because it ignores previous attempts to describe and understand the process under study. Most people begin by reading what others have written on the topic.

For most of us, the library is the best source of materials concerning our topic. With the advent of the World Wide Web, the library and its resource materials may no longer be totally in one physical location but stored virtually around the world. Reference material that at one time could be found only in the library is now available from almost any computer, as well as some cell phones and PDAs. For example, at one time, a primary reference source for locating books and journals related to psychology was ***Psychological Abstracts.*** The print version of *Psychological Abstracts* was discontinued at the end of 2006 and replaced totally by an online version called **PsycINFO.** Although this type of information is available from almost any location, you will still find the expertise of such people as reference librarians valuable in your search. Your librarian will be particularly helpful in determining what is available to you because a variety of methods are used for storing information, including books, journals, CDs, and DVDs. Also search services such as PsycINFO have modified their offerings to better fit the needs of different institutions, and thus what is available at the various institutions may be different. In this section we discuss both the traditional sources of information, such as books and journals, and their electronic versions. We end with a discussion of the Internet as a source of information, referring you to specific web pages throughout the following sections.

■ Journals and Books

Journals are the major outlet in which scientists describe their research. A scientific journal is a collection of experimental reports and other articles written by scientists. There are journals both for broad areas, such as the journals *Science* and *Nature,* and for more specific areas, such as the journal *The Behavioral and Brain Sciences.* The latter is different from others in that it includes commentaries from other scientists at the conclusion of each article. Psychologists publish their research in such journals as the *Journal of Experimental Psychology, Journal of Abnormal Psychology, Developmental Psychology, Journal of Personality and Social Psychology, Psychological Science, Psychophysiology, Health Psychology, Journal of Applied Psychology,* and *Psychosomatic Medicine*. These are just a few of the large variety of journals related to psychology. Your reference librarian can tell you which journals your library carries or has access to.

One important point to keep in mind in regard to journals is whether or not they are peer-reviewed. The journals that are peer-reviewed tend to be highly reputable sources of information. *Peer review* generally means that two or more scientists who are experts in the author's particular field read the paper and gave the author comments and suggestions for changes to be made before the article was published. In this way, the journal ensures that the research and information presented in the article will reflect the current scientific understanding of a topic. As we noted previously, many pseudoscientific claims are not reported in peer-reviewed journals, and thus lack expert scrutiny and represent the opinion of only one person.

When you examine a particular journal, you will notice that the articles cover various topics within the given area. However, you probably want to examine articles on a particular topic. One way to do this is to use one of the large computer databases available at many libraries. The major indexes that cover psychological research are PsycINFO (which replaced *Psychological Abstracts*), the Web of Science (which contains *Science Citation Index* and *Social Science Citation Index*), and PubMed (which replaced *Index Medicus*).

■ Computer Databases

With the development of computers and media able to store and access large sets of data, it has become possible to search a large database and retrieve bibliographic information in a few seconds. A number of libraries offer computerized searches, and you should check with your reference librarian to see what is available to you. One of the major databases for psychology is PsycINFO. PubMed performs the same service for the medical literature and also includes a number of psychological journals. Although we include examples of these databases in this chapter, some universities use different versions of the software. Thus, what is available to you may differ from what we show.

The basic principle behind computer searches is simple. It allows you to find research on a particular topic or by a particular author. One real advantage is speed. The computer can quickly perform a variety of search procedures. For example, if we were to search articles published during the past 10 years and ask which of them discussed the topic of psychotherapy, we would see on the computer screen that there are more than 10,000 such articles. If we now requested the psychotherapy articles that were descriptions of research in psychotherapy, we would find the number of articles available to be fewer than 200. If we asked for only those that studied patient-therapist matching ("Is psychotherapy more effective if patients and therapists are matched on particular characteristics such as age, sex, race, and therapeutic orientation?"), we would find that there are only a few articles. At this point we could ask the computer to print out the titles and the journals in which these articles were published. Some databases also contain a summary of each piece of research, which also can be printed. Computer databases are particularly useful for their ability to search for categories of research that normally might not be indexed. Many databases allow you to search for a particular word within the title or summary of the article.

PsycINFO   PsycINFO can be used for most searches related to topics of interest to psychologists. This system contains basically the same information as the older *Psychological Abstracts* and also includes some foreign journals and dissertations. Because most university libraries subscribe to such computer systems, students generally can perform these searches for no cost. PsycINFO is maintained by the American Psychological Association, and you can find recent information on this database including how to use it by going to their home page (http://www.apa.org/psycinfo). By using the electronic version, you can have the computer do the searching and sorting for you.

How would you do such a search? You first need to determine how to access PsycINFO. Once you have access to PsycINFO, you will be asked to choose which years you want to search and to enter a keyword for which the computer will search. If you were to search for research on emotions in PsycINFO, you might discover that more than 103,000 different articles and books were published on the topic. Thus, you would need to limit your search. One way to do this is to consider what aspect of the topic you are interested in studying.

For example, you may be interested in emotional regulation. You could then enter the term *emotional regulation* and see that your search has yielded few articles. At this point you could begin to examine the entries of interest to you. You might discover that even the topic *emotional regulation* is not specific enough. If you were interested in emotional regulation in children, you would need to specify this also. But how would you do that? You could enter the phrase "emotional regulation in children." You could also limit the search to recent years. Box 3.1 shows a search in PsycINFO for the term "emotion* regulation" in articles

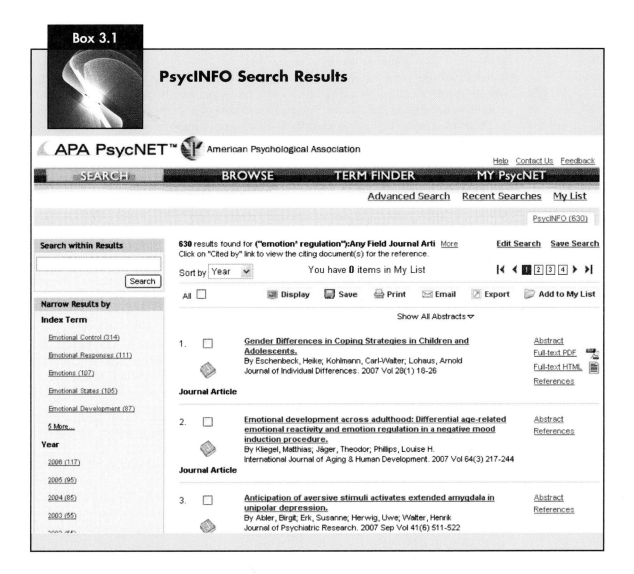

Box 3.1

PsycINFO Search Results

published in the years 2002–2005. Note: emotion* includes all words that begin with emotion, such as emotional; only the page for 2007 is shown.

National Library of Medicine   Whereas PsycINFO covers published material of interest to psychologists, PubMed performs the same function for medical journals. PubMed assesses a larger database called MEDLINE, which is part of the U.S. National Library of Medicine. Most topics of interest to psychological researchers, such as Dr. Shotland's research on bystander intervention, are not found in MEDLINE. However, at times there are overlaps; some research could be published in either a psychological journal or a medical one, as would be the case with social support and its relation to cancer or how one measures quality of life. At these times, PubMed is a source for research literature that may not be listed in PsycINFO.

PubMed is published by the U.S. National Library of Medicine (http://igm.nlm .nih.gov), which is part of the National Institutes of Health (http://www.nih.gov/) in Washington, D.C. PubMed can be accessed through a variety of sources, including the PubMed website (http://www.ncbi.nlm.nih.gov/PubMed/). There is also a MedlinePlus website (http://medlineplus.gov/), which contains a large variety of health-related information. Both PubMed and MedlinePlus are rich sources of information related to medicine and health, including U.S. government databases. Fortunately, these sources of information are free and can be accessed through any Internet connection. Both systems have extensive sets of instructions for use, including how to perform PubMed and MEDLINE searches. PubMed's search function is similar to that of PsycINFO. Box 3.2 shows a sample search (on psychoneuroimmunology).

Science Citation Index and *Social Science Citation Index*   The *Science Citation Index* (SCI) and the *Social Science Citation Index* (SSCI) list articles published in either the sciences (such as physics, chemistry, and biology) or the social sciences (such as sociology and economics). These two indexes are found in an online site entitled "Web of Science." The online site is able to search the *Science Citation Index* and the *Social Science Citation Index* individually or together. Areas of psychology are referenced in either or both indexes, depending on the area of study. Both list references by topic, by author, or by both. As with PsycINFO, it is useful to be specific, as this will help limit your search results. For example, depending upon what you are interested in, it would be better to search for terms such as *picture memory, recognition memory, autobiological memory,* or *rat memory* than to search just the term *memory.* You can also search by author, which will produce a list of all the publications that person has written. Since people in a variety of areas have the same name, you can limit the search by noting the name of the university with which the author is affiliated.

One advantage of the SSCI over other indexes is that it includes in a separate volume a list of all studies that have cited a particular study (hence the name *Social Science Citation Index*). This would be particularly useful to a researcher such as Dr. Newcombe. As she was beginning to plan her study examining the relationship between gender and speech types according to the theory of Robin Lakoff, she would want to know whether anyone else had tested this theory. As you will see later, in their articles scientists refer to the research and theories of others, so it would be possible to find all the studies that had referred to Lakoff's work. To do this, Dr. Newcombe would look up "R. T. Lakoff" and note all the articles that cited her work. Dr. Newcombe then could check these articles to see whether any other scientists had asked the specific question in which she was interested.

CONCEPT CHECK 3.4   You are interested in determining whether Gordon Bower's original mood and emotion experiment has been replicated by another researcher. Which library resource would help you?

■ The Internet

You can access a great variety of information via the Internet from professional organizations such as the American Psychological Society (http://www.psychologicalscience .org/), the American Psychological Association (http://www.apa.org), and the Canadian

Box 3.2

PubMed Search Results

A service of the National Library of Medicine and the National Institutes of Health

My NCBI
[Sign In] [Re

NCBI

Pub Med
www.pubmed.gov

| All Databases | PubMed | Nucleotide | Protein | Genome | Structure | OMIM | PMC | Journals |

Search | PubMed | for | psychoneuroimmunology | Go | Clear | Save S

Limits   Preview/Index   History   Clipboard   Details

About Entrez

Text Version

Display | Summary | Show | 20 | Sort by | Send to |

All: 862   Review: 387

Entrez PubMed
Overview
Help | FAQ
Tutorials
New/Noteworthy
E-Utilities

Items 1 - 20 of 862   Page | 1 | of 44 Next

☐ **1:** Eccles R.   Related Articles, Links

The power of the placebo.
Curr Allergy Asthma Rep. 2007 May;7(2):100-4.
PMID: 17437679 [PubMed - in process]

PubMed Services
Journals Database
MeSH Database
Single Citation Matcher
Batch Citation Matcher
Clinical Queries
Special Queries
LinkOut
My NCBI

☐ **2:** Goehler LE, Lyte M, Gaykema RP.   Related Articles, Links

Infection-induced viscerosensory signals from the gut enhance anxiety:
Implications for psychoneuroimmunology.
Brain Behav Immun. 2007 Apr 9; [Epub ahead of print]
PMID: 17428636 [PubMed - as supplied by publisher]

Related Resources
Order Documents
NLM Mobile
NLM Catalog
NLM Gateway
TOXNET
Consumer Health
Clinical Alerts
ClinicalTrials.gov
PubMed Central

☐ **3:** Goncharova LB, Tarakanov AO.   Related Articles, Links

Molecular networks of brain and immunity.
Brain Res Rev. 2007 Feb 22; [Epub ahead of print]
PMID: 17408562 [PubMed - as supplied by publisher]

☐ **4:** Kendall-Tackett K.   Related Articles, Links

A new paradigm for depression in new mothers: the central role of
inflammation and how breastfeeding and anti-inflammatory treatments
protect maternal mental health.
Int Breastfeed J. 2007 Mar 30;2:6.
PMID: 17397549 [PubMed - in process]

☐ **5:** Irwin MR, Miller AH.   Related Articles, Links

Depressive disorders and immunity: 20 years of progress and discovery.
Brain Behav Immun. 2007 May;21(4):374-83. Epub 2007 Mar 13.
PMID: 17360153 [PubMed - in process]

☐ **6:** Jensen SE, Lehman B, Antoni MH, Pereira DB.   Related Articles, Links

Virally mediated cervical cancer in the iatrogenically
immunocompromised: Applications for psychoneuroimmunology.
Brain Behav Immun. 2007 Feb 7; [Epub ahead of print]
PMID: 17291716 [PubMed - as supplied by publisher]

☐ **7:** Aubert A.   Related Articles, Links

Invertebrate studies and the evolution of comparative
psychoneuroimmunology.
Brain Behav Immun. 2007 Mar;21(3):290-1. No abstract available.

Psychological Association (http://www.cpa.ca/). Government agencies, such as the National Institutes of Health (http://www.nih.gov/), the National Institute of Mental Health (http://www.nimh.nih.gov/), the National Science Foundation (http://www.nsf.gov/), and the National Academy of Sciences (http://www.nas.edu/), also have websites.

Most colleges and universities have home pages that describe their programs and provide resources for psychology. For example, both Hanover College (http://psych.hanover.edu/) and Skidmore (http://psych.skidmore.edu/resources.htm) have pages that describe a variety of resources on the web. The Hanover site has links to tutorials and demonstrations, journals on the web, psychological software, and similar materials. The Skidmore resources page lists a variety of sites related to general psychology, biological psychology, clinical psychology, sensation and perception, and statistics. At these websites, you can view tutorials in psychology and other materials, for example, demonstrations of visual illusions. Also, you can access many journals through these college web pages. In addition, books that describe psychological resources on the web are available (Kardas, 1999; Varnhagen, 2002).

Some home pages are limited to a specific area of interest. For example, you can find a variety of neuroscience websites. These home pages include both general reference pages, such as ones addressed to neurosciences (http://www.neuroguide.com/), as well as specific pictures of brain images. The neuroscience general home pages can also send you to other sets of information related to the neurosciences, neurology, psychiatry, psychology, cognitive science, and artificial intelligence. If you click on an area related to academic centers, you will find a list of home pages from universities and researchers around the world.

Because the Internet makes it possible for any computer to be connected to any other computer and because anyone can set up a home page, there is no guarantee that the information you receive is always correct or unbiased. Although such search engines as Google have made more information available to us, it is not always easy to know which sites present accurate information. There are many pseudoscience sites on the web, so it is necessary to carefully consider the information you are being given. However, when you go to sites maintained by major institutions such as the National Institutes of Health or the National Library of Medicine, you are more likely to find accurate information.

CONCLUSION

We have discussed developing a hypothesis, the use of operational definitions, how various scientists have arrived at their ideas for research, and some library resources that you will use as you begin to explore your own ideas. At this point, you should be able to begin developing research studies of your own.

All experiments begin with an idea about the world in which we live. This consideration or idea is first formulated as a general statement or question. Whatever your idea, you must translate it into a specific research question or hypothesis; that is, you must develop a testable statement that points out what specific variables are to be examined and what the hypothesized relationship is between them, relying on operational definitions. At this point you should have stated clearly (1) your independent and dependent variables, (2) how each is measured, taking into account reliability and validity, (3) the hypothesized relationship between the independent and dependent variables, and (4) how this hypothesized relationship is to be tested. Before we turn to the question of experimental design, we want to review the major points of descriptive and inferential statistics in the next chapters.

KEY TERMS AND CONCEPTS

1. **Making hypotheses concrete**
   A. Operational definition
   B. Construct validity
2. **Types of reasoning**
   A. Inductive
   B. Deductive
3. **Measurement**
   A. Reliability
   B. Validity
4. **Developing ideas**
   A. Jude Cassidy
   B. Lance Shotland
   C. Nora Newcombe
   D. Jeffrey Parker
   E. Andreas Keil
5. **Strong inference**
   A. Four steps according to Platt
   • Develop alternative hypotheses
   • Perform the crucial experiment

   • Obtain clear-cut results
   • Repeat with supported hypothesis
6. **Wallas's four stages**
   A. Preparation
   B. Incubation
   C. Illumination
   D. Verification
7. **Library tools**
   A. PsycINFO
   B. MEDLINE
   C. *Science Citation Index*
   D. *Social Science Citation Index*
   E. Computer databases
   F. Internet
   G. World Wide Web

SUMMARY

1. Unlike Humpty Dumpty, who said to Alice in *Through the Looking-Glass,* "When I use a word it means just what I choose it to mean—neither more nor less," a researcher needs to present ideas in a form that others can understand. Creating an operational definition is one way researchers clarify their ideas and make their hypotheses more concrete. An operational definition presents a hypothesis in terms of observable operations that others can see and repeat.

2. Construct validity is the degree to which the procedure we are using is an adequate definition of the construct we are measuring. For example, a person could define *intelligence* operationally as the time required to respond to a stimulus. The question of construct validity would then arise, asking whether response time was a valid measure of the construct of intelligence.

3. Inductive and deductive forms of reasoning, also discussed in Chapter 2, were reviewed in relation to hypotheses.

4. We discussed the problem of measurement and the concerns of reliability and validity. *Reliability* is the consistency of a measuring instrument. *Validity* is its accuracy.

5. Scientists obtain ideas for research from a variety of sources. Dr. Shotland explained how reading the newspaper and listening to his class helped him to develop a productive line of research. Dr. Newcombe explained how talking to a friend led to her thinking about the manner in which men and women ask for what they want. Dr. Parker drew from his own history. Passages from Einstein and Kekulé suggest that ideas and solutions may also come in terms of vague bodily sensations or even dreams.

(continued)

SUMMARY (*continued*)

6. Wallas was interested in how scientists solve problems. He suggested four stages: preparation, incubation, illumination, and verification.

7. Because science represents a history of observation and theory development, it is important to know what others have observed and said about a particular topic. Reference libraries contain important tools for helping us find articles related to our interests. Library tools that are important in psychological research are the *Science Citation Index,* the *Social Science Citation Index,* and computer databases such as PsycINFO, MEDLINE, and Web of Science (which contains online versions of the *Science Citation Index* and the *Social*

Science Citation Index). Also, information is available on the Internet.

8. In performing research, you begin with an idea or theory. Through operational definitions, this idea must be turned into a testable hypothesis. This can be seen as a four-part process: (a) the definition of the independent and dependent variables; (b) a statement of how the independent and dependent variables are to be measured, considering issues of reliability and validity; (c) a statement of the hypothesized relationship between the independent and dependent variables; and (d) a statement of how this relationship is to be examined or tested.

REVIEW QUESTIONS

1. What are *operational definitions*? Give some examples.
2. What is *construct validity*?
3. Describe Dr. Shotland's study in terms of the independent variable, the dependent variable, and operational definitions.
4. How do intuition and revelation play a role in research?

5. What is meant by the term *strong inference*?
6. Name the reference work in which you would find a summary of most psychological articles.
7. Using a bathroom scale as an example, describe the difference between reliability and validity.

DISCUSSION QUESTIONS AND PROJECTS

1. Give some examples of inductive and deductive reasoning from newspapers, magazines, or television.
2. Discuss the topics you are most interested in researching and describe how you might construct an experiment to study these areas.
3. Discuss some important and interesting topics that may be difficult or impossible to research experimentally.
4. Find the reference section of your library and list five studies performed in the past 10 years that look at the relationship between watching television and aggression.

5. Design a study to determine whether people who take vitamins get better grades. What are the steps necessary to design such a study? What control groups would you need? What might some rival hypotheses be in such a study?
6. How might you design a study that would still be useful even if your hypothesis were refuted?
7. Assume that there exists a construct related to achievement called *motive to achieve*. Describe a way to measure this construct that would be reliable but would have no validity whatsoever.

INFOTRAC COLLEGE EDITION: EXERCISES

 William McGuire in a 1997 *Annual Review of Psychology* article suggests that most students are taught more about hypothesis testing than hypothesis generation. Look up his article "Creative hypothesis generating in psychology:

some useful heuristics" in InfoTrac College Edition and use one of his 49 heuristics to develop a hypothesis.

Others have been interested in mental imagery and creativity. Nicholas LeBoutillier and David Marks

(*continued*)

INFOTRAC COLLEGE EDITION: EXERCISES (*continued*)

reviewed a variety of papers concerning imagery and creativity in the February 2003 issue of the *British Journal of Psychology*. Their paper was titled "Mental imagery and creativity: a meta-analytic review study." You can find it quickly in InfoTrac College Edition by entering Nicholas LeBoutillier's name in the search window.

To help you better understand the material in this chapter, you can go to the Wadsworth's research methods workshop web page at http://www.wadsworth.com/psychology_d/templates/student_resources/workshops/resch_wrk.html. There you will find workshops related to research methods and statistics. One of the research methods workshops discusses the idea "Getting an idea for a study." As you go through this workshop, you will see many of the concepts that you just read about in this chapter.

☑ Answers to Concept Checks

3.1 Only the score on the verbal part of the SAT can be considered an operational definition. The other alternatives do not tell us how to measure verbal ability. However, just because we have an operational definition does not mean that it provides a good measure of the construct; it only specifies clearly how to make the measurement.

3.2 The lab clock would be a reliable instrument to use if you only wanted to time 30 minutes of free play.

3.3 Change professors, we hope. Both have an incorrect view of science. Research has to do with taking an idea, restating it as a testable hypothesis, and then designing an experiment or series of experiments to test the hypothesis. The origin of the initial idea is not important in terms of this process.

3.4 The *Social Science Citation Index* would be a good start. It would list others who referenced Bower's work, including those who replicated it.

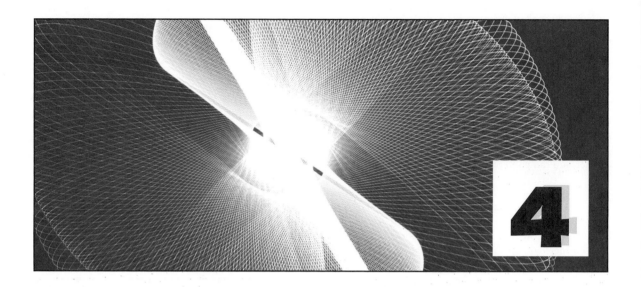

ETHICS

ETHICAL CONSIDERATIONS OF PSYCHOLOGICAL EXPERIMENTATION

THE RIGHTS OF THE SCIENTIST AND THE RESEARCH PARTICIPANT

THE EXPERIMENT AS AN ETHICAL PROBLEM

INGREDIENTS OF THE INITIAL SCIENTIST–PARTICIPANT DIALOGUE
Voluntary Participation
Informed Consent

THE RIGHTS OF THE RESEARCH PARTICIPANT AND THE RESPONSIBILITIES OF THE EXPERIMENTER

WHAT IS HARMFUL TO A RESEARCH PARTICIPANT?

ETHICAL GUIDELINES OF THE AMERICAN PSYCHOLOGICAL ASSOCIATION

INSTITUTIONAL REVIEW BOARD

DECEPTION STUDIES
Obedience-to-Authority Research
It's Not a Crime the Way I See It
Bypassing the Bypass

DEBRIEFING: WHEN IS ENOUGH ENOUGH?

THE PARTICIPANT AS COLLEAGUE

ANIMALS AS SUBJECTS

In this chapter we shift our focus. Previously we have discussed science and its methods. We also have discussed some ways in which individuals get ideas for research and how they begin to turn these ideas into hypotheses. In this chapter we discuss one aspect of how you interact with the participants in your research, that of ethics. Remember, an experiment is just another form of human interaction. There are three aspects or perspectives for understanding and experiencing research: that of the scientist, that of the participant, and that of the observer or witness. In this chapter, we examine the participant-scientist relationship from the viewpoint of the witness. As we said previously, it is the task of the witness to observe and evaluate the nature of the interaction between the scientist and participant in the research. In emphasizing the important issue of human ethics, we move from the world of observation and theory to the world of human values. This means that we use different criteria for making decisions than we do in the world of science. The new criteria are based on human values. Yet how do we make value judgments? On what criteria do we base our ethical behavior? The study of ethics offers some answers to these questions.

Ethics is the study of proper action. Ethics examines relationships between human beings and provides principles regarding how we should treat each other. The ultimate decision in ethical questions resides in judgments of value. Most people have either explicitly or implicitly formulated principles that reflect their values and give direction to their actions. Some of these principles may be based on a religious tradition. One example of such a principle is the Golden Rule, which states that you should do unto others as you would have them do unto you. Other principles may have a philosophical basis, such as *Kant's imperative.* Immanuel Kant, an 18th-century philosopher, suggested that one should "act so as to treat humanity, either yourself or others, always as an end also and never as a means only." Although rules of action may be useful in the abstract, problems often arise when one begins to apply these principles to concrete situations. In this chapter we look at one particular concrete situation—the scientific experiment—and attempt to determine some guidelines for making ethical decisions within this context.

Before we begin we need to make clear four points. First, the scientist has responsibilities to the world at large, which relies on the accuracy of the findings. Thus, to lie or commit fraud (as we will discuss in Chapter 11) would clearly be unethical. However, in this chapter our emphasis is on the experimental situation itself. Second, although most research scientists are concerned about ethics, actual ethical problems are minimal in most psychological experimentation. As we shall see, however, sometimes a scientist designs an experiment that unknowingly brings psychological distress to the participants. Preventing such situations requires careful consideration. Third, ethical decisions are regulated somewhat in our society by the federal government and by professional societies, such as the American Psychological Association (APA). In this chapter we present some of their recommended guidelines and procedures. Fourth, although there are guidelines, there are no hard-and-fast rules for every situation. *Whether in the role of scientist or research participant, you as a human being ultimately must decide how you will act and then assume responsibility for that action.*

"WE'LL ONLY DO 72% OF IT, SINCE IT'S BEEN REPORTED THAT 28% OF ALL SURGERY IS UNNECESSARY."

ETHICAL CONSIDERATIONS OF PSYCHOLOGICAL EXPERIMENTATION

Ethical considerations of psychological experimentation have at their heart the idea that people participating in research should not be harmed or affected in a way that would result in a lower level of any aspect of human functioning. In addition, ethical considerations must point out the scientist's right to know and to seek answers to questions; that is, it would also be considered unethical to prevent a scientist from seeking knowledge without considering his or her rights. Thus, we begin with the rights of the scientist to know and to pursue knowledge and the rights of the participants to be protected from undue harm.

In most cases the scientist has a question that he or she wants to ask and that the participant is willing to help answer. In some cases the participants learn something about themselves or about psychology from the experience, and they are glad to have participated. In psychophysiological experiments, for example, participants often report that they enjoy seeing their brain activity (for example, fMRI, EEG) and heart activity (electrocardiogram, EKG) displayed. Thus, they are willing to participate in research in exchange for these types of experiences. Other participants, like some travelers to a foreign country, enter the world of experimentation and leave it again without ever realizing the underlying structure of the place they have been. Although ignorant of the underlying structure, they still leave with the experience of the event and may be changed by it.

If these experiences were always pleasant and any changes in the participant always positive, participants would participate gladly in experiments, and scientists would face few ethical questions. However, at times the scientist may want to answer a question that requires that the participant experience psychological or physiological discomfort. These situations raise a number of questions: What are the responsibilities of the scientist toward the participant? What are the rights of the participant? Are there guidelines for reconciling conflicts between the rights of the participants to pursue happiness and the rights of the scientist to pursue knowledge? What type of relationship or dialogue would be most productive for helping the scientist and participant to fulfill their needs and desires? These are the questions we approach in this chapter.

Before concluding this introductory discussion, we want to point out that if we are not careful, how we view those involved in research can depersonalize the human qualities of those involved in the scientific enterprise—both the participants and the scientists. Although both the participant and the scientist have particular roles to play in science, they are first and foremost human beings. In performing psychological research, it is imperative that we value this fact.

THE RIGHTS OF THE SCIENTIST AND THE RESEARCH PARTICIPANT

In our society people have the right to search for the things that are important to them. The Declaration of Independence includes a reference to the individual's right to "life, liberty, and the pursuit of happiness." We begin with the idea that people, whether they are scientists or participants, have the right to pursue the activities that are important to them. However, some activities may infringe on the rights of others. Such activities range from the extreme case of murder, which violates the victim's right to life, to less harmful types of activities, such as someone's creating noise outside your bedroom window or throwing a cream pie at you across the cafeteria. When a conflict develops between my rights and your rights, we are forced to find a means of arriving at a solution to the problem. The traditional solutions are those of ethics and law; that is, people seek to establish ethical principles to guide their behavior, and society may adopt these ethical guidelines in the form of legal sanctions.

What does all this have to do with psychological experimentation? This is exactly the problem. We do not understand completely the relationship between ethics and experimentation, nor do we agree on the manner in which involvement in a scientific experiment infringes on someone's personal rights. For example, one researcher collected data online (for example, through Internet groups) by viewing habits of college students, faculty, and staff, especially in relation to pornographic material, without their knowledge (reported in the American Association for the Advancement of Science Professional Ethics Report, http://www.aaas.org/spp/dspp/sfrl/per/per.htm; look in archives for Summer 1995, and the article by Fowler). Is this acceptable research? Is it ethical to gather information about another person without his or her knowledge?

Science itself can give us few answers to the question of ethical relationships because science has focused on observation and theory. Thus, we are forced to look outside science.

In this book we use the concept of the witness to help us to gain this broad perspective. In this chapter we imagine ourselves to be the witnesses and examine in more detail the ethical relationship between the scientist and the participant. To accomplish this goal, let's now examine some specific experimental situations and bring forth some of the possible ethical considerations that must be examined.

THE EXPERIMENT AS AN ETHICAL PROBLEM

Let's begin with an extreme case of conflictual experimentation: the Nazi medical experiments during World War II. In several concentration camps, such as Ravensbrueck, Dachau, and Buchenwald, prisoners were injected with a virus or bacterium and then received drugs to determine the drugs' effectiveness against the injections. Although medical knowledge was gained from these experiments, the world as a witness judged the experiments to be unethical and criminal. During the trials of these scientist–physicians, held at Nuremberg, it was determined that they were guilty of war crimes; seven of them were later hanged, and eight received long prison sentences. As a result of these trials, a code of ethics for medical experimentation with human participants (called the Nuremberg Code) was adopted as a guideline for future research.

What was unethical about the experiments at the Nazi concentration camps was not that human beings were given a virus. Almost all of our current procedures of preventive medicine (the polio vaccine, for example) require that the procedure eventually be tested on human beings. These physicians were convicted of conducting experiments *without the consent of their participants.* One of the first principles of research is that the participants must consent to being part of an experiment. Furthermore, they must also be informed of the experiment's purpose and its potential risks. Thus, major ingredients that the witness looks for in the dialogue between the scientist and the research participant are *voluntary participation* and *informed consent.*

In the United States, one critical turning point was the publication of the article "Ethics and Clinical Research" by Henry Beecher in the *New England Journal of Medicine* in 1966. In this paper, Beecher presented some 22 examples of experiments that were not consistent with the Nuremberg Code, especially in terms of the participants not knowing that they were in an experiment or not giving consent. This eventually led to a variety of government reports in the 1970s on the protection of humans in biomedicial and behavioral research, which in turn led to the establishment of institution review boards (IRBs), which we will discuss more later in this chapter.

Although a variety of studies worldwide have ignored basic participant rights, one particularly troubling study was begun in 1932 by the U.S. Public Health Service. The participants of the study were African American men in Macon County, Alabama, who had syphilis. The people involved in the experiment were not told that they had syphilis and were kept away from any form of treatment. The study was originally designed to understand the long-term effects of syphilis. Although treatments for syphilis in the 1930s were not very effective, this study continued even after effective treatments were developed in the late 1940s. In fact, the study was not terminated until its existence was publicly exposed in a Washington newspaper in 1972, some 40 years later. This study not only violated basic ethical principles such as informed consent, but also put others, such as the participants' families, at risk. It came to be called the Tuskegee experiment (http://www.tuskegee.edu/Global/Story.asp?s=1207586). This study illustrates clearly the need for voluntary participation and informed consent, which we describe in the next section.

INGREDIENTS OF THE INITIAL SCIENTIST–PARTICIPANT DIALOGUE

■ Voluntary Participation

In the initial dialogue between the scientist and the prospective participant, the scientist must ask the participant to be a part of the experiment. This is the principle of *voluntary participation.* Information released in 1995 by the U.S. Department of Energy suggested that this principle was not followed in the United States in about four decades of radiation studies with approximately 1,600 people, including mental patients and prisoners. One of the major questions raised was whether the people involved were aware of and consented to being part of an experiment rather than believing they were receiving medical treatment. Did these people agree to participation in the radiation research, and did they know they could leave the study at any time? In essence, the voluntary participation principle suggests that a person should participate in an experiment only by free choice. In addition, this principle states that a participant should be free to leave an experiment at any time, whether or not the experiment has been completed.

The concept of voluntary participation involves a number of issues. One issue has to do with what is meant by the term *voluntary.* For example, is it ethical to use prisoners in an experiment? That is, is it really possible for a captive audience to say no without fear of reprisal? One answer to this problem has been to reduce the participants' sentences as a reward for participation in the research. Yet it has been argued that if a prisoner agrees to be in an experiment because he or she is seeking a reduced sentence, then this agreement is made not with free will but rather under a form of duress. In the same vein, it has been argued that giving a college student extra credit (points toward the final grade) for participation in psychological experimentation is unethical.

As you think about this issue, you will become entangled in the question of whether anyone can ever make a free decision and, if so, under what circumstances. As you might have realized already, this question becomes even more complicated for someone interested in developmental psychology, which requires research with children, or for someone interested in psychopathology, which requires research with patients who are mentally impaired. In terms of ethical concerns involving research with children, a number of recommendations have been put forward by the National Academies of Science, including how to obtain informed consent and ensure voluntary participation in research (Field & Behrman, 2004).

■ Informed Consent

Assuming for a moment that someone can agree freely to participate in research, the scientist in the initial dialogue should inform the prospective participant about what will be required of him or her during the study. The scientist must also inform the prospective participant about any potential harm that may come from participation. Thus, the prospective participant must be given complete information on which to base a decision. This is the principle of *informed consent*. As you can imagine, the principle of informed consent raises the issue of how much information about an experiment is enough.

Can you ever tell prospective participants enough so that they could fully understand the study? It has been suggested that *informed* consent may not be the same as *educated* consent and that participants can never really be given enough information. Additional problems are raised when the research involves some form of deception, as when a new drug is being tested against a placebo to determine its effectiveness. Although there are many problems being debated in relation to informed consent, the working procedure at this time is for the scientist to tell prospective participants, as fully as possible without jeopardizing the value of the experiment, what will be required of them and to inform them of any possible risks they might be taking by participating in the experiment.

From the principles of voluntary participation and informed consent, one can see that it is the initial task of the scientist to fully discuss the experimental procedure with prospective participants and to remind them that they are human beings who do not give away their rights just because they are taking part in a psychological experiment.

THE RIGHTS OF THE RESEARCH PARTICIPANT AND THE RESPONSIBILITIES OF THE EXPERIMENTER

In our society, research participants have the same rights during an experiment that they have outside the experimental situation. One major one is the *right to privacy*. Most of us at first think of the right to privacy as the right to spend time by oneself or with others of one's choosing, without being disturbed. This is the external manifestation of the right to privacy. But there is also an internal or intrapersonal manifestation of this right (see Raebhausen & Brim, 1967). This is the right to have private thoughts or, as it is sometimes called, a *private personality*. This means that the thoughts and feelings of a participant should not be made public without the participant's consent. It also means that a conversation between a participant and a scientist should be considered a private event, not a public one.

But how can the scientist ever report her or his findings? There are two considerations that are part of the scientist's responsibility to the participant: *confidentiality* and *anonymity*. The principle of confidentiality requires that the scientist not release data of a personal nature to other scientists or groups without the participant's consent. The principle of anonymity requires that the personal identity of a given participant be kept separate from his or her data. The easiest way to accomplish this is to avoid requesting names in the first place; however, there are times when this may be impossible. Another alternative is to use code numbers that protect the identities of the participants and to destroy the list of participants' names once the data analysis has been completed.

WHAT IS HARMFUL TO A RESEARCH PARTICIPANT?

As stated earlier, it is the right of a participant not to be harmed. In most psychological research, physical pain and harm present no problems, either because they are absent completely or because the participant is fully informed of the particular procedure that will be used, such as making a loud noise or placing the participant's hand in cold water to measure physiological responsiveness. However, the question of psychological harm presents a much larger issue, one that will continue to be debated for years to come. Is it harmful to show participants something true but negative about themselves? Is it harmful to create situations in which participants feel negative emotions such as fear or anger? Is it harmful to make participants feel like failures in order to determine how this affects their performance? These are the types of questions that are being debated currently.

As a scientist, where do you go for help? There are two major sources: the APA's guidelines on ethics and the institutional review board (IRB, also known as the human subjects committee or office of research compliance) at the institution in which you study or work. In addition, many specialty organizations have adopted guidelines for specific populations. For example, the Society for Research in Child Development has established ethical standards for research with children.

 CONCEPT CHECK 4.1   Professor Doolittle was running an experiment in which she examined undergraduates' attitudes toward drinking on campus. She very carefully designed the experiment so that her control and experimental groups were randomly selected and assigned. However, on the last day one of her participants said, "I don't feel comfortable in this situation. You are asking me to tell you the names of all my friends who drink. I wish to leave." Dr. Doolittle said, "You are my last participant and school is over tomorrow. Please don't leave until you finish the experiment; you only have a few more questions to go. And besides, you need the experimental credit for your grade." Is there an ethical problem with this response?

ETHICAL GUIDELINES OF THE AMERICAN PSYCHOLOGICAL ASSOCIATION

Because it may be difficult to determine how to resolve conflicts between the scientist's right to know and the participant's right not to be harmed by participating in an experiment, the APA first developed in 1953 a set of guidelines to help scientists determine their responsibilities toward participants and the manner in which the scientist–participant dialogue should be conducted. These have been updated and are part of a larger set of ethical principles that were published in the December 2002 issue of the *American Psychologist*. The APA developed the guidelines after much consideration and many revisions by the members of the association. The detailed ethical guidelines, titled *Ethical Principles of Psychologists and Codes of Conduct,* may be ordered from the APA (750 First Street N.E., Washington, DC 20002-4242) or can be found on their website (http://www.apa.org/ethics/) along with other related information on ethics. We now present the ethical guidelines directly related to research.

8. Research and Publication

8.01 Institutional Approval

When institutional approval is required, psychologists provide accurate information about their research proposals and obtain approval prior to conducting the research. They conduct the research in accordance with the approved research protocol.

8.02 Informed Consent to Research

a. When obtaining informed consent as required in Standard 3.10, Informed Consent, psychologists inform participants about (1) the purpose of the research, expected duration, and procedures; (2) their right to decline to participate and to withdraw from the research once participation has begun; (3) the foreseeable consequences of declining or withdrawing; (4) reasonably foreseeable factors that may be expected to influence their willingness to participate such as potential risks, discomfort, or adverse effects; (5) any prospective research benefits; (6) limits of confidentiality; (7) incentives for participation; and (8) whom to contact for questions about the research and research participants' rights. They provide opportunity for the prospective participants to ask questions and receive answers. (See also Standards 8.03, Informed Consent for Recording Voices and Images in Research; 8.05, Dispensing With Informed Consent for Research; and 8.07, Deception in Research.)

b. Psychologists conducting intervention research involving the use of experimental treatments clarify to participants at the outset of the research (1) the experimental nature of the treatment; (2) the services that will or will not be available to the control group(s) if appropriate; (3) the means by which assignment to treatment and control groups will be made; (4) available treatment alternatives if an individual does not wish to participate in the research or wishes to withdraw once a study has begun; and (5) compensation for or monetary costs of participating including, if appropriate, whether reimbursement from the participant or a third-party payor will be sought. (See also Standard 8.02a, Informed Consent to Research.)

8.03 Informed Consent for Recording Voices and Images in Research

Psychologists obtain informed consent from research participants prior to recording their voices or images for data collection unless (1) the research consists solely of naturalistic observations in public places, and it is not anticipated that the recording will be used in a manner that could cause personal identification or harm, or (2) the research design includes deception, and consent for the use of the recording is obtained during debriefing. (See also Standard 8.07, Deception in Research.)

8.04 Client/Patient, Student, and Subordinate Research Participants

a. When psychologists conduct research with clients/patients, students, or subordinates as participants, psychologists take steps to protect the prospective participants from adverse consequences of declining or withdrawing from participation.

b. When research participation is a course requirement or an opportunity for extra credit, the prospective participant is given the choice of equitable alternative activities.

8.05 Dispensing With Informed Consent for Research

Psychologists may dispense with informed consent only (1) where research would not reasonably be assumed to create distress or harm and involves (a) the study of normal educational practices, curricula, or classroom management methods conducted in educational settings; (b) only anonymous questionnaires, naturalistic observations, or archival research for which disclosure of responses would not place participants at risk of criminal or civil liability or damage their financial standing, employability, or reputation, and confidentiality is protected; or (c) the study of factors related to job or organization effectiveness conducted in organizational settings for which there is no risk to participants' employability, and confidentiality is protected or (2) where otherwise permitted by law or federal or institutional regulations.

8.06 Offering Inducements for Research Participation

a. Psychologists make reasonable efforts to avoid offering excessive or inappropriate financial or other inducements for research participation when such inducements are likely to coerce participation.

b. When offering professional services as an inducement for research participation, psychologists clarify the nature of the services, as well as the risks, obligations, and limitations. (See also Standard 6.05, Barter With Clients/Patients.)

8.07 Deception in Research

a. Psychologists do not conduct a study involving deception unless they have determined that the use of deceptive techniques is justified by the study's significant prospective scientific, educational, or applied value and that effective nondeceptive alternative procedures are not feasible.

b. Psychologists do not deceive prospective participants about research that is reasonably expected to cause physical pain or severe emotional distress.

c. Psychologists explain any deception that is an integral feature of the design and conduct of an experiment to participants as early as is feasible, preferably at the conclusion of their participation, but no later than at the conclusion of the data collection, and permit participants to withdraw their data. (See also Standard 8.08, Debriefing.)

8.08 Debriefing

a. Psychologists provide a prompt opportunity for participants to obtain appropriate information about the nature, results, and conclusions of the research, and they take reasonable steps to correct any misconceptions that participants may have of which the psychologists are aware.

b. If scientific or humane values justify delaying or withholding this information, psychologists take reasonable measures to reduce the risk of harm.

c. When psychologists become aware that research procedures have harmed a participant, they take reasonable steps to minimize the harm.

8.09 Humane Care and Use of Animals in Research

a. Psychologists acquire, care for, use, and dispose of animals in compliance with current federal, state, and local laws and regulations, and with professional standards.

b. Psychologists trained in research methods and experienced in the care of laboratory animals supervise all procedures involving animals and are responsible for ensuring appropriate consideration of their comfort, health, and humane treatment.

c. Psychologists ensure that all individuals under their supervision who are using animals have received instruction in research methods and in the care, maintenance, and handling of the species being used, to the extent appropriate to their role. (See also Standard 2.05, Delegation of Work to Others.)

d. Psychologists make reasonable efforts to minimize the discomfort, infection, illness, and pain of animal subjects.

e. Psychologists use a procedure subjecting animals to pain, stress, or privation only when an alternative procedure is unavailable and the goal is justified by its prospective scientific, educational, or applied value.

f. Psychologists perform surgical procedures under appropriate anesthesia and follow techniques to avoid infection and minimize pain during and after surgery.

g. When it is appropriate that an animal's life be terminated, psychologists proceed rapidly, with an effort to minimize pain and in accordance with accepted procedures.

8.10 Reporting Research Results

a. Psychologists do not fabricate data. (See also Standard 5.01a, Avoidance of False or Deceptive Statements.)

b. If psychologists discover significant errors in their published data, they take reasonable steps to correct such errors in a correction, retraction, erratum, or other appropriate publication means.

8.11 Plagiarism

Psychologists do not present portions of another's work or data as their own, even if the other work or data source is cited occasionally.

8.12 Publication Credit

a. Psychologists take responsibility and credit, including authorship credit, only for work they have actually performed or to which they have substantially contributed. (See also Standard 8.12b, Publication Credit.)

b. Principal authorship and other publication credits accurately reflect the relative scientific or professional contributions of the individuals involved, regardless of their relative status. Mere possession of an institutional position, such as department chair, does not justify authorship credit. Minor contributions to the research or to the writing for publications are acknowledged appropriately, such as in footnotes or in an introductory statement.

c. Except under exceptional circumstances, a student is listed as principal author on any multiple-authored article that is substantially based on the student's doctoral dissertation. Faculty advisors discuss publication credit with students as early as feasible and throughout the research and publication process as appropriate. (See also Standard 8.12b, Publication Credit.)

8.13 Duplicate Publication of Data

Psychologists do not publish, as original data, data that have been previously published. This does not preclude republishing data when they are accompanied by proper acknowledgment.

8.14 Sharing Research Data for Verification

a. After research results are published, psychologists do not withhold the data on which their conclusions are based from other competent professionals who seek to verify the substantive claims through reanalsis and who intend to use such data only for that purpose, provided that the confidentiality of the participants can

be protected and unless legal rights concerning proprietary data preclude their release. This does not preclude psychologists from requiring that such individuals or groups be responsible for costs associated with the provision of such information.

b. Psychologists who request data from other psychologists to verify the substantive claims through reanalysis may use shared data only for the declared purpose. Requesting psychologists obtain prior written agreement for all other uses of the data.

8.15 Reviewers

Psychologists who review material submitted for presentation, publication, grant, or research proposal review respect the confidentiality of and the proprietary rights in such information of those who submitted it.

As stated, these principles should not be considered laws that a scientist follows, thereby handing over the problems of ethics to the group that makes the laws. Rather, these principles may be considered *guidelines that should direct one's thinking when ethical matters are considered.* In fact, the principles emphasize that the responsibility of research is always with the individual scientist, and it is the scientist who must make decisions about how to respond to the ethical considerations of an experiment.

INSTITUTIONAL REVIEW BOARD

The U.S. Department of Health and Human Services requires that each scientist whose institution receives federal funds must seek a review of the ethical considerations of research with human participants, whether or not there is a deviation from the APA guidelines. This type of review is required not only of psychological research but of any type of research with human participants. The committee that reviews the research is to be made up of people who work at the same university, hospital, school, or other institution with the scientist, and also members of the community where the institution is located.

The main task of the institutional review board (IRB) is to determine whether the participants are adequately protected in terms of both welfare and rights. Box 4.1 illustrates the types of questions required by a typical IRB report. One major question that the committee asks is, "Are there any risks—physical, psychological, or social—associated with participating in a given piece of research?" Almost everything we do each day involves varying degrees of risk, so the committee attempts to determine when a risk is unreasonable.

The committee also considers the potential long-term effects of a particular treatment on a person. For example, asking a participant to run a mile, to give a small sample of blood, to have his or her heart rate measured, or to discuss his or her sexual preference or childhood involves some risks in the way the term is used by most internal review committees. However, the committee may decide that, in light of the information that

Box 4.1

Typical Format for Institutional Review Boards

1. Provide a brief description of the proposed study (for example, purpose, problem to be investigated).

2. What are the qualifications of the investigator(s) for conducting the study? (If students, who will be supervising the research?)

3. What are the requirements for and characteristics of the participants (gender, age range, health, medical or psychological status, prisoners, institutionalized, and so on)?

4. How will the participants in the research be sampled or recruited?

5. Describe the method of the study.

6. Describe the personnel, materials, equipment, or other resource requirements for your study.

7. Describe the procedure for obtaining informed consent from the participants (for example, how and when the study will be explained to participants). How will participants indicate their consent?

8. What are the potential risks to the participants, and what is the likelihood and seriousness of these risks? (Risks can be physical, psychological, social, and so on. Risks may result from experimental procedures or methods of obtaining, handling, or reporting data.)

9. Will deception be used in the research? Why is it necessary?

10. Describe any alternative methods that would reduce or eliminate risks and discuss why these were not used. If applicable, how and by whom was the electrical or mechanical equipment checked for safety?

11. What procedures are used to protect the confidentiality of a participant and his or her data?

12. How is the participant to be debriefed?

13. What are the potential benefits to the research participants or society of the proposed research?

14. List names and addresses of experts in the field with whom the IRB could discuss the risks involved in this research if necessary.

would be gained, these risks are not sufficient to prevent the study from being performed. Thus, a second major question that a review committee asks is, "Are the risks to the participants outweighed by the potential benefits to them or by the estimated importance to society of the knowledge to be gained?" If the committee determines that the answer to this question is yes, a third question is asked: "Has the experimenter allowed the prospective participants to determine freely whether they will participate in the experiment?" And finally, "Has the experimenter obtained the participants' informed consent?"

Although everyone agrees that it is imperative that the scientists involved protect research participants, there has been recent concern that IRBs may be moving beyond their original mandates and interpreting regulations too literally. For example, one researcher who wanted to study language in a preliterate tribe was instructed to have them read and sign a consent form (reported in the *American Association for the Advancement of Science Professional Ethics Report,* http://www.aaas.org/spp/dspp/sfrl/per/per.htm; look in archives for Spring 2002 and the article by Sieber). A variety of conferences are bringing together researchers, government officials, and legal experts to consider some of the larger questions raised with the goals of both protecting research participants and performing meaning-ful science (see also the Spring 2003 issue of *Professional Ethics Report* for a discussion of "Human Subject Regulations").

In terms of doing meaningful science, it should be pointed out that a complete descrip-tion of a study may actually eliminate the very phenomenon being studied. For example, in one study using a traditional verbal conditioning paradigm, Resnick and Schwartz (1973) found that giving the participants a complete description of the experiment resulted in the participants not demonstrating conditioning. These authors also reported that although the informed participants took part in the study, they did so in a more uncooperative man-ner. Another argument against fully informed consent is that of Loftus and Fries (1979), who argue that fully informed consent may be more harmful than helpful (Box 4.2).

One consequence of adopting a strict definition of informed consent is that it becomes very difficult to perform research that involves deception (that is, research in which the par-ticipant is not told the complete purpose of an experiment). Let's now examine deception studies and some of the ethical questions involved.

Box 4.2

Informed Consent May Be Hazardous to Your Health

The following was an editorial in *Science,* the journal of the American Association for the Advancement of Science. In this editorial, the authors suggest that informed consent may actually harm the subject in some cases (Loftus & Fries, 1979). Read the edito-rial and see what you think.

Before human subjects are enrolled in experi-mental studies, a variety of preliminary rituals are now required. These include an explana-tion of the nature of the experimental proce-dure and a specific elaboration of possible adverse reactions. The subjects, in turn, can either withdraw from the experiment or give their "informed consent." These rituals are said to increase the subjects' understanding of the procedures but, perhaps more important, they came into existence because of a strong belief in the fundamental principle that human beings have the right to determine what will be done to their minds and bodies.

Some, on the other hand, consider that the pur-pose of informed consent is not protection of subjects, but rather protection of investigators and sponsoring institutions from lawsuits based on the charge of subject deception should a misadventure result. But lawsuits arise in any case; subjects simply claim that they did not understand the rituals. It is reasonable, then, to ask whether the putative beneficiary, the sub-ject, might be harmed rather than helped by the current informed consent procedure.

A considerable body of psychological evidence indicates that humans are highly suggestible. Information has been found to change people's attitudes, to change their moods and feelings, and even to make them believe they have ex-perienced events that never in fact occurred. This alone would lead one to suspect that adverse reactions might result from information given during an informed consent discussion.

An examination of the medical evidence demonstrates that there is also a dark side to the placebo effect. Not only can positive therapeutic effects be achieved by suggestion, but negative side effects and complications

(continued)

(continued)

can similarly result. For example, among those subjects who participated in a drug study after the usual informed consent procedure, many of those given an injection of a placebo reported physiologically unlikely symptoms such as dizziness, nausea, vomiting and even mental depression. One subject given the placebo reported that these effects were so strong that they caused an automobile accident. Many other studies provide similar data indicating that to a variable but often scarifying degree, explicit suggestion of possible adverse effects causes subjects to experience these effects. Recent hypotheses that heart attack may follow coronary spasms indicate physiological mechanisms by which explicit suggestions, and the stress that may be produced by them, might prove fatal. Thus, the possible consequences of suggested symptoms range from minor annoyance to, in extreme cases, death.

If protection of the subject is the reason for obtaining informed consent, the possibility of iatrogenic harm [harm brought on by diagnosis or suggestion] to the subject as a direct result of the consent ritual must be considered. This clear cost must be weighed against the potential benefit of giving some people an increased

sense of freedom of choice about the use of their bodies. The current legalistic devices, which are designed in part to limit subject recourse, intensify rather than solve a dilemma.

The features of informed consent procedures that do protect subjects should be retained. Experimental procedures should be reviewed by peers and public representatives. A statement to the subject describing the procedure and the general level of risk is reasonable. But detailed information should be reserved for those who request it. Specific slight risks, particularly those resulting from common procedures, should not be routinely disclosed to all subjects. And when a specific risk is disclosed, it should be discussed in the context of placebo effects in general, why they occur and how to guard against them. A growing literature indicates that just as knowledge of possible symptoms can cause those symptoms, so can knowledge of placebo effects be used to defend against those effects. A move in this direction may ensure that a subject will not be at greater risk from self-appointed guardians than from the experiment itself.

Source: Loftus, E. F., & Fries, J. F. (1979). Informed consent may be hazardous to your health. *Science, 204,* 11.

DECEPTION STUDIES

Deception research is any study in which the participant is deceived about the true purpose of the experiment or the experimental procedures. For example, if an experimenter wanted to examine the effects of anxiety on performance in college students, he or she might create an anxiety-provoking situation followed by a performance measure. One method used to create anxiety in college students is to administer a so-called IQ test that cannot be completed in the allotted time and to state that most college students who later go to graduate school have no trouble finishing this test.

Another type of deception often used in medical research is the placebo treatment. For example, participants are given a pill made up of sugar or other inactive ingredients and told that it will cause certain physiological changes such as reducing the number of headaches they have been experiencing. It should be noted that as participants have become more sophisticated concerning medical research, the current trend is to acknowledge the existence of a placebo control.

Because it is impossible to obtain informed consent in deception research, is it unethical to perform this research? This is not an easy question to answer, and the professionals in the field currently fall into two camps. The first group suggests that any deception is unethical, and thus no deception research is possible; the second group argues that certain types of deception research are necessary. The second group further argues that given appropriate safeguards, deception research is the only way to answer certain questions. We do not attempt to determine which group is ethically correct here, but we present some important questions raised by deception research and discuss the ways in which some of these questions have been answered. To do this we present three deception studies in further detail.

■ Obedience-to-Authority Research

One of the classic deception research studies is Milgram's (1963, 1977) obedience-to-authority study. Using as a background such authority situations as the Old Testament story of God (the authority) commanding Abraham to kill his son and the situation of war, where one person (the authority) tells another to go out and kill the enemy, Milgram asked the question, "Under what conditions would one person (who is not the authority) obey an instruction to harm another, and how is this related to authority?"

To examine this question in a concrete situation, Milgram chose the setting of a psychological experiment. Milgram had argued in an earlier study that there was a difference in conformity between people from Norway and those from France. In his next study, he wanted to compare participants from Germany and the United States. He sought to determine whether participants would be willing to harm other participants on the authority of the experimenter. However, as you will see, Milgram stopped the study after running only the initial American studies.

The participants in this experiment were people who varied in age and occupation. The general procedure was to have a participant come into the laboratory for a *learning experiment*. The participant met the experimenter and another participant, who was really an associate of the experimenter. It was explained to the participant that little is known about the effects of punishment on memory and that in the experiment one participant would be the learner and one would be the teacher. A rigged drawing was held in which the associate of the experimenter drew the role of learner and the participant drew the role of teacher. Following this, the learner was taken to another room and strapped into a chair with what appeared to be shock electrodes. The participant did not know that the electrodes were not connected.

The participant was told that it was his or her job to teach the learner a series of words and to administer a shock as punishment whenever the learner made a mistake. The participant was further instructed to increase the shock with each error made by moving a switch on the control box. Voltage levels were marked on the control box, and at the higher voltage levels there were labels such as "Danger: Severe Shock."

Once the experiment began, the learner started making mistakes. The participant, following the instructions of the experimenter, administered shocks. As the voltage levels were increased, the participant began to hear moans coming from the learner. With more increases in voltage, the learner cried out in pain and later refused to answer any more questions. The experimenter told the participant to treat any nonresponse as a wrong answer and to administer additional shocks. When the participant refused to administer additional shocks, the experiment was concluded. The voltage level reached on the shock machine was used as a measure of the participant's willingness to obey authority even in the face of pressure from the learner not to inflict pain.

As you might imagine, objections have been raised to this research. One of the first objections to Milgram's work concerned whether the participants were protected in the experiment. In particular, Baumrind (1964) refers to the Milgram study as a case in which the participants were not treated with respect but rather were manipulated and made to experience the discomfort of emotional disturbance. Milgram responded that he did not foresee the emotional distress experienced by the participants. He stated that colleagues and psychiatrists with whom he discussed the proposed experiment all expected that most participants would terminate the experiment at an early stage by refusing to give shocks once the learner began to complain. Milgram agreed that once a number of participants had been run he could have terminated the experiment; however, he decided that "momentary excitement is not the same as harm." Thus, Milgram chose to continue the experiment.

Once the experiment had been concluded, it would have been unethical to allow a participant to leave the experimental situation without a true understanding of what had taken place. The process of explaining the true purpose of the experiment afterward is called **debriefing.** In the debriefing procedure, the experimenter, in accord with the APA principles 8.07 and 8.08, removes any misconceptions and offers a full discussion of the experiment. Although the APA's ethical principles had not been fully developed when Milgram first ran his experiment, he appears to have followed its principles. First, the participants all were told the nature of the hoax and that the learner never received any electric shock. Second, each participant had a friendly reconciliation with the learner and an opportunity to discuss the experiment. Third, participants were assured that their behavior was normal and other participants also felt the tension or emotion that they felt.

After the entire study was completed, all participants received a report of the experiment. According to Milgram, in this follow-up report the participants' behavior was treated in a dignified manner. As suggested by the APA principles, Milgram also conducted follow-up evaluations. Together with the report, all participants received a questionnaire that allowed them to express their thoughts and feelings about their participation in the experiment. In response to these questions, Milgram reports that 84% of the participants were glad to have participated in the experiment, 15% were neutral, and 1.3% expressed negative feelings about their participation. In addition, 80% of the participants believed that this type of research should be carried out, and 74% said they had learned something of personal importance from their participation. A psychiatrist interviewed selected participants to check for any negative long-term effects of the experiment; he found none.

Although some people have been critical of Milgram's work, it is important to note that people who knew Milgram speak of his deep concern for people and his integrity as a human being and scientist. In fact, some of his follow-up procedures were not required in his day. In many ways his procedures have helped us to consider in some detail the ethical treatment of participants and to establish appropriate guidelines. Today, it is not easy to follow the APA principles when it comes to deception research because it requires as much, if not more, work to follow up the participants as it does to run the original experiment. However, when there is a possibility of psychological or physiological long-term harm, it is necessary that this type of follow-up be performed.

■ It's Not a Crime the Way I See It

When reading newspaper reports of the break-in at the Watergate building as told by the press and by the Nixon administration, some people felt that they were hearing reports of two different events. West, Gunn, and Chernicky (1975) pointed out the manner in which the differing reports fit into current theory in social psychology. As suggested by the theory of Jones and Nisbett (1971), those involved in Watergate tended to focus on environmental determinants of behavior; for example, they claimed that the break-in was necessary because of the violent nature of the radical left. Members of the press were observers and tended to explain the break-in in terms of the characteristics of the participants.

Other events in history have also given rise to such conflicting interpretations, according to West and colleagues (1975). For example, those involved in Nazi war crimes claimed that they had to follow orders or they would have been shot. They emphasized situational factors, whereas those who judged these people for war crimes saw the problem in terms of the characteristics of the people involved. Likewise, in reading about the case of Kitty Genovese in Chapter 3, you may have thought to yourself, "Why didn't anyone help?" or "What was wrong with those people?" You, as an outside observer, were reacting to the characteristics of the people involved, whereas the people involved seem to have been reacting to the situational characteristics.

Although the three cases of Watergate, Nazi soldiers, and Kitty Genovese lend support to the theory of Jones and Nisbett, a scientist would still like to see the theory tested in a laboratory situation. West and colleagues (1975) decided to do this. They reasoned that if situational factors were important variables in the Watergate crime, then a significant percentage of people would agree to break the law if the situational pressure were high. Likewise, others, when being told of the crime, would attribute the event to the person involved and not to the situation. These authors designed the following experiment.

In a field study, participants were invited to participate in an illegal burglary. To determine the role of situational variables, rationales for the burglary varied across groups. The first rationale stated that the crime was being sponsored by a government agency. The second rationale offered the participants in that group a large amount of money for committing the crime. The third rationale offered immunity from prosecution for committing the crime. The fourth rationale, which served as a control for compliance, offered no money or immunity from prosecution. This last group was used to give the researchers some indication of how often participants would agree to be part of a crime without any particular inducement. Thus, it was used to assess the *demand characteristics* of the experiment.

A second experiment was performed with another group of participants. Each participant was given a booklet describing in detail one of the four conditions from the field experiment. These participants were asked to estimate how many people out of 100 would agree to participate in the burglary as described in the booklet. They were also asked whether they would participate and were given the opportunity to describe some characteristics of a person who would or would not participate. Based on the theory of Jones and Nisbett (1971), it was predicted that those who participated in the field experiment would attribute their actions to the situational cues, whereas those in the second experiment would focus on the characteristics of the person who agreed or refused to take part in the crime.

Imagine yourself in the field study. You do not know you are part of a study. As you go about your business, someone whom you believe to be a local private investigator approaches you. He says to you that he has a project that you might be interested in and suggests that you meet him at his home or a local restaurant. When you meet the private investigator, he has another person with him. They discuss a plan to burglarize a local advertising firm. The break-in is explained to you in terms of one of the four rationales just presented.

Some professionals believed this study violated the APA ethical principles; Cook (1975) suggested that the ethical principles were violated in two major ways. First, the study had a potential for negative effects on participants who went beyond their personal moral standards. Second, because the study paralleled the Watergate scandal, it would receive wide publicity.

The authors of the study responded to these concerns. Cook pointed out, and the authors agreed, that the participants should leave the experiment feeling that they had helped to gain new knowledge and that the experimenters were concerned for the welfare of the participants at all times. The authors described the procedures that they included to protect the participants. First, the field study was carried out so that the participants could not leave the experiment feeling that they had become involved in an illegal activity. The participants in the study were debriefed about the real nature of the meeting and the concerns of the experimenters over having used deception. Second, the experimental meeting was not forced on any participant but took place only after an initial agreement to meet at another location. Third, alternative experimental procedures that did not involve deception were considered and rejected. For example, a study in which people role-played the situation might have been used. However, because the study was to determine the difference between observing and actually participating in the situation, such alternative designs were considered unsuitable. Fourth, a lawyer-psychologist served as a consultant during the planning and implementing of the field study to protect the rights of the participants and the experimenters. Also, the state attorney's office found the procedure to be legally acceptable. If you are interested in the actual results, you may look up Cook's article in the library (Cook, 1975).

Bypassing the Bypass

Let's examine one other study that required deception. It raised a number of interesting issues, particularly the question of when the information gained is important enough to violate normal ethical standards. This particular study deals with medical research to determine the effectiveness of a heart operation for the treatment of angina (Cobb, Thomas, Dillard, Merendino, & Bruce, 1959). However, the same questions raised by this study are also applicable to studies dealing with evaluating new techniques in psychotherapy, biofeedback, behavioral medicine, and other fields. This study was reported in 1959; with the adoption of human participant review committees, such a study probably would not be permitted today. However, you must decide for yourself whether this is an important study.

In the study 17 patients with angina pectoris (pains in the chest) attributed to coronary artery disease were invited to participate in an experimental evaluation of an operation to relieve the angina. The patients knew that they were part of an experimental evaluation of the operation, but they did not know the nature of the evaluation. Furthermore, most patients knew from the popular press that the operation was considered to be a new and exciting treatment for angina. It should also be pointed out that the angina was severe enough to limit the activities of the patients, with the majority of them reported to be unable to work.

Once the patient was in the operating room and the anesthesia had been given, the surgeon opened an envelope that told him to which experimental group the patient belonged. For half the patients, the operation was carried out as usual; that is, there was a ligation of the internal mammary artery. For the other half of the patients, the chest was cut open and the artery of the heart was found, as in the normal procedure, but the artery was not cut and tied in the usual manner. Rather, the cardiac system was left untouched and the patient's chest closed. Both groups of patients were cared for normally, without the attending physician knowing to which group each belonged. Would you consider this experiment a violation of ethics?

Most people would consider it unethical to operate on another human being without his or her consent about the nature of the operation. Before you decide let's look at the results of the study. During the first 6 months following the operation, the same number of patients in both the experimental (ligation) and the control (incision only) groups showed "significant participative improvement." Just opening and closing the chest was shown to be associated with the same improvement rate as actually performing the operation. Positive changes were also noted in EKG evaluations. For example, one patient, who before the operation showed irregular heart wave patterns on an EKG during exercise, showed no irregularities after the operation. Surprising as it may seem, this patient was in the control group.

We are now faced with some difficult questions. For example, how can we go about testing the value of new therapeutic procedures, whether they be surgical or psychotherapeutic, without violating the rights of the participant? Are there times when we might consider it ethical to deceive a participant so that knowledge about a procedure might be gained? That is, are there times in which the savings in patient distress and economic resources justify less than full disclosure? Should the patients in the control group have been debriefed if they were reporting a significant improvement in their symptoms?

A current debate centers around placebo treatments. One side suggests that it is unethical to give a person a placebo when that means withholding active treatments for his or her disorder. The other side suggests that placebos offer an important method for testing new treatments. This debate and its ethical implications have been covered in such journals as *Science* (Enserink, 1999, 2000). What complicates this debate even more are the reports that placebos result in psychological and physiological changes as measured by objective methods such as brain imaging and psychopharmacological assays and may be reversed once the participant is told that they were part of the placebo group. What do you think about this type of research in general?

DEBRIEFING: WHEN IS ENOUGH ENOUGH?

Whether or not deception is used in an experiment, the experiment does not end without completing the dialogue between the scientist and the participant begun at the start of the experiment. Some researchers call this concluding dialogue *debriefing*. It is the goal of this dialogue to ensure that participants leave the laboratory with at least as much self-esteem and as little anxiety as when they came to the experiment (Kelman, 1968). The debriefing process consists of two major aspects. First, the debriefing is an opportunity for the participants to tell the experimenter how they felt about being part of the experiment. This not only is good feedback for the experimenter but also allows the participants to express any self-doubt about their performance and deal with thoughts and feelings that arose during the experiment. Second, the debriefing is an opportunity for the experimenter to explain the study to the participants in greater detail.

It often is difficult for the experimenter to determine how much information should be conveyed to the participants. For example, the design of the study might be too complex to describe in detail. When children are used as participants, it might be difficult to convey to the child what was being asked, and the experimenter might rely on the parents to help with this task. In the case of deception research, Carlsmith, Ellsworth, and Aronson (1976) suggest that just telling the truth is not enough and may even be more harmful than no explanation at all. These authors suggest that the experimenter include a discussion of why the deception was necessary and that the experimenter express regret for using deception. Furthermore, they suggest that the experimenter explain that the experiment was designed to deceive anyone and that it is normal to feel foolish or silly after being taken in by a deception. These authors also suggest that the participants be given the opportunity to develop and express their own reactions to deception research in general and to the present experiment in particular.

THE PARTICIPANT AS COLLEAGUE

Throughout our discussion of ethics, we have suggested that the experimenter value the participants and respect their rights. A useful metaphor is to consider the participant as a colleague, as someone who helps with the experiment. As with any colleague, you as a scientist would discuss with the participant what you were interested in doing and the manner in which you would go about doing it. Once the experiment was completed, you would discuss with your colleague-participant the results of the study. This would allow not only the participant to learn more about the experimentation but also you as a scientist to understand the participant's *experience* of the experiment and thus aid in your interpretation of the results.

This model could also be used in performing deception research, although with more difficulty. For example, if one were using college students in a deception study, Campbell suggests that the students might be told at the beginning of the term that some of the research being performed that term involved some deception. The general nature of the whys and hows of deception studies could be discussed at this time, and the potential participant could be allowed to see the importance of this type of research, whether it be of the placebo type or more direct deception. Those who did not want to participate in a deception study could ask to be excluded from studies of that type.

In summary, a participant should be treated as one treats a colleague, as someone who is valued and respected for the information that he or she can offer. If you use this approach, many ethical questions of psychological research will remain in the background and arise only in rare and special circumstances.

 CONCEPT CHECK 4.2   A student was conducting an EEG study in which he noticed that the participant's brain activity on one side looked different from that on the other. At the end of the experiment, he said to the participant, "I think you should see a physician because your EEG looks funny to me." Are there any problems with this experimenter's attempt to help the participant?

ANIMALS AS SUBJECTS

One of the more difficult issues on which to achieve consensus is the use of animals in experimental research. Much of what you learned in your introductory psychology course, especially in the areas of physiology and health, stress, and coping, may have come from animal research (compare Domjan & Purdy, 1995). Of course, human beings are also by definition animals, but in this section we use the word *animal* to refer to nonhuman animals. The debate over animal experimentation is broad based and requires that we examine our fundamental assumptions about the nature of animal life. There are many extreme positions in this debate. Some people question whether it is ever ethical for us to use animals for experiments.

It has been argued that the ethical issues go beyond pain and suffering to that of control. This position has led some to suggest that all animals should be able to run wild and that leash laws are a form of slavery. Do you consider it ethical to have a pet? As you think about this question, you might think of the strongest cases for using animals. For example, do we want to use dogs as aids for blind people?

Concerning the use of animals in research, it is clear that there are a number of emotional and polarized positions. The February 1997 issue of *Scientific American* offers a series of articles relating to animal research that illustrate well the opposing positions. For example, one position suggests that information learned from animal research is often redundant and unnecessary and may be misleading (Barnard & Kaufman, 1997). On the other hand, other researchers suggest that at least since the time of Pasteur, animal research has offered important breakthroughs in the treatment of disease for both humans and animals (Botting & Morrison, 1997).

In psychological research one position suggests that our goal should be to eliminate all animal research because animals are exposed to pain and suffering in the form of shock, stress, heat, cold, withdrawal of food, and even mutilation. Of course, it is not routine to subject animals to pain and suffering in research. Those who support it point out that animal research is crucial to meet the goals of society and, if anything, we should be increasing, not decreasing, animal research. One propaganda poster points out that animal research has added 20 years (through medical research) to the lives of the people who protest against it. This debate reminds us of the role of values in shaping our position on this topic.

Of course, there is no one right answer for all situations. We seek to present you with some of the basic questions and considerations that must be pondered with regard to animal research. In this way we hope to help you become an informed consumer, able to consider and evaluate the extreme positions you hear, both pro and con, concerning the question of animal experimentation.

Various fields of the behavioral sciences perform research with animals. These include learning, psychopathology, behavioral genetics, neurosciences, and health psychology. It is partly our concern for animals that has led us to perform animal research so that we can understand other species and, in turn, ourselves. We have gained valuable information on the manner in which bats navigate through dark spaces with echolocation, the manner in which animals communicate with one another, and the social systems within given species. We have used animals to understand how patterns of infant development lead to later emotional or addictive patterns and how diets rich in fats lead to atherosclerosis in animals who live in unstable environments.

Although it has been estimated that animal research represents less than 10% of total psychological research, some areas such as biological psychology have a larger percentage. Kalat (1992) suggests there are five reasons for studying animals in biological psychology. First, we are interested in animals for their own sake. For example, the naturalistic observation studies of Lorenz, as well as many bird and insect ethological studies, were designed to learn about a particular species of animal for its own sake. Veterinary research, like human medical research, has benefited pets, farm animals, and wildlife. Second, what we learn about animals sheds light on human evolution. Recent fieldwork with finches in the Galápagos Islands has helped to clarify Darwin's original theories of evolution (Weiner, 1994). Third, a certain process may be highlighted or exaggerated in animals and therefore easier to notice than it is in humans. For example, pigs have a cardiovascular system similar to that of humans and have been used in health psychology research. Thus, animal models of disease processes have led to real progress in such areas as the development and treatment of heart disease. Also, many insects have a short reproductive cycle that allows the study of genetics. Fourth, the underlying mechanisms of behavior are similar across species and sometimes are easier to study in a nonhuman species. For example, mechanisms such as nerve cell membranes, synapses in insects, and operant conditioning processes are similar in humans and various animals. And fifth, certain experiments are impossible with humans because of legal or ethical restrictions. One of the major reasons for conducting such research is the ability to gain experimental control over the situation. For example, with animals it is possible to regulate exactly such factors as diet, sleep patterns, housing situations, and exercise, which would be difficult or impossible with humans. Also, certain types of animals are more susceptible to diseases such as cancer or hypertension and thus offer a way of determining which factors slow down or speed up the onset of the disorder.

Overall, it is this last category that brings forth the real concerns with animal research. The question asks whether it is acceptable to use animals in research that would not be acceptable using humans. Gray (1990) maintains that one answer to this question is to distinguish between ethical and moral issues. If it is an ethical principle not to inflict pain unnecessarily, then it is unethical to inflict pain unnecessarily regardless of the species. It would not matter ethically whether it is a human being, a cat, or a cockroach. However, the moral choice may place us in opposition to the ethical principle.

For example, if there were two children in a burning house, their mother might discover that she could save only one at a time and thus risk pain to and loss of the second. She would be forced to make a moral decision. Gray likens this example to the situation of animal research: If certain experiments are not carried out, then people who might have benefited from the knowledge gained through those experiments may be forced to endure suffering or pain that could have been avoided. Although the clearest examples are in medical research, examples in psychological research also exist.

Gray argued that in the end we, like the mother who saves her own son or daughter, will perform research that saves our own species. However, at some point the amount of suffering inflicted on animals may not represent a reasonable balance with the avoidance of human pain and suffering, and thus it may not be morally defensible. The extreme cases are easy, but the real conflict arises when one is unsure whether an experiment will indeed lead to a cure and thus less suffering. These are difficult situations for scientists and for internal review committees.

The bond between humans and animals is of long standing. Historical records suggest that animals have been kept as pets and used for herding sheep, plowing fields, and transportation for thousands of years. To protect their welfare, various organizations have been formed over the years, including the Society for the Prevention of Cruelty to Animals (SPCA), formed in England in 1824 and in the United States in 1866. (Child abuse cases in the 19th century were brought to court under the laws against cruelty to animals because there were no similar laws for children.)

Greek physician Galen, who lived in the second century AD, is credited with the first documented use of living animals for research. Galen was able to demonstrate that arteries contain blood and not air. Until the 18th century, there was little if any ethical concern about animal research. However, by the 19th century, groups were formed in England to abolish painful animal research. Near the end of the 19th century, a committee of the British Association for the Advancement of Science presented a set of guidelines that contained four major points. First, medical experiments should be performed under anesthesia when appropriate. Second, a painful experiment is not justified if it merely demonstrates a fact already known. Third, if pain is involved, skilled researchers should perform the research with sufficient instrumentation in a properly regulated laboratory. Fourth, veterinary operations should not be performed only for the purpose of becoming more proficient at the operation.

Presented in 1871, these four principles formed the basis of many of the ethical considerations that were to be debated throughout Europe during the latter part of the 19th century and into the 20th century. In a paradox of history, it was under Hitler's government that federal laws pertaining to the protection of animals, especially as related to tormenting or rude treatment, were established in Germany in 1934. Phillips and Sechzer (1989) have published this history, along with a contemporary discussion of ethical approaches to animal research worldwide. We have drawn on this scholarly presentation for part of our discussion.

In the United States, contemporary regulation began with the publication of the *Guide for Laboratory Facility and Care* by the federal government in 1962. In 1966 the Animal Welfare Act was enacted. The Public Health Service issued regulations in 1985, which were revised in 1986 and again in 1996 (Box 4.3). Phillips and Sechzer maintain that, as a nation, our view of animal research changed during the two decades between the 1966 regulations and the 1985–1986 regulations, with both scientists and laypeople becoming more concerned about animal experimentation. For a discussion of how one large research institution, Harvard, balances the tension between animal research and animal care, see Lauerman (1999).

An important consideration has been the use of research to help us to scientifically understand animals and thus make more informed ethical decisions about them. For example, Dawkins (1990), in the journal *Behavioral and Brain Sciences,* asks how we can study animal welfare empirically. She suggests that, to answer this question, we need an objective basis for deciding when an animal is suffering. To answer this question, Dawkins suggests that we need to direct our attention to the inner experience of animals. This is an important challenge for behavioral scientists because at present the only good way we have to gain access into the experiential world of animals is through behavioral research. For example, animals can be trained to respond differentially according to their subjective experience of a drug. Because an animal can make choices, we can begin such a dialogue, albeit in a limited way.

Box 4.3

Public Health Service Principles for the Care and Use of Animals

The issue of animal research has raised a number of questions over the past couple of decades. A 1997 essay in *Scientific American* suggests that concern for animals has greatly changed the manner in which animals are treated in research and has resulted in an overall drop in animal research over the past 20 years (Mukerjee, 1997). To protect animals from undue suffering or harm, a number of professional organizations have issued guidelines concerning the care and use of laboratory animals, which are described in the text. Here we describe the federal guidelines issued by the Public Health Service (PHS) in 1985 and updated in 1996. In this policy statement, the PHS describes the manner in which animals are to be used and cared for. Further information about the policy can be obtained from the Office for Protection from Research Risks, National Institutes of Health, 6100 Executive Boulevard, MSC 7507, Rockville, MD 20892-7507 and the Office of Laboratory Animal Welfare website (http://grants.nih.gov/grants/olaw/olaw.htm).

Principles for the Care and Use of Animals Used in Testing, Research, and Training

The principles below were prepared by the Interagency Research Animal Committee. This committee, which was established in 1983, serves as a focal point for federal agencies' discussions of issues involving all animal species needed for biomedical research and testing. The committee's principal concerns are the conservation, use, care, and welfare of research animals. Its responsibilities include information exchange, program coordination, and contributions to policy development.

U.S. Government Principles for the Utilization and Care of Vertebrate Animals Used in Testing, Research, and Training

The development of knowledge necessary for the improvement of the health and well-being of humans as well as other animals requires in vivo experimentation with a wide variety of animal species. Whenever U.S. Government agencies develop requirements for testing, research, or training procedures involving the use of vertebrate animals, the following principles shall be considered; and whenever these agencies actually perform or sponsor such procedures, the responsible Institutional Official shall ensure that these principles are adhered to:

I. The transportation, care, and use of animals should be in accordance with the Animal Welfare Act (7 U.S.C. 2131 et seq.) and other applicable Federal laws, guidelines, and policies.[1]

II. Procedures involving animals should be designed and performed with due consideration of their relevance to human or animal health, the advancement of knowledge, or the good of society.

III. The animals selected for a procedure should be of an appropriate species and quality and the minimum number required to obtain valid results. Methods such as mathematical models, computer simulation, and in vitro biological systems should be considered.

IV. Proper use of animals, including the avoidance or minimization of discomfort, distress, and pain when consistent with sound scientific practices, is imperative. Unless the contrary is established, investigators should consider that procedures that cause pain or distress in

(continued)

(continued)

human beings may cause pain or distress in other animals.

V. Procedures with animals that may cause more than momentary or slight pain or distress should be performed with appropriate sedation, analgesia, or anesthesia. Surgical or other painful procedures should not be performed on unanesthetized animals paralyzed by chemical agents.

VI. Animals that would otherwise suffer severe or chronic pain or distress that cannot be relieved should be painlessly killed at the end of the procedure or, if appropriate, during the procedure.

VII. The living conditions of animals should be appropriate for their species and contribute to their health and comfort. Normally, the housing, feeding, and care of all animals used for biomedical purposes must be directed by a veterinarian or other scientist trained and experienced in the proper care, handling, and use of the species being maintained or studied. In any case, veterinary care shall be provided as indicated.

VIII. Investigators and other personnel shall be appropriately qualified and experienced for conducting procedures on living animals. Adequate arrangements shall be made for their in-service training, including the proper and humane care and use of laboratory animals.

IX. Where exceptions are required in relation to the provisions of these Principles, the decisions should not rest with the investigators directly concerned but should be made, with due regard to Principle II, by an appropriate review group such as an institutional animal care and use committee. Such exceptions should not be made solely for the purposes of teaching or demonstration.

---

[1]For guidance throughout these principles, the reader is referred to the *Guide for the Care and Use of Laboratory Animals* prepared by the Institute of Laboratory Animal Resources, National Academy of Sciences.

Although we are far from having a simple answer to this question, the empirical approach of Dawkins and others offers an important start.

The ethical guidelines of the APA described earlier include a section on the care and use of animals. This version was published in the December 2002 issue of the *American Psychologist* and is presented here. An expanded version can also be found on the APA website (http://www.apa.org/science/anguide.html).

8.09 Humane Care and Use of Animals in Research

a. Psychologists acquire, care for, use, and dispose of animals in compliance with current federal, state, and local laws and regulations, and with professional standards.

b. Psychologists trained in research methods and experienced in the care of laboratory animals supervise all procedures involving animals and are responsible for ensuring appropriate consideration of their comfort, health, and humane treatment.

c. Psychologists ensure that all individuals under their supervision who are using animals have received instruction in research methods and in the care, maintenance, and handling of the species being used, to the extent appropriate to their role. (See also Standard 2.05, Delegation of Work to Others.)

d. Psychologists make reasonable efforts to minimize the discomfort, infection, illness, and pain of animal subjects.

e. Psychologists use a procedure subjecting animals to pain, stress, or privation only when an alternative procedure is unavailable and the goal is justified by its prospective scientific, educational, or applied value.

f. Psychologists perform surgical procedures under appropriate anesthesia and follow techniques to avoid infection and minimize pain during and after surgery.

g. When it is appropriate that an animal's life be terminated, psychologists proceed rapidly, with an effort to minimize pain and in accordance with accepted procedures.

The APA has further described the manner in which they consider animal research essential for its contribution to psychological science. This overview can be found at their website (http://www.apa.org/science/animal2.html). The American Association for the Advancement of Science (AAAS), which publishes the journal *Science,* has also considered the question of animal research, which they considered "to be essential not only in applied and clinical research, but also in research that furthers the understanding of biological processes." Further discussions by the AAAS on the use of animals in research, testing, and education can be accessed on the AAAS website (http://www.aaas.org). Finally, just as there are IRBs for human participants in research, there are also institutional animal care and use committees for examining the care and use of animals in research.

As we conclude our considerations, let's remind ourselves that ethical questions have at their base issues of relationships and traditions. As scientists we ask what *is* and what *ought to be* our relationship with our participants and our society with regard to research. To answer this question, we stress that part of our ethical responsibility is to consult with others about our research. In this context, we described the manner in which internal review committees evaluate the ethics of research and the guidelines (for example, those of the APA and the federal government) used to direct our evaluations. With both humans and animals, we are only beginning to develop methods for the study of inner experience that can help to inform our ethical considerations.

CONCEPT CHECK 4.3

Jim does not believe that animals should be used in experiments. To make his point, he goes into one of the animal labs and modifies the equipment to make the experiment give false results. If he really believes in his values, is what he did unethical?

KEY TERMS AND CONCEPTS

1. **Ethical considerations in research**
2. **Participants' rights**
   - **A.** Voluntary participation
   - **B.** Informed consent
   - **C.** Right to privacy
     - Confidentiality
     - Anonymity
3. **Scientists' rights**
4. **Guidelines of the American Psychological Association**

5. **Use of deception in research**
   - **A.** Milgram
   - **B.** West et al.
   - **C.** Cobb et al.
6. **Debriefing**
7. **The participant as colleague**
8. **Animals as subjects**
   - **A.** APA ethical principles
   - **B.** Ethical versus moral questions

SUMMARY

1. Although the purpose of research is to gain understanding and knowledge, the search for knowledge takes place in the context of an interaction between the scientist and the participant. This being the case, it is necessary to ask what the obligations of the scientist and the participant are toward each other. This leads to a study of proper action and values: the study of ethics.

2. Three important points were presented. First, although actual ethical problems are minimal in most psychological experiments, there are exceptions that require careful consideration. Second, ethical considerations are partly regulated both by federal agencies and by professional societies such as the APA. Third, whether you are a participant or a scientist, you must decide how you will act and assume responsibility for that action.

3. Ethical consideration of psychological experimentation has at its heart the idea that a person participating in psychological research should not be harmed or negatively affected in a way that would result in a lower level of any aspect of human functioning.

4. Two ways in which participants' rights are ensured are through the principles of voluntary participation and informed consent. The principle of voluntary participation requires that the participant not be coerced into taking part in an experiment and that the participant be able to leave at any time during the experiment.

The principle of informed consent requires that the participant be informed about what is to take place in an experiment and about any potential harm, either physical or psychological, that may result from participation in the research.

5. The principle of privacy requires the scientist to maintain the participant's anonymity and to not release any personal information about a particular participant without that person's consent.

6. Questions of an ethical nature arise mainly from research that involves deception. Examples of these studies, such as the Milgram obedience study, point out the problems and promises of such research.

7. In all research except certain deception research, debriefing is a necessary component. In a debriefing session, participants are told about any deception that occurred as well as the importance of their participation in the research.

8. A recommended attitude to adopt as a researcher is to treat participants as colleagues who are there to help give valuable information about important psychological processes.

9. The use of nonhuman animals in research requires similar considerations as with human participants. To help with these considerations, the federal government and the APA have developed guidelines for the care and use of animals in research.

REVIEW QUESTIONS

1. What are the rights of the scientist and the participant in an experiment?
2. Why are the medical experiments conducted by the Nazis during World War II considered unethical?
3. What do you see as the difference between *informed* and *educated* consent?
4. What are the main themes of the APA guidelines on ethics?
5. What is an *internal review committee?*
6. What are the pros and cons of deception research?
7. What is *debriefing,* and why is it important?
8. In the final analysis, who is responsible for ethical concerns in an experiment?

DISCUSSION QUESTIONS AND PROJECTS

1. Discuss the participant's rights and the scientist's rights in performing research.
2. In performing an experiment that uses heart rate as a measure, you notice that the record of one of the participants looks different from every other one you have seen. Although the person told you at the beginning of the experiment that his heart was normal, you think

there might be a medical problem. What should you do about your concern?
3. Discuss the ethics of the heart surgery study presented in this chapter. What are the benefits and problems with such research? You could also look in your library for the research published in 1992 and 1993 on the effectiveness of the heart bypass operation. Does

(continued)

DISCUSSION QUESTIONS AND PROJECTS (*continued*)

knowing the effectiveness of the operation 25 years later make the earlier research more or less ethical?

4. One study not discussed in this chapter that has raised some ethical questions is the prison experiment conducted by Zimbardo in the 1970s (Zimbardo, Haney, Banks, & Jaffe, 1975). In this study, students were assigned the role either of guard or of prisoner for a week. Before the experiment could be completed, it was stopped because the guards were beginning to treat the prisoners in a cruel manner and prisoners began to obey the guards in what has been called a demeaning manner. Before the experiment began, it is unlikely that any of the students would have predicted they would act as they did. Discuss the ethics of conducting this research and what safeguards should be required. In what ways could it be considered unethical to show someone something true but unpleasant about himself or herself? What harm could have been done by this study?

5. Are there times when deception research might be useful, or should it be banned altogether?

6. What ethical considerations would one need to consider in using children as research participants?

7. How might you design a study to allow animals to choose the type of housing (for example, individual versus group) that they preferred? What ethical objections might there be to performing this research?

INFOTRAC COLLEGE EDITION: EXERCISES

InfoTrac College Edition can be used to learn more about research ethics. If you enter "research ethics" into the search, you will see a variety of articles in both the popular press and in scientific journals. One advantage of such an approach is that you can learn about how ethical concerns are being addressed in other fields and in other countries. For example, you can see the problems faced by the institution review boards (IRBs) in Britain in an article entitled "Meeting the challenges facing research ethics committees: some practical suggestions," which was published in the January 1998 issue of the *British Medical Journal*. You can also read about the need for research ethics in consumer research in an article by J. Jacoby and his colleagues in the 1998 *Annual Review of Psychology*.

To help you better understand the material in this chapter, you can go to Wadsworth's research methods workshop web page at http://www.wadsworth.com/psychology_d/templates/student_resources/workshops/resch_wrk.html. There you will find workshops related to research methods and statistics. The research methods workshop on "Ethical Issues" discusses the material presented in this chapter.

☑ Answers to Concept Checks

4.1 There are ethical problems with both the response and the situation. One aspect of an experiment is that participants have the right to object to or withdraw from any procedure in which they do not want to engage. Voluntary participation requires that a participant be able to leave at any time during an experiment. Many people would consider it unethical to require that a person's participation in an experiment be a required part of the grade for a course. That is, the participant must have an alternative to the experimental situation for participation to be voluntary.

4.2 Yes, there are a number of problems with the student's sharing his reaction with the participant. Because the student was not a neurologist or someone trained to diagnose abnormal brain activity, his conclusion that the EEG was abnormal may have been false. Thus, he may have created undue concern in the participant without just cause. In fact, the problem may have come from bad equipment or laboratory procedure and be unrelated to the participant. If it were determined that the record was accurate, a better procedure would be to take the record anonymously to a qualified specialist, who in turn could make an informed decision. Because many participants accept an experiment's conclusions as true, it is necessary to be especially careful not to make evaluations of participants' responses that are unrelated to the experiment.

4.3 It is unethical (and in some cases illegal) to falsify data. Science requires that experiments be run honestly and data collected accurately. If one does not believe in using animals in experiments, there are a number of places for making this point, including the review board of one's institution.

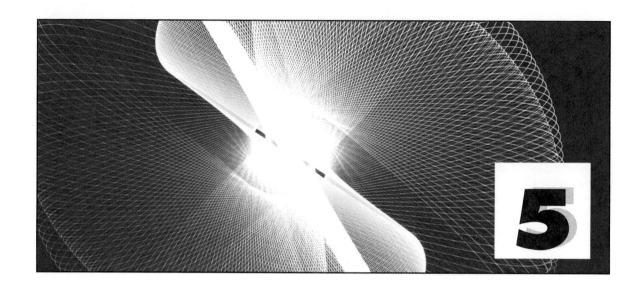

DESCRIPTION OF BEHAVIOR THROUGH NUMERICAL REPRESENTATION

MEASUREMENT

SCALES OF MEASUREMENT
Nominal Measurement
Ordinal Measurement
Interval Measurement
Ratio Measurement
Identifying Scales of Measurement

MEASUREMENT AND STATISTICS

PICTORIAL DESCRIPTION OF FREQUENCY
INFORMATION

DESCRIPTIVE STATISTICS
Measures of Central Tendency
Measures of Variability

PICTORIAL PRESENTATIONS OF
NUMERICAL DATA

TRANSFORMING DATA

STANDARD SCORES

MEASURE OF ASSOCIATION

Behavior can be described in many ways. In naturalistic observation studies, descriptions may consist of simple lists of behaviors or behavior sequences. For example, an ethologist might describe the detailed movements in the feeding behavior of some common fish. A developmental or clinical psychologist might describe the manner in which a family interacts. In experimental studies, behaviors usually are expressed in more quantitative terms. Some examples of quantitative measurements are the number of millimeters by which an observer overestimates the length of a line in a visual illusion experiment, the number of words recalled in a memory experiment, the change in a person's heart rate as a result of watching an emotionally charged film, and the results of an IQ test taken under different conditions.

As we pointed out in Chapter 3, there are a variety of ways to measure a particular process. If you were interested in emotional responding, for example, you could videotape facial expression; measure psychophysiological activity, such as EMG (electromyography), facial muscle activity, electroencephalographic (EEG) brain activity, or heart rate; obtain self-reports of internal states; and so on. Even when you decide which measure or measures to obtain, you still must decide whether to record the frequency of response, the intensity of response, the duration of response, the reaction time to the first response, or some combination of measures most appropriate to the question being asked. But how do we determine the appropriateness of a measure? One answer to this question is related to the conceptual question being asked. We discussed this aspect in Chapter 3, in relation to operational definitions and hypotheses.

Another answer comes from understanding basic statistical properties and operations. An introduction and review of descriptive statistics are the focus of this chapter. First, numbers are used in science to represent something beyond themselves, so we start the chapter with the concept of measurement. Second, it is important to know how to view data in terms of their underlying distribution, so we introduce simple pictorial methods of describing data and simple graphing. Third, it is important to be able to create the major statistical descriptors that describe a set of data; we therefore introduce the ideas of central tendency and variability. Fourth, we discuss the manner in which data may be transformed; in this context we present the idea of a standard score. Fifth, we discuss a simple way of describing the relationships within a set of data, using measures of association and particular correlational procedures. It should be noted that even in today's environment—when computer programs are readily available for describing, graphically representing, and analyzing data—it is still important that one have a fundamental understanding of how these processes work and their advantages and disadvantages.

MEASUREMENT

How we measure things is part of the field of study called measurement theory (Krantz, Luce, Suppes, & Tversky, 1971; Luce & Narens, 1987). Two of the first questions we are faced with in doing research are "What can we measure?" and "What do the measurements mean?" A number may be used in a variety of ways. Sometimes numbers are used to identify particular objects or events, as when a friend tells you she lives at 56 Walnut Spring

Lane. Sometimes numbers are used to mean "more than," as when a child says that a bike must cost $1 million more than a candy bar. As adults, we do the same thing when we tell someone that we woke up in the middle of the night and stayed awake for hours. Numbers can also be used to indicate an exact relationship. We know that the difference between 700 and 900 is the same as the difference between 300 and 500. Finally, numbers can be used to specify a unit of measure, such as 25¢.

We have just discussed four different ways in which numbers may be used in terms of four specific properties: identity, magnitude, equal intervals, and absolute zero. We can use these properties to help us to define levels of measurement, or scales of measurement as they are sometimes called.

SCALES OF MEASUREMENT

We commonly discuss four basic levels or **scales of measurement.** These are nominal, ordinal, interval, and ratio. They are summarized in Table 5.1 and discussed in this section. Our discussion will be somewhat brief; for more technical presentations see Coombs, Raiffa, and Thrall (1954), Roberts (1979), and Stevens (1946, 1951, 1957).

 ## Nominal Measurement

Nominal (sometimes called *categorical*) *measurement* occurs when people are simply placed into different categories. This form of measurement is a classifying or naming activity (hence the term *nominal*). For example, you can classify your research participants as men

Table 5.1

Scales of Measurement		
	Properties	Examples
Nominal	Identity	Telephone numbers, numbers on uniforms, brands of soup, employment statuses, diagnostic categories (schizophrenic, paranoid, neurotic, etc.)
Ordinal	Identity, magnitude	Class standing, results of races, weekly college football polls
Interval	Identity, magnitude, equal intervals	Temperature (Fahrenheit or Celsius), scores on intelligence tests, scores on personality adjustment inventories
Ratio	Identity, magnitude, equal intervals, absolute zero point	Length, weight, time, reaction time, number of responses made by an individual

or women, as right-handed or left-handed, as Catholic or Protestant. The differences between categories are of kind (qualitative) and not of degree (quantitative). In many research problems, it is sufficient to determine simply whether the number of individuals in a given category varies as a function of some treatment in which you are interested. For example, you might want to determine whether a particular type of advertising alters the percentage of people willing to try a new product. Your behavioral measure would then be whether an individual is willing to try a new product. Numbers themselves sometimes can be used as nominal categories. For example, the numbers on baseball jerseys, telephone numbers, and ZIP codes illustrate nominal uses of numbers, as do coding data (for example, male = 1, female = 2).

■ Ordinal Measurement

In the case of *ordinal measurement,* a single continuum usually underlies a particular classification system. College football standings, pop-music charts, and class standings are examples of ordinal measurements. In a psychological experiment, you might divide up your research participants on the basis of creativity and end up with three categories: noncreative, creative, and highly creative, which can be given the values 1, 2, and 3, respectively. These scores reflect an underlying continuum: the *relative amount* or *magnitude* of creativity. An ordinal scale represents some degree of quantitative difference, whereas a nominal scale does not.

Ordinal scales can be obtained whenever you rank research participants or events along a single dimension. With ordinal measures you are making statements only about order; the differences between consecutive values are not necessarily equal. Notice that numbers used in ordinal measurement have no mathematical properties other than providing categories and rank. Nothing is implied about the magnitude of the intervals between the categories. For example, in the case of the top 20 football teams, there is no assumption that the difference in excellence between the number 1 team and the number 4 team is the same as that between the number 6 team and the number 9 team. Furthermore, it does not make sense to say that the number 1 and 4 teams together equal the number 2 and 3 teams.

What we are really doing is transforming information expressed in one form to that expressed in another. For example, think of the food that you ate for supper last night. One way of presenting this information is to name the foods: pizza, soft drink, salad, green stuff (no one really knows what green stuff is, but every college cafeteria has a large supply of it). We can take this list of food and transform it into numerical representations. One simple method uses the property of identity. We can assign numbers to our food items to identify or distinguish single foods or groups. For example, we might let 1 represent all food that we feel better after eating and 0 stand for all food that we feel worse after eating. Pizza, soft drink, and salad would get a 1, and green stuff would get a 0. We have mapped the aspects of one set onto another set. All this means is that we have found another way (other than just listing) to represent our data.

This is not the only way that we can represent our data, however. We could also assign numbers to refer to how much we like the food. We could assign pizza a 1, salad a 2, soft drink a 3, and green stuff a 4. We have now presented the data in terms of the characteristic of magnitude. From this you know that pizza is ranked higher than a soft drink, but, as with a list of finishers in a race, you do not know anything about how much distance exists between them.

■ Interval Measurement

In *interval measurement* the scale values are related by a single underlying quantitative dimension (like ordinal data), and there are also equal intervals between consecutive scale values. *Equal intervals* means that there are equal amounts of the quantity being measured between every two successive numbers on the scale. Thus, on an interval scale, the interval between 1 and 4 equals the interval between 6 and 9. The household thermometer is an example of an interval scale. The degree lines are equal distances apart and reflect equal volumes of mercury; the difference between 20° and 40° is equivalent to the difference between 50° and 70°. When we say it is 0° outside, we do not mean that there is no temperature; we mean only that 0° is assigned a certain place on the scale.

■ Ratio Measurement

In *ratio measurement,* scores are related by a single quantitative dimension (as with interval or ordinal measurement). Also, they are separated by equal intervals (as with interval measurement), *and* there is an absolute zero. The most common ratio scales are found in the measurement of the physical attributes of objects, such as weight or length. There is no length shorter than 0 inches, no weight lighter than 0 pounds.

For example, if we were to represent our list of foods according to calorie content, we would know that the relationship between the 300-calorie salad and the 150-calorie soft drink was the same as that between the 300-calorie salad and the 450-calorie pizza; there is a 150-calorie difference between each pair.

We could also describe the food in terms of nutritional value, such as its ability to support life or its vitamin content. As you begin to make this mapping, you realize the need to have an absolute zero point. There is no way that green stuff could ever support life, much less contain vitamins. Thus, we could use numbers to represent the amount of a particular vitamin in the food. Pizza might have 33 units, the soft drink 12 units, salad 52 units, and of course, green stuff would have 0 units. Zero in this case means that the vitamin is not present at all; 0 represents an actual quantity.

■ Identifying Scales of Measurement

Frequently, the scale of measurement depends on the device (for example, scale or questionnaire) used for measuring the particular concept being studied. Even clear examples from the physical sciences (for example, temperature or length) that are normally viewed as being an interval or ratio measure could not be so called if the measuring instrument itself were not well constructed. In turn, the design of the measuring instrument depends on a theoretical understanding of the underlying concept. For example, until the development of the kinetic theory of heat, the measurement of temperature was inconsistent. There were many devices, each giving different results that could not be converted from one scale to another as they can now (for example, Celsius to Fahrenheit). Once a theoretical description of heat was developed, the problems of measurement were reduced. This may also be the case in psychology, with our many concepts lacking well-developed theory (for example, anxiety or intelligence).

Scales of measurement are related to how a particular concept is being measured and the questions being asked. For example, if we were to record the order of finish in a marathon, we would have an ordinal scale, whereas if we were to record times for the race, we would have a ratio scale. Although beyond the scope of our present discussion, we must also consider the relationship between physical measures and psychological characteristics. That is to say, a 100-watt light bulb may not be perceived to be twice as bright as a 50-watt one even though twice as much energy is being used. Similarly, recording times during a race is clearly a ratio scale, but that does not necessarily mean that running ability as measured by times during a race is. Thus, we need to both be aware of the nature of our measurements and consider the constructs that we are attempting to understand. We begin with the numbers and note that the devices that measure these should be both reliable and valid. As you remember, these concepts were discussed in Chapter 3 and we will continue to refer to them throughout this book.

 CONCEPT CHECK 5.1   Which scale of measurement best describes the following: telephone numbers; distances from Budapest to cities in the United States; temperatures throughout the year in Tuscaloosa, Alabama; and the ranking of basketball teams in the Big Ten?

MEASUREMENT AND STATISTICS

Mitchell (1986) tried to place the question of measurement scales and statistics in a historical and a philosophical context. He suggested that there are different theories or paradigms of measurement. For example, when we were in college taking methods courses, it was commonly taught that a direct relationship existed between the particular scale of measurement (nominal, ordinal, interval, or ratio) that we were using and a statistic (for example, *t* test or sign test) that was appropriate to use with it. S. S. Stevens introduced this idea, along with the idea of scales of measurement, in the 1940s (Stevens, 1946). The basic idea as traditionally taught is that the statistics used must be appropriate to the scale of measurement used.

Statisticians, as well as present-day experimentalists, no longer hold this view, and they continually point out that where a number comes from does not determine the appropriate statistical test. Gaito (1980) has presented a brief but clearly stated review of this issue. If you are interested in pursuing this further, you should consult Gaito's *Psychological Bulletin* article (1980) as well as Mitchell's *Psychological Bulletin* article (1986).

The main point is that no statistical reason exists for limiting a particular scale of measurement to a particular statistical procedure. The numbers do not care what you do to them. Lord (1953) illustrated this in a humorous manner with football numbers on the backs of players' jerseys. One could find the mean of all the players' numbers on a football team, but keep in mind that, as Lord pointed out, "the numbers do not remember where they came from." Like a computer, a statistical technique does not care what numbers it uses or where the numbers come from. Numbers are numbers as far as a computer or statistic is concerned. However, if you want to make reasonable conceptual decisions based on your numbers, then you must be concerned about where your numbers came from, and this is an issue of measurement, not statistics.

To this end, some researchers make a pragmatic distinction between qualitative measures and quantitative measures. Using measurement theory, we try to assign numbers in a manner in which we can make sense out of what we are doing. But to restate, your statistics do not know and do not care where your numbers come from. It does not matter to a statistic whether your numbers mean what you claim they do, much less whether your experiment was performed well or poorly. However, as a researcher you should care greatly about your inferences and logic. But, as we discuss in this chapter, statistics *do* tell us about numbers.

PICTORIAL DESCRIPTION OF FREQUENCY INFORMATION

A useful way to begin analyzing the results of any experiment is to convert your numerical data to pictorial form and then simply look at them. One way to depict the results of an experiment is to draw a frequency distribution. In a **frequency distribution,** you simply plot how frequently each score appears in your data. Suppose you were interested in dreaming. One initial baseline measurement might be to ask 20 people to write down their dreams for a week. To get an idea of how often people dream, you might begin your analysis by seeing how many dreams each person recalls.

Table 5.2 demonstrates such an experiment and shows the number of dreams each person remembered dreaming. To create a pictorial representation, a first step would be

Table 5.2

Hypothetical Dream Study

Participant	Number of Dreams Recalled	Participant	Number of Dreams Recalled
1	1	11	7
2	4	12	1
3	5	13	2
4	2	14	5
5	0	15	6
6	2	16	5
7	0	17	2
8	6	18	6
9	1	19	7
10	3	20	5

Figure 5.1

Bar graph of
dream data

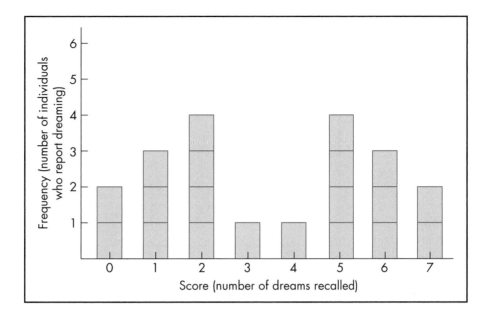

to find the smallest number of dreams recalled (0 in our case) and the largest number of dreams recalled (7). You could then list all the numbers between 1 and 7. Going through all the responses recorded in Table 5.2, you could make a mark by the number of dreams recalled for each person in your study. Now you have two variables (number of dreams recalled and number of people who recalled a certain number of dreams). This information can be plotted on a graph. Figure 5.1 shows such a graph, which represents a frequency distribution for these data. The vertical, or *y* axis **(ordinate),** labeled "Frequency," is the number of people who fall into each category; the horizontal, or *x* axis **(abscissa),** labeled "Score," is the number of dreams recalled. This type of presentation is called a *bar graph.*

In Figure 5.1 the two blocks above a 0 score mean that two people reported no dreams during the week. Counting the other blocks, we learn that three people reported only one dream, four people reported two dreams, and so forth. Because the measurements along the *x* axis may be treated as interval data, we could also present them in the form of a *frequency polygon.* Figure 5.2 presents a frequency polygon of the dream data.

On closer inspection, it appears that measurements for most people tend to be clustered either to the left or to the right on the *x* axis. This means that, for these 20 people, dreams were recalled either infrequently (one or two dreams) or frequently (five, six, or seven dreams). This particular type of distribution, in which the people tend to fall into two groups, is called a **bimodal distribution.** Figure 5.3 illustrates some common types of distributions you might encounter.

For our purpose, we call a distribution *normal* if it approximates a *bell-shaped* distribution (see Figure 5.3a). We will present a more exact definition later, but for now we will say that a distribution is normal if most of the scores are concentrated in the center of the abscissa, with few at the extremes. Intelligence test scores for 1,000 randomly selected

Figure 5.2

Frequency polygon
of dream data

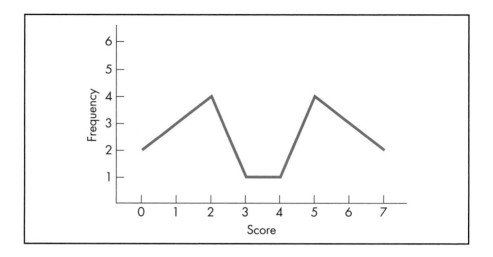

Figure 5.3

Four types of
frequency
distributions:
(a) normal,
(b) bimodal,
(c) positively skewed,
and (d) negatively
skewed

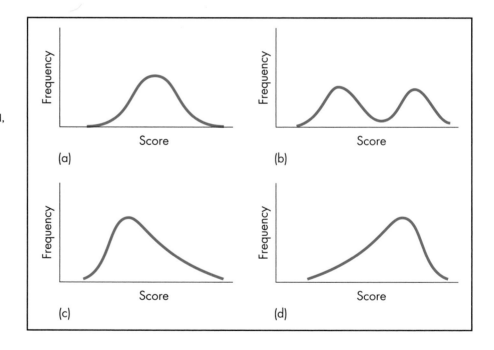

people approximate a normal distribution. In a bimodal distribution, the scores tend to be concentrated at two points along the abscissa (see Figures 5.2 and 5.3b). The distribution of heights for an equal number of men and women tends to be bimodal.

    A *skewed distribution* occurs when more scores occur at either end of the abscissa (see Figures 5.3c and 5.3d). For example, a distribution of verbal Scholastic Aptitude Test (SAT) scores among honors English majors would be skewed because few people with low verbal SAT scores would be included in this group. A skewed distribution can be skewed in either a positive or a negative direction. The slopes of the curves indicate whether the distribution is positively or negatively skewed. Simply said, if we begin at the point of our graph where the x and y axes meet (the left side of the graph), we can ask whether the values represented in the graph increase faster than they decrease. If this were the case, then we would say that a steeper slope on the ascending curve indicates that the distribution is positively skewed. A steeper slope on the descending curve indicates that the distribution is negatively skewed. Of course, in a normal distribution, the slopes of the ascending and descending curves are equal.

DESCRIPTIVE STATISTICS

◼ Measures of Central Tendency

We discuss three measures of central tendency in this section. These are the mean, the median, and the mode. If you listen carefully to the television news, you will notice that these measures often are used to describe the way we "typically" live. You will hear one report discussing the median income of college professors; another report may discuss the mean price of a new house in different cities in America. Modal (mode) descriptions are used less often.

Mean   Of the three measures of central tendency, the mean is used most often. The **mean** of a set of scores is the arithmetic average of those scores. It is obtained by adding the scores and dividing the total by the number of scores. In our dream data, 20 people reported a total of 70 recalled dreams:

$$\text{mean} = \frac{\text{sum of scores}}{\text{number of scores}} = \frac{\text{number of dreams recalled}}{\text{number of individuals}} = \frac{75}{20} = 3.75$$

In this particular example, 70 divided by 20 equals exactly 3.75. However, other times the answer may give us a recurring decimal, which must be rounded off to a given number of decimal places. For example, if the total score for 7 participants were 100, the mean would equal 14.285714285714. . . . The simple rule used by most researchers is to round up if the number is greater than or equal to 5 and to round down if it is less than 5. In this case, if we were to round to four decimal places, the mean would be 14.2857, whereas if we were to round to two decimal places the mean would be 14.29. We follow this rounding rule for any calculation performed in this book.

Median   The **median** of a set of scores is the middle score—that is, the score that has an equal number of scores both above and below it. To calculate the median of a set of scores, list all the scores in order of magnitude (from largest to smallest or vice versa); the median is the middle score or, in the case of an even number of scores, the score halfway between the two middle scores. In our dream data, the two middle scores are 3 and 4. Consequently, the median is 3.5.

A slight problem in calculating the median arises when the median interval contains a large number of scores. In this case we must interpolate so that an equal number of scores are above and below the median. This procedure is not required in this book. It is discussed in various statistics books, such as McCall (1980, pp. 64–66).

Mode   The **mode** is the most frequently occurring score. The only mathematical calculation required to compute the mode of a distribution of scores is to count the frequency of each score. The score that occurs most frequently is the mode. If there are two scores with the same frequency, we report two modes. For example, the dream data presented earlier had two modes: one at two dreams and one at five dreams recalled.

Choice of Measures   Given these three measures, you may be wondering which provides the best estimate of central tendency. There is no clear-cut answer. The appropriate choice varies with the particular frequency distribution and the intent of the researcher. For example, in a normal distribution the mode, median, and mean all have the same value (Figure 5.4a). This is not the case in a skewed distribution (Figure 5.4b). In a skewed distribution, extreme scores affect the mean.

For example, before you take a job in a company where the mean salary is $100,000 a year, you might want to find out the median salary; a mean of $100,000 could be produced

Figure 5.4

Mean, median, and mode of (a) a normal distribution and (b) a skewed distribution

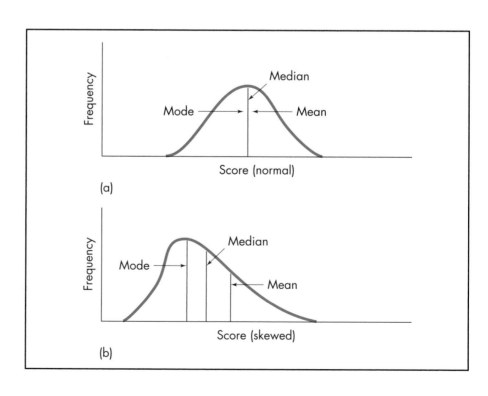

by 10 people making $10,000 each and 1 person making $1,000,000 (1,100,000/11 = 100,000). If you were a stock market analyst concerned with how much a company pays out in salaries, however, the mean would be the appropriate measure. In other words, if you are interested in the scores of a whole group, then the mean is the most appropriate measure.

However, if you are more interested in a representative individual score, then the median is more appropriate. In psychological research, we tend to use the mean most often both for historical reasons and because it fits into already developed statistical theory. In summary, the measure of central tendency that you use depends on the question that you are asking. In the final analysis, you must use your judgment to determine which measure of central tendency to use.

 CONCEPT CHECK 5.2
You have just graduated from college and you are applying for a job at three companies. Widget, Inc., tells you that its mean salary is $50,000. Fast Foods, Inc., tells you that its median salary is $50,000. And Deals-Are-Us, Inc., tells you that the modal salary of its workers is $50,000. If salary were your only concern in taking a job, which company would you be most interested in, and what additional information might you want to know?

■ Measures of Variability

You probably have completed a science course assignment requiring you to make measurements of some physical dimension, such as the length of a line. The exact readings among students probably differed. Thinking about this, we can gain some intuitive understanding concerning an important concept: **variability.** If we were to plot each measurement, we would see that the measurements varied around a particular point. We could also imagine that contained within these measurements was the actual length of the line or the true score. Thus, we can imagine any measurement to be composed of a true measurement plus the variability associated with that measurement. From this understanding, we can move to a more general notion that processes themselves may vary. For example, your weight may change from day to day while still remaining constant when viewed over a series of measurements. Thus, to describe a set of measurements more accurately, we need the concept of variability.

As we have seen, a measure of central tendency gives us some information concerning a set of scores; however, it does not give any information about how the scores are distributed. To obtain a more complete description of a set of data, we use a second measure in addition to the measure of central tendency. This is a measure of variability. Measures of variability are merely attempts to indicate how spread out the scores are. We can also call this variability *dispersion.* One common measure of dispersion is the **range,** which reflects the difference between the largest and smallest scores in a set of data. The actual computational formula given for the range in most introductory statistics books is the largest score minus the smallest score. (In the dream data presented earlier, the range is 7; that is, 7 − 0 = 7.) This is technically called the *exclusive range* (Keppel & Saufley, 1980). Although computing the range is easy, the range tells us only about the two extreme scores; it provides no information about the dispersion of the remaining scores if we know nothing about the underlying distribution.

Let's now demonstrate this graphically. Consider the following two sets of data for Group A and Group B.

Group A	Group B
2	2
3	5
4	5
5	6
6	6
7	6
8	7
9	7
10	10

In these two distributions, the ranges are the same (8), and the means are the same (6), yet the actual shapes of the distributions are very different (Figure 5.5). The scores in Group B appear more concentrated in the center of the distribution, yet our estimate of range does not reflect this. To provide a more sensitive description of the dispersion of *all* the scores, we use a second measure of the variability of data. This measure is called the variance.

Figure 5.5

Two different distributions with the same range and mean but different dispersions of scores

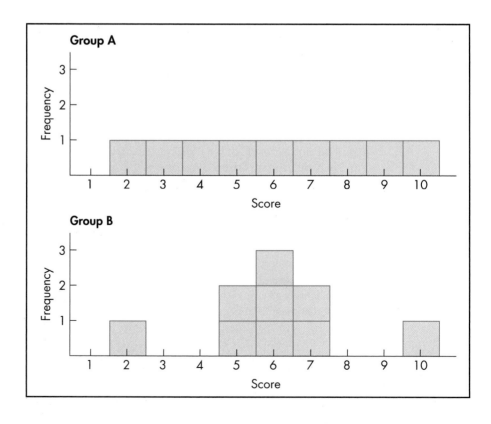

Simply stated, the variance is a description of how much each score varies from the mean. One way to describe the dispersion of *all* the scores would be to subtract each score from the mean and then add these deviations and divide the total by the number of scores. Unfortunately, for both technical and practical reasons, this approach does not give us the type of information that we need. Because the sum of the positive deviations is always equal to the sum of the negative deviations from the mean, adding these deviations gives a sum of 0. Instead, we square each deviation, add the squares, and then divide the total by the number of deviations. This gives us a description of how much each score varies from the mean. From this we arrive at the definition of *variance:* the average of the squared deviations from the mean.

To determine variance, we must first calculate what is called the **sum of squares;** that is, we add the numbers squared. The sum of squares is often abbreviated as *SS*. The first formula for *SS* that we will describe is called the *deviation method:* The sum of squares is equal to the sum of the squared deviation scores. Thus,

$$SS = \sum (X - \overline{X})^2$$

where $\sum$ = sum of, X = the individual score, and $\overline{X}$ = the mean of scores.

The deviation method is a useful teaching device because it requires that you compute the actual deviations for each score. The method is cumbersome, however. Once you master the concept, you might want to consider a second way to calculate the sum of squares. This is called the *computational formula* and sometimes is used simply because it requires less work, particularly on hand-held calculators:

$$SS = \sum X^2 - \frac{(\sum X)^2}{N}$$

where X = individual score and N = number of observations.

In Table 5.3 the sum of squares, *SS*, of a set of data is calculated by the deviation method. In Table 5.4, the sum of squares for the same set of data is calculated by the computational method. The difference in *SS* for the two methods reflects the rounding of the data to two decimal places during computation. As you remember the definition of variance—the average of the squared deviations from the mean—you will realize that we must now determine the average of the sum of squares. However, in determining the variance, we divide by *N* for a description of a single population. Remember we are discussing descriptive statistics at this point. As you will learn in the next chapter, $N - 1$ will be used with inferential statistics because this has been shown to be more accurate.

$$\text{variance} = \frac{\sum \text{of squares}}{\text{number of scores}} = \frac{SS}{N}$$

Using the example in Table 5.4, in which the sum of squares equals 93.75, we determine variance by dividing this sum by the number of scores (20). Thus,

$$\text{variance} = \frac{SS}{N} = \frac{93.75}{20} = 4.69$$

Table 5.3

Deviation Method			
Individual Score (X)	Deviation $(X - \overline{X})$	$(X - \overline{X})^2$	
1	−2.75	7.56	
4	0.25	0.06	
5	1.25	1.56	$\overline{X} = 3.75$
2	−1.75	3.06	
0	−3.75	14.06	$SS = \sum (X - \overline{X})^2$
2	−1.75	3.06	
5	1.25	1.56	$= 93.70$
6	2.25	5.06	
1	−2.75	7.56	
3	−0.75	0.56	
7	3.25	10.56	
1	−2.75	7.56	
2	−1.75	3.06	
5	1.25	1.56	
6	2.25	5.06	
5	1.25	1.56	
2	−1.75	3.06	
6	2.25	5.06	
7	3.25	10.56	
5	1.25	1.56	
Sum $(\sum) = 0$		Sum $(\sum) = 93.70$	

This calculation formula for variance now appears as

$$\text{variance} = \frac{\sum X^2 - \frac{(\sum X)^2}{N}}{N}$$

At this point, let's return to the two sets of data used in Figure 5.5. We saw that even though these distributions look quite different, the range for each distribution is the same. Granting for the moment that variance is a more sensitive measure of dispersion, let's see whether it provides a more useful tool than range for describing the dispersion about the mean of a group of scores. Table 5.5 shows the calculation of the variance for Group A, using the deviation method; Table 5.6 shows the calculation for Group B.

We see that Group B has a lower variance (4) than Group A (6.67). This supports our earlier subjective analysis, which indicated less variability, or dispersion, in Group B than in Group A. Because variance uses squared scores, however, the variance does not describe the amount of variability in the same units of measurement as the original scores; that is, a variance of 6.67 exceeds the greatest absolute deviation in either sample. Consequently, many researchers prefer to use the square root of the variance

Table 5.4

Computational Method

Individual Score (X)	X^2	
1	1	
4	16	
5	25	
2	4	$SS = \sum X^2 - \dfrac{(\sum X)^2}{N}$
0	0	
2	4	
5	25	$= 375 - \dfrac{(75)^2}{20}$
6	36	
1	1	
3	9	$= 375 - \dfrac{5625}{20}$
7	49	
1	1	
2	4	$= 375 - 281.25$
5	25	
6	36	
5	25	$= 93.75$
2	4	
6	36	
7	49	
5	25	
Sum ($\sum$) = 75	Sum ($\sum$) = 375	

Table 5.5

Group A Variance

Individual Score (X)	Deviation ($X - \overline{X}$)	$(X - \overline{X})^2$
2	−4	16
3	−3	9
4	−2	4
5	−1	1
6	0	0
7	+1	1
8	+2	4
9	+3	9
10	+4	16
	$\sum = 0$	$\sum = 60$

$$\text{Variance} = \frac{\sum (X - \overline{X})^2}{N} = \frac{60}{9} = 6.67$$

Table 5.6

Group B Variance		
Individual Score (X)	Deviation ($X - \overline{X}$)	$(X - \overline{X})^2$
2	-4	16
5	-1	1
5	-1	1
6	0	0
6	0	0
6	0	0
7	$+1$	1
7	$+1$	1
10	$+4$	16
	$\sum = 0$	$\sum = 36$

$$\text{Variance} = \frac{\sum (X - \overline{X})^2}{N} = \frac{36}{9} = 4$$

as their estimate of variability. The square root of the variance is called the **standard deviation (SD):**

$SD = \sqrt{\text{variance}}$

For Group A (variance = 6.67),

$SD = \sqrt{6.67} = 2.58$

For Group B (variance = 4),

$SD = \sqrt{4} = 2$

By making this transformation, we return to the original units of measurement and can therefore make meaningful comparative statements.

CONCEPT CHECK 5.3	Given the numbers 6, 5, 7, 9, 4, and 5, what are the mean, the variance, and the standard deviation?

PICTORIAL PRESENTATIONS OF NUMERICAL DATA

In addition to using numerical descriptions of data—such as frequency counts, measures of central tendency, and variance—it usually is helpful to use graphs to present our results pictorially.

Figure 5.6

Effects of room
temperature on
response rates in
rats

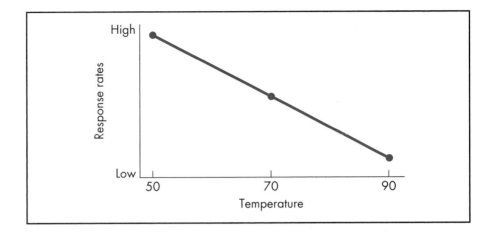

Figure 5.7

Effects of different
forms of therapy

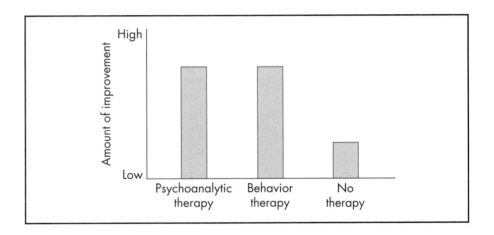

In psychology we have borrowed graphing procedures from other fields, such as mathematics, and we use many of their conventions. For example, the independent variable is placed on the *x* axis and the dependent variable on the *y* axis. Two main types of graphs are used: line graphs and bar graphs.

A *line graph* is used when the values of the independent variable correspond to points along a continuum. For example, you could graph the data from a study of the effects of room temperature on response rates in rats, as shown in Figure 5.6.

A *bar graph* is used to depict information that is categorical. For example, the results of a study that examined the effects of different forms of therapy could be illustrated, as shown in Figure 5.7. It would not be appropriate in this case to construct a line graph because these types of therapy do not lie along a continuum. (However, a line graph would be appropriate if the independent variable was the amount of a particular drug given because dosage levels of the *same* drug would form a continuum.)

TRANSFORMING DATA

After collecting the data, a researcher may discover that the numbers are too large or too small to work with comfortably. At this point the question arises, "How can I change these data to make them easier to work with?" The procedure is to transform the data. There are a variety of techniques for accomplishing this goal, depending on the type of data and the desired outcome of the transformation. In this section we introduce the topic briefly.

If you were to travel to Canada, Mexico, or Europe, you might be surprised to look at the temperature listed and see that it was only 30° when you were sweating. The explanation, of course, is that these countries use the Celsius scale, whereas the United States uses the Fahrenheit scale. Water freezes at 0° on the Celsius scale and boils at 100°. To convert to Fahrenheit, you multiply the Celsius reading by 9/5 and add 32. Thus, our reading of 30° would equal 86°.

When we converted the temperature from Celsius to Fahrenheit, we performed what is called a *linear transformation*. This means that if we were to draw a graph of the relationship between temperatures expressed in Fahrenheit and in Celsius, the resulting figure would be a straight line. You might try this for yourself by looking in a newspaper and recording the temperatures from around the world, then converting these into Celsius and plotting the relationship between Celsius and Fahrenheit. Using the example of temperature, we can see that there is a general formula that describes a linear transformation. Using three values that remain constant (*A*, *B*, and *C*), the formula is

$$\text{new number} = \frac{A}{B}(\text{old number}) + C$$

Because the values *A*, *B*, and *C* may be either positive or negative, we can add, subtract, multiply, or divide the values or perform a combination of these operations in a linear transformation.

Transformations are important for several reasons. The first is simply that researchers can use transformations to compare data collected using one scale with those collected using another. For example, in a biofeedback study designed to determine how well participants can raise their hand temperature, some researchers might report their data using Fahrenheit and others Celsius. Transforming the reported data makes it possible to compare the results.

Another reason for the importance of data transformation relates to statistical assumptions that are suggested for performing inferential statistical comparisons. If the researcher violates one of the assumptions, the results sometimes are difficult to interpret; one can sometimes avoid this problem by transforming the data so that the assumption is not violated. (This topic is discussed in some advanced statistical textbooks.)

We can now introduce a concept that Roberts (1979) calls *meaningfulness.* He holds that a statement is meaningful if the truth or falsity of the statement remains unchanged when one scale is replaced by another. To understand this better, let's look at an example. Imagine that you have performed a study in which you measured people's weights after a certain amount of exercise. One group received more exercise than the other. If we were to transform our data from weight in pounds to weight in kilograms, we still could make meaningful statements concerning the relationship between the two groups. However, in other cases this might not be true. For example, one measure (and underlying theory) of anxiety such as self-report might reflect a scale construction different from that of another, such as observed anxiety as rated by a professional, and thus prevent meaningful comparative statements because the scores from one anxiety scale could not be transformed to the other.

STANDARD SCORES

We are often interested in understanding a score in terms of its relationship to other scores. For example, just knowing that a friend scored a 76 on a chemistry test and a 62 on a physics test does not tell the complete story. When one examines the distribution, it might turn out that the 62 would actually be the higher grade if these tests were graded on a curve. That is, if the mean of the chemistry test were 85 with a standard deviation of 5 and the mean of the physics test were 50 with a standard deviation of 10, then our friend would be above the mean on the physics test but below the mean on the chemistry test. We could not compare the scores of the two tests unless we could present each of them in terms of its relative position on a particular distribution.

By asking the relative position of a particular score in terms of its mean and standard deviation, we create what is called a standard score. We also could transform all the scores of a particular set (for example, the chemistry test) into standard scores. The most common transformation of this kind is the z-score transformation. In more formal language, a z score for one particular measurement is a deviation score that is calculated by subtracting the mean of the distribution from that score and then dividing the difference by the standard deviation (which is the same as the square root of the variance). The formula is written as

$$z = \frac{score - mean}{SD} = \frac{score - mean}{\sqrt{variance}}$$

It is possible for a z score to be either positive or negative, depending on whether it is greater or less than the mean. There are two important characteristics of the z score. First, if we were to transform a set of data to z scores, we would find that the mean of these scores would equal 0. Second, the standard deviation of this set of z scores would equal 1. Being able to make this transformation has a number of advantages, which we discuss more fully later. For example, once we transformed our friend's chemistry and physics test scores, we could make a statement comparing how well he was doing relatively in each class.

For ease of presentation, z scores sometimes are transformed. For example, negative z scores can be transformed so that the negative numbers are removed. The SAT exams that are required for admission to some colleges can be viewed as transformed z scores based on a mean of 500 and a standard deviation of 100 for each portion of the test. For your information, the actual formula of the SAT score is 100 times the z score plus 500. A similar

$$\int_a^b f(x)\,dx + \int \sum_{i=1}^{i+n} \Delta_y$$

s.harris

"THIS IS THE PART I ALWAYS HATE."

transformation of the *z* score that also allows all the numbers to be positive is the *T* score. In this case the formula is 10 times the *z* score plus 50. *T*-score information is commonly seen in psychometric presentations such as intelligence tests.

MEASURE OF ASSOCIATION

Psychologists have long been interested in the question of whether our behavior and our self-reports go together—that is, whether we actually do what we say we will. To understand this question better, we could develop a questionnaire that asked people how often they would help people in need of assistance. We could also set up a situation in which there were many opportunities to help another person. If we had conducted this study, we could plot our data as shown in Figure 5.8. In this graph, called a *scatter diagram* or scatterplot, the score on the helpfulness questionnaire is on the *x* axis and the number of times the person actually helped someone is on the *y* axis. Each point on the scatter diagram represents one person and two scores: the score on the questionnaire and the number of times that the person helped someone in the experiment.

Note that those who score high on one measure also score high on the other measure. Likewise, those who score low on one also score low on the other. A useful statistic to apply to this type of analysis is the correlation. A correlation helps us to understand the relationship or degree of association between two measures. When we perform a correlation, we derive a correlation coefficient, which ranges between $+1$ and -1. A positive correlation represents a linear relationship between two factors, such that large values of one measure are associated with large values of the other.

Figure 5.8

Scatter diagram
showing positive
relationship
between two
measures

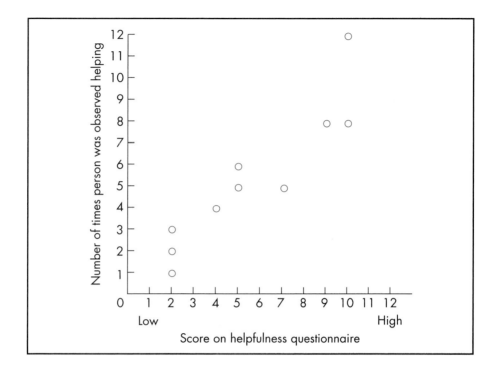

In our example a positive correlation would show a positive association between reporting that one would help in a situation and actually helping in a situation (see Figure 5.8). A zero correlation would show no relationship; that is, how a participant filled out the questionnaire would not be related in any way to how he or she actually behaved. A negative correlation would be found for people who either said they would help but did not or said they would not help but did. Figure 5.9 shows an illustration of a negative association. Figure 5.10 illustrates various relationships between two variables.

One of the most common correlation coefficients is the Pearson product moment correlation coefficient, or r. A *moment* measure is the distance between the mean and a score. In determining the correlation, we standardize the scores as z scores, which would include determining the moments (the differences between the scores and the mean) and using these to calculate correlation. The advantage of this procedure is that the two measures that you are correlating do not have to be in the same units of measurement because each is standardized. The exact formula is

$$r_{xy} = \frac{\sum z_x z_y}{N}$$

We begin by showing you this formula to help you to gain an intuitive understanding of the correlation coefficient. However, this is not the formula that you will see most commonly because rarely has the z score of your measures been calculated previously. Using the most common formula that begins with raw (non-z) scores, we will create a set of data to illustrate how you would determine the Pearson r using hypothetical measures of helping

Figure 5.9

Scatter diagram
showing negative
relationship
between two
measures

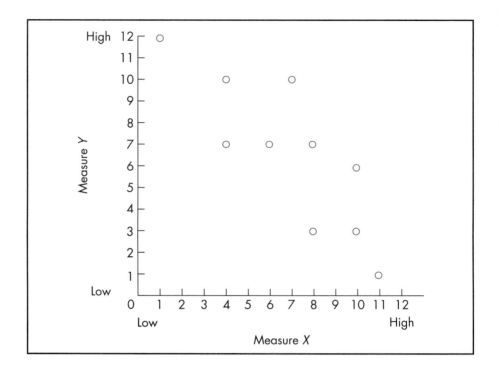

behavior (Box 5.1). In your own class, you might measure everyone's height and weight and then compute a similar correlation coefficient.

An important question now arises: What can you say about the underlying causal relationship between the two measures under study (for example, height and weight, or self-report and observed measures of helping)? Nothing! Correlations have to do with associations between two measures; they tell us nothing about the causal relationship between the two variables. We do not know whether either variable caused the other or even whether both variables were influenced by a third, extraneous variable.

For example, we could tell you our latest theory, stating that the size of your feet determines how fast you read. We could then show you data, collected from thousands of children, showing that as foot size increases, so does reading speed. Great theory, right? Although it may be a great theory, a positive correlation coefficient will do nothing to support it. Correlations do not help us to understand causality because there are numerous factors that are not in any way considered. In our example, the size of the feet and the reading speed were both related to development and had nothing to do with each other.

 CONCEPT CHECK 5.4 It was found that as the temperature increases, the sales of fur coats decrease. Would such a relationship result in a positive, negative, or zero correlation? If you were to draw such a scatter diagram, making up your own numbers, how would the graph look?

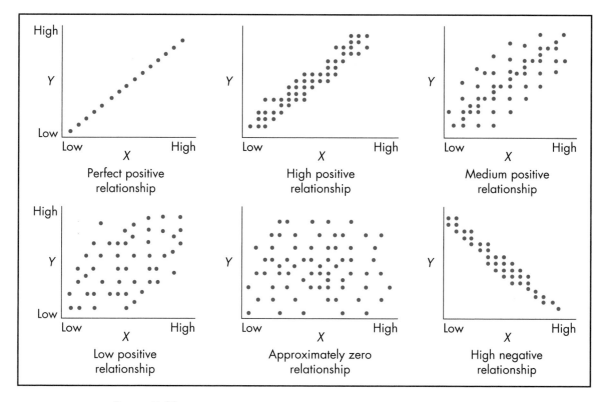

Figure 5.10

Scatter diagrams showing various relationships that differ in degree and direction

Additional information can be derived from the correlation coefficient. When you square the correlation coefficient (referred to as r^2) and multiply this number by 100, you have the amount of the variance in one measure due to the other measure. For example, in a study relating EEG functioning and spatial ability performance, Ray, Newcombe, Semon, and Cole (1981) found a −.71 correlation between hemispheric activity and spatial performance for males with high spatial abilities and a .20 correlation for a similar group of females. From this, one could calculate r^2 [$(-.71)^2$ = approximately .50; $.20^2$ = .04] and multiply by 100. We can then say that for males, 50% of the variability of the spatial performance is due to EEG activity; for females, 4%. Where we used the phrase "due to," others will say "explained" or "accounted for" or "predicted," but not "caused." Because correlations may go in either direction, you could also say that for males, 50% of the EEG activity is accounted for by spatial performance.

We can discuss not only the amount of variability accounted for but also the amount not accounted for. For example, if EEG activity explains 4% of the variability on spatial performance for high–spatial-ability females, then 96% of the variability is not explained by EEG activity and must be related to other factors. Although it is beyond our present discussion, it should also be noted that you could determine the amount of variance explained by multiplying the total variance by 4% in this example. The same procedure (for

Box 5.1

Pearson Correlation Coefficient

Using hypothetical scores from the helping experiment, we will compute a Pearson correlation coefficient. In this example there are 10 people with two scores each. We will call the score on the helpfulness questionnaire X and the score derived from the observation of the person Y.

More information concerning this and other types of correlation coefficients can be obtained in most statistical textbooks. There are also statistical "cookbooks" that show you how to perform these calculations step by step (Bruning & Kintz, 1968; Linton & Gallo, 1975).

| | Questionnaire | | Observation | | |
Participant	Score (X)	X^2	Score (Y)	Y^2	XY
1	2	4	3	9	6
2	10	100	12	144	120
3	9	81	8	64	72
4	4	16	4	16	16
5	7	49	5	25	35
6	10	100	8	64	80
7	1	1	2	4	2
8	5	25	6	36	30
9	2	4	1	1	2
10	5	25	5	25	25
$N = 10$	$\sum X = 55$	$\sum X^2 = 405$	$\sum Y = 54$	$\sum Y^2 = 388$	$\sum XY = 388$
	$(\sum X)^2 = 3025$			$(\sum Y)^2 = 2916$	

$$r = \frac{N\sum XY - (\sum X)(\sum Y)}{\sqrt{N[\sum X^2 - (\sum X)^2][N\sum Y^2 - (\sum Y)^2]}}$$

$$= \frac{(10)(388) - (55)(54)}{\sqrt{[(10)(405) - (3025)][(10)(388) - (2916)]}}$$

$$= \frac{3880 - 2970}{\sqrt{(4050 - 3025)(3880 - 2916)}}$$

$$= \frac{910}{994.03} = .915$$

example, 96% times total variance) could be used for determining the amount of variance not explained. In doing this, we would say we have *partitioned* the total variance into that explained and that not explained. Although we are getting ahead of ourselves, what you should remember is that the statistical technique *analysis of variance,* which we discuss later in the book, and that of *regression,* which we discuss in the next few paragraphs, are both mathematically and conceptually related to the degree of association between two variables in terms of the amount of variance accounted for.

As a digression, we should point out that a low r^2 in itself does not mean that the finding is not important. For example, Rosenthal (1990) pointed out that although some studies show that psychotherapy accounts for only 10% of the variance, this is still higher than what was initially called "the dramatic effects of AZT" in the treatment of AIDS, which accounts for approximately 5% of the variance. As we discuss later in this book, the value of a finding goes beyond a simple descriptive statement of the numbers. But we always need to consider how the numbers were derived.

However, at times we may want to go beyond just knowing the degree of association between two variables and actually predict how one variable influences the other. Of course, we need a good theoretical reason for doing so, but we will talk about that later. Suppose we want to predict someone's grade on a research methods exam based on how many hours he or she studied. One statistical technique to accomplish this goal is called *regression.* Conceptually, regression begins with a scatterplot and, like correlation, seeks to draw the best straight line through all the data points. It then asks: For every corresponding change in X (hours studied), what would be the change in Y (grade)? In this example, X is the independent variable, and Y is the dependent variable. If the correlation between studying and grades is high (close to 1), then for every change in study time there should be an equal change in grade received, although on a different scale. If there is no correlation between studying and grades, then a change in studying would have no effect on the grade.

Regression is a mathematical way to use our data to estimate how well we can predict that a change in one variable (studying) will lead to a change in another variable (grade). Although beyond this current discussion, the formula for predicting our dependent variable (grade) from our independent variable (study time) is composed of two terms. The first term is called a *regression coefficient* or *slope* because it estimates the change in grade (dependent variable) for each additional hour studied (independent variable). The term is nothing more than the standard deviation of the dependent variable divided by the standard deviation of the independent variable, which is then multiplied by the correlation of our independent and dependent variables. The second term is a *constant* that simply asks what would be our grade (dependent variable) if we did not study at all (independent variable). That is, we might expect that we would get some points on the test from going to class or reading the textbook even though we did not study for the test, and this amount must be added when taking into account the effects of studying. Thus, the actual regression equation states that our estimation of the dependent variable is equal to the dependent variable times the regression coefficient plus the regression constant.

Based on these ideas, additional important statistical techniques (such as path analysis and causal modeling) also focus on making statements concerning causal connections. For example, Plomin, Corley, DeFries, and Fulker (1990) sought to determine the role of genetics and environment on television viewing in young children. By examining the correlations between the viewing habits of children and those of their biological siblings and parents, and the same correlations for adopted children, the researchers concluded that individual differences in television viewing are influenced by both genetic and environmental factors.

Let's return again to the underlying distribution, as can be illustrated by a scatterplot (see Figures 5.8–5.10). Sometimes just a single value that lies outside the normal pattern (often called an *outlier*) can change the magnitude of a correlation drastically. Furthermore, if the relationship of the two variables that we are studying is not linear, then the correlation that we obtain will not adequately reveal the underlying relationship between them. In this case a graphic representation would be an important first step to supply us with valuable information and help us to determine immediately whether there are outliers or whether the underlying distribution is not linear.

For example, if we were to plot age in months against the number of words that a very young child speaks, we would see that there is a sudden and dramatic shift at a certain age, which of course would produce a nonlinear relationship. Another example of a nonlinear relationship would be the U-shaped curve that is said to relate motivation and performance. In this example one would perform poorly under conditions of high motivation or low motivation. The best performance would occur when there is a moderate amount of motivation. A correlation would not represent this *curvilinear* relationship accurately. Thus, for a correlation to give us the information that we desire, the underlying relationship between the variables must be a linear one. Visually inspecting a scatterplot is an important first step in determining the nature of the relationship between two variables.

In closing, it should be noted that there are other correlation coefficients in addition to the Pearson *r*. These are designed for use when data are based on rank orders (for example, Spearman *D*) or dichotomous data (for example, point-biserial). These and other types of correlation coefficients are included in many textbooks and handbooks on statistics.

KEY TERMS AND CONCEPTS

1. **Measurement**
   A. Scales of measurement
      - Nominal
      - Ordinal
      - Interval
      - Ratio
   B. Measurement and statistics
   C. Meaningfulness
2. **Pictorial description of frequency distribution**
   A. Bar graph
   B. Frequency polygon
   C. Bimodal distribution
   D. Positive skew
   E. Negative skew
   F. Normal distribution
3. **Measures of central tendency**
   A. Mean
   B. Median
   C. Mode

4. **Measures of variability**
   A. Range
   B. Variance
   C. Sum of the squares
   D. Standard deviation
5. **Graphs**
   A. Line graphs
   B. Bar graphs
6. **Transforming data**
   A. Transformations
   B. *z* scores
   C. SAT scores
   D. *T* scores
7. **Measure of association**
   A. Scatter diagram
   B. Positive correlation
   C. Negative correlation
   D. Amount of variance accounted for (r^2)
   E. Regression

SUMMARY

1. An important question in research is what we measure and what these measurements mean. One aspect of this question is the realization that a number does not always mean the same thing. When we use a nominal scale of measurement, differences between categories are qualitative but not quantitative. Ordinal data reflect amount or magnitude along a continuum. Interval data reflect magnitude in terms of equal intervals between successive scale values. For ratio data, scores are related by a single continuum (like interval and ordinal data), have equal intervals (like interval data), and have an absolute zero.

2. A pictorial or graphic presentation of data is an important first step. The vertical axis of a graph is called the *y* axis, or *ordinate*. The horizontal axis is called the *x* axis, or *abscissa*. There are several kinds of graphs; one of the more commonly used is called a *bar graph*.

3. Common distributions have special names. Those presented in this chapter were normal, bimodal, positively skewed, and negatively skewed.

4. Three important measures of central tendency are the mean (determined by adding the scores and then dividing by the number of scores), the median (the middle score), and the mode (the most frequently occurring score).

5. Some scores may be transformed from one scale to another, as when a temperature on the Fahrenheit scale is transformed to a temperature on the Celsius scale. If such a transformation can be made, statements made about the original data also apply to the transformed data. This is called *meaningfulness*.

6. Measures of variability are important in psychological research. Variability, or dispersion, is related to how spread out a set of scores is. The most common measures of variability are range, variance, and standard deviation.

7. Special statistical techniques have been developed to determine how two sets of data are associated with each other. One such technique is correlation. A correlation aids us in understanding how two sets of scores are related, but it does not tell us whether one score influences the other or whether both scores were influenced by a third, unmeasured factor. Certain distributions, such as curvilinear ones, are not reflected accurately in a correlation coefficient.

REVIEW QUESTIONS

1. What is *measurement*?
2. What are the four scales of measurement? Give an example of each.
3. Describe the bar graph presented in Figure 5.1 and name the type of distribution shown (for example, normal curve or bimodal).
4. What is the formula for a *mean*?
5. What is a *median*?
6. What is a *mode*?
7. What is the simple definition of *variance*?
8. What is meant by the term *SS*, and how is it calculated?
9. What is the relationship between *standard deviation* and *variance*?
10. Describe the different types of data you would use with a line graph and with a bar graph.
11. What is a *z* score?
12. What does r^2 mean?

DISCUSSION QUESTIONS AND PROJECTS

1. Find out the number of dreams the people in your class remember having had this week. Using these data, construct a frequency distribution and present it graphically.
2. Determine the mean, median, and mode as well as variance and standard deviation for the maximum daily temperatures in your area for April.
3. Construct a set of numbers in which the mean, median, and mode are the same, and another set in which they are different.
4. Why do some people say you can lie with statistics?
5. What are the differences between *measurements* and *statistics*?

(continued)

DISCUSSION QUESTIONS AND PROJECTS (*continued*)

6. Why do some people say that, in science, if you cannot measure it, it does not exist? What do you think?

7. Ask the people in your class to write two things on a piece of paper: the populations of their high schools and a rating of how well they enjoyed their first weeks at college. How might you do this in such a way that you can obtain a measure of association between the two? Would this prove (or disprove) that coming from a small high school makes one enjoy college more in the first weeks? What are the problems with making such a statement?

8. For 2 weeks, record two numbers from a newspaper each day. For example, you might pick out the daily Dow Jones Industrial Average and the daily temperature in Redwood City, California. Determine the correlation between these two variables and discuss what conclusions you can draw.

9. A study reports that smoking is associated with cancer, with a correlation coefficient of .86. Discuss the amount of variability in cancer rates that is accounted for by smoking. Discuss what can be concluded from the study.

INFOTRAC COLLEGE EDITION: EXERCISES

Researchers use graphs for showing patterns and exploring relationships. In a 2001 *Annual Review of Psychology* article entitled "Statistical graphics," Howard Wainer and Paul Velleman describe the use of graphical presentations throughout the history of science and some new ideas for psychology's future use of graphics. You should look up this article and other recent *Annual Review* articles in InfoTrac College Edition. (*Hint:* Because there are a number of articles on statistical graphics, it would be easiest to use "Howard Wainer" as your keyword search term.) Using the advanced search feature, you can also search the journal name "Annual Review of Psychology" and see the articles published in this journal.

As you look at some of these articles, note each graph in the article (you may need to click on the graph to

make it larger). What type of graph is it (for example, line graph, bar graph, etc.)? What is the graph telling you? As you read the article, note when statistics were used to make a particular point.

To help you better understand the material in this chapter, you can go to Wadsworth's research methods workshop web page at http://www.wadsworth.com/ psychology_d/templates/student_resources/workshops/ resch_wrk.html. There you will find workshops related to research methods and statistics. A number of the statistics workshops discuss the concepts presented in this chapter. These workshops include the following: Scale of Measurement, Central Tendency and Variability, z Score, and Correlation.

☑ Answers to Concept Checks

5.1 Telephone numbers represent nominal measurements, distances from Budapest represent a ratio scale, temperatures throughout the year represent an interval scale, and a team ranking represents an ordinal scale.

5.2 Of course, the best additional information to know is what your salary would be. Barring that information, the shape of the distribution of salaries of the company would also give you important information to evaluate the meaning of the particular mean, median, and mode of salaries. If the distribution were normally distributed, then you would know that the salary distribution of each company was the same. If this were not the case, then the mean, median, and mode would have different meanings for each company. For example, many fast-food companies have

most of their employees making the least amount of money. In this situation, you might want to know the mode. Given the information presented in the question, we would go with Fast Food, Inc.

5.3 The mean is the sum divided by the number of entries. In this case the sum is 36 divided by 6, which equals 6. The variance equals the sum of squares, which is 16 divided by 6, which is 2.67. The standard deviation is the square root of the variance, which equals 1.63. The relationship is a negative correlation. Such a graph is found in the lower right-hand corner of Figure 5.10.

5.4 The relationship between temperature and sales of fur coats would result in a negative correlation. The graph would look similar to Figure 5.9 or the bottom right figure (high negative relationship) in Figure 5.10.

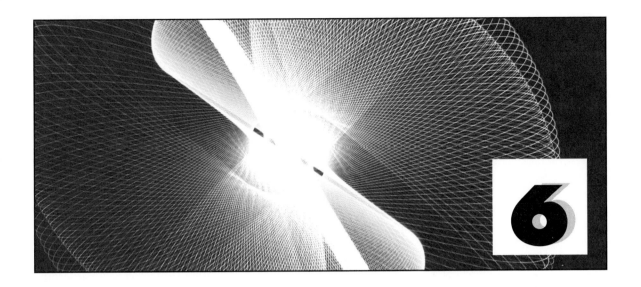

INFERENTIAL STATISTICS: MAKING STATISTICAL DECISIONS

PROBABILITY

THE NORMAL DISTRIBUTION

HYPOTHESIS TESTING

EXAMPLE OF INFERENTIAL STATISTICS: THE t TEST

ANALYSIS OF VARIANCE

Most of us can learn from experience. Like the child who touches a hot stove, we make decisions concerning future events based on past experiences. And like the child, we create for ourselves subjective probabilities about what the future will bring and what will happen if we touch the same hot stove again. We can do the same in regard to research. As we will see, one way to view research statistically is to ask what results we could expect if we ran the same experiment over and over again. The answer most of us would give is that we would expect the results to be similar. This answer reflects a long heritage of science, best exemplified by the Newtonian approach to physics. When we use such a classic approach, it does not matter where or when we conduct an experiment, as long as certain conditions are met. As Newton suggested in his second law, force is always related in the same manner to mass and acceleration. Thus, to infer that the results of one experiment will be similar to those of similar experiments poses no major problem.

Likewise, in simple chemical studies, it does not matter which actual sample of a pure element one uses. There is little question that the results found with one piece of pure gold would generalize to all pieces of pure gold. In such situations, there is little reason to invoke an inferential statistical procedure; to do so would be like trying to predict what card would be drawn from a deck of all aces.

However, there are situations in which we have reason to believe that the particular sample we are working with may *not* be like every other possible sample and that it may contain more or less of some measure. Most of the measures we study in psychology may be described in this way. Because the variables we study can be influenced by a wide variety of factors, there is generally variability in our measures across samples. In such situations we attempt to understand the properties of all possible samples (called the *population*) by looking at the particular sample with which we are working. This process requires **inferential statistics.**

In more technical language, inferential statistics is used to infer, from a given sample of scores on some measure, the parameters for the set of all possible scores (that is, the population) from which that sample was drawn. Implicit in this statement is the assumption that the sample we are discussing is the result of random sampling or some systematic form of sampling. That is, each element (for example, each person in the population of all people) is equally likely to be included in the sample, with some known probability. We will have more to say about random sampling later. For now, the important thing to remember is that inferential statistics constitutes a set of tools for inferring from a particular sample to larger populations. One way of viewing this conceptually is to ask how the statistics of our sample (that is, the mean and the standard deviation) match the parameters (the actual mean and standard deviation) of the entire population (the population values). The purpose of inferential statistics is to estimate these population characteristics.

Another way of viewing the inferential process conceptually is to assume that the same experiment was run an infinite number of times, each time with a different sample of individuals chosen from the entire population. If we were to plot the statistics from each experiment, the population of estimates would then represent all the possible outcomes of the experiment. For our purposes it does not matter which conceptual approach that you use; they are equally valid for understanding the logic of inferential statistics. To understand the logic of inferential statistics, we must introduce the related topic of probability.

PROBABILITY

We want to get ahead of ourselves for a moment and discuss how probability is used in the experimental report. We all have a sense of probabilities. For example, we do not plan to picnic in midwinter or to go snow skiing in midsummer.

A weather forecast may say that there is a 9 out of 10 chance it will rain tomorrow. This means that 9 out of 10 times the weather in the past has been the same as that predicted for tomorrow: It has rained. Mathematically speaking, this can be described as a 9/10 chance, a .9 chance, or a 90% chance. They are all the same, but the traditional way is to see probability running on a continuum from 0 (0% chance) to 1 (100% chance) and to use the decimal notation, as you will see in psychological articles.

Whether in science or in life, we accept that we live in an uncertain world and that even the best predictions can be influenced by accidents. There are risks in all that we do. We know that there is a possibility that the results of a study could have come out differently if we had performed the same study several times. But how do we assess this possibility? In empirical research we usually do this by assuming that the study was run many times and try to guess how the results would have come out each time. This helps us to understand the results of a particular study. As you will see in published articles, the results of a study usually contain a probability statement. For example, in a study on how children inhibit negative facial expression, Cole (1986) reported that preschool girls aged 3 to 4 displayed more negative facial expressions when the experimenter was not present than when the experimenter was present.

Included in Cole's report were the means and standard deviations for the frequencies of various types of facial expressions, as well as statistical statements that compared one type of expression with another (for example, positive versus negative emotions) in various conditions (for example, with and without the experimenter present). Included in these statistical statements were probability estimates of the form $p < .001$. The statement $p < .001$ means that if a large number of similar experiments were conducted, we would expect to replicate these results *by chance alone* (that is, to obtain the same results without the experimental manipulation) less than 1 time in 1,000. In making such a statement, we create a degree of certainty on which to rest our conclusions concerning particular experimental results. Because an understanding of probability is at the heart of this endeavor, it is important to have some understanding of its origins and theoretical basis.

Questions of probability date back thousands of years. Roman author Cicero (106–43 BC) tried to understand how one should interpret the event in which four dice were thrown and all came up the same. Was this an act of the gods or a rare event of chance? You might read *De Divinatione* for his answer. You might also want to look into the modern-day roots of probability theory: gambling. In fact, much of what we know about probability came about because some people wanted to make games of chance less chancy for themselves. It may also interest you to know that making better beer was one of the practical problems that led to the development of one popular statistical technique, Student's *t*. Actually it was William Gosset who wrote under the name Student. He worked for the Guinness Brewery in Dublin and asked what could be inferred about an entire batch of beer from sampling a small portion of it (Student, 1908). In other words, what is the probability that this particular sample is similar to the entire batch?

A traditional illustration of probability is tossing a coin. Let's assume that you watch me toss a coin and record whether it lands heads or tails. On the first throw, it lands heads. Which way will the coin land the next time? It may be heads, or it may be tails. The coin has no memory. It does not remember how it just landed; thus, every toss is like starting all over again. If you think coins remember, you are committing what is called the *gambler's fallacy.* You are failing to realize that coins have no memory; neither do games of chance. Every time the coin is tossed, it is starting over and thus is equally likely to come down heads or tails. In more technical terms, we say that each outcome is *independent;* that is, the outcome of one toss is not influenced by that of any previous toss.

Suppose on the second throw the coin lands tails. Now we have described two events. The first is that the coin lands heads, and the second is that the coin lands tails. We could call the first event A and the second B. For any given throw, what would be the probability of event A (the coin landing heads)? It is 1 out of 2, or .5. What is the probability that A will not happen? Formally, we can determine the probability of not-A by subtracting the probability of A from 1. The answer is .5. If A represented rain tomorrow and the probability were .9, then the probability of its not raining (not-A) would be .1 $(1 - 9 = .1)$, or 1 out of 10. In sum, to discover the probability that an event will not occur, subtract the probability of that event occurring from 1.

What if we want to know the probability of two events rather than just one? For example, we might ask the probability of tossing heads on the first throw and tails on the second. To answer this question, we must first ask the relationship of these two events; that is, does one event influence the other? In this case, the answer is no; these events are independent. The rule for determining the probability of two independent events is to multiply the probability of the first by that of the second. In our example of a heads throw followed by a tails throw, we would multiply the probability of the first event (.5) by that of the second (also .5): .5 × .5 = .25. Thus, there is a .25, or 25 out of 100, chance of having two coin tosses land as heads followed by tails. The rule is stated as

probability (A and B) = probability (A) × probability (B)

if A and B are independent.

Another method is to list all the possible results and see how many ways each result could be reached. The following list shows all the possibilities for two coins (or two consecutive tosses of one coin):

Coin 1	Coin 2
heads	heads
heads	tails
tails	heads
tails	tails

There are four outcomes: heads-heads, heads-tails, tails-heads, and tails-tails. Each outcome has a 1 in 4 chance of occurring on any trial. Once again, the probability of heads followed by tails is 1/4, or .25.

What if the order is not important to us, and we want only to know the probability of one heads and one tails in any order? In other words, the outcome could be either heads followed by tails or tails followed by heads. We use what is called the additive rule:

probability (A or B) = probability (A) + probability (B)

In our example, event A is the result heads-tails (with a probability of 1/4) and event B is tails-heads (also with a probability of 1/4). Thus, probability A + probability B = 1/4 + 1/4 = 1/2. Figure 6.1 shows in graph form the probabilities of the various combinations that result from tossing two coins.

Let's make the story more complicated by using three coins. Assume that the outcome of throwing three coins is one heads and two tails. What is the probability of throwing three coins and having them land heads-tails-tails? The probability of obtaining heads on the first toss is 1 out of 2, or .5, as is the probability of obtaining tails on the second toss, as is the probability of obtaining tails on the third toss. Multiplying the

Figure 6.1

Probability distribution for combinations resulting from tossing two coins

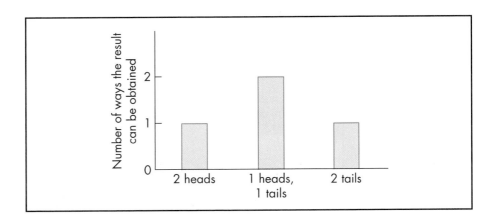

three probabilities, .5 × .5 × .5 = .125, or 1/2 × 1/2 × 1/2 = 1/8. As before, we can list all the possible results:

Coin 1	Coin 2	Coin 3
heads	heads	heads
heads	tails	heads
tails	heads	heads
tails	tails	heads
heads	heads	tails
heads	tails	tails
tails	heads	tails
tails	tails	tails

Looking at this list, we see that there is only 1 out of 8 possible results that will give the sequence heads-tails-tails. Therefore, the probability of this result is 1/8.

If we do not care about the order and just want to know how many results have one heads and two tails, we see that the answer is three: tails-tails-heads, heads-tails-tails, and tails-heads-tails. Figure 6.2 shows the probabilities. We also could have obtained the answer mathematically by the additive law of probability. The probability of tails-tails-heads is 1/8, as is the probability of heads-tails-tails and that of tails-heads-tails. The probability of two tails and one heads in any order is thus 1/8 + 1/8 + 1/8 = 3/8.

However, there is more to the additive formula. What we have told you thus far works only as long as it is impossible for the events to occur at the same time. For example, it is impossible to throw three coins and obtain on one toss both the sequence heads-tails-tails and the sequence tails-tails-heads. If it is possible for the events to occur together, then the additive formula must be modified. For example, suppose you counted the number of people in your class and specified how many are male and how many are female and specified how many are 20 years of age or older and how many are under 20. Let's assume that the numbers came out as shown in Table 6.1. If you were to put everybody's name in a hat and draw one name, what would be the probability of picking a male? If, out of 40 students, 20 are male, then the probability of picking a male would be 20/40, which equals 1/2, or .5.

Figure 6.2

Probability distribution for combinations resulting from tossing three coins

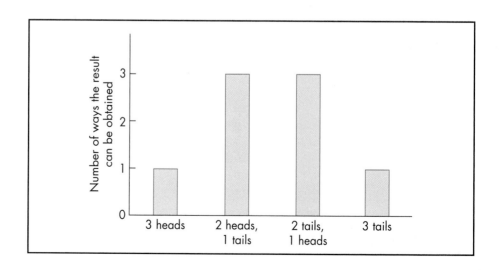

Table 6.1	Number of Students in Class, Grouped by Age and Sex		
	Male	Female	Total
Age 20 or older	5	7	12
Under 20 years of age	15	13	28
Total	20	20	40

What would be the probability of picking someone under 20 years old? There are 28 people in the class of 40 who are under 20 years of age, so the probability would be 28/40, which equals 7/10, or .7.

What about the probability of picking someone who is either under 20 years old or male? Notice that unlike the coin-tossing experiment, these two results can both occur at the same time: Someone can be both under 20 and male. Technically, we say these events are not mutually exclusive; that is, one event does not exclude the other. We must take this into account to determine the probabilities. When we want to find the probability of drawing the name of someone who is either male or under 20, we add the probabilities of each event occurring alone and then subtract from that the probability of both events occurring together. In our example, the probability of drawing the name of someone male or under 20 equals the probability of drawing someone male ($p = 20/40$, or .5) plus the probability of drawing someone under 20 years of age ($p = 28/40$, or .7) minus the probability of drawing a male under 20 years of age ($p = 15/40$, or .375). Thus, the probability of drawing a male or someone under 20 is $.5 + .7 - .375 = .825$.

 CONCEPT CHECK 6.1   If you were to toss a coin 50 times and, in the last 30 of these, you received heads each time, what would be the probability of having the next coin toss be tails?

 CONCEPT CHECK 6.2   In the example of having a coin land on heads for the previous 30 times (Concept Check 6.1), what would be the probability of having the next 3 coin tosses each be heads?

THE NORMAL DISTRIBUTION

Let's imagine that you toss a coin a large number of times. What would you expect the results to be? Of course, we would expect to have an approximately equal number of heads and tails over a large number of throws. If, rather than one coin, you had two or three coins,

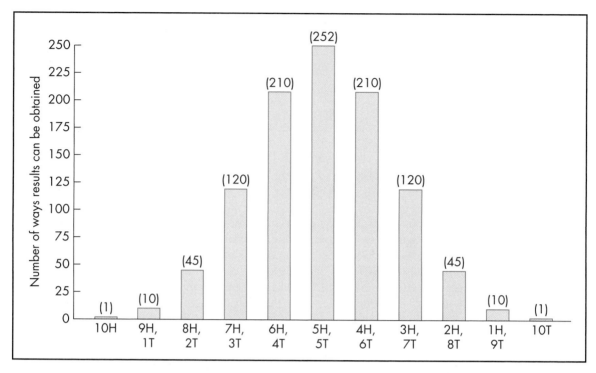

Figure 6.3

Probability distribution for combinations resulting from tossing 10 coins

what would you expect? In Figures 6.1 and 6.2, we saw a graphic representation of the number of possible ways each combination could be obtained. In fact, the two graphs are distributions of probability. If we were to extend our study to include 10 coins, we would find that there are 1,024 possible combinations. Figure 6.3 shows a probability distribution of the combinations resulting from tossing 10 coins. If we were to continue this process and develop probability distributions for even larger numbers of coins, we would eventually arrive at a distribution like the one shown in Figure 6.4. This distribution is similar to a normal probability curve, or normal distribution.

The normal distribution has a number of interesting practical and mathematical properties. For example, some characteristics of humans, such as height, intelligence, and even shoe size, tend to occur in this distribution. In other words, the majority of people wear similarly sized shoes, with only a few wearing very large or very small sizes. To obtain a graph of this distribution, we would plot shoe size along the *x* axis (horizontal axis) and the number of people who wear that size along the *y* axis (vertical axis). If we were to identify the places where the curve changes direction (the points of inflection) and draw lines from these points perpendicular to the *x* axis, we would find that these lines divide the *x* axis into segments, each equal to 1 standard deviation (*SD*) from the mean. If we let the area under the curve equal 100%, or the whole population, then we can describe how much of the population is found in each standard deviation (Figure 6.5). You can approximate this

Figure 6.4

Probability distribution for combinations resulting from an extremely large number of coin tosses

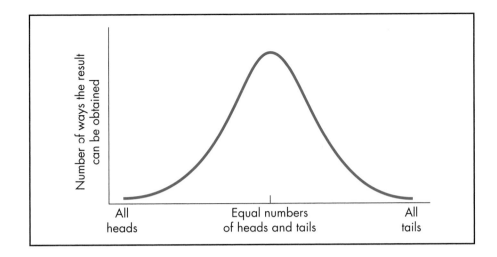

Figure 6.5

Normal distribution showing standard deviations

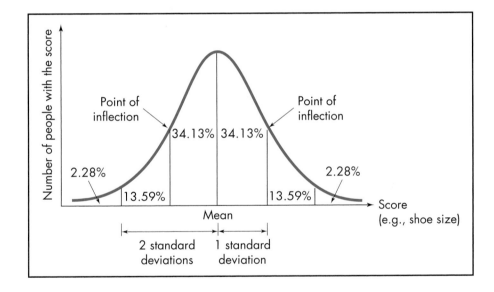

information by plotting a probability distribution for tossing a coin a large number of times and then counting the numbers that fall under these areas.

Let's assume that shoe size distribution constitutes a normal curve. You would then know that 68.26% of all people wear a shoe size that falls within 1 standard deviation in each direction from the mean. We could also say that for any person (randomly chosen) there is a 68.26% chance that he or she would wear a shoe size within 1 standard deviation of the mean size. More than 95% of all people fall within 2 standard deviations of the mean (in both directions); that is, choosing any person at random, you would have more than a 95% chance of finding that that person's shoe size falls within 2 standard deviations of the mean.

Figure 6.6

Distribution
derived from
giving a
standardized test
to a number of
students

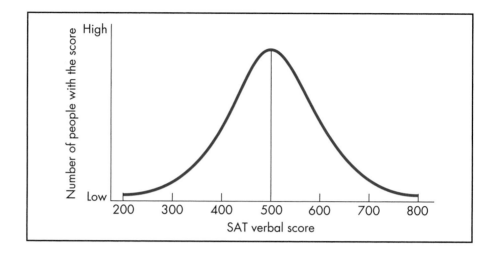

Unless you run a shoe company, however, you probably do not care very much about shoe sizes. But we can use this normal distribution for making inferences from our research. We could generate a graph of what the possible outcomes would be if we performed the same study over and over again (similar to assuming a normal distribution for people who wear different size shoes). For example, most of you took some type of college admission test, such as the Scholastic Aptitude Test (SAT). Let's assume that we have access to all the verbal scores on this test from students across the country. Then we could have a computer randomly select a sample of names and determine the mean and standard deviation of this sample. A given sample could appear as in Figure 6.6. The *x* axis represents the scores available on the test, and the *y* axis represents the number of people who received a particular score on the test for a given sample.

Let's now move from talking about a distribution of individual scores to a distribution of means. Because computers do not care what they do or how often, we might have the computer randomly select a sample of names a large number of times. We could then determine the mean and standard deviation of each sample. We could create a graph such as Figure 6.6 for each sample that would represent a distribution of individual scores for each sample. We could also draw a plot of the distribution of the means found in all the samples. It would look much like the normal curve presented in Figures 6.4 and 6.5. This finding is based on what is technically called the *central limit theorem* and lies at the heart of inferential statistics. It simply states that if a number of samples are drawn from a population at random, then the means of the samples tend to be normally distributed. As you can imagine, the larger the number of people in each sample, the less variability there will be in the means. Using the SAT example, we would expect to see means varying only slightly from 500 if the sample sizes were large, but more variability if the sample sizes were small.

If this were represented graphically, the bell-shaped curve would be skinny if the sample sizes were large but broad at the bottom if the sample sizes were small (Figure 6.7). Ask yourself why this is so. As you do, you will realize that, if you had only a few people in each

Figure 6.7

Hypothetical distribution of means derived from giving a standardized test to either a large or a small number of students a large number of times

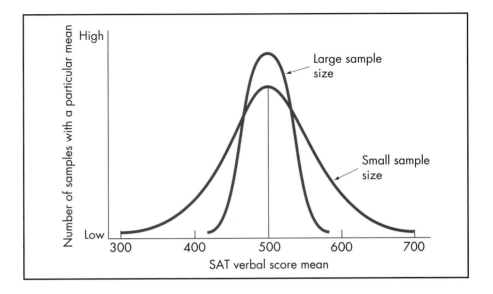

of your many, many samples, an extreme score from any person would have more influence on the mean. Thus, when you plot your means, you would expect more variability in the scores than if you had many people in each of your many, many samples. This is an important idea that lies at the heart of determining the probability levels of such statistics as the *t* test, which we illustrate at the end of this chapter. Said simply, if you reran the same experiment a large number of times with only 5 people, you would expect the mean of the 5 participants found each time the experiment was run to vary more than if you reran the experiment with 100 people each time. In fact, when you look at probability levels, which we discuss later, you are examining such a hypothetical situation.

To return to the central limit theorem, it should be noted that it is not a requirement of this theorem that the individual samples be randomly distributed. Even samples of numbers from a table of random numbers (in which every number from 1 to 100 appears equally often) would give a normal distribution of means, although the graphic illustration of any one sample would look more like a rectangle (no one number would be picked any more often than any other number). Thus, it is the sample of samples (also called the sampling distribution) that we are discussing. Furthermore, we can find the mean of all our means and the standard deviation of all our means. The standard deviation of all our means has a special name: the *standard error of the mean*.

If we had just one sample of students who took the SAT, what would be the best guess regarding the mean of all students who took the test? Of course, our best guess would be the mean of our sample. It is fortunate that we do not have to stop at this point; we can also estimate how far off we might be from where the population mean would be. To do this we estimate the standard error of the mean using the data from our sample. The formula is as follows:

$$\text{standard error} = \frac{\text{standard deviation}}{\text{square root of the number of scores}}$$

For example, if our sample of scores had a mean of 505 and a standard deviation of 100 and we had given the test to 900 people, then the standard error would be 100 divided by 30 (30 = $\sqrt{900}$), or 3.33. Because the central limit theorem says that the sampling distribution is normally distributed, we can now make the same type of statements about our research that we made previously about shoe size. Thus, we can say that 68.26% (percentage of cases within 1 standard deviation of the population mean; see Figure 6.5) of all means will be within 1 standard error (3.33 in our example), or 95.44% of all sample means will be within 2 standard errors (6.66). Or we can say, in probability terms, that we are more than 95% confident that the population mean is between 498.34 (mean of 505 − 6.66) and 511.66 (mean of 505 + 6.66). This is the idea of *confidence intervals,* or the area in which you expect a certain mean to be found. What if someone asked you whether it is more probable that, in your next sample of SAT scores, the mean would be about 500 or about 750? If you said "750," you should put your money in a bank and never place a bet. It would be more probable for the mean to be about 500. This is the basic logic of inferential statistics in general and hypothesis testing in particular.

HYPOTHESIS TESTING

Hypothesis testing is one of the main branches of inferential statistics. Underlying hypothesis testing are the ideas that we have just discussed in talking about the normal distribution. We assumed that if we tossed many coins we would expect to find heads on half of the tosses and tails on the other half. Thus, we began with the idea that the probability of heads is the same as that of tails. In other words, we assumed that there would be no differences between the number of times heads would come up and the number of times we would see tails. The idea of no differences is going to form the basis of the null hypothesis, which was developed by Sir Ronald Fisher (1935) who sought to determine whether a set of results differed from what would be expected. What would be expected, you might ask? In the example of the coin toss, we would expect an equal number of heads and tails.

To draw upon another of our previous examples, what would be expected if we measured the shoe size of a number of individuals? We would expect the average size to be the mean shoe size of all individuals. To remind you of what we said at the beginning of this chapter, when we talk about all possible individuals or all possible samples, we are referring to the statistical term *population.* Let's look at another example of SAT scores. Suppose you claim that the students in your class scored higher on the SAT than students around the country. You are essentially claiming that the students in your class come from a population (the population of high-scoring students) that is different from the population of all students taking the SAT. We can use what we have learned so far to test this assumption. The mean of your sample should be similar to the population mean of all students taking the SAT. This particular hypothesis, that the population mean is the same as the sample mean, is called the **null hypothesis.** If the null hypothesis cannot be rejected, then we cannot claim that your class comes from a different population.

On the other hand, what if we can reject the null hypothesis? If the null hypothesis can be rejected, then we make a statistical statement concerning the null hypothesis. Assume that the mean of your class was 750 on the verbal SAT while the mean of all people taking the verbal SAT is 500. The probability of finding a mean of 750 in a random sample drawn from the population of all people taking the test would be low, but it would be possible. In the same way that we could determine the probability of tossing 10 coins and having them all be heads, we can make a statement of probability that a sample mean is associated with a certain population mean some percentage of the time given a certain sample size. We might say that a sample mean of 750 could have been drawn from a population with a mean of 500 less than 1 time in 1,000. Thus, if we found a sample mean of 750, we would reject the null hypothesis and make this rejection with a conditional statement about the probability that this could have happened by chance.

In the psychological literature, the null hypothesis has taken on a broader meaning, resulting from the common practice of using two or more groups to test a particular treatment. For example, in the cereal experiment described in Chapter 2, we wanted to know whether the cereal affected one group more than the other. In such a situation, the null hypothesis as commonly used states that no differences exist between the two groups. Most students then assume that we are testing to see whether a difference exists between the means of the two groups (that is, does the mean of Group 1 equal the mean of Group 2?). This may appeal to our common sense, but statistically we are asking whether these two groups came from the same population. *Inferential statistics always refer to a population.* Although we discussed only the mean, a number of other parameters, such as the population variance (which we discussed in Chapter 5) and the size of the sample, are also important considerations and play a role in statistical hypothesis testing.

Let's use the logic that we have just developed on probability, distributions, and the null hypothesis to discuss some particular statistical techniques. One statistical technique, the t test (which we describe in the next section), uses the null hypothesis that two samples were drawn at random from identical populations. Let's imagine that someone was interested in comparing the effects of coffee and tea on memory. Such a researcher might give coffee to one group and tea to another group and then have both groups learn particular words. We would have one score—the number of words remembered—for each person. If we were to find the mean number of words remembered for each group, what would we expect? We begin as R. A. Fisher suggests with the idea that coffee and tea did not influence the number of words recalled, thus the null hypothesis. However, if the null hypothesis were not true, then we would expect that the number of words remembered in one group would be higher than those in another. For example, if coffee were associated with remembering more words, then the coffee group would show a higher score. Statistically, the t test examines the difference between the scores of the two groups and helps us to determine whether to accept or reject the null hypothesis.

 # EXAMPLE OF INFERENTIAL STATISTICS: THE t TEST

We have discussed the idea of statistically testing the null hypothesis, which states that two samples come from the same population. Although we discuss this in more detail throughout the book, we want to move at this time from a more conceptual to a more computational approach. We now present one of the more popular inferential statistical techniques: the *t* test. Theoretically, there are a variety of ways to view the *t* test. One way to view it is related to the correlation procedures that we discussed previously and say that the size of the *t* statistic is related to the size of the association between two variables and the number of people studied. Conceptually, we could say

$$t = \frac{\text{association}}{\text{lack of association}} \times \text{sample size}$$

Because we know that r^2 equals the variance accounted for, we could be more precise and say

$$t = \frac{\sqrt{\text{variance accounted for}}}{\sqrt{\text{variance not accounted for}}} \times \sqrt{\text{size}}$$

Or, in numerical terms,

$$t = \frac{r}{\sqrt{1 - r^2}} \times \sqrt{df}$$

The term *df* stands for degrees of freedom, which we discuss a bit later.

From your statistics course, you may be more familiar with considering the *t* test as the standardized difference between group means, which is the same as determining the difference between sample means divided by the standard error. Conceptually, we might consider how knowing the standard error of each of your groups would help you to decide whether your two groups were different. As we move to the computational formula, recall the meaning of some basic terms. Throughout this chapter, we have discussed a population and a sample from that population. In Chapter 5 we discussed the mean, variance, and standard deviation. We use different symbols to refer to the mean, variance, and standard deviation of the population as opposed to those characteristics of the sample. We speak of *population parameters* and use the following Greek letters:

population mean	μ
population variance	σ^2
population standard deviation	σ

In discussion of the sample, we say *sample statistics* or *characteristics* and use italic letters as follows:

sample mean	M or X
sample variance	S^2
sample standard deviation	S

When we find the variance of the sample, we use a slightly different formula from that used for population variance, which was presented in Chapter 5 in our discussion of descriptive statistics. Rather than divide the sum of the squares by the number of scores (N), we divide by $N - 1$. Statistical theory tells us that with repeated sampling using $N - 1$ gives us more accurate inferences. Thus, the formula becomes

$$\text{sample variance} = \frac{\text{sum of squares}}{\text{number of scores}} - 1$$

Since the denominator is technically called the *degrees of freedom,* the formula can also be written

$$S^2 = \frac{SS}{df}$$

Although a formal discussion of degrees of freedom is beyond the scope of this presentation, the basic idea is simple. *Degrees of freedom* refers to the number of scores that are free to vary. To illustrate this imagine that you and two friends are eating out and you are waiting for your order. One of you has ordered chicken salad on rye, another has ordered a yogurt and fruit cup, and the third has ordered pastrami on white bread with mayonnaise. The waiter comes with the food, but he has forgotten who ordered what. From his standpoint, he has a number of degrees of freedom in that he can place the dishes in any of several different combinations. However, if you were to remind him that you ordered chicken salad and the friend on your right the yogurt and fruit cup, this would limit his degrees of freedom. Once you had fixed the order in two of the three selections, the third was determined and not free to vary. The same is true with numbers. What if someone asked you to pick three numbers that added up to 20. You could pick any number you wanted for the first number. Say you pick the number 7. You could also pick any number you wished for the second. Perhaps you picked 8. However, once you picked the first two numbers, the third number could only be one number. In this example, the number must be 5. Thus, the general idea behind the term *degrees of freedom* reflects how many scores are free to vary.

Let's assume that we had run the cereal experiment discussed in Chapter 2 and obtained the results presented in Table 6.2. We could then perform a *t* test on the posttreatment scores for the experimental and control groups. From Table 6.2 we can see that there are seven people in each group; the mean weight gain in Group 1 was 7.857 pounds, and in

Table 6.2

Cereal Experiment Results: Weight Gain

	Group 1 (Experimental Group)			Group 2 (Control Group)	
		Weight Gain			Weight Gain
Person	X_1	$(X_1)^2$	Person	X_2	$(X_2)^2$
1	10	100	1	0	0
2	10	100	2	3	9
3	7	49	3	2	4
4	6	36	4	1	1
5	5	25	5	7	49
6	8	64	6	6	36
7	9	81	7	2	4
	$\sum X_1 = 55$	$\sum(X_1)^2 = 455$		$\sum X_2 = 21$	$\sum(X_2)^2 = 103$
	$\overline{X}_1 = 7.857$			$\overline{X}_2 = 3$	

Group 2 it was 3.00 pounds. We can use the computation formula for determining the sum of the squares (see Chapter 5):

$$SS = \sum X^2 - \frac{\left(\sum X\right)^2}{N}$$

Substituting the values from Table 6.2,

$$SS_1 = 455 - \frac{55^2}{7} = 22.857$$

$$SS_2 = 103 - \frac{55^2}{7} = 40$$

The particular formula we use for t is as follows:

$$t = \frac{\bar{X}_1 - \bar{X}_2}{\sqrt{\dfrac{SS_1 + SS_2}{(N_1 - 1) + (N_2 - 1)}\left(\dfrac{1}{N_1} + \dfrac{1}{N_2}\right)}}$$

Substituting our numbers from Table 6.2 into this formula, we have

$$t = \frac{7.857 - 3}{\sqrt{\dfrac{22.857 + 40}{(7 - 1) + (7 - 1)}\left(\dfrac{1}{7} + \dfrac{1}{7}\right)}} = \frac{4.857}{\sqrt{1.497}} = 3.97$$

What does the value of t mean? The next step is to look up this value of t in a t table. (See Table D2 in Appendix D.) The degrees of freedom are listed down the side of this table; across the top, the various probability (p) levels for one- and two-tailed tests. *One-tailed* refers to a unidirectional prediction (for example, "The experimental group is larger than the control group"); *two-tailed* refers to a bidirectional prediction (for example, "The experimental group is either larger than or smaller than the control group"). Using the list for two-tailed tests and looking up the value 3.97 with 12 degrees of freedom, we see that it is significant at the .01 level. In more formal notation, this would be written as $t(12) = 3.98$, $p < .01$. This means that if the cereal experiment were conducted a large number of times, we would expect the results to occur by chance fewer than 1 in 100 times.

Because most researchers use standard computerized statistical packages (for example, SPSS, SAS, BMDP, Minitab), it is now easier to report the exact statistical probability associated with our value of t. Table 6.3 shows the cereal experiment results as analyzed by BMDP statistical software. From this table, we can see that with a t value of 3.97 and 12 degrees of

Table 6.3

t Test for Cereal Experiment

Group	Exp.	Control	Test	Statistics	*p* Value	*df*
Mean	7.857	3.000				
Standard deviation	1.9518	2.5820				
S.E.M.	0.7377	0.9759	t	3.97	.0019	12

Figure 6.8

Graphic illustration of cereal experiment

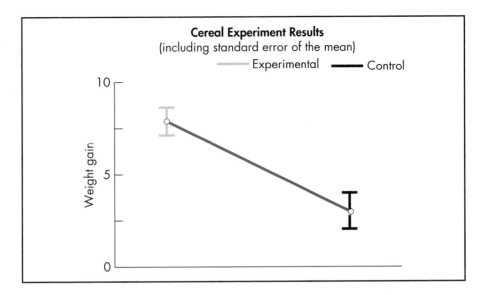

freedom (7 − 1 plus 7 − 1), the exact p value is .0019. Thus, we would have expected these results to have occurred by chance fewer than 19 times in 10,000. In the common language of research, we would say that the difference between the two groups in the experiment is statistically significant. As you may have guessed, *SEM* in Table 6.3 stands for *standard error of the mean*. Often, graphs of results include the standard error plotted, as shown in Figure 6.8. If you think about the meaning of the standard error, you also may discover how looking at the graph can give you a visual estimate of the differences between the groups in the experiment and help you to understand intuitively the statistical differences present.

For completeness, we should point out that the t test that we have just discussed is formally called the t test for independent groups; it assumes that the participants were assigned randomly to groups. (We discuss random assignment to groups in Chapter 8.) However, when the groups were matched according to some characteristic or composed of the same participants (for example, tested before and after a particular treatment), then a t test for matched scores would be used.

ANALYSIS OF VARIANCE

We just discussed comparing the experimental and control group in our cereal experiment with the t test. The t test works well when we have two groups to be compared. What if we had more than two groups? For example, we could have had a third group that received two bowls of the cereal being tested. Thus, Group 1 would receive no cereal; Group 2, one bowl; and Group 3, two bowls. Using t tests, you could compare Group 1 with Group 2,

Table 6.4

ANOVA Gain					
	SS	df	Mean Square (MS)	F	Sig.
Between Groups	82.571	1	82.571	15.764	.002
Within Groups	62.857	12	5.238		
Total	145.429	13			

then Group 2 with Group 3, and then Group 1 with Group 3. A better alternative is to use a statistical procedure referred to as **analysis of variance** (ANOVA). ANOVA uses an **F ratio** named after its developer, Sir Ronald Fisher, rather than a t ratio. However, the logic is the same. In fact, there is an exact relationship such that $F = t^2$. If we were to square the formula for t, then we obtain direct measures of variance rather than standard deviations—thus the name analysis of variance. The statistical formula for ANOVA allows us to compute the variation between our two or more groups (between-groups variance) and then to divide this by the naturally occurring variation within our groups (within-groups variance). Table 6.4 shows the results of the cereal experiment analyzed with an ANOVA procedure using SPSS. As you can see, the within-groups sum of squares (SS) is the same as we found in the t-test example with the cereal data (that is, $SS_1 + SS_2$; 22.857 + 40 = 62.857). We divide this by the degrees of freedom, which is 12. That is, the number of subjects in each group minus 1 (7 − 1) or 6 + 6 = 12. The between-groups sum of squares is actually an estimate of the population variance derived from the variance between group means and the number of participants in the study. The result is an F ratio of 15.764, which is equal to the t ratio that we found previously squared (3.79 × 3.79 = 15.76).

In the next chapter, we expand on the logic behind ANOVA and give you a conceptual understanding. In following chapters, we show some additional advantages of using ANOVA. One of these advantages is the ability to compare levels of two different independent variables in the same experiment. We describe this procedure is more detail in Chapter 9, as well as introduce the terminology and statistical techniques required.

 CONCEPT CHECK 6.3   What is the difference between the variance formula for descriptive statistics and that for inferential statistics?

As we show in Chapter 7, there is more to research than just the statistical decision related to the null hypothesis. We hope that you are beginning to understand why random sampling is an important aspect of the experimental method. We discuss this idea in more detail in the next few chapters. We also consider the ways in which we decide what can be inferred from our data on a number of levels.

KEY TERMS AND CONCEPTS

1. **Inferential statistics**
   A. Sample
   B. Population
2. **Probability**
   A. Independent events
   B. Mutually exclusive events
   C. Additive law of probability
   D. Multiplicative law of probability
3. **Normal distribution**
   A. Distribution of probability
   B. Distribution of scores
4. **Hypothesis testing**
   A. Null hypothesis
5. ***t* test**
6. **ANOVA**

SUMMARY

1. Using inferential statistics, we attempt to understand the characteristics of a population (all possible samples) from looking at a particular sample.
2. We discussed the multiplicative and additive laws of probability mathematically.
3. In the same way that we can create a distribution of scores, we can also create a distribution of probability. For example, if we were to flip coins repeatedly a large number of times and plot the results, we would create a distribution curve that looks similar to that of a normal distribution.
4. The fundamentals of probability can be used to aid researchers in testing statistical hypotheses. The major

statistical hypothesis tested is the null hypothesis, which states that no difference exists between the population mean and a particular sample mean.

5. Using the example of SAT scores, the question was asked whether a sample with a mean of 750 could be drawn from a population with a mean of 500. The answer was that it is possible but rare.
6. One of the more common statistical tests used in psychological research is the *t* test, the procedure for which was illustrated in the chapter.

REVIEW QUESTIONS

1. What is *inferential statistics*?
2. What is the *gambler's fallacy*?
3. Describe events that are independent of each other.
4. In what situations would you use the additive law of probability?
5. What is the *multiplicative law of probability*?
6. What does it mean for events to be *mutually exclusive*?
7. Describe the *normal distribution*.
8. In the SAT score example, which would be more likely: to draw a sample with a mean of 400 or one with a mean of 502?
9. Describe *hypothesis testing*.
10. Discuss the *null hypothesis*.

DISCUSSION QUESTIONS AND PROJECTS

1. Name some common uses of inferential statistics in everyday life.
2. Discuss some ways in which you see others using the gambler's fallacy in their everyday lives.
3. If you put all the names of the people in your class in a hat, what would be the probability of your name being drawn? What would be the probability of drawing the name of someone who has heard of your professor's favorite musical group? What would be the probability

of drawing the name of someone who has one brother but no sister? Of someone who has one brother and one sister? Of someone who has either one brother or one sister?

4. Plot the number of hours of sleep the people in your class reported having last night. Draw one graph for men and one for women. Determine how you would test statistically the hypothesis that there is a sex-determined difference in the amount of sleep people report.

INFOTRAC COLLEGE EDITION: EXERCISES

In this chapter, we discussed probability and statistical tests. Using InfoTrac College Edition, you can obtain more information about these concepts. For example, if you enter the term "normal distribution" in the InfoTrac College Edition search system, you will see how statistical principles are being applied in a variety of fields. As an example, in the May 2000 issue of the *American Statistician*, Paramjit Gill discusses how to think about later game reversals by first assuming that basketball and football scores are normally distributed. (You can find this article by either looking up "normal distribution" or the author Paramjit Gill.) You can also read a study asking "Are babies normal?" In this case Traci Clemons

and Marcello Pagano wanted to know if the birth weight of babies formed a normal distribution (*American Statistician*, Nov. 1999).

To help you better understand the material in this chapter, you can go to Wadsworth's research methods workshop web page at http://www.wadsworth.com/ psychology_d/templates/student_resources/workshops/ resch_wrk.html. There you will find workshops related to research methods and statistics. A number of the statistics workshops discuss the concepts presented in this chapter. These workshops include the following: Sampling Distribution, Central Limit Theorem, Independent Versus Repeated *t* Tests, and One-Way ANOVA.

☑ Answers to Concept Checks

6.1 The probability of having the coin land on tails the 51st time would be .5, or 50%. Because each coin toss is an independent event, it does not matter how the coin has landed in the past.

6.2 The question is "What is the probability of having three coins in a row all land on heads?" It is the probability of first heads, or .5, times the other probabilities, or $1/2 \times 1/2 \times 1/2 = 1/8$.

6.3 In descriptive statistics, variance is found by dividing the sum of the squares by the number of scores. In inferential statistics, the sum of the squares is divided by the number of scores minus 1.

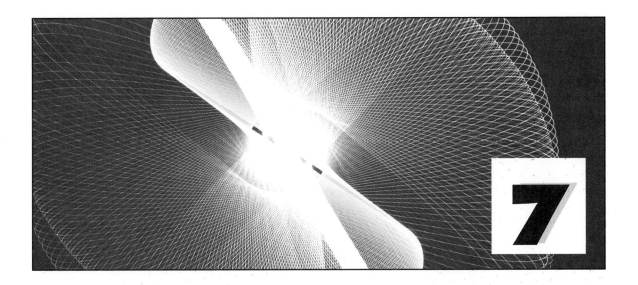

TESTING THE HYPOTHESIS:
A CONCEPTUAL INTRODUCTION

THE CONTEXT OF EXPERIMENTATION: AN EXAMPLE

TYPES OF VARIATION
Chance Variation
Systematic Variation Due to the Independent
    Variable
Systematic Variation Due to Confounds

STATISTICAL HYPOTHESIS TESTING

THREATS TO INTERNAL VALIDITY
History
Maturation
Testing

Instrumentation
Statistical Regression
Selection
Mortality
Selection–Maturation Interaction
Diffusion or Imitation of Treatments

CONCLUSION

Once you have developed your research hypothesis, what do you do next? Most students answer, "I perform an experiment to prove that my hypothesis is correct." It is true that the hypothesis must be evaluated in the light of an actual experiment. However, contrary to the manner in which science is sometimes portrayed, the evaluation of a hypothesis is a complex process that takes place on a number of levels. In fact, you need to ask three basic questions in order to evaluate your original research hypothesis. The first question is related to statistics and asks whether the numbers found in an experiment could be due to chance alone. The second question is related to alternative explanations for the research findings and asks whether the results of the study could be due to factors other than the independent variable as hypothesized; that is, are there threats to the internal validity of the study? The third question concerns the research hypothesis and asks what support exists for assuming that the independent variable is directly related to the results.

Thus, we are like detectives who sort through one set of clues and then another, hoping to determine how a particular situation occurred. What caused this event? Who did it? Although the detective might start by suspecting the butler, in research we begin with the possibility that *no one did it;* that is, we ask whether the experimental results, as we found them, happened not because of a crucial factor (the independent variable) but because of chance. Once we determine that chance alone did not produce the results, we are ready to look for other factors. "If it was not chance, then it was the independent variable," Watson might suggest to Sherlock Holmes. "Not yet," the sage of experience admonishes. "Let us first look to unknown factors that might be responsible for our experimental outcome." "But how can we know the unknown?" Watson might ponder. "Through logic, common sense, and knowledge of the literature" is the answer.

Interpreting the results of an experiment is a three-stage decision process. The first stage does not directly involve our research hypothesis at all. Instead, it involves the possibility that chance fluctuations between the performances of our groups might be solely responsible for any differences. The possibility that no differences exist between the groups makes us consider the null hypothesis. Because chance is always involved in our sampling and observations of the world, the null hypothesis is *always* one possible interpretation of even the most striking differences between our groups that must be evaluated. Regardless of how great the differences are between our groups, according to whatever dependent measure we are using, it is always possible that the results are due to chance fluctuations. Thus, when we make a statement about cause and effect in a psychological experiment, we never state that the independent variable *certainly* caused the effect on the dependent variable. Rather, we make the probabilistic statement that we can be relatively certain that our results were not due to chance alone.

It was a realization of the probabilistic nature of experimental outcomes that led to the development of statistical procedures at the beginning of the 20th century. Because of the central importance of chance in modern science, we will have much to say about chance, the null hypothesis, and the importance of statistics (see also Chapter 6). In the meantime, an essential idea to keep in mind is that the initial phase of interpreting the outcome of any experiment is a statistical decision process. Thus, when confronted with differences between our groups, we first use statistics to determine the probability that these differences are due to chance (the null hypothesis).

Once we have satisfied ourselves that our results are unlikely to be due to chance, we must turn to the second stage and examine another possibility: that our results are due to some systematic but unplanned factor, which we call a **confound.** If our results are indeed due to some factor other than our independent variable, then the internal validity of the experiment is threatened (see Chapter 2). In the fictitious series of breakfast cereal experiments described in Chapter 2, we saw that the weight gain that occurred in the experimental group was not due to the new cereal, as the manufacturers had hoped, but to the cream, bananas, and sugar that the participants ate along with the cereal. In confounded experiments like this one, the treatment effect is due not to the independent variable but to one or more overlooked factors. Thus, *we seek to eliminate sources of uncontrolled variance that operate in a systematic manner.* It is not necessary to control every possible factor that could influence our study but only to control the factors that we know influence our results in a systematic way. Otherwise, we would be paralyzed and would never be able to perform even a simple experiment.

One way that we learn which factors may influence our research systematically is through reading the published literature and examining our own research. Because it is always possible that the internal validity of an experiment is weakened by some unknown factor causing the observed differences, we routinely scrutinize both the published experiments of others and our own work for the possibility that confounds are present. However, it is in the nature of science that even with careful scrutiny we can never be certain that some unknown factor (other than the independent variable) is not responsible for the experimental results.

Once we have rejected the null hypothesis and considered various confounds as influencing our results, we can turn to the third consideration. We then can assume that our results reflect an action on the part of the independent variable; that is, there is now a greater probability that our research hypothesis is accurate. At this point we are ready to interpret our data in relation to the research hypothesis. Many people who are not familiar with the process of science tend to view it as consisting of only this third consideration. However, most scientists do not speak so much about "proving a hypothesis" as they do about "drawing inferences" and "controlling and seeking alternative explanations." In fact, many research scientists argue that the heart of experimentation lies in ruling out alternative explanations. In this chapter we emphasize the process of minimizing the likelihood of alternative explanations through a discussion of the null and confound hypotheses. In Chapter 8 we emphasize experimental control through a discussion of techniques for controlling, reducing, and eliminating various potential confounds.

Before we continue, let's emphasize that throughout this and the next chapter, we discuss experimental design and the interpretation of experimental results from the standpoint of the *scientist.* We present the experimental method in its ideal form. However, although internal validity and eventual statistical analysis are important determiners of experimental design, they are by no means the only factors to consider when conducting research. Other factors such as ethical considerations or cultural factors will be discussed in greater detail in other chapters.

In this chapter we wish to emphasize design and the types of interpretations that we can make. As discussed by well-known statistician John Tukey (1962), we are more concerned with data analysis than with statistical analysis. That is, we are like detectives using critical thinking to guide our understanding of the relationship between our variables rather than just paying attention to the statistical tests themselves, as important as they are. Now let's turn to an actual experiment and observe how we evaluate the three possible interpretations of experimental results.

CONCEPT
CHECK 7.1   Name the three considerations that are taken into account in evaluating the results of an experiment.

 THE CONTEXT OF EXPERIMENTATION: AN EXAMPLE

Bransford and Johnson (1972) performed an experiment to explore some of the factors that influence how we remember and encode what we hear. In particular, they were interested in the role of context in the comprehension and recall of information. That is to say, do you remember information differently if you can put it in a particular context of frame of reference? Imagine that you are a participant in that experiment and you are asked to listen to and later recall the following passage:

> If the balloons popped, the sound wouldn't be able to carry since everything would be too far away from the correct floor. A closed window would also prevent the sound from carrying, since most buildings tend to be well insulated. Since the whole operation depends on a steady flow of electricity, a break in the middle of the wire would also cause problems. Of course, the fellow could shout, but the human voice is not loud enough to carry that far. An additional problem is that a string could break on the instrument. Then there could be no accompaniment to the message. It is clear that the best situation would involve less distance. Then there would be fewer potential problems. With face-to-face contact, the least number of things could go wrong.

After the passage was read, the participants in the experiment were asked to rate it for comprehensibility; that is, they were asked to rate how well they understood the passage, with a rating of 7 meaning it was highly comprehensible. You might try this yourself. If you are like the participants in the experiment, you will rate the material as incomprehensible. Their actual average rating was 2.3 on the 7-point scale. The next task for the participants was to recall what they had read. Here they were instructed to write the main ideas that they remembered from the passage. How many ideas did you remember? The research participants in the experiment recalled, on the average, 3.6 ideas out of a possible 14.

A second group of participants was shown Figure 7.1 before they heard the passage. As with the group that did not see a picture, their task was to recall as many ideas from the story as possible. If we were to discuss these two groups in terms of levels of the independent variable (the picture), we would say that one group received the complete treatment and the other group received a zero level. One could also present other levels between the total picture and no picture. Bransford and Johnson actually did this in their complete experiment, but that is beyond the scope of this discussion.

After you have seen the picture, go back and read the passage. How would you rate its comprehensibility now? The participants in the group that saw the picture rated comprehensibility more than twice as high as those in the group that did not see the picture; they gave it a mean rating of 6.1 (versus 2.3 for the first group) on the 7-point scale. The second group also recalled many more ideas than the first group (8 versus 3.6 ideas). It is clear that having a context or schema in which to understand the information changes our ability to remember information. Although the Bransford and Johnson experiment was much more

Figure 7.1

Complete context picture

Source: Bransford, J. D., & Johnson, M. K. (1972). Contextual prerequisites for understanding: Some investigations of comprehension and recall. *Journal of Verbal Learning and Verbal Behavior, 11,* 717–726.

complex than we have presented it thus far, we draw on this simplified version to illustrate the task of evaluating the null, confound, and research hypotheses. We begin with a discussion of types of variation.

TYPES OF VARIATION

For centuries, philosophers have told us that everything varies, and in psychology we know this all too well. Some things vary a little; some things vary a lot. Some factors vary systematically; some factors vary by chance. In the process of experimentation, we have set the goal of understanding what part of our results may be attributed to **systematic variation** (for example, the influence of the independent variable on the dependent variable) and what part is due to nonsystematic or **chance variation.**

■ Chance Variation

Chance variation may also be called *error variation.* In this context, the words *chance* and *error* have a similar technical meaning. Chance or error variation refers to factors that influence the performance of the research participants in a nonsystematic manner. This means that *within the frame of reference of the experiment,* chance variation cannot be ascribed to any particular factors. This is not to say that we cannot find an explanation for the observed performance of the individual research participants. It does say, however, that the explanation given for any one individual cannot be ascribed to the group as a whole.

Consider a memory experiment like the one conducted by Bransford and Johnson. One person in the experiment might have performed poorly because he did not sleep well the night before. Another person might have done well because she had just received some good news from home. Another might have had too much coffee, whereas another could have been anxious because of a test the next period. Each factor would be considered as a chance factor or error factor *from the standpoint of the group* of participants who took part in the experiment.

■ Systematic Variation Due to the Independent Variable

Let's continue with the Bransford and Johnson example, in which one group of participants heard the description without seeing the picture and another group heard the description after being shown the picture. Once we have collected the results, we are faced with the task of interpreting them in relation to three possibilities: (1) There are no differences between our groups (the null hypothesis), (2) the results were produced by some systematic influence other than the independent variable (a confound), and (3) the results were produced in a systematic fashion by the independent variable.

Ignoring the question of confounds for the moment, let's discuss our results in terms of the effects of the independent variable and of chance or error. In evaluating the Bransford and Johnson study, we are trying to determine how much influence seeing the picture had on remembering the passage. To answer this question, we begin with what some students feel is a backward approach. We ask the questions, "What if seeing the picture had no effect on memory? What would the results look like then?" We already know the answer theoretically. The results from the two groups would look alike. Because the groups presumably were chosen to be similar, they would continue to be similar if the independent variable (and confounds) did not influence them.

We can present this point in a more technical way. First, let's use a more statistically oriented language, that of the F ratio. We introduced this in the last chapter, but let's repeat it here. The F stands for (Sir Ronald) Fisher, the man who developed the statistical technique of analysis of variance (ANOVA). The particular terms we use in discussing the F ratio are *within-groups variance* and *between-groups variance*. Within-groups variance reflects the factors of chance or error variance.

For example, in the Bransford and Johnson study, factors such as mental alertness, physical health, and emotional state are expected to have a random or chance effect on the groups as a whole. They do not contribute to any systematic differences between the two groups, which were selected *randomly*. (Random selection is discussed in detail in Chapter 8.) Factors that systematically influence a group of research participants, such as showing one group the picture before the memory task, are reflected in the between-groups variance. In other words, between-groups variance reflects the difference between the experimental group and the control group (that is, the effect of the treatment). Chance factors also contribute to the total between-groups variance (although when that term is used conceptually, we are referring mainly to the effect of systematic variations). Thus, between-groups variance equals the effect of treatment plus error variance, whereas within-groups variance is a result of chance or error variance alone. Thus, the F ratio is

$$\frac{\text{between-groups variance}}{\text{within-groups variance}} = \frac{\text{treatment effect} + \text{chance variance}}{\text{chance variance}}$$

Consider the relationship of between-groups variance and within-groups variance if the independent variable has no effect in a study. That is, if showing one group the picture had no effect on the participants remembering the passage, what is the relationship of between-groups variance and within-groups variance? They are the same. If there are no treatment effects, then

$$\frac{\text{between-groups variance}}{\text{within-groups variance}} = \frac{0 + \text{chance variace}}{\text{chance variance}}$$

Still ignoring confounds, if the independent variable has no effect on the dependent variable, the F ratio is roughly equal to 1. Thus, if the independent variable and confounds do not systematically influence the results, then

$$\frac{\text{between-groups variance}}{\text{within-groups variance}} = \text{approximately 1}$$

Systematic Variation Due to Confounds

Another aspect of the total variance in any experiment is related to confounds. Kerlinger (1973) called this **secondary variance,** or *uncontrolled systematic variance,* because it results from secondary variables (that is, variables other than the independent variable) that can affect the experiment in a variety of ways. Confounds may occur along with the independent variable and thus differentially affect the performance of the two groups. This chapter focuses on some of these confounds.

What is a confound? Almost anything can be a confound. A confound is something that systematically biases the results of our research. It may be the fact that on the day before we ran the experimental group in a social psychology experiment on conformity there was a television special on how we always do what other people tell us. Or a confound may be introduced into a weight-reduction experiment if one group is asked to lose weight at a time of the year when people eat less and their gastrointestinal systems work faster (summer), whereas another group was started at a time when people eat more (winter). A confound may be introduced when one group is made up of more men than women.

In one behavioral medicine study, the control group was instructed by young, inexperienced technicians, whereas the experimental group was instructed by an older, more experienced physician. This difference may have produced a confound in the results. As you consider these and other possible confounds, you will quickly realize that some confounds can be prevented or controlled. In the next chapter, we emphasize techniques for controlling systematic bias. However, other factors can never be controlled. You cannot control world events, but you can ask whether there is any reason to believe that a particular event that took place inside or outside of the laboratory could have influenced one group more than another and thus introduced a confound.

In addition to confounds that influence our groups differently, you also should consider the possibility that **extraneous variables** may occur independently of the independent variable. In this book we differentiate confounds from extraneous variables by referring to confounds as factors that influence the groups in an experiment differently, whereas extraneous variables tend to have a similar impact on the performance of all research participants.

Another way of saying this is that confounds vary systematically with the independent variable. Thus, confounds are a special case of extraneous variables. For example, if a memory experiment is run during a period when the building next door is being renovated, then we will expect the noise of the renovation to influence all participants in a similar fashion. We call this an extraneous variable because it can influence everyone's memory score, but not a confound because it will not influence our groups differentially. Some examples of such extraneous variables include the season of the year, consistent sounds from an adjacent room (for example, an air conditioner), the color of the room, or the temperature in the experimental setting. These are variables that can be controlled by the experimenter but are not (a point on which we elaborate in Chapter 8). Sometimes they are unknown; sometimes we realize their existence but decide they are not worth eliminating.

Because these extraneous variables affect both groups, they do not influence the internal validity of our experiments. Hence, they often are ignored. However, as we will see, they do contribute to the overall individual variability (that is, nonsystematic variation) and thereby affect the acceptance or rejection of the null hypothesis.

Thus, on a conceptual level, the variability in an experiment can be divided into three parts: (1) systematic variation due to the independent variable (treatment effect), (2) systematic variation due to confounds, and (3) variation due to chance, error, or nonsystematic variation. All sources of variation can be described in terms of these sources, although many terms are used to refer to these same concepts (for example, Kerlinger, 1973).

STATISTICAL HYPOTHESIS TESTING

Let's consider how the null hypothesis is related to the ratio of between-groups variance to within-groups variance. If the ratio is close to 1, then we will not be able to reject the null hypothesis. If the ratio is a large number, however, then we can reject the null hypothesis and explore the possibility that real differences exist between our groups. The meaning of the ratio must also be understood in relation to the sample size. Given the same sample size, as a general rule, the larger the ratio, the more certain we can be that there are real differences between our groups that are not caused by chance alone. The smaller the ratio, the less certain we can be that the results are not due to chance.

Actually, we are never fully certain that our results are or are not due to chance. Instead, we use statistics to help us make a best guess by assigning a probability to the statement that our results are not due to chance alone. That is, we may say that results from our study could have happened by chance only 1 time out of every 100. In the published literature, you will see this written as $p < .01$. You will see the F ratio in published papers as F equals some number (for example, $F = 5.8$). In the "Results" section of an article quoted in Chapter 15, you will see "$F = 21.54, p < .001$." In that example we would expect that the particular differences between the groups would occur by chance less than 1 time in 1,000. To be complete, it should be noted that you may also see the F ratio written as "$F(1, 48) = 21.54, p < .001$." The 1 and 48 represent the degrees of freedom for the between- and within-groups variance.

The current convention in the published literature is to use a probability level of less than .05, which is a chance of less than 5 times in 100, as the accepted level of statistical significance. The use of the .05 level of acceptance has been traced to Sir Ronald Fisher, and its history has been reviewed by Cowles and Davis (1982). As with any bet based on probability, we can be wrong, and we do make mistakes. Rejecting and failing to reject the null hypothesis are given special names. We call them Type I and Type II errors (see Box 7.1).

Box 7.1

Type I and Type II Errors

Suppose we reject the null hypothesis and assume that our results are not simply due to chance. Our decision may reflect the world accurately (correct rejection of the null hypothesis) or it may not (incorrect rejection of the null hypothesis). An incorrect rejection of the null hypothesis is called a Type I error.

A Type I error occurs whenever we incorrectly reject the null hypothesis and the true state is that chance fluctuations are solely responsible for the differences between our groups. Suppose that we accept the null hypothesis and bet that our results are merely due to chance. Our decision may reflect the world accurately (correct acceptance of the null hypothesis) or it may not (incorrect acceptance of the null hypothesis). An incorrect acceptance of the null hypothesis is called a Type II error.

A Type II error occurs when factors other than chance (e.g., the independent variable) are responsible for the differences between our groups, and we conclude that they are not.

True state of affairs

		Chance is responsible	Chance is not responsible
Null hypothesis decision	Fail to reject	Correct acceptance	Type II error (incorrect acceptance)
	Reject	Type I error (incorrect rejection)	Correct rejection

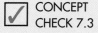 **CONCEPT CHECK 7.2**   Name some factors that might increase chance or error variation in an experiment in which students learn nonsense syllables.

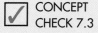 **CONCEPT CHECK 7.3**   Describe the *F* ratio in terms of variance.

A **Type I error** occurs when we reject the null hypothesis as being false when it is actually true. In other words, if we think that there are differences between our groups because of our experimental manipulation (and thus we reject the null hypothesis that no differences exist) when in fact the differences were the result of chance and not our independent variable, then we would have made a Type I error. We all have had problems with the luck of the draw. What is the actual chance of making this mistake? It is the probability or p level (for example, $p < .01$), also called the **alpha level,** symbolized by α. Thus, when we see in a research article that $F = 5.89$, $p < .01$, we know that the chance of making a Type I error is less than 1 in 100. In general, the larger the F ratio, the lower the chance of making a Type I error.

A **Type II error** occurs when we fail to reject the null hypothesis when it is actually false. In other words, if we think there are no differences between our groups but in fact our independent variable did have an influence, then we have committed a Type II error. In such a situation, chance has influenced our results such that the influence of the experimental manipulation is not apparent statistically. The probability of making a Type II error is called the **beta level,** symbolized by β. The real importance of β is that its inverse $(1 - \beta)$ equals the probability that a researcher will correctly reject the null hypothesis when it is false. This probability, $1 - \beta$, is called the **power** of a statistical test.

The concept of power has gained importance in the past decade and is becoming a common word in the research vocabulary. In fact, some journals and government agencies that provide grants require the inclusion of measures of statistical power (see Wilkinson and Task Force on Statistical Inference, 1999). Consider the situation in which you have a great research idea for a class project. What do you want to happen? Of course, you want to be able to demonstrate that your independent variable influenced the data you collected. You want to be able to reject the null hypothesis that, for example, your two groups were drawn from the same population and thus were not different from one another. A strong effect—one in which the between-groups variance is much larger than the within-groups variance and thus the F ratio is large—will help you reject the null hypothesis. From a personal standpoint, you particularly do not want to commit a Type II error. That is, you do not want to conclude that your two groups were not different when in fact they were.

Why might you make such a mistake? One reason might be that your *within-groups variance* (that is, chance variance) was large in comparison to the *between-groups variance,* which includes the influence of your independent variable. Another way of saying this is that you did not run the study very well. You also might make a Type II error if you used too few research participants to show the effect you wanted to demonstrate. That is to say, if the independent variable you are studying has only a minor effect on the dependent variable, then you would need to add more participants in the study to demonstrate this effect. If the effect were a strong one, then you would need fewer participants to show the effect statistically.

Thus, you need to be concerned about power. In essence, power calculations help us to understand how many research participants we need, depending on the magnitude of change—called the **effect size**—that our independent variable has on our dependent variable. The goal is to reduce the chance of Type II errors. If we are studying a phenomenon that is strong and our manipulation has a definite effect, we will need fewer participants to avoid Type II errors than if the phenomenon we are studying is weak.

One common measure of effect size is that of Cohen's *d,* which is basically the difference in the mean score in two groups divided by standard deviation of the measure from both groups. Alternatively, you can consider effect size in terms of the F ratio and discuss the amount of variance associated with a particular treatment effect, which is referred to as eta squared, or η^2 (see Murphy & Myors, 1998, for an extended discussion of power in relation to the F test). As you read the scientific literature, you will note that articles may include both a statement of probability and a measure of effect size. Thus, three factors— effect size, the alpha level (for example, $p < .05$), and the number of participants in a research study—define power, which is the probability that a study will correctly reject the null hypothesis when it is false.

In summary, on a statistical level we must decide whether our groups are equal (null hypothesis). Many kinds of inferential statistics can be used in a variety of situations. In the final analysis, these statistical manipulations boil down to a consideration of the size of our treatment effect and the amount of individual variation in our experiment. This comparison takes the form of the F ratio. As discussed previously, the numerator of this ratio reflects the difference between the scores of the experimental and control groups on the dependent variable. This difference, also called the *treatment effect,* is assumed to result in part from the independent variable. The difference between the experimental and control groups on the dependent measure is reflected in the statistical measure of between-groups variance.

The denominator of the F ratio reflects the amount of variability on our dependent measure among the research participants in this experiment. Because the individual variability is calculated by determining the amount of variation of our research participants within each group, it is sometimes called the *within-groups variance.* If there is a lot of individual variability on the dependent measure within our experimental and control groups, we would say that the within-groups variance is high; as a matter of common sense, we would insist that the treatment effects be quite large before assuming that any treatment effects were due to any cause other than chance.

In contrast, if there were only small individual differences on the dependent measure among the research participants in each group (low within-groups variance), it would be reasonable to assume that smaller differences between the experimental and control groups were not caused by chance. Thus, our confidence that the treatment effect is not due to chance fluctuations in the performance of the participants in our two groups is directly related to the size of the treatment effect and inversely related to the variability of scores within our groups.

On a concrete level, you can draw some important practical conclusions related to the F ratio that should help you design your experiments. It is important to understand that a large F ratio can be produced mathematically by *increasing the between-groups variance,* by *reducing the within-groups variance,* or by some variation of both. The practical implication of this fact is that positive experimental results can be obtained both by having a strong independent variable (that is, maximizing treatment variance) and by *controlling* the error variance (that is, minimizing error variance). The presentation of the independent variable may be made stronger by using extreme levels of the independent variable; for example, a zero level of a drug might be given to one group and a high dosage level given to another. Likewise, controlling error variance, which we discuss in the next chapter, offers another way of influencing the size of the F ratio and our rejection of the null hypothesis.

In accepting or rejecting the null hypothesis, we can make mistakes. These mistakes are called Type I and Type II errors, and the probabilities associated with these are symbolized by α and β, respectively. Power is the probability $(1 - \beta)$ of avoiding a Type II error and is related to effect size, the alpha level (for example, $p < .05$), and the number of participants in a research study. From a logical standpoint, even when the null hypothesis is not rejected, we cannot conclude, however tempting it may be, that we now have proof that there are no effects of the treatment. As we pointed out in Chapter 2, we would have confirmatory evidence but not proof.

The question now arises regarding how to interpret our results. If we have not rejected the null hypothesis, which states that our groups are equal after treatment, we interpret our data theoretically to mean that the independent variable did not affect the dependent variable. If we reject the null hypothesis, then we must decide what did produce the results of our experiment. Because the F ratio cannot tell us whether the systematic variation reflects the independent variable or a confound, we must logically and conceptually deduce the source of the systematic influence. To do this, we turn first to the question of confounds and then to our independent variable. At each stage of this process, we are attempting to become more and more certain of whether the independent variable affected the dependent variable.

 CONCEPT CHECK 7.4   In an experiment with no confounds, the treatment had no effect on the dependent variable. What would be the F ratio in such a case?

 CONCEPT CHECK 7.5   Imagine a study in which the independent variable was drinking coffee (2 cups versus 0 cups) and the dependent variable was emotional mood. If you were to run five participants (in each group) in such an experiment, should you be more concerned about a Type I or a Type II error?

 # THREATS TO INTERNAL VALIDITY

In determining internal validity, we ask what contributes to the treatment effects that we see. Is it our independent variable or perhaps one or more confound variables? To help researchers answer this question, Campbell and Stanley (1963) and Cook and Campbell (1979) presented a list of possible threats to internal validity that must be considered. We discuss this list for two reasons. First, we want to introduce you to some of the possible confounds that can influence the groups in our experiments differently. However, the list does not include every possible confound because many confounds are related to the specific type of research being performed and cannot be listed in a general manner. Second, we want you to begin thinking about ways in which you might control the effects of these confounds. You already know one way: the use of appropriate control groups. This discussion should help to set up your thinking in preparation for an introduction to experimental design. Let's now turn to several examples of threats to internal validity.

History

History refers to events that take place between measurements in an experiment that are not related to the independent variable. Sometimes these are large events such as 9/11, and other times these are lesser events such as changes in the weather. A closely followed political election or media event, for example, could influence the cognitions, emotions, and actions of participants. If your participants are college students, then winning an important sporting event could influence the results. In general, the longer the time between two measurements—a pretest and a posttest, for example—the greater the possibility that outside events will influence the situation. In the cereal experiment described in Chapter 2, the availability of other foods made it impossible to know whether the experimental cereal caused the weight gain. Some confounds are subtle and difficult to detect. For example, in a long-term treatment study with psychiatric patients, such factors as new staff or a change of diet could influence the outcome. Cunningham (1979) has shown that the amount of sunshine present during a helping behavior experiment can influence the degree to which participants aid an interviewer.

Even more subtle confounds may be introduced simply by a person taking part in research. For example, in clinical research studies in which participants come in for the treatment of some specific disorder, such as alcoholism or anxiety, it has been noted that once a person is defined as a patient under treatment, that person's family and friends begin to act differently toward him or her. Thus, it is impossible to know whether any change came about because of the treatment or because of relationships outside the treatment setting.

Maturation

Maturation refers to problems of interpretation resulting from the research participants' growing older, wiser, stronger, and healthier, as well as more tired, more bored, and so forth. The cartoon illustrates this problem. If a scientist is conducting a study that lasts for a period of time, it is imperative that maturational factors be controlled. This is accomplished

© Sidney Harris, ScienceCartoonsPlus.com

"OF COURSE I'VE BECOME MORE MATURE SINCE YOU STARTED TREATING ME. YOU'VE BEEN AT IT SINCE I WAS FOURTEEN YEARS OLD."

by the use of a control group. Confounds of this type plague many inexperienced researchers because they often have their research participants perform too many tasks over too long a time. The research participants become bored and frustrated, and then the results can be attributed to boredom and not to the independent variable in the study.

■ Testing

Testing refers to the problems that result from repeated measurement of the same person. For example, if a participant is given the same math test repeatedly, then both the practice of taking the test and the memory of certain items could influence the results. Another example is when blood pressure is taken once a minute for 30 minutes. With the standard cuff method of measuring blood pressure, each inflation and deflation of the cuff results in temporary changes in the tissue of the arm itself. Thus, just taking repeated measurements during a short time results in a change in blood pressure readings. Another example of testing as a confound occurs when participants are monitored for certain behaviors and after repeated observations they become aware of what behaviors the experimenter is recording.

■ Instrumentation

The problem of *instrumentation* is related to changes that occur in the measuring device, be it a person or a machine, during the course of an experiment. For example, if you were measuring aggressive behavior in children, you would become more accurate at making ratings as the study continues, and this could influence your results. To avoid this problem, Newcombe and Arnkoff (1979), in the study of speech styles discussed in Chapter 3, had more than one rater of the same material and compared the ratings for consistency. If possible, the ratings for each group should be made concurrently so that any improvement in ratings does not systematically influence the groups in the study. You can also have an instrumentation threat if raters in a study are influenced by previous ratings that they have made. For example, if you were rating aggression in children, and you first saw a very aggressive child and then saw a less aggressive one, you might rate the second child differently than you would have had you seen a very loving child first.

Another possible source of confounds is the use of machines. Many believe that machines are more reliable than people, but this does not mean that machines are always perfect. For example, some computer screens leave a slight afterimage once the screen is cleared. Thus, a stimulus that the experimenter believed to be presented for 250 milliseconds actually may have remained visible to the participant for a longer period. This would become a critical problem if a number of different computers were used for the experiment, each with a slightly different screen type.

■ Statistical Regression

A simple example of *statistical regression* occurs when participants are selected because of some score or measurement that turns out to be extreme. On the next testing, the score may return to normal. If this had happened during an experimental treatment, we might conclude that the change in the score was the result of the treatment, when in fact it represented only a regression to the mean or average score. Statistical regression thus occurs when extreme scores (very high or very low) change over time (low scores become higher and high scores become lower) without any treatment. A related problem is found in medical, psychotherapy, biofeedback, and drug studies that focus on people who come to a professional's office. Most people go to see a professional when a given disorder, such as a cold, is at its worst. With such disorders, some improvement can be seen over time without any treatment, and we may conclude incorrectly that the improvement is related to the treatment alone. Many promoters of pseudoscientific treatments exploit the fact that we seek treatment when we are feeling most ill. A website may say, for example, that if you wear a particular metal necklace, you will feel better in three days. Of course, with many minor disorders such as a cold, you would feel better in three days no matter what the treatment was or even if there were no treatment at all.

■ Selection

Selection confounds occur when the participants in one group differ initially from those in another group. Suppose you were testing a new technique to help you read better. For the experimental group, you used people who came to the reading clinic; these people received the treatment. For the control group, you used students in a psychology course. There are at least three possible problems with this design. First, there could be a difference (in IQ, reading level, achievement, and other factors) in the types of people who come to a reading clinic and those in a psychology class. Second, those who come to the clinic might have a lower reading score initially and be able to improve more than the psychology students, who may already be reading at their optimal level. Third, the people who come to the clinic probably would be more motivated and work harder at learning to read faster, no matter what technique was used. This third type of problem must be guarded against in any treatment study (for example, a study of the effects of a drug, relaxation training, or meditation) when the group receiving the treatment seeks the treatment and the control group does not.

In each of these cases, some characteristics of the participants might initially constitute important differences in the groups even before the independent variable is introduced. Thus, it is best to have both the experimental and the control groups consist of people seeking treatment. In this way, the groups are more likely to be similar at the beginning of the experiment.

■ Mortality

The problem of *mortality* occurs when participants drop out or refuse to take part in an experiment. The problem is greatest when participants differentially drop out of one group. For example, suppose you want to measure whether children are more creative after playing with dull toys than after playing with fun toys. You first classify the toys as dull or fun and then establish your measure of creativity. As you run the experiment, some of the children who are given dull toys to play with might leave the experiment or not return for other sessions. Thus, after a period of weeks, the fun-toy group might be composed of all the children who began the experiment, whereas the dull-toy group is composed of only half of the original children from that group. If you try to analyze these results, you are faced with the possibility that only a certain type of child remained in the dull-toy group. The dull-toy group would then consist of a different population from the fun-toy group, thus making your conclusions invalid.

■ Selection–Maturation Interaction

Selection–maturation interaction refers to the situation in which one group of participants changes along a given dimension faster than another group. For example, children whose families have lower-than-average incomes tend to develop cognitive abilities at different rates from children whose families have average incomes. If this difference is not taken into account, the experimenter could ascribe the difference to a specific treatment. Likewise, girls tend to develop verbal abilities before boys; when working with preschool children, this differential development must be taken into account.

Another possibility in this broad category is selection-testing interaction. For example, Fry and Greenfield (1980) examined job-related attitudes in a Midwestern city. They collected data from 529 policemen and 21 policewomen. Assume that this represented the total police force of the city and that other researchers were also collecting various data from these people. It could occur that every policewoman would be called on in each study, whereas only some of the 529 policemen would be called on in every study. This could cause each policewoman to become sophisticated and experienced at being a participant in an experiment, whereas it would remain a new experience for any given policeman. Thus, experimental results that compared policemen and policewomen in this city could be biased because of the policewomen's greater participation in psychological research. Cook and Campbell (1979) expand this category to include selection–history and selection–instrumentation interactions.

■ Diffusion or Imitation of Treatments

Participants in an experiment may communicate with each other, and by this communication they may reduce the differences between the groups. This phenomenon is called *diffusion.* If the difference between the experimental and control groups is that one group has information that the other does not have, then if the participants communicate with each other it is possible that this difference may be reduced or even removed completely.

Consider what would happen if a participant in the picture condition of the Bransford and Johnson study mentioned to a friend that he was in a psychology experiment and described the experiment and the picture he saw. If the friend were later in the experiment and assigned to the no-picture group, her results would be influenced greatly by her previous knowledge. The sharing of information among participants is a problem, particularly when they are drawn from a group that has daily contact. In his simulated attack study, outlined in Chapter 3, Dr. Shotland avoided this problem by helping the participants to understand the importance of his research and the necessity that they tell no one of the experiment until the study was completed. This may take place in the debriefing process, which we discussed in Chapter 4.

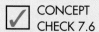 **CONCEPT CHECK 7.6**   Consider a school district that gives its students a particular achievement test each month to see how well they are learning. Describe one of the major threats to internal validity in such a situation.

CONCLUSION

After ruling out the null hypothesis and the confound hypothesis, we can assume that the results reflect the action of the independent variable. We can then go back and reexamine our numerical results in light of the assumption that our independent variable is the crucial agent. We begin to generalize from our set of data and consider both the implications of our results for other groups of people and the theoretical implications of the data. Sometimes we are led to new ideas, which in turn generate new research hypotheses, which can be interpreted with additional experiments.

Figure 7.2 presents a simplified outline of this procedure, which reflects the evolutionary nature of science. The steps include (1) the development of the hypothesis, (2) the translation of this hypothesis into a research design, (3) the running of the experiment, and (4) the interpretation of the results. You will notice that there is also an arrow from step 4 back to step 1. Researchers take the results and interpretations of their studies and create new research studies that refine the previous hypotheses.

Although Figure 7.2 shows a circular process, it would be represented better by a spiral in which each rotation adds additional information. This is the idea of the self-correcting nature of science, discussed in Chapter 1. The goal of the process is to help us to understand more about what we are studying and to lead us in new directions that we could not have discovered by reasoning alone. That is, experimentation gives us an interaction with reality that is not available solely through reason.

Figure 7.2

Schematic representation of the four major steps in the experimentation process

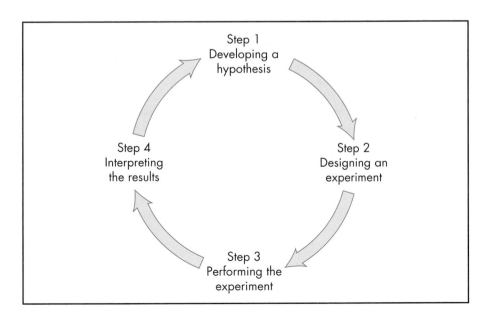

KEY TERMS AND CONCEPTS

1. **Types of hypotheses**
   A. Statistical (null hypothesis)
   B. Confound hypothesis
   C. Research hypothesis
2. **Variation**
   A. Chance or error variation
   B. Variation due to confound
   C. Variation due to independent variable
3. **Variance**
   A. Within-groups
   B. Between-groups
   C. Ratio of between-groups and within-groups variance
   D. F ratio
   E. Factors that influence ratio of between- and within-groups variance

4. **Type I and Type II errors**
   A. Effect size
   B. Power
5. **Threats to internal validity**
   A. History
   B. Maturation
   C. Testing
   D. Instrumentation
   E. Statistical regression
   F. Selection
   G. Mortality
   H. Selection–maturation interaction
   I. Diffusion or imitation of treatments

SUMMARY

1. Interpreting the results of an experiment may be seen as a three-part process, each part consisting of a separate hypothesis. The first consideration relates to the null hypothesis and is concerned with a statistical decision process, such as the one we discussed in Chapters 3 and 6. The second consideration relates to the possibility of rival hypotheses, such as confounds, that influenced the results in our research. The third consideration relates to the manner in which the independent variable influenced the dependent variable.

2. Variation is an important concept in research. We hope that systematic variations between groups in an experiment are planned and result from the influence of the independent variable on the dependent variable. Variations in an experiment may also be nonsystematic and result from chance; these are also called error variations.

3. The F ratio is a common inferential statistic in research. This ratio reflects the effect of the independent variable plus chance, divided by the effects of chance variation alone. In more technical language, this is called between-groups variance divided by within-groups variance. If there were no treatment effects, this ratio would be equal to 1.

4. An F ratio equal to 1 would not allow us to reject the null hypothesis. To reject the null hypothesis, we would need an F ratio larger than 1; how large depends on a number of factors, such as the number of participants in each group. Conceptually, a researcher could increase the size of the F ratio in two ways. The first way would be to decrease the amount of chance or error variance. This may be accomplished through careful control. The second way would be to increase the size of the treatment effect.

5. Even if the null hypothesis is rejected, it is still necessary to consider factors other than the independent variable that might have influenced the results. These other factors—confounds—have been called threats to internal validity by Campbell and Stanley. These threats include such possibilities as history, maturation, testing, instrumentation, statistical regression, selection, mortality, selection–maturation interactions, and diffusion of treatments.

6. The conclusion that the independent variable influences the dependent variable is considered only after the null hypothesis and the confound hypothesis have been ruled out.

7. The process of experimentation may be considered as a spiral that consists of four major steps, continually repeated. These include (1) the development of the hypothesis, (2) the translation of the hypothesis into a research design, (3) the running of the experiment, and (4) the interpretation of the results, which leads back to step 1, the development of a better hypothesis.

REVIEW QUESTIONS

1. How are a scientist and a detective alike?
2. Describe the hypotheses that a researcher must consider in performing research.
3. Describe the Bransford and Johnson study in terms of the independent variable, the dependent variable, and the hypotheses.
4. What is the meaning of *error* when discussing error or chance variations?
5. What factors influence within-groups variance?
6. What factors influence between-groups variance?

7. If no systematic variation affected the results of a study, what would the following ratio equal?

$$\frac{\text{between-groups variance}}{\text{within-groups variance}} = ?$$

8. What is the difference between a Type I error and a Type II error?
9. What is meant by the term *power*?
10. List Campbell and Stanley's threats to internal validity.

DISCUSSION QUESTIONS AND PROJECTS

1. Discuss the meaning of *chance* in science. In an experiment, how is chance related to the individual? To the group?
2. Use the Bransford and Johnson study as an example for the following questions: (1) How could between-groups variance be increased? Decreased? (2) How could within-groups variance be increased? Decreased?
3. A company gives its employees money if they lose weight. Records of weight loss are kept over a 6-month period. A control group also tries to lose weight but is not given money. The results will determine whether it will become part of company policy

to reward employees for weight loss in the future. What would a Type I error mean in this study? A Type II error?
4. The president announces on television that he has just completed a study in which he applied his economic program to the economy and found positive results. He presents a graph showing that the economy is improving, starting from the time he introduced his economic policy. Discuss the president's presentation in terms of possible confounds.
5. Discuss the Bransford and Johnson study in terms of threats to internal validity.

INFOTRAC COLLEGE EDITION: EXERCISES

In this chapter, we discussed three different hypotheses: the null hypothesis, or the possibility that the results are due to chance; the confound hypothesis, or the possibility that the results are not due to the independent variable; and the research hypothesis, which suggests that the results are due to the independent variable. Using InfoTrac College Edition, find the article by Robert Sternberg and his colleagues entitled "If you changed your name and appearance to those of Elvis Presley, who would you be?" published in the Fall 1998 issue of the *American Journal of Psychology*. (*Hint:* You can just type in the name of the article, and you obtain a full copy of it.) In the pilot study and the four experiments that these researchers describe, what is the research hypothesis, and what is the null

hypothesis? Can you think of any alternative hypotheses or confounds that could influence each experiment? (You could also consider the threats to internal validity discussed in the chapter.)

To help you better understand the material in this chapter, you can go to Wadsworth's research methods workshop web page at http://www.wadsworth.com/ psychology_d/templates/student_resources/workshops/ resch_wrk.html. There you will find workshops related to research methods and statistics. The research methods workshop on "Confounds—Threats to Validity" highlights the concepts presented in this chapter. Two of the statistics workshops, "Hypothesis Testing" and "Statistical Power," discuss the concepts introduced in this chapter.

☑ Answers to Concept Checks

7.1 The three broad considerations that must be evaluated include the null hypothesis, the confound hypothesis, and the research hypothesis.

7.2 Many different factors could influence the results in a nonsystematic manner. Some of these could include how particular participants felt that day, whether they had arguments with their boyfriends or girlfriends, a grade they may have received that day, or the amount of sleep they had the night before.

7.3 The F ratio equals the between-groups variance divided by the within-groups variance.

7.4 The F ratio would be equal to 1.

7.5 If we expected that coffee would have a positive but small effect on mood, there would be a greater chance of a Type II error with five participants. That is, with a few participants and a small effect, we would be more likely not to reject the null hypothesis. This is why the concepts of effect size and power are so important.

7.6 There are many problems in such a study, but one of the major threats is that of testing. Because the students see the same test each month, the improvement in results may be a consequence of simply recognizing the questions on the test and learning their answers, rather than of a general improvement in ability.

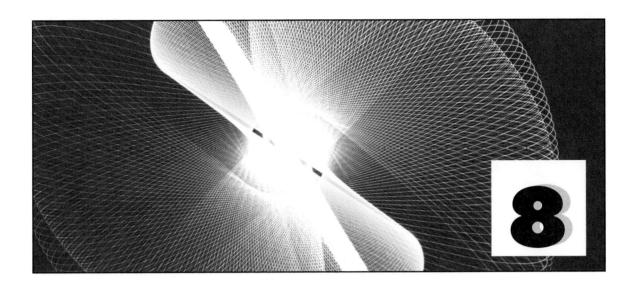

CONTROL: THE KEYSTONE OF THE EXPERIMENTAL METHOD

CONTROL ACHIEVED THROUGH PARTICIPANT ASSIGNMENT AND SELECTION

RANDOMIZATION
Random Sampling
Random Assignment

CONTROL ACHIEVED THROUGH EXPERIMENTAL DESIGN

CONTROL AS RELATED TO THE LOGIC OF EXPERIMENTATION

In the preceding chapters, we have followed the transformation of an idea into a research hypothesis. We have also begun the process of interpreting experimental results in terms of three separate hypotheses: (1) the chance hypothesis (the results are influenced by chance) and its inverse, the null hypothesis (each group is drawn from the same population, and thus the effects of the conditions are not different one from another); (2) the confound hypothesis (the systematic results are influenced by a factor other than the independent variable); and (3) the research hypothesis (the results are related to the independent variable). We also developed the conceptual thinking underlying the F ratio and pointed out how this ratio is related to differences between groups in an experiment (between-groups variance) and error or chance variation (within-groups variance). Our ultimate goal, both conceptually and practically, is to understand what influence, if any, the independent variable has on the dependent variable. In our experiments we want to be reasonably certain that once we reject the null hypothesis, the observed difference between our groups is indeed a result of the independent variable and not of other factors such as confounds.

In psychological research, we have some powerful techniques to help us to achieve this goal. Unlike the detective, who must always reconstruct events after the fact, the researcher has the advantage of being able to create a new situation in which to test ideas. This is comparable to a homicide detective's being able to bring a dead man back to life and place him in the presence of each suspect until the murder is reenacted. Such a reenactment might lack suspense and not make it in prime time, but it would increase the certainty of knowing who committed the murder. Increased certainty is a large part of the experimental process. Scientists increase certainty by creating an artificial situation—the experiment—in which important factors can be controlled and manipulated. Through **control** and manipulation, participant variables may be examined in detail, and the influence of one variable on another may be determined with certainty.

However, the experiment is an artificial environment created to answer a small number of specific questions, and it may not mirror the real world. When it does not, we are faced with a problem of generalizability and a threat to the external validity of our research. We approach these questions in Chapter 11. For now, however, we assume that our research does reflect the real world. In this discussion we present research in its more ideal form from the standpoint of the scientist, with an emphasis on techniques for reducing threats to the internal validity of an experiment. We emphasize the theme of control in three ways: (1) control as related to participant assignment, (2) control as related to experimental design and the assurance of internal validity, and (3) control as related to the logic of experimentation.

CONTROL ACHIEVED THROUGH PARTICIPANT ASSIGNMENT AND SELECTION

To illustrate some techniques available for participant assignment, let's begin with the simple illustration of a class designing an experiment. This particular class began with the idea that people can be taught to estimate time more accurately if they are given feedback about their performance. From this idea came a formal research hypothesis followed by a discussion of how to conduct the experiment. We pick up the discussion as someone suggests that the experiment should use two groups. One group of participants would receive verbal feedback on the accuracy of their estimates of a given time interval, and the other group would not be given feedback. Thus, we would have two levels of the independent variable: a zero level and a high level.

The first question asked is, "How do we go about assigning participants to the groups in this experiment?" It is suggested that someone could contact an equal number of male and female participants. They could then place the male participants in one group and the female participants in the other. After thinking about this for a moment, the rest of the class disagrees. They argue that there might be a difference between men and women in their ability to estimate time. This inherent difference might create unequal groups before the experiment even begins. Indeed, one student points out that in her recent readings in psychological literature on time estimation, she found a study indicating that there are sex differences in people's ability to estimate time. More specifically, she found that men are more accurate in estimating intervals of time than women.

As it turns out, this student had seen only one part of a larger and somewhat confusing story. Some of the published literature reports that there are sex differences in time estimation, and some reports that there are not (see Roechelein, 1972, and Rammsayer & Rammstedt, 2000, for some examples and a discussion of this literature). Faced with this ambiguity, the students need to decide how to control for possible sex differences. Note that the objection stemmed from common sense—namely, that men and women *might* differ in their ability to estimate time. The fact that one student was familiar with experimental evidence supporting this commonsense idea greatly strengthened the objection to dividing the participants into groups according to sex.

In view of this objection and the evidence supporting it, the class decides not to have all the women in one group and all the men in another group. If they did this, they could not be sure whether any difference between the two groups was a result of feedback or of a difference in men's and women's abilities to estimate time. The experiment would be confounded because they would not know which of the variables—that is, feedback or sex differences between the groups—caused any treatment effects they might observe. Although they might be able to obtain a treatment effect, they could not be sure what the causal factor was.

"Wait a minute!" someone in class yells out. "All of you are getting ahead of yourselves. Even before assigning participants to groups, we have to establish who our participants are and how many we should use, and only then how we are going to select them." The question of who our participants are is of course related to the topic that we are studying. If we are interested in time estimation in college students, then college students are the appropriate population. If we decide to use our own college, then we have to ask whether it is in any way different from colleges across the nation. Although this consideration does *not* affect the internal validity of our results, it does influence the generalizability or external validity of our results. The question of how many participants to use depends in part on the question being asked. We suggest that the literature is the best guide for this consideration. Although using a number of participants similar to those used in other experiments is not infallible (they can be wrong), it is a good guide. The class decides on 20 participants, 10 men and 10 women.

"We could select our participants by just calling them on the phone," one student suggests. "That's true," someone says, "but you may just call your friends, and they may not be a representative sample of all college students. Also, you would probably start calling and just keep on calling until you found 10 men and 10 women. The set of people you find in their dorm rooms at a given hour might be different from the set of college students in

Box 8.1

Random Number Table

A random number table is a table of numbers ordered in such a manner that their occurrence cannot be predicted from a mathematical formula. There are entire books of such numbers that researchers can use for selecting subjects randomly. An example of a random number table is given here.

Because there is no order to random number tables, it does not matter whether you read up the page, down the page, across the page, in either direction, or even diagonally. All that matters is that you state beforehand how you will use the table. A simple example would be to use the table to pick out 10 subjects from a possible 63 for use in the study. First, you might decide that you will use only the last two digits in each number. Second, you might decide you will read the numbers from the bottom to the top of the page. Third, you might decide you will ignore any number greater than 63.

Assume you turned to the page shown here. You would begin by closing your eyes and placing your finger on some part of the page, or any other method you wish to use. Once you have your first number (91511), you read up the page, using only the last two digits. The first 10 numbers are as follows: 11, 95, 24, 45, 25, 75, 50, 18, 06, and 71. Because you cannot use numbers larger than 63, you ignore 95, 75, and 71 and keep reading upward until you find three numbers smaller than 64. These are 54, 33, and 25. Because 25 occurred twice, you need to pick one final number, which is 05. At this time you could take your list of 63 possible participants and pick participants who are listed in positions 11, 24, 45, 25, 50, 18, 06, 54, 33, and 05. You now have a group of randomly selected subjects.

A larger random number table is reproduced in Appendix D.

69298	82732	38480	73817	32523	41961	44437
54224	35083	19687	11052	91491	60383	19746
35552	35970	19124	63318	29686	03387	59846
75366	76554	31601	12614	33072	60332	92325
20801	72152	39339	34806	08930	85001	87820
39908	05607	91284	68833	25570	38818	46920
73823	73144	88662	88970	74492	51805	99378
88815	16553	51125	79375	97596	16296	66092
31355	86064	29472	47689	05974	52468	16834
56302	00033	67107	77510	70625	28725	34191
34537	33310	06116	95240	15957	16572	06004
42080	97403	48626	68995	43805	33386	21597
60397	16489	03264	88525	42786	05269	92532
93454	68876	25471	93911	25650	12682	73572
15263	80644	43942	89203	71795	99533	50501

Last number

(continued)

(continued)

14486	29891	68607	41867	14951	91696	85065
06878	91903	18749	34405	56087	82790	70925
48542	42627	45233	57202	94617	23772	07896
73923	36152	05184	94142	25299	84387	34925
49071	39782	17095	02330	74301	00275	48280
05422	13442	78675	84081	66938	93654	59894
95348	78662	11163	81651	50245	34971	52924
17869	45349	61796	66345	81073	49106	79860
86482	05174	07901	54339	58861	74818	46942
42865	92520	83531	80377	35909	81250	54238
64816	51202	88124	41870	52689	51275	83556
62570	26123	05155	59194	52799	28225	85762
29789	85205	41001	12535	12133	14645	23541
54990	71899	15475	95434	98227	21824	19585
18611	47348	20203	18534	03862	78095	50136
						First number
86367	21216	98442	08303	56613	(91511)	75928
25651	83325	88428	85076	72811	22717	50585
26113	99447	68645	34327	15152	55230	93448
74014	64708	00533	35398	58408	13261	47908
09013	07832	41574	17639	82163	60859	75567

Source: Random Number Table. From *Handbook of Tables for Probability and Statistics*, 2/E, by William Beyer (Ed.). © 1968 Chemical Rubber Company (CRC Press, Inc.). Reprinted with permission.

general. Thus, you could select a biased group of participants: those who spend a lot of time near their phones." Our technique for avoiding this last criticism is to use a procedure known as random selection or random sampling (discussed in detail in the next section). With random selection, every person in the potential participant pool is equally likely to be selected for the study.

There are a number of ways in which random sampling can be accomplished. Box 8.1 illustrates the most common technique: the use of a **random number table,** which is available on many computers today. Random selection helps to control systematic confounds that could be introduced unknowingly into the participant-selection process, and it helps ensure that the participants reflect the population of the people who we are studying. After the 20 participants have been selected randomly, the next question is how to assign them to groups.

The class wants to avoid the potential confound created by sex differences. Someone points out that one way to eliminate this potential confound would be to limit the participants to one sex. Then, quite correctly, he points out that if they used this *elimination procedure* to remove the potential confound due to sex differences, they would be limiting the generality of the finding tremendously because any new facts they uncover would pertain to only one sex. (This person's concern about the generality of the results is very important; we return to a more extended discussion of its importance in Chapter 11.)

Someone else suggests that they could assign participants so that an equal number of men and women are in each group. We describe this process as an *equating procedure* and save the term *matching* for use in its more traditional sense, in which participants are matched in terms of a pretest (discussed later in this chapter and in Chapter 12). In this particular experiment, equating for sex differences consists of placing the same number of men and women in each group; alternatively, sex difference could be controlled by proportional assignment. Because we know there may be sex differences in the ability to estimate time, equating provides an important control. We do not want to mistake a difference in men's and women's abilities to estimate time for a difference caused by our independent variable: verbal feedback.

Before proceeding, it is important to understand exactly how equating controls for a possible confound due to sex differences. This procedure *does not eliminate sex differences,* as does the elimination procedure, which would limit the experiment to only men or only women. Instead, *we control for any sex differences.* By placing an equal number of men and women in each group, we ensure that any sex differences in time estimation affect both groups equally—that they do not differentially affect our experimental and control groups. Thus, equating for sex differences eliminates a potential confound from this experiment. The original experimental design and the revised design are contrasted in Figure 8.1.

One member of the class then suggests that they could ask all 20 participants to report to the laboratory at 2 P.M. As the participants arrive, they could simply assign the first 5 men and the first 5 women to the experimental group and the second 5 men and the second 5 women to the control group. After a moment's hesitation, someone points out that

Figure 8.1

Experiment to discover the effect of verbal feedback on subjects' estimation of time: (a) original experimental design and (b) revised experimental design

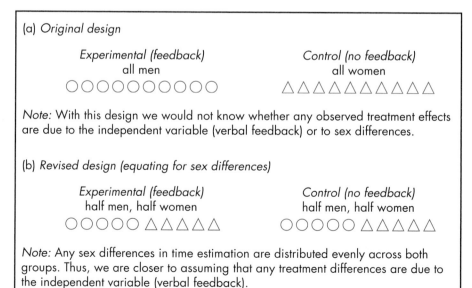

(a) *Original design*

Experimental (feedback)
all men
○○○○○○○○○○

Control (no feedback)
all women
△△△△△△△△△△

Note: With this design we would not know whether any observed treatment effects are due to the independent variable (verbal feedback) or to sex differences.

(b) *Revised design (equating for sex differences)*

Experimental (feedback)
half men, half women
○○○○○ △△△△△

Control (no feedback)
half men, half women
○○○○○ △△△△△

Note: Any sex differences in time estimation are distributed evenly across both groups. Thus, we are closer to assuming that any treatment differences are due to the independent variable (verbal feedback).

one group would then be made up of the participants who arrived on time and the other of participants who arrived somewhat later.

If a relationship exists between one's ability to get to an experiment on time and the ability to estimate time, another confound would be introduced. Although no one had encountered any published evidence of a relationship between one's ability to get to an experiment on time and ultimate accuracy in estimating time, it is reasonable to suspect that there might be a correlation. If there were, we would not know whether any observed treatment effect is due to the feedback or to the fact that there are punctual people in one group and tardy people in the other group. Consequently, it is agreed to control for a possible confound due to the participants' arrival time as well as controlling for sex differences.

As to exactly how the class might do this, one student suggests that, as the participants arrive, they should be assigned to either the experimental group (E) or the control group (C). With this alternating assignment procedure, participants would be assigned in the pattern "ECECECEC. . . ." Another student disagrees, saying that because E always precedes C, this would create a small but possibly relevant bias. He suggests assigning participants the way he and his friends used to choose players for baseball teams in fifth grade: The first choice goes to one team, the second and third choices go to the other team, the fourth and fifth choices go to the first team, and so on, until all players are chosen. Although he did not realize it at the time, he and his fifth-grade teammates had reinvented a commonly used *counterbalancing procedure*. With this procedure, participants would be assigned in the pattern "ECCEECCE. . . ." Like simple alternation this ensures that each condition (early versus late arrival) appears equally often, and it has the additional advantage that each condition precedes and follows the other condition an equal number of times. In Figure 8.2 this design is contrasted with the previous design, which controlled for sex differences but ignored the potentially confounding influence of arrival time.

By using these equating and counterbalancing procedures, our students arrive at the final experimental design depicted in Figure 8.2b. This design is superior to the original plan because it adequately rules out two potential confounds: that time estimation performance may be different for men and women and that time estimation may be related to a participant's ability to get to an experiment on time. By using equating and counterbalancing, the students feel confident that they have a confound-free design and decide to go ahead with their experiment.

Pause for a moment and think about their final design. Can you think of any other factors that might constitute potential confounds in an experiment designed to determine the effect of verbal feedback on time estimation? If you suspect that some factor may constitute a potential confound, you will strengthen your argument greatly if you can find some evidence supporting your concern (as the student did when she cited evidence that men and women differ in their ability to estimate time). In the absence of direct evidence, however, common sense can be a useful tool. For example, it makes sense to suppose that participants who get to an experiment on time might be better time estimators, so it is reasonable to control for this factor. However, our common sense tells us that factors such as where the participant was born are probably not related to the ability to estimate time; consequently, we would not bother to control for the place of birth of our participants.

As you become increasingly familiar with conducting experiments and with a particular research area, you will gain a better idea of what factors are reasonable to control for and what factors can be ignored safely. As we pointed out in Chapter 1, although common sense can be a useful tool, it can sometimes mislead even seasoned researchers. For example,

Figure 8.2

Effect of feedback on estimation of time: (a) revised experimental design and (b) final experimental design using equating and counterbalancing procedures

(a) *Revised design (equating for sex differences but ignoring arrival time)*

| Experimental (feedback) half men, half women | Control (no feedback) half men, half women |

○○○○○ △△△△△   ○○○○○ △△△△△
1 2 3 4 5   1 2 3 4 5   6 7 8 9 10   6 7 8 9 10

The numbers represent the arrival order of each man and woman.
Note: With this design, although we have controlled for sex differences, we do not know whether any eventual treatment differences are a result of the independent variable or of some relationship between the ability to get to an experiment on time and the ability to estimate time.

(b) *Final design (equating for sex and counterbalancing for arrival time)*

| Experimental (feedback) half men, half women | Control (no feedback) half men, half women |

○○○○○ △△△△△   ○○○○○ △△△△△
1 4 5 8 9   2 3 6 7 10   2 3 6 7 10   1 4 5 8 9

The numbers represent the arrival order of each man and woman.
Note: Both sex differences and arrival time differences are now evenly distributed across our two groups. Because this design balances for both sex and arrival time differences, any experimental effect can be assumed with greater probability to be a result of the independent variable.

in reaction time experiments, very few researchers bother to control for eye color or recent coffee drinking. Yet studies indicate that people with dark eyes tend to have slightly faster reaction times than people with light eyes (Landers, Obermier, & Patterson, 1976) and that certain levels of coffee drinking may influence sex differences in time estimation (Botella, Bosch, Romero, & Parra, 2001). Because of such possible confounds, random assignment of participants to groups is generally the best procedure to follow, as we see in the next section.

RANDOMIZATION

In the preceding discussion, when considering sex differences or arrival time differences, the students proposed using equating and counterbalancing procedures. These procedures would ensure that either sex differences or arrival time differences between the two groups would be controlled. Otherwise, we would not know whether any observed difference between our experimental and control groups was a result of verbal feedback (the independent variable) or of sex or arrival time differences (confounds) in the groups. Thus, if either of these variables were permitted to affect the groups differently, a serious confound would result. To control the impact of these potentially confounding variables, we typically use such procedures as equating groups and the counterbalancing of participant selection. However, as we will see, randomization is our most powerful tool to distribute potential confounds between our two groups.

The most powerful technique we have for eliminating unintended participant assignment confounds from the design of experiments is *randomization.* Randomization is the compilation of participant assignments solely on the basis of chance. For example, a simple way to assign participants randomly to either of two groups is to flip a coin. If the outcome is heads, we assign the participant to one group; if it is tails, we assign the participant to the other group. We would continue this process until one group is completely filled, and then place the remaining participants in the other group. Another common method of making random assignments is to use a random number table (see Box 8.1).

Let's take a moment to differentiate between two terms that are sometimes confused. These are random sampling and random assignment. **Random sampling** is the selection of participants from a larger population to participate in a piece of research. **Random assignment** is the assignment of selected participants to groups—for example, an experimental group and a control group—in an experiment. Let's now discuss these in more detail.

■ Random Sampling

Random sampling is the selection of the entire group of participants who will participate in an experiment. As we emphasize later in our discussion of external and ecological validity, when we conduct an experiment we want our conclusions to have relevance for more people than just those who took part in the experiment. One way we ensure this relevance is to have our participants constitute a representative sample of the entire population in which we are interested. By *representative* we mean that our sample is similar, in all major aspects, to the overall population from which it is taken.

For example, if I am interested in the time estimation ability of adult men, I must randomly sample my participants from the entire adult male population in such a way that all men in the population have an equally likely chance of being selected. I would want to be sure that the local lawyer has just as much chance of being selected as the local sanitation worker. In a similar way, I would want to be sure that a given 21-year-old man is just as likely to be selected as the town's only World War I veteran.

In our psychological experiments, the random sampling of a large population of participants to obtain the sample we work with is crucial if we want to generalize from the data we obtain in the laboratory to the entire population. For example, as many of you know, most research conducted in experimental psychology has used college sophomores as participants. In a sense, our psychology is a psychology of college sophomores and may not generalize to the entire adult population. We return to this consideration later in this book.

■ Random Assignment

After we have randomly selected our participants from the larger population that we are studying, we can randomly assign them to our experimental and control groups as a way of equating the groups before the experimental treatment. Randomly assigning participants has an important advantage over other procedures for equating groups: *Randomization controls for both known and unknown potentially confounding variables.* Unlike the equating and counterbalancing procedures, which attempt to equate our two groups directly on known relevant dimensions, randomization leaves solely to chance the assignment of our participants to a group. In this way not only will any *suspected* participant selection biases between our two groups (such as sex or arrival time or eye color differences) be nullified, but any other differences, even unknown or unsuspected differences, will also be nullified by being randomly distributed between our two groups. Indeed, it is not an overstatement to say that *randomization randomizes everything.*

As with equating and counterbalancing, it is important to realize that randomization does not remove the differences among the people in our experiment. The differences are still there. However, these differences are no longer differentially affecting either group. They affect both groups equally. Randomization thus provides a powerful tool for control because the impact of both known and unknown potentially confounding assignment biases can be distributed evenly between our experimental and control groups.

 CONCEPT CHECK 8.1 A newspaper article suggested that people who eat breakfast are healthier than those who do not. When this research was criticized, the researchers replied, "What's the problem? All of our participants were randomly selected." How might you respond to these researchers?

CONTROL ACHIEVED THROUGH EXPERIMENTAL DESIGN

As we emphasize throughout this book, science is a way of asking questions about the world. The quality of the answers we receive is influenced by several factors, one of the most important being the structure that we use to reach our answers. In research this structure is determined by our experimental design. Somewhat like a blueprint, the experimental design directs our procedures and gives form to the experiment. In essence, an experimental design is a plan for how a study is to be structured. In an outline form, a design tells us what will be done to whom and when. To be evaluated favorably, a design must perform two related functions. First, it must provide a logical structure that enables us to pinpoint the effects of the independent variable on the dependent variable and thus answer our research questions. Second, it must help us to rule out confounds as an alternative explanation for our findings. In this section we discuss experimental designs and introduce you to three specific designs that meet these criteria. In later chapters we discuss experimental design in greater detail.

A sound design must allow us to determine logically the effect of the independent variable on the dependent variable and to rule out alternative explanations. We informally introduced you to this idea in Chapter 2 with the cereal experiment. As you remember, the cereal company first tried to demonstrate the value of the cereal by giving it daily to a group of children and weighing them after several months to determine their weight gain. If we were to diagram the design of this study, it would be

Select the group   Give them cereal   Measure their weight gain

We could diagram the design in a more generalized manner as

Group A   Treatment   Measurement

Such a design would not be much help in pinpointing the effect of the independent variable on the dependent variable, nor would it rule out confounds. As was pointed out in Chapter 2, a stronger design would use a control group. This design would appear as

Experimental group   Cereal   Measurement
Control group   No cereal   Measurement

Again, we could diagram this in a more generalized manner, using T as an abbreviation for *treatment* and M for *measurement*:

Group A T M
Group B T (zero level) M

This new design helps us to determine the effects of the independent variable. However, it does not help us to rule out some of the threats to internal validity presented in Chapter 7. In particular, we could not rule out the possibility of biased participant selection unless we had randomly assigned participants to the two groups. To denote random assignment of participants, we place an R before each group in the diagram. Campbell and Stanley (1963) call this design a *posttest-only control group design.* The design is diagrammed as

R Group A T M
R Group B T (zero level) M

Let's now consider a modification of this design that is similar to the final cereal experiment discussed in Chapter 2. This new design adds a measurement before the treatment. Such a measurement before the treatment is called a **pretest,** whereas a measurement after the treatment is called a **posttest.** In the terminology of Campbell and Stanley (1963), this design is called a *pretest–posttest control group design.* It is diagrammed as

R Group A M T M
R Group B M T (zero level) M

This design would allow us to determine the effects of the independent variable on the dependent variable, as well as to control for the threats to internal validity discussed in Chapter 7. Let's briefly review the threats to internal validity presented by Campbell and Stanley (1963) in relation to the pretest–posttest control group design. History is controlled by including a control group; any effects of history on one group would apply equally to the other group. Maturation is similarly controlled in that any changes during the course of experimentation would affect both groups equally. Likewise, testing would affect both groups similarly. Notice that when we use the word *controlled,* we use it in the sense of being constant and not just in the sense that we can manipulate some factor. Controlling a factor in experimentation is the same as holding the effect of that factor constant for all groups throughout a research study. Such threats as participant selection and statistical regression would be controlled because the groups were randomly assigned in the first place. Mortality, or the dropping out of participants, would likewise not be expected to occur more often in one group than the other because the participants were randomly assigned. Random assignment would also control for the participant–maturation interaction. As you can see, this same design without random assignment would be much weaker.

Although Campbell and Stanley (1963) recommend the designs presented in this section as being useful for controlling threats to internal validity, the designs are not perfect. Confounds such as history can be introduced easily if participants are not treated consistently throughout a study. Common sense would say that if you are nice to one group of participants and nasty to another group, a confound will be introduced that could affect the results. In a rating study, if you rate the entire control group before the experimental group, an instrumentation confound may be introduced if your rating ability improves over time. The point is that designs serve their function only if used correctly.

A design such as the pretest–posttest control group design has been used by social psychologists in studying the persuasive effects of movies and lectures on participants' attitudes. Using this design, the researchers randomly assign participants to one of two groups. The participants are given a questionnaire concerning their attitudes toward a certain topic (being politically conservative, for example). The experimental group may be shown a movie supporting an extremely conservative position, whereas the control group sees no movie. The participants in each group then receive a questionnaire concerning their attitudes toward conservatism. Using this design, it is possible to measure the amount of attitude change brought about by the movie by comparing the mean change in the experimental group's scores (on the pretest and posttest questionnaires) with the mean change in the control group's scores.

As researchers used this type of design, it became apparent that the administration of a pretest alone could influence the persuasiveness of a movie or lecture; that is, if someone were asked his or her views on being conservative and were then shown a movie encouraging agreement with an extreme conservative position, the questionnaire itself could influence the attitude change produced by the movie. To control for this problem, Solomon (1949) suggested the use of a four-group design. Although we see this design used less often today, it does help us to consider the logic of experimentation, and we include it for this reason. In this design Groups 1 and 2 would be the experimental and control groups described previously. Groups 3 and 4 would be like the experimental and control groups, except that neither Group 3 nor Group 4 would receive the pretreatment questionnaire. The design could be outlined as

R	Group 1	Pretest	Treatment	Posttest
R	Group 2	Pretest		Posttest
R	Group 3		Treatment	Posttest
R	Group 4			Posttest

By using the *Solomon four-group design,* researchers can determine not only the effects of the treatment but also the interaction of the treatment with the presence or absence of a pretest. One can also use this design to determine the effects of maturation and history by comparing the posttest results of Group 4 with the pretest results of Groups 1 and 2.

The three designs presented in this section (posttest-only, pretest–posttest, and Solomon four-group) are considered by Campbell and Stanley (1963) to be examples of experimental designs that lead to a *true experiment.* According to Campbell and Stanley, a true experiment includes at least three characteristics and sometimes a fourth.

The first characteristic is that participants are assigned randomly to groups, such that a given participant is equally likely to be assigned to any of the groups. As we already mentioned, there are a number of procedures for accomplishing this goal, including the use of a random number table. In certain cases you may want to equate the participants before they are randomly assigned to groups. A simple procedure after the equating has been done is to flip a coin and allow the heads or tails to determine in which group the first participant of the pair is placed.

The second characteristic of a true experiment is that there are at least two levels of the independent variable. One level can be zero, as in the Bransford and Johnson study cited in Chapter 7; that is, not presenting one group with the picture is the same as presenting a zero level of the independent variable.

The third characteristic of a true experiment is that it controls for the major threats to internal validity (discussed in Chapter 7), such as history and selection.

Sometimes a fourth, theoretical characteristic is included. Although all researchers do not agree on it, this characteristic requires that a true experiment compare two alternative theoretical positions. We introduced you to this idea in Chapter 3, with Platt's discussion of strong inference. We used the example of falling weights lending support to either Galileo's theory or Aristotle's theory. This example illustrates the fourth criterion.

In this section we presented the most ideal cases of experimental design. Specifically, we presented three designs that can lead to true experiments and reduce the threats to internal validity. However, a general point must be made, which we continue to develop throughout this book: Research designs are created in response to the needs of researchers as they attempt to answer specific questions and rule out alternative explanations. This being the case, designs are not sacred in themselves but are valuable only insofar as they allow us to make accurate interpretations of experimental results. Thus, an experimental design is never a replacement for an understanding of your research area. With such an understanding, it is important to create useful experimental designs that actually control for the factors involved. Although true experimental designs aid greatly in our search for understanding, they can never replace logic, common sense, and a thorough knowledge of our research area.

CONCEPT CHECK 8.2   Name one advantage of the pretest–posttest design over the posttest-only design.

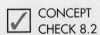

CONTROL AS RELATED TO THE LOGIC OF EXPERIMENTATION

In this section we want to pull together some of the themes related to the logic of experimentation. Figure 8.3 is a summary of the four conceptual steps in experimentation. Imagine an experiment in which participants are selected and then randomly assigned to one of two groups (steps 1 and 2 of Figure 8.3). The experiment is diagrammed as

$$R \quad \text{Group A} \quad T \quad M$$
$$R \quad \text{Group B} \quad \quad M$$

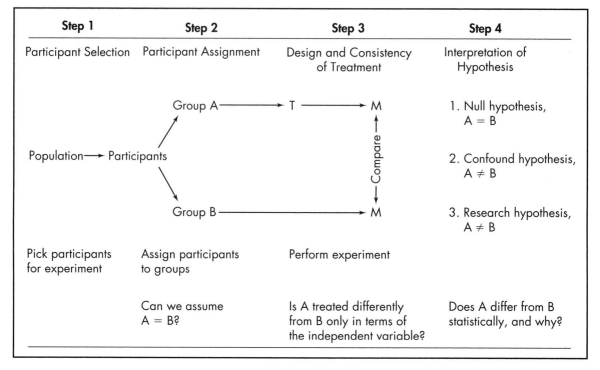

Step 1	Step 2	Step 3	Step 4
Participant Selection	Participant Assignment	Design and Consistency of Treatment	Interpretation of Hypothesis

Group A ⟶ T ⟶ M

Population ⟶ Participants

Group B ⟶ M

|Compare (vertical)

1. Null hypothesis, A = B

2. Confound hypothesis, A ≠ B

3. Research hypothesis, A ≠ B

| Pick participants for experiment | Assign participants to groups | Perform experiment | |
| | Can we assume A = B? | Is A treated differently from B only in terms of the independent variable? | Does A differ from B statistically, and why? |

Figure 8.3

The four conceptual steps in experimentation

To help us to determine logically the effect of the independent variable on the dependent variable, we must first ask whether Group A is equal to Group B before any treatment (independent variable) is introduced. We can assume that this is the case if we have randomly assigned participants to these two groups. The *F* ratio conceptually would equal approximately 1 at this point (assuming that we have a measure of the dependent variable in each group). If the two groups are chosen to be equal, then we can assume that there are no systematic effects on one group compared with the other *before* the independent variable is introduced. There should only be variations due to chance. As you remember, between-groups variance is influenced by differences between the groups as well as by chance variation; within-groups variance is influenced mainly by chance variation. The *F* ratio is

$$F = \frac{\text{between-groups variance}}{\text{within-groups variance}} = \text{approximately } 1 = \frac{\text{treatment effect} + \text{error}}{\text{error}}$$

If, for some reason, the two groups were unequal at the beginning of the experiment, then the *F* ratio would be greater than 1 *before* the independent variable is ever introduced. In this situation we might find ourselves rejecting the null hypothesis (Group A = Group B) and drawing an inappropriate conclusion. Thus, for the logic of experimentation to be valid, it is imperative that we control the participant assignment to the groups. The best method for ensuring that the participant groups are equal is through the random assignment of participants to groups. This is especially true when our design lacks a pretest measure from which our assumption of equal groups can be verified.

Having selected the participants and assigned them to groups, we proceed to step 3 of Figure 8.3: introducing the independent variable. In relation to the logic of experimentation, the main question that we ask here is, "Are the different levels of the independent variable the *only* way in which Group A is treated differently from Group B?" If the answer is no, then we face a possible confound, which makes interpretation of the data difficult, if not impossible. Thus, we must be able to control the experimental situation at step 3, or the logic of our experimental design falls apart. Statistics cannot help us at this point because any systematic change in Group A as compared with Group B because of either the independent variable or a confound will increase the between-groups variance, and it may cause us to erroneously reject the null hypothesis.

If an extraneous variable affects *both* Group A and Group B, then the within-groups variance is increased, thus making it more difficult to reject the null hypothesis and to see the effect of the independent variable on the dependent variable. For example, if a study with an independent variable that provoked anxiety was performed at the same time that college students (both men and women) were being called into the army on short notice, some students (those who could be drafted) might show higher anxiety scores, which would lead to greater variability than normal, making it more difficult to see changes related to the independent variable. As pointed out earlier, the more variability in an experiment, the greater the within-groups variance. However, if we treat all our participants the same and every participant is exposed to exactly the same experimental situation, then the within-groups variance is minimized. The simple rule is that the more consistently participants are treated in every way, the less the within-groups variance will be.

A simple rule for internal validity is to achieve as much control as possible over the experimental situation and to use this control to make the experiment as similar as possible for all participants. The first type of control that we exercise at step 3 is the control gained by a good experimental design. A design with sound structure helps us to rule out possible confounds or threats to internal validity. The second type of control that we exercise at this point is consistent treatment of our participants. Consistency of treatment helps us to reduce needless variation.

Step 4 in Figure 8.3 represents the interpretation of our experimental results. We discussed this in detail in Chapter 7. If we have achieved control in steps 1–3 of our experiment, then interpretation of the experimental results becomes an easy task. That is, once we have controlled group differences by randomly assigning participants and have controlled confounds by designing good experiments and minimizing needless variability among participants, we can assume that our results are due to the independent variable.

CONCEPT CHECK 8.3   Using Figure 8.3, describe the main consideration at each of the four stages of experimentation.

KEY TERMS AND CONCEPTS

1. **Participant assignment**
   A. Equating
   B. Counterbalancing
   C. Random assignment
2. **Participant selection**
3. **Random number table**
4. **Difference between random sampling and random assignment**
5. **Experimental designs**
   A. Posttest-only

   B. Pretest–posttest
   C. Solomon four-group
6. **True experiments**
   A. Participants randomly assigned
   B. At least two levels of independent variables
   C. Controls for major threats to internal validity
7. **Control as related to the logic of experimentation and the *F* ratio**

SUMMARY

1. Controlling the experimental situation is an important way that the researcher can make more accurate inferences about how the independent variable influences the dependent variable.
2. There are a variety of methods for equating groups to ensure that differences in an experiment are not a result of biased participant assignment. Three of these are equating, counterbalancing, and randomization.
3. Two terms sometimes confused are *random sampling* and *random assignment*. Random sampling is the selection of participants from a larger population. Random assignment is the assignment of selected participants to a particular group in an experiment.
4. Strong experimental designs help to rule out alternative factors that may account for the results in an experiment. Although no design is perfect, the

posttest-only design, the pretest–posttest design, and the Solomon four-group design help to rule out a number of potential threats to internal validity. Because of this ability, they are called true experimental designs by Campbell and Stanley (1963). Three characteristics (and sometimes a fourth) are seen as representative of a true experiment: (1) participants are randomly assigned to groups, (2) there are at least two levels of the independent variable, (3) the design can control for the major threats to internal validity, and (4) the experiment compares two alternative theoretical positions. (Some researchers do not require the fourth characteristic.) Figure 8.3 schematically presents the major steps in experimentation once the hypothesis has been developed. These are participant selection, participant assignment, experimental design, and the interpretation of the hypothesis.

REVIEW QUESTIONS

1. Describe a random number table and explain how it is used.
2. What are the disadvantages of using equating as an assignment procedure?
3. What is the difference between *random assignment* and *random sampling*?
4. What is the purpose of random assignment of participants to groups?

5. Diagram a posttest-only control group design.
6. What threats to internal validity does a Solomon four-group design control for?
7. Name three characteristics of a true experiment.
8. In terms of the null hypothesis, why is it important that all groups be equal at the beginning of the experiment?

DISCUSSION QUESTIONS AND PROJECTS

1. A university sets up a computer lab that students can use as they wish. At the end of the year, the administration decides to determine whether using the lab helps to increase a student's grade point average. To answer this question, the administration divides the students into two groups: those who have used the computer lab and those who have not. They determine the mean grade point averages of the two groups and conclude that using the computer results in a student's making better grades. Discuss this conclusion.

2. Assume another university was about to install a computer lab and asked you to help them design a study for determining its effect on grades. How might you design such a study?

3. If you could either randomly select participants or randomly assign participants to groups in an experiment, which would be the better procedure? What would be some of the problems in the interpretation of the data in each case?

4. How might one determine on what factors participants need to be equated? Give an example of a situation in which equating might offer an advantage over randomization. What would be some of the problems in making inferences from such a study?

5. A large corporation wants to develop a long-term project to test a series of leadership training courses that it is designing. These training courses are to be offered after work for low-level employees. The courses are to be run on a volunteer basis, and the workers will not be paid for staying late to attend. To evaluate the effectiveness of the courses at the conclusion of 5 and 10 years, the corporation decides that the measure of effectiveness will be how many of the employees who took the course had assumed levels of leadership in comparison to those who did not take the course. Discuss this design. Assume that, after 10 years, it is found that those who took the leadership course were in higher positions of leadership than those who did not. The corporation concludes that the leadership course produced leaders. Comment on this conclusion.

INFOTRAC COLLEGE EDITION: EXERCISES

This chapter discussed control as an important aspect of the experimental method in order to prevent biased results. Using InfoTrac College Edition, you can read research articles to determine how control is achieved. Search for the words "pretest posttest control group design" to see how other researchers have used this design. (*Hint:* Limit the search to looking for these words in the title, citation, and abstract and limit the search to peer-reviewed journals.)

You can discover how David Johnson and his colleagues used a pretest–posttest control group design in a study entitled "The effects of conflict resolution training on middle school students," published in February 1997, or how a study published in 2004 titled "Addressing stress with social work students: a controlled evaluation" sought to determine if providing a seminar on handling stressful situations would change the responses of those students who received the seminar as compared to those who did not receive it.

You can also search for the Solomon four-group design. For example, John Spence and Chris Blanchard, in a 2001 study titled "Effect of pretesting on feeling states and self-efficacy in acute exercise," used the Solomon four-group design to control for pretest effects.

To help you better understand the material in this chapter, you can go to Wadsworth's research methods workshop web page at http://www.wadsworth.com/psychology_d/templates/student_resources/workshops/resch_wrk.html. There you will find workshops related to research methods and statistics. The research methods workshop on "Controls" extends the material presented in this chapter.

 ☑ Answers to Concept Checks

8.1 You might respond by saying that although it is important to select participants randomly, it is also important to assign them randomly to groups. In the breakfast study, there may have been preexisting reasons why people did not eat breakfast, such as feeling sick in the morning, which would have differentially influenced the results. That is, people who did not eat breakfast may have been sicker before the experiment began.

(continued)

☑ Answers to Concept Checks *(continued)*

8.2 One of the major advantages is that it is possible to accurately measure the changes (from pretest to posttest) that the treatment had. It is also possible to see whether there were changes (between pretest and posttest) in the no-treatment condition that can further help to evaluate the changes in the treatment condition.

8.3 At step 1 we want to select participants randomly in such a way that our population under study is well represented. At step 2 we want to assign participants randomly to Groups A and B in such a way that we can assume Group A equals Group B before the experiment begins. At step 3 we want to perform the experiment in such a way that the only difference between Groups A and B is that Group A receives the experimental treatment. Finally, at step 4 we ask whether the two groups differ statistically (null hypothesis) and, if they do, whether this difference results from our research hypothesis or from some confound.

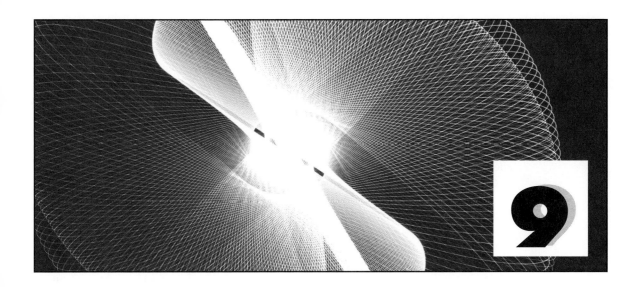

APPLYING THE LOGIC OF EXPERIMENTATION: BETWEEN-SUBJECTS DESIGNS

BETWEEN-SUBJECTS DESIGN TERMINOLOGY

COMPLETELY RANDOMIZED DESIGN

MULTILEVEL COMPLETELY RANDOMIZED DESIGNS

FACTORIAL DESIGN

FACTORIAL DESIGNS: THE LOGIC OF EXPERIMENTATION AND THE INTERACTION EFFECT

EIGHT POSSIBLE OUTCOMES OF 2 × 2 FACTORIAL EXPERIMENTS

INTERPRETATION OF SUBJECT VARIABLES WITH FACTORIAL DESIGNS

ADVANTAGES OF FACTORIAL DESIGNS

In Chapter 8 we emphasized the importance of control in experimentation and presented concepts underlying the design of experiments. We also introduced the idea of the true experiment and its advantages in helping us to infer causation. Specifically, we presented the blueprints for three designs that give a large degree of control over the experimental situation. In this manner potential confounds are reduced, thus limiting the threats to the internal validity of experiments. We want to build on that discussion in this chapter. By using more than two levels of the independent variable, we show how the potential usefulness of experimental designs can be increased. We also introduce designs that examine the effects of more than one independent variable on the dependent variable; these are called factorial designs.

From the onset of this discussion, it is important to remember that no design is perfect. Each design has its own strengths and weaknesses in relation to the specific scientific questions being asked. Part of your task as a scientist is to learn which designs are best suited to which types of questions and how existing designs may be modified to answer future questions. Whenever possible we will make specific suggestions about the appropriateness of designs and point out potential problems with certain designs. However, without an exploration of the specific context in which a given design is to be used, it is impossible to evaluate fully its appropriateness.

BETWEEN-SUBJECTS DESIGN TERMINOLOGY

Between-subjects designs are a general class of designs in which different research participants are used in each group. To be more precise, these designs involve comparisons *between* different groups of participants. In the illustrations of research presented thus far in this book, we have emphasized between-subjects designs. For example, the cereal experiment presented in Chapter 2 compared the weight gained by a group of children who ate cereal with that gained by a group that did not. The true experimental designs presented in Chapter 8 are also between-subjects designs. One characteristic of the between-subjects design is that any given participant receives only one level of the independent variable. Another characteristic is that only one score for each participant is used in the analysis of the results. Although the children in the cereal experiment were weighed more than once (before and after the treatment), the comparison between groups was based on the differences between these two measurements; a single score reflected the amount of weight gained.

The alternative to between-subjects designs is within-subjects designs. These present different levels of the independent variable to the same group of participants. For example, we could use a within-subjects design to determine the value of feedback in shooting baskets by having participants shoot baskets blindfolded (no feedback or zero level of feedback) and then without the blindfold (high level of feedback). In this case each participant would receive both levels of the independent variable and would have more than one measure of the dependent variable. We examine these designs in much greater detail in Chapter 10.

COMPLETELY RANDOMIZED DESIGN

One of the simplest between-subjects designs is the **completely randomized design,** which is also called the *simple randomized design* or the *simple random subject design.* In this type of design, the assignment of participants is completely randomized between groups. In its simplest form, it is composed of two levels of the independent variable. In Chapter 8 we used the following type of diagram:

R	Group A	*T* (high level)	*M*
R	Group B	*T* (zero level)	*M*

As you remember from that chapter, Group A received a high level of the independent variable, and Group B received a zero level. Let's quickly go through the procedure for using this design. Assume that we have already chosen 50 participants for our experiment, for two groups of 25 each. The next task is to assign randomly 25 participants to Group A and 25 to Group B. As mentioned earlier, this may be accomplished in several ways (for example, with a random number table), with the outcome being that every participant is as equally likely to be placed in Group A as in Group B. This process of randomization initially equates our two groups, and it enables us ultimately to infer that the independent variable influenced the dependent variable. The next task prescribed by the design is for Group A to receive a high level of the independent variable and Group B to receive a zero level. The task then is the measurement of the dependent variable for each group. Finally, the dependent variable is compared between the two groups; this comparison gives us our treatment effect.

MULTILEVEL COMPLETELY RANDOMIZED DESIGNS

The completely randomized design can contain more than two levels of the independent variable. Such a design is called a *multilevel completely randomized design* and can be diagrammed as

R	Group A	Level 1	*T*	*M*
R	Group B	Level 2	*T*	*M*
R	Group C	Level 3	*T*	*M*
R	Group D	Level 4	*T*	*M*

As an example of a completely randomized design with four levels of the independent variable, consider a study of the effects of drinking coffee on the performance of airplane pilots. Participants in four groups would be given a prescribed number of cups of coffee and then tested in a laboratory equipped with a flight simulator. The number of errors made by the participants in each group would be the dependent variable. In this hypothetical example, Level 4 could equal 6 cups of coffee, Level 3 could equal 4 cups, Level 2 could equal 2 cups, and Level 1 could equal 0 cups. If you actually were to run this study, you would of course need to consider a number of possible confounds (for example, the amount of liquid consumed is not equal in the four groups), so you might design the actual study differently.

In Chapter 7 we presented the Bransford and Johnson (1972) study in a simple two-group form, with one group seeing the entire picture before hearing the passage and the other group seeing no picture. That was an incomplete description of the study. In the actual study, there were five groups; the study thus was based on a multilevel completely randomized design. In addition to the two groups described previously, Bransford and Johnson included three other groups. As you remember, the independent variable was the amount of context (prior knowledge), with the appropriate picture representing total context. Group 1 saw this picture before hearing the passage. Group 2 also saw a picture before hearing the passage, but the picture presented to Group 2 represented only a partial context for the passage, although the individual components were the same as those presented to Group 1 (Figure 9.1). The third group was presented with a zero level of the independent variable and saw no picture before hearing the passage. There were also fourth and fifth groups that served as controls. Group 4 saw the picture representing the total context but not until after the passage had been heard. Group 5 heard the passage twice but did not see the picture.

Another illustration of a between-subjects design comes from clinical research. Strupp and Hadley (1979) asked how important technical skills are for the therapist in the process of psychotherapy; that is, does a professional psychotherapist learn certain skills or techniques that are required for a successful outcome in psychotherapy? To answer this question, these researchers compared the psychological improvement of clients seeing experienced psychotherapists with that of clients seeing college professors chosen for their ability to form good human relationships. Notice how Strupp and Hadley were attempting to control for the relationship factor in their study. In essence, they were asking whether something more than a good relationship is needed for successful psychotherapy to take place.

For research participants in the study, they used college students who requested therapy and who scored high on certain scales of a traditional psychological test (the Minnesota Multiphasic Personality Inventory). On the basis of traditional diagnostic systems, the research participants were classified as having neurotic depression or an anxiety reaction. The design of the study called for students to be assigned randomly to one of three groups. Group 1 was treated by experienced psychotherapists, Group 2 talked with college professors chosen for their ability to form good relationships, and Group 3, called a *minimal treatment group,* was told that treatment would be delayed. Group 3 thus served as a no-treatment control during the time the first two groups received therapy. The design of the study was

R	Group 1	M	T (experienced therapist: therapy skills plus good relationship)	M
R	Group 2	M	T (college professor: good relationship)	M
R	Group 3	M	T (waiting list no treatment)	M

As you can see, this is a multilevel completely randomized design with pretest–posttest measures. In the actual study, a number of dependent variables were measured. These included changes in psychological tests and ratings of change by the therapists, students, and outside clinicians. Strupp and Hadley thus were able to assess changes over time. This study is a good example of how to perform clinical research, and it illustrates some factors

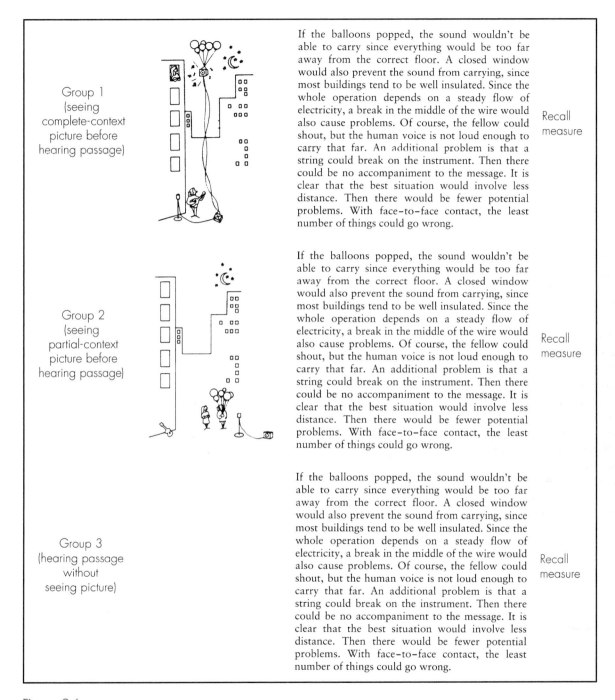

Group 1
(seeing
complete-context
picture before
hearing passage)

If the balloons popped, the sound wouldn't be able to carry since everything would be too far away from the correct floor. A closed window would also prevent the sound from carrying, since most buildings tend to be well insulated. Since the whole operation depends on a steady flow of electricity, a break in the middle of the wire would also cause problems. Of course, the fellow could shout, but the human voice is not loud enough to carry that far. An additional problem is that a string could break on the instrument. Then there could be no accompaniment to the message. It is clear that the best situation would involve less distance. Then there would be fewer potential problems. With face-to-face contact, the least number of things could go wrong.

Recall measure

Group 2
(seeing
partial-context
picture before
hearing passage)

If the balloons popped, the sound wouldn't be able to carry since everything would be too far away from the correct floor. A closed window would also prevent the sound from carrying, since most buildings tend to be well insulated. Since the whole operation depends on a steady flow of electricity, a break in the middle of the wire would also cause problems. Of course, the fellow could shout, but the human voice is not loud enough to carry that far. An additional problem is that a string could break on the instrument. Then there could be no accompaniment to the message. It is clear that the best situation would involve less distance. Then there would be fewer potential problems. With face-to-face contact, the least number of things could go wrong.

Recall measure

Group 3
(hearing passage
without
seeing picture)

If the balloons popped, the sound wouldn't be able to carry since everything would be too far away from the correct floor. A closed window would also prevent the sound from carrying, since most buildings tend to be well insulated. Since the whole operation depends on a steady flow of electricity, a break in the middle of the wire would also cause problems. Of course, the fellow could shout, but the human voice is not loud enough to carry that far. An additional problem is that a string could break on the instrument. Then there could be no accompaniment to the message. It is clear that the best situation would involve less distance. Then there would be fewer potential problems. With face-to-face contact, the least number of things could go wrong.

Recall measure

Figure 9.1

Pictorial representation of the Bransford and Johnson (1972) study

Source: Bransford, J. D., & Johnson, M. K. (1972). Contextual prerequisites for understanding: Some investigations of comprehension and recall. *Journal of Verbal Learning and Verbal Behavior, 11,* 717–726.

Group 4 (seeing complete-context picture after hearing passage)

If the balloons popped, the sound wouldn't be able to carry since everything would be too far away from the correct floor. A closed window would also prevent the sound from carrying, since most buildings tend to be well insulated. Since the whole operation depends on a steady flow of electricity, a break in the middle of the wire would also cause problems. Of course, the fellow could shout, but the human voice is not loud enough to carry that far. An additional problem is that a string could break on the instrument. Then there could be no accompaniment to the message. It is clear that the best situation would involve less distance. Then there would be fewer potential problems. With face-to-face contact, the least number of things could go wrong.

Recall measure

Group 5 (hearing passage twice)

If the balloons popped, the sound wouldn't be able to carry since everything would be too far away from the correct floor. A closed window would also prevent the sound from carrying, since most buildings tend to be well insulated. Since the whole operation depends on a steady flow of electricity, a break in the middle of the wire would also cause problems. Of course, the fellow could shout, but the human voice is not loud enough to carry that far. An additional problem is that a string could break on the instrument. Then there could be no accompaniment to the message. It is clear that the best situation would involve less distance. Then there would be fewer potential problems. With face-to-face contact, the least number of things could go wrong.

If the balloons popped, the sound wouldn't be able to carry since everything would be too far away from the correct floor. A closed window would also prevent the sound from carrying, since most buildings tend to be well insulated. Since the whole operation depends on a steady flow of electricity, a break in the middle of the wire would also cause problems. Of course, the fellow could shout, but the human voice is not loud enough to carry that far. An additional problem is that a string could break on the instrument. Then there could be no accompaniment to the message. It is clear that the best situation would involve less distance. Then there would be fewer potential problems. With face-to-face contact, the least number of things could go wrong.

Recall measure

Figure 9.1

(*Continued*)

that must be controlled to achieve a scientific understanding of such clinical processes as psychotherapy.

Let's turn to the logic of hypothesis testing as it is related to multilevel between-subjects designs. As with the simple two-level completely randomized experiments presented earlier in the book, we still must answer three questions: (1) Are the results due to chance? (2) Are the results due to a confound? (3) Are the results due to the independent variable? The first question is approached through a statistical test of the null hypothesis, which states that no differences exist between the groups. Thus, the null hypothesis for a three-level design states that Group 1 = Group 2 = Group 3. Again, we evaluate this through the F ratio. If the F ratio is statistically significant, then we know there is a difference between the groups; however, we do not know which group or groups caused this difference.

To determine whether there is a statistically significant difference between any combinations of groups, we must use a **post hoc test** that compares each group to another in a pairwise manner. A variety of post hoc tests, such as the Newman-Keuls procedure or Tukey's HSD post hoc test, can be found in the standard statistical computer packages. Performing a post hoc test is similar to performing a t test between Group 1 and Group 2, and then a t test between Group 2 and Group 3, and then a t test between Group 1 and Group 3. As you read advanced statistics books describing these tests (for example, Ramsey & Schafer, 2002; Winer, 1971), you will see that the number of tests that you do influences the probability of significant results and must be included in your analysis. That is to say, if you perform a large number of post hoc tests, you would expect more of them to be significant by chance than if you performed only a few tests, and this needs to be taken into account when you perform the statistics. Technically, this is referred to as *familywise error rates*. The error is the possibility of a Type I error as discussed previously, which can result from performing multiple tests that can lead us to reject the null hypothesis when it is true.

The alternative to using post hoc tests is to plan particular comparisons *before* the study is performed. Planned comparisons do not take advantage of chance in the same way as post hoc comparisons. Planned comparisons are called **a priori tests.** This is the statistical approach Bransford and Johnson took. They compared the "context before" condition (Group 1 in Figure 9.1) with each of the four other conditions. (For this comparison, they used something called *Dunnett's test,* which is beyond the scope of this book.)

The most common way to analyze a completely randomized design is to use a single-factor analysis of variance (ANOVA). In this case the null hypothesis would state that each research participant group was drawn from the same population, and thus the effects of the conditions would not be different from one another. If we did reject the null hypothesis and found that one or more groups differed significantly, we would then need to apply post hoc tests and compare the differences between the groups taken as pairs. In the hypothetical study of the effects of drinking coffee on airplane pilots, we would want to know not only whether the groups as a whole statistically differ from one another but also which particular groups differ from which other groups. After doing such a post hoc analysis, we might find that 6 cups of coffee cause different results from 0 cups of coffee but do not cause any statistical differences compared with 2 or 4 cups of coffee.

After you have rejected the null hypothesis, you turn to the question concerning confounds and use the logic presented in Chapter 7 to track down factors that might have played a role in the results. As you can see, if we could not assume that our groups were equal before we began the treatment, it would be impossible to conclude what effect, if any, the independent variable had on the dependent variable. Even if you do not read the random number table every night before you go to bed, we hope you have come to understand the extreme importance of the random assignment of research participants to your groups in an experiment. When we are reasonably sure that no significant confounds are present in our study, we can consider the third question concerning the independent variable. If we reject the null hypothesis and rule out confounds, then we may conclude that the independent variable influenced our results, and we may interpret this relationship theoretically.

 CONCEPT CHECK 9.1   Students told a professor that they learned foreign language words best in the morning after drinking coffee. To test this possibility, one morning in class, the professor gave students foreign words to learn and tested them on these words. The professor then asked the students whether they had drunk coffee that morning. At this point, the professor compared the scores of words learned by the two groups (drank coffee versus did not drink coffee). Can you think of a better way to perform this study?

FACTORIAL DESIGN

An early survey of published psychological research reported that most research using inferential statistics relied on more complex designs, such as **factorial designs** (Edgington, 1974), and this remains true today. The popularity of factorial designs seems related to our acceptance of the fact that there are few, if any, isolated cause-and-effect relationships in psychological processing. Rather, most psychological processes have several causes that interact with each other in various ways and cannot be determined from simple experimental designs such as those we have discussed thus far. The advantage of factorial designs is that they allow us to examine scientifically the effects of more than one independent variable, both individually and collectively, on the dependent variable.

An easy way to conceptualize factorial designs is to view them as a composite of several simple completely randomized designs, such as those we have discussed previously. Let's illustrate this point. Consider a completely randomized design to determine the effect of money on memory in psychological experiments. A simple design would be to randomly assign research participants to two groups. Each group would hear the same passage. The participants in one group would receive 1¢ for every idea remembered, and those in the other group would receive $1 for every idea remembered. This would be diagrammed as

R   Group 1   T (1¢)   M (recall task)
R   Group 2   T ($1)   M (recall task)

Now consider a second completely randomized design such as the two-treatment version of Bransford and Johnson's study presented in Chapter 7. We described this study as consisting of a zero level of the independent variable (no picture) and a high level of the independent variable (complete-context picture). This single-factor experiment can be diagrammed as

| R | Group 1 | T (picture: high context) | M (recall task) |
| R | Group 2 | T (no picture: zero context) | M (recall task) |

We could perform these two studies separately; however, then we could not determine the collective effect of both independent variables (money and context) on the dependent variable. Let's see how we might go about combining these two separate studies into one experiment.

An alternative to performing these studies separately would be to combine them into a factorial design. For ease of representation, let's diagram the first experiment in a horizontal fashion as

Money

Level 1 (1¢)	Level 2 ($1)
Group 1	Group 2

Likewise, we can diagram the second experiment in a vertical fashion:

Prior Knowledge

Level 1 (no picture)	Group 1
Level 2 (picture)	Group 2

Now, if we simply combine our graphic representations of these two studies, the diagram appears as

Money Factor

	Level 1 (1¢)	Level 2 ($1)
Prior Knowledge Factor — Level 1 (no picture)	Group A	Group C
Prior Knowledge Factor — Level 2 (picture)	Group B	Group D

Notice that with this design we have four separate groups, with each participant receiving a specified level of *each* independent variable. Group A will receive 1¢ for each correct idea recalled and will be given the minimum context: no prior knowledge (that is, no picture). Group B will be given 1¢ for each correct idea recalled and will be given the maximum context or prior knowledge (the picture). Group C will receive $1 for each idea recalled and minimum context (no picture). Group D will receive $1 for each idea recalled and maximum context (the picture).

This type of design is called a 2 × 2 (read "two by two") factorial design. In this notation, 2 × 2 refers to the two levels of one independent variable and two levels of another. The independent variables are also called *factors*. If we had a design involving six levels of Factor A and two levels of Factor B, then it would be called a 6 × 2 factorial design. Similarly, a design that consisted of two levels of Factor A, three levels of Factor B, and four levels of Factor C would be called a 2 × 3 × 4 factorial design. To summarize, in this notation, each factor represents a different independent variable. Thus, 2 × 3 would represent two different independent variables with the first having two levels and the second having three levels.

The treatment differences (between levels of a given factor) in a factorial design are called **main effects.** It is possible to determine the main effect for each factor. In our previous example, this would be equivalent to performing two single-factor experiments; one would compare the amounts of money given for recall, and one would compare the levels of pictorial context. However, in factorial designs the independent variables may combine in various ways in their effects on the dependent variable. Such a combined effect is called an **interaction effect.** Interaction effects cannot be determined by performing separate single-factor studies and thus are unique to factorial designs.

An interaction effect is the result of two independent variables combining to produce a result different from that produced by either variable alone. An interaction effect occurs when the effect of one independent variable depends on the level of another independent variable. For example, an interaction would be present if the two independent variables had a greater influence in combination than would be expected from adding the main effects of each variable together.

To illustrate, imagine a study measuring physiological reactivity (such as an increase in blood pressure) with one independent variable being that of social role (whether or not one were required to be a leader) and the other independent variable being stability of situation (whether the social environment was stable or always changing). In this study an interaction might appear such that social role had a greater influence when there was an unstable environmental situation.

To create a more extreme example, on a biological level we might find that two drugs in combination (for example, alcohol and a barbiturate) would create a greater effect (illness or even death) than would be expected from statistically adding the main effect of alcohol and the main effect of the barbiturate. Thus, it is only in combination that the interaction effect is produced.

This is only one type of interaction. We present other possible interaction effects later in this chapter. We should note that there has been some debate concerning how interaction effects should be presented (for example, Petty, Fabrigar, Wegener, & Priester, 1996; Rosnow & Rosenthal, 1995, 1996). Rosnow and Rosenthal (1995, 1996) note that statistically the interaction represents the residuals remaining after the influence of the main effects have been removed and suggest that interactions be presented in this manner. However, most research journals present interactions in terms of cell means, which include both the influence of the main effect and the interactions, and we follow this convention.

Before we leave the question of terminology, let's look at schematic diagrams of three different factorial designs (Figure 9.2). The blocks in the diagram are called cells. Notice

Figure 9.2

Schematic representation of 2 × 2, 3 × 3, and 2 × 3 × 2 factorial designs. Note that the total number of treatment conditions in each design can be obtained by multiplying the number of levels of each factor.

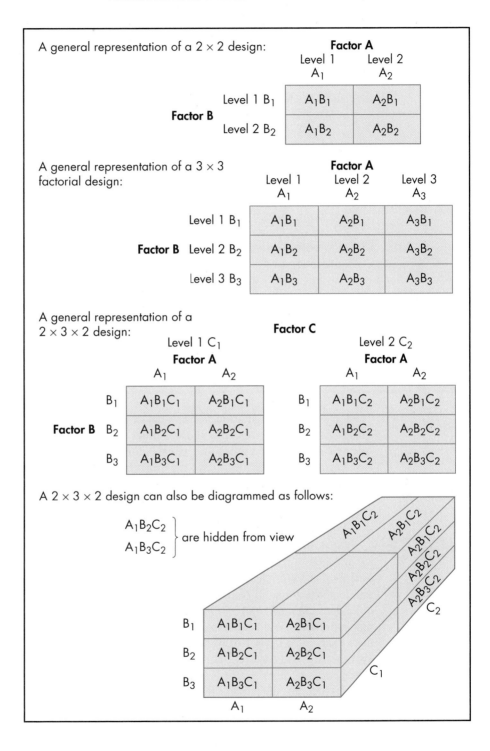

that the individual cells are labeled according to the level of each independent variable that affects the cell. For example, the group of research participants that receives Level 1 of Factor A and Level 2 of Factor B is labeled A1B2. Remember that in between-subjects designs, which we are discussing here, each cell represents a different group of research participants that has been randomly assigned to that cell.

CONCEPT CHECK 9.2   Recall Concept Check 9.1, in which students told a professor that they learned foreign language words best in the morning after drinking coffee. Having thought more about the study, the professor randomly assigned students to one of four groups. These groups included (1) learn words in the morning and drink 2 cups of coffee, (2) learn words in the afternoon and drink 2 cups of coffee, (3) learn words in the morning and drink no coffee, and (4) learn words in the afternoon and drink no coffee. Diagram and describe this study as a factorial design, noting the independent and dependent variables.

FACTORIAL DESIGNS: THE LOGIC OF EXPERIMENTATION AND THE INTERACTION EFFECT

The logic of experimentation for factorial designs is similar to that already described for single-factor experiments. As with these other experiments, in factorial designs we must be able to assume that the groups are equal before any of the treatments are presented. Once we can make this assumption, we may turn to an evaluation of our hypotheses. As with other designs, we seek the role of chance, confounds, and the independent variable in the results of our experiment. Because a factorial design involves the simultaneous evaluation of two or more factors and their interactions, the evaluation process is more involved than in a single-factor design.

For example, in a factorial design there are many null hypotheses, one for each factor of our design. As in a simple design, these null hypotheses state that the effects of the treatment at a given level are equal to those at every other level. In our 2×2 example, one null hypothesis would concern the main effect of Factor A. It would state that the effect of the treatment of Level 1 of Factor A is the same as that of Level 2 of Factor A. A second null hypothesis would concern the main effect of Factor B. It would state that the effect of the treatment of Level 1 of Factor B would equal that of Level 2 of Factor B. A third null hypothesis is also required. This null hypothesis would state that there are no interaction effects.

It is theoretically possible for any combination of these three null hypotheses in a 2×2 design to be accepted or rejected. Once we have made this determination, we can then continue to look for confounds, and eventually we can conclude what effects, if any, the independent variables have on the dependent variable. With more than one independent variable, the logic of searching for confounds is similar to that of the single-factor study, although the complexity is greater.

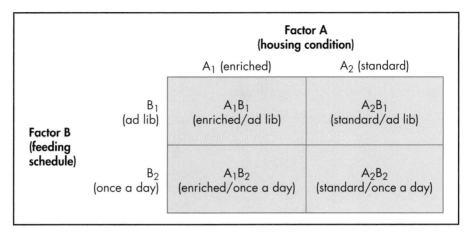

Figure 9.3

Matrix showing the four possible combinations of each of the two levels of a 2 × 2 factorial random-subject design. Notice that each cell contains one of the four possible combinations of our two independent variables (housing condition and feeding schedule).

Let's continue to illustrate factorial designs and their evaluation with a hypothetical experiment. In this experiment we want to study two factors and their effects on the learning ability of old mice (see Warren, Zerweck, & Anthony, 1982, for an actual study in this area). The dependent variable will be the number of errors in running a maze. One factor is whether the mice live in an enriched environment, with other mice and many playthings, or live alone in a standard laboratory cage. The second factor is the feeding schedule of these old mice. More specifically, we want to determine whether unlimited access to food and water (called an *ad libitum,* or *ad lib schedule*) affects these mice differently from a feeding of enough food once a day to maintain normal body weight. In our tentative design, we have designated the living environment as Factor A (with A_1 = enriched housing, A_2 = standard housing), and the feeding schedule as Factor B (with B_1 = ad lib, B_2 = once a day). Consequently, in this design there are four possible combinations of the two independent variables: A_1B_1, A_2B_1, A_1B_2, and A_2B_2. The matrix in Figure 9.3 represents this particular design. Each cell of the matrix contains one of the four possible combinations of our two independent variables.

In executing such a factorial design, we would follow the procedure shown in Figure 9.4. We would first obtain, say, 40 mice to participate in our experiment. Our research subjects would then be randomly assigned to any one of these four possible combinations of independent variables until an equal number of participants were in each cell of the matrix. Next, the subjects in the upper left-hand cell would receive the first level of both independent variables, A and B (A_1B_1 = enriched housing/ad lib feeding). Consequently, their performance on our dependent measure (the number of errors in running a maze) would reflect a combined effect of enriched housing and ad lib feeding. The participants in the upper right-hand cell of the matrix would receive the second level of independent variable A and the first level of independent variable B (A_2B_1 = standard housing/ad lib feeding).

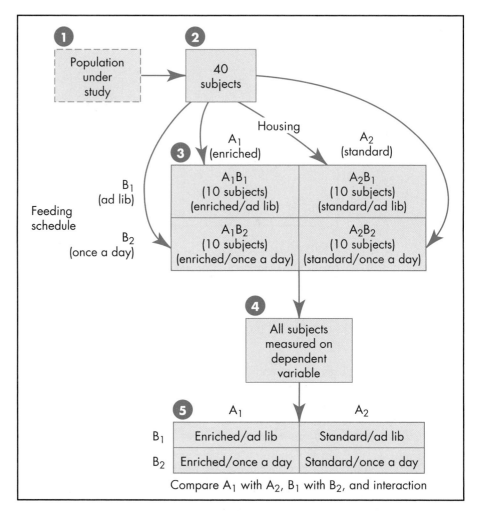

Figure 9.4

Schematic representation of the five steps involved in a factorial random-subject design involving two levels of each of two independent variables. (1) The entire group of 40 mice is obtained from a commercial animal supplier. (2) These 40 mice are randomly assigned to four groups of 10 each. (3) Each group is exposed to the appropriate level of each factor. (4) All subjects are measured on our dependent variable. (5) We determine whether the interaction effect and the main effects are statistically significant.

Their performance would reflect the influence of standard housing and ad lib feeding. The participants in the two lower cells would receive, respectively, the combinations A_1B_2 (enriched housing/fed once a day) and A_2B_2 (standard housing/fed once a day).

In analyzing the outcome of any factorial design, we are interested in two major questions. First, does either of our independent variables produce a statistically significant treatment effect? As mentioned earlier, in a factorial design we call the treatment effect of each

Table 9.1

Hypothetical Results of Maze-Running Experiment with 40 Old Mice			
	Type of Housing		
	Enriched	Standard	Row Mean
Ad lib feeding	6	21	
	4	23	
	8	22	
	5	22	
	7	24	
	7 $\bar{x} = 6$	20 $\bar{x} = 22$	14
	5	20	
	6	24	
	4	22	
	8	22	
Once-a-day feeding	13	14	
	15	14	
	15	13	
	13	15	
	18	12	
	16 $\bar{x} = 14$	16 $\bar{x} = 14$	14
	10	14	
	12	14	
	14	15	
	14	13	
Column mean	10	18	28

independent variable the *main effect* of that variable. In the preceding experiment, we have two independent variables: (1) type of housing and (2) type of feeding schedule. To determine the extent of the main effect of each independent variable, we compare the different performances at the two levels of each of our two independent variables. We calculate the performance on our dependent measure for each row and column of our matrix.

For example, Table 9.1 presents hypothetical data from 40 old mice tested on our dependent variable following a 6-month period of living under our two experimental conditions. To determine the main effect of the type of housing, we compare the mean score for all animals housed in the enriched condition with the mean score for all animals housed in standard cages (10 versus 18 errors; see Table 9.1). To determine the main effect of the type of feeding schedule, we compare the mean score for all animals who were fed ad lib with the mean score for all animals who were fed once a day (14 versus 14 errors; see Table 9.1). Just from glancing at these data, it appears that the type of housing had a definite effect on the final performance of the old mice on our dependent variable, whereas the type of feeding schedule apparently did not result in differences in performance. These data must be subjected to appropriate statistical tests before any final conclusions can be drawn regarding the null hypotheses.

With a factorial design, the second question we want to ask is, "As our two independent variables occur together, do they influence each other or do they remain independent of one another in their influence on the dependent variable?" The extent to which the impact of one independent variable on the dependent variable varies as a function of the level of the other independent variable in the experiment is called the *interaction effect*. To assess the interaction effects, we determine whether the difference between the means of the results pertaining to the two levels of one independent variable changes with the level of the other independent variable.

Consider the hypothetical data shown in Table 9.1 for the 40 mice tested on the learning task. As we pointed out, animals housed in the enriched environment learned the maze with fewer errors than animals housed in standard cages (10 versus 18 errors). In contrast, the type of feeding schedule did *not* have an effect on overall maze performance (14 versus 14 errors).

Although there was no overall difference in the mean number of errors for the mice on ad lib versus once-a-day feeding schedules, the performance of these mice was quite different depending on whether they lived in enriched or standard cages. More specifically, the animals fed once a day all performed about average regardless of housing (14 versus 14 errors). In contrast, the mean performance of the ad lib animals ranged from very good (only 6 errors) for the mice that lived in enriched housing to very poor (22 errors) for the mice that lived alone in standard cages. Thus, performance on the learning task showed a strong interaction effect. In this particular case, the ad lib animals were affected differentially by the type of housing, whereas animals fed once a day were affected uniformly by their living conditions.

Let's now turn to an example of an interaction from the research literature. This interaction occurred in an experiment dealing with intimacy, summarized by Rubin (1974). In this experiment the researchers wanted to know what effect the amount of perceived freedom or spontaneity has on both high or low levels of intimate behavior. To answer this question, they conducted a laboratory experiment involving written exchanges of self-disclosure statements between dating couples. The study relates to how you would respond if your boyfriend or girlfriend sent you a message (either very intimate or not very intimate) when you believed that the experimenter told him or her to write the message versus how you would respond when you believed that your boyfriend or girlfriend sent the message spontaneously. As you might predict, the return message (the message back from the boyfriend or girlfriend) was related both to the level of intimacy of the first message and to whether the person believed that the boyfriend or girlfriend had produced the message spontaneously or under the direction of the experimenter. See whether you can draw a graph to illustrate this interaction, making up your own numbers.

When interpreting the results of a factorial experiment, *always interpret the interaction effects first*. If there is an interaction effect, then the main effects cannot be discussed without a qualifier. If you consider the example of barbiturates and alcohol, you can see that an interaction effect makes it impossible to discuss the effects of either drug alone without qualifying the statement to include the interaction. That is, you can say that moderate drinking does not immediately lead to illness, but you should include the qualifier that this is true only when barbiturates are not taken simultaneously. To give another example, if you look at the data in Table 9.1, you can see that it would be inaccurate to conclude that type of housing is an important independent variable without qualifying the statement to say that this is true only if the feeding schedule is ad lib. Thus, the interaction effect must be interpreted before the main effects so that any necessary qualifiers can be added to a statement of the main effects.

Table 9.2

Analysis of Variance *F* Table for the Mouse Study					
Source of Variance	*df*	*SS*	*MS*	*F*	*p*
Housing (Factor A)	1	640	640	245.21	.001
Feeding (Factor B)	1	0	0	0	ns
A × B (interaction)	1	640	640	245.21	.001
Error (within groups variance)	36	94	2.61	—	—

Let's examine a table summarizing an ANOVA, such as we might see when reading a report of an experiment using a factorial design (Table 9.2). For our present purposes, we are concerned only that you know how to read such a table; it is not necessary that you understand the calculative procedures. In the first column, we see listed the sources of the variance. In a simple experiment, such as the cereal experiment described in Chapter 2, two sources would be listed in this column. The first would be the treatment variance as a result of eating cereal (between-groups variance), and the second would be the error variance (within-groups variance). In a factorial experiment, this column would list the treatment variance as a result of each independent variable and the interactions. The second column would list the degrees of freedom (*df*), discussed in Chapter 6. The third column would list the sum of the squares (*SS*). The fourth column would list the mean square (*MS*). *Mean square* is what we call a variance when it comes from the statistical analysis of variance. The fifth column would depict the *F* ratio, which, as we discussed, is the between-groups variance divided by the within-groups variance (error variance). In a factorial design, you must evaluate the treatment effect for each independent variable and for the interactions involved. Thus, you will have an *F* ratio for each main effect and interaction. The error term (within-groups variance) remains the same for each *F* ratio. Often there is an additional column listing the probability (*p*); "ns" indicates that it is nonsignificant. It is on the basis of this probability that we either accept or reject the null hypothesis (see Table 9.2).

Table 9.2 is the analysis of variance *F* table for the mouse study. On the basis of this table, we would reject the null hypothesis for Factor A (housing) and for the A × B interaction (the interaction of housing and feeding schedule). We would not reject the null hypothesis for Factor B (feeding schedule). It is rare in actual practice that we obtain an *F* ratio of less than 1, although it is possible in actual calculations, as was the case for Factor B (feeding schedule). After the null hypotheses have been evaluated for the interaction of A × B, the main effect of Factor A, and the main effect of Factor B, then conceptually one turns to the role of confounds and the independent variable in causing the results. (By the way, there is a possible confound in the mouse study that we just presented; see whether you can find it.)

Because factorial designs are used frequently in published reports, it is helpful to have some idea of how the main effects and interaction effects are manifested in data. With this goal in mind, the next section describes a hypothetical series of eight factorial experimental outcomes. In each case the outcome is depicted in two ways: numerically and graphically. Allow yourself several careful readings to get an understanding of the main effects and interaction effects.

CONCEPT
CHECK 9.3

Recall Concept Check 9.2 concerning learning foreign words, in which a professor randomly assigned students to one of four groups as follows: (1) learn words in the morning and drink 2 cups of coffee, (2) learn words in the afternoon and drink 2 cups of coffee, (3) learn words in the morning and drink no coffee, and (4) learn words in the afternoon and drink no coffee. What are main effects and interaction effects in this design, and what questions do we want to ask in order to evaluate these effects?

EIGHT POSSIBLE OUTCOMES OF 2 × 2 FACTORIAL EXPERIMENTS

The purpose of this section is to clarify the ideas of main effects and interactions in factorial designs. To achieve this goal, we will work directly with specific and hypothetical examples (Figures 9.5–9.12). First, we describe some actual examples of main effects and interactions from the research literature and then, using hypothetical data, present the eight possible outcomes of a 2 × 2 factorial experiment. We also plot the cell means. Let us begin with actual examples.

The first example involves eyewitness identification of suspects in videos of a mock crime. Stewart and McAllister (2001) examined the manner in which mug shots were presented to eyewitnesses and used the number of false positives (incorrectly identified the person) as the dependent variable. In one experimental condition, mug shots were presented one to a page whereas, in the other condition, pictures were presented 12 to a page. These two conditions made up the first factor. The second factor was picture arrangement in that the mug books were either arranged by how similar the person in the picture looked to the perpetrator or the pictures were randomly arranged in the book. Thus, the first factor was grouping (1 versus 12 to a page) and the second was picture arrangement (similar versus random). If you were to look up this article in the *Journal of Applied Psychology,* you would see their first graph similar to that of Figure 9.12 (page 222) (A_1 = random presentation, A_2 = grouped by similarity, B_1 = 12 to a page, B_2 = 1 to a page). They found that when the pictures were arranged by similarity more false positives were present when the pictures were presented one at a time as compared to 12 on a page. There was no difference in false positives when the pictures were randomly arranged.

The next example involves a series of experiments reported in the *Journal of Experimental Psychology: Learning, Memory and Cognition,* in which Fendrich, Healy, and Bourne (1991) studied long-term repetition effects. As part of the research, participants were asked on a number of days to enter a list of three-digit numbers using a computer keypad. On a separate day, participants were asked to rate whether the list that they were entering was a new list or one that they had seen previously. Participants were also asked to rate how certain they were of their rating. In terms of speed of entry into the computer, a significant 2 × 2 interaction was found for list type (old, new) by recognition rating (correctly identifying the list, incorrectly identifying the list). That is to say, old lists were entered faster than new lists when the old lists were recognized correctly, but more slowly when they were

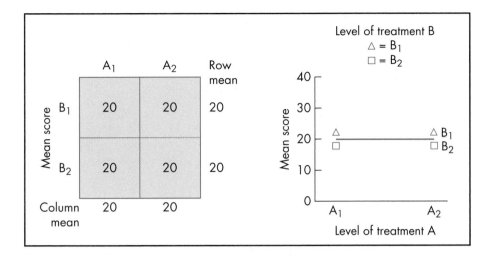

Figure 9.5

The main effects
and interaction
effect of treat-
ments A and B
are all nonsignifi-
cant.

identified incorrectly. This relationship corresponds to Figure 9.8 (A_1 = correct recognition, A_2 = incorrect recognition, B_1 = new list, B_2 = old list).

When the authors measured time to the first keystroke (which they assumed to be equal to encoding time), they found an interaction similar to that described in Figure 9.10 (page 221). In this case the average latency to the first keystroke for the old list was faster than for the new lists if the old lists were recognized correctly. Old lists were entered only somewhat more slowly than new lists if the lists were identified incorrectly.

If the time to the second keystroke is measured, then neither an interaction nor a main effect is present (as illustrated in Figure 9.5). In the actual article, this figure was presented in the form of a bar graph. You may want to redraw the results in this way to see how an interaction is represented in the form of a bar graph. Box 9.1 presents additional examples of interactions from the literature.

In each of the following examples (Figures 9.5–9.12), a different hypothetical outcome is described, in which either the main effects or the interaction effects may be assumed to be statistically significant. Figure 9.5 presents the first outcome, in which the same results are shown in two different ways: first numerically and then pictorially. In the left-hand portion of this figure is a matrix. The numbers inside the box represent the outcomes for each of the four groups in a hypothetical experiment.

For example, the group that received treatment combination A_1B_1 is represented in the upper left-hand cell of the matrix, the group that received condition A_1B_2 is in the lower left-hand cell, the group that received A_2B_1 is in the upper right-hand cell, and the group that received A_2B_2 is in the lower right-hand cell of the matrix. The numbers to the right of the box represent the means for conditions B_1 and B_2, respectively, and the numbers below the box represent the means for conditions A_1 and A_2, respectively. In the right-hand portion of the figure, the outcome is represented in graph form with the cell means plotted. The x axis of this graph (the horizontal axis) indicates groups A_1 and A_2. The y axis (the vertical axis) gives the values 10, 20, 30, and 40.

In this first example, the outcomes for the four groups are 20, 20, 20, and 20. Obviously, there was no main effect and no interaction effect. This same outcome is represented pictorially in the right-hand portion of Figure 9.5. Participants who received treatment

Box 9.1

Research Examples of Interaction Effects

Bower (1981) summarized a series of studies on mood and memory. The following graphs are from this 1981 paper.

An experiment by Bower, Monteiro, and Gilligan (1978) produced an interaction similar to that portrayed in Figure 9.8. In this study, college students were hypnotized and put in a happy or sad mood. Once the mood induction had been completed, the students memorized a list of 16 words. After the list was memorized, the opposite mood was induced. The students then learned a second list. At a later time (either 10 minutes or one day later), the original mood was again induced and the students recalled the first list. The results are shown in the following graph. (Figure based on Bower et al., 1978.)

Does the graph show that participants could learn more or fewer items when they were in the same mood as when they first learned the list?

A later study by Bower and Gilligan (1979) resulted in an interaction similar to that portrayed in Figure 9.9. In this study, participants were asked to remember personal experiences in either a positive or a negative mood. In the description of the remembered event, participants were asked to rate the event as pleasant or unpleasant. These data are presented graphically here. (Figure based on Bower and Gilligan, 1979.) In what type of mood would unpleasant events be most completely remembered?

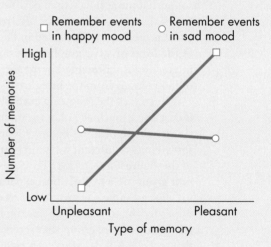

combination A_1B_1 responded with a dependent variable measure of 20, and this outcome is represented by the triangle above A_1 on the x axis. In a similar way, the outcome of group A_2B_1 is represented by a triangle above A_2 on the x axis. The line connecting these points is intended to highlight the total effect of the first level of condition B. The outcomes from groups A_1B_2 and A_2B_2 are represented by squares above A_1 and A_2 on the x axis and are joined by lines to show the total effect of the second level of condition B. In this example the

Figure 9.6

Treatment A is significant; treatment B and the interaction are nonsignificant.

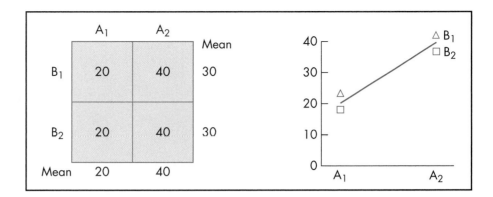

results are the same for all groups. Neither the main effects nor the interaction effects are statistically significant. In the graph this is indicated by the lines representing conditions B_1 and B_2 falling directly on top of one another. This shows that no difference exists between the main effects of B_1 and B_2. The fact that A_1 and A_2 are both equal to 20 is shown by the corresponding points falling at 20 on the y axis, so in this case nothing is significant.

Figure 9.6 shows a hypothetical condition in which the main effect of A is statistically significant, whereas the main effect of B and the interaction between A and B are nonsignificant. In the left-hand portion, the mean for condition B_1 and the mean for condition B_2 are both 30; that is, no difference exists between these two levels of factor B. In contrast, the mean effect of A_1 is 20, and the mean effect of A_2 is 40. Looking at the figure at the right in Figure 9.6, we see this graphically. The two lines overlapping indicate the fact that no difference exists between B_1 and B_2. Furthermore, the fact that the midpoint of each line corresponds to a value of 30 on the y axis reflects that 30 is the mean for both levels of condition B. In contrast, the values for A_1 and A_2 are quite different, which accounts for the slope in the lines between 20 and 40 along the y axis. In this case, then, the main effect of A is significant, whereas the main effect of B and the interaction effect are nonsignificant.

Figure 9.7 shows a case in which the main effect of B is significant and the main effect of A and the interaction effect are nonsignificant. A large difference exists between the values of B_1 and B_2 across conditions A_1 and A_2. The mean value of B_1 is 40. The mean value of B_2 is 20. The mean values of A_1 and A_2 across both conditions of B are the same: 30. The

Figure 9.7

B is significant; A and the interaction are nonsignificant.

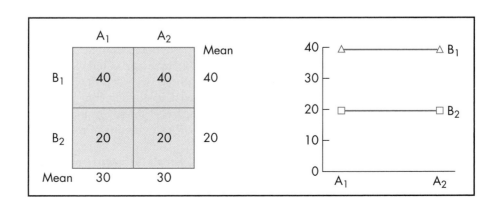

Figure 9.8

The interaction is significant; A and B are nonsignificant.

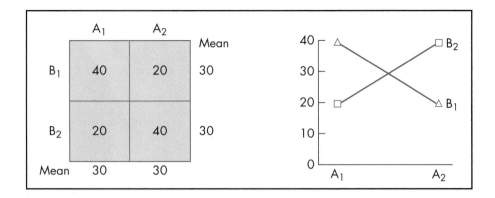

right-hand portion of Figure 9.7 graphically depicts these same results. Two parallel lines occur at 20 and 40 along the y axis. Note also that no difference appears in the mean value of A. The average of both levels is 30.

Figure 9.8 shows a hypothetical example in which the interaction effect is significant and neither A nor B is statistically significant. In this case the means of levels A_1, A_2, B_1, and B_2 are exactly the same: 30. This means that A_1 and A_2 and B_1 and B_2 are not statistically different from one another. Thus, the main effects of A and B are both nonsignificant. However, notice that the effect of B_1 in the presence of A_1 is 40, whereas the effect of B_1 in the presence of A_2 is 20. For B_2, exactly the opposite occurs; for B_2 in the presence of A_1, the value is 20, whereas in the presence of A_2, the value of B_2 is 40. Although the mean of each group is the same, the actual value of both levels of B is highly dependent on which level of A is involved. This is what we mean by a strong interaction effect. The right-hand portion of the figure shows the same thing. In this case, the line for B_1 slopes downward as you move from A_1 to A_2. In contrast, the line for B_2 slopes upward from A_1 to A_2, illustrating that B_2 is larger in the presence of A_2, so that the effect of B_1 and B_2 varies depending on whether it occurs in the presence of A_1 or A_2. Again, this is exactly what we mean by a significant interaction.

Hamann (1996) reports such an interaction in an implicit memory study in which blind people listened to or read in Braille a list of words (study phase). The participants then listened to or read in Braille the beginning of a word and were asked to complete the word (test phase). Although there were no main effects for percentage correct in terms of how the word was initially presented during the study phase (auditory or Braille) or how the word was presented during the test phase, there was an interaction.

Before proceeding, note that in Figures 9.5, 9.6, and 9.7, the lines representing B_1 and B_2 are parallel. In Figure 9.5 they are parallel and superimposed in the horizontal direction. In Figure 9.6 they are parallel and superimposed in an inclined direction. In Figure 9.7 they are not superimposed but are parallel in the horizontal direction. In each case the interaction is nonsignificant. In Figure 9.8, however, when the interaction is statistically significant, the lines are not parallel. Indeed, a useful guideline is that whenever the outcome of a factorial experiment involves nonparallel lines, you may have a significant interaction effect, although there are exceptions. This same sort of result can be seen in several of the following examples.

In the next case (Figure 9.9), an example is shown in which the main effect of A and the interaction effect are statistically significant, but the main effect of B is nonsignificant. The means for the two levels of A are 30 and 10, and the means for the two levels of B are 20 and 20.

Figure 9.9

A and the interaction are significant; B is nonsignificant.

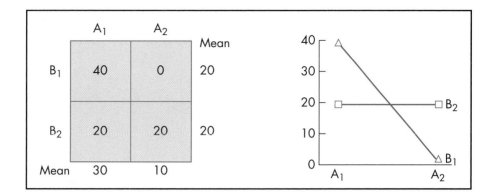

There is also an interaction effect illustrated by the fact that B_1 in the presence of A_1 and A_2 is markedly different from B_2 in the presence of A_1 and A_2. In one case there is no decrease, and in the other case there is a decrease. The right-hand portion of the figure depicts the same outcome. Note that B_2 is the same whether in the presence of A_1 or A_2, whereas the effect of B_1 varies considerably depending on whether it is occurring in the presence of A_1 or A_2. Note also that the lines are not parallel, which, as mentioned previously, is a clue that perhaps we are dealing with a significant interaction effect. Remember, *interaction* simply means that the manner in which the various levels of the one independent variable influences the dependent variable depends in part on the levels of the other independent variable.

Figure 9.10 shows a case in which B and the interaction effect are significant and A is not. The means for B_1 and B_2 are 10 and 30; the means for A_1 and A_2 are 20 and 20. In the right-hand portion of the figure, two lines divergent from one another represent the data. Note that once again the two lines are not parallel, suggesting a possible interaction effect.

In Figure 9.11 the main effects of A and B are statistically significant, and the interaction effect is nonsignificant. The mean differences between levels B_1 and B_2 are 10 and 30, and the means for levels A_1 and A_2 are also 10 and 30. In the right-hand portion of this figure, two parallel lines rising from left to right depict this outcome. The fact that the lines are parallel demonstrates the lack of an interaction effect.

Figure 9.12 shows an outcome in which all main effects and the interaction effects are significant. The means for B_1 and B_2 are 20 and 30, respectively. The means for A_1 and A_2 are

Figure 9.10

B and the interaction are significant; A is nonsignificant.

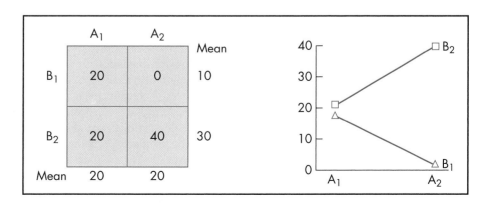

Figure 9.11

A and B are significant; the interaction is non-significant.

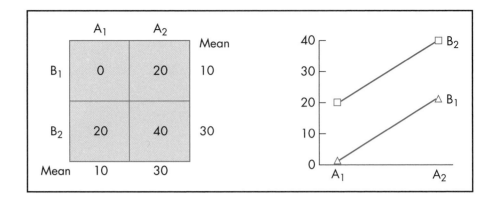

Figure 9.12

A, B, and the interaction are all significant.

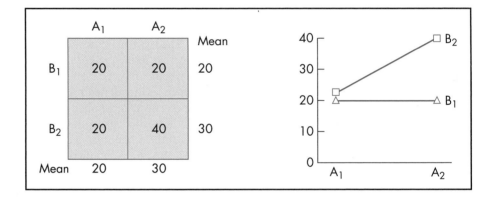

also 20 and 30, respectively. In the right-hand portion of the figure, we see two nonparallel lines; B_1 is the horizontal line representing the scores 20 and 20, and B_2 is a rising line from 20 to 40. The fact that at A_2 the effect of B_1 and B_2 is quite different from the effect of B_1 and B_2 at A_1 is consistent with the idea that we are working with a statistically significant interaction.

INTERPRETATION OF SUBJECT VARIABLES WITH FACTORIAL DESIGNS

In this section we offer a warning based on the type of research in which some students try to use factorial designs, although this warning is equally true for single-factor or multifactor designs. For the logic of experimentation to work best, you must be able to randomly assign participants to groups in such a way that any participant may be placed in any cell of the factorial design. This is not possible if one of the factors in the design is what has traditionally been called a subject variable. A **subject variable** is a characteristic or condition that a participant is seen to possess in a relatively permanent manner (that is, relative to the time frame of the experiment).

In the broadest sense, any physical or mental characteristic of a participant that can be measured is a subject variable. Some common examples of subject variables used in research are sex of the participant, eye color, being shy or outgoing, having cancer, being schizophrenic, and being intelligent. We could perform a study and choose our participants according to any of these characteristics. For example, we might ask whether feedback concerning accuracy improves basketball scores differently for men and women. Such a factorial study could be diagrammed as

	No Feedback	Feedback
Males		
Females		

Such a design could examine the effect of feedback on making basketball shots. Because the participants could be assigned randomly to either the feedback or the nonfeedback condition, it would be logical to conclude that feedback did (or did not) affect performance. However, we could not assign participants randomly to either the male or female condition because sex is a subject characteristic. Thus, if we found a difference between the performance of men and women, it would not be logical to conclude that the difference was due to sex. For example, the men and the women might have had different amounts of practice in basketball before the study. As an exercise you might note other possible confounds that could account for differential results between men and women in such a study.

When we cannot randomly assign participants to groups, it is difficult to control for the past experiences of the participants. Thus, the logic of our conclusions becomes weakened, and causality is impossible to specify. With this word of caution, we must also point out that the study of subject variables is an important part of psychology. For example, at times we may be particularly interested in differences between groups of people especially in such areas as sex differences, psychopathology, or cross-cultural research. For example, in a series of studies, Shinobu Kitayama and colleagues wanted to know if what one says about the types of choices one makes could be related to the culture in which one has lived (Kitayama, Snibbe, Markus, & Suzuki, 2004). Other social psychology research had shown that after people make choices, they often increase their liking of the chosen object and decrease their liking of the one not chosen. Could this be related to how their cultures view the role of the self in making choices? To answer this question, these researchers chose individuals who lived in Japan and in the United States because previous research had suggested that U.S. students view the self as independent, whereas Japanese students see the self as less independent and more connected with one's society and culture. Indeed, these researchers reported that Japanese students justify their choices in rating music differently than do U.S. students. In such studies as this, the interaction factor would be between groups (Japanese versus U.S.), and the experimental condition to which both groups were randomly assigned. Thus, using subject variables in factorial designs help us to answer questions when characteristics of our participants in the research are being addressed.

Many studies in psychology are devoted to such differences as between schizophrenic and nonschizophrenic participants, or men and women, or high-anxiety and low-anxiety participants, or even children and adults. In such comparisons, the logic of experimentation is considerably weakened and additional control measures are required for a meaningful interpretation of the results. We return to this point in Chapter 10.

ADVANTAGES OF FACTORIAL DESIGNS

Before concluding this discussion of factorial designs, it will be useful to point out several strengths of such designs. One major strength that we have already seen is that we can examine simultaneously more than one hypothesis or factor. This is important because human behavior often is influenced by more than one factor. A second advantage is that, because factorial experiments simultaneously evaluate each factor, they are much more economical in the number of participants and the total experimenter effort than studying each factor separately.

For example, suppose we want to investigate two independent variables, each of which has two factors (Figure 9.13). Furthermore, suppose we want 20 participants to experience each condition. If we use two separate, completely randomized designs, a total of

---

(a) *Two completely randomized design experiments*

	Experiment 1 (money)		**Experiment 2 (prior knowledge)**	
	Level 1 (1¢) 20 participants	Level 2 ($1) 20 participants	Level 1 (no picture) 20 participants	Level 2 (picture) 20 participants
Total number of participants for each experiment	40		40	
Overall total		80		

(b) *One 2 × 2 factorial design experiment*

	Money		Total participants across factor A
	Level 1 (1¢)	Level 2 ($1)	
Prior knowledge — Level 1 (no picture)	10	10	20
Level 2 (picture)	10	10	20
Total participants across factor B	20	20	
Overall total		40	

Figure 9.13

Participant requirements for (a) two completely randomized experiments and (b) a single 2 × 2 factorial design experiment. Note that the factorial design experiment requires half as many participants.

80 participants will be required (Figure 9.13a). If we use a single 2×2 factorial design, only 40 participants will be required (Figure 9.13b). The third, and perhaps most important, advantage of factorial designs is that by examining the extent of interactions between the different levels of the factors, we can see how the various causal factors influence performance.

KEY TERMS AND CONCEPTS

1. **Between-subjects design**
2. **Completely randomized design**
   A. Bransford and Johnson (1972)
   B. Strupp and Hadley (1979)
3. **Factorial designs**
   A. 2×2
   B. Main effects

    C. Interaction effect
    D. Cells
4. **Interpretation of**
   A. Interaction effects
   B. Main effects
5. **Advantages of factorial designs**

SUMMARY

1. Between-subjects designs are those that involve comparisons between different groups of participants.
2. One of the simplest between-subjects designs is the completely randomized design, also called the simple randomized design. When such a design contains more than two levels of the independent variable, it is called the multilevel completely randomized design. The Bransford and Johnson memory study (Chapter 7) is one illustration of this design.
3. A factorial design allows for the simultaneous assessment of more than one independent variable on the dependent variable. It is one of the most popular designs in psychology.
4. An important aspect of factorial designs is that they allow for the assessment of the combined influence of two or more independent variables on the dependent variable. This is called an interaction effect. An inter-

action effect reflects the extent to which one independent variable varies as a function of the level of the other independent variable.
5. Table 9.2 presents an ANOVA table illustrating the null hypotheses for each independent variable and the interactions between the independent variables.
6. In a factorial design with two independent variables, there are three separate null hypotheses: one for each independent variable and one for the interaction effect. A statistically significant interaction may result from a variety of numerical relationships. Figures 9.5–9.12 present these graphically.
7. Three advantages of factorial designs are (1) the simultaneous examination of more than one independent variable, (2) economy in the number of participants and total experimental effort, and (3) the determination of interactions between different levels of the factors.

REVIEW QUESTIONS

1. What is a *between-subjects design,* and how is it different from a *within-subjects design*?
2. What are *post hoc tests*?
3. What is a *factorial design,* and what is a *2 × 2 design*?
4. Describe a 2×2 design and explain the terms *main effects* and *interaction effects.*
5. In what order should main effects and interaction effects be interpreted? Why?
6. Describe the different aspects of the ANOVA table presented in this chapter (Table 9.2).
7. Draw a graph that would reflect a significant interaction effect.
8. What are *subject variables,* and how should they be interpreted in relation to changes in the dependent variable?

DISCUSSION QUESTIONS AND PROJECTS

1. Look up the Strupp and Hadley (1979) or the Bower research in your library, and note how these researchers controlled for possible confounds. (*Note:* For a review of the Bower research, see Bower, 1981.)
2. Develop rules for determining from a graph whether an interaction effect might be present.
3. Develop an experiment in which participants learn a series of sentences. Before presenting the sentences, give one group something pleasant to drink (for example, orange juice) and the other group nothing. Graphically present the results and discuss how these data would support the hypothesis that a pleasant experience before a memory task helps recall. What are some alternative ways of interpreting the data that point out potential confounds?
4. Take the design you constructed for the recall experiment in Question 3 and add the variable of the sentences being either simple or complex in meaning. Diagram this study and discuss potential outcomes. Would there be any advantage in performing two separate studies, one looking at the effects of pleasant experiences on recall and one looking at the level of complexity and its effect on recall? Would there be any disadvantage?
5. Construct a study examining factors related to helping behavior. For example, you might ask whether the physical appearance of the person in need of help influences how many people offer help and then ask whether physical appearance influences men and women differently. How would this study be designed, and what conclusions could you draw from the data? What other factors might you need to consider?

INFOTRAC COLLEGE EDITION: EXERCISES

In this chapter we discussed factorial between-subjects designs. As you read the published literature, you will see this type of design used often. For example, Jean Underwood and her colleagues were interested in the perception of road risk in children (*British Journal of Psychology,* 2007). Looking at the "Design" section of the experiment, notice the factors included in the 2 × 2 × 2 between-subjects factorial design. Amina Memon, Lorraine Hope, and Ray Bull sought to study how long someone saw a face as it relates to eyewitness accuracy and duration (*British Journal of Psychology,* 2003). Looking at the "Design" section of the experiment, notice the factors included in the 2 × 2 × 2 between-subjects factorial design. To which factors can participants be randomly assigned and to which can they not be randomly assigned? Notice the manner in which the results from the ANOVA are presented, as well as the graphs that are presented.

To help you better understand the material in this chapter, you can go to Wadsworth's research methods workshop web page at http://www.wadsworth.com/psychology_d/templates/student_resources/workshops/resch_wrk.html. There you will find workshops related to research methods and statistics. The Statistical Workshop on "Factorial ANOVA" extends the material presented in this chapter.

☑ Answers to Concept Checks

9.1 The major problem with the study is that participants were not assigned randomly to groups, and thus it is impossible to know whether the two groups were equal before the study began. A better study would be a completely randomized design in which students were assigned randomly to either a coffee-drinking or a non–coffee-drinking group and then tested for learning foreign language words.

9.2 Two independent variables are in this study. The first independent variable is the amount of coffee drunk (0 cups versus 2 cups). The second independent variable is the time of day at which the experiment was conducted (morning versus afternoon). The dependent variable is the number of words learned. The study can be diagrammed as

Time-of-Day Factor

	Morning	Afternoon
Level 1 (0 cups)	Group A	Group C
Level 2 (2 cups)	Group B	Group D

Coffee Factor

9.3 One main effect would be the coffee factor (0 versus 2 cups). One could ask whether there was any difference between students who received 2 cups and those who received none, regardless of the time of day. The other main effect would be time of day (morning versus afternoon). Likewise, one could ask whether there was any difference between when the students learned the material (morning versus afternoon), regardless of the amount of coffee drunk. However, the two main effects could combine in a variety of ways. For example, students might perform best with 2 cups of coffee in the morning or no cups in the afternoon. The graph in Figure 9.8 shows such a relationship, with A being coffee (A_1 = 0 cups and A_2 = 2 cups) and B being time of day (B_1 = afternoon, B_2 = morning). This would be one example of an interaction effect.

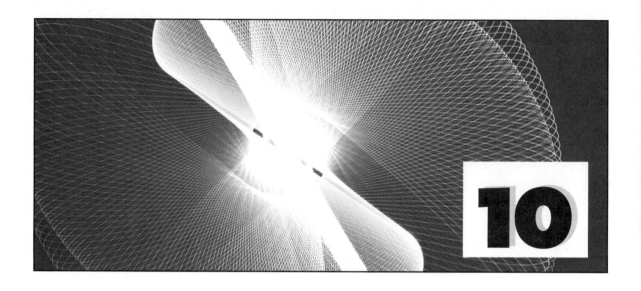

EXTENDING THE LOGIC OF EXPERIMENTATION: WITHIN-SUBJECTS AND MATCHED-SUBJECTS APPROACHES

WITHIN-SUBJECTS DESIGNS
An Illustration of Within-Subjects Research
Advantages and Disadvantages of Within-Subjects
  Designs
Counterbalancing
Repeated Measures

MIXED DESIGNS

MATCHED-SUBJECTS DESIGNS
Matching as a Control Procedure
Matching as an Experimental Procedure
Terminology

228

From the beginning of our discussion of experimental design in Chapter 7, we have stressed two themes. First, we stressed the logical necessity of beginning our experiments with groups that can be assumed to be equal. Second, we stressed the statistical importance of reducing variation, especially the within-groups variation (error variance) component of the F ratio. In relation to the need for beginning an experiment with equal groups, we suggested that the random assignment of participants is one of the best techniques for ensuring that no systematic differences are present at the onset of our experiment. In Chapters 8 and 9, we discussed a number of experimental designs, the logic of which was based on the random assignment of participants to groups. However, as we will see in this chapter, there are times when random assignment alone may not be the most appropriate approach.

In this chapter we discuss two approaches to experimental design that do not use random assignment alone. In the first section, we discuss within-subjects designs, in which the same participant is exposed to different experimental conditions. Later in the chapter, we discuss what are called matched-subjects designs. We discuss how matching can be used both as a control procedure and as an experimental procedure for analyzing differences between groups. As in the previous chapters, we stress the need for beginning our experiment with equal groups and the importance of reducing the within-groups variance component of the F ratio. Although the overall logic of experimentation presented in this chapter is similar to that discussed previously, the specific techniques for achieving these goals are slightly different.

WITHIN-SUBJECTS DESIGNS

In previous chapters we discussed designs that compare the performance of one group of participants with the performance of a different group of participants. These designs are called between-subjects designs. In **within-subjects designs,** the participant's own performance is the basis of comparison; that is, every participant serves in every group and receives all levels of the independent variable. In these designs we compare the performances of the same set of participants on the dependent variable following different treatments.

Let's look at an experiment performed first as a between-subjects experiment and then as a within-subjects experiment. In a simple between-subjects experiment, the experimenter wants to determine the role of immediate feedback in, say, shooting basketballs. One group is instructed to shoot baskets while wearing a blindfold (zero level of feedback), and another group is told to shoot without a blindfold (high level of feedback). This design is diagrammed as

R	Group 1	T (feedback)	M (number of shots successful)
R	Group 2	T (zero level of feedback)	M (number of shots successful)

If we identify the individual participants, the design is

				M (number successful)
R	Group 1	Participant 1	T (feedback)	24
		Participant 2		15
		Participant 3		17
		Participant 4		26
		Participant 5		15
R	Group 2	Participant 6	T (zero level of feedback)	20
		Participant 7		12
		Participant 8		13
		Participant 9		14
		Participant 10		12

We can perform this same study as a within-subjects design in which each participant is exposed to both levels of the independent variable; that is, every participant in the study shoots baskets both with and without a blindfold. We can diagram such a study in a fashion similar to the previous two-group study except that Group 2 contains the same five participants as Group 1. Thus, the total experiment is composed of only five participants:

Group 1	Participant 1	T (feedback)	M (number successful)
	Participant 2		
	Participant 3		
	Participant 4		
	Participant 5		
Group 2	Participant 1	T (zero level of feedback)	M (number successful)
	Participant 2		
	Participant 3		
	Participant 4		
	Participant 5		

For simplicity, we usually list the participants only once in a within-subjects design:

Factor A

	Level 1 (zero feedback)	Level 2 (feedback)
Participant 1	20	24
Participant 2	12	16
Participant 3	13	17
Participant 4	14	26
Participant 5	12	15

Within-subjects designs accomplish both of our goals: equating groups before the presentation of the independent variable and reducing error variance. Because the same participants are used in each group, we can be certain that before any treatment has begun, the groups are exactly the same. A within-subjects design also increases the sensitivity of a study by decreasing the chance or error variance because it removes the variance that results from individual variability. Like other authors (for example, Kerlinger, 1973, 1986), in this book we call error variance within-groups variance. To be technically correct, however, we need to point out that a within-subjects design will not reduce the variability of scores in each condition. Thus, when we speak of a reduced within-groups variance, we are referring to the reduction of error variance. The logic behind the reduction of error variance with a within-subjects design is that we would expect the behavior of the *same* participant in a series of different conditions to be more similar than the behavior of *different* participants in different conditions.

The error variance term of the *F* ratio for a within-subjects design is statistically smaller than that of a comparable between-subjects design. This means that smaller treatment differences are adequate for rejecting the null hypothesis. Table 10.1 shows the analysis of variance (ANOVA) tables associated with the basketball experiment performed both as a within-subjects design and as a between-subjects design. As you can see, the *F* ratio is 3.99 for a between-subjects design, and in a within-subjects design the *F* ratio is 10.57. In this

| Table 10.1 | **Analysis of Variance *F* Table for the Basketball Study as a Between-Subjects Design and as a Within-Subjects Design** |

If we were to use the data in the basketball example, we would find that the mean number of shots that went through the basket was 14.2 for the condition with the blindfold and 19.6 for the condition without.

As a between-subjects design in which we used a different group of participants in the blindfold versus feedback condition, the summary table would appear as

Source of Variance	df	SS	MS	F	p
Between-groups variance	1	72.9	72.9	3.99	.081
Within-groups variance (error)	8	146	18.25	—	—

As a within-subjects design in which we use the same participants in both conditions, the summary table would appear as

Source of Variance	df	SS	MS	F	p
Treatment variance	1	72.9	72.9	10.57	.031
Error	4	27.6	6.9	—	—

From this, you can see that the error variance is reduced in the within-subjects design, resulting in a larger *F* ratio than in the between-subjects design. The reason for this is that variability as related to subjects is included with the between-subjects error term and thus influences the *F* ratio, but it is partitioned separately in the within-subjects design and does not influence the *F* ratio. For more discussion of this issue, you can consult almost any statistical textbook (e.g., Jaccard & Becker, 1990).

particular case, we would reject the null hypothesis with the within-subjects design but not with the between-subjects design using the $p < .05$ level.

Some of you probably have noticed a potential problem in our basketball study: The results from the no-feedback condition might have a potential carryover effect on the feedback condition. The act of shooting a basketball, even without feedback, might lead one to perform better in the next condition. Thus, practice could confound this design. One way to control for this potential problem would be to use a counterbalancing procedure, as described in Chapter 8. All participants would first shoot the basketball in the no-feedback condition, then in the feedback condition, then in the feedback condition again, followed by the no-feedback condition. This would generate an ABBA order and thus help to control for the effects that are carried over from one trial set to another. One could also use a BAAB order to accomplish the same effect. Regardless of the order, we call this type of counterbalancing procedure **intrasubject counterbalancing** to contrast it with intragroup counterbalancing, which we discuss later in the chapter. Let's now illustrate a within-subjects design with an actual experiment.

■ An Illustration of Within-Subjects Research

The Boeing 727 airplane was introduced in the fall of 1965. Although pilots liked the airplane and the early test flights were good, within a year there were four accidents involving the plane (Kraft, 1978). The first accident involved a 727 flying into Chicago from the northeast. This plane began an approach from 22,000 feet and continued to descend until it flew into Lake Michigan, some 19 miles from the shore. The second accident occurred as a 727 flew into the Cincinnati area from the east. To make the landing, the plane had to fly over the river at night and land on a built-up runway. Unfortunately, the plane attempted to land some 12 feet below the level of the runway. The third accident happened as a 727 approached Salt Lake City from the south. From the airplane, the lights of Salt Lake City could be seen past the runway and to the right. In front of the runway it was dark. This airplane attempted to land short of the runway. The fourth accident occurred as a 727 attempted to land in Tokyo. It was a clear night, so the pilot decided to use the flight rules for visual landings (VFR) rather than for instrument landings (IFR). The pilot began the descent over Tokyo Bay with the lights of the city visible. The descent was halted abruptly when the plane hit the water, 6 miles east of the runway.

What happened? Assume that you are a psychologist called in to help to determine what caused the accidents. How would you go about this? First, you need to rule out mechanical problems with the airplanes, especially the altimeters (instruments that indicate altitude). Assuming that various experts eliminate mechanical problems as a cause, you might look to the manner in which the pilots were flying the planes. You also might look for any pattern of events present at each of the accidents. The initial clues that you find are that (1) all accidents happened at night, (2) the pilots were all operating under visual rather than instrument flight rules, (3) the instruments did not appear to be malfunctioning, and (4) each approach required pilots to fly over dark areas with lights in the distance.

Conrad Kraft, a researcher for the Boeing Company, reported that from this information it was hypothesized that the problem was a miscalculation of space perception on the part of the pilots. This hypothesis suggested that the pilots saw the equivalent of a visual illusion, which resulted in their misjudging the location of the ground. An analysis of the accidents also suggested that for various reasons—for example, looking for another airplane—the pilots had been distracted from their instruments. In the factorial language presented in Chapter 9, we would guess that the plane crashes were the result of an inter-action effect: That is, they were caused by a visual illusion but only when the pilots were distracted from the instruments. To determine whether this was the case, we could perform a simple 2×2 design. One level of Factor A would be the necessary conditions for the visual illusion (a clear night, no lights before the runway, and lights in the distance), and a second level would be a zero level of these conditions. The first level of Factor B would be pilot distraction from the instruments, and the second level would be a zero level of distrac-tion. We could represent this factorial design schematically:

Conditions Necessary for Visual Illusion

		Presence A_1	Absence A_2
Distraction from Instruments	Presence B_1		
	Absence B_2		

The dependent variable in such a factorial design would be the amount of landing error. Because flying can be simulated on flight simulators, this entire study could be performed in the laboratory, which would not only save money but would also control for environmental factors, such as wind speed and pressure level. Using a between-subjects design, we would randomly assign pilots to one of the four possible conditions (A_1B_1, A_1B_2, A_2B_1, A_2B_2). We could then conduct the study and determine any main effects or interaction effects.

Let's think about the realities of this situation and see whether a between-subjects design is really the best alternative. One factor we must consider is the research participant population. In this example we are interested in a rather special population: pilots who fly 727 airplanes. Thus, it seems somewhat wasteful, in terms of both time and money, to bring a large number of research participants to the laboratory just to make one landing in the simu-lator. We probably would want to collect as much data as possible from each pilot. Another consideration is to make the experimental and control groups as similar as possible. Are there any factors that we want to vary systematically between our groups? Experience with night flying in general, or with the 727 aircraft in particular, might be such a factor.

One solution to both considerations would be to use a within-subjects design. This would answer our first consideration by having each pilot serve in every condition. It would address our second consideration by allowing each pilot to serve as his or her own control. Allowing each pilot to serve as a research participant in each of the groups would automatically equate the groups for such factors as total flying time and knowledge of the 727 airplane. We can represent such a within-subjects design schematically exactly as we would a between-subjects design, except that each cell is composed of the same participants.

◼ Advantages and Disadvantages of Within-Subjects Designs

Several advantages to within-subjects designs have been mentioned previously. Because the same participants serve in each group, this experimental procedure ensures that all groups are equal on every factor at the beginning of the experiment. An additional benefit derived from using a within-subjects design is that the total number of research participants can be reduced dramatically. For example, in the simulator study just described, suppose we wanted to have 12 research participants per cell. In a between-subjects design, 4 cells × 12 research participants = 48 total research participants. By using a within-subjects design, we would need only 12 research participants in the entire experiment. The advantage with regard to the number of research participants becomes even greater as the complexity of the design increases. (For example, a 2 × 3 × 2 between-subjects design would have 12 cells and would require 12 times as many research participants as the equivalent within-subjects design.)

Another advantage to within-subjects designs is that they are statistically more sensitive to changes in the treatment effect. Why is this so? Most of the error variance in psychological studies results from differences among participants in the study. Within-subjects studies reduce this source of variance by using the same research participants in every condition. Because of this, in the F ratio there is a smaller within-subjects variance term. The within-subjects variance term is derived by taking the within-subjects variance as it would be found in a between-subjects design and subtracting an estimate of how consistent research participants are over the different treatment conditions. This means that the F ratio for within-subjects designs is more *sensitive* to changes in the treatments; that is, given the same treatment difference, we would be more likely to reject the null hypothesis with a within-subjects design than with a between-subjects design.

Before you throw out Chapter 9 and build your research career around within-subjects designs, let's consider some of the disadvantages. Remember, experimental designs are plans for helping us to answer research questions, and some questions cannot be answered appropriately by a within-subjects design. For example, if a treatment has any lasting effect on the research participants, then a within-subjects design is inappropriate. To illustrate this point, consider the Bransford and Johnson (1972) study (discussed in Chapter 7) as a within-subjects design. Each research participant would both be shown the picture and not be shown the picture. Clearly, seeing the picture would have a carryover or residual effect when research participants were asked to remember the passage in the no-picture condition.

Clinical treatment studies, such as the Strupp and Hadley (1979) psychotherapy study (discussed in Chapter 9) or a drug treatment study, would be difficult to interpret with a within-subjects design. If the same participant in the Strupp and Hadley study received counseling from both an experienced therapist and a college professor, it would be difficult to determine which changes in the participant should be attributed to which counselor. Thus, the within-subjects design is not appropriate when the treatment has a lasting effect or when the purpose of the study is to test for a lasting effect.

Another disadvantage of within-subjects designs is that they are extremely sensitive to time-related effects. To illustrate, consider a simple learning study in which the independent variable is the complexity of the material learned. The participants could be given progressively harder sets of materials to learn. If the material is presented in this order, can you see any confound that would make interpretation difficult? One possible confound might be fatigue; that is, by the time the participants reach the difficult material, they may be tired. The results would then be a result not only of the complexity of the material (the independent variable) but also of participant fatigue (a confound).

Another confound that could give us a misleading result is practice; each time the participants perform the experimental tasks, they may become better through practice. The effects brought about through continued repetition of the tasks, whether they are increases or decreases, are generically called **order effects.** At times, the terms *fatigue effects* (to note a decline in performance) and **practice effects** (to note an improvement in performance) are used.

Counterbalancing

In many cases, order and time can be controlled (but not eliminated) through such procedures as counterbalancing. For *complete counterbalancing,* certain conditions must be met. First, each condition must occur equally often; second, each condition must precede and follow all other conditions an equal number of times. Counterbalancing ensures that every possible sequence appears at each presentation of the treatment. We will call this procedure **intragroup counterbalancing** to contrast it with the intrasubject-counterbalancing procedure discussed previously.

In the learning study mentioned earlier, assume that there are three levels of difficulty. We could counterbalance the easy, medium, and hard levels so that in the first presentation of the independent variable the first participant would receive the easy level, the second participant the medium level, and the third participant the hard level. In the second presentation, the first participant would receive the medium level, the second participant the hard level, and the third participant the easy level. The third presentation would have the first participant receive the hard level, the second the easy, and the third the medium, and so forth. This is diagrammed as

Participant 1	easy	medium	hard
Participant 2	medium	hard	easy
Participant 3	hard	easy	medium
Participant 4	easy	hard	medium
Participant 5	hard	medium	easy
Participant 6	medium	easy	hard

This type of design would control for such time-related effects as an improvement in performance through practice or a deterioration in performance through fatigue or boredom.

Note that there are only six possible orders when one has three conditions (for example, easy, medium, and hard). However, as the number of conditions increases (for example, learning a variety of paragraphs or geometric shapes), a greater number of participants is required for a complete design. For example, 120 participants would be required if there were five conditions. Most researchers at this point use an *incomplete counterbalancing* procedure. For example, rather than easy, medium, and hard, suppose we had six conditions that we will call a, b, c, d, e, and f. One such incomplete counterbalancing procedure is

Individual 1	a	b	c	d	e	f
Individual 2	b	c	d	e	f	a
Individual 3	c	d	e	f	a	b
Individual 4	d	e	f	a	b	c
Individual 5	e	f	a	b	c	d
Individual 6	f	a	b	c	d	e

In this example note that each condition occurs equally often, but it is unbalanced in that each condition does not precede and follow all other conditions (for example, condition a never follows b). With a large number of conditions, an incomplete design is the most appropriate. A special case of incomplete counterbalancing is the *Latin square design.*

To form a Latin square, we must have the number of rows equal to the number of columns, which equals the number of conditions. The selection of the conditions traditionally has been performed randomly in a Latin square design (compare Edwards, 1962; Fisher & Yates, 1948). That is, in a 6 × 6 matrix, a random six-digit number (including only the numbers from 1 to 6) would be chosen, and the rows rearranged in that order. If the random number was 514632, row 5 would be placed at the top of the matrix, then row 1, then row 4, then row 6, then row 3, then row 2. This procedure would then be repeated for the columns and the columns rearranged according to that particular random number.

One common use of the Latin square design is with psychopharmacological research. For example, Rush, Higgins, Hughes, and Bickel (1994) used a Latin square design to study the effects of caffeine and triazolam on learning and performance. By using nine participants, these researchers were able to give all possible combinations of the two drugs (three levels of each). They found that caffeine administered alone did not significantly affect learning or performance but that caffeine did attenuate the triazolam-induced decrements in learning and performance.

Counterbalancing will not control for a *differential order effect.* For example, presenting the picture condition before the no-picture condition in the Bransford and Johnson study would produce a different effect from presenting the no-picture condition first. Counterbalancing would not control for this confound. Such a possibility can be tested for through an examination of the *treatment-by-order interaction.* With such an interaction, the effects of the treatments would depend on the order of presentation. This type of confound would also be inevitable in drug or clinical treatment studies such as the Strupp and Hadley psychotherapy study.

■ Repeated Measures

One common application of within-subjects designs uses repeated measures as one factor in a factorial design. This design is useful in studying psychological processes that occur over time and is widely used in studying human and animal learning processes. We might present the same subjects with different levels of problem difficulty (for example, easy versus difficult problems), which would be one factor, and the other factor might be the number of trials (the repeated-measures factor). The dependent variable in such a study could be the number of problems solved correctly. This design would tell us whether there are differences in the number of problems solved over repeated trials—that is, whether the two levels of difficulty are mastered at different rates. In this case we use repeated measures to study the process of learning or practice effects directly. At other times, we use a repeated-measures design as a control technique to ensure that learning or practice effects are not present in our study. If, as in the previous example, we had presented the easy problems to one set of participants and the difficult ones to another, we would have what is called a mixed design.

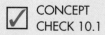 CONCEPT CHECK 10.1   Recall Concept Check 9.2 in which a professor randomly assigned students to one of four groups: (1) learn words in the morning and drink 2 cups of coffee, (2) learn words in the afternoon and drink 2 cups of coffee, (3) learn words in the morning and drink no coffee, and (4) learn words in the afternoon and drink no coffee. Describe this study as a within-subjects design. What effects would you have to consider with such a design?

MIXED DESIGNS

Probably the most common design used in psychological research combines a between-subjects design with a within-subjects design. Designs that include both "within" and "between" components are called **mixed designs.** For example, assume that we want to perform a biofeedback experiment to determine the effect of feedback on our ability to control heart rate. One factor is the amount of feedback (either total or partial feedback). Should we use a between-subjects or a within-subjects design? If one can learn the ability to control one's heart rate, there could be a carryover effect or a transfer of training from one condition to the other, especially if a research participant learned to control heart rate with total feedback first. This suggests that it would be better to use a between-subjects design and to assign research participants randomly to two groups: one that receives total feedback and one that receives partial feedback. We also might want to look at the effects of this training over a period of days. Thus, our second factor would be a repeated-measures component consisting of the number of days. Such an experiment is diagrammed as

		"Within" Factor (days)							
		1	2	3	4	5	6	7	8
Total Feedback	Participant 1								
	2								
	3								
	4								
"Between" Factor (feedback)	5								
	Participant 6								
	7								
Partial Feedback	8								
	9								
	10								

As with between-subjects designs discussed in Chapter 9, in mixed designs we are also interested in the main effects of each independent variable (for example, level of feedback and days) and the interactions among them. In terms of an interaction effect in the biofeedback study, we can ask whether one type of feedback produces a different learning rate than another. That is, we would ask whether the effects of feedback would depend on the time involved, or conversely, whether the effect of time would depend on the type of feedback presented.

The statistical analysis of mixed designs is complicated because they use different error terms in the F ratio. The error variance for the "between" comparison (level of feedback in our example) is computed differently from that of the "within" comparison (days in our example). Although a discussion of these statistical procedures is beyond the scope of this presentation, the logic of the *F* ratio remains the same, and you still must interpret the role of the independent variable and rule out the role of chance and confounds in the results.

Beilock and Carr (2001) in a *Journal of Experimental Psychology* article used a mixed design to determine the theoretical underpinning of choking under pressure. In one of their series of experiments, they examined the role of distraction (required to pay attention to additional stimuli) and self-consciousness (being videotaped) on putting errors (distance from target) in a golf game. Participants in the study were randomly divided into either the distraction group or the self-consciousness group and then given a series of 36 putts to perform, which were averaged into the first 18 and the second 18. In this 2 (distraction, self-consciousness) × 2 (errors in first series of putts versus errors in second series of putts) design, these authors found a main effect of practice but not of group. There was also no statistically significant interaction effect.

Because these authors were interested in choking under pressure, they created low- and high-pressure posttests. In the high-stress situation, participants were told that they could win money if their scores improved by 20% and that their score would influence the chance of a randomly assigned team member also winning money. The low-pressure posttest was just putting as normal. In this 2 (distraction, self-consciousness) × 2 (low-pressure posttest, high-pressure posttest) ANOVA, Beilock and Carr found a statistically significant interaction. Basically, there were no differences in errors between the distraction and self-consciousness condition in the low-pressure condition. However, in the high-pressure condition, there were more errors in the distraction condition as compared with the self-consciousness condition. Figure 10.1 shows the graph of this interaction.

Although one of the more common "within" factors in a mixed design is a temporal one, such as days or trials, there are other alternatives. For example, in social or industrial psychology, the dependent variable could be ratings along certain characteristics (for example, attractiveness, perceived ability, perceived motivation). Participants in the study would rate different groups of individuals (for example, White versus Black versus Asian or males versus females), which would be the "within" factor. Before the rating, participants in the study could be shown videos that would portray these groups in positive or negative ways (the "between" factor).

Figure 10.1

CONCEPT CHECK 10.2   A university administrator seeking to save money suggested that if faculty in all departments taught math skills, then there would be no need to have a math department. To prove this point, the administrator designed a within-subjects design in which students received math training from professional mathematicians and from other college faculty. The administrator reported that students showed improvement in math after training with college faculty as well as with professional mathematicians, and thus the math department was to be closed down. Comment on this finding.

 CONCEPT CHECK 10.3   The same experiment was performed as a between-subjects design and as a within-subjects design, with the same results. We know that the F ratio would be larger in the within-subjects design. What is the reason for this difference?

 # MATCHED-SUBJECTS DESIGNS

In this section we examine matching as a procedure for accomplishing the goals of equating groups in an experiment and reducing the within-groups variance (error variance). To help us in this discussion, we build on the logic of the within-subjects design. As you remember, within-subjects experiments equate groups by using the same participant in every treatment condition. Likewise, by using the same participants in each group, the within-groups variance is reduced because a participant will perform more consistently in different situations than different participants will perform in different situations. What if, rather than using the same participants in different groups, we use participants who are very similar? By using a **matched-subjects design,** we could reap some of the advantages of within-subjects designs and simultaneously take advantage of the random assignment of participants that is possible with a between-subjects design.

Our first task would be to find participants who are very much alike. We might use identical twins, for example, whom we would expect to perform more similarly on a variety of tasks than strangers because they are more alike physiologically. If we randomly assign one twin to the experimental group and the other twin to the control group, we should be able to equate our groups at the beginning of the experiment and reduce within-groups variance (error variance). However, because we cannot use identical twins in every study that we perform, an alternative is to match participants. If we pair participants along some factor and then randomly assign the members of each pair to two separate groups, we can assume that our groups are equal at the beginning of the experiment, and we can reduce within-groups variance (error variance). In terms of error variance, by this method we create a type of design that is a hybrid of within-subjects designs and between-subjects designs. We would not have as much error variance as in a between-subjects design or as little error variance as in a within-subjects design.

The characteristics we use to match our groups of participants obviously are of central importance to this design. In the broadest sense, any physical or mental characteristic of a participant that can be measured may be used for matching. Characteristics such as height, weight, intelligence, anxiety level, achievement motivation, hair color, and emotional sensitivity are all individual characteristics that can be measured. Consequently, they are all potential individual variables on which matching can be based. For a matching procedure to work, there must be a high correlation between the variable used for matching and the dependent variable. If the participants are matched on a factor that does not correlate with the dependent variable, then the within-groups variance will be no smaller than the variance obtained by random selection alone, and the amount of effort required for matching will have been wasted.

Matching can be used in either of two ways. First, it can be used as a control procedure. For example, if we were studying spatial ability, we might want to control for general intelligence. That is, we would want to make certain that each participant in one group would be matched with one in the other group who had the same IQ, but we would not analyze the intelligence factor itself. Second, if we were to analyze the intelligence factor, we would be using matching in the second way: as an experimental procedure. We discuss this use in more detail later in this chapter. Although it would be technically correct to refer to this second use of matching only as an experimental design, as contrasted with a control procedure, few researchers follow this procedure.

◼ Matching as a Control Procedure

When we know that a particular individual variable or characteristic has a high correlation with the dependent variable, equal groups may be obtained by matching along this characteristic. The task of forming matched groups of participants consists of two steps. First, pairs of participants are matched on some measure that is correlated with performance on the dependent variable. Second, one member of each pair is assigned randomly to either the experimental or the control group; the other member is then assigned to the other group. Such a design can be represented schematically as

MR	Group 1	T	M
MR	Group 2	T (zero level)	M

Notice that we placed an M before the R to denote that the participants were matched before they were assigned randomly to groups. In essence, we have a completely randomized design.

Let's look at another example of matching as a control procedure. Suppose we are interested in neurochemical changes that result from prolonged periods of sensory deprivation. For a number of reasons, we decide to use monkeys as subjects. Because monkeys are difficult to obtain, we decide to use as few as possible. To control for potential bias in the groups, we might decide to match along a dimension that is highly correlated with our dependent variable: a certain amino acid in the brain, for example. Figure 10.2 presents the overall procedure. We begin by performing a blood chemistry analysis of our monkeys and then rank order them on the basis of this analysis. After we complete the initial rank ordering, we pair the animals (for a two-group study) according to the rankings. We begin

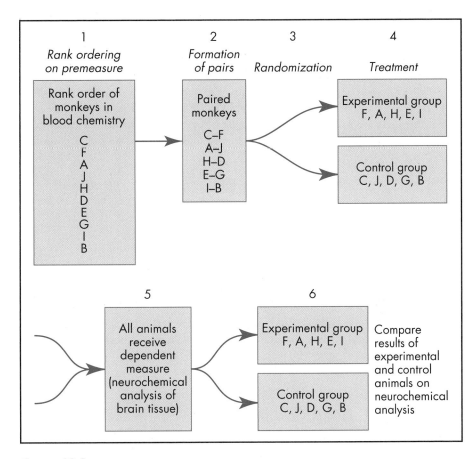

Figure 10.2

The six major steps in a matched-subjects design used to study changes in brain chemistry resulting from prolonged sensory deprivation. (1) Rank order all subjects on the aspect of blood chemistry that is known to be correlated with brain neuro-chemistry. (2) Form pairs of subjects on the basis of this rank order. (3) Randomly assign one member of each pair to the experimental group and one member to the control group. (4) Conduct the experimental treatments. (5) Conduct neurochemical analyses. (6) Compare the results for the experimental and control animals. Note that, except for our ranking and matching procedures, the design is similar to the completely randomized designs discussed previously.

with the two animals that have the highest rankings, then go to the next two, and so on. We randomly assign one member of each pair to one group and the other to the other group and then proceed with the experiment.

Matching as an Experimental Procedure

In the previous examples of matching as a control procedure, participants are matched according to some factor (individual variable), but the factor itself is not analyzed. It is possible to analyze the matching factor, however. When the matching factor is analyzed, the resulting procedure is traditionally called a *randomized block design.* The term *block* in this case refers to the development of the design by Sir Ronald Fisher when he studied agricultural procedures on different blocks of land.

Let's now discuss how the matching factor can be described and used experimentally. To begin, let's again schematically represent a randomized design in which matching is used as a control factor. Take the time estimation study, for example, in which an equal number of men and women are placed in each group. We might diagram such a design as

MR	Group 1 (males and females)	T	M
MR	Group 2 (males and females)	T (zero level)	M

We could further break down this design as

Group 1	Males	T	M
Group 1	Females	T	M
Group 2	Males	T (zero level)	M
Group 2	Females	T (zero level)	M

At this point it is possible to convert this experiment into a two-factor factorial design and analyze the factor of sex. Such a factorial design is diagrammed as

Factor A (feedback)

	Level 1	Level 2 (zero level)
Factor B (sex) Males		
Females		

We can now analyze for the main effect of Factor A, the main effect of Factor B, and the interaction of A and B. It must be remembered that the factor according to which the participants are classified is not a factor on which the participants are randomly selected, and it must be interpreted with caution. If there is a significant main effect for this factor, we may be able to conclude that a relationship exists between this factor and the dependent variable, but we cannot conclude that the relationship is a causal one. However, this does not mean that we want to ignore the classification factor. If there is an interaction between the classification variable and the treatment variable, there is much information to be gained. Such an interaction will tell us to which groups and under which conditions the findings of a particular study may be generalized.

For example, in a study of the effects of feedback on performance, Ray, Katahn, and Snyder (1971) divided participants into high- and low-anxiety groups and then randomly assigned them to either a high-feedback condition (feedback on the number of correct responses after each study trial) or a low-feedback condition (feedback only after a series of study trials). It was found in this study that there was no difference between the high- and low-anxiety groups when feedback was given at the end of a series of trials, but there was a difference when feedback was given at the end of each trial. With feedback after each trial, the low-anxiety group increased the number of items learned more than the high-anxiety group did. Such an interaction may be valuable in generalizing from this particular study to other studies concerning the role of feedback in learning.

In addition to the knowledge gained from the interaction effect, we have discussed two other advantages resulting from the prior matching of participants to groups. The first is that such matching ensures that the groups in a study are equal (on the measure by which they were matched) before the treatment is introduced. Equating groups in this way is especially valuable for situations in which we have a limited number of participants but cannot use a within-subjects design. The second advantage is that matching participants reduces the within-groups variance (error variance) and thus makes our design more sensitive to treatments than a comparable between-subjects design. However, this is possible only when the matching factor has a high correlation with the dependent variable.

■ Terminology

Before we leave this discussion of matching, let's briefly introduce a more sophisticated terminology concerning what traditionally has been called the randomized block design. Glass and Stanley (1970) suggest that we reserve the term **blocking** for cases in which the matching takes place on a nominal-scale factor such as sex. They also suggest that the use of twins likewise be considered matching on a nominal-scale factor. When the matching uses ordinal measurements such as ranking, they further suggest that the term *stratifying* be used.

Ranking participants into high-, medium-, and low-socioeconomic divisions is one example of using a stratifying variable. When interval or ratio scales are used, Glass and Stanley suggest that the term *leveling* be used. Some common examples are dividing participants according to intelligence levels (for example, IQs of 120+, 100–120, 80–100, <80), anxiety levels, or depression levels. It must be remembered that although the groups are developed in terms of individual variables—the members of each of the blocks, strata, or levels—it is still necessary to assign participants randomly to treatment conditions.

KEY TERMS AND CONCEPTS

1. **Within-subjects designs**
2. **Order effects**
3. **Counterbalancing**
4. **Repeated-measures designs**
5. **Mixed designs**
6. **Matched-subjects procedures**
   A. As a control procedure
   B. As an experimental procedure

7. **Randomized block design**
8. **Individual factors**
9. **Terminology of randomized block design**
   A. Blocking
   B. Stratifying
   C. Leveling

SUMMARY

1. Within-subjects designs are those in which every participant serves in every group and receives all levels of the independent variable. Performance on the dependent variable is compared following different treatments on the same set of participants.

2. Within-subjects designs have a number of advantages: (a) Because each participant serves in every group, all groups are equated at the beginning of the experiment, (b) fewer participants are needed than would be the case in a similar between-subjects design, and (c) within-subjects designs are statistically more sensitive to changes in the treatment effect.

3. There are two problems with within-subjects designs: (a) They are sensitive to time-related factors, and (b) they cannot be used when a treatment has a lasting effect on the participant.

4. A mixed design is one that combines both "within" and "between" designs, as illustrated by a study that compared differences between two different groups of participants over a number of days.

5. A matched-subjects procedure may be used either as a control procedure or as an experimental procedure, in which case the matching factor is analyzed statistically. Matching used as an experimental procedure traditionally has been called a randomized block design.

REVIEW QUESTIONS

1. Name some advantages of within-subjects designs.
2. In what situations would you *not* use a within-subjects design?
3. What is a *practice effect,* and why is it important?
4. For which effects will counterbalancing control? For which will it not control?

5. Give an example of the use of repeated measures.
6. What is a *mixed design*? Give an example.
7. Discuss matching as a control and as an experimental procedure.
8. Discuss random assignment to groups and the results from not assigning participants in this manner.

DISCUSSION QUESTIONS AND PROJECTS

1. Discuss the situations in which within-subjects designs are particularly useful.
2. Using an overhead projector and colored pens, it is easy to construct a transparency that demonstrates the Stroop effect. Construct an experiment to determine whether it is easier for students to read the names of the colors while they are tapping their right index fingers or their left index fingers. Discuss how you might design this experiment to look for sex differences.
3. What would be the advantages of performing the experiment in Question 2 as a within-subjects experiment?
4. Why is error variance reduced in a within-subjects experiment?

5. Discuss research areas in which within-subjects designs would be difficult to use and explain why.
6. Assume that a company is interested in finding which of three visual illusions airline pilots are most sensitive to and hires you to help construct such a study. How would you go about it? Would you want to counterbalance? Outline your study and then describe potential confounds and how you would control for them.
7. A company introduces a new beer. In three identical cups labeled A, B, and C, respectively, the new beer and two other brands are placed before the participant. The participant is instructed to taste each beer and state a preference. What would be the problems with using this procedure, and how could these be corrected?

InfoTrac College Edition: Exercises

Researchers have been interested in how humans read sentences that contain ambiguous statements such as "flying planes are dangerous." Keith Rayner and his colleagues reported such a study in the November 2006 issue of the *British Journal of Psychology*. As you read this study in InfoTrac College Edition, notice how the authors use counterbalancing. What was its purpose?

To help you better understand the material in this chapter, you can go to Wadsworth's research methods workshop web page at http://www.wadsworth.com/psychology_d/templates/student_resources/workshops/resch_wrk.html. There you will find workshops related to research methods and statistics. The research methods workshop on "Between Versus Within Designs" extends the material presented in this chapter.

✓ Answers to Concept Checks

10.1 As a within-subjects design, each participant would take part in every condition. Because of possible practice effects, you would want to counterbalance the order.

10.2 There is a good chance that students would show improvement, but it would be difficult to determine with a within-subjects design the source of the change. That is, if the students saw the math professors first, the students may have learned skills that they used when learning math from the other faculty. Thus, a within-subjects design is not appropriate when the possibility exists to carry over knowledge or skills from one condition to another.

10.3 The error term of the F ratio would be smaller in a within-subjects design, resulting in a larger F ratio.

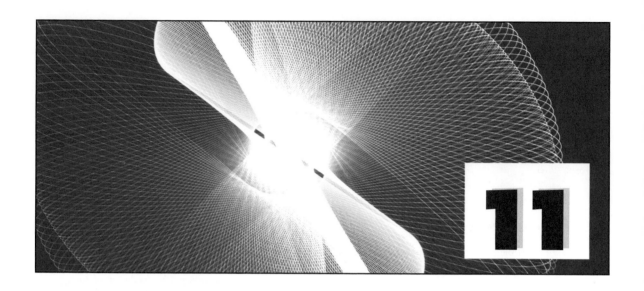

THE ECOLOGY OF THE EXPERIMENT: THE SCIENTIST AND RESEARCH PARTICIPANT IN RELATION TO THEIR ENVIRONMENTS

ECOLOGY

EXPERIMENTER FACTORS
Biased Data Collection
Biased Interactions with Research Participants
Some Ways to Avoid Experimenter Bias

SUBJECT FACTORS
Placebo Factors
Demand Characteristics

CULTURAL AND SOCIAL BIAS

In this chapter we want to move beyond our consideration of specific designs to a discussion of the context in which psychological research takes place. By *context* we mean not only the particular laboratory or setting in which the research is conducted but also the world in which scientists and research participants live outside the experiment. It is especially important to realize that the world in which we grew up may differ in significant ways from that of people of other cultures. It is this cultural context that we stress in this chapter.

Rogoff (1990), among others, argues that much of what we learn as children is really an apprenticeship to learning the thinking and doing of the culture in which we live. Thus, we cannot assume that our values or even our views of constructs such as intelligence, sanity, and competency are universally shared. This does not mean that these constructs can never be researched, but it does suggest the importance of agreed-on operational definitions and a willingness to examine the manner in which our previous cultural experiences shape our current views of psychological processes. Initial discussions in this book related to various perspectives of performing a science of behavior and experience. We suggested that science can be viewed from three separate perspectives: that of the scientist, that of the research participant, and that of the witness. In this chapter we extend that discussion to suggest the importance of the cultural context.

In the previous chapters, we emphasized the role of the scientist and the manner in which he or she interacts with the subject matter of psychology through research. The scientist plays an active role in science through the types of questions he or she asks, the methods by which he or she answers these questions, and the types of answers that are ultimately acceptable. We were particularly interested in one's ability to infer valid connections between variables using experimental procedures. In doing this we were speaking from the perspective of the scientist.

We are equally interested in one's ability to make valid statements from a broader perspective. Not only will we discuss methods for performing more valid experiments as seen from the perspective of the scientist, but we will also give you a clearer picture of how the humanity of both the scientist and the participant influences the actual conduct of the experiment. If these factors are not considered, the internal and external validity of an experiment may be threatened. To facilitate conveying these issues, we now shift our perspective to include that of the *witness*, who observes the interplay between the scientist and the research participant.

We realize that for some people, the perspective of the witness may be frustrating because it reminds us of aspects of science that are beyond our control and contradicts the picture of science as completely objective. It also shows us that our own culture may shape the manner in which we see the world and especially how we see people from cultures different from our own. However, as a careful reading of history will show, science has never been—and probably never will be—completely objective. As we have shown throughout this book, science is a means of helping us to explore, passionately at times, the world in which we live and to come to some understanding of this world. In our better moments, science may offer us a means of transcending some of our limitations as human beings. Yet, most often, science faithfully reflects our humanness and thus our limitations. The viewpoint of the witness, through an observation of the interactions of the scientist and the participant, helps us to understand the value and relevance, as well as the limitations, of any new information our research produces.

In this chapter we look at how some of these limitations affect science from the perspective of the witness. As scientists we can control for some limitations; others we can only accept. In this vein we consider the psychological worlds of the scientist and the participant and how these might influence, either collectively or separately, the outcome of psychological research.

The consideration of participant–scientist interactions is so important that some researchers believe all human experimentation is really a social event that should be viewed from a broad perspective (Petrinovich, 1979). As with any social event, each person may have a variety of reasons for participating. In an experiment certain social roles may be adopted; these roles, along with their historical origins, are discussed by Danziger (1985). In particular, Danziger suggests that two historical models dating from the 19th century have influenced psychological research in this country: the Leipzig model and the Paris model. The Leipzig model, typified by the research of Wilhelm Wundt and others about normal cognitive processes, makes little differentiation between the participant and the experimenter in terms of expected roles or social status. In fact, in the Leipzig model, the same person might serve in both capacities at different times. Psychophysics, in its study of the relationship between physical properties of a stimulus and our sensory experience of it, is one example of the Leipzig model in its methods.

The Paris model, typified by research about hypnosis and abnormal psychology, makes a clear distinction between the roles of the scientist and the research participant. In this model scientists and participants are different, and one would never play the role of the other. Danziger concludes his discussion by suggesting that American psychological

"You can't build a hut, you don't know how to find edible roots and you know nothing about predicting the weather. In other words, you do terribly on our I.Q. test."

experimentation has been influenced greatly by the Paris model and that this influence has shaped the type of information derived from the experimental context. He further suggests the importance of understanding the relationship between the social structure of knowledge-generating situations—experiments, for example—and the nature of their products.

Several themes involved in understanding the participant-scientist interaction are discussed in greater detail throughout this chapter. One theme is that all parties enter into an experimental situation with expectations that are in part directed by their cultures; thus, a complete understanding of the situation requires an exploration of these expectations and the cultures from which they arise. Another theme, perhaps the most important for our purposes, is that a mediating relationship exists between the social structure of an experimental situation and the type of information generated in this situation. Thus, experimental results are never just facts but require a broader understanding for their interpretation and the evaluation of inferential considerations. This focus is important both for the broad perspective it gives us of psychological research and as a means of understanding and perhaps eliminating or reducing the potential biases that enter into the process of research, with or without the knowledge of the scientist. To study the relationships among the scientist, the participant, and the experimental environment, we refer by analogy to the science of ecology.

ECOLOGY

The term *ecology* was coined more than 100 years ago. Ecology is the scientific study of the relationship of living organisms with each other and their environment (Miller, 1988). Most people are familiar with the word *ecology* as it is applied to the relationship between humans and their environment. For example, by following the food chain we may find that if certain chemicals are used to kill weeds on a farmer's field, the same chemicals might later appear in the breast milk that mothers feed their babies. In the 1970s, it was shown that when an atomic explosion took place in China, the fallout could be found in the cow's milk consumed by people in Philadelphia. Most recently, relationships have been reported between dust storms in Africa and certain medical problems (for example, asthma) in North America. We have also seen that decreases in the population of one type of animal—the lion, for example—have led to increases in that of another animal, such as deer. The general lesson we have learned from the study of ecology is that all parts of nature are closely interconnected and that it is impossible to make environmental changes without affecting the entire system, at least to some extent.

In the same way that we can discuss the ecology of nature by looking at the interrelationships between humans or animals and their environment, we can discuss the ecology of the psychological experiment by examining the relationships among the scientist, the research participant, and the experimental situation. By using the word *ecology*, we emphasize that there are ongoing dynamic interactions—among the scientist, the research participant, and the context—that must be considered before a complete understanding of experimental psychology is possible.

Bronfenbrenner (1979) has written extensively about the importance of including the ecological perspective in human development research. In particular, he stresses the importance of looking beyond the immediate observational or experimental situation. As an example, Bronfenbrenner suggests that to understand classroom development, one may need to study not only the types of teaching methods used but also the home environment, or even the employment situations of the parents, and how these affect the child's development.

The context of the experiment is also important; numerous studies in the past 50 years have shown that *where* the observation takes place plays an important role. For example, mothers play with their children differently in a laboratory setting than they do in a home setting. Also, it has been shown that blood pressure readings from the same person are higher when measured in a doctor's office than at the person's house. It follows that without an understanding of the ecological aspects of the scientific context, our conclusions and theoretical ideas may be invalid. From this perspective we can introduce the concept of *ecological validity*.

Ecological validity seeks to determine whether the impacts of the important relationships among the scientist, the participant, and the context have been considered fully in evaluating a given piece of research. As we see in this chapter, this evaluation includes examining the relationship of the scientist and the research participant to each other, to the particular research being conducted, and to the greater context of the society in which each lives and works. We discuss some of the possible threats to the ecological validity of research. We present these in a broad perspective but do not attempt an exact definition of the construct because it has been used in a variety of ways in the past. Probably the best-known historical usage of the term is that of Brunswik (1947), which we discuss later in this chapter. Our discussion is more from the perspective of the witness—a metaperspective of the experimental situation.

The witness's motivation is somewhat like that of a consumer protection agency. It is not to suggest that no scientific study can ever be acceptable but rather to offer considerations and at times outright warnings concerning the ecological validity of science. Just as no consumer product or service has been developed that gives perfect results each time, there will never be the perfect scientific experiment. Remember, our goal in science is not to perform a perfect experiment but *to use science to ask questions and to increase our understanding of a given phenomenon*. When used in an appropriate manner, science is one of the most powerful tools we have. When it is used out of context or in a haphazard manner, it is important that caveats and even warning labels be attached. Let's now turn to some of the considerations to keep in mind when assessing ecological validity.

EXPERIMENTER FACTORS

One initial warning in the acceptance and generalizability of research is the possibility of scientist or **experimenter effects.** To examine experimenter effects is to ask what portion of the results of an experiment can be said to be affected by the attitudes or behavior of the experimenter. Sometimes, just knowing that one group of participants has been assigned to a specific experimental condition may result in the experimenter scoring this group's behavior in line with expectations. As you will see throughout this chapter, scientists have developed a variety of means for limiting potential experimenter bias. In this section we discuss two types of experimenter effects: those due to biased data collection by the experimenter and those stemming from the experimenter's biasing the participant's performance.

■ Biased Data Collection

One potential source of experimenter **bias** in collecting data stems from our individuality: Two experimenters actually may see the world differently. In his history of psychology, Boring (1950) tells of an incident in the late 1700s and early 1800s that points up the importance of experimenter variability in scientific research. The story concerns an astronomer, Maskelyne, and his assistant, Kinnebrook. The method of noting star movement in those days was to look at a clock and then, listening to its ticking, count the ticks until a star crossed a wire in the telescope. Maskelyne dismissed his assistant when he discovered that the assistant timed the passing of stars almost a second later than Maskelyne did. Some 20 years later, after reading of this event, another astronomer named Bessel began to compare his own observations with those of others. Bessel found that different observers using the same method differed by a constant amount. However, Bessel did not fire his assistants. Rather, he became one of the first researchers to point out the effect that inherent differences in experimenters can have on the data they record.

The constant error in the observations of different scientists is what we call the **personal equation** in psychology. The personal equation suggests that because of one's physiological and psychological makeup, there are differences—albeit consistent differences—in the way we, as experimenters, observe the world. And these unique experimenter differences form a real source of experimenter bias. For this reason it is a common procedure in an observational or rating experiment for two or more independent observers to be used.

The use of a number of observers is particularly important in areas that might be culturally influenced. For example, what might be perceived as anxiety in one culture could be seen as shame or guilt in another. Thus, it is important that a piece of research begins with a clearly stated operational definition and that the observers be trained to code similar information in a similar manner. Fortunately, there is a way to check for inconsistent observations. The method computes a correlation of observations between two observers, using the correlational procedures we described in Chapter 5.

Another common statistic for computing this correlation, called *Cohen's kappa,* is described in a variety of sources (for example, Bakeman & Gottman, 1989). Whatever the actual statistical procedure, the logic for establishing agreement between the results recorded by different observers or raters is similar. The correlation between two raters is called **interrater reliability.** The higher the correlation between the ratings of two independent observers, the less the ratings represent inconsistent subjective factors of the raters. However, a high correlation may also result from different but consistent ratings from raters; Cohen's kappa attempts to correct for this difference. A low correlation suggests that better operational definitions are required or that additional training of the raters is needed. This is an important area; you should consult Bakeman and Gottman (1989) if you are interested in an extended discussion of interrater reliability and its measurement.

In addition to the inherent differences between experimenters in the way they perceive and respond to the world, personality may create a source of experimenter bias. Scientists are human and at times the desire to see their hypotheses supported outweighs their honest viewing of the world as it is. In most cases this temporary reversal of priorities asserts itself in an unconscious or unintentional manner. For example, psychologists have studied carefully other scientists conducting research and have learned that if an experimenter makes an error recording a single piece of data, that error is most likely to be in support of the research hypothesis (Rosenthal, 1979).

In addition, a scientist can subtly influence the outcome of an experiment. For example, any unintended variations from the experimental plan tend to favor the hypothesis, the decision about whether to accept or discard a participant's data tends to be influenced by whether the performance supports the hypothesis, and the use of inappropriate statistical techniques, such as unplanned ad hoc analyses, may be misleading. As it turns out, this confusion of priorities is by no means limited to modern researchers. In fact, Barber (1976) suggests that some of our more famous scientists, including Isaac Newton, John Dalton, and Gregor Mendel, may have presented their data as being more precise than was possible during the time in which they lived. Some of these scientists' assistants, like college students performing an experiment when they know what the results ought to be, may have helped the data to fit the predicted theory to please the person for whom they worked.

In the first half of the 19th century, a new and exciting field was emerging that sought to do what intelligence testing does today: The field was called *craniometry*. Proponents of craniometry believed that there was a relationship between brain size (calculated from measurements of the skull) and intelligence. Today we know that there is little relationship between brain size and intelligence in humans, but at that time it was part of the accepted beliefs. Millions of people are said to have had their heads measured in hopes of learning about their abilities.

One of the leading figures in this field in America was Samuel George Morton, a well-known physician and scientist. Morton expanded the work by studying the skulls of people from various races and countries. He measured the quantity of BB pellets that the skull would hold and used this as a measure of intelligence. Before you decide that he was crazy, you should realize that when he died, the *New York Daily Tribune* proclaimed that "probably no scientific man in America enjoyed a higher reputation among scholars throughout the world than Dr. Morton" (Gould, 1978).

Much of his reputation was based on his use of objective scientific measurements, in the spirit of modern-day empiricism. However, one of his major conclusions was that there is a difference in intelligence between the races of the world as well as within races. For example, Morton concluded that English and German people were more intelligent than Jewish people and that Jewish people were more intelligent than Hindu people. In terms of races, White people were seen as being at the top of the intelligence ladder, with Indian people in the middle and Black people on the bottom. Gould, a scholar interested in the history of science, reexamined Morton's data and the methods by which he came to his conclusions (Gould, 1978). Gould found that Morton "unconsciously" had selected his samples in such a way that the mean head sizes of the Indians were smaller than those of the Whites. Morton also made two errors in his mathematical computations; both favored the view of White supremacy, which was in vogue at that time.

There are other cases in which scientists did more than unconsciously or consciously push the data in the direction of their hypotheses; there are cases of outright fraud. Of course, these are problems of ethics, but we discuss them at this point. Two representative examples are the studies of Sir Cyril Burt and Walter Levy.

Burt was interested in demonstrating that intelligence is the result of genetic factors. One method of testing an idea such as this is to examine the intelligence of monozygotic twins (twins in which both individuals develop from the same egg and thus are genetically identical). Burt maintained that if twins who are genetically identical but have had different environmental influences have similar IQs, then it can be concluded that heredity has more effect on IQ than environment does. (These same types of studies are used for determining the genetic component of disorders such as schizophrenia.) However, when Burt's data were reexamined, the results of his studies were seen to present an almost impossible occurrence. The correlation between the IQs of monozygotic twins reared apart was .771 in the first sample of sets of twins, .771 in the second sample, and .771 in the third sample. As Burt found more and more twins who could be used in his study, he performed other correlations to measure how closely the IQs of the twins were similar, and whether the correlation was done using 21, 30, or 51 pairs of twins, the result was always .771. It is extremely unlikely that the correlations in all three studies would be exactly the same; most scientists familiar with Burt's work assume that his data were misreported to support his theory (for a discussion of this case, see Hearnshaw, 1979).

The second case is that of Walter Levy, who performed research in parapsychology. It came to light that Levy had altered data to support his previous research. He subsequently resigned and admitted that he had fudged the data. Barber (1976) not only discusses these cases but also points out that, in a number of studies, college students who have been asked to run laboratory experiments have been shown to change data or alter the instructions or procedure of the experiment. Whether these students wanted to get a good grade or were in a hurry to finish their midterm exams is not known.

The journal *Science* reports a case that resulted in the resignation of two scientists from two major medical centers and the retraction of 11 research reports from the scientific literature (Broad, 1980). The story began when a researcher submitted her paper to a scientific journal for publication. In the journal review process (which we discuss in Chapter 15), another scientist saw the paper and made a copy of it. During the next month, the second scientist wrote a paper that included passages from the first scientist's paper without reference to her. By chance, in the review process for this second paper, the first scientist saw the paper and realized that it included passages from her own work. She then wrote to the journal and to the dean of the medical school where the other scientist worked and accused the other scientist of plagiarism. According to the *Science* article, the dean at first felt that the scientist at the medical school had acted improperly in copying from the work of another, but that because the copying was not related to the actual data collection, it did not call into question the research itself. However, further investigation revealed that the original research had never been performed completely and that the results had been fabricated. In the process of the investigation, another scientist was implicated, and the results from 11 published papers were called into question.

During the 1990s renewed attention was directed to the question of scientific conduct. For example, a Commission on Research Integrity was established by the National Institutes of Health and held its first meeting in June 1994. Some purposes of this commission were to help define scientific misconduct and to gather experiences of scientists and others in terms of research fraud and misconduct. There is now a permanent Office of Research Integrity within the U.S. Department of Health and Human Services (DHHS), which has a website (http://ori.dhhs.gov/). In 2004 the department issued more formal guidance to clarify cases in which scientists had financial interest in the outcome of research.

International journals such as *Science* and *Nature* also have addressed these issues. For example, the journal *Science* devoted a section of its June 23, 1995, issue to the question of conduct in science. With increased competition for funds and the human need for recognition, this report emphasizes the importance of helping students to understand early in their careers the overall ecology of the scientific research enterprise, as we are doing in this chapter. Noting that little research has been directed at understanding research integrity issues, the DHHS funded a series of new projects beginning in 2002. Additional information about the freedom and responsibilities of scientists in relation to society and how they apply to beginning scientists like you can be found in the online publication *Professional Ethics Report* (PER) at the American Association for the Advancement of Science website (http://www.aaas.org/spp/sfrl/per/per.htm).

Experimenter bias not only can affect the data the experimenter records but also can exert a strong influence on the theoretical interpretation of the findings. Like any other human beings, scientists may consciously or unconsciously choose to view their own and other scientists' results from a biased position that supports their earlier viewpoints. Although few people would consider this type of behavior fraudulent, it is important to be aware of its possibility when evaluating published theories, reviewing papers, or even just reading the discussion sections of published papers.

■ Biased Interactions with Research Participants

To understand one way that an experimenter might unintentionally bias the interactions with research participants, consider yourself a participant in an experiment in which the scientist is testing the hypothesis that more college men than women dream about violating social taboos. Imagine what type of person (male or female, attractive or unattractive, old or young) you would be most willing to tell your uncommon dreams to. Imagine what type of person you would be least likely to tell your dreams to. As you realize that you react differently to different people in your life, you can also see how research participants in a psychological experiment might react differently to different experimenters. With some experimenters, participants would be reticent, and with others they would talk freely. Such experimenter characteristics as gender, attractiveness, dress, race, and age are known to influence many types of psychological experimentation and should be considered in evaluating a set of studies.

Once the experimenter begins to interact with participants in the actual experiment, additional factors are likely to influence the research. If you have performed research, remember your first experiment. Otherwise, imagine what it would be like to ask people to serve as participants in an experiment. In the real or imagined experiment, did you feel anxious? Did you feel that you were imposing on these people? Did you want one group to respond differently from another? Most experimenters do want their experimental groups to be different from their control groups. It is only natural, but it is also a source of bias if the experimenter communicates to the participants that they are expected to respond in a certain manner or if the experimenter treats one group differently from another. Let's now consider two examples of biased interactions with participants.

Animals can be bred for certain characteristics, such as color, temperament, and predisposition for specific diseases. In the first study, students were given rats to train in running a maze. Half the students were told that they had received specially bred maze-bright rats and the other half were told that they were given maze-dull animals. In reality all the animals were bred the same and were randomly assigned to the two groups of student experimenters. At the end of the study, the authors reported that the rats trained and tested by experimenters expecting bright behavior showed statistically significant superior learning over that of the rats run by the experimenters expecting dull behavior (Rosenthal & Fode, 1963). A second study using a Skinner box showed the same findings with other experimenters and animals (Rosenthal & Lawson, 1964).

Similar work has also shown expectancy effects with humans. In a classic study by Rosenthal and Jacobson (1966), teachers were told that certain students, who were actually chosen at random, had shown great promise on a newly developed IQ test. Indeed, these students did show increased achievement gains some 8 months later. Clearly, the teachers treated the randomly selected group in a different manner than those who were not named by the researchers as having great promise. Rosenthal and Rubin (1978) have reviewed 345 studies of interpersonal expectancy, and it is now apparent that scientists, like people everywhere, have expectations and that these expectations may influence the outcomes of their studies. They may even influence the type of interaction that a research participant is required to complete. For example, a persuasion study examining sex differences might report inaccurate results if the male experimenter selected topics on which he could perform well and ignored those that he did not understand but were part of the working knowledge of women.

This same type of bias may appear as we attempt to study the behavior and experience of people from cultures other than our own. For example, researchers are only beginning to understand the factors that influence how ethnic minority college students experience emotional distress (Okazaki, 1997) or factors that determine how Asian Americans, African Americans, Mexican Americans, and White clients use and respond to mental health services (Sue, Fujino, Hu, Takeuchi & Zane, 1991).

As we begin to study other species with which we cannot communicate directly, an even more difficult situation occurs. Often, we attempt to modify the methods that we have used with humans and apply them to animal populations. This is especially problematic when we assume that animals are exactly like humans and ignore important differences in nervous systems or, conversely, when we say that animals are totally different from humans and ignore the great similarities. As we move toward more cognitive and experiential types of research with animals (for example, Budiansky, 1998; Ristau, 1991), we also move toward a greater potential for biased attributions regarding animal cognition, be it language, emotion, or mental imagery. The problem of this bias is that it may divert the discussion from the real breakthroughs in our understanding of animal cognition toward an argument concerning a few overinterpreted issues such as *animal language* or *animal consciousness*.

Although we all like to think of ourselves as objective in our research, it is important to realize that our passionate commitment to our own hypotheses may lead us to give special attention to the outcomes that we expect from our research. In this way we create self-fulfilling prophecies; that is, we expect something to happen and look for confirmation of our expectations. Even researchers who study self-fulfilling prophecies may have self-fulfilling prophecies, as suggested by some who have tried to replicate Rosenthal's research.

In this and the preceding section we have discussed two major sources of experimenter bias: biased data collection by the scientist and biases conveyed by interactions between the experimenter and the research participant. Although research has described various possible sources of experimenter bias, this issue is complex, and our understanding of these sources of bias is far from complete. Consequently, it is difficult to say exactly how various situations bring forth bias. Thus, it becomes the task of the scientist when designing a new study—and of the witness when evaluating research—to ask whether experimenter bias might influence either the treatment of participants or the collection of the data. Perhaps the best way we can minimize the effects of this problem is to remind ourselves that the only way that we will ever understand human behavior and experience is to examine it in its complexity, which includes the manner in which scientists and participants interact.

■ Some Ways to Avoid Experimenter Bias

A number of possible procedures can help to reduce experimenter bias. As suggested, one of the most common is to use several different experimenters, and even to include this as a factor in the study. Maher (1978a) suggests that it may be necessary, especially in clinical psychology research, to expose the participants to a number of different experimenters and experimental situations. This suggestion is based on Brunswik's notion that we should sample not only from research participant populations but also from a number of stimuli situations (Brunswik, 1947). By this Brunswik meant that the psychological phenomenon under study should be presented not only to a representative sample of research participants but also in a representative sample of situations.

Another way to reduce experimenter bias is to keep the person who is interacting with the participants blind to the hypothesis and to the particular groups with which he or she

Box 11.1

Recommendations for Research

In an attempt to improve psychological research, Theodore Barber (1976) suggests 13 changes that must be made in the way research is performed. This is a summary of these changes.

- In light of Kuhn's analysis of the importance of paradigms, researchers need to be aware of their underlying assumptions and state them explicitly when possible.

- Less bias will occur if the person who plans the study (the investigator) is not the same person who analyzes the data.

- Less bias will occur if the person who plans the study (the investigator) is not the same person who actually performs the study (the experimenter).

- Researchers should be pilot participants in their own experiments, to understand the actual experience of experimentation as encountered by the research participants.

- Investigators (those who plan studies) should specify *exactly* what the experimenters (those who run the studies) should and should not do and when.

- Pilot studies carried out by experimenters should be run and supervised carefully by investigators to ensure correct and rehearsed procedures before the actual experimental phase begins.

- Researchers should be trained in the complexity of data analysis and the manner in which different types of analyses may lead to different conclusions.

- Students should be taught more the value of good research methods in answering questions and less the importance of finding significant results.

- Teachers in beginning experimental courses should emphasize the importance of following research procedures to the letter and recording the data honestly.

- When investigators use experimenters to run the experiment, the investigators should monitor carefully to see that the procedures are being followed.

- Investigators should use multiple experimenters, who vary in personal attributes, to collect the data.

- Whenever possible, experiments should be performed blind; if possible, the experimenter giving the treatment should be different from the experimenter recording the results.

- One should not rely on any one study for the answer but seek replications performed by different experimenters in different locations. For the student, a replication of a previous experiment should be encouraged and rewarded as a worthwhile activity.

is working. For example, blind studies often are used in drug research in which behavioral ratings are made after a certain drug is administered. In this type of study, the raters are not told which participants received which drugs or even whether they received a drug at all. In this way the experimenter's expectation cannot be conveyed to the participants, nor can it affect the manner in which the data are recorded. For more recommendations for improving research, see Box 11.1. (We discuss double-blind studies in more detail later in the chapter.)

The most useful way to begin eliminating experimenter bias from your own experiments is to try consciously to see the experiment from varying perspectives. We are in a stronger position if we accept that we all are human and make mistakes. The important point for science is not that we were wrong but that we are willing to change.

CONCEPT CHECK 11.1 Four developmental psychologists each watched and rated the same set of videotapes of children expressing aggression while playing. From these tapes, the psychologists concluded that boys are more aggressive than girls when they play. What additional information would you want before you accepted this conclusion?

SUBJECT FACTORS

Another potential source of misinterpretation traditionally has been called subject factors. **Subject factors** are present when the research participants are not behaving *in the way we expect them to behave.* Some of these factors occur because we have not considered how a particular participant might experience our study. Subject factors boil down to the realization that research participants are human. In some cases participants are highly motivated to please the experimenter. In other cases they may try to figure out the experiment and behave in a way that will support or sabotage the experiment.

In many psychology departments, introductory students serve as participants in experiments to earn extra points on their final grades. Scientists working in these settings will be quick to tell you that near the end of the term, when students are working under increased pressure, participant bias can become a real problem. At exam time the available participants may feel harassed, anxious, tired, and generally negative toward participating in research. From a broader ecological perspective, it is clear that such a participant has little motivation to be part of a psychological experiment. Thus, it is the task of the scientist to consider how the participant experiences the experiment and to look for personal and social factors that might bias the results of the experiment.

One classic example of an initially overlooked subject factor occurred in an experiment conducted in the 1930s. The experiment took place at the Hawthorne plant of Western Electric and was designed to determine how factors such as lighting and working hours affect productivity. The participants were a group of women who worked at the plant; they were asked to work under varying conditions. The productivity of these women was compared with general productivity. When the data were analyzed, a strange finding emerged. In many cases the productivity of these women increased. It even increased under a condition in which the lighting in the experimental condition was not as good as that in the actual plant. From an experimental design standpoint, it was difficult to understand the data until the experimenters examined how they had treated these women. The answer they came up with was that the women in the experiment had been given special attention just by being in an experiment. This attention caused the women to consider themselves *special,* and this feeling was reflected in the work they performed.

Today the **Hawthorne effect** remains a warning to experimenters that being given attention and considering oneself special may produce, either directly or indirectly, results much stronger than those of the experimental independent variables. This is not to suggest that you treat the research participants of your experiments in a cold, impersonal manner, but you should take into account the way in which the research participants experience your experiment. In some cases you may need a control group that is treated just as "special" as the experimental group. The easiest way to evaluate participants' perceptions of their treatment is simply to ask a few people to be participants in your study and then ask them how they felt and how they reacted to your study.

Another example of participant bias took place during the Depression and involved a group of dental students who were paid to be research participants. The study had been designed to examine a new type of toothpaste and its effects on bacterial concentration and tooth decay. Participants with high bacterial concentrations were sought. To qualify for the study and earn some needed money, the students ate candy bars to increase their bacterial concentrations. Once the study was over and the participants were paid, they quit eating candy, and the bacterial counts decreased. The experimenters did not realize that the participants had been eating candy bars, and in their analysis of follow-up reports they stated that the decrease in bacterial concentration was due to the new experimental toothpaste (Simon, 1978). This story demonstrates that in research we are dealing with human beings, whose behavior may be motivated by any number of factors, many of which we do not even suspect. The dental study illustrates that the participants were reacting not only to the demands of the experimental environment by using the new toothpaste but also to the demands of a larger environment, in this case an economic one.

In psychological experiments the witness reminds us that it is not enough to watch the behavior of human beings as one would watch inanimate objects. Although people may *just* react to the experiment as designed, their reactions may also reflect many factors of which we are not aware. It is our delightful human complexity that makes psychological research both difficult and exciting. Psychological scientists have had to learn that participants are not passive robots; they are active, creative people with definite motives. It is impossible for any experimenter to know exactly which aspects of the study the participants are responding to and what their motives are. For example, when a participant takes part in a psychological experiment, it is impossible to predict (regardless of the design of the study) whether the participant will react to the experimenter as someone to make contact with, as someone to talk to, as a neutral person just doing a job, or as a person who is keeping the participant away from some important work such as studying for an exam.

Because the participant in an experiment is an active, creative, complex human being, he or she may decide not to follow the instructions of the experiment and to second-guess the experimenter by acting in a certain manner. Consider an experiment in which the participants are shown erotic films, and then a physiological measure such as pulse rate is taken. In reality the participants might find the films boring, but because they like the experimenter and want to help him or her, they might decide to think about someone who does make them feel erotic and thus give the experimenter more interesting results. Unfortunately, the results have nothing to do with the research as it was designed.

Let's now examine three possible ways that participants might respond in such an experiment. If the experimenter asks participants to watch an erotic film, they might (1) just watch the film and react naturally; (2) react, out of humanness, more to the experimenter than to the film; or (3) consciously construct what they think the experiment is about and respond to the thought rather than to the film. Restated in broad terms, participants may react to the experimental situation, to the experimenter, or to themselves. What makes the interpretation of scientific research even more difficult is that these three possibilities may be brought forth systematically and thus bias the results in a number of complex ways. In the erotic film example, we might find a gender and experimenter interaction in which men and women react differently to a female experimenter.

As we will see, participants may react differently not only to the experimenter but also to the experimental situation itself. In this section we consider two important phenomena: the placebo effect and demand characteristics. These two phenomena remind us of the importance of having a broad ecological understanding of the relationships among the scientist, the research participant, and the experimental situation.

 CONCEPT CHECK 11.2   A famous psychologist comes to campus. As part of her visit, she selects a small group of research participants and conducts a demonstration of a new cognitive self-help technique with the group. When asked about the new procedure at a meeting of the psychology club, the students all give testimonials about how the new technique changed their lives. What different factors might have led to such testimonials?

■ Placebo Factors

One potential problem in an experiment is the influence of **placebo** effects. Imagine that you have just picked up your newspaper and there is a story that says, "Scientists have found a new cure for headaches." As you continue to read the story, you are told of a technique called biofeedback, in which information about physiological changes from a person's body is fed back to the person; it is through the use of this feedback that headaches are being cured. As a consumer of scientific research, how would you go about evaluating this story? First, you might use common sense and note that it seems reasonable that as one learns to relax there should be a decrease in muscle tension and that the number of headaches that are thought to be related to tension should also decrease. Second, you might check the experimental design to see whether the study included a baseline condition in which the number of headaches per person was recorded before biofeedback was administered. If you have headaches yourself, you might be ready to run out to the local biofeedback practitioner and sign up. But even if the biofeedback treatment worked for you as it did for the people in the study, it still would not have been demonstrated scientifically that biofeedback was the ingredient that caused your headaches to decrease. Both the consumer and the scientist would need to consider the placebo factor.

The term *placebo* comes from the Latin verb *placere,* "to please." It refers to the phenomenon that some people show physiological changes just from the suggestion that a change will take place. For example, in a number of studies that have attempted to treat tension headaches with a variety of procedures, it has been shown that 60% of the people report signs of improvement when given only placebo treatments, such as a pill containing nothing but sugar or other inert ingredients (Hass, Fink, & Hartfelder, 1963). In recent years research has suggested that endorphins (naturally occurring chemical compounds with analgesic properties) may be released internally on the expectation of change. This finding may contribute to our understanding of the placebo effect.

The placebo phenomenon is so strong with some people that a placebo operation (opening up the chest but not performing a heart operation) has been shown to result in recovery rates for patients with angina pectoris (pains in the chest) similar to those following an actual coronary bypass operation (Cobb, Thomas, Dillard, Merendino, & Bruce, 1959). To control for the placebo effect in research, various procedures have been used. One is to use a control group that receives either no treatment or a treatment previously shown to be ineffective for the particular disorder under study.

A more powerful control is to use a **double-blind** experiment in which the experimental group is divided into two groups. One group is given the actual treatment, and the other is given a treatment exactly like the experimental treatment but without the active ingredient.

© Sidney Harris, ScienceCartoonsPlus.com

"IT WAS MORE OF A 'TRIPLE-BLIND' TEST. THE PATIENTS DIDN'T KNOW WHICH ONES WERE GETTING THE REAL DRUG, THE DOCTORS DIDN'T KNOW, AND, I'M AFRAID, NOBODY KNEW."

For example, in a study of medication, the placebo group would receive a medicine that looks and tastes like the experimental one but does not contain the substance being tested. Neither the placebo group nor the experimental group would know which medication they were receiving, and in this way these research participants are said to be **blind controls.** The term *double blind* indicates that the physicians or nurses giving the medication also do not know which medication is experimental and which is placebo. A more sophisticated version of this design would allow for the placebo and experimental research participants to be switched systematically during the study; thus, the same participant would receive at times the active treatment and at times the placebo treatment (for an overview, see Shapiro, 1997; White, Tursky, & Schwartz, 1985). Placebo research continues to be an important topic as evidenced by a National Institutes of Health conference on the Science of Placebo devoted to the topic. The conference was held in 2000 with a book (*The Science of the Placebo*) published in 2002 (for information, see http://placebo.nih.gov/).

■ Demand Characteristics

A phenomenon similar to the placebo effect is that of demand characteristics in psychological research. **Demand characteristics** occur when a participant's response is influenced more by the research setting than by the independent variable. For example, in a test on the effect of marijuana on behavior or on the effects of hypnosis, most participants have some idea of how they will be expected to act, and they may respond in this manner. The response may include actual faking on the part of the participant. If demand characteristics play an important role in the experiment, then they pose a significant threat to internal validity and offer an alternative explanation for understanding the influence of the independent variable.

Orne and Scheibe (1964) sought to understand the role of demand characteristics in a sensory deprivation experiment. Sensory deprivation research has focused on the effects of reducing the amount of stimulation a person receives from the environment. In such an experiment, participants are asked to lie in a room with pads on their arms and legs and goggles over their eyes, which blocks out stimulation. Early descriptions of this research reported in the popular press suggested that without sensory stimulation, research participants would hallucinate, feel disoriented, and have a difficult time working on any type of task.

Orne and Scheibe set up a sensory deprivation experiment without any sensory deprivation. They divided participants into two groups. Participants in the first group received a physical exam and gave a short medical history. Although they were told that the experiment was safe, they were allowed to see a tray labeled "Emergency Tray" that had drugs and medical instruments on it. This group was asked to report any problems that they might have in concentrating, as well as any unusual visual imagery, fantasies, or feelings (including disorientation) that they might have. The participants were told that during the experiment they were to work on an arithmetic task. They were then placed in a special room with food, water, and the materials needed for the arithmetic task. Inside the room was a button marked "Emergency Alarm" that they could press if they wanted to get out of the room.

The control group was not given a physical exam or shown the "Emergency Tray." The people in the control group were told only that they were to perform the arithmetic task and that if they needed to get out of the room, they should knock on the window.

In actuality neither group received any type of sensory deprivation. However, the results reported by the experimental group were similar to those reported in the previous sensory deprivation experiments. This study suggests that the previous results may have been related to the expectations of the research participants—expectations based on either their own knowledge or an experimenter's leading questions—rather than sensory deprivation alone. Thus, in any type of research that asks for a participant's reaction (such as studies using alcohol, drugs, or hypnosis), it is important to consider the possible influence of demand characteristics. If possible, a demand-characteristics condition should be built into the experiment.

Orne reported one study of hypnosis that attempted to control for demand characteristics (Orne, 1969; Orne & Evans, 1966). The purpose of the study was to find out what would happen if a hypnotist left the room after deep hypnosis had been induced. This particular experiment had theoretical importance because one theory of hypnosis suggested that the research participants would return to their normal state of awareness rapidly, whereas another predicted that it would take some time. The study was designed to see which of the two theories more accurately reflected reality. In the study a group of hypnotic participants was compared with a control group in which research participants were asked to simulate hypnosis and act as if they were hypnotized. Orne and Evans called their control group a *quasi-control group* because the control group was being used more to check out the experimental conditions than to compare directly with the experimental group.

The experimenters wanted to design a study in which the hypnotist left the room in an apparently accidental manner, in order to avoid breaking the implicit agreement that the hypnotist would remain with and take care of the hypnotized research participant. To accomplish this end, the experimenters staged a power failure. During the second of two sessions, after the experimental participants had been hypnotized and were tapping their feet to imagined music, a tape recorder in the room stopped and a desk light went off. The experimenter said that a fuse had blown and left the room.

The findings of the study were apparently clear. The quasi-control group continued to act as if hypnotized until the experimenter returned some 30 minutes later. However, the experimental participants brought themselves out from the hypnotic trance. This required varying amounts of time, and, once out from under the trance, they appeared somewhat confused.

During the postexperimental interviews, it was learned that the quasi-control research participants believed that the power failure was not real. The experimental group did not seem to suspect the deception. Because the quasi-control research participants were aware of the deception, it was difficult to conclude anything directly from the study. The experimenters then considered ways to make the power failure seem more real. They reexamined the experimental situation and realized that although the tape recorder and the desk lamp had gone off, the room lights and a small polygraph continued to be on. Also, the room had a one-way mirror, and this suggested to the research participants that they were being observed, which they were.

A new study was designed. This study also used an experimental and a quasi-control group, but the room was changed. There was no one-way mirror, and when the pretended power failure occurred, all the equipment and the lights in the room went off. The experimenter was blind as to which was the real hypnotic group and which was the simulated one. Under the new conditions, the results for the experimental group were the same. However,

"WHAT IT COMES DOWN TO IS YOU HAVE TO
FIND OUT WHAT REACTION THEY'RE LOOKING
FOR, AND YOU GIVE THEM THAT REACTION."

the quasi-control group showed quite different results. As soon as the experimenter left the room, the great majority of these participants stopped simulating and acted as if they were not being observed.

Orne and Evans concluded from the second study that both groups considered the power failure real and that their experimental manipulation was therefore meaningful. Without a control for demand characteristics, an experimenter might have concluded that the theories were correct when in fact the results might have been due to the research participants' acting as they believed they should.

When evaluating research, it is important to consider the role of placebo factors and demand characteristics. It is also important for the researcher to check through such techniques as the quasi-control group and the credibility of the experimental manipulations. *It is not enough to assume that the participants in an experiment believe what is being said and accept rationales as true; this must be verified, especially in any study that uses deception.*

 CONCEPT CHECK 11.3   A researcher interested in the manner in which vitamins help a person feel better devised a study in which she gave vitamins along with orange juice to one group of research participants and orange juice alone to another group. How might you design this study to reduce placebo and other similar effects?

CULTURAL AND SOCIAL BIAS

You may think it strange to suggest that the society and environment in which you live could cause significant bias in scientific research. Yet science is not immune to a shared cultural view, whether it be that a certain racial group is inferior or that one type of science is better than another. Sometimes a scientist may perform a research study and not realize that his or her data are biased.

For example, a number of studies have shown that people who go to an outpatient psychiatric facility for intervention often receive treatment based not on their disorders but on other factors such as their ethnic backgrounds. In general, in these studies African Americans tended to receive psychopharmacological interventions and Caucasians tended to receive verbal psychotherapy. If a researcher were to conduct a study using past medical records, there would be an unintended confound of race because the two types of treatment used different populations. It is also the case that health psychology and other medical studies previously relied heavily on male participants, which could bias the results.

To combat such bias, in 1994 the U.S. National Institutes of Health implemented a policy that required all federally funded research involving human participants to include women and members of minority groups. In response to this requirement, the *Journal of Consulting and Clinical Psychology* devoted a special issue (October 1996) to the recruitment and retention of minorities in clinical research. Not only do we see an emphasis to perform research that more adequately reflects the characteristics of our own society but we are also beginning to see a greater emphasis of understanding worldwide processes in terms of cross-cultural research methods (Lyons & Chryssochoou, 2000).

One common way in which scientific research may be influenced is through a shared paradigm (Kuhn, 1970). A **paradigm** is an accepted worldview; it may include ideas about the value of what one is doing as well as specific assumptions about how the world is. Because a paradigm shapes the way in which you see the world, when it changes, everything seems to change. A number of paradigm changes in science have altered the manner in which scientists see the world. One of the first was the change from seeing the earth as the center of the universe to seeing it as just another planet. Once the earth was seen as just another planet, a new scientific cosmology became possible, as did a new idea about the place of humans in the universe.

In psychology we have seen changes in scientific viewpoints that have allowed research never considered possible. For example, at one time it was considered impossible to have a scientific study of consciousness. However, consciousness has now become an important focus for the neurosciences with research journals devoted to this topic. Today there are a number of research projects in which chimpanzees are being taught to communicate either through a computer or through sign language, thus opening an entirely new field of research that a few years ago was considered impossible. Likewise, we are gaining a new view of both young people and old people that suggests they are capable of far greater potential than we had assumed previously. Whereas the previous paradigm emphasized the negative and pathological, today's view is currently being expanded to include a positive psychology. We now are beginning to realize that children can interact with their external environment—for example, by recognizing faces—immediately after birth. Not only our children but also we ourselves are beginning to be seen in a new light.

We are also beginning to realize that the body and its physiology are influenced directly by emotional and cognitive factors previously thought to have little influence. For example, we now know that brain connections can be modified, which was previously thought impossible. We need to keep in mind that by limiting ideas, important questions are not asked and productive relationships are left unexplored. We introduce a bias into our scientific research by letting the believed limitations of our time restrict the scope of our vision. Consequently, we never consider certain aspects of behavior that lie beyond our limited view. Every scientist and every society holds limited views of the world. That is not the point; rather, the point is to *realize* that this is the case.

KEY TERMS AND CONCEPTS

1. **The role of the witness in science**
2. **Ecology**
3. **Experimenter factors**
   A. Personal equation
   B. Interrater reliability
   C. Experimenter bias
4. **Subject factors**
   A. Hawthorne effect
5. **Placebo factors**
6. **Demand characteristics**
7. **Double-blind experiment**
8. **Cultural and social bias**

SUMMARY

1. All research takes place in a specific context, which extends beyond the laboratory. This context includes the scientist–research participant interactions during an experiment, the world of the scientist when he or she is not performing science, and the world of the research participant when he or she is not being part of an experiment.

2. Ecology as a science interested in the relationship of living organisms and their environment offers a model for studying the overall contextual relationships between the scientist and the research participant. Ecological validity depends on whether the relationships among the scientist, the research participant, and the context have been fully considered in evaluating a piece of research.

3. Experimenter effects are changes in the dependent variable produced by the attitude or behavior of the experimenter and not related to the independent variable. These effects may be a result of biased data collection by the experimenter or by experimenter influence on the research participant's performance.

4. Using multiple experimenters and having the experimenter not know (be blind to) a research participant's group can reduce the threat of experimenter bias.

5. Research participants may also bias an experiment. They live in their own psychological worlds, and this factor must be considered, as illustrated by the Hawthorne experiment. In that experiment, the research participants felt themselves to be special and responded accordingly. Some research participants may want to help an experimenter and in so doing give the data that they think the experimenter wants. Other research participants may try to sabotage an experiment.

6. The word *placebo* comes from the Latin word for "to please." The placebo effect is the phenomenon (especially likely in drug or psychotherapy studies) in which a suggestion of change actually produces a change. Recent research suggests there may be a biochemical basis to the placebo response.

7. The term *demand characteristics* refers to the research participants' being more influenced by the experimental setting than by the independent variable. An example of this would be the case in which research participants who have been told to consume a large quantity of alcohol produce behaviors that they believe someone who is drunk would produce.

REVIEW QUESTIONS

1. How can the concept of ecology be applied to the experimental situation?
2. Give some examples of experimenter bias. How would you attempt to reduce this bias?
3. What are *placebo effects*?
4. How might a drug company control for placebo effects?
5. Discuss demand characteristics.
6. What potential experimental biases might result from the interaction between the research participant and the experimenter?

DISCUSSION QUESTIONS AND PROJECTS

1. Discuss how research results depend on the context in which they are derived. How do they transcend the context?
2. It is said that experimenter bias does not affect the internal validity of an experiment. What does this mean? In what cases is this statement true and in what cases false?
3. How could the Hawthorne effect play a role in the experiments that you perform in class?
4. When does a research participant in an experiment know what the independent variable is?
5. Design your own double-blind study. What information would you give to the research participants, and what information would you give to the experimenters?
6. A researcher is interested in the effects of alpha-wave feedback on feelings of well-being. The researcher develops an experiment in which the experimental group receives alpha biofeedback and fills out a "feeling of well-being" questionnaire before and after the experimental session and again the next day. The control group is shown a cartoon book and also fills out the questionnaire before and after the session and on the next day. Both the control and experimental groups showed similar positive scores after the session, but only the alpha-feedback group reported more positive well-being on the next-day questionnaire. The researcher concludes that alpha biofeedback has lasting effects on a person's well-being. Discuss this conclusion.

INFOTRAC COLLEGE EDITION: EXERCISES

When researchers code videotapes or rate participants' responses, using more than one coder helps to control for bias. It is important to determine how similar two coders are in their classification of events or responses. One method is to determine the correlation between two judges' responses. Mary Ann Foley and her colleagues had two judges rate imagery responses in terms of self-references. You can read this study using InfoTrac College Edition by looking up either the author or the study ("Self-referencing: how incessant the stream?") that was published in the *American Journal of Psychology* (Spring 1999).

In terms of biased data, we discussed the work of Sir Cyril Burt. You can read more about the papers of Burt in an article ("Some further observations concerning Sir Cyril Burt") by Brian Butler and Jennifer Petrulis, which was published in the *British Journal of Psychology* (February 1999). Another article by R. B. Joynson in the August 2003 issue of the *British Journal of Psychology* reviews the evidence against Cyril Burt in the light of selective bias.

We also discussed how research participants might give biased results as illustrated by the Hawthorne effect. Using InfoTrac College Edition, you can see how current human factor researchers control for the Hawthorne effect in a study ("Workplace changes associated with a reduction in musculoskeletal symptoms in office workers") by Nancy Nelson and Barbara Silverstein, published in the journal *Human Factors*.

To help you better understand the material in this chapter, you can go to Wadsworth's research methods workshop web page at http://www.wadsworth.com/ psychology_d/templates/student_resources/workshops/ resch_wrk.html. There you will find workshops related to research methods and statistics. The research methods workshop on "Controls" discusses single- and double-blind studies.

☑ Answers to Concept Checks

11.1 One important piece of information would be the interrater reliability, using the specific operational definition of aggression. If this correlation were low, you might conclude that the operational definition of aggression was not a good one. You might also want to know the sex of each rater and whether there were any systematic errors in the manner in which the ratings were made.

11.2 A variety of factors might have influenced the students' testimonials. First, the cognitive self-help technique might actually have changed their lives. However, before you would want to accept this conclusion, you should rule out a number of other factors. Some of these include being associated with a famous psychologist, the changes that result from being selected to be part of a small elite group, and the desire to please.

11.3 One obvious problem with the initial study is that the results could be influenced by the manner in which the experimenter gave participants the vitamins. That is, she could convey additional encouragement or expectancy that would bias the results. A simple improvement would be to run the study as a double-blind placebo study, such that one group received a vitamin and the other group a placebo pill that was similar in appearance to the vitamin tablet. In addition, neither the research participants nor the experimenter would know which were the actual vitamin pills and which were the placebos.

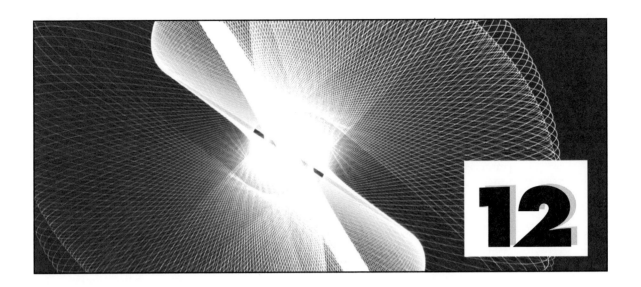

QUASI-EXPERIMENTAL, CORRELATIONAL, AND NATURALISTIC OBSERVATIONAL DESIGNS

CLOSED AND OPEN SYSTEMS

QUASI-EXPERIMENTAL DESIGNS
Time Series Design
Interrupted Time Series Design
Multiple Time Series Design
Nonequivalent Before–After Design
Retrospective and Ex Post Facto Designs

CORRELATIONAL PROCEDURES

NATURALISTIC OBSERVATIONS
Concerns While Making Naturalistic Observations
To Conceal or Not to Conceal; To Participate or Not
  to Participate
Strengths and Weaknesses of Naturalistic
  Observation

In the previous chapters, we presented a more idealized approach to experimentation, one in which the experimenter has a high degree of control over the experimental manipulation. Such experiments play an important role in making inferences because few variables are uncontrolled by the experimenter. However, one cannot always construct an experimental situation with a great deal of control—for example, when we study the psychological reaction to natural disasters such as earthquakes. There are other times when the researcher is faced with a situation in which uncontrollable or unpredictable factors influence the experimental outcomes. Even a well-designed study may be compromised by problems such as unequal attrition rates, in which randomization can no longer be assumed. For example, a researcher may discover that a data collection device did not function properly on a particular day or that an unequal number of participants in one condition did not complete the experiment.

The design task for all these situations is still to help support inferences of the greatest strength possible. Although the logic remains the same, the methods for accomplishing this task may vary somewhat, hence the designation quasi-experimental design. Quasi-experimental designs are one focus of this chapter. A second approach we examine is that of correlational procedures. We conclude with a discussion of naturalistic observation. Because these three procedures often are used in research conducted outside the laboratory, we illustrate their use in such a context. However, moving a study to the field does not preclude the use of tight experimental control or the use of designs centered on the manipulation of variables. Many of the designs that we have discussed previously may be applied in the field, depending on the questions asked.

Throughout the chapter we discuss the more philosophical issue of when one would want to give up rigorous experimental controls in order to better study real-world processes and thus collect data more relevant to our everyday lives. Such a debate in relation to memory was presented in *American Psychologist* in January 1991. In considering the general issue of tight design as opposed to more real-world research, we discuss the relationship between internal and external validity as we seek to design research that is both sound and relevant.

CLOSED AND OPEN SYSTEMS

Throughout the history of science, experimental control of the research situation has been a prime objective. You can see this desire for control in classic studies in the physical sciences as well as in psychological research. Scientists try to create a research environment in which they can control the important factors that influence the topic under study. That is, they try to create a closed system. For our purposes a *closed system* is one in which the important factors that influence the environment are controlled by the experimenter. For example, the technique of studying falling objects such as feathers and weights in the closed system of a vacuum chamber illustrates the great degree of control achieved in classical physics. Likewise, B. F. Skinner's use of the Skinner box and the precise caring for and feeding of animals offers the experimenter a high degree of control over the environment to which an organism is exposed and makes possible detailed studies of animal learning.

When we have a high degree of control over the environment, the types of designs we discussed in Chapters 9 and 10 are extremely important. With these experimental designs, we have the greatest confidence that our dependent variable truly reflects the effect of our independent variable. In particular, these designs help us to rule out alternative explanations and rival hypotheses, and in this manner they ensure a greater degree of internal validity.

Sound experimental control and the resulting high degree of internal validity are extremely desirable features in any experiment. Yet whatever the importance of internal validity, it is equally important that our designs reflect other issues as well. For example, our research findings should be generalizable. Can the results of an experiment be generalized beyond our particular research setting to ongoing life situations? For example, would waiters perform the same on a laboratory memory task—in which they have little personal investment—as they would when they take your order in a restaurant? Such questions are important as we seek to generalize our results beyond one specific setting to a broader context. The generalizability of an experimental outcome is called its **external validity.** When Campbell and Stanley (1963) first used the term *external validity,* they were asking to what other groups, settings, treatment variables, and measurement variables an experimental outcome could be generalized.

Today, many scientists and nonscientists are insisting that research findings should have direct relevance to everyday psychological issues that affect us all. This growing concern for the applicability of our research findings to the real-life situations that we all face influences our research efforts in two ways. First, the theoretical questions and hypotheses we generate increasingly deal with complex, relevant psychological issues and processes. Second, our research participants and settings increasingly reflect real-life situations.

One method for increasing the generality and relevance of our research is to move the research from the laboratory to the setting in which the phenomenon that we are studying occurs naturally. For example, in a laboratory you could not study the psychological effect of experiencing some unplanned event such as an inner-city riot, the bombing of the Federal Building in Oklahoma, the nuclear reactor accident at Three Mile Island, the destruction of the World Trade Center in New York City, or a natural disaster such as an earthquake. Neither can you study in the laboratory the impact of some large-scale intervention policy such as the Head Start Program. If we were studying the effect of anxiety on final examination performance, a possible natural setting would be the actual final examination session of a college course. If our theoretical issue deals with interpersonal relationships between strangers in a large city, then the natural setting is the streets of that city.

Although moving research into the field does not preclude rigorous experimental designs, it is often the case that as we move outside the laboratory and its highly controlled environment, we find ourselves able to control fewer of the factors that influence the behavior of our participants and thus less able to rule out alternative hypotheses. Whereas we often consider the laboratory a closed system, the world outside the laboratory is an open system in which the participants are influenced by a number of factors over which experimenters have little control.

In some cases, we cannot manipulate the levels of the independent variable; in others, we cannot adequately eliminate potentially confounding variables; and in most we have little real control in terms of participant selection and assignment. Outside the laboratory we have little influence over what humans do, feel, or think as they move about in the everyday world. In these situations we cannot achieve the same degree of control that we accomplish in a closed system. Thus, we need research designs that are appropriate to situations in which we have greater difficulty ruling out alternative explanations and that give us less certainty that the changes in the dependent variable were really the result of changes in the independent variable. In these situations (which also may include some laboratory situations), we may find ourselves relying more on reasoning and logic than on direct control of the experimental situation.

In fact, in some cases the time required for developing control of the experimental situation brings about unforeseen consequences. Let's consider one striking anecdote told by developmental psychologist Dale Harris. When Harris was teaching at the University of Minnesota, one student decided to perform an experiment that enlisted the participation of elderly people in retirement homes around Minneapolis. To sample participants randomly, the student collected the names of all the residents of the retirement homes and began random selection in such a way that each resident had an equal chance of being selected for the study. However, the time required to complete this sampling process correlated with an event that was unforeseen by the student. During the time in which this random sampling was taking place, 12% of the residents in the retirement homes died! This points up the importance of reducing tight experimental controls when the phenomenon under study occurs in a changing environment. Additional examples of such studies are those performed in a changing work environment or clinical studies performed in hospitals and clinics, where both patients and staff change frequently. These changes make tight experimental controls impractical.

It is possible to perform useful research in the field even with lowered control. For example, one applied study asked whether rear-end collisions could be reduced by adding a warning device to the backs of cars (Voevodsky, 1974). The independent variable was an amber light that indicated the rate of deceleration and was affixed to the rear ends of taxicabs. A group of cabs that did not have the device served as a control group. At the end of the experimental period, the group of cabs with the device had a rear-end collision rate lower than that of the control group.

What types of questions might you ask in evaluating this study? One question would relate to the Hawthorne effect, which we discussed in Chapter 11. Might the drivers in the experimental group have seen themselves as part of an experiment and been more careful in their driving? The author of the research suggested that if there were such an effect, then we would expect to see an overall reduction in accident rates for the cabs. That is, one might expect that both the control and experimental groups would have had lower accident rates during the experimental period than during similar periods in previous years. The rate for front-end accidents, in which the taxi runs into another car, was the same for both the experimental taxis and the control taxis. Also, there was no reduction in front-end accidents. The only reduction in accidents was for those caused by other cars running into the taxis from behind, and that reduction occurred only in the experimental group. Thus, it could be assumed that driving a cab with the device did not influence how carefully the driver of the cab drove, but that it did influence the driving of those who were following the cabs.

This taxi study offers an example of a valid and useful study performed with less control than found in the laboratory. In this study reasoning and logic were used to arrive at the conclusions drawn from the research results. Such research may have a direct influence on our lives because all new cars sold in this country come equipped with a third rear brake light, mounted at eye level (generally above the trunk).

Sometimes significant events that change our lives cannot be predicted and make designing research more difficult. However, as we will see, there are procedures for helping us to answer research questions. As you look into the psychological literature, you will see that a variety of tragedies and natural phenomena have been researched. The critical issue in such situations is formulating the research question and logically ruling out alternative explanations. The attacks on the World Trade Center on September 11, 2001, came as a surprise. Yet, even such a tragic event can offer us insights into human behavior as well as appropriate methods for treating those who experience such tragedies.

For example, suppose we were interested in studying the psychological effects of a disaster such as the World Trade Center in 2001, the nuclear accident at Three Mile Island in 1979, or the Loma Prieta earthquake in 1989. There is no way we could control the onset or even the site of such an occurrence, nor could we randomly assign some people to a *potential meltdown* or *earthquake group* and others to a *no-meltdown* or *nonearthquake group.*

In the case of the World Trade Center, it would be difficult to find someone who was not affected in some manner including fear of flying or desire to learn more about certain areas of the world or religious movements. Furthermore, when dealing with the people affected, it would be difficult to eliminate other factors that may have coincided with the disaster itself. Some of these influences may have been positive, such as the concern expressed by friends, relatives, and strangers all over the country. Others were probably more negative, such as fear of future terrorist attacks and concern over local and national security.

Let's assume that you are interested in some of the effects of the 1989 Loma Prieta earthquake. It occurred at the time when much of the country was watching a World Series game being broadcast from San Francisco, and thus the earthquake was witnessed by a large part of the population. Let's examine briefly a few different approaches, which we can discuss in more detail later. One approach would be to ask *retrospective* questions and simply look for changes in such factors as psychological well-being, physical health status, or accident rates before and after the event. In a retrospective study, as the name implies, we simply look back at an event. For example, Berkowitz (1970) reported an increase in violent crime following the assassination of President John F. Kennedy in 1963.

Social psychologist James Pennebaker (1991) wanted to find out whether the 1989 Loma Prieta earthquake had an effect on conflict levels in the population in general. He collected data from the San Francisco police department on reported assaults occurring before and after the earthquake. We refer to such research as **archival research** because it uses existing records collected before the time of the study and not for the purpose of the study. Figure 12.1 shows the percentage change in the number of reported assaults, from 4 weeks before the earthquake to 20 weeks after the earthquake.

What can we say about these data? And more important, what can we *not* say? We can say that after the earthquake there was an increase in the number of assaults reported to the police. However, we can say nothing about which factors actually produced the increase. Moreover, we do not know whether the increase in assaults was produced by a small percentage of the population or represented a larger phenomenon throughout the population.

Pennebaker designed a second study to find out whether people reported more arguments with their coworkers or families after the earthquake than before. To answer the question, Pennebaker used a device that randomly telephoned people within the community. He found that by the third week after the quake, the percentage of people who reported having arguments with family or coworkers had increased from 40 to 60%. Could this increase have been a chance occurrence? To help rule out the possibility that the results were not related to the earthquake, Pennebaker at the same time addressed the same question to people from three other cities, two in California and one in Texas. Figure 12.2 presents the results.

Figure 12.1

Number of assaults reported in San Francisco before and after the 1989 Loma Prieta earthquake

Source: Pennebaker (1991).

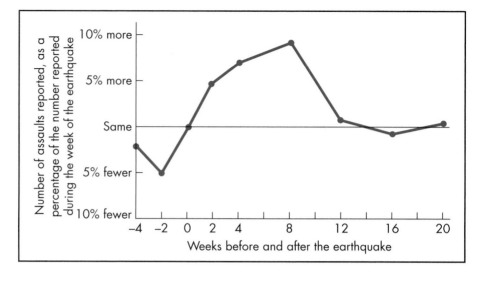

Figure 12.2

Percentage of individuals reporting conflict after the 1989 Loma Prieta earthquake

Source: Pennebaker (1991).

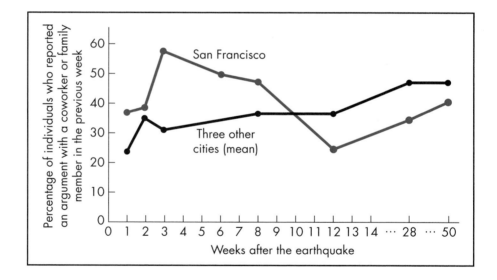

In a third study, people in San Francisco were asked whether they had dreamed about the earthquake during the previous week. These dream data were compared with dreams in response to another significant event: the Persian Gulf War. Figure 12.3 presents the results. As a footnote we can point out that Pennebaker had previously been conducting research in the San Francisco Bay Area on questions related to health and social psychology. Thus, his ability to conduct these three studies was in place when the earthquake took place. He just needed to act quickly and shift his focus to study this chance event.

More recently, Pennebaker has been interested in how events affect a person's language. For example, do you use different words or phrases when you are under stress than when you are not? We would expect individuals to use more positive or negative words to reflect

Figure 12.3

Percentage of individuals reporting dreams about the 1989 Loma Prieta earthquake and the 1991 Persian Gulf War

Source: Pennebaker (1991).

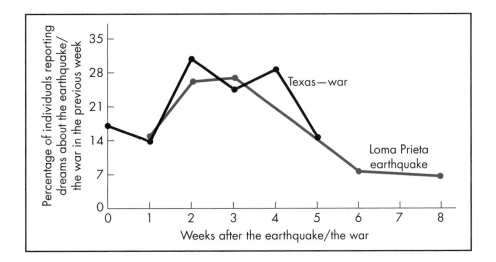

their internal state. But are there other differences in language use? Research suggests that individuals will use more first-person singular pronouns when depressed or dealing with a personal crisis (Pennebaker & Lay, 2002) and more inclusion of others including saying "we" to establish a sense of community. The lack of using the pronoun "I" might reflect also an attempt to distance one's self from an experience.

If you were interested in examining linguistic qualities during times of stress, how might you do it? What Pennebaker and his colleagues did was to use the Internet. The Internet is a fast-growing phenomenon that attracts a wide variety of individuals. What these researchers chose to use were sites that allow individuals to share online diaries and focus on the period before and after 9/11 (Cohn, Mehl, & Pennebaker, 2004). In specific, these researchers downloaded the diaries of 1,084 U.S. individuals for a 4-month period including the 2 months before and the 2 months following 9/11 with the average individual updating their diary every 2 days, resulting in some 71,800 entries overall. What did they find? In the short term following 9/11, individuals expressed more negative emotions and were both more socially and cognitively engaged based on a linguistic analysis. One idea is that during times of collective stress such as 9/11, individuals will use more plural pronouns such as "we." Although the study examined a variety of measures, Pennebaker separately determined the use of first-person singular and first-person plural words and emotional reactions at baseline (pre-9/11) and approximately 2 months following 9/11. Figures 12.4 and 12.5 present these data that show a drop in first-person singular words and an increase in first-person plural words on 9/11 and the next few days afterward. Notice how the use of the first-person pronouns parallels emotional expression.

Whenever we attempt to study real-life events or to increase the external validity of our inquiries by studying phenomena in real-life situations, we run a strong risk of decreasing the internal validity of our experiments. In most cases the internal validity of our research is jeopardized or even decreased as we move from the laboratory to more natural settings. Yet the overall applicability and relevance of our research may be increased greatly, and this may enhance the value of our work. Thus, we are always faced with a trade-off between (1) precision and direct control over the experimental design

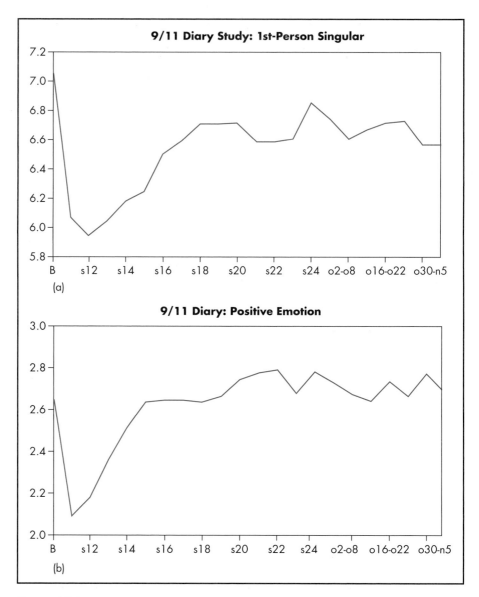

Figure 12.4

Number of (a) first-person singular and (b) positive emotional references made in Internet diary entries at baseline and following the World Trade Center attack on September 11, 2001 (s11). The x axis of the graph shows the dates for September (s), October (o), and November (n).

Source: Pennebaker (2004).

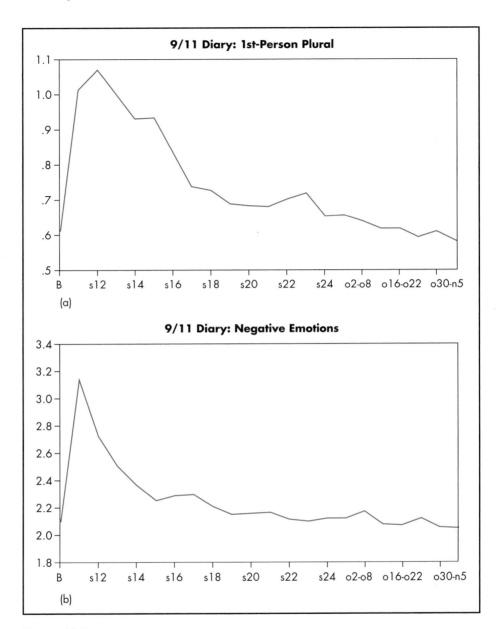

Figure 12.5

Number of (a) first-person plural and (b) negative emotional references made in Internet diary entries at baseline and following the World Trade Center attack on September 11, 2001 (s11). The x axis of the graph shows the dates for September (s), October (o), and November (n).

Source: Pennebaker (2004).

and (2) generalizability and relevance to real-life situations. The process of conducting sound and relevant research requires a balance between our concerns for internal and external validity.

One solution to the difficulties faced when studying real-life events, although somewhat ambitious, is to combine naturalistic observation with more experiment-like procedures in a real-life situation. We present one set of such studies that took place over a number of years, beginning in the late 1940s. The initial study in the series was designed to explain the development and nature of prejudice. Later studies refined the procedure and may be familiar to you from introductory psychology books as the Robbers' Cave Experiment (see Sherif, Harvey, White, Hood, & Sherif, 1961). A portion of our discussion is based on an interview that we had with one of the researchers, Carolyn Wood Sherif.

The impetus for performing the research was the experimenters' dissatisfaction with the theoretical notions of that time relating to the development of prejudice. The example of prejudice that many people were attempting to understand during that period was that of some German people against Jewish people. Some of the writers of the day tried to explain the behavior of Nazis during World War II by suggesting that the German people involved were somehow different from other people. The researchers of this study were not satisfied with that answer. The questions remained: What is the nature of prejudice, and how does it develop? How might you go about studying prejudice?

The initial hypothesis was that normal, healthy people would develop all earmarks of prejudice when (1) they found themselves in situations of strong group identification and (2) their group was placed in such circumstances that it had to destroy the aspirations of another group in order to reach its most cherished goals. To test such a hypothesis, it was necessary to set up a situation involving groups in which only one group could win. Many alternatives might come to mind (a college sports event or a business competition between companies, for example). Because these researchers wanted as much control as possible over the experiment and were interested in the formation of group prejudice, they chose a summer camp. To better understand what naturally happens in a summer camp, one of the researchers, Muzafer Sherif, spent the summer of 1948 visiting camps and watching daily activities. Unlike such other group environments as businesses or universities, a summer camp offered the potential for few outside influences except letters from home or visits from parents and thus extended to the researchers the possibility of a high degree of control in a naturalistic setting.

Once a camp was chosen for the experiment, the staff of the camp were trained in observational techniques, some of which we discuss later in this chapter. To allow for access and observation, some of the researchers became part of the staff. For example, one became a handyman and thus was able to wander around camp without being noticed. The counselors recorded observations twice a day. For ethical purposes, the parents were told of the experiment before they chose that particular camp.

To ensure reliability, additional measures were taken by independent raters; that is, when a counselor observed a boy behaving in a certain way over a period of time (he became a leader or a clown, for example), an independent observer was asked to observe that boy. To further validate the observations, miniexperiments were designed. For example, the researchers at one time created a baseball practice in which each camper threw a baseball at a target and the other campers rated the accuracy of his throw. Because it was difficult to judge exactly where the ball hit, the researchers wanted to know whether there was a systematic error related to status in the group; that is, were the most popular campers in the groups seen as being better at throwing? By using these mini-experiments and additional observations, the researchers could base their conclusions not just on a single set of data but on a combination of measures obtained in different situations.

In the third of the series of camp experiments that has come to be called the Robbers' Cave Experiment (Sherif et al., 1961), the researchers observed the formation of group leadership structures. As the researchers had postulated, a group culture formed even when participants had no idea of the existence of another group. After about a week, each group learned of the existence of another group of campers, and the staff arranged a sports competition between the two groups. What the researchers were most interested in was whether prejudice would develop between the groups and, if so, how it would develop. Carolyn Wood Sherif describes this development:

> When they found out there was another group in camp, they said they would like to compete with them. So the camp staff arranged this event so that they could compete. They set up a tournament in which there were a series of events and points to be gained cumulatively. Great prizes offered—loving cup, Swiss Army knife for each boy on a winning team, and so on—lots of motivational things. The tournament went on for three or four days. The boys . . . would say "we will beat you," but in a very friendly way. They greeted one another, and after the first events they would give the cheer "Two, four, six, eight, who do we appreciate?" name the other team, and all of these good-sportsman sort of things.

> But this started to evaporate very quickly. The extent of the rivalry—the concern that the other group was doing them in, that they weren't playing fair, that things were being stacked against them, and so on—began to appear very quickly. So when those things would happen, they would then start to behave more aggressively toward the other group. These sorts of aggressive actions, in turn, would feed the fuel, if you will, of the images that they had of the other boys. So that very shortly, rather clear-cut stereotype views of the other group developed. They were cheats, stinkers, you know. And we, of course, are brave, honorable, and true. [After the tournament, each group said] they would just as soon never see those guys again.

At this point the researchers sought to intervene and reduce the conflict that had developed. In the first study, they arranged for a sporting event with another camp nearby, thus requiring that the two teams work together. This intervention was effective, and it represents a case in which outside competition reduced group conflict. This result permitted a clearer hypothesis for two later studies. To quote Sherif, "So the hypothesis stated that in order to reduce intergroup conflict and prejudice once it was generated, it would be necessary to have conditions in which there were goals strongly desired by members of both groups, but absolutely not obtainable without the resources and efforts of both groups together." Those were called superordinate goals. In the first study, the researchers used a sporting event with another camp to bring the two groups together; in the third study, they used a water shortage for the same purpose.

The researchers describe a complex series of interactions in the development and reduction of group prejudice. The findings supported the notion that given the right situation, prejudice can be found in any person, not just in those with psychological problems. Such a conclusion offers us the possibility of generalizing these findings to the present-day situation and the prejudice that one ethnic group faces from another. For our purposes this series of studies presents one approach to using naturalistic settings in answering psychological questions. We have touched only on the surface of the studies, and we recommend that you read them yourself for an interesting account of conducting psychological research in the field.

We hope to encourage you to see the potential of psychological research for asking important theoretical and practical questions when tight experimental control is not possible. To this end we introduce research designs in this chapter that offer alternatives to the designs presented previously in this book. With the first group of designs, we lack sufficient experimental control over the variable under study and over potentially confounding variables to make logical statements about the relationship between the independent and dependent variables. We rely instead on logically discounting alternative interpretations of the data. To emphasize that these designs are less rigorous, many researchers call them **quasi-experimental designs.** Because these designs often are used to evaluate the impact of some variable on an ongoing process, they are also called **evaluation research designs.**

Although there are many ways in which quasi-experimental designs approximate true experimental designs, when using them we still cannot be as confident about the relationship between the independent and dependent variables as with true experimental designs. Nevertheless, they are extremely useful in uncovering potential relationships in complex psychological phenomena in a variety of settings. Consequently, because of our growing interest in studying complex psychological processes, these designs can play an important role. In a similar fashion, these designs are useful in showing where a relationship does not exist, thus reducing the need to perform more highly controlled designs. For example, if a new form of psychotherapy is shown not to work in quasi-experimental situations in which a variety of placebo and suggestibility factors would help its effectiveness, it would be difficult to argue that the therapy would work better in highly controlled situations.

Another type of procedure we consider is that of correlational designs. **Correlational designs** attempt to describe the relationship between two variables. Although a researcher may use these designs for confirming predictions, they do not allow one to infer causation. However, they are useful for disconfirming potential causal relationships. For example, if smoking cannot be shown to be correlated with cancer, then it would be impossible to infer that smoking causes cancer.

The final class of designs we examine is **naturalistic observation** techniques. These techniques provide an important tool for describing an ongoing process in its natural setting. In this chapter we describe some of the traditional ways in which these approaches have been used. We can point out that many researchers also use modified observational techniques in such areas as emotional expression (facial expression, for example), content analysis of conversations, and bodily reactions. Our overall purpose in this chapter is to point out that one not only generates data in an experimental situation but finds data in everyday situations, and there are techniques for studying these found data.

CONCEPT CHECK 12.1   Professor Rigid taught his class that if you could not randomly assign participants to groups, then you could never do science. How might you respond to such a position?

QUASI-EXPERIMENTAL DESIGNS

■ Time Series Design

A **time series design** is a within-subjects design; that is, the performance of a single group of participants is measured both before and after the experimental treatment. Before we continue it should be noted that although it is similar to this design, we describe the single-case example of this procedure in Chapter 13. Overall, this design is useful when we are interested in the effects of an event that has happened to all members of the population that we are studying.

For example, suppose you decide to become a college guidance counselor and, after obtaining your Ph.D., you take a job at a small college. One day you are talking to your friend, the gymnastics coach, and she mentions that her gymnasts perform very well in practice and during warm-ups but seem to fall apart during actual competition. As a psychologist you know that certain relaxation training and simple imagery concentration exercises have been shown to improve performance in other test situations. You mention this to the coach, and she immediately asks you to try these relaxation exercises with the team. You agree and for the next week you spend time working with each athlete during daily practice. The entire team enjoys the exercises and feels that they are helpful. To evaluate the effectiveness of these relaxation procedures more objectively, you decide to compare the team's total score at the next meet with its total score at their previous meet. This particular design, which involves comparing a single pretest measure (total score at the first meet) with a single posttest measure (total score at the second meet), is called a *single-group pretest–posttest design.*

During their next meet, the gymnasts' composure is much improved, and their total score is better than in the previous meet. Because the coach kept a record of each athlete's apparent composure during each performance, it is also possible to rate each gymnast's composure at each of these two meets. Figure 12.6 shows the hypothetical results for these

Figure 12.6

Hypothetical results of a single-group pretest–posttest design studying the effects of relaxation exercises on (a) the total points scored by a gymnastics team and (b) the coach's estimate of the gymnasts' composure

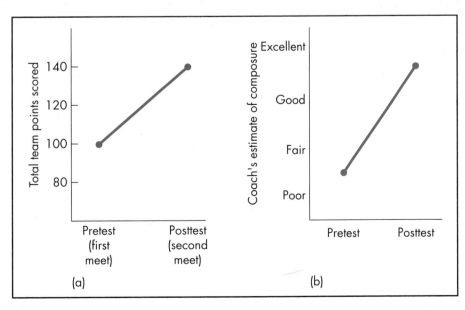

two variables—performance and composure. Both the total score and the coach's estimate of composure increased markedly following the relaxation and concentration exercises. Before concluding that the exercises caused these changes, however, we should keep in mind that we have used only a single pretest–posttest measure; we have no idea how much fluctuation would normally occur between any two meets. Perhaps the sharp increase in the score and the shift in composure ratings are independent of the relaxation exercises. Not knowing the normal amount of fluctuation between any two measures is a serious weakness of the single-group pretest–posttest design.

■ Interrupted Time Series Design

One way to overcome the weakness of the single-group pretest–posttest design is to use an *interrupted time series design,* which is discussed under the topic of single-case designs in Chapter 13. This design involves making several pretest and several posttest measurements. The basic idea behind this type of design is that the additional pretest and posttest scores give us a better estimate of the normal fluctuation from test to test. Once we know the amount of normal fluctuation, we can better interpret the impact of the phenomenon that we are studying. Figure 12.7 is a schematic representation of an interrupted time series design.

As an example of a time series design, let's again consider the hypothetical experiment dealing with the effect of relaxation procedures on the performance of gymnasts. In this case a time series design could incorporate the scores for several meets before and after the introduction of the relaxation and concentration exercises. Consider for a moment the three possible outcomes depicted in Figure 12.8. In Figure 12.8a, the pretest and posttest scores are fairly constant; it would be reasonable to assume that the apparent change in performance reflected a real shift. In Figure 12.8b, there is considerable fluctuation in the pretest and posttest scores, so our best bet is to assume that the sharp increase in performance after introducing the relaxation procedures was simply chance fluctuation that would have occurred anyway. In each case we interpret the effect of the phenomenon under study by comparing its impact with the normally occurring fluctuations of weekly meet scores. An interrupted time series design can also provide some estimate of how long-lasting the influence of the phenomenon is. For example, Figure 12.8a shows a hypothetical outcome that would lead us to suspect a fairly long-lasting impact of the relaxation procedures. Figure 12.8c shows a hypothetical outcome consistent with the idea that the gymnasts' performance was improved only temporarily.

Pretests	Phenomenon under study	Posttests
O_1, O_2, O_3, O_4	X	O_5, O_6, O_7, O_8

Figure 12.7

Interrupted time series design. In this figure, O represents each observation or test score and X represents the occurrence of the phenomenon under study. Note that the phenomenon under study, X, interrupts the periodic measurement of our group of subjects (after Campbell & Stanley, 1963).

Figure 12.8

Hypothetical outcomes of an interrupted time series design examining the effects of relaxation exercises on the total points scored by a gymnastics team in 10 weekly meets. X marks the point at which the exercises were introduced. (a) Outcome in which the pretest and posttest scores are fairly consistent. (b) Outcome characterized by much variability in the pretest and posttest scores. (c) Outcome in which what might be a transient effect is superimposed on a more constant background.

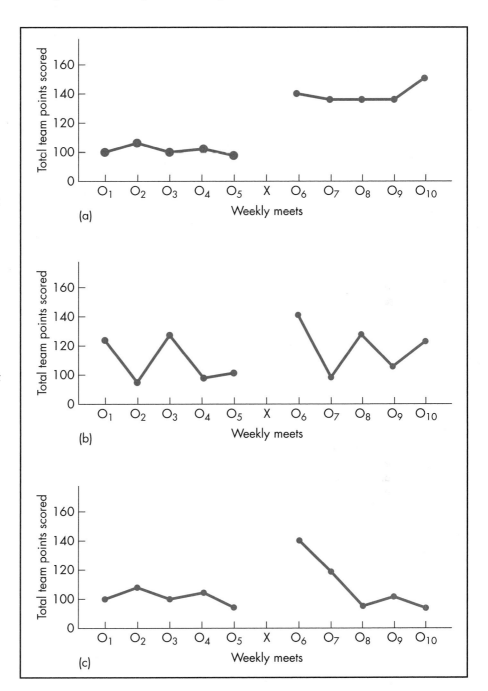

In the research literature, the interrupted time series design has been used to study changes before and after major changes in legislation (for example, increasing speed limits). Carrington and Moyer (1994) examined suicide rates before and after the 1977 changes in the Canadian federal gun control law to better understand whether availability of guns was related to suicide rates, which it was. A number of studies have examined the introduction of various drunk-driving laws using interrupted time series designs. For example, Hilton (1984) found little effect of such laws on fatal accidents in California. West, Hepworth, McCall, and Reich (1989) found that after a reduction in vehicular fatalities following the introduction of driving-while-intoxicated (DWI) laws in Arizona and California, the fatality rate returned to prelaw levels. Likewise, Ross and White (1987) found that publishing names in the newspaper of people convicted of crimes had no effect on drunk driving but did reduce the incidence of shoplifting. This type of design is also used for examining health psychology interventions in a community by examining changes prior to and after an intervention (Biglan, Ary, & Wagenaar, 2000).

Although the interrupted time series design is a great improvement over the simple pretest–posttest design, it still leaves us far short of a clear statement of how one variable influenced the other. For example, if the results were those shown in Figure 12.8a, you could certainly feel confident that a real shift in team performance occurred at about the time you introduced your relaxation procedures. However, any number of other events might be contributing to this unusually abrupt shift in team performance. Perhaps the increased care and attention given to each athlete were responsible, not the exercises themselves; maybe some campus event that occurred about that time caused the shift; or perhaps there was a television special on gymnasts bound for the Olympics.

In an ideal situation, we could control for many of these alternative interpretations by including a control group of some sort. However, because *all* members of the population under study have been exposed to the relaxation procedure, it is impossible to select a control group. This is an important limitation of the interrupted time series design, and it must be kept in mind when we are interpreting the outcome. As it turns out, it is sometimes possible to redefine the population that we are studying to make use of control participants who were not directly exposed to whatever phenomenon is being studied. In this case we might see whether there was a shift in the performance of gymnasts from a nearby college. This expanded form of the interrupted time series design is called a multiple time series design.

■ Multiple Time Series Design

A *multiple time series design* attempts to rule out some alternative interpretations by including a control group that does not receive the experimental treatment. Because it uses a second group of participants, the multiple time series design is not a within-subjects design like the interrupted time series design; rather, it is a between-subjects design. Figure 12.9 schematically represents a multiple time series design.

In our study of the effectiveness of relaxation procedures on the performance of gymnasts, it might be helpful to use a control group of gymnasts from a neighboring college. We could use their total weekly team scores as control data. To the extent that these participants are similar to our original participants in any relevant individual difference variable and are living under similar social and environmental influences, we can assume that the two groups are equal for factors other than the experience of the relaxation training itself. Figure 12.10 shows two sets of hypothetical data for each team.

Pretests	Phenomenon under study	Posttests
Experimental group		
O_1, O_2, O_3, O_4, O_5	X	$O_6, O_7, O_8, O_9, O_{10}$
Control group		
O_1, O_2, O_3, O_4, O_5		$O_6, O_7, O_8, O_9, O_{10}$

Figure 12.9

Multiple time series design. In the figure, O represents each periodic observation or test score; X represents the occurrence of the phenomenon under study. Note that the phenomenon under study, X, interrupts the periodic measurements of the experimental group but not of the control group (after Campbell & Stanley, 1963).

Figure 12.10a shows the hypothetical scores from Figure 12.8c for the gymnasts who received the relaxation exercises, along with the total team scores for the gymnasts from the neighboring college who did not receive the special training. The difference between the scores of the two teams in the two meets following the special training is certainly consistent with the idea that the relaxation procedures had a definite but transient influence on the overall performance of the gymnasts. Before accepting this conclusion, however, keep in mind that we may have overlooked some social or environmental influence that affected our experimental group and not our control group. For example, it is quite possible that some local campus event or even some independent event among the team members at about the same time influenced their team spirit and consequently their performance. This latter interpretation is *always* a real possibility when using the multiple time series design to study complex phenomena in their natural settings.

In Figure 12.10b the hypothetical weekly scores for both teams show a sharp increase following the relaxation training. Because the gymnasts from the neighboring college did not receive the relaxation training, it is likely that some factor other than the relaxation training is responsible for this improvement. One possibility is that both teams were affected by some common event. Can you think of any common events that could account for this parallel performance? It should be increasingly evident that the interpretation of quasi-experimental designs is a tricky business and that there is always a danger that unknown variables may be contributing to the performance differences between our experimental and control groups. This adds to the difficulty of deciding which of several possible interpretations of our final outcome best reflects the true causal factor. In many cases we will never know which interpretation is correct.

On September 12, 1983, New York State put into effect a bill that required a 5¢ deposit on bottles and cans. To test the effectiveness of this law, Levitt and Leventhal (1986) noted the number of bottles and cans found along a highway exit in New York and in a similar site in New Jersey, which did not have a returnable law. These researchers made seven observations 2 weeks apart before the enactment of the law and seven times after the enactment of the law. These researchers reported a decrease from 260 items of litter in New York before the enactment of the law to 145 items after the enactment. The litter in New Jersey showed a

Figure 12.10

Hypothetical outcomes of a multiple time series design examining the effects of relaxation exercises on the total points scored by a gymnastics team in 10 weekly meets. *X* marks the point at which the exercises were introduced to the experimental group. (a) Outcome in which the experimental group's performance improved and the control group's did not. (b) Outcome in which both groups' performance temporarily improved.

much less drastic change (221 items before and 214 after the New York law). These authors made their multiple time series design stronger by measuring nonreturnable litter at both sites, which showed no changes in relation to the law, and by doing a follow-up at both sites 1 year later that showed a continuing decrease in litter for the New York site but not for the New Jersey site. Figure 12.11 presents these results.

◼ Nonequivalent Before–After Design

A *nonequivalent before–after design* is used when we want to make comparisons between two groups that we strongly suspect may differ in important ways even before the experiment begins. Because the two groups in this design are initially unequal, there is an unusually

Figure 12.11

Amount of litter before and after the passage of New York's bottle and can deposit law.

Source: Campbell & Stanley, 1963.

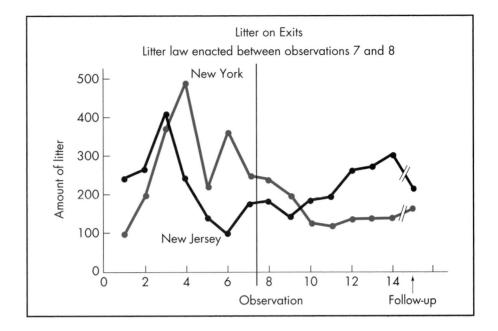

Litter on Exits

Litter law enacted between observations 7 and 8

	Pretreatment measure	Treatment	Posttreatment measure	Difference
Experimental group	O_1	X	O_2	$O_1 - O_2$
Control group	O_1		O_2	$O_1 - O_2$

Figure 12.12

Nonequivalent before–after design. In this figure, O_1 and O_2, respectively, represent the pretreatment and posttreatment dependent measures for each group; X represents the treatment or independent variable. Note that for this design, group comparisons are made between the differences in the scores for each group rather than directly between posttreatment scores (after Campbell & Stanley, 1963).

high risk of ultimately confusing the initial differences with the effects of the independent variable. Consequently, in this design we avoid simply comparing both groups on a single dependent measure. Instead, each group is given a pretest and a posttest, and we compare the amount of change in the test scores for the experimental and control groups. By comparing the differences in scores rather than single dependent measures, we attempt to control more directly for the fact that we are dealing with initially unequal groups. Each group's pretest score serves as a **baseline** from which we estimate the amount of change from pretest to posttest. Then we compare the magnitude of the change for each group by comparing the difference in that group's scores. Figure 12.12 schematically represents this design.

The nonequivalent before–after design is widely used in educational research, in which we often are interested in comparing different schools, classes, or programs. As an example, let's assume that you have just completed your Ph.D. and have taken a job teaching psychology at the college level. One day your department head asks whether you would be willing to develop a new course in human sexuality and, if so, whether you could teach a morning and afternoon section next fall. Having never taught a course on sexuality before, you would like to know whether a lecture or discussion format would be more effective in influencing student attitudes concerning human sexuality. Because you will teach two sections, you could begin to answer this question by teaching the morning session with a discussion format and the afternoon session with a lecture format. Then at the end of the term, you could give an attitude questionnaire to each section and directly compare their scores.

Because teaching is still a new experience for you, you decide to ask one of the senior professors what she thinks about your idea. To your surprise she points out that students who voluntarily schedule 8:00 A.M. classes are very different from those who take 4:00 P.M. classes. She warns that a direct comparison of attitudes at the end of the term may reflect these initial participant differences as well as the effects of your discussion and lecture formats. Impressed by her comments, your initial impulse might be simply to assign students randomly to each class, as you would do in an experiment you were conducting in the laboratory. In this case, however, you are not in the laboratory, and because your students voluntarily select which section of your course they will enroll in, you have no control over the assignment of participants. Consequently, you cannot control for these potentially confounding individual differences by randomly assigning participants to each group.

At this point, while on the verge of abandoning the whole idea, you recall that quasi-experimental designs often can be used in real-life situations where experimental designs cannot. In this particular case, your major problem is that you strongly suspect that the two groups will be different at the onset of the experiment. Therefore, you decide to use the nonequivalent before–after design, which was developed for situations in which we cannot randomly assign participants to groups and are faced with having to compare groups that may differ at the onset of the experiment. Figure 12.13 depicts the final design that you might choose.

The nonequivalent before–after design often is used in such areas as evaluation research (see Mark, Cook, & Cook, 1984, for more detail). Many of the threats to internal validity, such as history, are ruled out by this design, but there are problems, such as the threat of selection-maturation. The selection–maturation threat occurs when one group changes at a different rate from the other. For example, suppose a television program to help learning is shown to disadvantaged children, and their progress scores are compared to those of children from higher socioeconomic levels who are not shown the television program. It might be difficult to show a treatment effect for the disadvantaged children because it is

Figure 12.13

Example of a nonequivalent before–after design

Source: Adapted from Levitt and Leventhal (1986).

	Pretreatment	Treatment	Posttreatment	Difference
Experimental group	Attitude questionnaire	Discussion	Attitude questionnaire	Pretest score – posttest score
Control group	Attitude questionnaire	Lecture	Attitude questionnaire	Pretest score – posttest score

common for children from a higher socioeconomic level to progress faster during a given time period. Thus, we might conclude that the treatment did not have an effect when in fact it did. One of the best ways of ruling out alternative explanations when using this type of design is to have a thorough knowledge of the groups being used and of each group's expected rate of change on the variables being measured.

Retrospective and Ex Post Facto Designs

In the designs that we have discussed thus far, the experimenter planned a study that would take place in the future. The **retrospective designs** and **ex post facto designs** attempt to use empirical procedures for suggesting meaningful relationships between events that have occurred in the past. Some researchers see this procedure as important for suggesting how a significant event in the past (for example, growing up under Hitler or watching television) might have influenced people. Schnelle and Lee (1974) used an ex post facto time series analysis when they studied the manner in which transferring problem prisoners to another prison affected the number of offenses committed by the prisoners who were not transferred. From prison records these authors created an ex post facto ABA design, with B being the transfer of problem prisoners and A being the measurement of offenses by the prisoners not transferred. As with other quasi-experimental designs, such studies as this can say *whether* a change took place, but it is impossible to state *why* the change took place.

The use of the term *ex post facto design* historically has referred to a particular type of quasi-experimental design in which a relationship is identified between an earlier event (such as being on a school sports team or not) and some later event (such as being successful in business). However, today we see the term used in a broad manner to include a variety of retrospective approaches, such as attempts to determine which of many previous factors (for example, anger, depression, eating certain types of foods) are associated with a given condition (for example, cardiovascular problems). Consistent with this change in terminology, the studies in this section are referred to by the general term *retrospective,* and traditional *ex post facto designs* are included within this term.

The most common use of retrospective designs is in studies of educational techniques, disease, and psychopathology. For example, Barthell and Holmes (1968) studied the number of listed activities of students in a high school yearbook to determine whether there were differential rates of high school activity between people identified later in life as schizophrenic and nonschizophrenic. Because the study took place after the fact, these researchers had to determine a possible control group after the fact. For their control group, they chose the students whose pictures appeared next to those of the schizophrenic students in the yearbooks. In one sense you are working backward in the ex post facto procedure; you know the outcome and want to determine the antecedents of this outcome. Thus, one of the important questions is, "Did you select the correct measure (for example, high school activities) to compare the two groups?" Of course, this question is unanswerable, and for this reason the procedure produces only a weak form of inference.

Let's consider another example of retrospective research, one that points out some additional interpretation problems. You might be interested in people who have a particular disease. If you have a theory that nutrition is important, you might study what healthy and diseased people ate for breakfast. You then might find that the people with the disease did not eat breakfast. Eating may or may not have been the important factor in the disease; you cannot know from a retrospective design. The same results may have been brought about because the people with the disease did not feel good when they woke up in the morning and hence chose not to eat breakfast. Thus, participants may have been self-selected on the treatment variable, and in this way invalidate your conclusion that the treatment variable affected the groups. In a true experiment, this objection would have been avoided because you would have selected the participants and assigned them to groups.

Although retrospective and ex post facto designs are weak forms of inference, Kerlinger (1973, 1986) suggested that these designs can be used to good advantage in one type of case: the testing of alternative hypotheses. His ideas are based on those of Chamberlin (1890/1965) and Platt (1964; see Chapter 3). Using retrospective procedures, one can examine *alternative dependent variables.* For example, retrospectively, cigarette smoking might be shown to be associated with lung cancer more than with brain tumors. Although the research still cannot make causal statements, testing alternatives can lead to a greater understanding of the phenomenon under study. Many retrospective designs also may be considered types of correlational studies, and we now turn to this topic.

 CONCEPT CHECK 12.2   The governor of a large state pointed to the results of an interrupted time series design in which, following an increase in the legal age at which one could buy alcohol (the treatment), the number of highway accidents was lower in the next 5 years than in the year before the drinking age was increased. How might you comment on such a conclusion?

CORRELATIONAL PROCEDURES

Sometimes we have a process, be it trauma, AIDS, or intelligence, that we as scientists believe is important to study and understand. However, because of lack of knowledge or level of analysis, it is impossible or impractical to design a highly controlled experiment. In such a situation, there are a number of alternative solutions. One of the most common is identifying a situation in which the variables of interest occur and passively observing their occurrence. For example, if someone were interested in the relationship between how often a baby was held and how often it cried, a first step might be to collect data about these variables for a number of babies. Once data were collected for the two variables—amount of time crying and amount of holding—the correlational statistic (discussed in Chapter 5) would be one means of defining the degree of relationship between them. However, in this book we use the term *correlational designs* in a generic manner that does not imply that a particular statistical procedure is required or was used in the analysis.

It should be noted that there are a number of more advanced procedures built on describing the association between two variables and our ability to predict one variable based on another. These advanced procedures include regression, path analysis, and causal modeling; the interested reader should consult one of the general introductions to this area (Bentler, 1980; Connell & Tanaka, 1987).

Research studies developed with the goal of describing a relationship between two variables but not attempting to show how one variable influences the other are called *correlational studies* in psychology. This is because the statistic commonly used for establishing a degree of association is that of the correlation coefficient, which we presented in Chapter 5. In correlational studies, as with correlational statistics, the researcher is interested in asking whether there is a relationship between two variables. For example, a psychophysiologist might be interested in asking whether there is a relationship between electroencephalogram (EEG) activity and age. Assume that you discover that the frequency of EEG activity slows down in a fairly regular fashion as one ages from 30 to 70 years old. You cannot conclude that a decrease in EEG activity causes one to grow older because a number of processes remain unmeasured and uncontrolled in such a study. You should carefully note this point, since many media reports will report a correlational relationship as if it represents causation, which it does not.

Given a more bizarre relationship—such as the famous correlation between stock market prices and the length of women's skirts—one quickly realizes the importance of seeking unknown factors that influence both variables and thus produce the relationship. As you consider these for yourself, the meaning of the often-quoted statement "Correlation does not imply causality" becomes clearer.

Correlational procedures are an efficient alternative and an important initial step in the inferential process. For example, Bremner and Narayan (1998) were interested in the manner in which stress influences brain development and memory. The particular area of the brain of interest was the hippocampus, which is related to memory processes. As an initial step, they reviewed the literature and found that veterans with combat-related post-traumatic stress disorder (PTSD) showed a significant correlation between levels of combat exposure and hippocampal volume, as shown by brain-imaging techniques as well as lower recall scores on a memory task. Although you might want to conclude that combat stress reduces the size of the hippocampus, these researchers point out that it could be the opposite situation: People who from birth have a smaller hippocampus may experience stressful situations as more traumatic and be at greater risk for PTSD. These researchers were able to strengthen their case that trauma influences hippocampal changes by using matched controls in additional studies of PTSD and examining survivors of childhood abuse and through animal studies that show that positive handling (the opposite of trauma) is protective.

However, before any statement of causation could be established, it was first necessary to establish that an association existed.

As pointed out in Chapter 2, one of the traditional requirements for establishing causation is a degree of association. Establishing such an association was one of the first tasks biomedical researchers attempted when they sought to show a causal link between smoking and cancer. If they could not have demonstrated a degree of association between the two variables, then it would have been impossible to conclude that one variable affected the other. With correlational designs no variables are manipulated, and thus there are no independent and dependent variables. However, some individuals, as might be seen on pseudoscientific websites, have attempted to portray a correlational design as if it were of an experimental nature.

To illustrate, assume that a researcher was interested in the question of how depression and study habits are related. Some people might try to answer this question by dividing participants at the median into high- and low-depression groups (based on some measure of depression, such as the Beck Depression Inventory) and then treating depression as an independent variable and the amount of study time as the dependent variable. Skinner (1984) suggested that there are a number of problems with this approach. First, following such a procedure, information is lost because one has created an artificial categorization—high- and low-depression groups—that was not present in the selection device and may not exist in the underlying population. Second, from a statistical standpoint, an analysis of variance or *t*-test procedure would be less sensitive than a correlational one in such a design. Third, the results, which should be interpreted in correlational terms, may be interpreted as if one variable (depression) had caused the changes in the other variable (study habits).

Let's discuss this third problem in more detail. In the example of depression and study time, no variable was manipulated; it is therefore not possible to infer that depression affected the amount of study time. In fact, one might just as well draw the opposite inference: The amount of time spent studying influences how depressed a person feels. There is also another alternative, called the *third-variable problem,* in which a third, unmeasured variable influences the other two.

Consider the correlation between the number of schools in a city and the amount of alcohol consumed in that city. This correlation is a high-positive one. However, there is no causal relationship between the amount of drinking and the number of schools. A third variable, that of population, influences both: Where there are more people, there are both more schools and more drinking.

As another example, consider the correlation between outdoor swimming and depression. Suppose such a correlation were highly negative; how would you interpret this result? You might conclude either that depression kept people away from swimming or that exercise including swimming cured depression. Either or both of these hypotheses might be true, but the correlation does not justify any causal representation. It is possible that swimming and depression are related, but it is also possible that there is a third variable. For example, more people swim in the summer, and there is a lower incidence of depression in the summer. Research suggests that some types of depression (for example, seasonal affective disorder) are related to lack of sunshine; therefore, sunshine could be the third variable.

In conclusion, correlational research does not demonstrate that there is any causal relationship between two variables, however intuitively appealing such a relationship might be. However, a lack of correlation does rule out any possibility of causality.

 CONCEPT CHECK 12.3   A newspaper article suggested that drinking fine wine was associated with health. If you wanted to study this possibility in more detail, what possible hypotheses might you entertain?

NATURALISTIC OBSERVATIONS

In the first two chapters we stressed that our basic scientific methods are direct extensions of ways we normally learn about and interact with the world. In many ways the method of naturalistic observation derives from what may be our most primitive way of learning about the world: simply paying attention and observing what happens. One elegant example of this approach sought to determine how men and women carry objects, which was part of a larger theoretical question about gender differences (Jenni & Jenni, 1976). These researchers simply observed male and female college students as they carried books around campus. In this study, which was published in *Science,* it was found that 92% of the women carried books in front of their bodies, with one or both arms wrapped around the books, whereas 95% of the men carried the books at their sides using one hand.

In addition to offering a method to study a focused question such as gender and posture, the method of naturalistic observation can also be useful in extremely complex situations, such as studying animals in the wild or the early stages of investigating a phenomenon. If little is known about the phenomenon, we can benefit tremendously from a detailed description of it. Natural scientists have used this technique for many years. They initially focused on simply classifying and describing a wide variety of plant and animal life on our planet. More recently, they have used a similar technique to study animal behavior.

Perhaps the greatest single application of the technique of naturalistic observation was Darwin's 5-year voyage on HMS *Beagle,* during which he compiled many detailed descriptions of plant and animal life over a large part of the world. As he observed and recorded his observations, ideas came to him about how this great abundance of plant and animal life developed. He later synthesized these ideas to form the foundation of the modern theory of organic evolution. Darwin's early work demonstrates two functions of naturalistic observation. First, it allows us to amass descriptive knowledge about a phenomenon. Second, as we become more familiar with it, we may gain insight about general patterns or lawful relationships in the phenomenon.

Researchers continue to rely on naturalistic methods today. The initial research may consist of recording descriptions of the behaviors that are observed. From these initial observations, new hypotheses and theories may be developed and further explored through observation. In one such study, Tinbergen (Lehner, 1979) observed young herring gulls obtaining food from their parents' bills. He was impressed particularly by how fast the young chicks could learn to peck the parents' bills, and he wondered how the chicks could distinguish them from other objects in their environment.

Tinbergen returned to the literature and discovered two conditions that would bring forth the pecking. The first was that a red object must be placed in front of the young bird; the second was that the red object must be kept low to the ground. By means of simple quasi-experimental designs, it was shown that the young bird would peck at many objects that were both red and low to the ground, including cherries and the red soles of bathing shoes. This understanding led Tinbergen into more experimental studies, using carved birds as stimuli. It also led to some beginning hypotheses concerning the sensory apparatus of herring gulls.

In this work Tinbergen moved from naturalistic observation to experimental studies. This refinement of ideas is a natural process; scientists often begin with a broad perspective and then focus on a more narrow experimental question. However, it is important to return to the broad perspective of naturalistic observation to add validity to the experimental findings. Both Tinbergen (1972) and Lorenz (1973) argue that in the study of animal behavior it is necessary to create a balance between naturalistic and experimental methods.

As we begin to use naturalistic methods to study human beings, we are faced with greater complexity both in subject matter and in the scientist's own role in what is being observed. In some cases the observer may choose to remain undetected or can just blend into the background. Krantz (1979) used this approach when he observed obese and nonobese people eating with others in a university cafeteria. In a study of family interactions during a child's second year of life, or the "terrible twos," Belsky, Woodworth, and Crnic (1996) made observations in the family's home during dinnertime. By choosing this time, these researchers sought to blend into the background as the parents were preoccupied with preparing dinner and feeding their 2-year-olds.

In other cases the scientist may find it more useful to become a participant in the situation under study. In an early study of doomsday cults, Festinger, Riecken, and Schachter (1956) became members of a cult whose leader, Marion Keech, claimed to hear messages from outer space that predicted the end of the world the following December 21. These researchers were able to observe not only the behavior of the members as they prepared for the end of the world but also their reactions to and relationship with their leader as nothing happened on December 21.

Another classic and controversial example of scientists acting as participants in a naturalistic study is Rosenhan's 1973 study, titled "On Being Sane in Insane Places." Rosenhan's research focused on the manner in which mental hospital staff distinguish sane people from insane ones and on the types of experiences that patients in these hospitals face. In this study eight sane people gained admission to 12 different hospitals across the country. Each of these "pseudopatients" called a hospital and reported that he or she heard voices. Initial interviews were established for admission. Except for the initial complaint of voices and the false names and occupations that were given, all the information given at these interviews was correct. Once admitted to the hospital, the pseudopatients ceased to simulate any symptoms, and they followed all instructions from the staff.

Surprising as it may seem, in none of the hospitals were the researchers treated in any way other than as insane patients, and their true identities were never realized. This was true even though most of the researchers openly took notes and attempted to have normal conversations with the staff. In the published report, Rosenhan discussed his observations and the subjective experiences of powerlessness and depersonalization that the researchers felt. Although there are a variety of criticisms about the methods and conclusions of this report, it is extremely interesting reading and often-debated research that points out the role of the scientist as investigative reporter using the methods of naturalistic observation.

■ Concerns While Making Naturalistic Observations

Although naturalistic methods do not tell us how one variable influences another, questions of validity are still important. In these designs we want to know whether our observations are valid and what factors might account for their not being accurate. In this section we consider possible problems in both steps in naturalistic observation: data collection and data analysis.

Data Collection　One problem any observer faces is that if the participants realize that they are being observed, they may behave differently. When a participant's behavior is influenced by the mere presence of the observer, it is called **reactive behavior.** Reactive behaviors tell us what people are like when they know they are being observed; they tell us nothing about behavior under normal circumstances. To keep our observations free from reactive behaviors, we attempt, by concealing our identity as researchers, to avoid interfering in any way with the process that we are studying. These undetected observations, which are called *unobtrusive observations,* greatly facilitate the task of interpreting observations. (See Webb, Campbell, Schwartz, & Sechrest, 1966, for an excellent discussion of unobtrusive measures.)

Researchers attempt to make unobtrusive observations in a variety of ways. In some cases they attempt to conduct their observations without being seen by the participant. Some use one-way mirrors; some use hidden, closed-circuit television cameras. In some cases ethologists and comparative psychologists have surgically implanted tiny radio trans-mitters in wandering animals such as wild wolves to study their natural migratory patterns. This procedure obviously would not provoke any reactive behaviors on the part of the wolves, as would occur if they were tracked across the Arctic by howling dogs pulling a sled or by a noisy helicopter.

As we mentioned in Chapter 2, simply observing can be difficult. Part of the difficulty is that we do not usually observe for prolonged periods of time without somehow interfering with the process because our natural tendency is to jump in and participate in some way. For example, try simply listening to a friend with no interference other than an occasional supportive statement. Another reason it is difficult to observe accurately is that we are influ-enced by *selective perception;* that is, the observations of untrained observers are markedly influenced by what they expect to see. The extent to which our observations are restricted by our selective perceptions has a great impact on the accuracy of our observations.

Fortunately, it is possible to teach observers to observe more accurately. One common first step is simply to emphasize the dangers of selective perception. Once we realize that what we expect to see acts as a filtering device, we have come a long way toward seeing things as they really are. The use of additional observers can also be a good way to increase the accuracy of observations, particularly if their expectations or selective perceptions are different from our own.

Another common problem, especially for new observers, is boredom. When you feel bored, you are observing boredom, not the phenomenon you are supposed to be observing. Use boredom as a warning sign that you are not focusing. A useful technique for minimiz-ing selective perceptions and boredom is to pretend every few seconds that you have never before witnessed the setting you are observing. In this way you are constantly looking at the scene with a fresh perspective or with a beginner's mind. With this attitude you are con-stantly reopening yourself to any subtle changes or surprises.

The process of recording observations is crucial. Careful, immediately recorded, leg-ible notes are of great value. If you cannot record your observations as they occur, then take sketchy notes and, after the observation session is over, use these highlights to assist you in recalling as much detail as you can. Mechanical devices such as video- and audiotape recorders can be useful aids. Remember that these devices are limited; they capture only a portion of what is going on. Even miles of tape will never have a single theoretical insight.

Data Analysis   The task of processing and analyzing field study data may initially seem monumental. Many data are redundant, so the task of analyzing them usually is not as in-volved as it initially appears. A good way to begin is to review all your data several times so that you get the whole picture of what happened. Next, it may be helpful to describe the major patterns of behavior. This initial emphasis on common or invariant behavior is helpful be-cause it provides a baseline of the relevant behavior. Once these primary behavior patterns are outlined, it may be profitable to examine instances of atypical behavior. For example, if you are observing the play behavior of a group of children, ask, "Do a small number prefer not to play? What do they do instead?" Sometimes you will find situations in which no clear patterns of behavior emerge. In such cases it is useful to develop a complete behavioral taxonomy: an organized list of the behaviors observed and the relative frequency of each behavior.

"OUR REPUTATION FOR LONGEVITY IS BASED ON SEVERAL FACTORS! HARD WORK, SIMPLE FOOD, LACK OF STRESS AND THE INABILITY TO COUNT CORRECTLY."

Once the major results become apparent, you will have an excellent basis for evaluating any theoretical ideas you may have recorded while observing your participants. You may find that ideas that initially seemed fruitful do not reflect the major patterns of your overall empirical observations. Any incorrect notions can be disregarded easily and replaced by your empirical findings. As you process and analyze your data, you may get insights about what causal factors underlie the natural behaviors that you are observing. These can be added to any factors that you thought of while observing the participants in your study and can be evaluated later for possible study with formal experimental designs.

In some cases you may decide that a simple intervention in a future field setting may provide useful clues to how one variable influences another. If you decide to explore these issues in your field setting, keep in mind that you will no longer be using the method of naturalistic observation. Instead, you probably will be using one of the quasi-experimental designs discussed in the early part of this chapter. This is precisely what quasi-experimental designs were developed to do.

■ To Conceal or Not to Conceal; To Participate or Not to Participate

Every observer must face two issues. Both stem from the fact that in actual practice the basic method that we just outlined sometimes must be modified to fit the realities of the situation that we are attempting to study. The first issue is whether to conceal our identities as researchers; the second is whether to participate in the social process that we are observing.

Previously, we emphasized the importance of unobtrusive observation techniques as a means of minimizing the likelihood of reactive behaviors contaminating our observations. Sometimes, however, the phenomenon that we are studying dictates that there is simply no reasonable way to collect data without being seen. In these cases we can best observe the process that we are studying by concealing our identities as researchers and becoming actively involved in the process. For example, Alfred (1976) posed as a member of the Church of Satan for several years while he studied the sociology and psychology of its members. No one knew he was conducting research until he revealed his true purpose to their leader and requested permission to publish a summary of what he had learned.

Other researchers make no attempt to conceal themselves while collecting data. For example, anthropologists living among and observing people from other cultures typically do not attempt to conceal themselves. In her study of adolescents in Samoa, Margaret Mead (1928) made no attempt to conceal her identity from the people she studied. Mead found that Samoan adolescents do not experience psychological problems to the extent seen among adolescents in the United States. She suggested that their more open attitudes toward sexual behavior may underlie this difference; however, other researchers disagree with this suggestion.

The decision about whether to be an active participant in the process that we are observing also depends on the phenomenon that we are studying. In the cases of ethologists (such as Lorenz and Tinbergen) and anthropologists (such as Mead), data usually are collected without the researcher's becoming part of the process under study. In contrast, Alfred's valuable contribution was based on his active participation in the process that he was observing. There is always a danger that the researcher's participation may unintentionally alter the process being observed. On the positive side, participation enables the researcher to experience the process personally. These introspective data can provide a fruitful source of new ideas about psychological processes.

Deciding whether to remain concealed or to reveal your identity depends to a large extent on whether you are observing highly reactive behaviors. If you suspect that the behavior of your participants will be different if they know they are being observed, then use some sort of concealed-observation strategy. If you suspect that there is much to be gained by personally experiencing the process that you are studying and if you feel the overall process would not be significantly influenced by your participation, then you might consider participating.

■ Strengths and Weaknesses of Naturalistic Observation

It may be helpful to mention briefly some strengths and weaknesses of the method of naturalistic observation. One advantage is that it attempts to describe behavior as it naturally occurs in real-life settings. This emphasis on observing how things naturally occur enables us to begin our study of a new process with an accurate description of naturally occurring behaviors. As our observations unfold, new ideas about possible relationships or the possible survival value of the behavior that we are observing may occur to us. Another advantage to naturalistic observation is that it studies behavioral processes as they unfold over a period of time. This emphasis on observing sequences of behavior provides an important temporal dimension to studying human behavior. This consideration of the flow of ongoing behavior is a valuable complement to experimental and quasi-experimental designs, which tend to focus on discovering the factors that may be influencing behavior at a given time.

One disadvantage of naturalistic observation is that it tends to be qualitative and to rely more on the subjective judgment of the observer than do other research methods. Consequently, selective perception can pose a serious threat to the validity of our data. Another disadvantage is that if we study a single instance of a process extensively, the representativeness of our sample may be compromised. Unless we also examine other instances of the same phenomenon, we run the risk of making inappropriate generalizations, and this is a serious threat to the external validity of our observations. Finally, naturalistic observations do not provide information about how one variable influences another. Of course, this is not really a weakness, any more than Beethoven is weak compared with Bach. Instead, it reminds us that no single technique answers all our questions. We return to this point later; in the meantime, keep in mind that science is a fluid yet pragmatic process that makes use of a variety of techniques and approaches to answer our questions about reality.

KEY TERMS AND CONCEPTS

1. **Field research**
   A. External validity
   B. Voevodsky taxi study
   C. Sherif et al. camp study
2. **Quasi-experimental designs**
   A. Time series design
   B. Interrupted time series design
   C. Multiple time series design
   D. Nonequivalent before–after design
   E. Retrospective and ex post facto designs
3. **Correlational procedures**
4. **Naturalistic observation**
   A. Tinbergen
   B. Rosenhan
   C. Problems of data collection and analysis
   D. The role of the scientist (to observe, to participate, to do both)
   E. Strengths and weaknesses

SUMMARY

1. This chapter points out some distinctions that have been made between various types of research. One of these distinctions reflects whether research is run in a laboratory or out in the field. Another distinction refers to whether the design of the study is a true experimental design or a quasi-experimental design. Although these are separate dimensions, it is often more difficult to conduct true experiments in the field. Thus, quasi-experimental designs often are used in field research.

2. Quasi-experimental designs are a set of designs that do not have the necessary controls to rule out important threats to internal validity, as true experimental designs do. Lacking strong experimental control, researchers in quasi-experimental designs attempt to discount alternative explanations logically.

3. Some types of quasi-experimental designs are time series designs, interrupted time series designs, multiple time series designs, and nonequivalent before–after designs.

4. An ex post facto design or retrospective design attempts to use empirical procedures for suggesting meaningful relationships between events that occurred in the past.

5. Correlational designs focus on describing a relationship between two variables. Although such designs cannot establish that causation does exist, they can be an important means of demonstrating that it does not.

6. Naturalistic observation is the process of observing organisms, usually in their natural environment. It is a descriptive procedure and is illustrated by the work of Lorenz and of Tinbergen.

REVIEW QUESTIONS

1. What is gained and what is lost when an experiment is conducted outside the laboratory?
2. What does it mean to say that there is a trade-off between external and internal validity in any experiment?
3. What are some of the problems and threats to internal validity with a simple time series design?
4. What is *ex post facto research*, and what problems are associated with it?
5. How are data collected and how are analyses performed in a naturalistic observation study?
6. What are the strengths and weaknesses of naturalistic observation methods?

DISCUSSION QUESTIONS AND PROJECTS

1. Discuss the advantages and disadvantages of time series designs.
2. Design a naturalistic observation study in which you would observe a child at play. What different roles might you take in relation to the child, and how might they affect your results?
3. Discuss medical research that uses an ex post facto design and give examples reported in the newspaper.
4. How are the explorations of Tinbergen and Rosenhan similar, and how are they different? How could experimenter bias have influenced these studies?
5. What are some of the problems of interpretation in a multiple time series design?

INFOTRAC COLLEGE EDITION: EXERCISES

At times, we want to determine whether results found in a more experimental situation would also be similar in a more real-world situation. Thomas Dingus and his colleagues were interested in which factors influence driving using a navigational display. After conducting two studies in which drivers were required to drive a predetermined route, a third naturalistic study was performed using rental car drivers without an experimenter present. You can read this study, entitled "Effects of age, system experience and navigation technique on driving with an Advanced Traveler Information System," in the journal *Human Factors* (June 1997).

In the chapter we discussed the Robber's Cave Experiment as an example of a quasi-experimental design that examined the manner in which prejudice could be induced in normal individuals. In the 50 years since this study was conducted, a variety of studies have contributed to an understanding of intergroup process. You can find a review of this work in the 1998 *Annual Review*

of Psychology in an article entitled "Intergroup contact theory" by Thomas Pettigrew.

You may also want to read the 1999 issue of the *Annual Review of Psychology* in which S. Mark Kopta and his colleagues discuss how to evaluate psychotherapy ("Individual psychotherapy outcome and process research: Challenges leading to greater turmoil or a positive transition"). In this discussion, they consider questions of research design, which we have discussed in the last three chapters.

To help you better understand the material in this chapter, you can go to Wadsworth's research methods workshop web page at http://www.wadsworth.com/ psychology_d/templates/student_resources/workshops/ resch_wrk.html. There you will find workshops related to research methods and statistics. The research methods workshop on "Nonexperimental Approaches" discusses the material presented in this chapter.

✓ Answers to Concept Checks

12.1 You might begin by saying that it is accurate that if you cannot randomly assign participants to groups, then the study may not be called a *true experiment.* However, you might also want to point out that with Professor Rigid's definition, a number of important topics, such as the reaction of people to earthquakes, to power plant meltdowns, and to war, would be beyond the methods of science. You might also point out that it is possible to use a different type of design—quasi-experimental design—that relies on logic to rule out alternative explanations to the hypotheses.

12.2 Although you could not argue with the actual data, you could question the interpretation that the results were due to changing the drinking age. For example, in the same year that the drinking age was increased, the speed limit may have been reduced, which could contribute to a lower accident rate.

12.3 One might research the possibility that fine wine is associated with good health in several ways; three possibilities follow. One possibility is that the newspaper stressed only one side of the correlation in inferring that wine was associated with health. The correlation may have resulted from a situation in which more people who are healthy drink wine. Perhaps unhealthy people do not like or want wine. Another possibility is that because a higher standard of living is required to buy fine wines, a third variable—the ability to afford better health care—could be the causal factor. That is, people with a higher standard of living may also take better care of themselves and use health care facilities in a more preventive manner. Finally, one could always look for particular causal factors (for example, a biochemical substance found in wine) that might be associated with health.

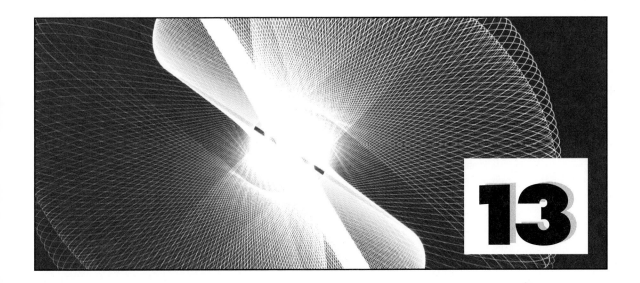

SINGLE-SUBJECT DESIGNS

TYPES OF SINGLE-SUBJECT DESIGNS

CASE STUDY DESIGNS
Naturalistic Case Studies
One-Shot Case Studies

EXPERIMENTAL SINGLE-SUBJECT DESIGNS
Reversal Design
Multiple-Baseline Design

Multielement Design
Making Sense of Single-Subject Experimental
  Results

**ALTERNATIVE TYPES OF SINGLE-SUBJECT
RESEARCH**

Single-subject designs in their various forms are an important tradition in the history of science that is experiencing a resurgence in interest (Blampied, 2000; Jones, 1993). In discussing single-subject designs, we use a broad definition that extends from the more naturalistic single-subject designs to the more experimental single-subject designs. These designs historically have been used to study such areas as perception, learning, memory, and psychophysics. Examples of research directed at understanding a particular characteristic of an individual (such as a particular psychological or neuropsychological impairment) typically have been called case studies, although this distinction has lost its meaning over the years.

It should also be understood that single-subject designs may involve more than one participant in the research. Thus, you might see the term *small-N designs* being used in a manner similar to how we use the term *single-subject designs*. The general characteristic of these approaches is that the individual's data are not averaged with those of other participants. Thus, single-subject experimental research uses a somewhat different underlying philosophy from that of the designs previously discussed, which use the calculus of probability and inferential statistics to help make decisions. The emphases with these previous designs have been on such topics as the sampling of individuals and the averaging of experimental results to arrive at group means. Single-subject approaches do not require that emphasis.

The underlying philosophy of **single-subject designs** assumes that the process under study is found within that single subject and can be controlled appropriately. Thus, a sampling of research participants is not necessary. However, this is not to suggest that the ability to control variables or to specify operational definitions is no longer important. Quite the contrary, these factors are still critical in establishing a relationship between an independent variable and a dependent variable. Although somewhat different in single-subject designs, the issues of internal and external validity also must be considered (Mace & Kratochwill, 1986). To better understand single-subject research, let's consider briefly the history of these designs.

If you think about it, you will realize that most of the physics and chemistry experiments that you performed in high school were single subject in nature. You may have measured physical quantities—mass or acceleration, for example—using the same subject (for example, a ball rolling down an inclined plane) a number of times. Or you may have done experiments to determine the chemical characteristics of a particular element. In doing this research, you never considered randomly choosing the particular sample of the element from all possible samples but simply used whatever sample of the element was available.

In the traditional physical science approach, one is not concerned with sampling of participants, nor does one expect large variations in the data. For example, to measure speed and acceleration in classic physics, a person simply rolls a steel ball down a measured incline and makes the necessary measurements. The scientist may repeat this procedure a number of times, but in the end he or she is able to make a precise or *point prediction* (within certain limits) about the speed and acceleration of a steel ball rolling down the inclined plane. Likewise, to determine the properties of a particular chemical element, one simply takes a sample and makes the measurement. It is assumed that every sample of the element—gold, for example—will have the same chemical properties. Because each sample is the same, there is no advantage to performing the same experiment on more than one sample of the element.

Psychology and the behavioral sciences have borrowed broadly from the approach and philosophy of the physical sciences, especially the approach associated with

Sir Isaac Newton's classic physics. For example, Sigmund Freud, in his *Project for a Scientific Psychology* (1895/1966), set forth the task of making psychology scientific in a like manner to the physics and chemistry of his day. Wilhelm Wundt—who, along with William James, is credited with being the founder of modern psychology—used the experimental study of a few participants in depth as the appropriate method for psychological investigation.

In the late 19th century, Hermann Ebbinghaus conducted some of the most often described single-subject experiments in which he learned nonsense syllables and began the systematic study of memory processes (Ebbinghaus, 1885). Ebbinghaus was able to show that memory is influenced by such factors as the number of words on a list and the time between learning the list and being asked to recall the syllables—factors still studied today in memory research. Lest you think this is a dead tradition, you should know that for 6 years beginning in 1972, Marigold Linton recorded at least two events from her life each day. Every month she tested her ability to remember, order, and date a sample of the events she had recorded previously (Linton, 1982).

To continue the history of single-subject research, Thorndike (1898) studied intelligence by examining the ability of individual cats to solve problems. The psychophysical tradition of Ernst Weber and Gustav Fechner, whose physical measures were shown to represent a different scale from those of psychological experience, is another example of using single-subject research designs. In Russia, Ivan Pavlov conditioned single dogs in his classic conditioning studies. During the 1930s, B. F. Skinner began a series of conditioning experiments that emphasized the virtues of single-subject designs. Skinner's work used a method that came to be called *experimental analysis of behavior.* This approach often used a single pigeon, rat, or other organism as both the experimental and the control participant. Additional animals were used to replicate the previous research. One hallmark of these approaches was that the data from a single participant remained separate and were not statistically averaged with those of other participants.

As we have seen, the idea of single-subject designs has existed since the beginning of modern psychology at the end of the 19th century. In fact, it was not until the 1920s and the statistical work of R. A. Fisher with farming plots that psychology began to shift to larger sample sizes with statistical evaluation between groups. However, even Fisher included single-subject research in his original book. Based on the methods of Fisher, the idea of a control and an experimental group with generalizable results became the hallmark of psychology.

One problem with the Fisher approach was that individual differences became error variance and generally were ignored and averaged out. In the Fisher approach, as we have discussed in previous chapters, stability is achieved by averaging data from a number of participants. Based on this tradition, a negative view arose toward single-subject approaches, that to study an individual participant was somehow unscientific and that real science was performed only with groups of individuals. But even during this period, a minority of researchers emphasized the importance of knowing well the behavior of single individuals. Because the minority was largely influenced by the operant conditioning approach of Skinner, for years the term *single-subject design* was almost synonymous with the study of operant conditioning. Today, this is no longer the case, and we use a much broader definition of *single-subject design* in this chapter.

Although the philosophy of science concerning the experimental designs underlying these different approaches is extremely important, an in-depth discussion is beyond the scope of our present discussion. For an important and informative discussion of the

Box 13.1

Paul Meehl: Philosophy of Science and the Research Methods of Psychology

Paul Meehl was a psychologist interested in improving the methods of clinical research, which led him into philosophy of science. One of his frequently cited papers is called "Theoretical Risks and Tabular Asterisks: Sir Karl, Sir Ronald, and the Slow Progress of Soft Psychology" (Meehl, 1978). By this time you should realize that Sir Karl is Sir Karl Popper, whom we discussed early in this book in Box 2.2, and that Sir Ronald is Sir Ronald Fisher, for whom the F ratio is named and whom we discussed in Chapters 6 and 7. The asterisks refer to the way in which ANOVA tables are often portrayed in published articles, with one asterisk next to the F ratio denoting a significance level of $p < .05$ and two asterisks denoting $p < .01$.

Theoretical risk is the more interesting question for Meehl because he was concerned with what it takes for us to claim that a theory is false, especially in such areas of clinical, social, or developmental psychology in which individual differences may play a large role. The larger question for Meehl was, "Has significance testing actually advanced fields such as biology or psychology?" Historically, Fisher developed his techniques for studying the growing of agricultural products such as corn. Meehl suggested that in such fields as that the distance from our independent variable to our dependent variable

is not very far. That is, you can put a type of fertilizer on part of a field and not on another part and then it is possible to tell which corn grew larger or had more ears.

However, if you give someone therapy once a week and measure their level of depression after 3 months, there is a much larger distance between our independent variable (therapy) and the dependent variable (level of depression). Logically, we can think of a number of factors that might have influenced our results other than the therapy. Thus, statistical differences alone, even at the $p < .05$ level, are not enough to move the science of psychology forward. Meehl further suggested that it is always more valuable to show that the results of research agree with what is predicted theoretically than it is to compute a precise probability that something merely differs from something else. By this he means that it our task in psychology to develop theories that predict results more exactly than just saying that two groups are statistically different from one another at some level of probability. As we will see in this chapter, one approach is to demonstrate that you have achieved experimental control over the situation. According to Skinner and others, statistical tests become less important if you can show graphic changes that map directly onto your interventions.

underlying philosophy of science traditions in psychological research, especially the tradition of Fisher as opposed to that of Karl Popper, the interested reader should consult Meehl (1978), who we review in Box 13.1. Also, a comparison of single-subject analysis and inferential statistical analysis and a discussion of Type I and Type II errors are included in Parsonson and Baer (1978).

In the past few decades, a number of researchers have again sought to understand the individual participant within scientific psychology (for example, Franklin, Allison, &

Gorman, 1997; Hersen & Barlow, 1976; Kazdin, 1982; Kratochwill, 1978; Sidman, 1960; Valsiner, 1986). The task is not so much to ask which are better—single-subject or group designs—but to ask what kinds of questions each type of design is uniquely able to answer. Sanderson and Barlow (1991), for example, point out the value of single-case as well as other designs in answering particular questions in clinical psychology. Furthermore, the *Journal of Consulting and Clinical Psychology* devoted a special section to single-case methodologies in psychotherapy process and outcome research (Jones, 1993). One such use of the single-case design is quite practical. If it were your task to work with an autistic child over the next year, you might try a variety of means to maintain the child's attention and additional means to influence his or her behavior. Single-case designs offer a powerful method for determining which techniques work best with a given individual.

TYPES OF SINGLE-SUBJECT DESIGNS

In general, we can discuss two different purposes of single-subject designs. The first purpose is primarily descriptive and is represented by the case study method, which has been used throughout the history of psychology. Such a descriptive approach could be either a single-subject naturalistic observation approach or an approach in which a single variable is observed after the application of a particular treatment. On the other end of the continuum are single-subject designs that are more experimental in their intent. These designs represent the second purpose of single-subject designs. That is, when our primary goal is to focus on how the introduction of a particular factor influences a particular aspect of an individual's behavior, then single-subject experimental designs such as the reversal design and multiple-baseline design may be used.

Often, descriptive and experimental intents may be combined. A classic study from the history of health psychology illustrates early attempts to achieve experimental control. In 1895 a 9-year-old boy named Tom swallowed some scalding hot clam chowder. This led to his esophagus being closed by scar tissue. An operation was performed to create an opening in the abdomen that allowed food to be placed directly into the stomach. Some 46 years later, in 1941, Wolf and Wolff (1943) began to study directly the effects of Tom's emotional reactions on his stomach. In general, they found that negative experiences, such as frustration, resulted in increased stomach motility and secretion. During the next 17 years, they combined both the descriptive and the experimental single-subject approaches to understand stomach function and its relation to emotionality.

Such intense study of one person offers insight into the manner in which emotions influence physiological processes and has led to a variety of experimental studies. Thus, at times we describe a person's behaviors or psychological processes in detail with the purpose of scientifically modeling these behaviors or cognitive processes, which in turn can be used to direct experimental procedures. As with all the designs that we discuss in this book, the goal is to be able to understand a phenomenon, support our conclusions, and eliminate rival hypotheses. As we will see, there are times when single-subject designs are essential in this quest.

CASE STUDY DESIGNS

■ Naturalistic Case Studies

The *case study* is one of the most widely used methods for studying individual participants. It is based on the logic of describing, analyzing, interpreting, and evaluating a set of events and relationships within a framework or theory (Bromley, 1986). The typical descriptive case study focuses on either problematic or exceptional behaviors. Indeed, for years the case study approach has been the primary method for studying phenomena in clinical medicine, clinical psychology, and the neurosciences. Its advantage has been its ability to present the clinical implications of a particular disorder. One classic example that Freud discussed was the case study of Anna O. Another example is described in Morton Prince's book *The Dissociation of a Personality* (1913). Prince described a case of multiple personality (now called dissociative identity disorder) at a time when the existence of that diagnostic category was in question.

An advantage of such extended discussions is the ability to describe processes not easily reduced to a single variable. For example, Luria (1972) describes in great detail the attempt of one man to overcome a neuropsychological deficit that left him with "a shattered world." This is a story about a brilliant young Russian scientist, Zasetsky, who became a soldier in World War II and was shot in the head. Zasetsky's wound was such that areas of the brain that help us to move in space or understand complex language were damaged, whereas areas that allow one to reflect on one's condition were not. Luria's intriguing work describes both his and the patient's own experiences over a 25-year period.

Likewise, Oliver Sacks has used the case study approach to give insight into the world experienced by people with particular clinical disorders. Two of the most famous of these became part of the popular culture with the movie based on Sacks's book *Awakenings* (1973) and his book *The Man Who Mistook His Wife for a Hat* (1985).

Ramachandran (1998) summarized his case study work on phantom limb pain, the situation in which a person continues to experience the existence of a limb that has been lost. Because there is evidence of the remapping of brain areas that were associated with sensation in the arm that differs from person to person, the case study approach accounts for individual differences in an important way.

Case studies are used not only for studies of disorders but also for studies of potential. For example, Maslow (1970) used the case study technique to study exceptional people whom he considered to be self-actualizing. Likewise, since the 19th century, developmental psychologists have kept records of the development of their own children (Bolgar, 1965). In the case of Jean Piaget, these observations led to his later theories.

A case study is a narrative description of an individual or some aspect of an individual that brings together relevant aspects of the person's history and present situation. The value of such an approach is that it is possible to describe the individual case in its actual context. The information that makes up the case study may come from a variety of sources, including the patient's recollection of events, information from friends or relatives, and public records.

In one sense we all use case study techniques when we go to a professional complaining of a pain. The professional then diagnoses the problem and prescribes some form of

	Treatment	Response
Single subject	X	O

Figure 13.1

One-shot case study design. In the figure, *X* represents the treatment given to a single subject; *O* refers to the experimenter's observations.

therapy. After some time, we return and give the professional feedback on whether the pain decreased. Neither physical pain (such as headaches) nor psychological distress (such as feeling lost or without purpose) can be seen from behavior alone.

The case study is one of the oldest techniques of medical and psychological description. Case studies based solely on the reports of participants or patients are open to all the problems of self-report (such as selective forgetting, the desire to show ourselves in a positive light, and outright deception), but there are times when the case study can be a useful technique.

One-Shot Case Studies

In addition to the use of the case study method to provide a general description, there is a somewhat more specific use of the case study design. The case study is a narrative that summarizes an experimenter's direct observations of a participant's behavior after some sort of treatment has been performed. This design, sometimes called the *one-shot case study,* is represented in Figure 13.1. Gottmann (1973) suggests that systematic case study observation offers therapists a means of obtaining information about specific interventions in therapy during an ongoing series of sessions.

One could also use the one-shot case study, although less powerfully, in a retrospective manner to study the effects of an event that took place in the past. The study of reactions to various forms of trauma is one such retrospective study. For example, Scoville and Milner (1957) published a case study describing the effect of surgical removal of the hippocampal region of the brain from a man; that study has become a classic in the field (Box 13.2). As a result of the surgery, this man, although able to remember events from his past, had no memory of the present. He would read the same newspaper over and over without retaining the information he had read.

From this tragic case study, a wealth of information has been obtained about memory. This information has been discussed, and more recent case studies of naturally occurring memory problems such as amnesia have been reviewed (Squire & Zola-Morgan, 1991). In instances such as that described by Scoville and Milner, the case study can be a useful tool in research. The observations may suggest new hypotheses, demonstrate rare phenomena, or even show exceptions to established facts.

Thus, the case study design can provide valuable initial descriptions of new phenomena, which can then be studied carefully with more rigorous experimental methods. Likewise, the case study approach can lead to important models and perspectives not available with traditional experimental methods. For example, Kodak, Northup, and Kelley (2007) show how the single case study approach can be used to develop more effective treatments

Box 13.2

A Patient with Bilateral Temporal Lobe Damage

In 1957 Scoville and Milner first described a male patient (H.M.) who underwent bilateral temporal lobe surgery in 1953. The surgery consisted of the removal of tissue on the medial surface of both temporal lobes, including large portions of the hippocampi. The purpose of the operation was to relieve very frequent and severe epileptic seizures, which were unrelieved by anticonvulsant medication. (Scoville was encouraged to attempt this procedure because he had strong reason to believe that some abnormality of this region was responsible for the seizures and because evidence from nonhuman primates indicated no behavioral abnormalities following removal of this area.) Although the surgical procedure strikingly reduced the number of epileptic seizures, the operation had an unanticipated and awful consequence: The patient was unable to either learn or remember any new material!

Before the surgery, H.M. was a motorwinder who was unable to work because of his epileptic seizures. After the surgery he was pleasant and easygoing, as he had been before surgery. His measured IQ actually rose from 104 to 119 (presumably it was depressed before the surgery by the epileptic abnormality). However, H.M. exhibited striking memory deficits for events both before and after the surgery. For example, except for Scoville, whom he had known for many years before the surgery, he was completely unable to recognize members of the hospital staff; he could not even learn his way to the bathroom. He was unable to remember the death of a close uncle, even though he was reminded repeatedly and became genuinely upset every time he was informed.

As the years passed, his ability to remember events remained severely impaired. H.M. could not remember his new house address, even after living there for 6 years. He could not recognize neighbors and, when left alone, would invite strangers into his house, thinking they were friends whom he had forgotten. He was able to perform simple jobs such as mowing the lawn, but he could not remember where to find the lawnmower or that he had used it the previous day. He read newspapers over and over, forgetting that he had already read them. He spent many hours re-solving the same jigsaw puzzle without any sign of learning it. His memory deficit was paralleled by a total lack of appreciation of the passage of time. His deficit in registering new material remained severe many years later (Milner, 1966).

Over the years H.M. and his mother faithfully cooperated with a number of psychologists in the United States and Canada, who carefully examined the nature of his unfortunate deficit. Taken together, their findings provide a wealth of information about human temporal lobe function. Yet this case obviously raises moral issues, as Scoville (1968) stressed:

> This one case, so carefully studied, has demonstrated to many the grave danger of bilateral resection of the medial parts of the temporal lobes when the hippocampus is included in the removal. Even at this late date, however, scientific publications continue to propose the removal of the hippocampus bilaterally for relief of behavioral disorders, intractable pain, and other reasons; such proposals no longer seem justifiable in view of the profound anterograde amnesia which results.

Later case studies with naturally occurring memory problems such as amnesia have also led to a greater understanding of the role of the hippocampus in human memory. Squire and Zola-Morgan (1991) have reviewed this information, and the interested student should consult this paper.

for young children with behavior problems. Likewise, Longo and Bisconer (2003) show the effectiveness of a behavior program to reduce aggression in an individual with schizophrenia. However, as an experimental design, the case study does not give us the ability to make strong inferences. As with the single-group, pretest–posttest design, we have no assurance that the observations would not be exactly the same without the treatment or have not been influenced by confounding variables. Because of the lack of control procedures, we can say nothing about causal factors and may risk confusing any number of confounding variables with our treatment. To strengthen our conclusions, we consider ways to add more experimental control to our single-case designs.

Kazdin (1982, 2003b) provides an overview of single-case designs and suggests that the single-subject design is not only misnamed but also misunderstood. Kazdin believes that it is misnamed because at times a single-subject design may be used with a large number of participants. He believes that the single-subject design is misunderstood because some people believe that it is not a *true experiment* and thus cannot reveal *causal relationships* between variables or generalize beyond the few participants under study. Kazdin considers that view to be a misunderstanding of the design.

Campbell has also discussed this point by suggesting that the single-subject design "should not be demeaned by identification with the one-group posttest-only design" (Cook & Campbell, 1979, p. 96). Although the descriptive subject-study approach has this problem, the more experimental single-subject designs do not. Of course, there are limitations to single-subject experimental designs, as there are with any designs. However, there are situations in which single-subject designs offer an important alternative to traditional experimental design.

CONCEPT
CHECK 13.1   After reading the first section of this chapter, one student decides that single-subject designs are important to use in situations in which there are too few participants for real experimental control to be achieved and statistics to be used. How might you respond to this conclusion?

EXPERIMENTAL SINGLE-SUBJECT DESIGNS

With experimental single-subject designs, we want to determine the manner in which one variable influences another. Because single-subject designs are not based on the same methodological considerations as traditional experimental methods, the task of controlling for extraneous variables requires a different type of method. We have pointed out that even when more traditional means of experimental control are not used, we can reject some alternative hypotheses on logical grounds. One main way in which single-subject experimental designs accomplish this goal is through the use of a time series approach (see Kratochwill, 1978).

The logic of a *time series approach,* as we discussed in Chapter 12, is to establish a series of measurements over time. This series of measurements forms a basis of comparison with another series of measurements after the independent variable—a treatment, for example—is introduced. As you can imagine, the more stable the baseline measurement sequence, the easier it is to establish that the independent variable has influenced the dependent variable. Thus, establishing a baseline is extremely important; it serves as a reference point with which to compare changes associated with the introduction of the independent variable. Furthermore, the baseline gives us some sense of how stable or labile the dependent variable is when the independent variable is not present. Thus, if we can show a different pattern of responding when the independent variable is present from when it is not, we have some evidence to conclude that the independent variable influenced the dependent variable.

If the pattern is established with respect to a series of baseline and treatment conditions over time, then it is called **intrasubject replication** (the pattern is repeated within a single participant). As with the research methods discussed previously, it is important that the dependent variable be clearly described through *operational definitions*. Also, the data are dealt with differently in single-subject research. Unlike traditional designs, in which the data from a number of participants are averaged together, when more than one participant is used in it, single-subject research asks whether the data from each participant replicate the same pattern as the data of the other participants. This is sometimes called **intersubject replication** (the pattern is repeated between participants).

The case study may offer the best type of information when the goal is to note the change in a single individual. In that case the average change in all patients or participants would give an incorrect picture of change. To illustrate this point, consider a treatment that produced a beneficial change in half the patients and a negative change in the other half. If group means or averages were calculated, one might erroneously conclude that the treatment had no effect on patients. Thus, in some cases it is more accurate to record a number of systematic, single-case studies than to record group data. Moras, Telfer, and Barlow (1993) illustrate the use of a single-case design for the treatment of a person with both generalized anxiety disorder and depression. They offer this design also as a means of showing efficacy of new treatment approaches that would lend support for the possibility of large-scale investigations.

In another example of a single-subject design, Osborne, Rudrud, and Zezoney (1990) sought to determine whether adding an orange stripe to a baseball could help members of the baseball team learn to hit a curveball better. The direction of spin on a baseball tells the batter whether the pitcher pitched a curveball (downward spin), a fastball (backward spin), or a knuckleball (no spin). However, the batter has only a little more than one tenth of a second to decide whether to swing. These authors reasoned that if you could see the seams on the baseball better, then it would be possible to know more quickly the type of pitch.

To test this possibility, the authors designed a single-subject study. To add control to the study, a pitching machine was used. The marked baseballs had either 1/4-inch or 1/8-inch orange stripes marking the seams of the baseball. The dependent variable was the number of *well-hit balls* as operationally defined by seven criteria, including the distance the ball traveled after being hit. Graphs were constructed for each player, charting the number of balls hit from each of the three types (no marking, 1/8-inch orange stripe, or 1/4-inch orange stripe). The authors concluded that adding a marking to the ball improved the batters' performance. Let's now examine some particular types of single-subject designs.

Reversal Design

One common type of single-subject design is the *reversal design*. The term *reversal* comes from the shifting in this design of the baseline and treatment conditions. The rationale behind the reversal design is simple: If a participant behaves one way before a given

	A Baseline	B Treatment	A Baseline	B Treatment
		X		X
Single subject	O_1	O_2	O_3	O_4

Figure 13.2

This figure represents an ABAB single-subject reversal design. X represents the administration of the independent variable; O represents the behavioral observations made on the subject. Note that O_1 and O_3 represent the observations of the dependent variable in the absence of the treatment condition, and O_2 and O_4 represent the observations of the dependent variable in the presence of the treatment condition.

treatment is presented, then behaves quite differently when it is presented, then returns to the original state when the treatment is removed, and finally changes again when the treatment is presented a second time, it is reasonable to suspect that this fluctuation in the participant's behavior is due to the treatment. It is hard to imagine how an extraneous variable might vary in a manner parallel with the treatment to produce a similar fluctuation in the participant's behavior; however, this possibility can never be ruled out completely.

Reversal designs may use any number of reversals. For example, a design that measures a participant's behavior before, during, and after a treatment is called an ABA design. The *before* and *after* conditions are designated the *A conditions,* and the treatment is designated the *B condition.* During the A conditions, baseline behavior is monitored in the absence of the treatment. (You should note that the single letter *A* or *B* generally represents numerous observations across time.) The purpose of the baseline period is to allow the aspect of interest to be monitored over a period of time without any type of intervention. During the B phase of the design, the participant's behavior is monitored during the intervention or treatment. As in any experimental design, it is necessary to clearly define and state the treatment. By recording observations made over time periods in which a treatment is and is not introduced, one is able to determine the effect of introducing that treatment. Figure 13.2 depicts an ABAB reversal design, briefly described in the previous paragraph. Figure 13.3 shows a diagram of the same design in two different ways. You will discover that some areas of research prefer one method of diagramming over the other, but they both represent exactly the same design.

A variant of the general ABAB design is to compare two treatment conditions against each other rather than against a baseline. Dyer, Dunlap, and Winterling (1990) used such a reversal design with students from three schools for students with autism or mental retardation in order to study the participants' problem behaviors. In particular, these authors wanted to determine whether giving the students a choice of tasks and reinforcers would reduce problem behaviors, such as aggression, self-injury, and tantrums. The dependent variable in the study was the percentage of intervals that included instances of problem behaviors that were specified individually for each child. Because it is important that the measurement of the dependent variable show reliability, these authors had observers rate a videotape of the sessions. They found that the agreement among the raters was 92% for noting problem

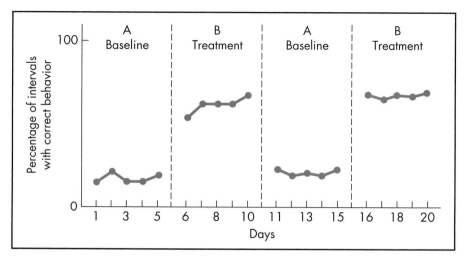

Figure 13.3

This figure represents an alternative method of diagramming an ABAB single-subject reversal design. Depending on the dependent variable, the change from baseline to treatment may be seen either as an increase (e.g., percentage of intervals with correct behavior) or as a decrease (e.g., percentage of intervals with problem behavior).

Source: Dyer, Dunlap, and Winterling (1990).

behaviors. Figure 13.4 shows the results for the three students. This design would be described as an ABA design for the first student, a BABA for the second, and an ABABA for the third (where A = student has choice; B = teacher has choice, student has no choice).

It is also possible to treat a group as if it were a single participant and use a reversal design. For example, in Iceland, Ragnarsson and Björgvinsson (1991) studied the effects of placing signs along a highway on reducing drivers' speeds. These authors used an ABCA reversal design, with A being the baseline, B being the placement of a single sign along the highway, and C being the placement of two signs. The first sign read "YESTERDAY ____% DROVE THROUGH HERE AT THE RIGHT SPEED," and the second sign read, "BEST RECORD SO FAR ____%." The percentages were selected randomly from numbers between 85 and 95 and were not based on actual observations. The dependent variable was the speed of the cars passing the signs. To ensure accuracy, a radar device measured the cars' speeds. In this study the initial baseline (A) lasted for 10 sessions over 5 days. The single-sign condition (B) lasted for 8 sessions over 4 days, and the double-sign condition (C) lasted for 24 sessions over 12 days. Following the sign conditions, both signs were removed and speeds were measured for 10 sessions over 5 days. The results indicated that posting the signs reduced the percentage of drivers exceeding 70 km/hr from 41% during baseline to around 20%. The percentage of speeders again increased during the second baseline.

In considering the reversal design, it is important to keep in mind that we are using the phenomenon of reversibility of some behavior in the presence or absence of the treatment condition to study the way that this behavior may be influenced by our treatment condition. One limitation of the reversal design is that it will work only when we are studying the effect

Figure 13.4

Results of an ABA study of three students

Source: Dyer, Dunlap, and Winterling (1990).

of treatment conditions on behaviors that return quickly to baseline levels once the treatment is over. The influence of all treatments is not this transient. When we are dealing with treatments that result in more permanent shifts in behavior, this particular design cannot be used. When we are interested in studying the long-lasting effects of various independent variables on single participants, one solution is to use a multiple-baseline design, which we discuss next.

CONCEPT
CHECK 13.2   Jim decides that he is going to perform an experiment using a single-subject design on his roommate, John. Jim wants to know whether playing music by Radiohead or Bob Marley or Beethoven piano sonatas influences John's decision to study at the library. How might Jim perform this experiment?

Multiple-Baseline Design

Like the reversal designs just discussed, the *multiple-baseline, single-subject design* relies primarily on logic to gain its degree of experimental control. With the multiple-baseline design, we monitor several behaviors of a single subject simultaneously. Once baseline levels are established for each behavior, we apply our treatment to one of these behaviors. The likelihood of a causal relation is inferred from the fact that, of the several monitored behaviors, *only* the behavior exposed to the experimental treatment changes, whereas all nontreated behaviors remain unchanged. Once this first behavioral shift is noted, the treatment is applied to the next behavior, and so on. The idea behind this design is that the baseline behaviors would be unlikely to shift by chance alone as each behavior received the treatment. To use the terminology of the first half of this book, each participant serves as his or her own control.

Consequently, in the multiple-baseline design, the successive shifting of baseline levels as the treatment is applied gives us reason to suspect a relationship with the treatment. Unlike the reversal designs, which work only for behaviors that are readily reversible, multiple-baseline designs can be used for behaviors that are permanently changed by the experimental treatment. Figure 13.5 depicts a schematic representation of a multiple-baseline, single-subject design.

Hersen and Bellack (1976) used a multiple-baseline design to demonstrate the effects of a treatment program for a schizophrenic patient. The patient made little contact with others, rarely engaged in conversation, and was compliant even to unreasonable requests. The treatment consisted of training in the development of assertiveness skills and skills for making contact with others. The measures taken over the baseline and treatment sessions were the amount of eye contact while talking, the amount of speaking without prolonged pauses,

Several	A	Baseline	*Treatment*	Baseline	Baseline	Baseline
behaviors	B	Baseline	Baseline	*Treatment*	Baseline	Baseline
of a single	C	Baseline	Baseline	Baseline	*Treatment*	Baseline
subject	D	Baseline	Baseline	Baseline	Baseline	*Treatment*

Figure 13.5

Multiple-baseline design. In this design, several behaviors (A, B, C, and D) are monitored simultaneously. The treatment is applied successively to each of these behaviors. The continuation of baseline measures after treatment sometimes is omitted. Note that evidence suggestive of a causal relationship would consist of a successive shift in baseline activity as each successive behavior receives the treatment condition.

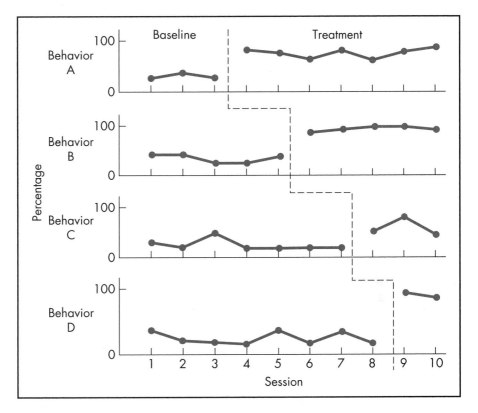

Figure 13.6

Multiple-baseline design. This type of representation is an alternative to the one presented in Figure 13.5. In this case the baseline measures were not continued after the treatment condition was introduced. The letters A, B, C, and D could represent either different behaviors of a given participant, the same behavior of one participant in different situations, or the same behavior of different participants.

the number of requests made of another person, and the number of unreasonable requests not complied with. This design requires that baselines be taken for the four measures and that treatments be introduced at different sessions for each of the behaviors to be changed, while measurements of all behaviors are continued. This type of design helps us to determine whether the treatment was specific to a particular behavior (Figure 13.6).

Concerning the limitations of the multiple-baseline design, it is important to keep in mind that each behavior being monitored must be *independent* of the others. The behaviors that we are monitoring must not be so highly interrelated that a change in one behavior results in parallel changes in other behaviors even though the participants did not receive the treatment conditions. If the behaviors under investigation were interdependent, then the successive unfolding of baseline shifts due to the successive application of our treatment condition would be destroyed, and this design would lose much of its usefulness. For example, Kazdin (1973) notes that this design may be of limited value in studying inappropriate classroom behaviors because many of these behaviors are interrelated and any treatment that is effective for one behavior is likely to influence other behaviors as well. Although the interrelatedness of these behaviors may eventually facilitate whatever intervention program is implemented, the fact that several of the behaviors may be altered simultaneously by the treatment of any one makes the multiple-baseline design of little use in studying interrelated classroom behaviors.

■ Multielement Design

In a *multielement design,* one is comparing different levels of a given variable (for example, treatment versus no treatment) or different treatments. This design is also called the *alternating treatment design* or *simultaneous treatment design* because it tests alternative treatments (Hains & Baer, 1989). For example, a teacher could ask, "What is the best procedure for helping a child with learning disabilities to pay attention?" Each procedure would form a different treatment, and these could be studied on alternate days or at different periods within the same day. Likewise, a researcher could study the effects of three different drugs on memory in an elderly participant, each on a different day. If we were studying two treatments, then the design would be similar to the ABAB reversal designs that we discussed previously. However, the key element of the multielement design is that it incorporates *many reversals,* which may be fast-paced.

Hains and Baer (1989) suggest that there are a number of advantages to this design. One advantage is that by having frequent reversals of the treatments, one is able to examine the changes within the context of background variables that are difficult or impossible to change. In a school setting, such background variables might include the weather, the cycle of extracurricular activities, and changes in class composition. Another advantage of this design is that any differences in the effects of different treatments seem to emerge quickly.

The limitation of such a design is that it is best suited to changes that are short-lived. For example, a study of the effects of different drugs on memory would be possible only if none of the drugs had a lasting effect on the participant. Thus, both the treatment and its effect cannot be long-lasting for this design to be useful. If there were long-lasting effects, then there would be a carryover problem similar to that discussed in Chapter 10. A similar problem, which we discussed in other chapters in terms of sequence or order effects, appears when one has multiple treatments (for example, drug A, drug B, drug C) such that one treatment is influenced by the treatment that precedes it. Thus, it is possible that our measurement of the effects of drug B is influenced by the fact that drug A preceded it. One answer to this problem is to counterbalance the treatments.

As we said previously, counterbalancing does not eliminate an order effect. However, with a single-subject design, any order effect would be visible across the time series. For example, if we were to perform the memory study using three drugs over a period of time, we would have an initial baseline condition followed by the drugs' being compared to each other followed by a final baseline condition, in a counterbalanced order. That is, on each day an experimenter could give a single participant either one of the drugs or a baseline condition in a counterbalanced order over a period of time. From such a time series, we could observe not only which drug increased memory but also whether one particular counterbalanced order gave a different effect. That is, we might discover that drug B produced an overall increase in words remembered when given after drug C or no drug (the baseline condition) but not when given after drug A.

Making Sense of Single-Subject Experimental Results

Once you have conducted your single-subject experiment, you must make a decision concerning what you have found. One of the first steps is to present the data visually in a graphic form, as illustrated throughout this chapter. Carr and Burkholder (1998) explain how to present single-subject design graphs using currently available spreadsheets. To aid in the interpretation of such graphic presentations, a number of guidelines have been suggested to ensure consistency of presentation and interpretation (Franklin, Gorman, Beasley, & Allison, 1998).

How do you know that the particular pattern of results that you collected is meaningful? The main tool that you have is logic. As we said previously, if the dependent variable changes when the treatment is added, then we have evidence that our treatment influenced our dependent variable. A further tool that we use is that of **replication.** The ability to reproduce the same relationship a number of times suggests that the relationship is stable. In fact, researchers who use single-subject designs suggest that they obtain more stable relationships by performing the same experiment on one participant (or a few participants) 100 times than by using 100 participants, with each receiving the experimental procedure once.

As we suggested, a reversal type of design works only in areas (for example, vision or operant conditioning) in which the experiment does not permanently modify the organism under study. Unlike traditional experimental procedures based on inferential procedures, traditional experimental single-subject designs do not offer a cutoff level such as the .05 probability level, so the researcher must determine the meaning of the pattern observed. For this reason single-subject researchers often specify the criterion of change sought before the experiment begins and continue the treatment section until this degree of change is found.

✓ CONCEPT CHECK 13.3   A clinical psychologist was working with a psychotic patient in a state hospital. It was her desire to develop experimental conditions that would make permanent changes in a number of harmful behaviors. However, she read that reversal designs would not work in this situation because the behavior changes were to be permanent. What should she do?

ALTERNATIVE TYPES OF SINGLE-SUBJECT RESEARCH

We have focused in this chapter on the more traditional single-subject designs, which do not rely on inferential statistics; however, one recent trend is to use inferential procedures in single-subject studies (Gorman & Allison, 1998). Many researchers have reported using single-subject approaches with group designs. For example, Ericsson and Polson (1988a, 1988b) combined a variety of research traditions to better understand everyday memory processes. They wanted to study the memorizing ability of a particular waiter who was able to remember dinner orders from more than 20 people sitting at different tables without writing them down. To gain greater experimental control, Ericsson and Polson reconstructed a restaurant-like situation in the laboratory. There they studied in greater detail the manner in which the waiter (J.C.) memorized orders, and they compared J.C.'s results with those of untrained control participants.

The research addressed three issues. First, by having J.C. verbally describe his thoughts while memorizing orders in the restaurant, the researchers began to develop a scientific model of his skills, which they intended to model on a computer. Second, to help determine the nature of J.C.'s memory ability, the researchers compared his performance with that of college students who had no experience waiting on tables. And third, the researchers sought to determine whether J.C.'s memory skills could be compared with theoretical models in the field of cognitive psychology. This work is an example of how research with a single participant may be combined with group studies to approach basic psychological questions.

Another trend is to use single-subject approaches conceptually as an aid in describing theoretical cognitive models. For example, Chi and Koeske (1983) studied for more than a year the knowledge structure and memory of a 4-year-old boy. This boy was very interested in dinosaurs, and the researchers used that interest to understand how he processed cognitive information. They constructed a map of how items of dinosaur information (for example, types of dinosaurs and the foods they ate) were related in this child's mind and how these relationships influenced his memory for dinosaur names.

Likewise, Landau, Gleitman, and Spelke (1981) sought to determine which types of spatial and geometric information a 2-year-old child processed. The intriguing aspect of this study was that the child was blind from birth, so the manner in which vision played a role in spatial development could also be considered. Through a series of experiments, the researchers studied this child's spatial knowledge and geometric representation. They concluded that sight was not required for developing such skills as moving around and navigating through one's environment.

KEY TERMS AND CONCEPTS

1. **History of single-subject research**
2. **Case study designs**
   A. Naturalistic case studies
   B. One-shot case studies
3. **Experimental single-subject designs**
   A. Types of replication
      • Intrasubject replication
      • Intersubject replication

   B. Reversal design
   C. Multiple-baseline design
   D. Multielement design
4. **Alternative types of single-subject research**

SUMMARY

1. This chapter briefly describes the history of single-subject research and its importance in psychology. A distinction is made between the descriptive case study approach and the experimental single-subject design.
2. The naturalistic case study has been a traditional means of describing an individual, especially in areas

such as clinical psychology, medicine, and neuropsychology. Although important in its descriptive abilities, the naturalistic case study is weak in its ability to draw causal relationships or to make sound inferences.

3. Experimental single-subject designs use a series of measurements over time to establish stability. Within

(continued)

SUMMARY (*continued*)

this context, stability is shown either within the same participant (intrasubject replication) or among different participants (intersubject replication).

4. Types of experimental single-subject designs include the reversal design, the multiple-baseline design, and the multielement design.

5. Some alternative types of single-subject designs use traditional inferential statistics.

REVIEW QUESTIONS

1. Name some important points in the history of single-subject research.
2. How is the descriptive single-case approach different from the more experimental types of single-subject designs?
3. Describe a naturalistic case study.
4. What is the logic of experimental single-subject research that seeks to establish a relationship between the independent and the dependent variables?

5. What is the difference between *intrasubject replication* and *intersubject replication*?
6. Describe some of the most popular experimental single-subject designs and give an example of when each might be used.
7. What are some strengths and weaknesses of single-subject approaches?

DISCUSSION QUESTIONS AND PROJECTS

1. Discuss how you might design a single-subject experiment to determine whether eating breakfast influences alertness during the day.
2. Diagram an ABABA single-subject design and discuss some types of dependent variables that could be used in such a design. Name some dependent variables that could not be used in such a design.

3. A student is interested in determining whether people become more tired when using a color or a monochrome computer screen. How might she design such a study using the single-subject method?
4. In the study referred to in Question 3, how might the experimenter control for such factors as beginning and end of term?

INFOTRAC COLLEGE EDITION: EXERCISES

We pointed to the case study approach as important in understanding particular disorders. In an article in the *Journal of Cognitive Neuroscience* (May 1998), Price et al. used brain-imaging techniques to study individuals with deep dyslexia, a disorder in which individuals make semantic errors in reading single words aloud. In terms of single-subject designs, we pointed out that these designs were often used in studies of conditioning. For example,

Chris Ninness and colleagues used four single-subject ABA designs to study which computer voices individuals preferred. Using InfoTrac College Edition, you can find this article in the Fall 2001 issue of the *Psychological Record*. In this same journal, you can read a discussion concerning how single-subject experiments are described in experimental texts and a general discussion of these designs.

☑ Answers to Concept Checks

13.1 You would send the student back to reread the first section of this chapter. Although descriptive case studies lack experimental rigor, there are experimental single-subject designs that are valid experimental tools. The main theme of single-subject designs is the ability to study a single participant or group of participants in depth rather than making limited observations with more participants. With the more experimental types of single-subject designs, conclusions are based more on logically demonstrating a relationship between the independent and dependent variables through repeated observations.

13.2 A reversal design (for example, ABAB) would be one possibility. However, one would still need to be careful that one particular condition did not always appear during special times (for example, midterms and finals) when John would normally be going to the library. It should be noted that each condition (A or B) in the ABAB design represents a number of individual presentations over time.

13.3 Because she is working with a single patient, a single-subject design would be most appropriate. It is also true that if the behavior change were permanent, the reversal design would not work. However, a multiple-baseline design that monitored a variety of behaviors would be useful. The most common procedure would be to establish a baseline for each behavior under study and then apply the treatment condition to each of these, one at a time. The logic of this would be that we would expect only the behaviors exposed to the independent variable to change.

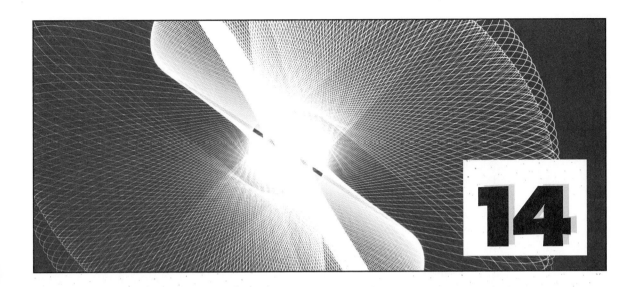

QUESTIONNAIRES, SURVEY RESEARCH, AND SAMPLING

QUESTION CONSTRUCTION
AND FORMATS
Types of Questions
General Considerations
Special Techniques for Reactive Questions

METHODS OF ADMINISTERING A SURVEY
Face-to-Face Interviews
Telephone Interviews
Mail Questionnaires

Computer Questionnaires
Internet Research
Surveys: Conclusion

SAMPLING
Probability Sampling
Nonprobability Sampling

SAMPLE SIZE

RELIABILITY AND VALIDITY

A psychotherapist might notice that more of the clients coming to see her with problems of depression are women. Puzzled by this observation, she could conduct a research project to help her to understand the relationship between gender and depression. That is, she might want to know whether being depressed is statistically related to gender. One beginning approach would be to gather data from a variety of sources, such as hospitals, counseling centers, and private practitioners, concerning the problems that people initially describe when they seek treatment. In fact, there are a number of sources detailing trends in the treatment of psychological disorders including depression (for example, Olfson et al., 2002). The therapist could then single out depression and simply note the number of men and women who seek help.

Let's assume that the psychotherapist is interested in the question of whether more women are depressed than men, using the standard psychiatric definition of depression as the operational definition. One potential problem is that such a study might not tell us whether there are more women than men who are depressed, but rather whether more women than men seek psychological help for any problem in general and depression in particular. The observation that our therapist made might reflect not that there are more depressed women than depressed men but that more women than men seek help for their depression. To rule out this alternative and to learn something about the incidence of depression in the general population, types of research techniques would be required that are different from those we have presented so far. One alternative would be to use survey research techniques. This chapter presents the main considerations in performing survey research. Survey research methods can help us to understand the characteristics of some particular group of people, which we call a *population*. A number of websites are available for learning about survey research. For example, the survey research center at the University of Michigan (http://www.isr.umich.edu/home/) offers a variety of details including data from surveys related to such topics as health, life development, and aging. For example, a set of surveys published in 2007 examined the mental health of immigrants matched to individuals who had been in the United States for a longer period of time in terms of ethnicity, gender, and other factors. These data suggest that immigrants have lower rates of mental disorders than native-born Americans. You can also see a survey designed to study midlife development supported by the MacArthur Foundation at http://midmac.med.harvard.edu. This site discusses not only the rationale for performing the study but also the specifics of sampling and data collection.

Other sites such as that of the Gallup Organization (http://www.gallup.com), the American Statistical Association (http://www.amstat.org), and the U.S. Census Bureau (http://www.census.gov) offer additional information on performing survey research as well as current surveys. For example, if you put "survey research" in the American Statistical Association search box, you will see that they have a survey research methods section with an online booklet called "What Is a Survey?" At these sites you can see how our attitudes about drafting women for the military have not changed in the last 10 years, read about the history of sampling as used in surveys, and view the latest U.S. census data. Other sites such as the Murray Research Center (http://vdc.hmdc.harvard.edu/VDC/) at Harvard contain the data from both survey and longitudinal research, including Mary Ainsworth's study of attachment, Lewis Terman's study of gifted children, and Jack Block's study of personality over the life span, as well as a variety of other studies. Let's look at one of these classic survey studies related to well-being and life satisfaction.

This large-scale survey research project focused on the well-being and life satisfaction of people in the United States at two times: 1957 and 1976 (Veroff, Douvan, & Kulka, 1981). The 1957 survey and its replicate in 1976 were designed to answer questions about average men and women. These questions included how well or how badly adjusted people consider themselves to be; how happy (or unhappy), worried (or not), and optimistic (or pessimistic) people are in their outlook; what troubles people in the United States and what they do about their problems; and to whom they turn for help and how effective that help is. Such information would help the researcher in our previous example to understand the relationship between seeking help and gender, as well as the specific issue of depression as it relates to differences between women and men. In this chapter we discuss the survey related to well-being as an exemplar of the types of questions to be considered and the particular steps to be accomplished in performing survey research.

As with any type of research, one of the first questions in designing a survey concerns the general purpose of the research (Box 14.1). Veroff, Douvan, and Kulka (1981, p. 6) report two distinct purposes for conducting their surveys. The first purpose was "to assess the subject mental health, the life experiences of American adults," and the second was "to determine in some detail how American people cope with problems of adjustment which arise in their lives." The second question was of practical concern to the U.S. Congress, which, through the National Institutes of Mental Health, helped to fund this study. Congress was interested in determining whether Americans would use mental health facilities if the government helped to provide them. Thus, in economic terms alone, the results of this survey would have far-reaching implications.

To fulfill the broad aims of the survey, the researchers addressed specific questions, such as how willing people are to seek psychological help and whether going to a mental health professional carries a stigma in people's minds. They also addressed more practical questions, such as how one decides whom to go to and how people decide whether the help they were given was good or bad. In relation to the broad aim of describing the life experiences of American adults, the researchers chose to examine feelings and sources of well-being, self-perceptions, marriage, parenthood, and work, as well as patterns of reported problems. The survey researchers also decided to differentiate the responses given by men and those given by women concerning the way in which people experience and report distress and satisfaction. Once the more specific aims have been determined, one is then faced with the task of developing the actual questions that will be used in the survey and deciding how to administer them.

The section that follows deals with the content of the survey: the actual questions asked and their construction. A later section focuses on the process of administering the survey: the manner in which questions are presented to a person, including both the manner of administration (for example, face-to-face interview versus mail survey) and the relationship between the interviewer and the respondent. These two aspects are highly interrelated; the manner of administration often influences the format of the questions being asked.

 CONCEPT CHECK 14.1   A number of studies have shown that women go to psychotherapists for depression more often than men. Does this mean that more women than men suffer from depression? What types of research methods would be useful to answer this question?

Box 14.1

Steps for Designing a Survey Research Project

Approximately 50 years ago, Campbell and Katona (1953) set up a simple nine-step flowchart describing the steps required for conducting a survey. These steps offer a review and checklist for any surveys you are designing.

1. *General objectives:* The first step is to state why the survey is necessary. What is the broad objective one is seeking to accomplish? For example, using the case of the psychotherapist presented at the beginning of this chapter, we would say that her overall objective was to describe the relationship between gender and depression.

2. *Specific objectives:* The second step is to be more specific—to state exactly what types of data will be collected and specify the particular hypotheses to be explored. Again using the example of depression, the specific objectives would include a statement of indicators of depression, such as feeling state (reporting that one feels blue, difficulty sleeping, and so on). The particular hypotheses could be (a) that women report depression or symptoms of depression more often than men, and (b) that women report seeking help for these symptoms more often than men.

3. *Sample:* Two main decisions are needed at this point. The first decision requires that you state which population you are addressing; that is, to which group do you wish to generalize your results? The population that one designates is related to the original question. For example, in a political survey, the population might be all the registered voters in a particular state. Once the population is established, the second decision is required. This decision relates to how large a sample one is to use, as well as how the sample is to be chosen. Particular techniques for sample selection are discussed in this chapter.

4. *Questionnaire:* This step requires a decision about how the sample is to be surveyed (in person, by telephone, or by mail) as well as the particular questions to be asked. The researcher at this point must decide on the types of questions and responses that will be included. Will the questions use an open-ended or fixed-alternative format or some combination of both? Once the actual questions are developed, it is important to pretest them to ensure clarity. With fixed-alternative questions, the pretest will help to determine whether adequate responses have been provided.

5. *Fieldwork:* This step is related to the people who will actually conduct the survey. The interviewers must be trained and thoroughly practiced. Other considerations such as the interrelationship between the sex, race, and socioeconomic level of the interviewer and the respondent also must be taken into account.

6. *Content analysis:* Some surveys return data in a qualitative form, and they must be transformed into a quantitative form. The information must be coded to ensure reliability across subjects—there must be a system of coding open-ended questions. Even if the data are presented in a numerical fashion, as on a Likert scale, there must be a systematic manner of grouping data for future analysis.

(continued)

(continued)

7. *Analysis plan:* Most surveys contain a large number of questions, each of which could be compared to every other, either singularly or in combination. Before the actual data are collected, it is important to specify a plan of analysis that will answer the research hypotheses. This does not preclude later reanalysis of the data for different purposes, but it is important to have an initial plan for data analysis.

8. *Tabulation:* This step is required in a large survey. The researcher must decide how the data are to be entered into the computer and in what form the data should be stored.

9. *Analysis and reporting:* The final stage is the preparation of a report, which would include not only how the data are related to the specific objectives but also such considerations as the reliability of the data from this study.

As Campbell and Katona point out, these nine steps may be interrelated; decisions affecting one step may also have important implications for another step. With this qualification, these steps offer guidelines for the design of survey research.

QUESTION CONSTRUCTION AND FORMATS

At first it may seem easy to construct a survey; you just ask questions. However, it becomes more complicated than that when we realize that not everyone thinks the same way we do. Simple changes in wording can significantly influence someone's response. For example, if you ask whether we should help the poor among us, you will get different responses than if you ask about welfare. With this in mind, you should realize that constructing a survey can be complicated, with each decision you make affecting every other decision. Should you ask people general questions, or should you have them compare one viewpoint with another? How should you word a question so that respondents will give you an honest response rather than one that they think is socially acceptable? This section offers guidance.

■ Types of Questions

Many types of questions may be used in a survey. One of the more common types is called an *open-ended question*. An open-ended question, as the name implies, has no fixed answer but allows the respondent to answer in any manner. For example, "What do you like best about college?" is an open-ended question. You could respond by naming a particular course or a good friend, by talking about being on your own, or by telling what you do on Saturday night. An open-ended question is flexible, and this flexibility carries a number of advantages. One advantage is that an open-ended question does not impose the researcher's point of view on the respondent. Another is that the person being interviewed may give you information that you had not considered previously, and this information may show you a new way of understanding the issue being investigated.

Open-ended questions also offer an important way to begin a survey. For example, the survey of life satisfaction and well-being, discussed previously, used a number of open-ended questions. One of these asked about leisure and was worded as follows (Veroff et al., 1981, p. 552):

> One of the things we'd like to know is how people spend their time. For instance—how do you usually spend your time when your work is done—what kind of things do you do, both at home and away from home?

However, open-ended questions can pose a problem when you analyze the data and try to establish meaningful patterns of responding. It is sometimes difficult to know how to translate the responses to an open-ended question into categories that fit the original research hypothesis. Of course, it is possible for researchers to impose their own points of view and thus defeat one of the advantages of open-ended questions. Therefore, it is important to select scoring categories carefully. The life satisfaction and well-being survey conducted by Veroff et al. made 55 distinctions in order to score responses to the item "What are some of the things you feel pretty happy about these days?"

Another type of question is called a *fixed-alternative question,* which limits the number of responses that a participant can make. This type of question is also called a *closed-ended question.* An example would be a question that asked

Do you believe that Puerto Rico should become a state?

Yes [   ]   No [   ]

With the fixed-alternative question, respondents are limited in their responses. Respondents cannot give a reason for their responses, as they could with the open-ended question. However, in constructing fixed-alternative questions, you are not limited to yes or no. For example, a town might ask whether college students should be allowed to vote in local elections. The question could be

Should students be allowed to vote?

1. Yes, under any circumstances.
2. Yes, but only if they pay local taxes.
3. No.

Qualified answers such as "Yes, but . . ." or "No, but . . ." permit the answering of additional questions that the researchers might be interested in while retaining an easy-to-score survey question. It is also possible to combine open- and closed-ended questions in a single item. For example, someone might ask what your favorite TV show is, listing specific choices and then "Other" followed by a blank for you to write in a choice of your own. Such an item would appear as

What is your favorite TV show?

[   ] *Seinfeld*

[   ] *24 Hours*

[   ] *The Simpsons*

[   ] Other: Please specify

It is not uncommon for open-ended and closed-ended questions to be used in the same questionnaire. One technique is to use open-ended questions followed by fixed alternatives to achieve more specific responses. For example, in the survey on American life satisfaction, the question concerning leisure time was later followed by this closed-ended question:

Next, how much of your free time do you spend doing things that challenge you? Would you say that you spend most, a lot, some, a little, or none of your free time doing such things?

1. Most   **2.** A lot   **3.** Some   **4.** A little   **5.** None

When a researcher begins a line of questioning with an open-ended question and then follows this with more specific items, as in the previous example, the process is called *funneling.* Like a funnel, the questions initially are very broad and then become more and more narrow. However, it is important to begin with open-ended questions; otherwise, the closed-ended questions will limit the information the respondent gives.

It is important to choose responses that fit with the category of the question being asked. If the question has to do with frequency, such as "How often do you . . . ," then the appropriate alternative answers might be "never," "rarely," "sometimes," "often," and "very often." If the question asks how true you believe a certain statement to be, the alternatives might be "very true," "somewhat true," "not very true," and "not at all true." Although the responses offered for each question usually are balanced, it is also possible to present an unbalanced response set. That is, in response to the question, "Have you ever been dishonest on an exam?" the answers "always" and "almost always" would receive few if any checks. It would be appropriate to offer respondents some alternatives that suggest that they almost never are dishonest or look at anyone else's paper. The responses might be "sometimes," "almost never," "once or twice," and "never." Another important point is that if the response categories ask for specific information, then the categories must not overlap. Consider the following question:

How many children do you have?

    a. 0–1 child
    b. 1–2 children
    c. 2 or more children

Which answer would you check if you have two children? Because the categories overlap, it is difficult to know how to respond. Although the problem may seem obvious in this example, it is sometimes seen in other surveys, such as those requesting salary information.

The types of items that we have discussed only begin to touch on the number of possible alternatives that can be used. In the concluding part of this section, we want to introduce briefly a variety of other response formats. We present them for illustration only and suggest that you consult more in-depth presentations if you design a survey using these formats (for example, Babbie, 2008; Edwards, Thomas, Rosenfeld, & Booth-Kewley, 1997; Fink & Kosecoff, 1998).

One alternative format is to use a nonverbal mode for describing preference. With special populations, such as children, it could be more appropriate to use graphic rather than verbal alternatives. For example, children might be asked to point to happy or sad faces to convey how much they like or dislike a certain game. Some other types of formats have been developed for particular purposes, such as analysis and scaling. We include them in this section because you may hear researchers describe their questionnaires as using *Likert-type items,* for example.

Likert (1932) published a technique for measuring attitudes. The general format is the same as that of the fixed-alternative items that we have presented. One item might be stated as

If I heard someone calling for help in a large city, I would help him or her.

Strongly agree	Agree	Uncertain	Disagree	Strongly disagree
(5)	(4)	(3)	(2)	(1)

As you can see, the format of the response is the same as that of items that we have discussed. However, Likert developed a method of scaling items. Each item is given a certain weight, represented by the number in parentheses. A number of scale items are then added together to form an index, such as an index of helping behavior. The original procedure was to perform an item analysis to determine which items contributed to the index consistently across participants. Items that did not contribute consistently could be eliminated from the final version of the questionnaire.

Another type of response format is called the *semantic differential.* The semantic differential uses bipolar adjectives (such as *good* and *bad, soft* and *hard, modern* and *old-fashioned, interesting* and *boring, hot* and *cold, slow* and *fast*) in relation to a particular concept or idea. These adjectives usually are placed at each end of a 7-point scale. The instructions ask the respondent to check an appropriate place between each pair of adjectives to rate a concept or thing. For example, you could be asked to rate a course you were taking:

Please rate your course in introductory psychology along the following dimensions.

easy ____:____:____:____:____:____:____ hard
fun ____:____:____:____:____:____:____ dull
sexy ____:____:____:____:____:____:____ not sexy
fast ____:____:____:____:____:____:____ slow

For clarity you could list categories such as "very much," "a lot," "somewhat," and so on, at the top of the semantic differential. Because the semantic differential was originally developed for measuring the meaning of objects, or what is called *semantic space of experience,* it is possible to use adjectives that may be related experientially to a concept. Thus, we can ask whether a musical recording is *hot* or a course *sexy* using this technique. When analysis is performed using a number of semantic response lines related to a single concept, it is possible to arrive at an overall profile (see Osgood, Suci, & Tannenbaum, 1957, for more information about the semantic differential).

■ General Considerations

Developing questions for a survey may be more difficult than you think at first, for a variety of reasons. One reason is the ambiguity of language. For example, we often say such things as, "I always eat with my friends," when we are trying to emphasize how close we are to our friends. However, if someone were to ask you the question, "Do you always eat with your friends?" on a survey, you would probably consider the question to be asking for specific information, and you might have some difficulty knowing exactly how to answer the question. In fact, in one poll in which respondents reported that the questions were clearly stated, the understanding of the phrase *over the last few years* was interpreted to mean less than 2 years by some of the respondents and more than 10 years by others. Thus, it is important in developing questions to be as clear as possible and to avoid unwanted ambiguity. Sometimes, the particular question you are asking may be difficult to phrase in a simple sentence, especially if you are asking about how someone feels or thinks about more global concepts, such as freedom, love, religion, country, or family.

Be careful, however, not to fall into the trap of asking double-barreled questions. Double-barreled questions are those items that combine two separate questions into one. For example, the question "Should people be allowed to use their cell phones in the airport but not on the plane?" asks two separate questions. The first question is whether people should be allowed to use their cell phones in the airport, and the second question is whether people should be allowed to use their cell phones on the plane. A double-barreled question is difficult to code. A "no" answer by a respondent, for example, could mean that people should not be allowed to use their cell phones either in the airport or on the plane, or it could mean that people should be allowed to use their cell phone either in the airport or on the plane, but not both places.

Another type of question that can reduce the validity of your survey is one containing negatives. For example, a negative question could ask, "Will you not be supporting an increase in tuition next year?" To answer that question may require a second negative, as in "No, I will not." There are at least two problems with this type of question. First, many individuals will just ignore the "not" as they read the question, as you may have done yourself. Second, many individuals have a difficult time knowing what a yes or no answer means. If you are asked whether you agree or disagree that Puerto Rico should not become a state, how do you answer? Negative and double negative questions take humans longer to process than positive questions and are more prone to misinterpretation.

Another consideration as you construct your survey is whether you are setting up an overall response set. That is, you do not want someone to be able to answer "yes" to every question. Once a response set is established, many individuals will continue along that line and pay less attention to the questions themselves. If you were doing a survey on gun control, for example, you would not want those in support of it always answering in the same way to each question, and vice versa. Some questions in such a survey could be of the form "The government needs to restrict the sale of guns" whereas others could be of the form "Individuals should have the right to buy guns as they wish." If you were studying speech anxiety, some questions could have the form "I feel anxious before I speak in front of a group" and others could have the form "I feel relaxed before I speak in front of a group." Thus, a response set could not be established. One way to accomplish this is to have some questions that are reverse scored.

Sometimes, you may be asking for information that people do not want to give. How you phrase your question may determine whether the person is willing to answer. For example, many people will say whether their income is between $10,000 and $29,999, between $30,000 and $59,999, or above $60,000, but they will not tell you the exact figure. If you do not need to know the exact figure, do not ask. One of the first rules for developing questions is to ask only what you need to know.

Another important consideration is the order in which the questions are asked. For example, the life satisfaction and well-being survey discussed previously would probe for positive responses before negative ones. That is, on open-ended questions, such as general questions on marriage, the interviewer would ask about the *nicest things* in marriage before asking about things that are *not quite as nice as you would like them to be.* Some researchers who have studied order effects suggest that a person's response to one question has an effect on his or her response to the next question (Schuman & Presser, 1981). These effects seem to be strongest when the questions are of a general or summary type.

Another important guideline is to consider what you are asking not only from your own perspective but also from the perspective of those responding to the survey. Questions that seem perfectly clear when we are developing a questionnaire may not appear as clear when asked in a survey. The respondent may have a different frame of reference. For example, if I asked you about your worth, you would not know whether I wanted to know how much money you had in the bank or how you valued yourself psychologically. Again, it is important to reduce any unwanted ambiguity. One way of doing this is to establish a context in which the question is presented. As you may have noticed, in the life satisfaction and well-being survey, the researchers began by saying that they wanted to know how people spend their leisure time. This is a better approach than just asking, "What do you do when you are not working?"

Context is also important when we ask people to give us information that may be at odds with either what is accepted in society or their public image. For example, a question designed to learn about parents' anger toward their small children might begin with the statement, "All parents become angry with their children from time to time. What do you do when you become angry?" The established context—that all parents become angry at times—enables the respondent to feel freer to disclose information in relation to his or her own angry feelings and actions. By creating a context in which the person can answer the question, we gain more accurate information. However, it is also important not to go to the extreme and create an introduction to your questions that leads the person to answer in a manner that does not reflect his or her real attitude.

You should also avoid *leading* in developing questions. To avoid potential bias based on their own perceptions, some researchers develop fixed-alternative responses based on the initial administration of an open-ended question. To ensure that you do not have leading questions in the survey, you might begin by asking the question in an open-ended fashion to a group of people. You would tabulate their responses and use these as a basis for fixed-alternative items.

At this point, it is time to consider one of the most important guidelines for survey research: *Pretest the survey!* It is imperative that you give the questions that you have developed to people and that you note any unwanted ambiguity in their responses or any misunderstanding of the items. One technique for understanding how those who take your survey understand the questions is to have them think out loud as they answer the survey. In this way you can determine that their understanding of the survey is the same as you intended. In the ideal situation, the survey should be pretested on the population to which it will be given. This is particularly important to help determine the adequacy of fixed-choice responses. Pretesting helps us to easily perceive that we have worded an item correctly (or incorrectly) and whether the alternatives offered actually represent the manner in which our target group would respond. It is not uncommon to pretest a survey more than once and to use the feedback from each testing to develop a better survey for answering the original research question.

☑ CONCEPT A music professor wanted to know what type of music undergraduates like to
CHECK 14.2 listen to. To answer this question, he conducted a survey in which he asked a
number of students the following three questions:

1. Do you like classical music? Yes _____   No _____
2. Do you like acid rock?   Yes _____   No _____
3. Do you like polka music?   Yes _____   No _____

The professor was surprised to find that after the survey he still did not know
what type of music undergraduates like to listen to. How might he have conducted this study to better answer his question?

■ Special Techniques for Reactive Questions

What if you were to ask someone a question about his or her sexual fantasies or whether he
or she had ever broken the law? How honestly do you think that the person would respond?
These are difficult questions to answer. Some people would answer honestly, and some
would not. Because it is not possible to know when someone is not answering a survey
honestly, techniques have been developed to ask potentially reactive or embarrassing questions. These procedures have been shown to have a more valid response rate than asking
the question directly.

One such technique is the *random response method* (Warner, 1965). We describe the
most simple version of the technique using a coin, but you could also use dice or other
methods that give equally randomized results. Using the coin, the person answering the
survey is told to flip a coin for each question. If the coin is heads, she or he is to answer yes.
However, if the coin is tails, the participant is to answer the question truthfully. Because the
researcher in this situation has no idea which questions the person answered honestly and
which questions he or she answered in terms of the coin flip, it is assumed that the participant is more willing to tell the truth. Shotland and Yankowski (1982) tested this assumption by having people *overhear* answers to a test. These researchers compared the random
response method to direct questioning of the participants. They found that the participants
told the truth 64 to 80% of the time using the random response method but only 10 to 27%
of the time using direct questioning.

How does the random response method work? It is simple: Assume that you gave each
of a large group of people a survey and a coin and told them to answer yes when the coin
landed on heads and no when the coin landed on tails. What would you expect to find?
The answer, of course, is that each question would have an equal number of yes responses
and an equal number of no responses. Now change the situation slightly; suppose they are
told to respond yes to heads but honestly to tails. What would the results be this time? The
answer is that any result different from 50% can be considered not the result of chance but
based on an *honest response*. Thus, if 80% of the responses to a hypothetical question ("Do
you like watching soap operas on TV?") were yes, we would assume that if everyone were
being honest when they were supposed to be, 60% of all respondents would have responded
yes to this question.

How do we determine the honest response when the responses we recorded were composed of both honest responses and coin flips? We determine this by subtracting 50% (the expected probability) from 80% (the percentage of yes responses) and dividing by 50% (the expected probability). In conclusion, when you have questions that produce reactive or embarrassing responses, such as asking one about sexual practices, the random response method offers a valid alternative to direct questioning or even anonymous questionnaires.

METHODS OF ADMINISTERING A SURVEY

■ Face-to-Face Interviews

When someone mentions the word *survey,* we may think of census takers coming to our house or of the exit polls that we see on television during political elections. In both of these cases, the interviewer presents the person with a series of questions face-to-face and records his or her answers. There are a number of advantages to this approach. One of the main advantages of face-to-face interviews, especially if the survey is somewhat complex, is that you are able to achieve a better idea of the psychological set from which the person is answering the questions. For example, you can determine how motivated the person may be to give you answers. You can also judge the respondent's comprehension and clear up any ambiguity or misunderstanding. With open-ended questions, it is possible to probe for additional information if the initial response is brief or incomplete. For example, in the survey question concerning what people do with their free time, if the person says only, "Have fun," it would be possible to follow up with a probe such as "Tell me more" or "Can you name some particular activities?" and thus produce a more specific answer. The interviewer can also make and record observations related to race, sex, socioeconomic level, and so forth, without having to ask these questions directly. Compared with other forms of survey administration, such as sending questionnaires through the mail, face-to-face interviews generally give higher completion rates and more complete information.

There are also disadvantages to face-to-face interviews. First, face-to-face interviews are expensive in terms of time and personnel, thus limiting the number of interviews that can be conducted compared with other methods, such as mail or telephone surveys. Second, although the interviewer may help the respondents to understand the questions and may clarify the responses, the interviewer can also bias the results, either consciously or unconsciously. For example, some interviewers may probe more with men than with women, or they may probe less with older than with younger respondents, and thus systematically bias the results.

It may also happen that the respondent would give different answers face-to-face than with a written questionnaire. As you can imagine, some people find it difficult to discuss sensitive issues (such as sexuality, drug or alcohol use, or behaviors that might be considered deviant) in person, whereas they might answer an anonymous questionnaire quite easily. It is also possible that the respondent will not like the interviewer's looks, clothing, race, or sex, and may give biased information. For example, one interviewer reported that, after a productive interview session, the respondent said that the interviewer was really a civil rights worker trying to integrate the neighborhood and that the respondent was not

Box 14.2

Verbal Report as Data: Can We Tell More Than We Know?

It is often said that if you want to know something, you should ask. In psychological research this simple suggestion has led to a great deal of debate. The debate centers on a number of themes, one of which asks whether there really is a relationship between attitudes and behaviors. Another asks whether a person can really know about himself or herself. For example, do you really know your attitude concerning the opposite sex? Can you really predict whether you will help someone in distress if you happen into such a situation walking through the streets of New York? Do you actually know how you think as you go about solving a problem, and can you report this to an experimenter? Although our tendency is to say that we know a great deal about ourselves, research has demonstrated that these questions represent complex considerations that cut across most of psychological research. They are particularly important to survey researchers because survey research relies heavily on self-report data.

Survey researchers have adopted two main approaches concerning self-report data. The first approach is to seek situations in which it can be assumed that survey responses will give a useful description of a person's attitudes, views, and behaviors. For example, it is assumed that people can report what they do in their leisure time or whether they would vote for a particular person in an election. The second approach disconnects the attitude from behavior and places an emphasis on attitudes in themselves. For example, it is possible to ask people about their optimism for the future, their views of capital punishment, or what they think about free trade, all without involving references to a particular behavior.

With regard to the second approach, it has been suggested that verbal data are important

in their own right and do not have to be related to nonverbal data (compare Galtung, 1967). This theoretical position suggests that it is not necessary to validate a questionnaire related to behavior by actually observing behavior. To expand on this position, it is important to understand that social and psychological relationships are complex and that all modes of behavior— cognitive, emotional, and physiological, as well as self-report—are not expected to show identical patterns in every situation. This complexity makes psychological research interesting, and it is often amazing to discover how widely particular aspects of behavior vary. For example, in one study the task was to listen to a tape recording of different voices and to report after each voice whether the voice was one's own or that of another person. It was shown that individuals would give a psychophysiological response (electrodermal) to hearing their own voices even though they reported that it was not their voice (Gur & Sackeim, 1979). This type of research suggests that people have multiple response systems and that self-report data cannot be expected to give a single, consistent picture across all of these. The research also suggests that when you tap the right channel, it is possible for people to tell you more than they know they know.

Whether people can tell you more than they know they know has been the topic of much debate. Nisbett and Wilson (1977), in a *Psychological Review* article, suggest that people may not be able to use introspection to describe their cognitive processes accurately. People may not actually know why they like someone or why they took a particular course or why they like one color of clothes as opposed to another.

(continued)

(continued)

According to Nisbett and Wilson, people also may not have access to how they go about making decisions. In particular, these authors suggest that research participants may be unaware of stimuli that importantly influence a response, may be unaware of the response itself, and may be unaware that a particular stimulus has actually influenced a particular response. If Nisbett and Wilson are correct, then researchers would need to rethink survey research that addresses itself to asking people why they do what they do or research that asks people how they go about solving certain problems.

In a later article, Ericsson and Simon (1980) suggest that psychology has always used verbal behavior as data even in nonsense-syllable experiments in which the participants report remembering which syllable was paired with which other syllable. That is, even in studies that claimed to measure only observable responses, self-report information was still considered valuable. Because Simon and his colleagues often use self-report data to study how people go about solving problems, it would be important to them if participants could not report how they went about solving problems. In Chapter 1 we discussed one of these studies using novice and expert chess players. Using an information-processing model, Ericsson and Simon suggest that situations do exist in which verbal reports may not be consistent with behavior, as suggested by Nisbett and Wilson, particularly situations that do not require memory processes. If you were asked how you would solve a particular problem had you been given the problem in a different manner, the self-report and the actual behavior—how you really would have solved the problem—might differ. You would have no actual behavior on which to base your self-report and thus would have to create a hypothetical situation and imagine hypothetical behavior. However, Ericsson and Simon would predict that if you had just solved the problem, then you would have this information in memory and self-report would be valid. Self-report may be consistent with behavior when the self-report describes an actual set of behaviors that have occurred in the recent past. However, there may be less consistency if the event has not occurred. This is only a statement of the idea that, whether it be solving a problem or responding to cries of help from a person on the streets of New York, we may not be able to predict our own future behavior.

With regard to survey research, the question ultimately becomes, "How will the data be used and why do we want the data in the first place?" If we are interested in attitudes, then self-report offers a historically important way of tapping into how people feel or think about a certain topic. Likewise, if we are interested in past behavior, self-report also offers a means of obtaining this information as perceived by the person giving it. However, if we want to know about future behavior, self-report may offer a good guess but not certainty. In addition, not everyone wants to give you the information you are seeking. Thus it may be important to include some type of question that assesses how readily that particular person has given out certain information in the past and to judge your results accordingly.

being fooled (Converse & Schuman, 1974). It is possible that this respondent's answers were biased by his or her perception of the interviewer. If you conduct interviews, you should consider the possibility that college students will be perceived as having values different from those of the surrounding communities. All of these possibilities must be considered when using face-to-face interviews. As with any piece of research, it is important to walk through each step and determine to the best of your ability whether there could be a potential problem or confound.

■ Telephone Interviews

One alternative to face-to-face interviews is the telephone interview. Telephone surveys have given us critical information concerning such areas as health practices and attitudes toward our world. Often, surveys that we read about in the newspaper are the result of telephone interviews. For example, in 1983 the *New York Times* interviewed by telephone 1,309 men and women, asking them about their attitudes toward work (Dowd, 1983). One of the questions asked was, "If you were free to do either, would you prefer to have a job outside the home, or would you prefer to stay home and take care of your house and family?" In this survey, 72% of the men and 45% of the women said they would prefer to have a job outside the home.

Surveys also help us to measure changing attitudes in response to particular events. In May 1999, for example, 1,000 individuals were telephoned and asked about reinstating the military draft in America; 22% were in favor at this time. However, after the attack on the World Trade Center on September 11, 2001, similar polls found 66% (Time/CNN), 77% (Gallup), and 76% (Fox Broadcasting) in favor of reinstating the draft. These and other telephone polls can be found in a polling database called Polling the Nation, which may be available in your library. You can also see current polls on the Gallup (http://www.gallup.com) and Zogby (http://www.zogby.com) websites.

A telephone interviewer can establish rapport, determine motivation, and clarify questions and responses while still being more cost-effective than a face-to-face interviewer. That is, it is possible in a given amount of time to conduct a larger number of telephone interviews than face-to-face interviews because face-to-face interviewing also requires time for traveling and finding a particular house or apartment. Also, in a telephone survey, if someone chooses not to participate, all one needs to do is to call the next number; in a face-to-face survey, one must walk away and look for the next participant.

At one time survey researchers avoided telephone interviews because telephones were associated with higher socioeconomic levels; this is no longer the case (Tourangeau, 2004). In the 1960s, 1970s, and 1980s, telephone interviewing became popular and accurate as over 90% of all households had a phone. Today, for the first time in at least 30 years, the number of households with a land line is beginning to decrease as individuals are replacing household phones with cell phones and computer phones. As expected, those with cell or computer phones reflect a different demographic than those people with only a land line. These changes are presenting problems that compromise some polls (see Kempf & Remington, 2007, for an overview). For example, some individuals use an answering machine and never answer their phone. It is also estimated that about 30% of residential phone numbers in the United States are unlisted numbers, and a number of people use cell phones as their only phone. Compared to the 1960s and 1970s, individuals are also less willing today to share information or attitudes over the phone, which in turn increases the refusal rate. These types of situations make finding a random sample a more difficult process. To avoid the potential bias of leaving out unlisted numbers, for example, some surveys use telephone numbers obtained by randomly choosing four digits and adding these to the three-digit code for the area. This avoids the problem of unlisted numbers, but it creates another problem: It includes business numbers and disconnected numbers. Another methodology is to identify working residential phone numbers and then call numbers similar to these. This approach is based on the way in which telephone companies distribute numbers, in blocks or clusters of consecutive numbers.

Telephone interviews also have a general time limitation. It is commonly known that interviews lasting more than 15 minutes make some people feel uncomfortable, and these people may actually end the interview by hanging up the telephone, whether or not you are finished. However, the MacArthur Foundation study on midlife development was able to use a 30-minute phone interview after an initial contact was established.

As with all areas of research, computers have created new possibilities in telephone interviews. It is now possible to have the computer randomly dial phone numbers from a preselected list; in addition, a computer can tell the interviewer what questions to ask and can record the responses. New technologies, such as voice mail, which automatically ask questions and direct calls in many large organizations, also may be used for telephone surveys. To increase response rates, some telephone surveys begin with human contact and then switch the respondent to a computer-directed one.

■ Mail Questionnaires

A different type of survey procedure uses self-administered questionnaires delivered through the mail. One of the major advantages of mail questionnaires is that they can be sent almost anywhere in the world for the cost of postage. As you can imagine, however, one of the disadvantages is that they may not always be returned. In fact, the return rate of mail surveys is typically very low in comparison to the completion rate of face-to-face interviews. If you obtain a return rate above 75%, you can consider yourself fortunate. A return rate of 50% should be considered acceptable. The typical mail survey has a return rate of below 50%. With a return rate below 50%, you need to reconsider the type of sample that is required, the purpose of the survey, and the manner in which the survey is to be used and then evaluate your data accordingly.

The problem with low-response rates is that the sample may not represent the desired population. However, there are times that a low-response rate may exactly reflect the desired population. For example, Visser, Krosnick, Marquette, and Curtain (1996) compared mail surveys and telephone surveys over a 15-year period in their ability to predict Ohio elections. Although the telephone surveys had a 60% response rate and the mail surveys only a 20% return rate, the mail surveys were better able to predict the outcome of the elections. How can this be? It appears that the people who took the time to fill out the survey were also people who would take the time to vote. Thus, the low-response rate actually made the sample more representative. Overall, you must consider the response rate in the context of the research in order to evaluate your findings. (See Krosnick, 1999, for a review.)

Because you want people to respond to a mail survey, it is important that you do everything you can to ensure that they read, complete, and return your questionnaire. Although it is more expensive, the survey should be sent by first-class mail; some people open only their first-class mail and throw away the rest. Most survey researchers supply postage-paid return envelopes; you would not want your survey to be lost for lack of a stamp. It is also important that the questionnaire look professional. The first impression should be that the questionnaire will be easy to complete and return. It is also important that the respondent understand the importance of the survey; to this end you should include a carefully prepared cover letter explaining the survey and placing it in an appropriate context. One means of increasing the response rate is to use follow-up letters reminding the respondent of the survey and to enclose another copy of the questionnaire.

Another means of improving response rate is to include a small payment such as a dollar with the questionnaire.

Some researchers have also increased response rates by including a shortened version of the original questionnaire in additional follow-up letters. They may lose some information with the less detailed version, but they are able to obtain the most important information. They are also able to obtain information on the type of respondent who did not initially fill out the questionnaire. Mail surveys lack some advantages of face-to-face interviews, such as personal contact and the ability to request additional information, but sometimes people are more open and honest with their answers in a mail survey. This is especially true if they believe themselves to be responding anonymously and are reporting areas of personal behavior, such as medical problems, sexuality, or attitudes not in keeping with currently held viewpoints.

■ Computer Questionnaires

Computers can be used for administering surveys in a variety of ways. For example, as previously mentioned, computers can be used in face-to-face interviews to aid in the data collection process. Although computer surveys have some of the same problems as mail surveys, they also have some advantages. For example, you might not initially think that taking the same survey on paper or via a computer would make a difference, but research suggests that people find a computer format both more enjoyable and faster than a paper survey (see Edwards et al., 1997). Computer administration of surveys also allows for easier branching or asking different questions depending on the answer to a specific question. For example, rather than saying "Skip the next two questions if you answered no to the present question" on a paper format, the computer can simply present the appropriate question. In this same manner, the survey can be restricted to questions that are relevant to that particular respondent.

■ Internet Research

Computers also can be used with mail surveys such that individuals are mailed a web address at which they can complete the survey. Given that many corporations, educational institutions, and individuals are connected to the web, it is also possible to perform web-based surveys. The Internet offers great opportunities for performing research, including questionnaire research (Kraut et al., 2004). The United States, for example, has gone from less than 10% of the households having computers with Internet access in 1985 to over 50% in 2001 to 75% in 2004. Even more individuals have access through schools, libraries, or work. Some Asian countries offer Internet access to almost all of their citizens. This gives researchers almost an unlimited access to individuals from around the world. Some researchers have reported data sets containing over 1 million individuals (compare Nosek, Banaji, & Greenwald, 2002). By working with established websites such as that hosted by the National Geographic Society, researchers can target individuals with particular interests or individual characteristics and make available thousands of respondents for surveys. Also, some psychology-related sites such as the Social Psychol- ogy Network (http://www.socialpsychology.org/expts.htm) list surveys and experiments available online. Although beyond our present discussion, there exist a variety of resources including books (for example, Birnbaum, 2001, 2004) and websites (for example, http://salmon.psy.plym.ac.uk/mscprm/forms.htm) that describe in detail how to set up questionnaires on the web. Although potentially valuable, Internet research also has many of the same problems as other methods plus problems of not knowing exactly who completed your survey and under what conditions (Nosek & Banaji, 2002). Additionally, because not everyone has access to or uses the Internet in the same way, your Internet survey could be biased. Thus, you should develop procedures ensuring that you are collecting a random sample of individuals for your study. We will discuss such issues in more depth when we discuss sampling procedures in the section "Sampling."

■ Surveys: Conclusion

In conclusion, there are a variety of methods for administering surveys. The four most popular methods are face-to-face, telephone, mail, and Internet surveys. There are advantages and disadvantages to each, as we have discussed. Typically, one is faced with a trade-off between response rate and cost. In deciding which form of administration you should use, you will need to determine what is important in your survey research. If it is important for you to have a high rate of return on your surveys, then face-to-face or telephone interviews will be good choices. As you will learn in the next section, the ability to have a representative sample is extremely important in some situations; in such situations, mail surveys are ruled out. Time may also be a factor, as in political surveys taken the day before an election. When cost is an important factor and you need a large number of responses, a mail or Internet survey may be more appropriate. As with any research, you need to consider why you are doing the research in the first place, as well as what type of information will best answer your research question. (See Babbie, 2008; Edwards et al., 1997; Fink & Kosecoff, 1998, for more information on types of surveys.)

SAMPLING

In discussions of research throughout this book, we have raised the question of generalizability and considered how the results from a particular experiment could be applied to a larger group. The question of generalizability or representativeness is also important for survey research. How can we ensure that the results obtained in giving our questionnaire or interview to a group of people will apply to some larger population? If we were developing a questionnaire for only one group—such as all senior psychology majors in your college—and if we gave it to every senior psychology major, then generalizability would not be an issue because our sample would represent the entire population. This type of survey is called a *census*. Like descriptive statistics, a census is aimed at obtaining descriptive information about a particular group of people and nothing more.

However, if we want to apply the results obtained beyond the specific group from which they were obtained, then we need to be concerned about generalizability. In laboratory experiments, one of the ways to accomplish this is through careful experimental controls and the selection of participants, as discussed in previous chapters. In survey research, for generalizability we place much of the emphasis on the selection of participants through sampling procedures. In this section we want to introduce you to sampling techniques. For additional information you can consult textbooks that specifically discuss sampling techniques (for example, Scheaffer, Mendenhall, & Ott, 1979).

You probably are familiar with the general idea of sampling in relation to television ratings or attempts to predict who will win a political race. You may have wondered how raters can say that a television show is highly rated when fewer than 2,000 people are sampled out of millions. You may also wonder what is meant by a statement such as, "Seventy-eight percent of the population really wants to take a course in methodology, with a sampling error of 4%" (besides wondering what weird population would have given that response). These types of sampling are covered in this section.

In 1936, asking over 2 million people for whom they would vote in the next presidential election led one magazine, *Literary Digest,* to conclude that Alfred Landon would beat Franklin Roosevelt (Gallup, 1972). To be precise, *Literary Digest* predicted that Landon would carry 32 states and 57% of the vote compared to Roosevelt's 43%. In fact, the results were very different, with Landon carrying only 2 states and receiving 37% of the vote in comparison to Roosevelt's 61%.

George Gallup conducted a much smaller survey of 5,000 voters, however, and correctly predicted the winner. Gallup's prediction was that Roosevelt would win 40 states with 56% of the popular vote. What was the secret of his success? How did he do more with less? The answer was in the sampling procedures. Although the magazine *Literary Digest* sampled 2,376,523 people, their names were drawn from automobile registration lists and telephone directories.

Realizing that this survey took place during the Depression, you can understand what the bias was in this sampling technique. During the Depression, many people did not have money for cars or telephones and thus would not have been included in the survey. Those who did have telephones and cars tended to be wealthy and also to be Republicans. Thus, wealthy Republicans completed the survey, saying they would vote for Landon and against Roosevelt and the New Deal. Gallup used a sampling procedure that did not exclude the poor, who were mainly Democrats and more likely to vote for Roosevelt. Gallup thus had the more accurate representation, and his prediction was right.

Other election predictions seem even more amazing. For example, using a sample size of fewer than 2,000 people, a *New York Times*/CBS poll in 1976 correctly predicted that of almost 80 million voters, 51.1% would vote for Jimmy Carter and 48.9% for Gerald Ford; the actual vote was 51.1% for Jimmy Carter and 48.9% for Gerald Ford—the same numbers as the prediction.

Of course, not every prediction is that good. In 1948 the Gallup Poll predicted that Dewey would beat President Truman, which was not the case. However, this may have had less to do with sampling than the decision to stop the polling 10 days before the election in a race that had a late swing of support for Truman and a misinterpretation of what undecided voters would do, which turned out to be giving their votes to Truman.

In the 1984 election, in which Ronald Reagan won 59% of the popular vote and almost all the electoral college votes, there were discrepant estimates of the victory margin even when different polls were taken simultaneously (Converse & Traugott, 1986). Thus, sampling is only one part of the survey picture, albeit a critical one. Let's examine sampling in some depth.

The basic idea behind sampling is that we would like to learn about the characteristics of a large group of people (called a *population*) by studying a smaller group (called a *sample*). If all people were equal in every way, then it would not matter which people we chose to study out of a large group. We could use any procedure that we wanted for selecting a sample. No matter how respondents were grouped, the results would always be the same. However, people are not the same in every way, and thus we try to find ways of choosing people from the larger group in such a way that the characteristics found in the smaller group reflect those of the larger group.

One of the first tasks is to define the population in which we are interested, and this is usually related to the research questions being asked. If we are interested in memory and learning across the life span, then we will want to define our population so that people of all ages are included. If we are interested in the drinking habits of female college students, then we will have a more narrowly defined population. Once the population is defined, a question arises about the appropriate sample that is needed. Because our goal is to per-form research—to examine a particular sample and from this sample make inferences about the larger population—it is important that our sample reflect the larger population. The more the sample reflects the larger population, the more confidence we have in any inference we make from our smaller sample to the larger population. A variety of sampling techniques are available, and we present some of the more popular ones, along with the major advantages and disadvantages of each. There are two main types of sampling: prob-ability sampling and nonprobability sampling.

CONCEPT CHECK 14.3 The *Happy Valley News* ran a front-page story proclaiming that residents were opposed to adding more forms of mass transit in the city. These results came from a call-in poll to a local radio station one morning. Based on this informa-tion, what could you conclude about the views of the citizens of this town?

■ Probability Sampling

In *probability sampling* the term *probability* refers to the predetermined chance of any indi-vidual's being selected for the study, given the particular constraints under study. There are several forms of probability sampling.

Simple Random Sampling   The main characteristic of a randomized procedure is that every member of the population has a known chance of being selected. In *simple random sampling,* each member has an equal chance of being selected. This is like putting the names of everyone in the population into a hat and drawing out a certain number of names. For example, if you were interested in how your campus radio station was rated, you might consider all students in your university as the population and then choose a sample from this population using a random number table (see Box 7.1). You could then conduct a survey on this sample.

Systematic Sampling   A variation on the random sampling procedure is to list the total population and then choose every *n*th person listed. For example, you might include every fifth person in your sample. This procedure, called *systematic sampling,* has the advantage of being more efficient than simple random sampling. However, it is important that the list you use contain the entire population in an unbiased order. Most alphabetical lists of a population would not introduce bias into a survey, but it is important to consider possible bias from a variety of sources. For example, if you sampled every fifth person in a classroom with 10 seats in each row, you might produce a biased sample without realizing it. In some classrooms the first seat in each row has a desk designed for someone who writes left-handed; thus, if you happened to sample every fifth person, beginning with the person sitting in the first seat, you might have 50% right-handed people and 50% left-handed people—probably not a representative sample of the population of students in that class. Of course, this is an extreme case of bias, but we include it to emphasize that there are types of bias that you might not anticipate but that can cause problems in the sample.

Stratified Random Sampling   At times, we may realize that, to answer the research question in which we are interested, we need to ensure that certain people are represented systematically in our sample, especially if we expect that differences exist in certain groups. For example, we might want to make sure that certain age groups are included or that both male and female participants are represented. To accomplish this we would use a *stratified random sampling* procedure. For example, if it were important to us that both male and female participants were included in our sample in a certain proportion, then we could divide the population according to this category and then take a separate random sample from each of the resulting divisions. Although stratification by sex is an easy example to understand, it is more common to stratify when a group of people is likely to be underrepresented because the actual numbers of that group are small. For example, if you conduct a survey requiring that the respondents include all minority groups, then stratification would be a useful procedure.

Cluster Sampling   There are situations in which the physical constraints, both in time and money, make it difficult to use a random sampling technique. For example, if you wanted to study language before the introduction of television, you would need geographic areas in which television had not yet been introduced. In areas that did not have television, it might be impractical to create a random sample from the entire area. It would be more economical to select a few villages and study them in some depth. Likewise, researchers interested in how people feel about the chance of their being the victims of crimes may choose to study the inhabitants of particular blocks in a large city. The general procedure in *cluster sampling* is to randomly select a certain number of population units (such as villages or city blocks) and then enlist the participation of the people who live in those units.

Multistage Sampling   A *multistage sampling procedure,* as the name implies, relies on sampling at different stages in the process. At times, we may use the same sampling technique but with different populations. For example, if we wanted to study U.S. college students, we might first randomly sample colleges throughout the country. Then we could randomly sample students in each selected college. Likewise, we might randomly sample cities in the country and then randomly sample people within these cities.

We might also change the type of sampling procedure from one stage to the next. For example, the study of life satisfaction and well-being discussed previously used a multistage sampling procedure. Before sampling, the researchers decided that the sample would be limited to private households, thus excluding prisons, hospitals, colleges, and other forms of group housing. In the first stage of the sampling procedure, standard metropolitan areas, single counties, and certain county groups within each region of the country were listed. Initial samplings were made proportional to population. That is, the sampling procedure was set up so that areas with larger populations would have a greater chance of being selected. This was changed to an equal probability in the final selection for location. Once specific addresses were selected, a single person at this address was chosen randomly to be interviewed.

■ Nonprobability Sampling

One common example of nonprobability sampling is the use of introductory psychology students for research. Because most students do not randomly take a course in introductory psychology unless it is a required course (that is, they self-select and in this way form a special group), the question of generalizability arises; that is, to what populations can research performed with introductory psychology students be generalized? This is an important question that should be considered whenever one is using this or any other convenient group for research.

Convenience Sampling   In *convenience sampling* we use the people who are available to us. Sometimes simple surveys use a convenience sampling procedure, as when people on the street or in shopping malls are interviewed as they happen to walk by the interviewer. Some students, for example, might choose their sample by picking every 10th person who comes into a snack bar over a 2-day period. Although this sample might be useful if the total population is snack-bar users, it would not be useful if the survey were to be generalized to all college students. A sample selected in this manner would exclude students who never come to the snack bar and would also overinclude those who come in more than once a day.

Quota Sampling   Another type of nonprobability sampling is *quota sampling*. A quota sample sets up a quota, or number, of specific types of people. For example, we might decide to include in our survey three biology majors, three psychology majors, and three faculty members.

Snowball Sampling   Another type of nonprobability sampling is called *snowball sampling*. This sampling procedure is used most often when no list of the population exists. For example, if a medical researcher were interested in health issues related to prostitution, it would be impossible to obtain a list of prostitutes on which to base the sample. A common procedure is to find one prostitute who would agree to be part of the research, and then ask that person to help locate others, and these people would help locate others, in a snowball fashion.

Sample Size

In this chapter we have said little about one very important matter: sample size. Sample size in survey research is based on the types of considerations that we discussed in Chapter 6 in our presentation of inferential statistics. We want to be able to choose a sample of people who have the same characteristics as the overall population. If we succeed with this goal, then we can generalize successfully from our sample to the overall population. Because research is expensive in terms of time and money, we want our sample to be as small as possible. But how do we go about deciding the actual size we need?

In simple terms we determine the size of the sample we need by asking two questions. The first question concerns the characteristics of the population to which we want to generalize. How many people are available to be used in the survey, and how homogeneous are these people? As you can imagine, if the population is homogeneous on the characteristic that we want to study, then fewer people will be needed for the sample to approximate the population. If there is a wide range of variation, then more participants will be needed. The second question asks how accurate is the answer that we need to the question that we are asking. That is, how much difference can we tolerate between the characteristics found in the sample and those of the overall population? These two questions together determine sample size. In general, the larger the population to which we want to generalize—or the greater the variability and the more exact we want the results to be—the larger is the required sample size.

Because we have little control over the size of the population in which we are interested, our main concern is with the second question—that of acceptable variations in the estimate of the population parameters. We establish an upper and lower bound within which we want the results to fall with some established probability; in other words, we make a statement of how much error we will tolerate. For example, if we were to conduct a survey as to how many students would want an outdoor café built onto the student union, we might decide that we would accept an error of 5%. Suppose the results of the survey indicated that 67% of the students were in favor of the outdoor café. We could then assume that if the entire student body had been questioned, the exact percentage in favor of the café would be in the range between 62% (the lower bound) and 72% (the upper bound). This range is called a *confidence interval*. In this example we would say there was a *sampling error* of plus or minus 5%.

The amount of sampling error that is acceptable is related to the original purpose of the survey. In the beginning of a political campaign, for example, you might be interested only in survey results that give ballpark figures on which candidate is leading. However, as the election draws nearer, it might become important to have more exact estimates of how the vote is expected to go. Thus, in an initial survey, you might be willing for your survey to report that 40% of the voters favored a particular candidate with a sampling error of plus or minus 5%. This means that if the election were held that day, up to 45% would have voted for that candidate. In a survey nearer the time of the election, it might be less acceptable to risk being off by as much as 5%.

Once we have some idea of the size of our population, how variable it is, and the amount of error that we are willing to tolerate, we can determine the sample size that we will need. The actual formula we use requires that we establish confidence levels. The 95% level is used traditionally. At this level the probability of the results happening by chance is 5 out of 100. The general formula is

$$\text{sample size} = \left(\frac{\text{confidence level} \times \text{variation in population}}{\text{desired precision}} \right)^2$$

Suppose we want to know how much the average college student pays for books. How many students will we need to survey? Using the formula, we can determine the appropriate number. The variation in the population that we use is the *standard deviation* (see Chapter 5). The standard deviation for a particular population is often known from previous surveys. (It also can be estimated from the sample standard deviation, although not before the survey is performed; for this figure, see advanced survey textbooks.)

Let's assume in this case that we know the standard deviation to be $20. The confidence level traditionally used is the 95% level, which is expressed in the formula as a standard score (z score) of $1.96. For the desired precision, assume that we want the error to be less than $2. Substituting these numbers in the formula, we determine that we need 384.16 participants to satisfy our conditions:

$$\text{sample size} = \left(1.96 \times \frac{20}{2} \right)^2 = 384.16 \text{ people}$$

We might also solve this equation using different levels of precision. For example, we will need 1,537 participants if we want the error to be less than $1, but only 96 participants if we accept an error of $4.

There are tables to aid researchers in determining the sample size for survey research (Yamane, 1967). These tables generally assume a large standard deviation and present the desired precision in terms of percentage error. From such a table, we would learn that if we were to perform a survey in a national election, we would need 10,000 respondents for a 1% error, 2,500 for a 2% error, 1,111 for a 3% error, 400 for a 5% error, and only 100 respondents for an error of 10% (Yamane, 1967).

 ## RELIABILITY AND VALIDITY

As with other types of research that we have discussed, questions of reliability and validity are also important for survey research. A survey is reliable if it can be given a number of times and produce the same results. Many of the issues that we have discussed in this chapter, such as carefully considering the wording of questions and pretesting the survey, help to increase the reliability. However, there is little doubt that if the 1936 *Literary Digest* survey that we discussed previously were to be given to the same or similar individuals, we would again obtain the same results that Roosevelt would lose the election. Thus, we not only want our surveys to be reliable but also valid. That is, the survey should accurately reflect what is being examined. Validity can be increased through sampling procedures as well as techniques to ensure increased response rates.

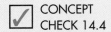

CONCEPT CHECK 14.4 A group of students from Moosesylvania State University wants to know whether the library should be open longer during final exam week. Would it be better to randomly sample 2,000 students from around the country or to take a census of the 500 students at the university?

KEY TERMS AND CONCEPTS

1. **Survey research**
2. **Question construction and formats**
   A. Open-ended questions
   B. Closed-ended questions
   C. Funneling
   D. Likert scale
   E. Semantic differential
3. **Special techniques for reactive questions**
4. **Methods of administration**
   A. Face-to-face interviews
   B. Telephone interviews
   C. Mail questionnaires
5. **Probability sampling**
   A. Simple random sampling
   B. Systematic sampling

   C. Stratified random sampling
   D. Cluster sampling
   E. Multistage sampling
6. **Nonprobability sampling**
   A. Convenience sampling
   B. Quota sampling
   C. Snowball sampling
7. **Sample size**
   A. Confidence interval
   B. Sampling error
8. **Reliability and validity**

SUMMARY

1. Survey research is gaining popularity in the social sciences. Such research allows experimenters to ask broad questions, such as "How do Americans view their mental health?"

2. An open-ended question is one in which respondents can respond in any way they wish. An example would be to ask someone, "What do you like best about college?"

3. A closed-ended question is one in which respondents are limited in their responses. A multiple-choice question is an example of a closed-ended question.

4. In developing questions for a survey it is important to be clear, avoid unwanted ambiguity, and ask questions in such a manner that the respondent is able to give the information that you need. It is especially important that you pretest the survey.

5. There are a number of methods for administering a survey. Three of the most common ways are

face-to-face interviews, telephone interviews, and self-administered questionnaires delivered through the mail.

6. The problem of generalizability is especially critical for survey research. To ensure that the results from a single group can be applied to other groups, sampling techniques are used. A broad distinction is made between probability sampling and nonprobability sampling. The more common forms of probability sampling are simple random sampling, systematic sampling, stratified random sampling, cluster sampling, and combining methods in a multistage format. Nonprobability sampling techniques include convenience sampling, quota sampling, and snowball sampling.

7. The sample size required is related to three factors: confidence level, variation in the population, and the desired precision (amount of error).

REVIEW QUESTIONS

1. What is the purpose of survey research? Give an example.
2. What is the value of an open-ended question?
3. How might open-ended and closed-ended questions be combined?
4. Give an example of a semantic differential.
5. Why must surveys always be pretested?
6. What are the major ways of presenting questionnaires to respondents? What are the advantages of each?
7. Why is sampling important?
8. Describe the major forms of probability sampling.
9. When would nonprobability sampling be appropriate?
10. What are the three major factors in determining sample size?

DISCUSSION QUESTIONS AND PROJECTS

1. Many students in experimental psychology classes are interested in how music affects their moods. Discuss how you might determine whether this is an interest mainly of people taking experimental psychology or of all college students.
2. Outline a way to determine how people believe music affects their moods.
3. What could you conclude about how music actually does influence mood from the research conducted in Question 2?
4. Why is sampling so important for surveys? Observe how political candidates or others use surveys and what types of sampling procedures they use.
5. How is it possible to know how millions of people will vote in a national election from speaking with only a few thousand? Why would it be no better to ask as many people as you could?
6. A university wants to know whether the student union should sell beer. How might you help them answer this question? What are some of the issues that would have to be considered from the standpoints of both the university and the students?

INFOTRAC COLLEGE EDITION: EXERCISES

The 1999 *Annual Review of Psychology* reviewed the empirical literature concerning survey research ("Survey research" by Jon Krosnick). Reading this article in InfoTrac College Edition will give you great insights into the factors that influence how people respond to surveys. For example, research suggests that individuals would rather answer yes than no to an item in a survey. Roger Tourangeau is a researcher who is interested in evaluating new technologies and their influence on survey results. Enter his name in InfoTrac College Edition and see some of his work on this topic, including the use of audio computer-assisted interviewing (*Public Opinion Quarterly*, 2003) and an overview of new technologies and their methodologies (*Annual Review of Psychology*, 2004).

To help you better understand the material in this chapter, you can go to Wadsworth's research methods workshop web page at http://www.wadsworth.com/psychology_d/templates/student_resources/workshops/resch_wrk.html. There you will find workshops related to research methods and statistics. The research methods workshops on "Designing a Survey" and "Surveys" discuss the material presented in this chapter.

☑ Answers to Concept Checks

14.1 Although it is possible that more women than men are depressed, it may also be the case that the numbers are the same. The actual finding was that more women than men seek help for depression, and thus it may be that the difference between men and women is in their help-seeking behavior rather than depression per se. One possible approach to answering the original question would be through the use of survey research that examined both help-seeking behavior and the incidence of depression in the population of interest.

(continued)

☑ Answers to Concept Checks (*continued*)

14.2 A number of approaches could answer the question better. One of these would be to reword the questions to allow for a greater variety of responses. Rather than just yes or no, the person could answer "not at all," "a little," "some," or "very much." The question could also be asked in terms of a behavior, such as

1. Compared with other music you listen to, how much time do you listen to classical music?

Never	A little	Some	A lot	All the time
(1)	(2)	(3)	(4)	(5)

14.3 Nothing can be concluded from this poll, other than that the people who called were opposed to the idea.

Although many radio stations and newspapers use these types of polls, they are highly biased and not representative. Ask yourself which people in a town would be listening to this particular radio station, have access to a telephone during the time of the survey, and make the effort to call. At the least you would probably be excluding most working people and most students from such polls.

14.4 If the question is when this particular library should be open, then the data from all 500 students of the university is the right choice. If one wanted to generalize these results to all college students in the country, then a random sample would be required.

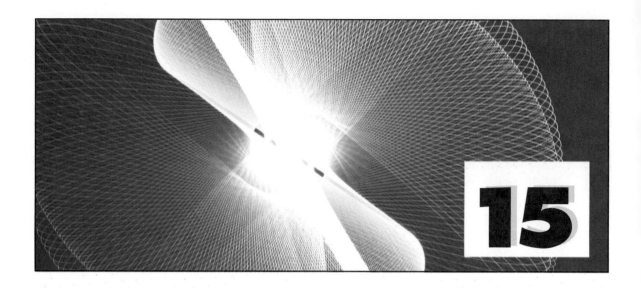

SHARING THE RESULTS

COMMUNICATION WITH OTHER
SCIENTISTS: THE SCIENTIFIC ARTICLE

PREPARING YOUR ARTICLE
Abstract
Introduction
Method

Results
Discussion
References

PUBLISHING YOUR ARTICLE

WHAT MAKES A GOOD ARTICLE?

In the preceding chapters, we traced the unfolding of an experiment from its initial conception through the analysis of the results. Once the final outcome is known, we can integrate these new facts into our understanding of the phenomenon that we are studying, and in this way we slowly expand our understanding of the world. One important responsibility of the scientist in this process is to communicate new facts to other scientists and, equally important, to nonscientists. In this way we not only expand our own understanding but also share our findings with others so that they, too, may integrate our new findings into their understanding of the world. The idea that science is a shared activity is by no means new. More than 2,000 years ago, Aristotle emphasized that science has two parts: *inquiry* and *argument*. *Inquiry* for us includes the actual experiments or observations that generate the new facts. *Argument* includes our responsibility to communicate our findings in oral or written form.

The particular manner in which we choose to communicate our findings is directed by the audience with whom we want to communicate. In psychology there are generally two types of audiences to whom we direct our communication. In the majority of instances, we are addressing other scientists who are studying related phenomena and might be interested in our findings. The availability of our findings to other scientists helps them to consider new questions and replicate our results in their own labs. As scientists from around the world experience similar findings, the pervasiveness of a phenomenon becomes apparent. With such an understanding, scientists can move on to studying a new aspect of the phenomenon.

In addition to making our findings available to other researchers, we have a responsibility to convey to nonscientists the essential direction of our findings and their ethical and moral implications. This second responsibility is particularly relevant to psychologists, whose findings may have direct bearing on how we relate to one another, interact with our children, and understand ourselves. In this chapter we describe how scientists communicate with each other by describing how a formal scientific paper is written.

COMMUNICATION WITH OTHER SCIENTISTS: THE SCIENTIFIC ARTICLE

There are many ways that we can share our findings with other scientists. In some cases new facts are shared in informal conversations with colleagues over a drink at the local coffee house or bar. In other cases new material is presented orally at scientific meetings, or perhaps an entire book is written describing a lengthy series of experiments. In most cases, however, formal communication between scientists takes the form of published journal articles.

Formal journal articles are different from everyday conservation. As you will see, scientists adopt a precision so that other people can know exactly how a particular piece of research was performed. Scientists also seek to describe carefully how their work relates to previous research and what their work may mean theoretically. As someone new to scientific writing, this may seem like a difficult and time-consuming task, and it is. At times, we may feel that someone in a previous article has already said what we want to say in a clear and concise way, and we may wonder why we should not just use their words. However, it is critical that you distinguish between someone else's ideas and your own. Thus, part of what you will learn in this chapter is how to cite someone else's work. To not cite others' work when you use their words is considered to be plagiarism. Most universities have material on their websites to help students learn about plagiarism, including Penn State (http://tlt.its.pus.edu/suggestions/cyberplagstudent.html), Georgetown University (http://gervaseprograms.georgetown,edu/hc/plagiarism_print.html), and the University of North Carolina (www.unc.edu.depts/wcweb/handouts/plagiarism.htm). Purdue University includes a discussion of plagiarism as part of its site to help students write better papers (http://owl.english.purdue.edu). These and other sites will help you better understand how to give others' words and ideas the credit they deserve. The main idea is that when you use the ideas or words of other people, you need to give them credit. We now describe the process of writing a scientific article and the steps by which an article is accepted for publication and published.

PREPARING YOUR ARTICLE

In simple terms a scientific article is the story of an experiment. It begins with a description of what is already known about the particular phenomenon being studied and a clear statement of the purpose of the experiment. Thus, your research article begins with what is already known in terms of research about the particular phenomenon that you are studying. You then describe the question that you want to ask based on this knowledge. It is important that you explain your rationale for doing the experiment at this point and the results that you expect to find. Next, you are ready to describe the manner in which the experiment was performed in enough detail so that others wanting to replicate your study can do so. You then describe the results of the experiment. Finally, you interpret the results in relation to themselves (are there any confounds or interpretation problems?) and then in relation to what we already know about the phenomenon under study. That is, how do your results fit into the established body of knowledge in the area? Your conclusion draws the reader back to the rationale for doing the experiment that you established in the beginning of your paper. You may also discuss how the results of your experiment might be related to other experiments in the area under study.

To facilitate this communication process, a specific format or outline for scientific papers has been developed. Scientific articles are divided into five parts: (1) abstract, (2) introduction, (3) method, (4) results, and (5) discussion. Detailed descriptions of what should be covered in each section and other guides to writing style are presented in the *Publication Manual of the American Psychological Association* (2001; available from APA, 750 First Street NE, Washington, DC 20002-4242). Websites also offer additional information on APA style. For example, Georgia Southern University has an overview of APA style (http://www.psychwww.com/resource/apacrib.htm) with reference to a variety of specifics. In addition, the APA website has a page devoted to information concerning APA style (http://www.apastyle.org), which also includes information on how to cite electronic resources (http://www.apastyle.org/elecref.html), and a frequently asked questions page (http://www.apastyle.org/faqs.html). A number of books also describe how to write papers in psychology (for example, Rosnow & Rosnow, 2005; Sternberg, 2003).

The current *Publication Manual* also includes three major guidelines for referring to individuals and groups. The first guideline is to describe at the appropriate level of specificity. This guideline suggests that scientific writing requires precision and thus there is more clarity if you say individuals in the study were 65 to 85 years of age rather than the study involved older individuals. Likewise, if your study used Mexican Americans or Chinese Americans, it would be more precise to say this rather than Hispanic Americans or Asian Americans. If you are referring to both men and women, your writing should reflect that (that is, not just "man" or "men"). The current *Publication Manual* also suggests that the term *gender* is cultural and should be used when referring to men and women as social groups. The term *sex,* on the other hand, is biological and should be used when a biological distinction is predominant.

The second guideline found in the *Publication Manual* is to be sensitive to labels. Rather than labeling individuals as "schizophrenic" or "gays," it is suggested that you use phrases such as "individuals diagnosed with schizophrenia" or "gay men" as a way to retain a person's individuality. Also, it is suggested that parallel forms be used when describing different groups of individuals. For example, rather than saying "man and wife" it would be more parallel to say "husband and wife" or "man and woman."

The third guideline is to acknowledge participation. This change, which began with the 1994 *Publication Manual,* directs researchers to refer to those who participate in research as *participants* and other more specific terms (*children, patients, clients, respondents,* etc.) rather than the older term *subjects.* The idea is that individuals actively participate in research and our language should reflect this. Thus, it is also more accurate to use the active voice and say "students completed the survey" rather than the passive "students were given the survey." Additional suggestions for referring to gender, sexual orientation, racial and ethnic identity, age, disabilities, and other descriptors of people are included in the *Publication Manual* and reproduced in Appendix A in this book.

According to the APA, one purpose of this change was to allow researchers to be more specific. It is important that you become familiar with both the APA format and the APA style because these are used by many scientific journals around the world. Once you are familiar with them, you will find it easier to read articles and locate information quickly in those you are just skimming. Furthermore, you will undoubtedly use the APA format as a model in preparing your own proposals or papers. We now briefly describe each of the five parts of a scientific article.

■ Abstract

Most scientific papers open with a brief 100- to 120-word **abstract,** or summary of the entire article. The purpose of the abstract is to give an overall description of the experiment. By reading the abstract, we can quickly decide whether we want to take the time to read the entire paper. In this way we avoid reading halfway through an article before we realize it is not the sort of experiment we thought it was simply from reading the title. The typical abstract provides a brief, clear statement of the purpose, method, and results of the experiment. It is written in a concise manner and describes the essential features of the article.

With the use of electronic databases, the abstract has taken on an even more important role. Because scientists around the world use electronic databases (such as PsycINFO, which includes the abstract), it is important that the abstract be written carefully. It is also important that the abstract include the key words that will allow for efficient computer searching of such databases. Because abstracts are being included in databases, abstracts currently are limited to 960 characters, including spaces. To give you an idea of how an abstract is written, an example follows. This abstract comes from an article published in the *Journal of Experimental Psychology: General* (Fox, Russo, Bowles, & Dutton, 2001).

> Biases in information processing undoubtedly play an important role in the maintenance of emotion and emotional disorders. In an attentional cueing paradigm, threat words and angry faces had no advantage over positive or neutral words (or faces) in attracting attention to their own location, even for people who were highly state-anxious. In contrast, the presence of threatening cues (words and faces) had a strong impact on the disengagement of attention. When a threat cue was presented and a target subsequently presented in another location, high state-anxious individuals took longer to detect the target relative to when either a positive or a neutral cue was presented. It is concluded that threat-related stimuli affect attentional dwell time and the disengage component of attention, leaving the question of whether threat stimuli affect the shift component of attention open to debate.

Another abstract is taken from an article published in the *Journal of Consulting and Clinical Psychology* (Hanson, Kilpatrick, Freedy, & Saunders, 1995).

> The impact of the 1992 Los Angeles (L.A.) civil disturbances on psychosocial functioning was assessed as part of a larger project investigating the views and attitudes of residents in L.A. County. Random digit dialing methodology identified a household probability sample of 1,200 adults (age 18 or older) from L.A. County. Respondents completed a telephone interview 6 to 8 months after the disturbances. Respondents' degree of exposure to the disturbances, mental health impact of the disturbances, and mental health effects of chronic versus acute exposure to violence were assessed. Consistent with hypotheses, the impact of the disturbances was the worst in the South Central communities. Higher rates of posttraumatic stress disorder (PTSD; both diagnostic level and subclinical symptomatology) were found among respondents who reported disturbance-related experiences. Exposure to an acute event (i.e., the disturbances) was predictive of current PTSD symptomatology after controlling for demographics, lifetime trauma, and other types of stressful events.

A third example of an abstract is from the work of Cooper, Frone, Russell, and Mudar (1995), which appeared in the *Journal of Personality and Social Psychology*. This research tested a particular model of alcohol use that suggests that people use alcohol in two separate ways: One is an attempt to reduce negative emotions, and the second is an attempt to enhance positive emotional experiences. These authors tested this model in a sample of adults and adolescents using the advanced statistical techniques of moderated regression and path analysis.

> The present study proposed and tested a motivational model of alcohol use in which people are hypothesized to use alcohol to regulate both positive and negative emotions. Two central premises underpin this model: (a) that enhancement and coping motives for alcohol use are proximal determinants of alcohol use and abuse through which the influence of expectancies, emotions, and other individual differences are mediated and (b) that enhancement and coping motives represent phenomenologically distinct behaviors having both unique antecedents and consequences. This model was tested in random samples (1 of adults, 1 of adolescents) using a combination of moderated regression and path analysis corrected for measurement error. Results revealed strong support for the hypothesized model in both samples and indicate the importance of distinguishing psychological motives for alcohol use.

The next example examines if how fast you can identify an angry or happy facial expression is related to the face being that of a male or a female. These authors (Becker, Kenrick,

Neuberg, Blackwell, & Smith, 2007) found that the people in their study were better able to detect angry expressions in males and happy expressions in females.

> Findings of 7 studies suggested that decisions about the sex of a face and the emotional expressions of anger or happiness are not independent: Participants were faster and more accurate at detecting angry expressions on male faces and at detecting happy expressions on female faces. These findings were robust across different stimulus sets and judgment tasks and indicated bottom-up perceptual processes rather than just top-down conceptually driven ones. Results from additional studies in which neutrally expressive faces were used suggested that the connections between masculine features and angry expressions and between feminine features and happy expressions might be a property of the sexual dimorphism of the face itself and not merely a result of gender stereotypes biasing the perception.

The final example comes from a study published in the *Journal of Abnormal Psychology* (Watkins & Teasdale, 2001) that examines what is referred to as overgeneral memory. Overgeneral memory is seen in depression and posttraumatic stress disorder that reflects a summary of repeated occasions rather than a single autobiographical event.

> Previous research has shown that, compared with a rumination induction, a brief distraction procedure reduces overgeneral autobiographical memory in depression. The authors investigated whether this effect depends on reduction in analytic thinking or reductions in self-focus. Focus of attention (high vs. low self-focus) and thinking style (high vs. low analytical thinking) were independently manipulated in depressed patients in a 2×2 design. Autobiographical recall was measured pre- and postmanipulation. Thinking style significantly affected overgeneral memory, whereas focus of attention significantly affected despondent mood. Reducing analytical self-focus reduced overgeneral memory, suggesting that high levels of naturally occurring ruminative analytic thinking may be important in the maintenance of overgeneral memory. Overgeneral memory in depression may be associated with chronic ruminative attempts to make sense of current or past difficulties.

◼ Introduction

The *introduction* of a scientific paper is designed to provide background information about the phenomenon that you are studying and to help the reader understand how you arrived at your hypothesis and the experiment you eventually performed. The key to writing a good introduction is to be clear in your own mind about the reasons you are performing the research before you begin. It is your task in the introduction to lay out the logic of the research that you conducted. A typical introduction begins with a simple sentence or two explaining the nature of the research problem in broad terms. It then describes what we already know about the phenomenon being studied. As this narrative unfolds, relevant facts and theoretical speculations are described.

Once this background information has been presented and the reader knows the present status of the research area, the introduction concludes with a clear statement of purpose, which may include the particular hypothesis being evaluated. For example, in the Watkins and Teasdale (2001) article just described, the introduction begins with this sentence:

> When asked to recall memories of specific autobiographical events, depressed patients are more likely than control to retrieve overgeneral, categoric memories that are summaries of repeated occasions—for instance, waiting at bus stops or making mistakes.

Wood and Cowan (1995) studied aspects of the *cocktail party phenomenon,* in which one is able to pay attention to a single conversation in the midst of a number of other conversations. Although the task in such a situation is to pay attention to a single conversation, these authors were interested in how much information is processed and recalled from the other conversations, which they refer to as task-irrelevant. They begin their introduction with the following sentence:

> A basic, yet unanswered, question in selective attention research is the extent to which task-irrelevant information is processed and recalled.

Becker et al. (2007), whose abstract we just examined, begin their introduction section by asking the reader to imagine an angry face and then consider if this face was that of a male or female.

> Close your eyes for moment, and imagine an angry face. In fact, try to conjure up the prototypical angry face. Is the face that of a man or a woman?

When Shotland and Straw (1976) wrote an article describing their research on bystander behavior (discussed in Chapter 3), they began their article like this:

> From time to time newspapers report that bystanders have witnessed an attack by a man on a woman without adequately helping the victim.

Shotland and Straw continued by describing some current theories that attempted to explain why bystanders do not help. Because the theories were derived from the reports of actual events and after-the-fact reports of witnesses, the authors sought to test empirically certain aspects of these theories. They concluded their introduction section with a statement of purpose and a hypothesis. Notice the clear statement of logical consequences in the following statement:

> The set of experiments we describe explores the implications and effects of a perceived relationship between a victim and her attacker on helping behavior. Specifically, the hypothesis for Experiment 1 was: If bystanders perceive a relationship between a woman and her attacker, they will be less likely to intervene than if the victim and attacker are perceived as strangers.

Likewise, Newcombe and Arnkoff (1979) begin the report on their research on speech styles and the sex of the speaker (also described in Chapter 3) with the following sentence:

> Our impressions of other people are derived from many sources: what they say, what they do, what others think of them, and so on.

The authors continue the introduction by discussing some important research that has been performed in this area, and they help the reader to understand why they performed this particular study. The introduction concludes with a statement of why the study was performed. In this particular study, the purpose is stated as follows:

> In these initial experiments, the concern was to evaluate the effects, if any, of a variable over which people have some control (speech style) as compared to the effects of a set of variables over many of which they have less or no control (the pitch of their voice, their sex).

Thus, the general form of an introduction is to begin with a broad conception of the problem, followed by a discussion of previous research related to the topic, and then to end with a specific statement of the hypothesis or purpose of the study. Notice that as an introduction unfolds there is a progression from a general topic to a specific purpose. You might think of an introduction as the simple story of relevant published experiments, which leads us from our general topic of interest to our specific purpose or rationale underlying the hypothesis.

Introductions may be brief, as we will see. The following is the introduction from a study on eating rate and obesity (Gaul, Craighead, & Mahoney, 1975). Note again how the last part of the introduction presents the purpose or hypothesis of the study.

> In their recent review Stunkard and Mahoney (in press) concluded that behavior modification techniques have demonstrated considerable effectiveness in the treatment of obesity. Many of these techniques were based in part on the behavioral analysis of eating patterns first presented by Ferster, Nurnberger, and Levitt (1962).
>
> An implicit assumption of many behavior modification programs has been that eating patterns differ for obese and nonobese people. Specifically, it has been presumed that overweight individuals eat faster and take fewer bites (cf. Stuart & Davis, 1972). However, virtually no empirical data regarding that assumption have been presented. The purpose of the present study was to determine if obese people consume their food more rapidly than nonobese people, and if consummatory behaviors (chewing and drinking) differ for two groups.

The next example of an introduction is from an exploratory study by Ravizza (1977) that examines the subjective experiences of athletes during sporting events. Again, you will see how the author first describes the focus of his study in relation to previous research. He helps the reader to understand how this specific research is both different from and similar to other studies and then concludes with a statement of purpose. Because the research is an exploratory study into an unknown area, the purpose is presented not in the form of a hypothesis but in the form of the goals of the study.

> The traditional emphasis of research on sports has been to develop techniques to improve physical performance. One result of this emphasis is that the major focus in sport research has been on motor performance. In contrast, the subjective experience of the athlete has been minimized (Kleinman, 1973; Park, 1973). One explanation for this emphasis on motor performance is that athletes' subjective experiences are difficult to measure and to study scientifically. Some progress has been made in studying nonpathological, yet extraordinary, psychological experience (Laski, 1961; Maslow, 1968). The limited research dealing with this aspect of sport reveals that participation provides the athlete with a wide domain of subjective experiences (Leonard, 1975; Metheny, 1968; Slusher, 1967; Thomas, 1972). Some of these studies have focused on specific aspects of the subjective experience of the athlete (Beisser, 1967; Csikszentmihalyi, 1975; Gallwey, 1974; Murphy, 1972, 1973; Ravizza, 1973).
>
> The purpose of the present investigation is twofold: first, to use the interview technique to ascertain the personal experiences of athletes; and second, to achieve a general characterization of at least one subjective aspect in sport, those experiences involved in an athlete's "greatest moment" while participating in sport.

Of course, not all studies have a brief introduction. At times, you must describe in some detail theoretical aspects of a model you are testing as well as how the model can be tested. For example, Bolger and Zuckerman (1995) seek to provide a framework for understanding the role of personality in terms of reactivity to stress. They begin their introduction with the following paragraph.

> Personality is an important determinant of health and psychological outcomes (Contrada, Leventhal, & O'Leary, 1990; Friedman, 1990). Although researchers do not fully understand how personality leads to these outcomes, it has become clear that stressful experiences and how people cope with them play an important explanatory role (Bolger & Schilling, 1991). In this article, we propose a framework that delineates this explanatory role, a framework that combines trait and process approaches to the study of personality (see Mischel & Shoda, 1994). Our framework specifies that personality may affect exposure to stressful events, reactivity to those events, or both, and that these processes can help explain how personality affects outcomes. Our framework also specifies that personality differences in reactivity to stressors can be due to differential choice of coping strategies, differential effectiveness of the strategies chosen, or both. Below, we elaborate on this framework and provide an empirical test of the alternative models it implies.

In summary, the introduction section can be viewed as being composed of five tasks. The first task is to tell the reader what the research is about—that is, to describe the particular topic you will be studying. The second task is to describe the relevant background, to

"I THINK YOU SHOULD BE MORE EXPLICIT HERE IN STEP TWO."

inform the reader about what is already known about a topic. Once the reader has the relevant background, then it is possible to move to the third task, to tell the reader why further research is necessary. In essence, at this point you justify your study to the reader, including how the study logically follows from the information that you have previously presented in the introduction. Following this, the fourth task is to state the purpose of the study. The fifth task is to make predictions or state hypotheses.

The manner in which each of these five tasks is accomplished has been illustrated in the previous examples. One thing you may notice is that the first time a reference is presented in the text, it is always presented in its entirety, with all authors (up to five) included. After the first presentation, publications with more than three authors may be referenced by the first author and the Latin phrase *et al.,* which is an abbreviation for "and others." For example, you might see (Ruiz, Pincus, & Ray, 1999) presented in any of the sections of the text initially but only (Ruiz et al., 1999) after this initial presentation. One exception to this rule is that if a publication has six or more authors, then *et al.* is used in the initial cite and thereafter.

Method

The third section of a scientific paper is called the *method* section and consists of a detailed description of how the experiment was conducted. The goal of this section is to provide enough detail for another researcher to conduct an exact replication of your experiment. In addition, the procedural details provided in the method section allow the reader to visualize exactly how you conducted your experiment. In this way a careful reader may spot design problems that escaped your attention. The APA *Publication Manual* suggests that the method section be divided into three parts: participants, apparatus (or materials), and procedure.

The method section typically begins with a description of the participants in the study—that is, whether they were males or females, college students or patients in a hospital, and so forth. It is important to include the number of participants who took part in the experiment as well as the manner in which they were recruited. The selection of the control group, if any, should be described as well. Two examples of how participants might be described follow. The first is from Stadler (1995).

Participants

One hundred students from introductory psychology courses at the University of Missouri–Columbia participated in return for course credit. Twenty students were randomly assigned to each of the five conditions by order of entry into the laboratory. All participants reported normal or corrected-to-normal vision and hearing.

The next example of a participants section comes from the clinical literature and was published in the *Journal of Abnormal Psychology* (March et al., 1999). Notice that this description not only tells how participants were selected but also gives the important characteristics of the groups.

Participants

Informed consent was obtained from 14 chronic schizophrenic inpatients and 16 nonpsychiatric comparison participants of similar age (patients = 39.6 ± 8.9 years; controls = 39.2 ± 7.0 years). All of the participants were of normal hearing by self-report. Participants with significant musical training were excluded. Schizophrenic participants were recruited from the inpatient units of the Bronx Psychiatric Center, a New York State inpatient treatment setting, and diagnosed according to criteria from the Diagnostic and Statistical Manual of Mental Disorders (3rd ed., rev.: DSM-III-R; American Psychiatric Association, 1987) by a board-certified attending research psychiatrist using semistructured clinical interview (DSM-III-R checklist) and other clinical materials as required. Participants with DSM-III-R Axis I disorders other than schizophrenia, including alcoholism or substance abuse, were excluded from the study. All but one patient were on antipsychotic medication at the time of testing (this patient had been prescribed haloperidol but was noncompliant with medication at the time of test). Of these, 5 were receiving typical antipsychotics and 8 were receiving atypical antipsychotics (2 clozapine, 2 risperidone, 3 sertindole, and 1 seroquel); 4 participants were receiving additional treatment with anticholinergics, 2 were receiving valproate, 1 was receiving lithium, and 1 was receiving fluoxetine. Control participants were recruited by personal contact from faculty, trainees, and staff of the Bronx Psychiatric Center. The schizophrenic and control groups differed significantly in sex distribution, with more women included among the controls (6 men, 10 women) than among the patients (12 men, 2 women). Control participants were also significantly higher than patients in the Quick Test (Ammons & Ammons, 1962; IQ: patients = 96.9 ± 10.2, controls = 110.7 ± 14.4). t(26) = 2.9, p <.01. All of the participants received a small honorarium for their participation.

Following the description of the participants in the experiment, there is a statement of the experimental situation and any equipment or apparatus that was used, including their brand names and model numbers. In physiological, psychophysiological, and other such studies, this would include a statement of the instrumentation settings (such as amplification and filters) that were used in the study.

For example, in an electroencephalogram (EEG) study reported in the *Journal of Experimental Psychology: Human Perception and Performance,* Bernstein, Scheffers, and Coles (1995) describe their psychophysiological procedures:

Psychophysiological Recording

The electroencephalogram (EEG) was recorded from midline and lateral scalp electrode sites: frontal midline (Fz), central midline (Cz), parietal midline (Pz), C3′ (4 cm left of Cz), and C4′ (4 cm right of Cz) according to the 10/20 system (Jasper, 1958), referenced to linked mastoids. Signals were amplified using Grass Model 7P122 (Quincy, MA) amplifiers set to a high-frequency cut-off of 35 Hz (3dB/Octave roll-off) and a time constant of 8 s. Horizontal and vertical eye movements were recorded from stand locations (see Gratton, Coles, Sirevaag, Eriksen, & Donchin, 1988) and extended by Miller, Gratton, and Yee (1988). Additional filtering was accomplished off-line using a digital low-pass filter (of a type described by Farwell, Martinerie, Bashore, Rapp, & Goddard, 1993) with a passband of 8 Hz, a stop band of 10 Hz, and a width of 39 points.

The final part of the method section is a statement of the procedure used in the study. In describing the manner in which the study was conducted, it is important to include everything that the participants were told or were led to believe. Because every experiment is a social situation, it is also important to include some statement of the manner in which the experimenters treated the participants, as well as the important social characteristics of each of the experimenters.

When your design calls for dividing participants into various groups, it is necessary to describe how group assignment was determined (random, matching, etc.). It is also necessary to describe how you operationally defined your independent and dependent variables and how your various groups were tested. For example, if you used an individual difference variable such as anxiety, you would want to include the mean scores and standard deviations on whatever anxiety scale you used in assigning participants to either low- or high-anxiety conditions. You also should state whether the experimenter who tested the participants knew to which group a given participant belonged and, if there was a scoring procedure, whether it was performed blind. For example, in a study that examined the content of dreams of anxious and nonanxious participants, it is important to know whether the dream coder knew whether a given dream belonged to a high- or low-anxiety participant.

In some psychology experiments, it is necessary to have an extended method section so that other scientists understand exactly what happened to a participant during the experiment and how particular behaviors were measured. This is particularly true in social psychology experiments in which any type of deception is used. The method section in a deception study should include not only the method but also the safeguards—such as debriefing and follow-up measures—that were used in the study. The following example of a method section is taken from the Shotland and Straw (1976) study on bystander behavior.

Method

The first procedure attempted was similar to the one used by Borofsky et al. (1971) in which a male attacked a female during a psychodrama. The fight was actually videotaped and played for each subject, who was told he or she had been arbitrarily selected to act in the next psychodrama pairing of the three subjects and was asked to leave the other two subjects (the confederates) so as not to inhibit them and to watch their psychodrama on television in the next room. This procedure proved unworkable as approximately 40% of the subjects thought the fight was staged.

A second procedure was needed that was more believable. The local police department was made aware of the impending experiment and their advice was sought. Three of the first author's colleagues in the Department of Psychology were asked to review the procedure for ethical considerations.

Subjects

The subjects were 51 male and female students who participated in order to receive course credit for either an introductory psychology or Man-Environment Relations course during the summer of 1974 at The Pennsylvania State University.

Procedure

Two couples with theatrical training were recruited through the cooperation of a faculty member in the Drama Department. One couple (Team 1) consisted of a man who was 1.70 m, 63.50 kg (5 feet 7 inches, 140 pounds) with brown hair conventionally cut, paired with a woman who was 1.57 m, 49.90 kg (5 feet 2 inches, 110 pounds) with shoulder-length black hair. The second couple (Team 2) consisted of a man who was 1.85 m, 90.72 kg (6 feet 1 inch, 200 pounds) with light brown hair conventionally cut, paired with a 1.70 m, 54.43 kg (5 feet 7 inches, 120 pounds) woman with long blonde hair. All of the college-age actors wore the usual jeans and shirts.

Each couple worked on alternate nights with subjects' being randomly assigned to conditions, the only provision being that the conditions contained an equal number of male and female subjects. The student came to take part in a study of attitudes in which he or she expected to answer a questionnaire and be interviewed. The student arrived at the appointed room and found a note explaining that the experimenter would arrive later to interview him or her and asking that the subject begin filling out the questionnaire. On the table with the questionnaires were what appeared to be a university phone with a standard sticker giving emergency telephone numbers, including the police. The telephone was not functioning and was rigged to provide a dial tone when it was appropriate, and to record any telephone number that the subject might try to call.

Other rooms on the floor had apparent activity in them. From the room across the hall emanated the sound of a computer printer, and in the room next to the experimental room a radio played.

After the subject entered the room 5 minutes passed, during which time the subject proceeded to fill out the questionnaire. The confederates, on a different floor of the building, received a signal by walkie-talkie and took the elevator to the proper floor. Before the doors opened, a loud verbal argument could be heard. The woman was accused by the man of picking up a dollar he claimed to have dropped. After approximately 15 sec of heated discussion, the man physically attacked the woman, violently shaking her while she struggled, resisting and screaming. The screams were loud piercing shrieks, interspersed with pleas to "get away from me." Along with the shrieks one of two conditions was introduced and then repeated several times. In the stranger condition the woman screamed, "I don't know you," and in the married condition, "I don't know why I ever married you." From the first designation of the condition the physical fight lasted a maximum of 45 sec, with the entire incident not lasting more than a minute.

The fight was immediately terminated with the attacker fleeing at any attempt by the subject to intervene. If no one intervened, the fight was terminated by a third confederate (male), who came out of a nearby room and demanded in a loud voice that the attacker stop beating up the woman. The attacker then ran away while the false intervener consoled the woman. Every effort was made to keep a direct intervener away from the actors to insure their safety. Two confederates were placed in concealed locations between the actors and the subject, one to falsely intervene, the other to inform the subject it was an experiment, if necessary.

A subject was considered an intervener if he or she called the police on our phone, asked a person in the computer room to help stop the fight, shouted at the attacker to stop, or acted to intervene directly. The fight was staged 15.85–16.15 m (52–53 feet) away from the room containing the subject. If the subject came down the hall toward the fight some 9.14 m (30 feet) and did not turn into an intersecting hallway, he or she was counted as intervening.

The subjects were interviewed immediately following the experiment and fully debriefed by the first author, who spent up to 45 minutes with each subject. The interviews were unstructured except for several standard questions. First, the subjects were asked to describe what they had seen. If they did not adequately describe the experimental condition to which they were assigned, they were asked: (a) What was the relationship between the two people fighting? (b) How do you know? Subjects were asked (c) What caused the fight? and (d) Did you think it was a rape? They were then asked to describe their thoughts and behavior in the sequence in which they had occurred while witnessing the fight. After the debriefing each subject was specifically asked: (e) Do you think we have done any harm to you by having you go through that experience? and (f) Do you think that the potential results and implications of the research are worth the experience you went through? Each subject was urged to call the first author if he or she wished to discuss any aspect of the experiment in the future.

Results

The fourth part of a research article is the *results* section. The chief purpose of this section is simply to state the outcome of the experiment and then indicate whether the outcome was statistically significant. For example, a results section might begin with the statement that the experimental and control groups did or did not differ significantly in terms of whatever dependent variable was measured. Following this general statement, the actual group scores may be presented, and then the manner in which the results were analyzed is briefly described. Quite often the results section also contains figures or tables that aid the reader in visualizing the outcome of the experiment (see Appendix B for examples).

Any hypothesis presented in the introduction should have the corresponding results presented in the results section. Although there are no hard-and-fast rules concerning discussion of or references to other studies in the results section, these usually are saved for the discussion section. Granholm, Asarnow, and Marder (1996) examined an attentional task with schizophrenic outpatients and a matched nonpsychiatric control group. The beginning of their results section follows.

> A 2 (group) × 2 (array sizes) × 2 (visual angles) × 4 (target quadrant locations) mixed model analysis of variance (ANOVA) was carried out on the percentage of correct detections. This ANOVA yielded significant main effects for group, $F (1, 48) = 21.54, p < .001$, array size, $F (1, 48) = 190.40, p < .001$, and target location, $F (3, 144) = 60.74, p < .001$, but not for visual angle, $F (1, 48) = 0.97$. Significant interactions were found between group and array size, $F (1, 48) = 7.06, p < .01$, group and visual angle, $F (1, 48) = 4.62, p < .05$, array size and visual angle, $F (1, 48) = 4.20, p < .05$, and array size and target location, $F (3, 144) = 29.09$, $p < .001$. No other two-way or higher order interaction was statistically significant.

Following the initial statement of the statistical results, Granholm et al. described the manner in which each group performed the task.

In Chapter 6 we discussed the concept of effect size and power and its relation to the number of individuals necessary to adequately test our hypotheses. Because of its importance, a number of publications including the latest edition of the APA *Publication Manual* are suggesting that these measures be included in the results section (Wilkinson & Task Force on Statistical Inference, 1999; available at http://www.apa.org/journals/amp/ amp548594.html). The measure of effect size or strength of relationship is generally placed after the probability level.

For example, Chang and Lenzenweger (2001) used a signal detection procedure to compare biological relatives of individuals with schizophrenia and control individuals. In such a task, if an individual reports the presence of stimuli that are not present, it is called a false alarm. Note that in describing the false-alarm rates, these authors present the mean and the standard deviation of their data and then the *t*-test results with the exact probability measure and then effect size (Cohen's *d*).

> The false-alarm rates for the two-point task are derived from the 60 one-point stimulation trials. The schizophrenia relatives false-alarm rate ($M. = 028, SD = .019$) did not differ from that of the control subjects ($M. = 027, SD = .021$), $t(67) = 0.115, p < .91$, Cohen's $d = .05$.

Öhman, Flykt, and Esteves (2001) sought to determine if individuals would be quicker to detect a fear-relevant stimulus (for example, spider or snake) surrounded by more neutral pictures (for example, flower or mushroom) or the other way around. Nine of these pictures were presented in a matrix (3 rows and 3 columns) for 1 second and could include either nine pictures of the same objects or different objects. In this reaction time (RT) study, the participant was asked to respond as quickly as possible as to whether the pictures were of the same object (spider, snake, flower, or mushroom) or contained different objects (some combination). The authors began their results section as follows.

Results

The mean RTs to fear-relevant and fear-irrelevant targets for all positions in the matrix are displayed in Figure 1. In agreement with the main hypothesis of the study, the analysis showed that the participants were clearly faster in detecting fear-relevant than fear-irrelevant targets, $F(1, 24) = 22.29, p < .0001$.

As mentioned, authors often present tables or figures to exhibit the results of a study. For example, McKenna and Sharma (1995) performed a series of experiments to explore the Stroop effect with emotional and neutral words. The traditional Stroop effect is produced when words for colors (for example, *red, green, blue*) are presented in different-color inks and the individual is asked to indicate the color of the ink. This produces an interference because the individual finds it difficult not to read the word itself. McKenna and Sharma asked whether emotional words (for example, *fail, fear, grief, death*) would also produce an interference effect. The dependent variable in this study was the reaction time (RT) required to indicate the color. The results section follows.

Results

An analysis of errors showed no significant differences. The mean number of errors were 4.33% and 4.34% for neutral and emotional words, respectively.

Analysis of emotional Stroop. The mean correct RT across blocks is presented in Figure 3. The RT scores were analyzed in a three-way ANOVA, with order as a between-subjects variable and emotional class and block as within-subject variables.

The analysis revealed that the color identification took longer for emotional words (931 ms) than for neutral words (901 ms), $F(1, 38) = 7.16, MSE = 9,511, p < .01$. As in the previous experiments, there was no main effect of order, and order did not interact with any other variable. There was a main effect of block, $F(3, 114) = 21.17, MSE = 8,297, p < .001$. Tukey multiple comparison tests showed that this was due to the first block showing significantly faster RTs than any of the other three blocks.

In graphing the results, the dependent variable is placed on the y axis (vertical axis) and the independent variable is placed on the x axis (horizontal axis) of the graph. In this study there are two independent variables: blocks and the nature of words (emotional versus neutral). If one of the independent variables involved time (order of presentation), then this is the variable that typically is plotted on the x axis. Figure 15.1 illustrates the graph depicting the results of this aspect of the experiment.

◼ Discussion

The final section is called the *discussion* section. In general, the discussion is in three parts. In the first part, you report the chief finding of the present experiment. In doing so you draw the reader back to the rationale that you established in the introduction

Figure 15.1

Mean reaction time (RT) to color name category—neutral and emotional words for the four blocks in Experiment 3

Source: McKenna and Sharma (1995). McKenna, F., & Sharma, D. (1995). Intrusive cognitions: An investigation of the emotional Stroop task. *Journal of Experimental Psychology: Learning, Memory, and Cognition, 21,* 1595–1607.

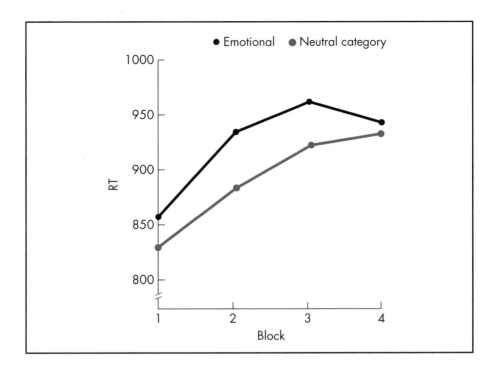

section of your article and conclude the manner in which your results support or refute the theoretical rationale that you developed previously. In the second part, you point out any limitations or potential confounds that might affect your interpretation of the results and restate them in light of these limitations. We believe that this is an essential step in any discussion, and we encourage you to make it a part of your scientific papers. In the third part of the discussion, you directly relate the results of your experiment to other published experiments on the same topic and describe how the present experiment expands our understanding of the phenomenon under study. For example, Ray et al. (2006) published an article in *Psychological Science* that examined individuals who had been previously tortured by repressive governments. The purpose of the study was to understand the manner in which psychological processes associated with the torture and current brain states were related in this group. The discussion section begins as follows.

Overall, we studied the relationship between dissociative experiences and a cortical measure, delta dipole density. Differential patterns of delta dipole density have been found in individuals experiencing a variety of pathological and psychopathological conditions. This suggests its usefulness in distinguishing pathological conditions across patient groups. We found the number of dissociative experiences reported to be significantly and positively related to the density of abnormal slow wave generators in the left ventral region of the anterior cortical structures and in the left hemisphere as a whole. The inverse relationship was found for the right hemisphere as a whole and for the right anterior superior areas. Statistically partialing out the level of post traumatic stress disorder did not influence these relationships suggesting that the level of dissociation contributes a separate component over and above PTSD symptoms to delta dipole density. This finding is also theoretically consistent with DSM-IV not including dissociation as a PTSD criterion. Further, the patient group was shown to have significantly more delta dipoles in the left ventral region than a culturally matched control group without torture experience. It should be noted that physical torture involving head injury will also influence slow wave activity, but this activity would appear different in both the pattern and location than we observed. Further, severe physical head trauma which results in loss of consciousness does not lead to PTSD (Glaesser et al., 2004).

In the discussion section, it is also important to discuss the way in which your results either do or do not support your hypotheses. For example, in the Hanson, Kilpatrick, Freedy, and Saunders (1995) study of the effects of the 1992 civil disturbances in Los Angeles on mental health, the authors included the following.

> In support of Hypothesis 2, higher rates of current PTSD, posttraumatic stress sequelae (i.e., reexperiencing, avoidance, and arousal criteria), and subthreshold symptoms of PTSD were found among respondents who reported that they had experienced disturbance-related violence or destruction, compared with those who did not. These findings are consistent with previous research that has examined rates of PTSD among victims of other types of traumatic events (Breslau et al., 1991; Kilpatrick et al., 1989; Resnick et al., 1993; Ullman, 1995). The results of this study indicated that exposure to the disturbances did negatively impact mental health.

At times you may present more than one experiment in a single paper. The basic procedure is to have a single introduction section, then a method, results, and discussion section for each experiment, followed by a general discussion section that interprets the results of all the studies in relation to your hypotheses. For example, the Öhman et al. (2001) article that examined reaction time to fear-related stimuli describes three different experiments. The general discussion section begins as follows.

> The results from the experiments reported in this article can be summarized in a number of broad generalizations. First, participants were consistently faster to find a fear-relevant stimulus (snake or spider) than a fear-irrelevant stimulus (flower or mushroom) against backgrounds of fear-irrelevant and fear-relevant stimuli, respectively. This finding suggests that humans share a predisposition to preferentially direct attention toward potentially threatening animal stimuli. Second, the latency of finding a fear-relevant target stimulus was independent of where in the matrix it was located.

Let's look at another example. Klein and Boals (2001) performed two experiments to determine the effects of emotional disclosure through expressive writing on working memory (WM). The final section of their paper was a general discussion that brought together the results of both studies.

> **General Discussion**
>
> The findings from these two experiments shed new light on available WM capacity and markedly expand the benefits of expressive writing to this widely studied cognitive process. We have shown that usable WM is not a static variable but can change as a function of a psychosocial manipulation, with such changes reflecting variations in intrusive and avoidant thoughts about offtask topics. . . .

To help you to grasp the fundamental differences among the sections of an article, we suggest that the method and results sections be written in an exact manner. The method section must be detailed enough to permit another scientist to perform an exact replication of your experiment; the results section must be an accurate statement of what actually happened in your experiment. In a sense, because these sections are a statement of how you performed your experiment and what your results were, they are a record of your experiment and can be expected to be an accurate description of what happened. In contrast, the discussion is a statement of what you think your finding means for our understanding of the phenomenon you are studying. Although your finding will last forever, your interpretation of your data may vary considerably as your understanding of the phenomenon grows with each successive experiment.

Once you have finished writing the five major sections of the article, the remaining steps are to find a title for your paper and to list your references. The title of your paper is important because, like the abstract, it describes the nature of your experiment. Consequently, many titles are written so that they describe the nature of the independent and dependent variables. For example, in 1958 Silverstein and Klee published an article in the *American Medical Association Archives of Neurology and Psychiatry* titled "Effects of lysergic acid diethylamide (LSD-25) on intellectual functions." The title of this paper tells us the independent variable (lysergic acid diethylamide) and the dependent variables (some measure of intellectual function).

■ References

The author, title, and reference information for every study you cite in your paper are listed in a *references* section at the end of the paper. The references section is important for the valuable information that it gives to other scientists. There are no hard-and-fast rules for referring to other studies, but general guidelines suggest that you do so for one of three purposes. The first purpose is to acknowledge a scientific fact, assumption, or working hypothesis. For example, a study by Castonguay, Goldfried, Wiser, Raue, and Hayes (1996) begins with the statement, "Despite support for the effectiveness of cognitive therapy for depression, researchers are still confronted with a high degree of uncertainty about its underlying processes of change." Following this sentence, the authors can give one or more references directing the reader to theoretical or research articles that have examined this question. A second purpose of the references section is to direct the reader to a more detailed discussion of a theoretical concept or a specific experimental or statistical procedure. Because a research report is by its nature short, it is important to direct others to extended discussions of the concept under study, as might be found in *Psychological Bulletin* or *Psychological Review*. The third purpose is to give credit to other scientists for developing an idea, technique, or line of research.

The latest version of the *Publication Manual* suggests that references be presented in the same manner as they would appear in a printed journal article, with each reference using a hanging indent (first line of reference is at the left margin and all lines below that are indented), and that titles of journals and books be presented in italic. However, the *Publication Manual* also allows for variations to this format if it cannot be accomplished by your word processing system. In either case the chosen format should be consistent throughout the references.

The following is an example of the APA style of citing books and journals, including Internet references. It should be noted that in 2007, APA updated section 4.16 of the publication manual, which describes references to electronic resources. The latest update to referencing of information found on the Internet can be accessed at the APA website, http://www.apastyle.org/elecref.html.

References

 American Psychological Association. (1995, September 15). *APA public policy action alert: Legislation would affect grant recipients* [Announcement posted on the World Wide Web]. Washington, DC: Author. Retrieved January 25, 1996 from the World Wide Web: http://www.apa.org/ppo/istook.html.

Bianchi, L. (1895). The function of the frontal lobes. *Brain, 18,* 497–522.

Darwin, C. R. (1965). *The expression of the emotions in man and animals.* Chicago: University of Chicago Press. (Original work published 1872)

Flynn, J. R. (1984). The mean IQ of Americans: Massive gains 1932 to 1978. *Psychological Bulletin, 95,* 3–28.

Leventhal, H. (1980). Toward a comprehensive theory of emotions. In L. Berkowitz (Ed.), *Advances in experimental psychology* (Vol. 13, pp. 139–207). New York: Academic Press.

Simpson, J. A., Collins, W. A., Tran, S., & Haydon, K. (2007). Attachment and the experience and expression of emotions in romantic relationships: A developmental perspective. *Journal of Personality and Social Psychology, 92,* 355–367.

A journal article as it was published is presented in Appendix B. For additional help with preparing papers in APA format, we have reproduced in Appendix C the typed copy of selected parts of this article showing the proper spacing, headings, and so forth. This shows both the format a student might use to submit a research paper to a class and the manner in which it *must* be submitted for publication in an APA journal or other journals. As you may have noticed, the five major parts of this study—the abstract, introduction, method, results, and discussion—along with the title and references are presented in Appendix B in their entirety. Also, if you look at the conclusion of the references section, you can see the date on which the journal received the article.

Now that you know the sections required in an article, we can turn to the next step: submitting the article for publication. Before we do this, we want to remind you that proposals for research may also follow the APA format. In a proposal, of course, you would not have actual data. Your results section would describe how your data would be quantified and which specific statistical tests you would use. Likewise, the discussion section could discuss possible outcomes and what these might mean scientifically. To aid you in preparing proposals, Box 15.1 presents a checklist for preparing a research proposal.

 CONCEPT CHECK 15.1   Describe the basic sections of a research paper.

CONCEPT CHECK 15.2   In which section would you find a statement of the hypothesis?

Box 15.1

Preparing a Research Proposal

For some students there is less emphasis on the writing of formal research papers for publication and more emphasis on the development of sound research proposals. In developing proposals many conceptual and procedural questions must be considered. In this process a checklist is helpful. Robert Holt developed the following checklist. Students who have particular problems with developing a research project will find Holt's clear-cut advice helpful and should consult his original article (Holt, 1965).

Checklist of Questions to Be Asked About a Research Proposal

1. What is the problem?
   a. Is it clearly stated?
   b. Is it focused enough to facilitate efficient work (that is, are hypotheses directly testable)?
2. What are the underlying objectives?
   a. Is the problem clearly related to the objectives?
3. What is the significance of the proposed research?
   a. How does it tie in with theory?
   b. What are its implications for application?
4. Has the relevant literature been surveyed adequately?
   a. Is the research adequately related to other people's work on the same or similar topics?
5. Are the concepts and variables adequately defined (theoretically and operationally)?
6. Is the design adequate?
   a. Does it meet formal standards for consistency, power, and efficiency?
   b. Is it appropriate to the problem and the objectives?
   c. Will negative results be meaningful?
   d. Are possibly misleading and confounding variables controlled?

e. How are the independent and dependent variables measured or specified?
7. What instruments or techniques will be used to gather data?
   a. Are the reliabilities and validities of these techniques well established?
8. Is the sampling of subjects adequately planned for?
   a. Is the population (to which generalizations are to be aimed) specified?
   b. Is there a specific and acceptable method of drawing a sample from this population?
9. Is the sampling of objects (or situations) adequately planned for?
   a. To what population of objects (situations) will generalizations be aimed?
   b. Is there a specific and acceptable method of drawing a sample from this population?
10. What is the setting in which data will be gathered?
    a. Is it feasible and practical to carry out the research plan in this setting?
    b. Is the cooperation of the necessary persons obtainable?
11. How are the data to be analyzed?
    a. What techniques of data reduction are contemplated?
    b. Are methods specified for analyzing data qualitatively?
    c. Are methods specified for analyzing data quantitatively?
12. In the light of available resources, how feasible is the design?
    a. What compromises must be made in translating an idealized research design into a practical research design?
    b. What limitations or generalizations will result?
    c. What will be needed in terms of time, money, personnel, and facilities?

Source: Holt (1965).

CONCEPT
CHECK 15.3

Lauren read an article about an experiment that related one's musical preference to IQ. She thought this would be a good study to replicate for her experimental psychology class. Although the ideas and data in the article were
well presented, she could not determine how the original study was conducted.
Which section of the original paper must be improved?

PUBLISHING YOUR ARTICLE

Now that we have discussed the basic form of a research article, let's talk about the process
of submitting an article for publication. One of the first questions a scientist asks is, "Who,
or what portion of the scientific community, do I want to read my article?" For example,
suppose someone has performed a study that examines the EEG changes in humans over a
period of years and how these changes correlate with the participants' education and psychological development. Depending on the particular hypothesis of the study and its focus,
the final article might be sent to a journal that reports physiological research, such as *Psychophysiology* or *Neuropsychologia;* to a journal emphasizing developmental processes, such
as *Developmental Psychology;* or even to a journal that discusses educational development.
Each of these journals is read by a different group of scientists, so publishing an article in
one journal will give you a different audience from publishing in another.

To help the potential author, most journals include a statement at the beginning about
the types of articles that they publish. If your study is a replication and continuation of some
of the articles cited in your introduction, probably the same journal that published the other
studies will be interested in your work. Once you have decided on an audience and a journal,
it is a good procedure to look through recent issues of the journal to see whether the particular style that is used deviates from the APA recommendation. For example, journals may
differ in the references and results sections. Thus, the particular form of reference citation
must be checked carefully, as well as the manner in which statistical significance is reported.

Another issue is the question of placing your work on the web. Sometimes, researchers
may want to place their newly found results on their web pages. However, there are some
precautions that should be considered. First, if it is placed on the web it should be clearly
noted as an unpublished paper. The APA (www.apa.org/journals/posting.html) suggests

that the following be placed on such a paper: "Draft version 4, 5/3/2005. This paper has not
been peer reviewed. Please do not copy or cite without author's permission." It should also
be noted that some journals will not consider publishing a paper if it has been placed on
the web because they consider this prior publication, although this is not the case with most
psychological journals. Of course, you should check with the journal to which you plan to
submit your paper before you place it on the web.

Once your paper is published, the requirements vary by journal. APA journals allow
you to post a copy of the final manuscript with three limitations: (1) The posted article
must carry an APA copyright notice and include a link to the APA journal home page;
(2) it cannot be archived with any other non-APA repositories; (3) APA will not provide

electronic copies of the APA-published version for this purpose, and authors are not permitted to scan in the APA-published version. Most journals allow authors to place abstracts on their web pages and to electronically send the full article to others.

Once you have written the article following the guidelines in the front of the journal, you send the number of copies requested to the editor of the journal and wait. Some journals give information about publication decisions quickly, and others take months. To understand why there is a delay before your article is accepted or rejected, let's examine what happens when an article is received by the editor of a journal. In most cases the editor is a scientist employed by a university or research laboratory who has agreed to be editor for a few years. The editor thus has another job on which he or she spends considerable time. A paid assistant generally performs the day-to-day processes of the journal. Once the editor receives the manuscript, he or she usually chooses two scientists who are studying phenomena similar to yours and asks them to recommend whether the article should be accepted for publication. The process of review by other scientists is called the peer review system.

Each reviewer reads your article and evaluates it in terms of the clarity of presentation, the logic of the experiment, the appropriateness of the data analysis used, and the meaningfulness of the discussion section. This is similar to the type of feedback that your professors give you about your research reports and proposals. (In the next section, we present in more detail some criteria that are used for research evaluation.)

After a reviewer has read and evaluated an article, she or he writes a review, which is sent to the editor. Usually these reviews are a couple of pages long and are designed to give feedback to the author. In some cases the reviewers point out limitations of the experiment itself or critique the way the article is written. Specific suggestions often are made to improve your paper. In each case a general recommendation is made about whether the article should be published. The editor reads these reviews, makes a final decision about whether to publish the paper, and then informs the author of the decision. Sometimes the reviewers differ over the quality of the article, and the editor must decide between the views of the reviewers. Other times the reviewers suggest publication only if the author will agree to rewrite or reanalyze part of the study. Thus, after some wait, you receive the reviews and the editor's disposition regarding publication of your article.

If the editor agrees to publish your article as it stands, there is still another wait for the article to be printed. This delay is called the publication lag. It is generally brought about because a journal accepts many good articles and is able to publish only a few of them in any given issue. The publication lag may range from a month or two to more than a year.

 # WHAT MAKES A GOOD ARTICLE?

One question students ask is, "What criteria do editors and reviewers keep in mind as they are reviewing papers for publication?" Obviously, the answer is important; it should give you an idea of what senior scientists consider both good research and a well-written experiment. Brendan Maher, editor of the *Journal of Consulting and Clinical Psychology*, reports that four out of every five articles submitted to the journal are rejected. Because most of these are rejected for methodological reasons, Maher produced a set of guidelines for publishing articles (Maher, 1978a). These guidelines have been reconsidered by Kazdin (1995), who poses a series of questions for authors and reviewers to consider. Box 15.2 reproduces these questions, which Kazdin designed to guide the preparation of journal articles.

Box 15.2

Major Questions to Guide Journal Article Preparation

Abstract

What were the main purposes of the study?

Who was studied (sample, sample size, special characteristics)?

How were participants selected?

To what conditions, if any, were participants exposed?

What type of design was used?

What were the main findings and conclusions?

Introduction

What is the background and context for the study?

What in current theory, research, or clinical work makes this study useful, important, or of interest?

What is different or special about the study in focus, methods, or design to address a need in the area? Is the rationale clear regarding the constructs to be assessed?

What specifically were the purposes, predictions, or hypotheses?

Method

Participants

Who were the participants and how many of them were there in this study? Why was this sample selected in light of the research goals?

How was this sample obtained, recruited, and selected?

What are the participant and demographic characteristics of the sample (e.g., gender, age, ethnicity, race, socioeconomic status)?

What inclusion and exclusion criteria were invoked (i.e., selection rules to obtain participants)?

How many of the participants eligible or recruited actually were selected and participated in the study?

Was informed consent solicited? How and from whom, if special populations were used?

Design

What is the design (e.g., longitudinal, cross-sectional) and how does the design relate to the goals of the study?

How were participants assigned to groups or conditions?

How many groups were included in the design?

How were the groups similar and different in how they were treated in the study?

Why were these groups critical to address the questions of interest?

Assessment

What were the constructs of interest and how were they measured?

What are the relevant reliability and validity data from previous research (and from the present study) that support the use of these measures for the present purposes? Were multiple measures and methods used to assess the constructs?

Are response sets or styles relevant to the use and interpretation of the measures?

(continued)

(continued)

How was the assessment conducted? By whom (as assessors or observers)? In what order were the measures administered?

If judges (raters) were used in any facet of assessment, what is the reliability (inter- or intrajudge consistency) in rendering their judgments or ratings?

Procedures

Where was the study conducted (setting)?

What materials, equipment, or apparatuses were used in the study?

What was the chronological sequence of events to which participants were exposed? What intervals elapsed between different aspects of the study (e.g., assessment occasions)?

What procedural checks were completed to avert potential sources of bias in implementation of the manipulation and assessments?

What checks were made to ensure that the conditions were carried out as intended?

What other information does the reader need to know to understand how participants were treated and what conditions were provided?

Results

What were the primary measures and data on which the predictions depend?

What are the scores on the measures of interest for the different groups and sample as a whole (e.g., measures of central tendency and variability)?

How do the scores compare with those of other study, normative, or standardization samples?

Are groups of interest within the study similar on measures and variables that could interfere with interpretation of the hypotheses?

What analyses were used and how specifically did these address the original hypotheses and purposes?

Were the assumptions of the data analyses met?

If multiple tests were used, what means were provided to control error rates?

If more than one group was delineated, were they similar on variables that might otherwise explain the results (e.g., diagnosis, age)?

Were data missing due to incomplete measures (not filled out completely by the participants) or due to loss of participants? If so, how were these handled in the data analyses?

Are there ancillary analyses that might further inform the primary analyses or exploratory analyses that might stimulate further work?

Discussion

What were the major findings of the study?

How do these findings add to research and how do they support, refute, or inform current theory?

What alternative interpretations can be placed on the data?

What limitations or qualifiers must be placed on the study given method and design issues?

What research follows from the study to move the field forward?

Note: Further discussion of questions that guide the preparation of journal articles can be obtained in additional sources (Kazdin, 1992; Maher, 1978a). Concrete guidelines on the format for preparing articles are provided by the American Psychological Association (2001).

Source: Preparing and Evaluating a Research Report, by Alan Kazdin in *Journal of Psychological Assessment,* 1995, 7, p. 232. Copyright © 1995 by the American Psychological Association. Reprinted with permission.

KEY TERMS AND CONCEPTS

1. **Parts of an article**
   A. Abstract
   B. Introduction
   C. Method
   D. Results
   E. Discussion
   F. References
2. **What makes a good proposal or article?**

SUMMARY

1. An important part of research is communicating the results to others, and for this purpose a particular format has evolved. This format includes five parts: (1) abstract, (2) introduction, (3) method, (4) results, and (5) discussion. Also included are references, tables, and figures as required.

2. The abstract is a 100- to 120-word summary of the article. The typical abstract provides a clear statement of purposes, method, and results.

3. The introduction of a paper is designed to review what is already known about the topic being studied, to explain the reason for the present study, and to outline the hypothesis.

4. The method section consists of a detailed description of what was done so that another scientist can precisely replicate the experiment. This description covers which participants were used and how they were selected, what the experimental situation was, any equipment that was used, and the procedures, including what the participants were told or led to believe.

5. The results section describes the outcome of an experiment and states what statistical procedures were used and the results of the analyses.

6. The discussion section describes the results of the study as they relate to previous research and theoretical interpretation as well as any potential limitations of the experiment.

7. An excellent set of guidelines for assessing research reports is reproduced in Box 15.2.

REVIEW QUESTIONS

1. What are the major parts of a research article?
2. What is an *abstract,* and where is it located in a paper?
3. How do you determine which references to include in a paper?
4. Where will the research hypothesis be located in a paper?
5. Statistical tests will be reported in which section of a paper?
6. What is the purpose of the discussion section?
7. Why are many articles rejected for publication in the *Journal of Consulting and Clinical Psychology*?
8. How are a proposal and a published article the same, and how are they different?

DISCUSSION QUESTIONS AND PROJECTS

1. Pick an article published in one of the APA journals (e.g., *Journal of Experimental Psychology, Journal of Personality and Social Psychology, Journal of Abnormal Psychology*) or an APS journal such as *Psychological Science*. Place a piece of paper over the abstract and read the article. Now write an abstract of your own. How did your abstract differ from the existing one?

2. Pick an article of interest to you. Read the article and write a summary of it. Look up this same article in PsycINFO and compare your summary with the existing one. What are the differences between your summary and the one in PsycINFO?

3. Discuss the function of the discussion section.

4. Why do people use references? What are the reasons for including or excluding a reference to a particular article?

5. Take a simple task such as balancing a ruler on the end of your finger in two conditions: (a) singing a song to yourself and (b) saying the alphabet backward. Measure the amount of time you can balance the ruler in each condition. Assume that you have used the appropriate control procedures, such as counterbalancing the order of conditions. Write the procedure section of a research article describing such a task with the various conditions.

InfoTrac College Edition: Exercises

In this chapter we discussed the necessary parts of a research article. Using InfoTrac College Edition, look up the article entitled "If you changed your name and appearance to those of Elvis Presley, who would you be? Historical features in categorization," by Robert Sternberg and his colleagues, which was published in the *American Journal of Psychology* (Fall 1998). As you go through the article, note what type of information is contained in each of the sections—abstract, introduction, method, results, discussion, and references. This article is different from the ones discussed in the chapter in that more than one experiment is presented in the report. How was this accomplished?

To help you better understand the material in this chapter, you can go to Wadsworth's research methods workshop web page at http://www.wadsworth.com/ psychology_d/templates/student_resources/workshops/ resch_wrk.html. There you will find workshops related to research methods and statistics. The research methods workshop on "APA Style" and "Evaluating Published Research" discusses the material presented in this chapter.

☑ Answers to Concept Checks

15.1 The basic sections of a research paper are (a) abstract, (b) introduction, (c) method, (d) results, and (e) discussion, followed by a references section.

15.2 A statement of the hypothesis traditionally is found at the end of the introduction section.

15.3 The method section. It is one purpose of the method section to describe the original study in enough detail so that another experimenter could conduct a similar study. Most method sections describe the participants in the experiment, the types of equipment or test materials used, if any, and the procedures that were followed.

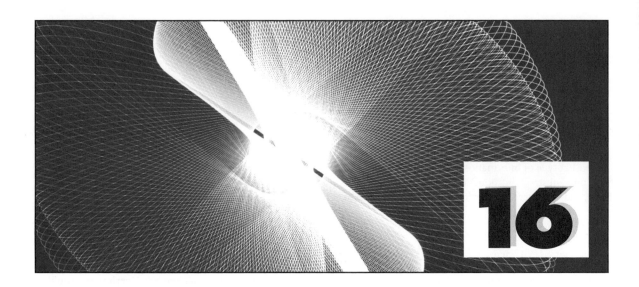

BEYOND METHOD

DIMENSIONS OF RESEARCH

BEGINNING WITH A QUESTION

LIMITATIONS TO FINDING ANSWERS
Our Tools
Our Shared View of the World
Our Psychological Limitations

SCIENCE AS A COMPLEX
HUMAN PROCESS

VALUE IN SCIENCE

RELEVANCE

SCIENCE AS A MEANS OF
TRANSCENDENCE

T hroughout this book we have considered more than just methods because we believe that the process of science is *more* than simply applying the scientific method to the study of human behavior and experience. In this chapter we intend to move beyond the specific application of particular designs, as important as these approaches are, and focus on some of the broad themes that we have presented throughout this book. The title of this final chapter, "Beyond Method," emphasizes this intention. Let's first review schematically the approaches to research we have presented thus far.

DIMENSIONS OF RESEARCH

In the preceding chapters, we discussed the contemporary research methods used to study human behavior and experience. Now we attempt to bring them together in a single schematic representation. To facilitate viewing them together, let's consider three dimensions of research approaches (Figure 16.1). Although we discuss the end points of these dimensions, it should be noted that each dimension represents a continuum. The first dimension is the extent to which we intervene directly in the phenomenon that we are studying. At one extreme is the true experiment. This is an active method that makes it possible to study relationships between variables by directly manipulating an independent variable and observing its effect on the dependent variable. Experimenters typically are interested in how one factor affects another at a given time. At the other extreme is the method of naturalistic observation. This typically is a passive method that makes it possible for researchers to attempt to describe a process as it unfolds.

Figure 16.1

Schematic representation of the three-dimensional nature of research approaches

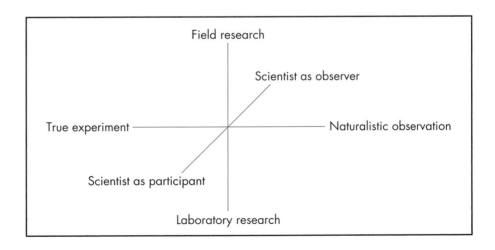

It is important to realize that something is gained and something is lost whenever we adopt either of these methods. When we use naturalistic observation, we find ourselves unable to test important relationships. Likewise, it is impossible to produce changes in the people who participate in our research; we must wait until new behaviors and experiences appear spontaneously. The experimental method gives us the advantage of increased control and thus the ability to infer important relationships between events. However, we have to know what we are looking for to use this method successfully. As soon as we choose a dependent variable, certain information is excluded. In general, the information that is excluded is *what we do not know to begin with*. For example, how many of us consider the weather (temperature, pressure, humidity) when we design experiments? We assume that weather is not an important factor. But some migraine sufferers, for example, report an increase of episodes before storms.

For these reasons we suggest using the experimental method and naturalistic observation simultaneously. When conducting a true experiment, we are interested not only in the dependent variable that is being collected but also in watching the total experiment. Likewise, when observing people in naturalistic research, we consider what variables might be related and what variables might affect others. Thus, as one is developing ideas concerning a topic, there is a continuous interplay between naturalistic and experimental methods. This is true both for research and for developing ideas.

The second dimension is the research setting: laboratory versus field research. Laboratory research creates an experimental situation that includes all the important variables that affect the phenomenon that we are studying. By moving our research into the laboratory, we obtain greater control over environmental factors. Field research gives us less control over environmental factors and allows for more ecologically valid behavior on the part of the person we are studying. By performing research in the field, many researchers believe the responses of the participants are more natural and thus less controlled by the demand characteristics of the experiment.

There is also a third dimension of research approach: the scientist's participation in the experiment. At one extreme is the scientist as observer; in this case it is assumed that the scientist is in no way involved in the experiment and only records data passively. At the other extreme is the scientist as participant; in this case the scientist is actually part of the study. There is no hard-and-fast determination about whether scientist-as-observer or scientist-as-participant gives the greater objectivity; it depends on the questions being asked. If you were studying the social psychology of a motorcycle gang, then being part of the group rather than observing the group as an outsider might obtain more accurate information. However, if you wanted to see how other people react to a motorcycle gang driving through their town, then it might be better to be an observer so that you could see the reaction of the town both during and after the event.

As you look at the dimensions of research approaches in Figure 16.1, you can see that you as a scientist have available a variety of methods and approaches to understand the questions you are studying. No one approach or method is superior. Methods are useful only in relation to a particular question being asked. To help illustrate this point, let's now divide the three-dimensional illustration in Figure 16.1 into two two-dimensional ones (Figure 16.2). As an exercise try to determine in which quadrant the various research studies discussed in this book should be placed. Depending on the particular topic that

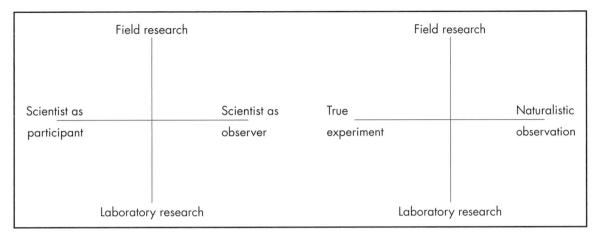

Figure 16.2

Two-dimensional diagrams for representing research approaches

you want to study and the particular questions that you ask, you will choose one of the research methods. This brings us to the next aspect of science that we want to address: the questions we study.

BEGINNING WITH A QUESTION

As we have stressed throughout our discussion, the process of science is more than the mere application of method. In fact, much of the important work of learning to be a scientist lies in the realm of remembering how to ask questions. We said *remembering* rather than *learning* because performing science is not some special activity that sets us apart from the rest of humanity; it is an activity that stems from it. To emphasize this point, in the beginning of this book, we described the scientist as being like a child out to discover the world. Part of your task as a scientist is to recapture that childlike perspective—to remember how to find the wonder and excitement of asking questions. Once you become fascinated with a process or phenomenon, then you naturally consider it, explore it, and begin to ask questions about it.

Excitement and wonder are not enough, however. Just as the child grows up and matures, the scientist moves beyond the initial excitement of a question and begins to formulate a systematic approach about how to answer the question. This usually means not just one experiment but also a series of directed research studies called a *research program* (Box 16.1). In formulating such an approach, the scientist draws on both the work of others and his or her own independent ideas. We discuss the scientist's reliance on others and himself or herself in greater detail later in this chapter. For now we only want to emphasize that being excited about an idea or research question is an important beginning, but it is only a beginning. The hard work comes next.

Box 16.1

Philosophy of Science: Imre Lakatos

Imre Lakatos suggests that the important advances in science are made through adherence to research programs. By saying this, Lakatos means that science is more than following trial-and-error hypotheses. A research program is the examination of a number of major and minor hypotheses about a topic. Some examples Lakatos gives of research programs are Newton's theory of gravity, Einstein's relativity theory, and the theories of Freud.

An important point is whether the research program is progressive or degenerating. How do you tell the difference? The main characteristic of a progressive research program is that it predicts novel facts. Thus, a progressive program leads to the discovery of new facts, whereas a degenerating program only reinterprets known facts in light of that theory. By this, Lakatos means that a degenerating research program only explains the results of already existing experiments, whereas a progressive research program leads in new directions and predicts new facts. In this way Lakatos proposes that science changes not by sudden revolutions, as Kuhn suggested, but through the replacement of degenerating research programs with progressive ones.

For more information on Lakatos, see Lakatos (1978) and Eysenck (1976).

LIMITATIONS TO FINDING ANSWERS

The scientist encounters many obstacles within the hard work of research that may limit the types of questions that can be asked. Three of the most important limitations are the tools that we have available to us, our shared view of the world, and our personal psychological limitations, such as fear of making mistakes or of being rejected by our colleagues and friends.

Our Tools

Many of the questions that we want to ask in science may be limited by the particular techniques available to us in the period in which we live. This is true of physical tools and technologies as well as methodological sophistication. In the same way that the telescope and the microscope allowed scientists to see worlds that were unknown, electronic developments such as the computer, the physiological amplifier, and various brain-imaging devices allow us to study worlds of human behavior and experience that were previously beyond our limits. With new tools come new methodological advances. However, it is a trap to "fall in love" with a particular tool or research technique, be it methodological, statistical, or mechanical. In such a situation, a scientist is apt to try to make all human behavior and experience conform to measurement by the favored tool. There is an old saying that if you give a child *only* a hammer, he or she will treat everything as if it were a nail. This is not the fault of the hammer but of the child's view of how a hammer should be used. The same is true for the scientist's view of the purpose of research tools, which leads us to our next point.

Our Shared View of the World

In science a number of approaches are available, yet what we study is largely a personal decision shaped by our shared conceptions and personal perceptions. At times these conceptions can be culture bound, leading us to believe that what we do is what people throughout the world do. For example, research in social psychology suggests that some traditional social psychology phenomena such as cognitive dissonance or the often-cited attribution error may not apply in non-Western cultures (Gilbert, Fiske, & Lindzey, 1998); the same is true for other types of attribution as well (Masuda & Kitayama, 2003). Even more interesting is the finding that East Asians and Americans actually pay attention to different aspects of such stimuli as photos. Asians are more sensitive to the relationship between objects and the entire photo while Americans are more sensitive to the attributes of the individual objects (Masuda & Nisbett, 2006). At other times our personal views or desires may influence our approach or conclusions. Research on reasoning shows that we are better at being critical of others' inferences than of our own and that we are more likely to construct models that support our own views rather than refute them (Johnson-Laird, 1999). Although we all think and act in accordance with our representations of reality, scientists are just beginning to study when children first come to realize that it is the representation of reality rather than reality itself that guides much of behavior and experience (Flavell, 1999).

One of the greatest problems for a scientist interested in discovering new truths is related to our views of the world. Some writers call these views *tacit* or *metaphysical,* as well as *unconscious.* We all have assumptions that guide and direct our behavior, such as "People are evil," "Humankind is an aggressive species," "All behavior is learned," or "All behavior is innate." Even the law of parsimony (which states that the best explanation in science is the least complicated) is itself an untested metaphysical assumption. Having assumptions is not the problem; the real problem, as biologist David Bohm suggests, occurs when a person confuses the assumptions with directly observed facts (Bohm, 1969). Take a common example of this problem: In the morning we *see* the sunrise, and in the evening we *see* the sunset. But the sun neither rises nor sets; it is we who are turning in space and move into sight of the sun and out of sight of the sun. Once this discrepancy is pointed out to you, you will agree, and you even may see the next sunrise or sunset differently.

A scientific example of the problem is that people once believed heavy objects would reach the ground faster than lighter ones. Two more recent examples are the belief that organs innervated by the autonomic nervous system (the heart, the stomach, and certain glands) are beyond self-regulation and the belief that our immune system is not influenced by psychological processes such as grief. These beliefs have been called into question, and we have come to recognize that our thoughts, feelings, and actions have a profound influence on our bodies. For example, experimental demonstrations show clearly the importance of psychological interventions in cancer survival (Baum & Posluszny, 1999; Cohen & Herbert, 1996; Spiegel, Bloom, Kraemer, & Gotthel, 1989).

From the discovery of the manner in which our emotions influence our biochemistry to the finding that jogging reduces depression, we are coming to discover important interactions between our behaviors and the physiological and biochemical processes of the brain. In fact, we are learning that experience is a major contributor to the manner in which the brain develops (Kolb & Whishaw, 1998; Pantev, Engelien, Candia, & Elbert, 2001).

Psychology is also gaining a new appreciation of genetics, a field largely ignored during a time when learning was thought to account for all behavior (McGuffin, Riley, & Plomin, 2001), as well as for what can be learned from ethology and evolutionary biology. For example, the New York Academy of Sciences published a volume (April 2000) on evolutionary psychology with an emphasis on human reproductive behavior. Traditional psychological journals such as *Child Development* (Bjorklund & Pellegrini, 2000) and *Journal of Abnormal Psychology* (August 1999 series of articles on "Evolutionary versus prototype analysis on the concept of disorder") have devoted recent issues to understanding their fields from an evolutionary perspective. Clearly, a variety of popular press books and scholarly works are reshaping the manner in which psychology examines the roles of nature and nurture (for example, Bjorklund & Pellegrini, 2002; Buss, 2005; Geary, 2005).

As we reconsider the questions that our organism is designed to answer, especially from the perspective of evolution, we find ourselves rethinking the nature of emotion, language, and even consciousness itself. Donald Campbell even suggests we should see the process of science itself from an evolutionary perspective (Box 16.2). This and other shifts in our views highlight the importance of new approaches to studying human functioning. Much traditional scientific research and thought have been directed at "normal behavior" and the pathological exception exemplified by neuroses and psychoses.

One area that is only beginning to be explored systematically is that of human potential and positive psychology (Seligman & Csikszentmihalyi, 2000). Csikszentmihalyi (2000) has been particularly interested in what he calls the "flow" state, which is the experience of being totally absorbed in a particular activity such as sports. One aspect of this experience may include the sense of time slowing down and the ability to make difficult moves with ease. Another aspect of positive psychology includes what it means to be psychologically healthy as well as the experience of positive emotions such as love, empathy, and altruism (see Snyder & Lopez, 2002, for an overview). Potential questions ask what a person can do in the *best of cases*. In relation to this question, researchers are exploring creativity, musical

Box 16.2

Donald Campbell: Evolutionary Epistemology

Donald Campbell helped to define the way in which researchers think about validity through his distinctions of internal and external validity. As we discussed in Chapter 7, he was interested in helping researchers logically rule out alternative explanations that are described as threats to internal validity. In the process he studied epistemology, which is the study of how people acquire knowledge and determine what is or is not valid. That is, how do we know what we know? Ruling out alternative hypotheses is one way that we make useful approaches to the accuracy of a proposition. As Campbell studied the search for truth in science, he came to see it as evolutionary in both content and process. In fact, he called his approach *evolutionary episte-mology*. He begins with a simple yet important idea: Evolution is a knowledge process. That is, contained within the natural selection process is a mechanism that increases an organism's ability to take in and process information. Thus, in the same way that particular physiological structures (such as the eye) and cognitive systems (such as memory) have been influenced by evolutionary processes, science as a human creation has also been influenced. From this perspective Campbell suggests that science is our most sophisticated mechanism for knowing about the world.

and artistic abilities, genius, and even what makes excellent scientists (see Runco, 2004, for a review of creativity research).

Scientists recently have begun to shift in their view of the world, from seeing processes as stable to asking how instability and fluctuations are a part of nature. Included in this shift is a renewed interest in patterns of behavior, complexity, and the manner in which processes evolve. One example of such an approach uses models based on nonlinear system analysis, or chaos (Elbert et al., 1994; Gleick, 1987; Ruelle, 1991). This approach has been applied to a variety of systems, including meteorology, physiology, and physical systems. The chaos approach suggests that small changes in initial conditions may produce large deviations in expected trajectories later. In developmental psychology, clinical psychology, and health psychology, it is easy to imagine situations in which initial brief exposures (for example, to a second language, abuse, health, or illness) would greatly influence one's later trajectory through life. Researchers are also considering new types of graphs and statistics for describing nonlinear change (for example, Cudeck & Harring, 2007). This is particularly important in longitudinal data in which change at one age occurs faster than that at another.

In a different context, Bandura (1982) argues that many of what we consider significant events in our lives (whom we marry, where we go to college, where we work, and so on) are often the results of brief chance encounters. Such thinking makes us reconsider what the "normal" trajectory is in terms of behavior, which in turn may give way to the possibility that our simple *view of regularity* may not offer the best alternative. For example, in Chapter 1 we brought to your attention the paper by Goldberger and Rigney (1991), in which the authors suggest that the normal heart pattern is chaotic and that a regular pattern may be a sign of pathology. Such work requires that we rethink our shared view of

"I HOPE WE GET TO COMMUNICATE WITH THEM. I'D JUST LIKE TO TELL THEM WE HAVE NO INTEREST IN COMMUNICATING WITH THEM."

the world. The chaos approach has been applied to a variety of other processes, including psychology in general (Abraham, 1990) and cognitive and sensory processes within the brain (Ray, Wells, Elbert, Lutzenberger, & Birbaumer, 1991) in particular.

■ Our Psychological Limitations

Emotional learning blocks have been of great interest to cognitive psychologists (Bransford, 1979). Such blocks may result from a fear of performing poorly, looking stupid in the eyes of others, or feeling foolish. Some authors (Horner, 1972; Maslow, 1971) suggest that some of us fear success. In all fairness, if the people in our learning experiments and other studies display these fears, then we must entertain the possibility that we as scientists possess the same fears. Thus, one major limitation to new discovery is our own fear of what the discovery might mean for us personally.

Some scientists have begun to record their psychological processing as they perform the work of science, giving us valuable insight into some of our psychological limitations. One famous example is Watson's *The Double Helix* (1968). This book records not only the scientific search for the structure of DNA but also the psychological jealousies and ego motivation that surrounded this search, as well as something of the manner in which they influenced science. In a formal study, Mitroff studied scientists and their psychological reactions to science. In particular, he examined how scientists who studied the composition of the moon reacted when rock specimens were brought back initially, especially when these rock formations were in conflict with the scientists' own theories. Mitroff also examined how scientists relate psychologically to their families and their work and how they express their emotions (Mitroff, 1974; Mitroff & Fitzgerald, 1977). Mitroff and Fitzgerald end their report by agreeing with Maslow's conclusion that science can serve as a defense and a way of avoiding life, or it can serve as a means of increasing psychological health (Maslow, 1966). Likewise, Mahoney (1976) attempted to examine our myths of the scientist and replace them with a more accurate picture of science as performed by real people who, like everyone else, have real emotions and limitations.

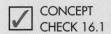

CONCEPT
CHECK 16.1
Professor Finn taught his class that in science, "Data speak for themselves," and that in research, "We leave our human problems behind." How might you respond?

Science as a Complex Human Process

In this section we want to make more explicit some of the themes that we have presented throughout this book. With many of these themes, we have emphasized that science is a complex human process involving a deep commitment to experiencing the world as it is, regardless of our preconceived notions or hypotheses about its nature; a strong concern for both the scientist and the research participant, involving both ethical and moral issues; and a profound desire to better understand the many issues and problems that confront us in our world. Thus, we are saying that science concerns itself with truth, value, and relevance.

In 1890 T. C. Chamberlin, a scientist and president of the University of Wisconsin, published a paper in the journal *Science* (Chamberlin, 1890/1965) in which he addresses many of the issues that we have been indirectly concerned with in this book. In particular, he discusses the means for transcending our own preconceptions and pet theories to arrive at a more accurate picture of reality. Chamberlin begins his article by suggesting that there are two fundamental approaches to learning about the world. The first consists of "attempting to follow by close imitation the processes of previous thinkers, or to acquire by memorizing the results of their investigations." By this Chamberlin means that you learn science by copying the experiments of previously successful scientists and that you come to learn the methods that they used. This type of study has constituted the majority of the material in this book. As a student of science, it is your first task to be able to replicate the successful procedures of others, and to do this you must know the accepted methods of study. We refer to many of these procedures in Figures 16.1 and 16.2.

The second approach Chamberlin calls *primary* or *creative study*:

> In it the effort is to think independently, or at least individually, in the endeavor to discover new truth, or to make new combinations of truth, or at least to develop an individualized aggregation of truth. The endeavor is to think for one's self, whether the thinking lies wholly in the fields of previous thought or not. It is not necessary to this habit of study that the subject-material be new; but the process of thought and its results must be individual and independent, not the mere following of previous lines of thought ending in predetermined results. (Chamberlin, 1890/1965, p. 754)

Einstein presents one clear example of this approach. In the early 1900s, physicists relied on either Newton's theory or Maxwell's equations to help them to understand the world. Einstein chose neither approach but began with what he considered a *thought* experiment. He imagined a person riding on a streetcar moving away from a town clock. What would happen, Einstein wondered, if the car traveled at the speed of light? Because the light reflected from the clock would be traveling at the speed of light and the person in the car was also traveling at the speed of light, the light reflecting from the clock would be traveling at the same speed as the person perceiving the clock. Thus, the person would always be *seeing* the same time on the clock; time would have stopped. If one imagines the person in the car going faster than the speed of light, he would actually be going faster than the light reflected from the clock, and thus he would see the clock going backward.

These thought experiments helped Einstein see the world in a new and independent way, of which he himself was unsure. Because these thought experiments made predictions that Einstein did not believe initially, he turned to philosophy to consider his predictions. The result was that Einstein realized that our concept of time comes out of the unconscious. That is, our concept of time is not something absolute but rather an unconscious conclusion of our mind based on the input of sensory information. We had always *assumed* time to be an absolute. The real absolute, as Einstein soon suggested, was not time but the speed of light. Later experimentation supported this conclusion.

Not only does the example of Einstein help us to understand Chamberlin's second, or creative, approach to science, but it is also a good illustration of the scientist's willingness to work through a problem logically and to consider surprising outcomes, even when the outcomes go against personal or traditional conceptions of the world.

Chamberlin suggests that a scientist's desire to see the world from a particular perspective can be transcended through a method he called *multiple working hypotheses.* This method is one that considers a family of hypotheses, each leading to different conclusions or interpretations. For Chamberlin this method could be applied both to one's thinking and to one's research. (In Chapter 3 we presented Platt's interpretation of this method in relation to research.) By considering two or more alternative hypotheses, we often are able to advance to more sophisticated questions. For example, in the early history of psychology, some scientists argued that all behavior was innate, and they were able to find support for this theory. Other scientists suggested that all behavior was environmentally determined, and they found support for this theory. Today, by considering both theories, it has been possible to move beyond either and to study how environmental *and* innate factors interact.

Here again, we do not want to consider just one hypothesis but rather a family of hypotheses that compete with each other and offer alternative views of reality. Chamberlin suggests that the method of multiple working hypotheses can be applied not only to hypotheses but also to methods themselves. We demonstrate this application later in the chapter. Chamberlin suggests that by adopting the method of multiple working hypotheses, one will not accidentally place one's motivation in the demonstration that a pet theory is true but rather will search for truth.

VALUE IN SCIENCE

The second theme that we have emphasized in this book is the role of value in science. As we have suggested, the domain of value is separate from the domain of science. However, this is not to say that there is no overlap between domains. Consider Figure 16.3. In this diagram the domain of science represents the world in which we test hypotheses and create theory. The domain of value cuts across the domain of science and thus influences science.

Figure 16.3

Intersection of the planes of science and value

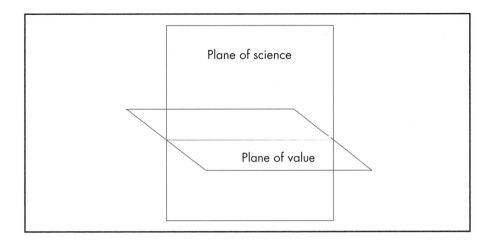

The question of ethical research and moral concern for the scientist and the research participant is one clear example of the manner in which the world of value influences science. We should remember that, although we are influenced in science by value, we in no way test the validity of our ethical and moral values; that is, every scientist brings with him or her specific values that remain unexamined in the process of science. However, based on our common heritage and collective statements of guidance, such as the APA's ethical principles, we hope that there is little actual difference between scientists in terms of ethical values.

As important as ethics are, there are other values that people bring to the scientific enterprise. Like ethics, these values are untestable from the standpoint of science, but they often enter into the choice of research questions as well as the interpretation of information. For example, many atomic scientists have been committed to the peaceful use of atomic energy, and some of these scientists have refused to work on projects that could lead to weapons of war. However, other scientists have felt that a strong defense system is necessary for maintaining their values, and they have engaged in scientific searches that could lead to better weapons of war. Likewise, in the behavioral sciences, some scientists suggest that behavior modification or particular drugs—or even hormone changes—offer important means of rehabilitating prisoners, whereas others see these techniques as a denial of freedom and refuse to support such efforts. In health care we also have seen a recent emphasis on the necessity of not just prolonging life but also evaluating the psychological quality of a prolonged life.

Beyond the question of applying scientific knowledge to technological advances, individual scientists also hold personal values not directly connected with their scientific work. For example, Jonas Salk, the developer of the Salk polio vaccine, concerned himself with humanity and worked to understand how we shape our own evolution (Salk, 1973). In particular, he stressed how our own ego gives human beings the possibility to destroy our species unless we are willing to become actively involved in trying to understand the value judgments facing us. Other scientists have stressed the importance of universal love or the nonviolent teachings of Gandhi. Einstein, for example, stressed the importance of opposing war. Still others have pursued music or poetry on a personal level. Newton spent much of his time reading the book of Revelation in the Bible, trying to understand its meaning and relevance for the future.

The important point is that the scientist has never been without values; there is no such person as a completely dispassionate scientist. *Science cannot be performed in a value-free way.* Science historian Jacob Bronowski (1965) argues "that the practice of science compels the practitioner to form for himself a fundamental set of universal values." An example of a scientist's attempt to describe his values in relation to science and the study of consciousness is Roger Sperry's 1983 book *Science and Moral Priority.*

RELEVANCE

The third theme that we want to discuss is that scientists possess a desire to better understand the world in which we live, as well as the organisms (including ourselves) that live in it. For many scientists, this desire has manifested itself in a cry for relevance. Some scientists have directed their research toward broad ecological concerns. Others have focused their explorations on understanding physical and mental disorders. Still others have attempted to explore new areas that hold promise for the future development of humans as a species.

In recent years, increasing efforts have been made not only to understand psychological disorders but also to develop and evaluate new methods of treatment. One example of such work is Skinner's early attempts, through applying learning theory techniques, to help neurotic and psychotic people. Another is Neal Miller's attempt to apply learning principles to modify physiological disorders.

Other psychologists have attempted to move beyond normal and pathological processing and ask, "What is a person's potential?" Maslow (1970) has studied people who are living up to their abilities. He calls these people *self-actualized* and has begun initial descriptive explorations into their behaviors and experiences.

Other researchers point out that because we study lessened states of awareness such as sleep and coma, we should also study hyperaware states or altered states of consciousness. In an article in *Science,* Tart (1972) suggests that we need to develop a state-specific science. By this he means that scientific methods and approaches that are appropriate to the study of one state of consciousness (such as sleep) may not be appropriate to the study of other states of consciousness (such as drug experiences or states of ecstasy). Thus, each state of consciousness may require different scientific approaches.

Not only does the question of relevance address broad concerns, but it also leads us to evaluate specific research efforts. One case in point is the need to distinguish *scientifically significant* results from results that are *statistically significant.* When researchers compare experimental and control groups in an experiment, it is possible to find statistically significant differences, suggesting that the variations were not the result of chance. *However, the differences themselves, even if statistically significant, may be so small as to have no significant scientific meaning.*

Let's look at a simple example. Suppose you developed a new technique for decreasing blood pressure through relaxation. After months of testing, you might find that your technique did result in statistically significant differences between experimental and control groups. However, on close examination, you might discover that members of the experimental group reduced their blood pressure by only 2 to 4 mm Hg and still showed blood pressures in the hypertensive range. Your results, although statistically significant, would not be clinically significant and thus could not be presented as a treatment for high blood pressure. Thus, it is possible to achieve statistically significant differences in science that are of such small magnitude as to be considered scientifically insignificant.

 CONCEPT
CHECK 16.2   "The way to get ahead is to work all the time, read every piece of literature, and perform study after study." Do you think this is good advice if you want to make a contribution to science?

SCIENCE AS A MEANS OF TRANSCENDENCE

In the previous sections, we suggested that scientists are influenced by considerations of truth, value, and relevance. Thus, science is and always has been something beyond mere methods. We approached these considerations from the standpoint of the scientist. However, science can serve another function besides expanding knowledge. It can aid us in our own growth and development both as individuals and as a society. We suggest that one value of science is its ability to aid us in transcending our personal and collective limitations. In the process of science, we commit ourselves to the search for truth over and above our personal beliefs. To begin a search for understanding carries with it the commitment to accept the answers that we find and to share these answers with others (Box 16.3).

In this manner, scientific knowledge represents a superior knowledge—a knowledge that remains constantly open to question and revision. Scientific knowledge represents superior knowledge not in the sense that it is correct but in the sense that it is open to question, rebuttal, and change. Without the willingness to reconsider, reexamine, and reevaluate knowledge, that knowledge—however valuable at the moment in which it is presented—becomes dogma and lacks the life to lead us to an increasing understanding of the world in which we live.

As Karl Popper (1959, 1972), G. Spencer-Brown (1979), Thomas Kuhn (1970), and others have shown us, we must consider that every theory is inadequate and will one day be refuted. This should cause not despair but hope—the hope that through science we can reduce the amount of ignorance that we collectively hold. With each new theory that we advance, we give ourselves the opportunity to understand the world in a new way. Each new approach and theory is somewhat like a pair of glasses that shapes our perspective and gives a certain focus to what we view. With a particular pair of glasses, we can view our world and draw a map of what we see. As useful as this process is for science, it is equally important that we remember that there is a difference between the map and the reality that the map represents. Herein lie both the hope and the limitation of science. The hope is that through science we can produce maps useful for our times. The limitation is that we may forget that there is a difference and confuse the map that we have drawn with the reality that we live with.

To point out that there is a distinction between the world that we live in and the manner in which we describe it scientifically, we have introduced three separate perspectives

Box 16.3

Lewis Thomas on the Nature of Science

It is hard to predict how science is going to turn out, and if it is really good science it is impossible to predict. This is the nature of the enterprise. If the things to be found are actually new, they are by definition unknown in advance, and there is no way of telling in advance where a really new line of inquiry will lead. You cannot make choices in this matter, selecting things you think you're going to like and shutting off the lines that make for discomfort. You either have science or you don't, and if you have it you are obliged to accept the surprising and disturbing pieces of information, even the overwhelming and upheaving ones, along with the neat and promptly useful bits. It is like that.

The only solid piece of scientific truth about which I feel totally confident is that we are profoundly ignorant about nature. Indeed, I regard this as the major discovery of the past hundred years of biology. It is, in its way, an illuminating piece of news. It would have amazed the brightest minds of the 18th-century Enlightenment to be told by any of us how little we know, and how bewildering seems the way ahead. It is this sudden confrontation with the depth and scope of ignorance that represents the most significant contribution of 20th-century science to the human intellect. We are, at last, facing up to it. In earlier times, we either pretended to understand how things worked or ignored the problem, or simply made up stories to fill the gaps. Now that we have begun exploring in earnest, doing serious science, we are getting glimpses of how huge the questions are, and how far from being answered. Because of this, these are hard times for the human intellect, and it is no wonder that we are depressed. It is not so bad being ignorant if you are totally ignorant; the hard thing is knowing in some detail the reality of ignorance, the worst spots and here and there the not-so-bad spots, but no true light at the end of any tunnel nor even any tunnels that can yet be trusted. Hard times, indeed.

But we are making a beginning, and there ought to be some satisfaction, even exhilaration, in that. The method works. There are probably no questions we can think up that can't be answered, sooner or later, including even the matter of consciousness. To be sure, there may well be questions we can't think up, ever, and therefore limits to the reach of human intellect which we will never know about, but that is another matter. Within our limits, we should be able to work our way through to all our answers, if we keep at it long enough, and pay attention.

Source: Thomas, L. (1979). The Medusa And The Snail: More Notes Of A Biology Watcher. New York: Viking.

in this book: the perspectives of the scientist, the research participant, and the witness. At this time we can reunite these perspectives and remind ourselves that they are not separate but actually highly interrelated. As single beings incorporating these perspectives, we can begin to understand our world from a multifaceted perspective. It is through the interplay of these three aspects that science comes alive. Just as we suggested at the beginning of this book that to understand life we must experience it, we suggest now that to know science we must fully perceive these three aspects—the scientist, the research participant, and the witness—within ourselves.

Figure 16.4

Four fields of
knowing

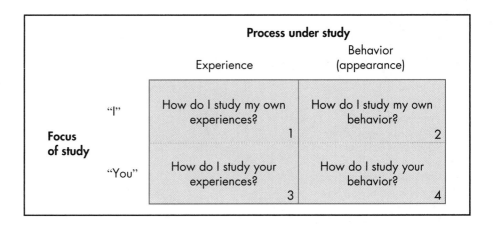

It is also important that we reexamine the domains of exploration as presented
in Chapter 1. Consider the matrix in Figure 16.4, which represents one way of studying
ourselves and others. On one side of the matrix are the categories "I" and "You," and across
the top are the categories "Experience" and "Behavior." Throughout the brief history of scientific psychology, we have focused our energy on the fourth cell—the study of external
behavior—although originally psychology also emphasized the first cell, personal experience. As the science of psychology developed, the early work directed at the first cell was
ignored or discarded, often in the name of being *scientific*. Psychology became almost a
battleground between those who were interested in behavior and those who were interested
in experience.

Today this has begun to change, and we are seeing a new group of scientists emerging
who are interested in the study of both behavior *and* experience, not only in others but also
in themselves. Whereas psychology had been attempting to reduce the specific cells in the
matrix that we were studying, the field is beginning to include topics and approaches from
all the cells.

We are just beginning to explore the behavior and experience available to us, and
many gaps in our knowledge need to be filled. We hope that you have come to see that
the topics that we study in psychology are complex and defy single-minded approaches.
It should be clear that the study of any cell of the matrix that we discussed in this section, although an important and useful beginning, can never give us a complete picture
of psychological functioning. It is your job to understand the traditional methods and
approaches and be able to replicate important work. However, it is also your job to look
to a fuller understanding of behavior and experience in the future.

 CONCEPT
CHECK 16.3   Throughout the history of psychology, we have gone through periods that
emphasized either the experience of the individual or the behavior of the individual. How might behavior and experience be considered together in any
future science of psychology?

KEY TERMS AND CONCEPTS

1. **Types of research and the relationship of the scientist and the research participant**
   A. Field research
   B. Laboratory research
   C. True experiment
   D. Naturalistic observation
   E. Scientist-as-observer
   F. Scientist-as-participant
2. **Limitations to knowing**
   A. Available tools
   B. Shared view of the world
   C. Personal psychological limitations

3. **Lakatos: research programs**
4. **Science as a complex human process**
5. **Chamberlin**
   A. Two types of science
      • Imitations
      • Primary or creative study
   B. Method of multiple working hypotheses
6. **Value in science**
7. **Relevance in science**
8. **Science as a means of transcendence**

SUMMARY

1. Research is a multifaceted process that can be divided along three dimensions. The first dimension relates to the research setting (laboratory versus field). The second dimension relates to the type of method used (naturalistic observation versus true experiment). The third dimension relates to the role of the experimenter (observer or participant). A given piece of research may lie anywhere along these three dimensions.
2. The process of science is more than merely applying methods. It is an important part of being human and as such requires that we consider both human limitations and human values.
3. Three important limitations are the tools available to us, our shared view of the world, and our personal psychological limitations.
4. In 1890, Chamberlin suggested two fundamental approaches to learning about the world. The first approach consists of learning by imitating other scientists. The second approach involves making an effort to think independently in the endeavor to discover new truth. Einstein, with his use of thought experiments, presents an example of this second approach.

5. Science cannot be viewed as value free. All scientists have values, and these values influence how they perform science and what topics they research.
6. The desire for relevance has directed some scientists to attempt a better understanding of our human condition. For example, many scientists have turned their attention toward the question of aging because more people are living longer. Other researchers are looking not only to questions of psychopathology but also to those of human potential.
7. A distinction can be drawn between results that are statistically significant and results that are scientifically significant.
8. We are only beginning to understand ourselves as humans. Many questions have yet to be answered, such as those related to consciousness and self-awareness. Many of these questions are complex and defy single-minded approaches.
9. Behavior and experience are two important aspects that must be included in any attempt to describe and understand human processes.

REVIEW QUESTIONS

1. Why do we have to know what we are looking for in order to use the experimental method?
2. Give an example of when it would be more useful for a scientist to be a participant in an experiment and when it would be more useful to be an observer.

3. What is a *research program*?
4. What does this chapter suggest are the major limitations to our learning about the world? Give examples of each type of limitation.

(continued)

REVIEW QUESTIONS (*continued*)

5. Describe the two approaches to knowing discussed by Chamberlin.

6. What is the difference between *statistical significance* and *scientific significance*?

7. According to Lewis Thomas, how has science changed since the 18th century?

8. In what way can it be said that science has the potential to be a superior knowledge?

9. Discuss the four fields of knowing (Figure 16.4).

DISCUSSION QUESTIONS AND PROJECTS

1. Give some examples of how untested assumptions have shaped what we study in psychology.

2. What is meant by the statement, "If you give a child only a hammer, he or she will treat everything like a nail"? How does this idea apply to research?

3. How are emotional blocks to learning, such as fear of failure or even fear of success, related to performing research?

4. Some people say that science is value free. Discuss this statement and describe ways in which values enter science.

5. What does Lakatos mean by the term *novel fact*?

6. What does Campbell mean by *evolutionary epistemology*?

7. What is similar about Lakatos's and Thomas's views of science?

8. What might the study of experience offer psychology?

INFOTRAC COLLEGE EDITION: EXERCISES

This chapter sought to move beyond questions of methodology per se and ask broader questions concerning human behavior and experience. Using InfoTrac College Edition, you can begin such a quest in the *Annual Reviews of Psychology*. For example, in the chapter, we referred to the Kolb and Whishaw (1998) article on brain plasticity ("Brain plasticity and behavior"), which describes the manner in which experience is able to shape the brain's development. We also discussed a psychology of potential that asks what a person can do in the best of cases. The *Annual Review of Psychology* (1998) article "Giftedness: An exceptionality examined" discusses the question of being exceptional. Another view of potential is to examine the question of well-being, which can be seen in the 2001 *Annual Review of Psychology* article "On happiness and

human potentials." The 1999 *Annual Review of Psychology* has an article entitled "Trust and distrust in organizations: Emerging perspectives, enduring questions" that discusses the question of trust and cooperation in organizations.

We also introduced you to questions of animal cognition. In the 1999 *Annual Review of Psychology* is an article reviewing the current theory and research in this area by S. Boysen and G. Himes. In this last chapter, we also returned to our theme of better understanding the individuals who do science. Fortunately, the *Journal of Cognitive Neuroscience* has published interviews with well-known neuroscientists such as Michael Posner, Larry Squire, Jon Kaas, and others. These can be found by searching for the *Journal of Cognitive Neuroscience* and looking for articles beginning with the word *Interview*.

☑ Answers to Concept Checks

16.1 Although some data do seem to make a point very clearly, these data are always interpreted within the context of a particular theoretical approach to the world. Thus, data are always interpreted within the context of a shared world and never in isolation. In addition, numerous studies have shown that our humanness enters into the process of science.

Although we seek through the scientific enterprise to transcend our limitations, on a very real level we always carry our humanness—and therefore our frailty—with us, even in science.

16.2 Actually, it is bad advice. Of course, it is important to understand the literature and to work hard. However, as Chamberlin suggested more than

(*continued*)

☑ Answers to Concept Checks *(continued)*

100 years ago, it is equally important to think. That is, it is important to reconsider the question that one is asking from a variety of perspectives and not to accept the interpretations of others. A colleague of ours suggests that his graduate students take some paper, go out into the woods, and just think about the questions they want to answer in their research.

16.3 Although we can tell you how it is being accomplished today, it becomes your job to tell us how you will accomplish this feat as you begin to direct psychological research that is relevant and accurate and reflects both the behavior and experiences of the people you study.

GUIDELINES FOR NONBIASED LANGUAGE IN APA JOURNALS

Over the years the issue of biased language in writing about individuals and groups has become an important consideration. For the past 30 years, the *Publication Manual of the American Psychological Association* has emphasized nonsexist language. Other task forces of the APA have developed guidelines in relation to sexual orientation, racial and ethnic identity, disability, and age. These can be viewed at the APA website (www.apa.org).

With the 5th edition of the *Publication Manual of the American Psychological Association,* work of the various task forces has been brought together in a single set of guidelines. These guidelines are designed to reduce ambiguity and bias in language in terms of gender, sexual orientation, racial and ethnic identity, disabilities, and age.

APA GUIDELINES TO REDUCE BIAS IN LANGUAGE

As a publisher, APA accepts authors' word choices unless those choices are inaccurate, unclear, or ungrammatical. As an organization, APA is committed both to science and to the fair treatment of individuals and groups, and this policy requires authors of APA publications to avoid perpetuating demeaning attitudes and biased assumptions about people in their writing. Constructions that might imply bias against persons on the basis of gender, sexual orientation, racial or ethnic group, disability, or age should be avoided. Scientific writing should be free of implied or irrelevant evaluation of the group or groups being studied.

Long-standing cultural practice can exert a powerful influence over even the most conscientious author. Just as you have learned to check what you write for spelling, grammar, and wordiness, practice reading over your work for bias. You can test your writing for implied evaluation by reading it while (a) substituting your own group for the group or groups you are discussing or (b) imagining you are a member of the group you are discussing (Maggio, 1991). If you feel excluded or offended, your material needs further revision. Another suggestion is to ask people from that group to read your material and give you candid feedback.

What follows is a set of guidelines, followed in turn by discussions of specific issues that affect particular groups. These are not rigid rules. You may find that some attempts to follow the guidelines result in wordiness or clumsy prose. As always, good judgment is required. If your writing reflects respect for your participants and your readers, and if you write with appropriate specificity and precision, you will be contributing to the goal of accurate, unbiased communication. Specific examples for each guideline are given in Table 2.1 on p. 399 at the end of this appendix.

■ Guideline 1: Describe at the Appropriate Level of Specificity

Precision is a necessity in scientific writing; when you refer to a person or persons, choose words that are accurate, clear, and free from bias. The appropriate degree of specificity depends on the research question and the present state of knowledge in the field of study. When in doubt, it is better to be more specific rather than less, because it is easier to aggregate published data than to disaggregate them. For example, using *man* to refer to all human beings is simply not as accurate as the phrase *men and women*. To describe age groups, it is better to give a specific age range ("ages 65–83") instead of a broad category ("over 65"; see Schaie, 1993). When describing racial and ethnic groups, be appropriately specific and sensitive to issues of labeling. For example, instead of describing participants as Asian American or Hispanic American, it may be helpful to describe them by their nation or region of origin (e.g., Chinese Americans, Mexican Americans). If you are discussing sexual orientation, realize that some people interpret *gay* as referring to men and women, whereas others interpret the term as including only men (for clarity, *gay men* and *lesbians* currently are preferred).

Broad clinical terms such as *borderline* and people *at risk* are loaded with innuendo unless properly explained. Specify the diagnosis that is borderline (e.g., "people with borderline personality disorder"). Identify the risk and the people it involves (e.g., "children at risk for early school dropout").

Gender is cultural and is the term to use when referring to men and women as social groups. *Sex* is biological; use it when the biological distinction is predominant. Note that the word *sex* can be confused with *sexual behavior*. *Gender* helps keep meaning unambiguous, as in the following example: "In accounting for attitudes toward the bill, sexual orientation rather than gender accounted for most of the variance. Most gay men and lesbians were for the proposal; most heterosexual men and women were against it."

Part of writing without bias is recognizing that differences should be mentioned only when relevant. Marital status, sexual orientation, racial and ethnic identity, or the fact that a person has a disability should not be mentioned gratuitously.

■ Guideline 2: Be Sensitive to Labels

Respect people's preferences; call people what they prefer to be called (Maggio, 1991). Accept that preferences will change with time and that individuals within groups often disagree about the designations they prefer (see Raspberry, 1989). Make an effort to determine what is appropriate for your situation; you may need to ask your participants which designations they prefer, particularly when preferred designations are being debated within groups.

Avoid labeling people when possible. A common occurrence in scientific writing is that participants in a study tend to lose their individuality; they are broadly categorized as objects (noun forms such as *the gays* and *the elderly*) or, particularly in descriptions of people with disabilities, are equated with their conditions—*the amnesiacs, the depressives, the schizophrenics, the LDs,* for example. One solution is to use adjectival forms (e.g., "gay *men*," "elderly *people*," "amnesic *patients*"). Another is to "put the person first," followed by a descriptive phrase (e.g., "people diagnosed with schizophrenia"). Note that the latter solution currently is preferred when describing people with disabilities.

When you need to mention several groups in a sentence or paragraph, such as when reporting results, do your best to balance sensitivity, clarity, and parsimony. For example, it may be cumbersome to repeat phrases such as "person with _____." If you provide operational definitions of groups early in your paper (e.g., "Participants scoring a minimum of X on the X scale constituted the high verbal group, and those scoring below X constituted the low verbal group"), it is scientifically informative and concise to describe participants thereafter in terms of the measures used to classify them (e.g., ". . . was significant: high verbal group, $p < .05$"), *provided the terms are inoffensive.* A label should not be used in any form that is perceived as pejorative; if such a perception is possible, you need to find more neutral terms. For example, *the demented* is not repaired by changing it to *demented group,* but *dementia group* would be acceptable. Abbreviations or series labels for groups usually sacrifice clarity and may offend: *LDs* or *LD group* to describe people with specific learning difficulties is offensive; *HVAs* for "high verbal ability group" is difficult to decipher. *Group A* is not offensive, but neither is it descriptive.

Recognize the difference between *case,* which is an occurrence of a disorder or illness, and *patient,* which is a person affected by the disorder or illness and receiving a doctor's care (Huth, 1987). "Manic-depressive cases were treated" is problematic; revise to "The patients with bipolar disorders were treated."

Bias may be promoted when the writer uses one group (usually the writer's own group) as the standard against which others are judged. In some contexts, the term *culturally deprived* may imply that one culture is the universally accepted standard. The unparallel nouns in the phrase *man and wife* may inappropriately prompt the reader to evaluate the roles of the individuals (i.e., the woman is defined only in terms of her relationship to the man) and the motives of the author. The phrase *husband and wife* or *man and woman* is parallel and undistracting. Usage of *normal* may prompt the reader to make the comparison of *abnormal,* thus stigmatizing individuals with differences. For example, contrasting lesbians with "the general public" or with "normal women" portrays lesbians as marginal to society. More appropriate comparison groups might be "heterosexual women," "heterosexual women and men," or "gay men."

■ Guideline 3: Acknowledge Participation

Write about the people in your study in a way that acknowledges their participation. Replace the impersonal term *subjects* with a more descriptive term when possible and appropriate—*participants, individuals, college students, children,* or *respondents,* for example. *Subjects* and *sample* are appropriate when discussing statistics, and *subjects* may also be appropriate when there has been no direct consent by the individual involved in the study (e.g., infants or some individuals with severe brain damage or dementia). The passive voice suggests individuals are *acted on* instead of being actors ("the students *completed* the survey" is preferable to "the students *were given* the survey" or "the survey was *administered* to the students"). "Participants completed the trial" or "we collected data from the participants" is preferable to "the participants *were run.*" Although not grammatically passive, "presented with symptoms" suggests passiveness; "reported symptoms" or "described symptoms" is preferred (Knatterud, 1991). Similarly, consider avoiding terms such as *patient management* and *patient placement* when appropriate. In most cases, it is treatment, not patients, that is managed; some alternatives are "coordination of care," "supportive services," and "assistance." If patients are able to discuss their living arrangements, describe them as such. *Failed,* as in "8 participants failed to complete the Rorschach and the MMPI," can imply a personal shortcoming instead of a research result; *did not* is a more neutral choice (Knatterud, 1991).

As you read the rest of this appendix, consult Table 2.1 on p. 399 for examples of problematic and preferred language. Section 9.03 lists references for further information about nondiscriminatory language and for the guidelines that the APA Publications and Communications Board received as working papers for the additions to this section; the full texts of these papers are available in updated form on an ongoing basis.

2.13 Gender   Avoid ambiguity in sex identity or sex role by choosing nouns, pronouns, and adjectives that specifically describe your participants. Sexist bias can occur when pronouns are used carelessly, as when the masculine pronoun *he* is used to refer to both sexes or when the masculine or feminine pronoun is used exclusively to define roles by sex (e.g., "the nurse . . . *she*"). The use of *man* as a generic noun or as an ending for an occupational title (e.g., *policeman*) can be ambiguous and may imply incorrectly that all persons in the group are male. Be clear about whether you mean one sex or both sexes.

To avoid stereotypes, use caution when providing examples:

> To illustrate this idea, **an American boy's** potential for becoming a football player might be an aggregate of strength, running speed, balance, fearlessness, and resistance to injury. [The manuscript was revised to *a child's.*]

There are many alternatives to the generic *he* (see Table 2.1), including rephrasing (e.g., from "When an individual conducts this kind of self-appraisal, *he* is a much stronger person" to "When an individual conducts this kind of self-appraisal, that person is much stronger" or "This kind of self-appraisal makes an individual much stronger"), using plural nouns or plural pronouns (e.g., from "A therapist who is too much like his client can lose *his* objectivity" to "Therapists who are too much like their clients can lose *their* objectivity"), replacing the pronoun with an article (e.g., from "A researcher must apply for *his* grant by September 1" to "A researcher must apply for *the* grant by September 1"), and dropping the pronoun (e.g., from "The researcher must avoid letting *his* own biases and expectations . . ." to "The researcher must avoid letting biases and expectations . . ."). Replacing *he* with *he or she* or *she or he* should be done sparingly because the repetition can become tiresome. Combination forms such as *he/she* or *(s)he* are awkward and distracting. Alternating between *he* and *she* also may be distracting and is not ideal; doing so implies that *he* or *she* can in fact be generic, which is not the case. Use of either pronoun unavoidably suggests that specific gender to the reader.

2.14 Sexual Orientation   *Sexual orientation* is not the same as *sexual preference.* In keeping with Guideline 2, *sexual orientation* currently is the preferred term and is to be used unless the implication of choice is intentional.

The terms *lesbians* and *gay men* are preferable to *homosexual* when referring to specific groups. *Lesbian* and *gay* refer primarily to identities and to the culture and communities that have developed among people who share those identities. Furthermore, *homosexuality* has been associated in the past with negative stereotypes. Also, the term *homosexual* is ambiguous because some believe it refers only to men. *Gay* can be interpreted broadly, to include men and women, or more narrowly, to include only men. Therefore, if the meaning is not clear in the context of your usage, specify gender when using this term (e.g., *gay men*). The clearest way to refer inclusively to people whose orientation is not heterosexual is to write *lesbians, gay men,* and *bisexual women or men*—although somewhat long, the phrase is accurate.

Sexual behavior should be distinguished from sexual orientation; some men and women engage in sexual activities with others of their own sex but do not consider themselves to be gay or lesbian. In contrast, the terms *heterosexual* and *bisexual* currently are used to describe both identity and behavior; adjectives are preferred to nouns. *Same-gender, male-male, female-female,* and *male-female sexual behavior* are appropriate terms for specific instances of sexual behavior in which people engage, regardless of their sexual orientation (e.g., a married heterosexual man who once had a same-gender sexual encounter).

2.15 Racial and Ethnic Identity   Preferences for terms referring to racial and ethnic groups change often. One reason for this is simply personal preference; preferred designations are as varied as the people they name. Another reason is that over time, designations can become dated and sometimes negative (see Raspberry, 1989). Authors are reminded of the two basic guidelines of specificity and sensitivity. In keeping with Guideline 2, authors are encouraged to ask their participants about preferred designations and are expected to avoid terms perceived as negative. For example, some people of African ancestry prefer *Black* and others prefer *African American;* both terms currently are acceptable. On the other hand, *Negro* and *Afro-American* have become dated; therefore, usage generally is inappropriate. In keeping with Guideline 1, precision is important in the description of your sample (see section 1.09); in general, use the more specific rather than the less specific term.

Racial and ethnic groups are designated by proper nouns and are capitalized. Therefore, use *Black* and *White* instead of *black* and *white* (colors to refer to other human groups currently are considered pejorative and should not be used). For modifiers, do not use hyphens in multiword names, even if the names act as unit modifiers (e.g., *Asian American* participants).

Designations for some ethnic groups are described next. These groups frequently are included in studies published in APA journals. The list is far from exhaustive but serves to illustrate some of the complexities of naming (see Table 2.1).

Depending on where a person is from, individuals may prefer to be called *Hispanic, Latino, Chicano,* or some other designation; *Hispanic* is not necessarily an all-encompassing term, and authors should consult with their participants. In general, naming a nation or region of origin is generally helpful (e.g., *Cuban* or *Central American* is more specific than *Hispanic*).

American Indian and *Native American* are both accepted terms for referring to indigenous peoples of North America, although *Native Americans* is a broader designation because the U.S. government includes Hawaiians and Samoans in this category. There are close to 450 Native groups, and authors are encouraged to name the participants' specific groups.

The term *Asian* or *Asian American* is preferred to the older term *Oriental.* It is generally useful to specify the name of the Asian subgroup: Chinese, Vietnamese, Korean, Pakistani, and so on.

2.16 Disabilities   The guiding principle for "nonhandicapping" language is to maintain the integrity of individuals as human beings. Avoid language that equates persons with their condition (e.g., *neurotics, the disabled*); that has superfluous, negative overtones (e.g., stroke *victim*); or that is regarded as a slur (e.g., *cripple*).

Use *disability* to refer to an attribute of a person and *handicap* to refer to the source of limitations, which may include attitudinal, legal, and architectural barriers as well as the disability itself (e.g., steps and curbs handicap people who require the use of a ramp). *Challenged* and *special* are often considered euphemistic and should be used only if the people in your study prefer those terms (Brown, 1992). As a general rule, "person with _____," "person living with _____," and "person who has _____" are neutral and preferred forms of description (see Table 2.1).

2.17 Age   Age should be defined in the description of participants in the Method section (see section 1.09). Be specific in providing age ranges; avoid open-ended definitions such as "under 18" or "over 65" (Schaie, 1993). *Boy* and *girl* are correct terms for referring to people of high school age and younger. *Young man* and *young woman* and *male adolescent* and *female adolescent* may be used as appropriate. For persons 18 and older (or of college age and older), use *men* and *women. Elderly* is not acceptable as a noun and is considered pejorative by some as an adjective. *Older person* is preferred. Age groups may also be described with adjectives; gerontologists may prefer to use combination terms for older age groups (*young-old, old-old, very old,* and *oldest old*), which should be used only as adjectives. *Dementia* is preferred to *senility; senile dementia of the Alzheimer's type* is an accepted term.

Table 2.1

Guidelines for Unbiased Language

Problematic	Preferred
Guideline 1: Use an appropriate level of specificity	
The client's behavior was typically female.	The client's behavior was [specify].
Comment: Being specific avoids stereotypic bias.	
Guideline 2: Be sensitive to labels	
Participants were 300 Orientals.	There were 300 Asian participants [perhaps adding "150 from Southeast Asia (Thailand, Laos, and Vietnam) and 150 from east Asia (North and South Korea)"].
Comment: Orientals is considered pejorative; use *Asian,* or be more specific.	
the elderly	older people
Comment: Use adjectives as adjectives instead of as nouns.	
girls and men	women and men
Comment: Use parallel terms; *girls* is correct if females of high school age or younger are meant.	
Guideline 3: Acknowledge participation	
Our study included 60 subjects.	Sixty people participated in our study.
Comment: Participants is preferred to *subjects.*	
	Gender
1. The client is usually the best judge of the value of his counseling.	The client is usually the best judge of the value of counseling.
	The client is usually the best judge of his or her counseling.
	Clients are usually the best judges of the value of the counseling they receive.
	The best judge of the value of counseling is usually the client.
2. man, mankind	people, humanity, human beings, humankind, human species
man a project	staff a project, hire personnel, employ staff
man-machine interface	user-system interface, person-system interface, human-computer interface

(continued)

Table 2.1

Guidelines for Unbiased Language (*continued*)	
Problematic	Preferred
manpower	workforce, personnel, workers, human resources
man's search for knowledge	the search for knowledge
3. males, females	men, women, boys, girls, adults, children, adolescents

Comment: Specific nouns reduce the possibility of stereotypic bias and often clarify discussion. Use *male* and *female* as adjectives where appropriate and relevant (*female experimenter, male participant*). *Males* and *females* may be appropriate when the age range is quite broad or ambiguous. Avoid unparallel usage such as 10 *men* and 16 *females.*

4. Research scientists often neglect their wives and children.	Research scientists often neglect their spouses and children.

Comment: Alternative wording acknowledges that women as well as men are research scientists.

5. woman doctor, lady lawyer, male nurse, woman driver	doctor or physician, lawyer, nurse, driver

Comment: Specify sex only if it is a variable or if sex designation is necessary to the discussion ("13 female doctors and 22 male doctors"). *Woman* and *lady* are nouns; *female* is the adjective counterpart to *male.*

6. mothering	parenting, nurturing [or specify exact behavior]
7. chairman (of an academic department)	chairperson, chair [use *chairman* only if it is known that the institution has established that form as an official title]

Comment: Department head may be appropriate; however, the term is not synonymous with *chair* and *chairperson* at all institutions.

chairman (presiding officer of a committee or meeting)	chairperson, chair, moderator, discussion leader

Comment: In parliamentary usage, *chairman* is the official term and should not be changed. Alternatives are acceptable in most writing.

8. foreman, mailman, salesmanship	supervisor or superintendent, postal worker or letter carrier, selling ability

Comment: Substitute preferred noun.

(*continued*)

Table 2.1

Guidelines for Unbiased Language (*continued*)

Problematic	Preferred
9. The authors acknowledge the assistance of Mrs. John Smith.	The authors acknowledge the assistance of Jane Smith.

Comment: Use given names.

10. cautious men and timid women	cautious women and men, cautious people
	timid men and women, timid people

Comment: Some adjectives, depending on whether the person described is a man or a woman, connote bias. The examples illustrate some common usages that may not always convey exact meaning, especially when paired, as in the first column.

11. Participants were 16 men and 4 women. The women were housewives.	The men were [specify], and the women were [specify].

Comment: Describe women and men in parallel terms, or omit description of both. Do not use *housewife* to identify occupation, a term that indicates sex and marital status and excludes men. Use *homemaker,* which can denote a man.

Sexual orientation

1. The sample consisted of 200 adolescent homosexuals.	The sample consisted of 200 gay male adolescents.
	The sample consisted of 100 gay male and 100 lesbian adolescents.

Comment: Avoid use of *homosexual,* and specify gender of participants.

2. Manuscript title: "Gay Relationships in the 1990s"	"Gay Male Relationships in the 1990s"
	"Lesbian and Gay Male Relationships in the 1990s"

Comment: Specify gender equitably.

3. Participants were asked about their homosexuality.	Participants were asked about the experience of being a lesbian or a gay man.

Comment: Avoid the label *homosexuality.*

4. The women reported lesbian sexual fantasies.	The women reported female-female sexual fantasies.

Comment: Avoid confusing lesbian orientation with specific sexual behaviors.

(*continued*)

Table 2.1

Guidelines for Unbiased Language (*continued*)

Problematic	Preferred
5. It was the participants' sex, not their sexual orientation, that affected number of friendships.	It was the participants' gender, not their sexual orientation, that affected number of friendships.

Comment: Avoid confusing gender with sexual activity.

6. participants who had engaged in sexual intercourse	participants who had engaged in penile-vaginal intercourse
	participants who had engaged in sexual intercourse or had sex with another person

Comment: The first preferred example specifies kind of sexual activity, if penile-vaginal intercourse is what is meant. The second avoids the assumption of heterosexual orientation if sexual experiences with others is what is meant.

7. Ten participants were married, and 5 were single.	Ten participants were married, 4 were unmarried and living with partners, and 1 was unmarried and living alone.

Comment: The preferred example increases specificity and acknowledges that legal marriage is only one form of committed relationship. Marital status is sometimes not a reliable indicator of cohabitation (e.g., married couples may be separated), sexual activity, or sexual orientation.

Racial and ethnic identity

1. The sample included 400 undergraduate participants.	The sample of 400 undergraduates included 250 White students (125 men and 125 women) and 150 Black students (75 men and 75 women).

Comment: Human samples should be fully described with respect to gender, age, and, when relevant to the study, race or ethnicity. Where appropriate, additional information should be presented (generation, linguistic background, socioeconomic status, national origin, sexual orientation, special interest group membership, etc.). Note that *African American* currently may be preferred.

2. The 50 American Indians represented. . . .	The 50 American Indians (25 Choctaw, 15 Hopi, and 10 Seminole) represented. . . .

Comment: When appropriate, authors should identify American Indian groups by specific group or nation; when the broader designation is appropriate, note that *Native American* may be preferred to *American Indian*. In general, American Indian, African, and other groups prefer *people* or *nation* to *tribe*.

(*continued*)

Table 2.1

Guidelines for Unbiased Language (*continued*)

Problematic	Preferred

3. We studied Eskimos. · We studied Inuit from Canada and Aleuts.

Comment: Native peoples of northern Canada, Alaska, eastern Siberia, and Greenland may prefer *Inuk* (*Inuit* for plural) to *Eskimo.* Alaska Natives include many groups in addition to Eskimos.

4. Table entries:

Race				Race			
White	21	15		White	21	15
Non-White	15	4		African American	10	1
				Asian	5	3

Comment: Non-White implies a standard of comparison and is imprecise.

5. the articulate Mexican American professor · the Mexican American professor

Comment: Qualifying adjectives may imply that the "articulate" Mexican American professor is an exception to the norm (for Mexican American professors). Depending on the context of the sentence, ethnic identity may not be relevant and therefore should not be mentioned.

Disabilities

1. *Put people first, not their disability*

disabled person	person with (who has) a disability
defective child	child with a congenital disability
	child with a birth impairment
mentally ill person	person with mental illness

Comment: Preferred expressions avoid the implication that the person as a whole is disabled.

2. *Do not label people by their disability or overextend its severity*

depressives	people who are depressed
epileptics	individuals with epilepsy
borderlines	people diagnosed with borderline personality disorder
neurotic patients	patients with a neurosis (or neuroses)
the learning disabled	children with [specify the learning characteristics]
retarded adult	adult with mental retardation

Comment: Because the person is *not* the disability, the two concepts should be separate.

(continued)

Table 2.1

Guidelines for Unbiased Language (*continued*)	
Problematic	Preferred
3. *Use emotionally neutral expressions*	
stroke victim	individual who had a stroke
person afflicted with cerebral palsy	person with cerebral palsy
population suffering from multiple sclerosis	people who have multiple sclerosis
individual confined to a wheelchair	individual who uses a wheelchair

Comment: Problematic expressions have excessive, negative overtones and suggest continued helplessness.

PRINTED ARTICLE

Child Development, November/December 2004, Volume 75, Number 6, Pages 1761–1773

Comparison of Sadness, Anger, and Fear Facial Expressions When Toddlers Look at Their Mothers

Kristin A. Buss and Elizabeth J. Kiel

Research suggests that sadness expressions may be more beneficial to children than other emotions when eliciting support from caregivers. It is unclear, however, when children develop the ability to regulate their displays of distress. The current study addressed this question. Distress facial expressions (e.g., fear, anger, and sadness) were examined in 24-month-old toddlers throughout 4 episodes as well as specifically during looks to their mothers. Consistent with hypotheses and the literature, toddlers expressed sadness more frequently and with more intensity than target emotions only during looks to their mothers. These findings indicate that toddlers as young as 24 months of age are using particular emotional displays to elicit support from the social environment.

Much research has explored young children's facial expressions and their abilities to modulate them. Research has shown that children's abilities to regulate and modulate their emotional expressions improve with age (e.g., Buss & Goldsmith, 1998; Fuchs & Thelen, 1988; Garber & Dodge, 1991; Saarni, 1979) but has not fully examined the early development and implications of developing skills. Toddlers, in particular, remain understudied.

The current study addressed this gap in the study of emotional expression. We aimed to demonstrate that toddlers display facial expressions of sadness more often than other distress facial expressions when looking at their mothers and that these expressions facilitate the communication of the need for support from their caregivers. Although we know of few studies specifically addressing to this question, the literatures on emotion regulation, the functionalist approach to emotion expressions, and

the socialization of facial expressions provide the rationale for the current study and are reviewed.

Emotion Regulation and the Function of Emotional Expression

Emotion regulation in general reflects "changes associated with activated emotions" (Cole, Martin, & Dennis, 2004) and more specifically reflects processes that facilitate reduction of distress, whether initiated by the individual (i.e., intrinsic) or by others (i.e., extrinsic) (Thompson, 1994). Young children rely on their mothers to assist in the regulation of their emotions before they acquire the skills to do so on their own; infants maintain emotional and physiological homeostasis after arousal by being comforted by their mothers (Hofer, 1994). To facilitate this extrinsic regulation in ambiguous or fear-eliciting situations, infants engage in behaviors that signal distress (e.g., crying) or requests for help (e.g., looks to mother), or both. The social referencing literature provides extensive evidence that infants look to their mothers for help and in turn modulate their behavior depending on their mothers' responses, in most cases displaying less distress (e.g., Buss & Goldsmith, 1998; Grolnick, Bridges, & Connell, 1996; Mangelsdorf, Shapiro, & Marzolf, 1995; Moses, Baldwin, Rosicky, & Tidball, 2001; Rothbart, Ziaie, & O'Boyle, 1992; Stifter & Braungart, 1995). Campos Mumme, Kermoian, and Campos (1994) argued that a child's change in facial expression connotes emotion regulation. The functionalist understanding of emotion expressions espouses a similar appraisal.

An important aspect of the functionalist approach to emotion is that facial expressions facilitate the

Kristin A. Buss and Elizabeth J. Kiel, Department of Psychological Sciences, University of Missouri-Columbia.

The project from which these data were derived was supported, in part, by three grants from the National Institute of Mental Health: the first to H. Hill Goldsmith (R01-MH50560), the Wisconsin Center for Affective Sciences (Richard Davidson, P50 MH52354), and a National Research Service Award to the first author (F31-MH11747). The second author was supported by a Huggins Graduate Fellowship from the University of Missouri-Columbia. Portions of this project were presented at the 2003 Society for Research in Child Development meeting. We extend special thanks to Kathryn Stern-Holmes, Paty Perez, Suzanne Welch, and Amy Hopper. We express our appreciation to the families and toddlers who participated in this project.

Correspondence concerning this article should be addressed to Kristin A. Buss, Department of Psychological Sciences, University of Missouri-Columbia, 210 McAlester Hall, Columbia, Missouri 65211. Electronic mail may be sent to bussk@missouri.edu.

individual's relational goals (e.g., increase closeness with caregivers) as well as signify the individual's internal state in the social environment (Campos et al., 1994). Specifically, distress expressions can elicit beneficial responses (Hortsmann, 2003; Huebner & Izard, 1988; Zeman & Garber, 1996), serving communication, attachment, and the evocation of helpful responses from the caregiver (Malatesta, Culver, Tesman, & Shepard, 1989). Thus, negative facial expressions serve instrumental purposes in a child's social world.

Differential emotions theory (Izard, 1977, 1991) suggests that each distress emotion has a distinct adaptive social function and elicits particular reactions from a social partner. Anger expressions, for example, tell another to withdraw or leave. Caregivers tend to respond to these expressions with discipline and feelings of annoyance or anger (Huebner & Izard, 1988). Fear expressions can communicate the cessation of activity, retreat, or help (Hortsmann, 2003), although there have been few studies of this sort examining fear expressions. Finally, sadness expressions convey requests for help, comfort, or support from significant social partners (Hortsmann, 2003; Shipman, Zeman, Nesin, & Fitzgerald, 2003) and evoke interaction (Huebner & Izard, 1988).

Particularly relevant to the current study are findings that sadness expressions seemed to be the least aversive and induced the most positive responses of support (Hortsmann, 2003; Huebner & Izard, 1988; Shipman et al., 2003). Huebner and Izard (1988) underscored the significance of mothers' differential responding to specific affective expressions: Even without vocal cues, sadness and anger facial expressions evoked specific reactions from caregivers. For example, sadness expressions elicited more talk, play, and interact responses than anger expressions. This research motivated the current study because it demonstrated that infants expressed sadness instead of the more typically elicited distress expression of anger. However, the question of whether infants express more sadness than fear expressions toward caregivers in fear-eliciting situations remains unanswered.

Socialization and Development of Emotion Regulation

Infants are thought to be unable to modulate their facial expressions intentionally because the minute muscle movements involved in these expressions are tightly linked to the physiological experience of emotions (Izard et al., 1995; Malatesta et al., 1989). Although most research suggests that children must have an explicit awareness of internal emotions to modulate affective expressions (e.g., Saarni, 1979), some may suggest otherwise. Preschoolers can express positive facial expressions to an experimenter when given an unwanted prize, even when other behaviors indicate they feel disappointed (Cole, 1986). These preschoolers, however, did not verbalize awareness of this response, indicating that the ability to modulate facial expressions develops before their ability to understand this response. Research in infants' expressions of pain indicated that infants between 3 and 18 months decreased their expressions of pain and increased their expressions of other negative emotions, such as sadness, after inoculations (Axia & Bonichini, 1998). Although infants' expressions may have reflected changes in their actual feelings, it is more parsimonious to conclude that the expression of sadness in this study served a relational goal. In other studies, mothers responded with more warmth and support to sadness expressions (Huebner & Izard, 1988), and mothers showed patterns of responding more contingently to sadness expressions, which connote better regulation (Huebner & Izard, 1988; Zeman & Shipman, 1998). It is more functional for an infant to display an expression that elicits support than to display an expression that evokes a negative reaction or nonreaction. Note, however, that research has not addressed what type of affective response a pain reaction would elicit.

Children learn to modulate their expressions through face-to-face interactions with their mothers, who reinforce certain expressions (e.g., positive expressions and specific distress expressions) with contingent responding (Huebner & Izard, 1988; Malatesta, Grigoryev, Lamb, Albin, & Culver, 1986; Malatesta & Haviland, 1982; Malatesta et al., 1986; Saarni, 1979; Zeman & Penza, 1997). Specifically, mothers start to socialize against anger expressions at a very early age by reacting negatively to them or completely ignoring them (Malatesta et al., 1986). Mothers do, alternatively, reinforce sadness expressions, which seem to reflect better regulation by the child (Huebner & Izard, 1988; Zeman & Shipman, 1998), as early as between 3 and 6 months (Malatesta & Haviland, 1982).

Current Study

Although past research has addressed infants' beginning facial affect modulation and the way preschool children display this skill, there is little work on the intervening period. The goal of the current study was to ask whether 24-month-old toddlers modulate their facial displays with their mothers. In addition, many earlier studies examined expressions of anger and sadness, though few studies addressed the expression of fear. This study examined the pattern of facial expressions (sadness, anger, and fear expressions) occurring in response to frustrating and threatening situations. Direct observation of these facial expressions revealed whether toddlers modulated their expressions when looking at their mothers and, specifically, whether they did so in the previously reported pattern of displaying sadness rather than the putative target emotion.

We addressed four questions in this study. First, what was the predominant distress expression in each episode? Each episode was designed to elicit a target emotion (fear or anger); therefore, we sought to confirm the presence of these emotions. Second, did toddlers express sadness more than the target emotion when looking at their mothers? Third, did the expression of sadness increase in frequency and intensity during looks to mother? Fourth, did the expression of sadness occur more when toddlers looked at their mothers than when they were not looking at their mothers? Across analyses, we predicted that sadness expressions would be more common than the target expression when toddlers looked to their mothers. Moreover, we predicted that sadness expressions would be more common during a look than when toddlers were not looking at their mother.

Method

Participants

Participants were 71 twenty-four-month-old children (35 female) recruited from local public birth records. Visits were scheduled within 1 month of the second birthday ($M = 24.50$, $SD = .40$, range = 23.03 to 25.57). Participants and families were not selected for any behavior or characteristic. Most of the participants were Caucasian (96%) and were from intact, middle-class families (Hollingshead index = 48.66).

Procedure

As part of a larger project, the children participated in a laboratory visit consisting of a series of modified Preschool Laboratory Temperament Assessment Battery (Lab–TAB) episodes (Goldsmith, Reilly, Lemery, Longley, & Prescott, 1994). For the current study, we concentrated on two threat contexts to elicit fear and two frustration contexts to elicit anger modified for use with children under 3 years (Buss & Goldsmith, 2000). Distress episodes were always separated by a positive or neutral episode. The order of episodes was the same for all children with one exception. The two stranger approach episodes were counterbalanced across children. All episodes were videotaped through one-way glass or a remote-controlled camera mounted near the ceiling in the corner of the room.

Threat episodes. For both stranger approach contexts, a male stranger entered the room and paused at least 8 ft away from the child; following a 10-s pause, he slowly approached the child, knelt down, and looked at the child without speaking for up to 2 min. The experimenter terminated the episode if the child became too distressed (i.e., crying for 20 s without calming) or upon request of the mother. The two contexts differed only in the restraint that was placed on the child's behavior. In the first approach (Stranger Highchair), the child finished a snack while sitting in a highchair. This episode was designed to limit the availability of coping behaviors such as escape. In the second approach (Stranger Free Play), the child played with a few toys on the floor, a context that allowed the child to escape. In both contexts, the mother was present, seated in the corner of the room about 6 ft from the highchair, but the experimenter instructed her not to interact with her child.

Frustration episodes. We observed children during two frustration tasks, Toy Removal and Toy in Locked Box. In both tasks, the child was seated at a child-sized table and the mother was positioned to the left of the child (about 4 ft away). The Toy Removal task was designed to evoke frustration directed at the mother. In this task, the experimenter demonstrated how to play with a toy and encouraged the child to play with it for a brief period. The mother, as previously instructed by the experimenter, removed the toy, stating she did not like it and did not want the child to play with it anymore. The removal lasted for 30 s, after which the mother stated she changed her mind and returned the toy to the child. The Toy in Locked Box task was designed to elicit frustration by hindering the child from playing with a toy within view. The experimenter showed the child a toy locked inside a transparent box but then gave the wrong keys to the child before leaving the room. The child was thus unable to attain the toy. After 2 min, the experimenter returned and stated she mistakenly gave the child the wrong keys. She then gave the child the correct key, and the child was allowed to play with the toy.

1764   Buss and Kiel

Looks and Affect Scoring

Facial affect was scored for maximum intensity every 10 s for the duration of each episode. After the initial scoring, we rescored facial affect occurring with a look to mother. All coders were blind to the study hypotheses and trained by the first author. Three trained coders recorded each time the child looked at the mother within each of the episodes. Looks to mother must have lasted more than 1 s to be coded; all shorter looks to mother were considered "checking in" and were not scored for distress expressions. The coders recorded the times of the looks to mother and constructed three segments: the 3 s before the looks to mother, the duration of the looks to mother, and the 3 s after the looks to mother. We used 3 s before and after the looks to mother because this matched the average duration of the looks to mother. Looks to mother ranged in duration from 2 to 9 s for each episode (Toy in Locked Box: $M = 2.35$, $SD = .95$; Toy Removal: $M = 2.89$, $SD = 1.94$; Stranger Highchair: $M = 2.36$, $SD = 1.35$; Stranger Free Play: $M = 2.79$, $SD = 2.77$).

After identifying the looks to mother, two new coders made a second pass to score facial expressions (as well as served for agreement on number of looks); they scored the presence and maximum intensity of anger, fear, sadness, and pleasure expressions for each segment. Note that each of the four emotions was scored for maximum intensity rather than choosing one emotion over the others. However, looks to mother with a pleasure expression were coded less than 1% of the time and therefore were not considered further. Intensity of facial affect was scored on a 4-point scale (spanning 0 to 3) using the AFFEX coding system (Izard, Dougherty, & Hembree, 1983). The definitions for the intensities were as follows: 0 = expression not present; 1 = expression barely present or fleeting typically reflected in only one facial region; 2 = clear expression, present in one facial region strongly or in more than one facial region; and 3 = clear and strong expression, present in at least two facial regions. Coders recorded the maximum intensity of each expression. Distress facial expressions were differentiated from each other by examining changes in the brows and eyes, cheeks, and mouth in the following ways. Anger was scored when brows were pulled in and down, eye lids tensed, and eyes narrowed. Anger in the mouth involved an open and squared mouth or lips pressed tightly and tensed. Sadness was scored when brows were pulled in and up, and eyes drooped at outside corners. A sad mouth was scored when corners were pulled down and lower lip re-

sulted in a pout. It is important to note that sadness was not scored if the child was crying or about to cry because the cry or precry mouth often resembles sadness. Fear was scored when brows were raised but not pulled together, lids were raised, and eyes were widened. Fear in the mouth was scored when lips were pulled back straight, often pulling cheeks back but neither up nor down. Reliabilities on type and intensity of affect for each episode were very good with agreement among raters scoring separately ranging from 83% to 96% and kappas ranging from .73 to .81. Recall that during the second pass of coding the presence of looks to mother was rescored and agreement for identification of looks to mother was 97%.

There were missing data for three of the four episodes. For the Stranger Highchair episode, 6 participants were not scored: 2 because mothers refused the episode, 1 because child refused to get into the highchair, and 3 because of equipment failure. Six participants also were not scored in the Stranger Free Play episode: 3 because the episode was not done, 2 because the child refused the episode, and 1 because the mother refused the episode. For analyses of the Toy in Locked Box episode, 1 child was not scored because of a poor tape. Thus, Stranger Highchair, Stranger Free Play, Toy in Locked Box, and Toy Removal had 65, 68, 70, and 71 participants, respectively.

Results

The frequency counts and descriptive statistics for facial affect and the looks to mother across each task are presented in Table 1. Note the discrepancy between total number of looks to mother and the number of looks to mother that were coded for facial affect. There were a number of looks to mother that were not coded because the face was not visible; therefore, these were not considered further. We tested for main effects of gender and found only one significant difference. Boys had a higher frequency of looks to mother with sadness facial expression ($M = 1.15$, $SD = .20$) than girls ($M = .55$, $SD = .15$) in the Toy Removal task, $t(64) = -2.42$, $p < .05$.

Comparison of Facial Expressions of Sadness and the Target Emotion

We conducted two sets of analyses comparing sadness to the target emotion (fear or anger depending on the episode). First, we compared sadness expressions to the target expression for the entire

Table 1
Mean (SE) Frequency and Intensity of Facial Affect and Number of Looks to Mother by Episode

	Stranger Highchair (*n* = 67)	Stranger Free Play (*n* = 68)	Toy Removal (*n* = 71)	Toy in Locked Box (*n* = 70)
Frequency target[a]	10.10 (0.89)	2.16 (0.31)	1.37 (0.54)	2.76 (0.31)
Frequency sadness	4.50 (0.87)	4.40 (0.57)	0.54 (0.12)	4.07 (0.44)
Intensity target[a]	0.74 (0.08)	.23 (0.04)	1.02 (0.12)	0.15 (0.02)
Intensity sadness	0.31 (0.05)	0.60 (0.05)	0.71 (0.08)	0.17 (0.03)
Total looks	351	216	173	385
Total coded looks[b]	330	171	158	359
No looks[c]	6	6	2	2
Mean no. of looks	5.13 (3.61)	3.04 (2.03)	2.54 (1.47)	5.17 (2.78)

[a]Target emotion was fear for Stranger Highchair and Stranger Free Play. Target emotion was anger for Toy Removal and Toy in Locked Box.
[b]Represents the number of looks where facial affect was coded.
[c]Represents the number of children who did not look to their mother during the episode.

episode (Table 1). Second, we compared sadness expressions to the target expression during looks to mother (Tables 2 and 3). For each set of analyses we examined data independently for each episode, observing both the frequency of expression and the intensity of the expression for each individual. Recall that an intensity score of 1 reflected a slight or fleeting expression. To be conservative in our determination of the presence of facial expressions for the frequency analyses, we counted only expressions that were intensities of 2 and 3. Frequency counts represent the total number of looks to mother associated with each affect expression for each participant. Likewise, for the intensity analyses we examined the whole scale of intensity of affect (0–3) for each child by creating a mean intensity score across each child's looks to mother. For all analyses we used repeated measures analysis of variance (ANOVA) or multivariate analysis of variance (MANOVA) to compare fear to sadness for the threat episodes and anger to sadness for the frustration episodes. We examined our frequency and intensity data for the presence of outliers and found no evidence; thus, we were confident that our results were not biased by extremes on frequency or intensity.

Comparisons of expressions across the entire episode. Recall that each episode was designed to elicit a target emotion (Buss & Goldsmith, 2000). The two stranger episodes were designed to elicit fear and the toy removal episodes were designed to elicit anger. We tested whether this was the case by examining the frequency and intensity of discrete facial expressions across the episodes, without considering looks to mother. We then compared the presence of the target versus sadness for all episodes. We counted the total number of fear and sadness facial

expressions across the stranger approach episodes (see means in Table 1). The facial expressions occurring during a look to mother were not counted for these analyses. For Stranger Highchair, fear facial expressions were approximately twice as frequent as facial expressions of sadness, $F(1, 59) = 24.46$, $p < .001$. The intensity of facial fear was also higher than the intensity of facial sadness during Stranger Highchair, $F(1, 60) = 32.83$, $p < .001$. In contrast, the opposite pattern emerged in Stranger Free Play. Fear facial expressions were observed half as often as sadness facial expressions, $F(1, 67) = 13.89$, $p < .001$. Finally, the intensity of sadness expressions was higher than the intensity of fear expressions, $F(1, 64) = 28.58$, $p < .001$. Note that although the frequency of sadness expressions remained the same across the two episodes, the frequency of fear was lower in the Free Play episode. Overall, this episode elicited less distress.

In Toy Removal, anger facial expressions were nearly 3 times more frequent than sadness facial expressions, $F(1, 69) = 14.68$, $p < .001$. The intensity of anger expression was also higher than the intensity of sadness expression during Toy Removal, $F(1, 69) = 6.99$, $p < .01$. In contrast, for Toy in Locked Box, sadness facial expressions were more frequent than anger facial expressions, $F(1, 69) = 5.32$, $p < .05$. There was not a significant difference in intensity between anger expressions and sadness expressions during the Toy in Locked Box episode.

Comparison of expressions during looks to mother. We examined whether sadness facial expressions were more common than either fear or anger facial expressions during a look (averaging across the before, during, and after segments). In follow-up analyses, we examined the data within each look segment

1766   Buss and Kiel

Table 2
Mean (SE) Frequency of Facial Expressions by Episode

| | Segments of looks to mother | | | | | |
	Before	During	After	F	η^2	Across segments
Stranger Highchair ($n = 65$)						
Sadness	0.43 (.15)	0.71 (.19)$_a$	0.72 (.20)$_a$	0.94	.02	0.78 (.20)$_a$
Fear	0.23 (.13)	0.10 (.08)$_b$	0.16 (.11)$_b$	00.31	.01	0.25 (.16)$_b$
Stranger Free Play ($n = 68$)						
Sadness	0.05 (.04)	0.05 (.03)	0.09 (.05)	0.84	.02	0.12 (.06)
Fear	0.02 (.02)	0.02 (.02)	0.02 (.02)	0.29	.00	0.02 (.02)
Toy Removal ($n = 70$)						
Sadness	0.53 (.11)$_a$	0.71 (.11)$_a$	0.63 (.12)$_a$	9.71***	.13	0.88 (.13)$_a$
Anger	0.18 (.06)$_b$	0.16 (.06)$_b$	0.15 (.06)$_b$	0.75	.01	0.28 (.08)$_b$
Toy in Locked Box ($n = 71$)						
Sadness	0.07 (.06)	0.05 (.03)	0.06 (.05)	3.69*	.05	0.12 (.08)
Anger	0.09 (.04)	0.10 (.04)	0.07 (.04)	1.75	.02	0.18 (.07)

Note. Numbers in parentheses are standard errors. Means in columns comparing sadness and fear and anger within each episode that do not share subscripts differ at $p < .01$ (with Bonferroni correction). F statistics represent the tests of differences among the discrete look segments. η^2 = effect size.
*$p < .05$. ***$p < .001$.

Table 3
Mean (SE) Intensity of Facial Expressions by Episode

| | Segments of looks to mother | | | | | |
	Before	During	After	F	η^2	Across segments
Stranger Highchair ($n = 65$)						
Sadness	0.33 (.07)$_a$	0.45 (.09)$_a$	0.40 (.08)$_a$	9.36***	.05	0.39 (.08)$_a$
Fear	0.16 (.04)$_b$	0.19 (.04)$_b$	0.15 (.05)$_b$	2.43†	.03	0.17 (.04)$_b$
Stranger Free Play ($n = 68$)						
Sadness	0.11 (.04)	0.16 (.05)	0.13 (.05)	1.14	.02	0.13 (.04)
Fear	0.11 (.05)	0.18 (.07)	0.10 (.04)	0.64	.01	0.15 (.05)
Toy Removal ($n = 70$)						
Sadness	0.78 (.09)$_a$	1.01 (.11)$_a$	0.98 (.11)$_a$	4.69*	.13	0.94 (.10)$_a$
Anger	0.28 (.07)$_b$	0.37 (.07)$_b$	0.32 (.07)$_b$	3.04†	.02	0.32 (.07)$_b$
Toy in Locked Box ($n = 71$)						
Sadness	0.10 (.02)	0.11 (.03)	0.07 (.03)	3.89*	.04	0.09 (.02)
Anger	0.13 (.03)	0.11 (.04)	0.09 (.02)	2.17	.01	0.12 (.03)

Note. Numbers in parentheses are standard errors. Means in columns comparing sadness and fear and anger within each episode that do not share subscripts differ at $p < .01$ (with Bonferroni correction). F statistics represent the tests of differences among the discrete look segments. η^2 = effect size.
$^\dagger p < .10$. *$p < .05$. ***$p < .001$.

independently. We conducted four planned comparisons of sadness versus the target emotion for each episode. To reduce the likelihood of Type I error, we used a Bonferroni correction to adjust familywise error. All p values reflect this correction. Results were largely consistent with our predictions.

Analyses conducted with frequencies are presented in Table 2. During Stranger Highchair, expressions of sadness were 3 times as frequent as expressions of fear during a look (i.e., averaging across the look segments), $F(1, 60) = 8.92$, $p < .05$ (Table 2, last column). This pattern of sadness greater than fear was evident during the look, $F(1, 60) = 12.91$, $p < .01$, and after the look, $F(1, 60) = 10.06$, $p < .05$ (Table 2, first three columns). The difference between sadness and fear was not significant before the look. Analyses of the intensity of expressions were consistent with the frequency analyses (Table 3). Expressions of sadness were twice as intense as expressions of fear during the look, $F(1, 60) = 7.57$, $p < .01$ (Table 3, last column). This pattern of higher intensities of sadness expressions than fear expressions was consistent across the three segments of the look: before, $F(1, 60) = 4.68$, $p < .05$; during, $F(1, 60) = 8.28$, $p < .01$; and after, $F(1, 60) = 8.53$, $p < .01$ (Table 3, first three columns). During Stranger Free Play, expressions of sadness were not statistically more frequent than expressions of fear after Bonferroni correction and there were no differences in intensity between sadness and fear expressions (see Tables 2 and 3, respectively).

During Toy Removal, sadness expressions were nearly three times as frequent as anger expressions during a look, $F(1, 67) = 18.35$, $p < .001$ (Table 2, last column). Sadness expressions were more frequent than anger expressions before the look, $F(1, 66) = 13.78$, $p < .01$; during the look, $F(1, 67) = 24.58$, $p < .001$; and after the look, $F(1, 67) = 18.83$, $p < .001$ (Table 2, first three columns). The analyses comparing the frequencies of sadness and anger were conducted separately by gender. Recall that across the episode boys had higher frequencies of sadness expressions than girls during Toy Removal. Therefore, we conducted these analyses separately for boys and girls. The frequency of sadness expressions ($M = 1.20$, $SE = .20$) was higher than the frequency of anger expressions ($M = .29$, $SE = .11$) for boys, $F(1, 32) = 18.17$, $p < .0001$. Although not statistically significant, the frequency of sadness expressions ($M = .55$, $SE = .15$) was higher than the frequency of anger expressions ($M = .27$, $SE = .10$) for girls, $F(1, 32) = 2.75$, $p = .11$. Analyses of the intensity of expressions were consistent with the frequency analyses. Expressions of sadness were more than twice as intense as expressions of anger during the look, $F(1, 66) = 41.38$, $p < .001$ (Table 3, last column). Again, this pattern of higher intensities of sadness expressions than anger expressions was consistent across the three segments of the look: before, $F(1, 66) = 31.34$, $p < .001$; during, $F(1, 66) = 30.68$, $p < .001$; and after, $F(1, 60) = 41.73$, $p < .001$ (Table 3, first three columns). Finally, the frequencies and intensities of sadness versus anger expressions for Toy in Locked Box were not significantly different (Tables 2 and 3, respectively).

Change in Affect Across Segments of Look

Does the frequency and intensity of sadness increase when toddlers look at their mothers? We examined the changes in frequencies of sadness expressions and the target emotion expressions across the three segments of the look: before, during, and after. Visual examination of these results is available in Figures 1 and 2 and test statistics are presented in Tables 2 and 3. We used repeated measures MANOVA and entered both sadness and the target emotion into the analyses to observe change in one emotion while controlling for change in the other emotion. In Stranger Highchair, we failed to observe a significant change in the frequency of sadness or fear expressions (Table 2, fourth column). We also conducted these analyses with the intensity of the affect expressions (Table 3, fourth column). There was a significant difference across the segments in the intensity of sadness. The intensity of sadness expression increased from before the look to during the look and remained higher after the look. The intensity of fear differed across the segments as well. The intensity of fear expression increased from before the look to during the look, then decreased after the look. We observed no significant changes in frequency of sadness expressions or fear expressions across the look segments in Stranger Free Play. Finally, change in the intensity of sadness during Stranger Free Play approached significance ($p < .10$), and there was no significant change in fear intensity across the look segments.

Turning to the frustration tasks, we observed significant changes in the frequency of sadness expressions for Toy Removal (Table 2). The frequency of sadness expressions increased from before to during the look and then decreased from during to after the look. However, the frequency of anger expressions did not change across the look segments. There was also a significant difference across the segments in the intensity of sadness and, although significant, less so for anger (Table 3). The intensity of sadness increased from before the look to during the look and remained higher after the look. We found a similar pattern with sadness during Toy in Locked Box. We observed significant changes in the frequency of sadness expressions for Toy in Locked Box. Finally, the intensity of sadness increased from before to during the look, then decreased after the look, whereas there was no significant change in anger intensity across the look segments.

Comparison of Affect Expressions When Looking and Not Looking to Mother

In a final comparison, we examined whether expressions of sadness (or the target emotion) were more common during a look to mother than when not looking at mother. The raw frequency counts could not be used for these analyses because the total

Figure 1. Frequency of sadness versus fear facial expressions in Stranger Highchair (top panel) and Stranger Free Play (bottom panel).

time spent looking at mother was significantly less than the total time spent not looking at mother. Therefore, we created proportion scores to control for this difference. For each episode, we compared sadness expressions during looks to mother to sadness expressions not during a look using repeated measures ANOVA. We repeated these analyses for the target expression as well. Results confirmed our predictions. For Stranger Highchair, sadness was more common during a look to mother than not during a look to mother, $F(1, 57) = 12.75$, $p < .001$. During a look to mother sadness occurred 14% ($M = 14.39$, $SD = 3.49$) of the time compared with only 4% ($M = 4.31$, $SD = 1.48$) of the time when the toddler was not looking at mother. The general pattern was reversed with fear occurring more when the toddler was not looking at the mother, although not

significantly different. There were no differences between looks and nonlooks for either sadness or fear during Stranger Free Play. In Toy Removal, sadness was more common during a look to mother than not during a look to mother, $F(1, 67) = 49.68$, $p < .0001$. During a look sadness occurred 39% ($M = 39.09$, $SD = 5.43$) of the time compared with only 2% ($M = 1.86$, $SD = .40$) of the time when the toddler was not looking at mother. The pattern for anger was the same with 13% ($M = 12.79$, $SD = 3.51$) of looks to mother and 5% ($M = 4.46$, $SD = .67$) of nonlooks to mother containing an anger expression, $F(1, 67) = 6.71$, $p < .05$. Finally, for Toy in Locked Box, the pattern of results was in the opposite direction for sadness, $F(1, 67) = 41.55$, $p < .001$, and anger, $F(1, 67) = 10.53$, $p < .01$, with expressions occurring more when the toddler was not looking at mother (sadness

Figure 2. Frequency of sadness versus anger facial expressions in Toy Removal (top panel) and Toy in Locked Box (bottom panel).

during look: $M = 1.91$, $SD = 1.10$; sadness during episode: $M = 13.97$, $SD = 1.49$; anger during look: $M = 3.71$, $SD = 1.42$; anger during episode: $M = 9.12$, $SD = 1.04$).

Follow-up Analyses

There were two possible explanations for the current pattern of findings (i.e., sadness > target) that needed to be addressed statistically. First, because sadness expressions can be associated with or mistaken for precrying and crying, it was possible that the increased frequency of sadness was due to crying. Although coders were instructed not to code a sadness expression if the infant was crying, we tested this assumption directly. There were few

toddlers who cried in each episode ($n = 6$ for Stranger Highchair, $n = 3$ for Stranger Free Play, $n = 6$ for Toy Removal). No toddlers cried during Toy in Locked Box. We compared toddlers who cried (criers) with toddlers who did not cry (noncriers) on the presence of sadness and the target emotion for each episode individually. For the two stranger approach episodes, sadness and fear were not significantly different for criers versus noncriers; in fact, there was a trend for noncriers to show more distress. In contrast, sadness and anger were more common in criers versus noncriers during Toy Removal; therefore, we performed all previous analyses without the criers. All the effects remained significant ($ps < .001$), such that sadness was more common than anger during a look to mother, and sadness increased across the segments of the look to mother. Therefore, we were confident that crying did not affect the pattern of results.

A second possible explanation for the pattern of findings was that toddlers' sadness increased with repeated looks to mother because the mothers were told not to respond. We tested this assumption by analyzing only facial expressions during the first look to mother for Stranger Highchair and Toy Removal. Comparison of the sadness to the target emotion during looks to mother remained significant and in the same direction for Toy Removal ($ps < .001$) but failed to reach significance for Stranger Highchair. That is, sadness expressions were higher than anger expressions, but there was no difference between sadness expressions and fear expressions. In the analyses of sadness across the segments of the looks to mother, results were unchanged for both Stranger Highchair ($p < .05$) and Toy Removal ($p < .001$). Sadness expressions increased across the segments of the look to mother, but the target emotion did not. Again, we were confident that the results were not primarily the result of repeated looks to mother.

Discussion

We investigated whether 24-month-olds were able to modulate their distress facial expressions when looking at their mothers. In particular, we tested whether sadness facial expressions were more likely to occur despite contextual pressure for anger or fear expressions to be predominant. Results largely supported our predictions.

Evidence for Sadness Expressions During Looks to Mother

We demonstrated that toddlers were more likely to display sadness expressions than either anger or fear expressions (i.e., the target expressions) during looks to their mothers and that these expressions of sadness were more intense than expressions of anger or fear under the same circumstances. These results were most pronounced for the Stranger Highchair and Toy Removal episodes and were consistent across the segments of the look (before, during, and after). We also conducted analyses to determine whether facial expressions of sadness increased from before to during the look to mother. Again, we examined both the frequency and intensity of sadness, fear, and anger across the different segments of the look (before, during, and after). Sadness was more intense and more frequent during and after the look

than before it, even after controlling for changes in anger and fear expression.

One could argue that these results were an artifact of sadness expressions being more likely than target expressions in general. Recall that for the threat episodes the target emotion, by design, was fear whereas for the frustration episodes it was anger. For Stranger Highchair and Toy Removal, we found that the target expression was more frequent and intense than sadness across the entire episode. In addition, we failed to find the predicted pattern of expressions (sadness > fear or anger) during looks to mother for the other two episodes, Stranger Free Play and Toy in Locked Box. One explanation was that sadness expressions were more common than the target expression across these episodes. Note also that the base rates of the target facial expressions were much lower in these two episodes, suggesting that they were not as likely to elicit distress.

Given these results, we were fairly confident that toddlers modulated their facial expressions when looking to their mothers. However, the final test of this hypothesis was to compare the frequency of sadness expressions when the toddlers looked at mother to sadness expressions when toddlers did not look at mother. As predicted, toddlers were more likely to express sadness when they were looking at mother than when they were not looking at mother.

As noted earlier, these effects were not consistent across all episodes. For Stranger Free Play and Toy in Locked Box, sadness expressions were not more likely during looks to mother, but they were more likely to be expressed than the target emotion across the entire episode. We contend that, because the predominant expression was sadness in these episodes, toddlers did not have to increase their sadness expression when they looked to their mothers. In addition, there were important differences between the two frustration episodes that may have resulted in the distinct pattern of results. In Toy Removal, compared with Toy in Locked Box, the mother was the source of the frustration, and when toddlers looked to their mothers they were more likely to express sadness. We argue that sadness is the most adaptive expression under these circumstances because directing anger toward the source of that anger (i.e., mother) would likely not result in a positive response.

Implications of Results for the Broader Literature

Although these results do not provide evidence for the intentional or effortful modulation of facial expressions they nevertheless raise the question of why toddlers displayed more sadness to mothers. In this section, we draw two conclusions addressing this question that map onto the literatures that framed our research questions. First, results support the functionalist theory of emotions (Campos et al., 1994) and differential emotions theory (Izard, 1977, 1991). These theories suggest that sadness expressions are more likely to elicit interaction and facilitate social support (Hortsmann, 2003; Huebner, & Izard, 1988; Shipman et al., 2003). To gain social support while feeling anger, therefore, children may change their expressions to sadness to serve this motivation best. Note, however, that toddlers may not understand the association between specific facial expressions and discrete responses from mother.

Although there is strong support for the adaptive function of sadness compared with anger, there is virtually no evidence that fear expressions are less adaptive than sadness expressions in seeking help. Fear expressions can communicate a variety of requests to the observer, including "back-off" and possibly "help" (Hortsmann, 2003). Our results are the first to demonstrate that sadness expressions are more common than fear expressions during a look to mother, at least under particular circumstances, but do not address the function of fear expressions explicitly. We suggest that toddlers may be merely generalizing from the anger situation to the fear situation. As Huebner and Izard (1988) demonstrated, mothers were more likely to respond to sadness expressions than to anger. Through socialization and repeated exposure to these situations, the toddler would learn the contingency between sadness and positive maternal response (Malatesta & Haviland, 1982; Malatesta, Grigoryev, Lamb, Albin, and Culver, 1986), which he or she may generalize to subsequent fear-inducing situations.

Second, recall that the functionalist approach to emotion posits that expressions serve several uses, including social goals that sometimes require separating facial expressions from internal feelings (Campos et al., 1994), as well as communicating felt emotion. With this in mind, we cannot be sure that the observed changes in facial expression were not accompanied by internal feelings of sadness. Although we cannot measure feeling states in young children, we suggest that examining in detail the changes in affect expressions across the different segments of the look may be a clue to feeling states. We argue that if the child was experiencing sadness, it would be more frequent and intense before the look to mother than during the look to mother. This would suggest that the child was experiencing sadness and was sharing that with the mother, in the

same way he or she might share pleasure with his or her mother in a positive situation. Support for this interpretation comes from the literature on affective sharing, the phenomenon of infant's looks to mother accompanied by a smile (e.g., Hornick & Gunnar, 1988; Mundy, Kasari, & Sigman, 1992), and anticipatory smiling. There is increasing evidence for the distinction between looks to mother preceded by smiles (anticipatory smiles), believed to reflect the intention of the infant to share affect, versus looks to mother followed by a smile (reactive smiles; Jones & Hong, 2001; Messinger, Cobo-Lewis, Fogel, Acosta, & Cassel, 2003). In the present study we demonstrated that sadness was less likely to precede the look, suggesting that the infants may not have been feeling sad before looking at their mothers. An important caveat here, however, is that there was not a complete absence of sadness before the look, and sadness did not decrease after the look. Nevertheless, sadness expressions did increase during the look, which is not consistent with an anticipatory expression explanation. Therefore, although the possibility remains that toddlers' internal states changed to sadness when looking to their mothers, we believe that the expression of sadness simply reflected attempts by the child to gain support from the mother.

Finally, although toddlers' use of sadness expressions over other distress emotions supports the functionalist perspective, the mechanisms by which toddlers do so remain unanswered. We speculate on one possible mechanism, that of the development of display rules. As defined by Ekman (1993, p. 384), display rules refer to "culture-specific predictions about who can show which emotions, to whom, and when." Although early research supposed that cognitive development and awareness of internal emotions were required for the use of display rules (e.g., Saarni, 1979), the results of the current study, together with research in infants' pain expressions (Axia & Bonichini, 1988) and preschoolers ability to mask disappointment with a smile (Cole, 1986), indicate that even infants and young children modulate their facial reactions seemingly without these abilities. School-age children have disclosed that they chose to express sadness when they expected comfort, soothing, and other positive reactions from their audience (Underwood, Cole, and Herbsman, 1992; Zeman & Garber, 1996; Zeman & Shipman, 1996). Because toddlers cannot report on feeling states we cannot know whether the child's display of sadness was consistent with his or her feeling state. Moreover, we do not know when this ability emerges. We believe that the current study's demonstration that older infants show sadness over other distress emotions is good evidence for affect modulation, albeit insufficient to fit a display rules explanation.

Limitations, Caveats, and Future Directions

The literature on modulation of facial expressions thus far has been piecemeal, with few studies in infancy and preschool-age children and then jumping to school-age children. The current study adds to the literature with toddlers, but again with cross-sectional findings. Therefore, we have little information about the development of this type of affect modulation ability.

It is important to note that mothers were instructed not to interfere with or interact with their toddlers, perhaps resulting in more distress or more looks to mother. Recall that we addressed this concern and found that selecting only the first look to mother resulted in the same pattern of results. An increase in sadness because of mothers' lack of responding, however, would not contradict our findings. As the emotion regulation literature suggests, children will seek out the help they need from caregivers when they are distressed. Increases in distress, therefore, should lead to increased help-seeking behaviors.

Finally, because mothers did not interact with their children, we were unable to determine whether mothers were more likely to pick up on the sadness signals and respond with help. We know from other work that mothers are more likely to respond to sadness than anger (Huebner & Izard, 1988), but what about fear? Although our work suggests that children were more likely to display sadness expressions than fear expressions, this may not be reflected in the responses mothers make following these displays. This remains an important question for future research.

Conclusion

These data are unique in providing evidence that toddlers are more likely to use certain distress expressions when seeking help from their mothers. Twenty-four-month-old children showed increased frequency and intensity of sadness expression when looking to their mothers despite situational pressure to display anger or fear expressions. As discussed throughout this article, there is a paucity of data on how and whether young children change their facial expressions to gain assistance from caregivers. The current results raise questions for the investigation of the mechanisms of facial affect modulation in young children.

References

Axia, G., & Bonichini, S. (1998). Regulation of emotion after acute pain from 3 to 18 months: A longitudinal study. *Early Development and Parenting, 7,* 203–210.

Buss, K. A. (2000). *The physiology of emotional reactivity in toddlers: Endocrine and cardiac considerations.* Unpublished doctoral dissertation, University of Wisconsin-Madison.

Buss, K. A., & Goldsmith, H. H. (1998). Fear and anger regulation in infancy: Effects on the temporal dynamic of affective expression. *Child Development, 69,* 359–374.

Buss, K. A., & Goldsmith, H. H. (2000). *Manual and normative data for the Laboratory Temperament Assessment Battery–Toddler Version* (Technical report). Madison, WI: University of Wisconsin, Department of Psychology.

Campos, J. J., Mumme, D. L., Kermoian, R., & Campos, R. G. (1994). A functionalist perspective on the nature of emotion. In Nathan A. Fox (Ed.), The development of emotion regulation: Biological and behavioral considerations. *Monographs of the Society for Research in Child Development, 59*(2–3, Serial No. 240), 284–303.

Cole, P. M. (1986). Children's spontaneous control of facial expressions. *Child Development, 57,* 1309–1321.

Cole, P. M., Martin, S. E., & Dennis, T. A. (2004). Emotion regulation as a scientific construct: Methodological challenges and directions for child development research. *Child Development, 75,* 317–333.

Ekman, P. (1993). Facial expression and emotion. *American Psychologist, 48,* 384–392.

Fuchs, D., & Thelen, M. H. (1988). Children's expected interpersonal consequences of communicating their affective state and reported likelihood of expression. *Child Development, 59,* 1314–1322.

Garber, J., & Dodge, K. (1991). *The development of emotion regulation and dysregulation.* Cambridge, England: Cambridge University Press.

Goldsmith, H. H., Reilly, H. H., Lemery, K. S., Longley, S., & Prescott, A. (1994). *Manual for Laboratory Temperament Assessment Battery* (Technical report). Madison, WI: University of Wisconsin, Department of Psychology.

Grolnick, W. S., Bridges, L. J., & Connell, J. P. (1996). Emotion regulation in two-year-olds: Strategies and emotional expression in four contexts. *Child Development, 67,* 928–941.

Hofer, M. A. (1994). Hidden regulators in attachment, separation, and loss. *Monographs of the Society for Research in Child Development, 59*(2–3, Serial No. 204), 192–207.

Hornick, R., & Gunnar, M. R. (1988). A descriptive analysis of infant social referencing. *Child Development, 59,* 626–634.

Horstmann, G. (2003). What do facial expressions convey: Feeling states, behavioral intentions, or action requests? *Emotion, 3,* 150–166.

Huebner, R. R., & Izard, C. E. (1988). Mothers' responses to infants' facial expressions of sadness, anger, and physical distress. *Motivation and Emotion, 12,* 185–196.

Izard, C. E. (1977). *Human emotions.* New York: Plenum.

Izard, C. E. (1991). *The psychology of emotions.* New York: Plenum.

Toddlers' Distress Expressions   1773

Izard, C. E., Dougherty, L. M., & Hembree, E. A. (1983). *A system for identifying affect expressions by holistic judgments (Affex)*. Newark, NJ: University of Delaware, Computer Network Services and University Media Services.

Izard, C. E., Fantauzzo, C. A., Castle, J. M., Haynes, O. M., Rayias, M. F., & Putnam, M. F. R. (1995). The ontogeny and significance of infants' facial expressions in the first 9 months of life. *Developmental Psychology, 31*, 997–1013.

Jones, S. S., & Hong, H. W. (2001). Onset of voluntary communication: Smiling looks to mother. *Infancy, 2*, 353–370.

Malatesta, C. Z., Culver, C., Tesman, J. R., & Shepard, B. (1989). The development of emotion during the first two years of life. *Monographs of the Society for Research in Child Development, 54* (1–2, Serial No. 219).

Malatesta, C. Z., Grigoryev, P., Lamb, C., Albin, M., & Culver, C. (1986). Emotion socialization and expressive development in preterm and full-term infants. *Child Development, 57*, 316–330.

Malatesta, C. Z., & Haviland, J. M. (1982). Learning display rules: The socialization of emotion expression in infancy. *Child Development, 53*, 991–1003.

Mangelsdorf, S. C., Shapiro, J. R., & Marzolf, D. (1995). Developmental and temperamental differences in emotion regulation in infancy. *Child Development, 66*, 1817–1828.

Messinger, D. S., Cobo-Lewis, A., Fogel, A., Acosta, S., & Cassel, T. (2003). *Patterns in time: The development of infant expressive coordination and infant–mother coordination*. Paper presented at the meeting of the Society for Research in Child Development, Tampa FL.

Moses, L. J., Baldwin, D. A., Rosicky, J. G., & Tidball, G. (2001). Evidence for referential understanding in the emotions domain at twelve and eighteen months. *Child Development, 72*, 718–735.

Mundy, P., Kasari, C., & Sigman, M. (1992). Nonverbal communication, affective sharing, and intersubjectivity. *Infant Behavior and Development, 15*, 377–381.

Rothbart, M. K., Ziaie, H., & O'Boyle, C. G. (1992). Self-regulation and emotion in infancy. *New Directions for Child Development, 55*, 7–23.

Saarni, C. (1979). Children's understanding of display rules for expressive behavior. *Developmental Psychology, 15*, 424–429.

Shipman, K. L., Zeman, J., Nesin, A. E., & Fitzgerald, M. (2003). Children's strategies for displaying anger and sadness: What works with whom? *Merrill-Palmer Quarterly, 49*, 100–123.

Stifter, C. A., & Braungart, J. M. (1995). The regulation of negative reactivity in infancy: Function and development. *Developmental Psychology, 31*, 448–455.

Thompson, R. A. (1994). Emotion regulation: A theme in search of definition. In N. Fox (Ed.), The development of emotion regulation: Biological and behavioral considerations. *Monographs of the Society for Research in Child Development, 59* (2–3 Serial No. 240), 25–52.

Underwood, M. K., Coie, J. D., & Herbsman, C. R. (1992). Display rules for anger and aggression in school-age children. *Child Development, 63*, 366–380.

Zeman, J., & Garber, J. (1996). Display rules for anger, sadness, and pain: It depends on who is watching. *Child Development, 67*, 957–973.

Zeman, J., & Penza, S. (1997). Preschoolers as functionalists: The impact of social context on emotion regulation. *Child Study Journal, 27*, 41–67.

Zeman, J., & Shipman, K. (1996). Children's expressions of negative affect: Reasons and methods. *Developmental Psychology, 32*, 842–849.

Zeman, J., & Shipman, K. (1998). Influence of social context on children's affect regulation: A functionalist perspective. *Journal of Nonverbal Behavior, 22*, 141–165.

Buss, K.A. and Kiel E., Comparison of sadness, anger, and fear facial expressions when toddlers look at their mothers. From *Child Development*, v75.i6, pp. 1761–1773, by permission of Blackwell Publishing.

ARTICLE MANUSCRIPT (SELECTED PAGES)

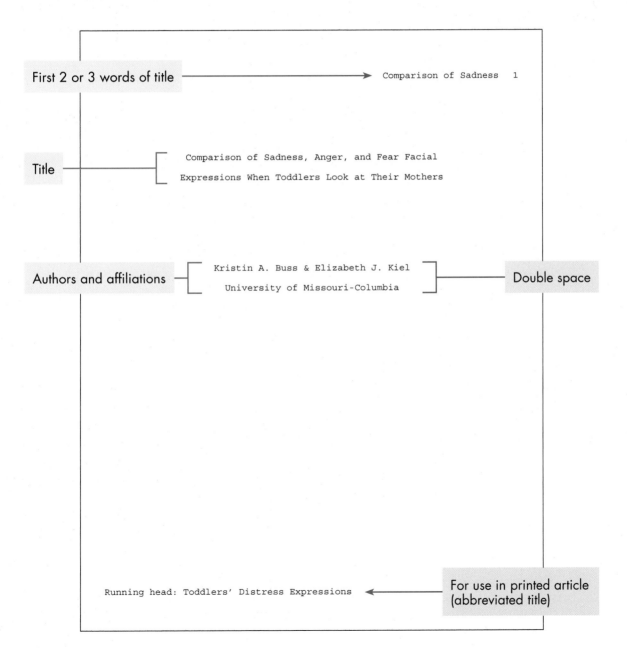

First 2 or 3 words of title   ⟶   Comparison of Sadness   1

Title —

Comparison of Sadness, Anger, and Fear Facial
Expressions When Toddlers Look at Their Mothers

Authors and affiliations —

Kristin A. Buss & Elizabeth J. Kiel
University of Missouri-Columbia   ⟶   Double space

Running head: Toddlers' Distress Expressions   ⟵   For use in printed article
(abbreviated title)

Abstract begins on new page

Abstract

Not indented

Research suggests that sadness expressions may be more beneficial to children than other emotions when eliciting support from caregivers. It is unclear, however, when children develop the ability to regulate their displays of distress. The current study addresses this question. Distress facial expressions (e.g., fear, anger, and sadness) were examined in 24-month-old toddlers throughout four episodes as well as specifically during looks to their mothers. Consistent with hypotheses and the literature, toddlers expressed sadness more frequently and with more intensity than target emotions only during looks to their mothers. These findings indicate that toddlers as young as 24 months of age are using particular emotional displays to elicit support from the social environment.

Single paragraph

First page of text

Comparison of Sadness   3

Title

> Comparison of Sadness, Anger, and Fear Facial

Expressions When Toddlers Look at Their Mothers

Indent and begin text

> Much research has explored young children's facial expressions and their abilities to modulate them. Research has shown that children's abilities to regulate and modulate their emotional expressions improve with age (e.g., Buss & Goldsmith, 1998; Fuchs & Thelen, 1988; Garber & Dodge, 1991; Saarni, 1979), but has not fully examined the early development and implications of developing skills. Toddlers, in particular, remain understudied.

Refer to articles and books by authors and year

The current study addresses this gap in the study of emotional expression. We aimed to demonstrate that toddlers display facial expressions of sadness more often than other distress facial expressions when looking at their mothers and that these expressions facilitate the communication of the need for support from their caregivers. Although we know of few studies specifically addressed to this question, the literatures on emotion regulation, the functionalist approach to emotion expressions, and the socialization of facial expressions provide the rationale for the current study and are thus reviewed below.

Emotion Regulation and the Function of Emotional Expression

Emotion regulation in general reflects "changes associated with activated emotions" (Cole, Martin, & Dennis, 2004) and more specifically reflects processes that facilitate reduction of distress, whether initiated by the individual (i.e., intrinsic) or by others (i.e., extrinsic) (Thompson, 1994). Young children rely on their mothers to assist in the regulation of their emotions before they acquire the skill to do so on their own; infants maintain emotional and physiological homeostasis after arousal by being comforted by their mothers (Hofer, 1994). In order to facilitate this "extrinsic" regulation in ambiguous or fear-eliciting situations, infants engage in behaviors that signal distress (e.g., crying) and/or requests for help (e.g., looks to expressions (sadness, anger, and fear expressions) occurring in response to frustrating and threatening situations. Direct observation of these facial expressions revealed whether toddlers modulated their expressions when looking at their mothers, and, specifically, whether they did so in the previously reported pattern of displaying sadness rather than the putative target emotion.

We addressed four questions in this study. First, what was the predominant distress expression in each episode? Each episode was designed to elicit a target emotion (fear or anger), so we sought to confirm the presence of these emotions. Second, did toddlers express sadness more than the target emotion when looking at their mothers? Third, did the expression of sadness increase in frequency and intensity during looks to mother? Fourth, did the expression of sadness occur more when toddlers looked at their mothers compared to segments when they were not looking at their mothers? Across analyses, we predicted that sadness expressions would be more common than the target expression when toddlers looked to mother. Moreover, we predicted that sadness expressions would be more common during a look compared to sadness expressions observed when toddlers were not looking at their mother.

Method is centered ⟶ Method

Participants is flush to left margin and in italics.

Participants ⟵

Participants were 71 twenty-four month old children (35 female) recruited from local public birth records. Visits were scheduled within 1 month of second birthday ($M = 24.50$, $SD = .40$, range 23.03-25.57). Participants and families were not selected for any behavior or characteristic. Most of the participants were Caucasian (96%) and were from intact middle class families (Hollingshead Index = 48.66).

Procedure

Comparison of Sadness   11

ranging from .73 to .81. Recall that during the second pass of coding the presence of looks to mother was rescored and agreement for identification of looks to mother was 97%.

There were missing data for three of the four episodes. For the Stranger High Chair episode, 6 participants were not scored: two mothers refused the episode, one child refused to get into the high chair, and three participants were not scored due to equipment failure. Six participants also were not scored in the Stranger Free Play episode: three because the episode was not done, two because the child refused the episode, and one because the mother refused the episode. For analyses of the Toy in Locked Box episode, one child was not scored because of a poor tape. Thus, Stranger High Chair, Stranger Free Play, Toy in Locked Box, and Toy Removal had 65, 68, 70, and 71 participants, respectively.

Results

The frequency counts and descriptive statistics for facial affect and the looks to mother across each task are presented in Table 1. Note the discrepancy between total number of looks to mother and the number of looks to mother that were coded for facial affect. There were a number of looks to mother that were not coded because the face was not visible, so these were not considered further. We tested for main effects of gender and found only one significant difference. Boys had a higher frequency of looks to mother with sadness facial expression ($M = 1.15$, $SD = .20$) than girls ($M = .55$, $SD = .15$) in the Toy Removal task, $t (64) = -2.42$, $p < .05$.

Comparison of Facial Expressions of Sadness and the Target Emotion

We conducted two sets of analyses comparing sadness to the target emotion (fear or anger depending on the episode). First, we compared sadness expressions to the target expression for the entire episode (Table 1). Second, we compared sadness expressions to the target expression during looks to mother (Tables 2 & 3). For each set of analyses fear were not significantly different for criers versus non-criers; in fact there was a trend for non-criers to show more distress. In contrast, sadness and anger were more common in criers versus non-criers during Toy Removal; therefore, we ran all previous analyses without the criers. All the effects remained significant (ps < .001), such that sadness was more common than anger during a look to mother, and sadness increased across the segments of the look to mother. Therefore, we were confident that crying did not affect the pattern of results.

A second possible explanation for the pattern of findings was that toddlers' sadness increased with repeated looks to mother because the mothers were told not to respond. We tested this assumption by analyzing only facial expressions during the first look to mother for Stranger Highchair and Toy Removal. Comparison of the sadness to the target emotion during looks to mother remained significant and in the same direction for Toy Removal (ps < .001), but failed to reach significance for Stranger Highchair. That is, sadness expressions were higher than anger expressions, but there was no difference between sadness expressions and fear expressions. In the analyses of sadness across the segments of the looks to mother, results were unchanged for both Stranger Highchair (p < .05) and Toy Removal (p < .001). Sadness expressions increased across the segments of the look to mother, but the target emotion did not. Again, we were confident that the results were not primarily the result of repeated looks to mother.

Discussion is centered ——————————▶ Discussion

We investigated whether 24-month-olds were able to modulate their distress facial expressions when looking at their mothers. In particular, we tested whether sadness facial expressions were more likely to occur despite contextual pressure for anger or fear expressions to be predominant. Results largely supported our predictions.

Evidence for Sadness Expressions during Looks to Mother

References are placed
on separate page.

References

Axia, G., & Bonichini, S. (1998). Regulation of emotion after acute
    pain from 3 to 18 months: A longitudinal study. *Early Development and
    Parenting, 7,* 203-210.

Buss, K. A. (2000). *The physiology of emotional reactivity in
    toddlers: Endocrine and cardiac considerations.* Unpublished doctoral
    dissertation, University of Wisconsin-Madison.

Buss, K. A., & Goldsmith, H. H. (1998). Fear and anger regulation in
    infancy: Effects on the temporal dynamic of affective expression. *Child
    Development, 69,* 359-374.

Campos, J.J., Mumme, D.L., Kermoian, R., & Campos, R.G. (1994). A
    functionalist perspective on the nature of emotion. In Nathan A. Fox
    (Ed.), *The development of emotion regulation: Biological and behavioral
    considerations. Monographs of the Society for Research in Child
    Development, 59 (2-3, Serial No. 240),* 284-303.

Cole, P. M. (1986). Children's spontaneous control of facial expressions.
    Child Development, 57, 1309-1321.

Cole, P. M., Martin, S. E., & Dennis, T. A. (2004). Emotion regulation as
    a scientific construct: Methodological challenges and directions for
    child development research. *Child Development, 75,* 317-333.

Ekman, P. (1993). Facial expression and emotion. *American Psychologist,
    48,* 384-392.

Fuchs, D., & Thelen, M.H. (1988). Children's expected interpersonal
    consequences of communicating their affective state and reported
    likelihood of expression. *Child Development, 59,* 1314-1322.

Garber, J., & Dodge, K. (1991). *The development of emotion regulation and
    dysregulation.* Cambridge: Cambridge University Press.

Journal Article

Book

Following the reference section, in order, are appendixes,
author notes, footnotes, tables, figure captions, and figures.
Each starts on a separate page.

Table 1

Mean (SE) Frequency and Intensity of Facial Affect and Number of Looks to Mother by Episode

	Stranger Highchair n = 67	Stranger Free Play n = 68	Toy Removal n = 71	Toy in Locked Box n = 70
Freq Target[1]	10.10(.89)	2.16(.31)	1.37(.54)	2.76(.31)
Freq Sadness	4.50(.87)	4.40(.57)	.54(.12)	4.07(.44)
Intensity Target[1]	.74(.08)	.23(.04)	1.02(.12)	.15(.02)
Intensity Sadness	.31(.05)	.60(.05)	.71(.08)	.17(.03)
Total Looks	351	216	173	385
Total Coded Looks[2]	330	171	158	359
No Looks[3]	6	6	2	2
Mean # Looks	5.13(3.61)	3.04(2.03)	2.54(1.47)	5.17(2.78)

[1] Target emotion was fear for Stranger Highchair and Stranger Free Play. Target emotion was anger for Toy Removal and Toy in Locked Box.

[2] Represents the number of looks where facial affect was coded.

[3] Represents the number of children who did not look to their mother during the episode.

Place each table including caption on a separate page.

Toddlers' Distress Expressions   37

Figure Captions

Figure 1. *Frequency of sadness versus fear facial expressions in Stranger Highchair (top panel) and Stranger Free Play (bottom panel).*

Figure 2. *Frequency of sadness versus anger facial expressions in Toy Removal (top panel) and Toy in Locked Box (bottom panel).*

Place figure captions on a separate page from the figure.

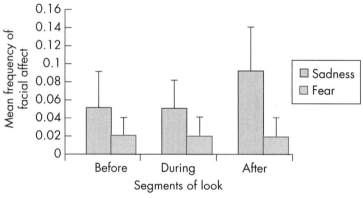

Place each figure without captin on a separate page.

TABLES

Table D.1 Random Numbers

10480	15011	01536	02011	81647	91646	69179	14194	62590	6207	20969	99570	91291	90700
22368	46573	25595	85393	30995	89198	27982	53402	93965	34095	52666	19174	39615	99505
24130	48360	22527	97265	76393	64809	15179	24830	49340	32081	30680	19655	63348	58629
42167	93093	06243	616580	07856	16376	39440	53537	71341	57004	00849	74917	97758	16379
37570	39975	81837	16656	06121	91782	60468	81305	49684	60672	14110	06927	01263	54613
77921	06907	11008	42751	27756	53498	18602	70659	90655	15053	21916	81825	44394	42880
99562	72095	56420	69994	98872	31016	71194	18738	44013	44840	63213	21069	10634	12952
96301	91977	05463	07972	18876	20922	94595	56869	69014	60045	18425	84903	42508	32307
89579	14342	63661	10281	17453	18103	57740	84378	25331	12566	58768	44947	05585	56941
85475	36857	53342	53988	53060	59533	38867	62300	08158	17983	16439	11458	18593	64952
29818	69589	88231	33276	70997	79936	56865	05859	90106	31595	01547	85590	91610	78188
63553	40961	48235	03427	49626	69445	18663	72695	52180	20847	12234	90511	33703	90322
09429	93969	52636	92737	88974	33488	36320	17617	30015	08272	84115	27156	30613	74952
10365	61129	87529	85689	48237	52267	67689	93394	01511	26358	85104	20285	29975	89868
07119	97336	71048	08178	77233	13916	47564	81056	97735	85977	29372	74461	28551	90707
51085	12765	51821	51259	77452	16308	60756	92144	49442	53900	70960	63990	75601	40719
02368	21382	52404	60268	89368	19885	55322	44819	01188	65255	64835	44919	05944	55157
01011	54092	33362	94904	31273	04146	18594	29852	71585	85030	51132	01915	92747	64951
52162	53916	46369	58586	23216	14513	83149	98736	23495	64350	94738	17752	35156	35749
07056	97628	33787	09998	42698	06691	76988	13602	51851	46104	88916	19509	25625	58104
48663	91245	85828	14346	09172	30168	90229	04734	59193	22178	30421	61666	99904	32812
54164	58492	22421	74103	47070	25306	76468	26384	58151	06646	21524	15227	96909	44592
32639	32363	05597	24200	13363	38005	94342	26384	58151	06646	21524	15227	96909	44592
29334	27001	87637	87308	58731	00256	45834	15398	46557	41135	10367	07684	36188	18510
02488	33062	28834	07351	19731	92420	60952	61280	50001	67658	32586	86679	50720	94953
81525	72295	04839	96423	24878	82651	66566	14778	76797	14780	13300	87074	79666	95725
29676	20591	68086	26432	46901	20849	89768	81536	86645	12659	92259	57102	80428	25280
00742	57392	39064	66432	84673	40027	32832	61362	98947	96067	64760	64584	96096	98253
05366	04213	25669	26422	44407	44048	37937	63904	45766	66134	75740	66520	34693	90449
91921	26418	64117	94305	26766	25940	39972	22209	71500	64568	91402	42416	07844	69618

Source: Beyer (1960).

Table D.1   Random Numbers (continued)

00582	04711	87917	77341	42206	35126	74087	99547	81817	42607	43808	76655	62028	76630
00725	69884	62797	56170	86324	88072	76222	36086	84637	93161	76038	65855	77919	88006
69011	65795	95876	55293	18988	27354	26575	08625	40801	59920	29841	80150	12777	48501
25976	57948	29888	88604	67917	48708	18912	62274	65424	69774	33611	54262	85963	03547
09763	83473	73577	12908	30883	18317	28290	35797	05998	41688	34952	37888	38917	88050
91567	42595	27958	30134	04024	86385	29880	99730	55536	84855	29080	09250	79656	73211
17955	56439	90999	49127	20044	59931	06115	20542	18059	02008	73708	83517	36103	42791
46503	18584	18845	49618	02304	51038	20655	58727	28168	15475	56942	53389	20562	87338
92157	89634	94824	78171	84610	82834	09922	25417	44137	48413	25555	21246	35509	20468
14577	62765	35605	81263	39667	47358	56873	56307	61607	49518	89656	20103	77490	18062
98427	07523	33362	64270	01638	92477	66969	98420	04800	45585	46565	04102	46880	45709
34914	63976	88720	82765	34476	17032	87589	40836	32427	70002	70663	88863	77775	69348
70060	28277	39475	46473	23219	53416	94970	25382	69975	94884	19661	72828	00102	66794
53976	54914	06990	67425	68350	82948	11398	42878	80287	88267	47363	46634	06541	97809
76072	29515	40980	07391	58745	25774	22987	80059	39911	96189	41151	14222	60697	59583
90725	52210	83974	29992	65831	38857	50490	83765	55657	14361	31720	57375	56228	41546
64364	67412	33339	31926	14883	24413	59744	92351	97473	89286	35931	04110	23726	51900
08962	00358	31662	2538	61642	34072	81249	35648	56891	69352	48373	45578	78547	81788
95012	68379	93526	70765	10592	04542	76463	54328	02349	17247	28865	14777	62730	92277
15664	10493	20492	38391	91132	21999	59516	81652	27195	48223	46751	22923	32261	85653
16408	81899	04153	53381	79401	21438	83035	92350	36693	31238	59649	91754	72772	02338
18629	81953	05520	91962	04739	13092	97662	24822	94730	06496	35090	04822	86674	98289
73115	35101	47498	97637	99016	71060	88824	71013	18735	20286	23153	72924	35165	43040
57491	16703	23167	49323	45021	33132	12544	41035	80780	45393	44812	12515	98931	91202
30405	83946	23792	14422	15059	45799	22716	19792	09983	74353	68668	30429	20735	25499
16631	35006	85900	98275	32388	52390	16815	69298	82732	38480	73817	32523	41961	44437
96773	20206	42559	78985	05300	22164	24369	54224	35083	19687	11052	91491	60383	19746
38935	64202	14349	82674	66523	44133	00697	35552	35970	19124	63318	29686	03387	59846
31624	76384	17403	53363	44167	64486	64758	75366	76554	31601	12614	33072	60332	92325
78919	19474	23632	27889	47914	02584	37680	20801	72152	39339	34806	08930	85001	87820

(continued)

Table D.1   Random Numbers (continued)

03931	33309	57047	74211	63445	17361	62825	30908	05607	91284	68833	25570	38818	46920
74426	33278	43972	10119	89917	15665	52872	73823	73144	88662	88970	74492	51805	99378
09066	00903	20795	95452	92648	45454	09552	88815	16553	51125	79375	97596	16296	66092
42238	12526	87025	14267	20979	04508	64535	31355	86064	29472	47689	05974	52468	16834
16153	08002	26504	41744	81959	65642	74240	56302	00033	67107	77510	70625	28725	34191
21457	40742	29820	96873	29400	21840	15035	34537	33310	06116	95240	15957	16572	06004
21581	57802	02050	89728	17937	37621	47075	42080	97403	48626	68995	43805	33386	21597
55612	78095	83197	33732	05810	24813	86902	60397	16489	03264	88525	42786	05269	92532
44657	66999	99324	51281	84463	60563	79312	93454	68876	25471	93911	25650	12682	73572
91340	84979	46949	81973	37949	61023	43997	15263	80644	43942	89203	71795	99533	50501
91227	21199	31935	27022	84067	05462	35216	14486	29891	68607	41867	14951	91696	85064
50001	38140	66321	19924	72163	09538	12151	06878	91903	18749	34405	56087	82790	70925
65390	05224	72958	28609	81406	39147	25549	48542	42627	45233	57202	94617	23772	07896
27504	96131	83944	41575	10573	08619	64482	73923	36152	05184	94142	25299	84387	34925
37169	94851	39117	89632	00959	16487	65536	49071	39782	17095	02330	74301	00275	48280
11508	70225	51111	38351	19444	66499	71945	05422	13442	78675	84081	66938	93654	59894
37449	30362	06694	54690	04052	53115	62757	95348	78662	11163	81651	50245	34971	52924
46515	70331	85922	38320	57015	15765	97161	17869	45349	61796	66345	81073	49106	79860
30986	81223	42416	58353	21532	30502	32305	86482	05174	07901	54339	58861	74818	46942
63798	64995	46583	09785	44160	78128	83991	42865	92520	83531	80377	35909	81250	54238
82486	84846	99254	67632	43218	50076	21361	64816	51202	88124	41870	52689	51275	83556
21885	32906	92431	09060	64297	51674	64126	62570	26123	05155	59194	52799	28225	85762
60336	98782	07408	53458	13564	59089	26445	29789	85205	41001	12535	12133	14645	23541
43937	46891	24010	25560	86355	33941	25786	54990	71899	15475	95434	98227	21824	19585
97656	63175	89303	16275	07100	92063	21942	18611	47348	20203	18534	03862	78095	50136
03299	01221	05418	38982	55758	92237	26759	86367	21216	98442	08303	56613	91511	75928
79626	06486	03574	17668	07785	76020	79924	25651	83325	88428	85076	72811	22717	50585
85636	68335	47539	03129	65651	11977	02510	26113	99447	68645	34327	15152	55230	93448
18039	14367	61337	06177	12143	46609	32989	74014	64708	00533	35398	58408	13261	47908
08362	15656	60627	36478	64648	16764	53412	09013	07832	41574	17639	82163	60859	75567

(continued)

Table D.1   Random Numbers (continued)

79556	29068	04142	16268	15387	12856	66227	38358	22478	73373	88732	09443	82558	05250
92608	82674	27072	32534	17075	27698	98204	63863	11951	34648	88022	56148	34925	57031
23982	25835	40055	67006	12293	02753	14827	23235	35071	99704	37543	11601	35503	85171
09915	96306	05908	97901	28395	14186	00821	80703	70426	75647	76310	88717	37890	40129
59037	33300	26695	62247	69927	76123	50842	43834	86654	70959	79725	93872	28117	12933
42488	78077	69882	61657	34136	79180	97526	43092	04098	73571	80799	76536	71255	64239
46764	86273	63003	93017	31204	36692	40202	35275	57306	5543	53203	18098	47625	88684
03237	45430	65417	63282	90816	17349	88298	90183	36600	78406	06216	95787	42579	90730
86591	81482	52667	61582	14972	90053	89534	76036	49199	43716	97548	04379	46370	28672
38534	01715	94964	87288	65680	43772	39560	12918	86537	62738	19636	51132	56947	

Table D.2	Distribution of t			
n	.05	.02	.01	.001
1	12.706	31.821	63.657	636.619
2	4.303	6.965	9.925	31.598
3	3.182	4.541	5.841	12.924
4	2.776	3.747	4.604	8.610
5	2.571	3.365	4.032	6.869
6	2.447	3.143	3.707	5.959
7	2.365	2.998	3.499	5.408
8	2.306	2.896	3.355	5.041
9	2.262	2.821	3.250	4.781
10	2.228	2.764	3.169	4.587
11	2.201	2.718	3.106	4.437
12	2.179	2.681	3.055	4.318
13	2.160	2.650	3.012	4.221
14	2.145	2.624	2.977	4.140
15	2.131	2.602	2.947	4.073
16	2.120	2.583	2.921	4.015
17	2.110	2.567	2.898	3.965
18	2.101	2.552	2.878	3.922
19	2.093	2.539	2.861	3.883
20	2.086	2.528	2.845	3.850
21	2.080	2.518	2.831	3.819
22	2.074	2.508	2.819	3.792
23	2.069	2.500	2.807	3.767
24	2.064	2.492	2.797	3.745
25	2.060	2.485	2.787	3.725
26	2.056	2.479	2.779	3.707
27	2.052	2.473	2.771	3.690
28	2.048	2.467	2.763	3.674
29	2.045	2.462	2.756	3.659
30	2.042	2.457	2.750	3.646
40	2.021	2.423	2.704	3.551
60	2.000	2.390	2.660	3.460
120	1.980	2.358	2.617	3.373
∞	1.960	2.326	2.576	3.291

Source: Fisher, R., & Yates, E. (1974). Statistical tables for biological, agricultural, and medical research (6th ed.). London: Longman Group Ltd.

Table D.3 The *F* Distribution (Values of $F_{.05}$)

Degrees of Freedom for Numerator

	1	2	3	4	5	6	7	8	9	10	12	15	20	24	30	40	60	120	∞
1	161	200	216	225	230	234	237	239	241	242	244	246	248	249	250	251	252	253	254
2	18.5	19.0	19.2	19.2	19.3	19.3	19.4	19.4	19.4	19.4	19.4	19.4	19.4	19.5	19.5	19.5	19.5	19.5	19.5
3	10.1	9.55	9.28	9.12	9.01	8.94	8.89	8.85	8.81	8.79	8.74	8.70	8.66	8.64	8.62	8.59	8.57	8.55	8.53
4	7.71	6.94	6.59	6.39	6.26	6.16	6.09	6.04	6.00	5.96	5.91	5.86	5.80	5.77	5.75	5.72	5.69	5.66	5.63
5	6.61	5.79	5.41	5.19	5.05	4.95	4.88	4.82	4.77	4.74	4.68	4.62	4.56	4.53	4.50	4.46	4.43	4.40	4.37
6	5.99	5.14	4.76	4.53	4.39	4.28	4.21	4.15	4.10	4.06	4.00	3.94	3.87	3.84	3.81	3.77	3.74	3.70	3.67
7	5.59	4.74	4.35	4.12	3.97	3.87	3.79	3.73	3.68	3.64	3.57	3.51	3.44	3.41	3.38	3.34	3.30	3.27	3.23
8	5.32	4.46	4.07	3.84	3.69	3.58	3.50	3.44	3.39	3.35	3.28	3.22	3.15	3.12	3.08	3.04	3.01	2.97	2.93
9	5.12	4.26	3.86	3.63	3.48	3.37	3.29	3.23	3.18	3.14	3.07	3.01	2.94	2.90	2.86	2.83	2.79	2.75	2.71
10	4.96	4.10	3.71	3.48	3.33	3.22	3.14	3.07	3.02	2.98	2.91	2.85	2.77	2.74	2.70	2.66	2.62	2.58	2.54
11	4.84	3.98	3.59	3.36	3.20	3.09	3.01	2.95	2.90	2.85	2.79	2.72	2.65	2.61	2.57	2.53	2.49	2.45	2.40
12	4.75	3.89	3.49	3.26	3.11	3.00	2.91	2.85	2.80	2.75	2.69	2.62	2.54	2.51	2.47	2.43	2.38	2.34	2.30
13	4.67	3.81	3.41	3.18	3.03	2.92	2.83	2.77	2.71	2.67	2.60	2.53	2.46	2.42	2.38	2.34	2.30	2.25	2.21
14	4.60	3.74	3.34	3.11	2.96	2.85	2.76	2.70	2.65	2.60	2.53	2.46	2.39	2.35	2.31	2.27	2.22	2.18	2.13
15	4.54	3.68	3.29	3.06	2.90	2.79	2.71	2.64	2.59	2.54	2.48	2.40	2.33	2.29	2.25	2.20	2.16	2.11	2.07
16	4.49	3.63	3.24	3.01	2.85	2.74	2.66	2.59	2.54	2.49	2.42	2.35	2.28	2.24	2.19	2.15	2.11	2.06	2.01
17	4.45	3.59	3.20	2.96	2.81	2.70	2.61	2.55	2.49	2.45	2.38	2.31	2.23	2.19	2.15	2.10	2.06	2.01	1.96
18	4.41	3.55	3.16	2.93	2.77	2.66	2.58	2.51	2.46	2.41	2.34	2.27	2.19	2.15	2.11	2.06	2.02	1.97	1.92
19	4.38	3.52	3.13	2.90	2.74	2.63	2.54	2.48	2.42	2.38	2.31	2.23	2.16	2.11	2.07	2.03	1.98	1.93	1.88
20	4.35	3.49	3.10	2.87	2.71	2.60	2.51	2.45	2.39	2.35	2.28	2.20	2.12	2.08	2.04	1.99	1.95	1.90	1.84
21	4.32	3.47	3.07	2.84	2.68	2.57	2.49	2.42	2.37	2.32	2.25	2.18	2.10	2.05	2.01	1.96	1.92	1.87	1.81
22	4.30	3.44	3.05	2.82	2.66	2.55	2.46	2.40	2.34	2.30	2.23	2.15	2.07	2.03	1.98	1.94	1.89	1.84	1.78
23	4.28	3.42	3.03	2.80	2.64	2.53	2.44	2.37	2.32	2.27	2.20	2.13	2.05	2.01	1.96	1.91	1.86	1.81	1.76
24	4.26	3.40	3.01	2.78	2.62	2.51	2.42	2.36	2.30	2.25	2.18	2.11	2.03	1.98	1.94	1.89	1.84	1.79	1.73
25	4.24	3.39	2.99	2.76	2.60	2.49	2.40	2.34	2.28	2.24	2.16	2.09	2.01	1.96	1.92	1.87	1.82	1.77	1.71
30	4.17	3.32	2.92	2.69	2.53	2.42	2.33	2.27	2.21	2.16	2.09	2.01	1.93	1.89	1.84	1.79	1.74	1.68	1.62
40	4.08	3.23	2.84	2.61	2.45	2.34	2.25	2.18	2.12	2.08	2.00	1.92	1.84	1.79	1.74	1.69	1.64	1.58	1.51
60	4.00	3.15	2.76	2.53	2.37	2.25	2.17	2.10	2.04	1.99	1.92	1.84	1.75	1.70	1.65	1.59	1.53	1.47	1.39
120	3.92	3.07	2.68	2.45	2.29	2.18	2.09	2.02	1.96	1.91	1.83	1.75	1.66	1.61	1.55	1.50	1.43	1.35	1.25
∞	3.84	3.00	2.60	2.37	2.21	2.10	2.01	1.94	1.88	1.83	1.75	1.67	1.57	1.52	1.46	1.39	1.32	1.22	1.00

Source: Merrington, M., & Thompson, C. (1943). Tables of percentage points of the inverted beta (F) distribution. *Biometrika, 33.* 73–88.

Table D.4   The F Distribution (Values of $F_{.01}$)

	Degrees of Freedom for Numerator																		
	1	2	3	4	5	6	7	8	9	10	12	15	20	24	30	40	60	120	∞
1	4,052	5,000	5,403	5,625	5,764	5,859	5,928	5,982	6,023	6,056	6,106	6,157	6,209	6,235	6,261	6,287	6,313	6,339	6,366
2	98.5	99.0	99.2	99.2	99.3	99.3	99.4	99.4	99.4	99.4	99.4	99.4	99.4	99.5	99.5	99.5	99.5	99.5	99.5
3	34.1	30.8	29.5	28.7	28.2	27.9	27.7	27.5	27.3	27.2	27.1	26.9	26.7	26.6	26.5	26.4	26.3	26.2	26.1
4	21.2	18.0	16.7	16.0	15.5	15.2	15.0	14.8	14.7	14.5	14.4	14.2	14.0	13.9	13.8	13.7	13.7	13.6	13.5
5	16.3	13.3	12.1	11.4	11.0	10.7	10.5	10.3	10.2	10.1	9.89	9.72	9.55	9.47	9.38	9.29	9.20	9.11	9.02
6	13.7	10.9	9.78	9.15	8.75	8.47	8.26	8.10	7.98	7.87	7.72	7.56	7.40	7.31	7.23	7.14	7.06	6.97	6.88
7	12.2	9.55	8.45	7.85	7.46	7.19	6.99	6.84	6.72	6.62	6.47	6.31	6.16	6.07	5.99	5.91	5.82	5.74	5.65
8	11.3	8.65	7.59	7.01	6.63	6.37	6.18	6.03	5.91	5.81	5.67	5.52	5.36	5.28	5.20	5.12	5.03	4.95	4.86
9	10.6	8.02	6.99	6.42	6.06	5.80	5.61	5.47	5.35	5.26	5.11	4.96	4.81	4.73	4.65	4.57	4.48	4.40	4.31
10	10.0	7.56	6.55	5.99	5.64	5.39	5.20	5.06	4.94	4.85	4.71	4.56	4.41	4.33	4.25	4.17	4.08	4.00	3.91
11	9.65	7.21	6.22	5.67	5.32	5.07	4.89	4.74	4.63	4.54	4.40	4.25	4.10	4.02	3.94	3.86	3.78	3.69	3.60
12	9.33	6.93	5.95	5.41	5.06	4.82	4.64	4.50	4.39	4.30	4.16	4.01	3.86	3.78	3.70	3.62	3.54	3.45	3.36
13	9.07	6.70	5.74	5.21	4.86	4.62	4.44	4.30	4.19	4.10	3.96	3.82	3.66	3.59	3.51	3.43	3.34	3.25	3.17
14	8.86	6.51	5.56	5.04	4.70	4.46	4.28	4.14	4.03	3.94	3.80	3.66	3.51	3.43	3.35	3.27	3.18	3.09	3.00
15	8.68	6.36	5.42	4.89	4.56	4.32	4.14	4.00	3.89	3.80	3.67	3.52	3.37	3.29	3.21	3.13	3.05	2.96	2.87
16	8.53	6.23	5.29	4.77	4.44	4.20	4.03	3.89	3.78	3.69	3.55	3.41	3.26	3.18	3.10	3.02	2.93	2.84	2.75
17	8.40	6.11	5.19	4.67	4.34	4.10	3.93	3.79	3.68	3.59	3.46	3.31	3.16	3.08	3.00	2.92	2.83	2.75	2.65
18	8.29	6.01	5.09	4.58	4.25	4.01	3.84	3.71	3.60	3.51	3.37	3.23	3.08	3.00	2.92	2.84	2.75	2.66	2.57
19	8.19	5.93	5.01	4.50	4.17	3.94	3.77	3.63	3.52	3.43	3.30	3.15	3.00	2.92	2.84	2.76	2.67	2.58	2.49
20	8.10	5.85	4.94	4.43	4.10	3.87	3.70	3.56	3.46	3.37	3.25	3.09	2.94	2.86	2.78	2.69	2.61	2.52	2.42
21	8.02	5.78	4.87	4.37	4.04	3.81	3.64	3.51	3.40	3.31	3.17	3.03	2.88	2.80	2.72	2.64	2.55	2.46	2.36
22	7.95	5.72	4.82	4.31	3.99	3.76	3.59	3.45	3.35	3.26	3.12	2.98	2.83	2.75	2.67	2.58	2.50	2.40	2.31
23	7.88	5.66	4.76	4.26	3.94	3.71	3.54	3.41	3.30	3.21	3.07	2.93	2.78	2.70	2.62	2.54	2.45	2.35	2.26
24	7.82	5.61	4.72	4.22	3.90	3.67	3.50	3.36	3.26	3.17	3.03	2.89	2.74	2.66	2.58	2.49	2.40	2.31	2.21
25	7.77	5.57	4.68	4.18	3.86	3.63	3.46	3.32	3.22	3.13	2.99	2.85	2.70	2.62	2.53	2.45	2.36	2.27	2.17
30	7.56	5.39	4.51	4.02	3.70	3.47	3.30	3.17	3.07	2.98	2.84	2.70	2.55	2.47	2.39	2.30	2.21	2.11	2.01
40	7.31	5.18	4.31	3.83	3.51	3.29	3.12	2.99	2.89	2.80	2.66	2.52	2.37	2.29	2.20	2.11	2.02	1.92	1.80
60	7.08	4.98	4.13	3.65	3.34	3.12	2.95	2.82	2.72	2.63	2.50	2.35	2.20	2.12	2.03	1.94	1.84	1.73	1.60
120	6.85	4.79	3.95	3.48	3.17	2.96	2.79	2.66	2.56	2.47	2.34	2.19	2.03	1.95	1.86	1.76	1.66	1.53	1.38
∞	6.63	4.61	3.78	3.32	3.02	2.80	2.64	2.51	2.41	2.32	2.18	2.04	1.88	1.79	1.70	1.59	1.47	1.32	1.00

Source: Merrington, M., & Thompson, C. (1943). Tables of percentage points of the inverted beta (F) distribution. Biometrika, 33, 73–88.

GLOSSARY

abstract A summary (of approximately 100 words) at the beginning of a research article; describes purpose, methods, and results of the research.

affirming the consequent A form of reverse confirmatory reasoning in which one case is used to draw the illogical conclusion relating to all similar cases.

alpha level The probability of making a Type I error.

analysis of variance (ANOVA) An inferential statistical technique used to compare differences between two or more groups with the purpose of making a decision that the independent variable influenced the dependent variable.

antecedent The first of two propositions in a logical argument of the form *If antecedent is true, then consequent follows.*

a priori test A statistical test that is planned before the experiment is performed and therefore is part of the design of the experiment. This test is contrasted with a post hoc test, which is decided upon after the data have been examined.

archival research Research using previously collected records that were not gathered for the purpose of the present study.

baseline A measure of a particular behavior or process taken before the introduction of the independent variable or treatment.

beta level The probability of making a Type II error.

between-subjects design A design in which comparisons are made between one group and another. Participants in a given group do not receive the same level of the independent variable or treatment as those in another group.

bias A prejudice in the design, performance, analysis, or presentation of a research project.

bimodal distribution The situation in which the scores of a distribution form two separate nodes or peaks, one at each end of the distribution (for

example, the distribution of scores from a class exam in which most students made either an A or an F).

blind control A participant in a research project who is not informed of the important factors in the procedure.

blocking The matching of groups before the beginning of the experiment according to some important variable that the participants possess (for example, placing an equal number of males and females in each group). Glass and Stanley (1970) suggest that the term *blocking* be used with nominal-scale variables.

chance variation The occurrence of events without any known antecedent as seen from the standpoint of the experiment.

completely randomized design Also referred to as the *simple randomized design* or the *simple random-subject design,* a design in which participants are randomly assigned to each of the possible groups in an experiment.

confound A factor that systematically biases the research but was not purposely introduced by the experimenter.

confounding variable A variable that systematically varies with the independent variable that could provide an alternative explanation for the influence of the independent variable on the dependent variable.

consequent The second of two propositions in a logical argument of the form *If antecedent is true, then consequent follows.*

construct A generalized concept, such as anxiety or gravity, that is constructed in a theoretical manner.

control A technique used to reduce the effects of extraneous variables on results and to ensure greater certainty that the changes in the dependent variable result from the independent variable.

control group Traditionally, the group that receives a zero level of the independent variable and that is used to assess the effects of the independent variable or treatment.

correlation A statistical technique for determining the degree of association between two or more variables.

correlational approach *See* correlational design.

correlational design A design used to establish the relationship between two variables without the ability to infer causal relationships.

debriefing The process of informing a participant after the experiment about the nature of the experiment, clarifying any misunderstanding, and answering any questions that the participant may have concerning the experiment; a necessary and important aspect of deception experiments.

deception research Research in which participants are led to believe that the purpose of the study or their performance in the experiment is something different from the actual case.

deduction Reasoning from the general to the particular, as in the case of creating an expected hypothesis for a particular experiment from a general theoretical statement. Opposite of *induction.*

demand characteristic The overall effect of the situation on a participant's behavior; generally used to denote aspects of an experiment that bias the results and prevent adequate influence of the independent variable.

denying the antecedent A form of reasoning in which a false premise is illogically concluded to result in a false consequent.

dependent variable In an experiment the variable that is said to depend on the action of another variable (the independent variable).

double blind The situation in which both the participant and the experimenter or agent of the experimenter are blind to certain key aspects of the experiment. Double-blind studies are often used in drug research in which neither the participant nor the person who administers the drug knows whether it contains the active ingredients or a placebo.

effect size The statistical magnitude of change that the independent variable has on the dependent variable.

empiricism An emphasis on using direct observation as a means of gaining information.

evaluation research See quasi-experimental design.

experimental group The group that receives the independent variable in an experiment.

experimental method A method based on strict control in experimentation, for making valid inferences concerning the relationships between one variable and another.

experimenter effect An effect upon participants in an experiment that can be traced to the behavior of the experimenter but is not designed to be part of the experimental manipulation.

ex post facto design A design in which the experimenter attempts to reconstruct the important factors in a situation after the fact.

external validity Generalizability of an experimental outcome to other groups, settings, treatment variables, and measurement variables.

extraneous variable A variable that is not directly related to the hypothesis under study and that the experimenter does not actively attempt to control (for example, time of day and the color of room are assumed to affect both groups equally and do not reduce the internal validity of the experiment).

factorial design A design in which there is more than one independent variable and each independent variable is present at every level of the other independent variable.

falsificationism The philosophical position that the goal of science is to falsify hypotheses. A major proponent of this position is Karl Popper. It is further suggested that, to be scientific, a hypothesis must be stated so that it can be falsified through research.

F ratio A statistic for comparing the variance attributed to chance with that attributed to treatment effects, calculated in an analysis of variance.

frequency distribution A set of scores organized according to frequency of occurrence.

generalizability The ability to extend a set of findings observed in one piece of research to other situations and groups.

Hawthorne effect The situation in which the participants' knowledge that they are part of an experiment influences the results differentially.

hypothesis A statement or expectation developed in relation to an explicit or implicit theory concerning potential outcomes of an experiment (that is, the relationship between the independent and dependent variable).

independent variable The variable defined by the experimenter and thus is outside the experimental situation (and therefore is independent).

induction The process of reasoning from a part to a whole, as might be performed when data from a particular study are used to develop a general theory.

inferential statistics Used to infer from a given sample of scores the parameters related to the set of all possible scores from which that sample was drawn.

interaction effect The situation in a factorial design whereby one variable influences another variable differently at different levels.

internal validity The ability to make valid inferences concerning the relationship between a dependent and an independent variable in an experimental situation.

interrater reliability The correlation between ratings of two or more raters in a research study.

intersubject replication The case in single-subject research in which a pattern of results is replicated between participants.

intragroup counterbalancing A procedure ensuring that every possible sequence appears at each presentation of the treatment.

intrasubject counterbalancing A procedure in which all participants receive the tasks in the same counterbalanced order.

intrasubject replication The procedure in single-subject designs in which the independent variable is introduced and removed in a manner to observe its influence within a single individual.

main effect A change in the dependent variable that is seen to have resulted from a change in the independent variable. See also treatment effect.

marker variable A variable that occurs with the construct under study and thus can index or indicate its presence.

matched-subjects design A procedure for equating groups in an experiment and reducing within-groups variance by using participants who are similar.

mean The average of a set of scores.

measurement The process of determining a dimensional or quantitative representation of a construct.

median The middle score in a distribution.

mixed design A design that includes both within-subjects and between-subjects components.

mode The score that occurs with the greatest frequency.

modeling A procedure using either a conceptual or a mathematical model to generate data.

modus ponens (confirmatory reasoning) Reasoning that a true premise leads to a true consequent.

modus tollens (disconfirmatory reasoning) Reasoning that a false consequent leads to a false premise.

naturalistic observation A scientific approach that focuses on observation and description; it is generally used with naturally occurring and ongoing phenomena, with little experimenter intervention.

null hypothesis The hypothesis that the differences between two or more population parameters are zero. Used nontechnically to refer to the condition that no differences exist between groups in an experiment.

operational definition A definition that presents a construct in terms of observable operations that can be measured and utilized in research.

order effect The effect in which participation in one condition of the experiment influences results in a later condition.

paradigm The worldview and set of assumptions that direct what a scientist examines, what measurements are made, and how these are to be understood.

personal equation A constant factor related to a person's psychology and physiology that results in individual differences in the measurement of variables.

placebo (Latin: "I shall please") Although the term is used in a variety of ways, it is common to speak of a placebo control, which controls for the effects of suggestibility (for example, in drug study, one group [the placebo control] receives an inert pill but is treated in every other way like the group that receives the pill with active ingredients).

post hoc test A statistical test that is conceived and performed after an experiment has been run.

posttest A measurement occasion that occurs at the conclusion of the presentation of the treatment or independent variable.

power The inverse $(1 - \beta)$ of the probability of making a Type II error; related to the number of individual results required to show a significant difference given a particular effect size.

practice effect The effect brought about by the continued repetition of a task.

pretest A measurement occasion that occurs prior to the introduction of the independent variable.

Psychological Abstracts A cumulative index that includes summaries and listings of past and current research of a psychological nature.

PsycINFO A computerized searching system available on CD or the Internet that includes summaries and listings of past and current research of a psychological nature.

qualitative method A method that emphasizes verbal descriptions and narratives rather than traditional statistical methods.

quantitative method A method that emphasizes measures using numbers and traditional statistical techniques.

quasi-experimental design Also called an *evaluation research design,* a design used when sufficient control over the variables under study and potentially confounding variables is lacking. Because of this lack of control, definite statements cannot be made about cause and effect.

random assignment Occurs when participants' chances of being assigned to each group in an experiment are equal.

random number table A table of numbers created so that their occurrence

cannot be predicted from a mathematical formula.

random sampling The selection of participants in an unbiased manner so that each potential participant has an equal possibility of being selected for the experiment.

range The measure of dispersion reflecting the difference between the largest and smallest scores in a set of data.

reactive behavior A change in the participant's behavior due to the mere presence of an observer.

reliability The requirement that a measure be consistent and reproducible.

replication Repeating a procedure under a similar set of conditions to check the outcome, thereby decreasing the likelihood that the results may have occurred by chance.

retrospective design *See* retrospective method.

retrospective method (post hoc method) A procedure by which a researcher examines data available prior to the beginning of the study (for example, medical records from the past 20 years) to answer the research question.

scale of measurement The type of information that a number conveys. Several basic types of scales include nominal, ordinal, interval, and ratio.

Science Citation Index A cumulative listing of articles published in the physical sciences (chemistry, biology, and physics) and in the social sciences (psychology and sociology).

secondary variance A variation in an outcome of an experiment that is due to variables other than the planned independent variables.

single-subject design A design based on a limited number of participants, usually one.

Social Science Citation Index a cumulative index of articles published in the social sciences.

standard deviation A measure of variability calculated by taking the square root of the variance.

subject factor A characteristic of the participant's behavior that causes

unexpected behavior in the experimental setting.

subject variable A variable that refers to an existing attribute of an individual (for example, sex) that an experimenter selects rather than manipulates.

sum of squares A number used in the determination of the variance; calculated by summing the squared values for the deviation of each data point from the mean of that data set.

systematic variation Variation due to systematic factors.

test–retest reliability A measure of consistency (usually the correlation coefficient) in which a measurement is conducted at two separate times and their similarity determined.

time series design A within-subjects design requiring the measurement of data both before and after an experimental treatment.

treatment effect The effect produced by the treatment or independent variable on the dependent variable.

Type I error The error of rejecting the null hypothesis when it is true.

Type II error The error of accepting the null hypothesis when it is false.

validity The accuracy of our ideas and our research; the degree to which these are true and capable of support.

variability The manner in which measurements vary within an experimental condition. The statistical measurements of variability are those of standard deviation and variance.

within-subjects design A design in which the participants receive more than one level of the independent variable.

x **axis** The horizontal axis of a graph also referred to as the abscissa. The independent variable is typically placed on the *x* axis.

y **axis** The vertical axis of a graph also referred to as the ordinate. The dependent variable is typically placed on the *y* axis.

BIBLIOGRAPHY

Abraham, F. (1990). *A visual introduction to dynamical systems theory for psychology.* Santa Cruz, CA: Aerial Press.

Alfred, R. (1976). The Church of Satan. In C. Glock & R. Bellah (Eds.), *The new religious consciousness* (pp. 180–202). Berkeley: University of California Press.

American Psychological Association. (2001). *Publication manual* (5th ed.). Washington, DC: Author.

Aserinsky, E., & Kleitman, N. (1953). Regularly occurring periods of eye motility and concomitant phenomena during sleep. *Science, 118,* 273–274.

Babbie, E. R. (2008). *The practice of social research* (11th ed.). Belmont, CA: Wadsworth.

Bakeman, R., & Gottman, J. (1989). *Observing interaction: An introduction to sequential analysis.* Cambridge, UK: Cambridge University Press.

Bandura, A. (1982). The psychology of chance encounters and life paths. *American Psychologist, 37,* 747–755.

Barber, T. X. (1976). *Pitfalls in human research.* New York: Pergamon.

Barefoot, J., Dahlstrom, G., & Williams, R. (1983). Hostility, CHD incidence, and total mortality: A 25-year follow-up study of 255 physicians. *Psychosomatic Medicine, 45,* 59–63.

Barnard, N., & Kaufman, S. (1997). Animal research is wasteful and misleading. *Scientific American, 276,* 80–82.

Barthell, C. N., & Holmes, D. S. (1968). High school yearbooks: A nonreactive measure of social isolation in graduates who later become schizophrenic. *Journal of Abnormal Psychology, 73,* 313–316.

Baum, A., & Posluszny, D. (1999). Health psychology: Mapping biobehavioral contributions to health and illness. *Annual Review of Psychology, 50,* 137–163.

Baumrind, D. (1964). Some thoughts on ethics of research: After reading Milgram's "Behavioral study of obedience." *American Psychologist, 19,* 421–423.

Bechara, A., Tranel, D., Damasio, H., Adolphs, R., Rockland, C., & Damasio, A. (1995). Double dissociation of conditioning and declarative knowledge relative to the amygdala and hippocampus in humans. *Science, 269,* 1115–1118.

Becker, D., Kenrick, D., Neuberg, S., Blackwell, K., & Smith, D. (2007). The confounded nature of angry men and women. *Journal of Personality and Social Psychology, 92,* 179–190.

Beilock, S., & Carr, T. (2001). On the fragility of skilled performance: What governs choking under pressure? *Journal of Experimental Psychology: General, 130,* 701–725.

Belsky, J., Woodworth, S., & Crnic, K. (1996). Trouble in the second year: Three questions about family interaction. *Child Development, 67,* 556–578.

Bentler, P. (1980). Multivariate analysis with latent variables: Causal modeling. *Annual Review of Psychology, 31,* 419–456.

Berkowitz, L. (1970). The contagion of violence: An S-R mediational analysis of some effects of observed aggression. Nebraska Symposium on Motivation, 18, 95–136.

Bernstein, P., Scheffers, M., & Coles, M. (1995). "Where did I go wrong?" A psychophysiological analysis of error detection. *Journal of Experimental Psychology: Human Perception and Performance, 21,* 1312–1322.

Beyer, W. H. (1960). *Handbook of tables for probability and statistics* (2nd ed.). Cleveland: Chemical Rubber Company.

Biglan, A., Ary, D., & Wagenaar, A. (2000). The value of interrupted time-series experiments for community intervention research. *Prevention Science, 1,* 31–49.

Birnbaum, M. (2001). *Introduction to behavioral research on the internet.* Upper Saddle River, NJ: Prentice Hall.

Birnbaum, M. (2004). Human research and data collection via the Internet. *Annual Reivew of Psychology, 55,* 803–832.

Bjorklund, D., & Pellegrini, A. (2000). Child development and evolutionary psychology. *Child Development, 71,* 1687–1708.

Bjorklund, D., & Pellegrini, A. (2002). *The origins of human nature: Evolutionary developmental psychology.* Washington DC: American Psychological Association.

Blampied, N. (2000). Single-case research designs: A neglected alternative. *American Psychologist, 55,* 960.

Bohm, D. (1969). Further remarks on order. In C. H. Waddington (Ed.), *Towards a theoretical biology* (Vol. 2). Edinburgh: Edinburgh University Press.

Bolgar, H. (1965). The case study method. In B. B. Wolman (Ed.), *Handbook of clinical psychology* (pp. 28–39). New York: McGraw-Hill.

Bolger, N., & Zuckerman, A. (1995). A framework for studying personality in the stress process. *Journal of Personality and Social Psychology, 69,* 890–902.

Boring, E. G. (1950). *A history of experimental psychology* (2nd ed.). New York: Appleton-Century-Crofts.

Botella, P., Bosch, F., Romero, F., & Parra, A. (2001). *Human Psychopharmacology Clinical and Experimental, 16,* 533–540.

Botting, J., & Morrison, A. (1997). Animal research is vital to medicine. *Scientific American, 276,* 83–85.

Bower, G. H. (1981). Mood and memory. *American Psychologist, 36,* 129–148.

Bower, G. H., & Gilligan, S. G. (1979). Remembering information related to one's self. *Journal of Research in Personality, 13,* 420–432.

Bower, G. H., Monteiro, K. P., & Gilligan, S. G. (1978). Emotional mood as a context of learning and recall. *Journal of Verbal Learning and Verbal Behavior, 17,* 573–585.

Bransford, J. D. (1979). *Human cognition.* Belmont, CA: Wadsworth.

Bransford, J. D., & Johnson, M. K. (1972). Contextual prerequisites for understanding: Some investigations of comprehension and recall. *Journal of Verbal Learning and Verbal Behavior, 11,* 717–726.

Bremner, J., & Narayan, M. (1998). The effects of stress on memory and the hippocampus throughout the life cycle: Implications for childhood development and aging. *Development and Psychopathology, 10,* 871–885.

Bridgman, P. W. (1927). *The logic of modern physics.* New York: Macmillan.

Broad, W. J. (1980). Imbroglio at Yale (I): Emergence of a fraud. *Science, 210,* 38–41.

Bromley, D. (1986). *The case-study design in psychology and related disciplines.* New York: Wiley.

Bronfenbrenner, U. (1979). *The ecology of human development.* Cambridge, MA: Harvard University Press.

Bronowski, J. (1965). *Science and human values.* New York: Harper & Row.

Brown, B. O. (1992). Portraying people with disabilities: Toward a new vocabulary. *The Editorial Eye, 15,* 1–3, 6–7.

Bruning, J. L., & Kintz, B. L. (1968). *Computational handbook of statistics.* Glenview, IL: Scott, Foresman.

Brunswik, E. (1947). *Systematic and representative design of psychological experiments.* Berkeley: University of California Press.

Budiansky, S. (1998). *If a lion could talk: Animal intelligence and the evolution of consciousness.* New York: Free Press.

Buss, D. (Ed.). (2005). *The handbook of evolutionary psychology.* Hoboken, NJ: Wiley.

Camic, P., Rhodes, J., & Yardley, L. (2003). *Qualitative research in psychology.* Washington, DC: American Psychological Association.

Campbell, A. A., & Katona, G. (1953). The sample survey: A technique for social science research. In L. Festinger & D. Katz (Eds.), *Research methods in the behavioral sciences.* New York: Dryden.

Campbell, D. T., & Stanley, J. C. (1963). *Experimental and quasi-experimental designs for research.* Chicago: Rand McNally.

Carlsmith, J. M., Ellsworth, P. C., & Aronson, E. (1976). *Methods of research in social psychology.* Reading, MA: Addison-Wesley.

Carr, J., & Burkholder, E. (1998). Creating single-subject design graphs with Microsoft Excel™. *Journal of Applied Behavioral Analysis, 31,* 245–251.

Carrington, P., & Moyer, S. (1994). Gun availability and suicide in Canada: Testing the displacement hypothesis. *Studies on Crime and Crime Prevention, 3,* 168–178.

Castonguay, L. G., Goldfried, M. R., Wiser, S. L., Raue, P. J., & Hayes, A. M. (1996). Predicting the effect of cognitive therapy for depression: A study of unique and common factors. *Journal of Consulting and Clinical Psychology, 64,* 497–504.

Chamberlin, T. C. (1965). The method of multiple working hypotheses. *Science, 148,* 754–759. (Original work published in 1890)

Chang, B., & Lenzenweger, M. (2001). Somatosensory processing in the biological relatives of schizophrenia patients: A signal detection analysis of two-point discrimination. *Journal of Abnormal Psychology, 110,* 433–442.

Chi, M., & Koeske, R. (1983). Network representation of a child's dinosaur knowledge. *Developmental Psychology, 19,* 29–39.

Cobb, L. A., Thomas, G. I., Dillard, D. H., Merendino, K. A., & Bruce, R. A. (1959). An evaluation of internal-mammary-artery ligation by a double-blind technique. *New England Journal of Medicine, 260,* 1115–1118.

Cohen, J. (1990). Things I have learned (so far). *American Psychologist, 45,* 1304–1312.

Cohen, J., Dunbar, K., & McClelland, J. (1990). On the control of automatic processes: A parallel distributed processing account of the Stroop effect. *Psychological Review, 97,* 332–361.

Cohen, L., & Holliday, M. (1982). *Statistics for social scientists.* London: Harper & Row.

Cohen, M., & Nagel, E. (1934). *An introduction to logic and scientific method.* New York: Harcourt.

Cohen, S., & Herbert, T. (1996). Health psychology: Psychological factors and physical disease from the perspective of human psychoneuroimmunology. *Annual Review of Psychology, 47,* 113–142.

Cohn, M., Mehl, M., & Pennebaker, J. (2004). Linguistic markers of psychological change surrounding September 11, 2001. *Psychological Science, 15,* 687–693.

Cole, P. (1986). Children's spontaneous control of facial expression. *Child Development, 57,* 1309–1321.

Connell, J. P., & Tanaka, J. S. (Eds.). (1987). Special section on structural equation modeling. *Child Development, 58,* 1–175.

Converse, J. M., & Schuman, H. (1974). *Conversations at random: Survey research as interviewers see it.* New York: Wiley.

Converse, P., & Traugott, M. (1986). Assessing the accuracy of polls and surveys. *Science, 234,* 1094–1098.

Cook, S. W. (1975). A comment on the ethical issues involved in West, Gunn, and Chernicky's "Ubiquitous Watergate: An attributional analysis." *Journal of Personality and Social Psychology, 32,* 66–68.

Cook, T. D., & Campbell, D. T. (1979). *Quasi-experimentation: Design and analysis issues for field settings.* Chicago: Rand McNally.

Coombs, C. H., Raiffa, H., & Thrall, R. M. (1954). Some views on mathematical models and measurement theory. *Psychological Review, 61,* 132–144.

Cooper, M. L., Frone, R., Russell, M., & Mudar, P. (1995). Drinking to regulate positive and negative emotions: A motivational model of alcohol use. *Journal of Personality and Social Psychology, 69,* 990–1005.

Copi, I. (1986). *Introduction to logic.* New York: Macmillan.

Cowles, M., & Davis, C. (1982). On the origins of the .05 level of statistical significance. *American Psychologist, 37,* 553–558.

Cronbach, L. J., & Meehl, P. (1955). Construct validity in psychological tests. *Psychological Bulletin, 52,* 281–302.

Csikszentmihalyi, M. (1990). *Flow: The psychology of optimal experience.* New York: Harper & Row, 1990.

Cudeck, R., & Harring, J. (2007). Analysis of nonlinear patterns of change with random coefficient models. *Annual Review of Psychology, 58,* 615–637.

Cunningham, M. R. (1979). Weather, mood, and helping behavior: Quasi-experiments with the sunshine samaritan. *Journal of Personality and Social Psychology, 37,* 1947–1956.

Cytowic, R. (1989). *Synesthesia.* New York: Springer-Verlag.

Danziger, K. (1985). The origins of the psychological experiment as a social institution. *American Psychologist, 40,* 133–140.

Dawkins, M. (1990). From an animal's point of view: Motivation, fitness, and animal welfare. *Behavioral and Brain Sciences, 13,* 1–61.

DeSchepper, B., & Treisman, A. (1996). Visual memory for novel shapes: Implicit coding without attention. *Journal of Experimental Psychology: Learning, Memory, and Cognition, 22,* 27–47.

Deutsch, F., & Saxon, S. (1998). The double standard of praise and criticism for mothers and fathers. *Psychology of Women Quarterly, 22,* 665–683.

De Waal, F. (2000). Primates—A natural heritage of conflict resolution. *Science, 289,* 586–590.

Dillman, D. A. (1978). *Mail and telephone surveys: The total design method.* New York: Wiley.

Domjan, M., & Purdy, J. (1995). Animal research in psychology: More than meets the eye of the general psychology student. *American Psychologist, 50,* 496–503.

Dowd, M. (1983, Dec. 4). Many women in poll equate values of job and family life. *New York Times.*

Dyer, K., Dunlap, G., & Winterling, V. (1990). Effects of choice making on the serious problem behaviors of students with severe handicaps. *Journal of Applied Behavior Analysis, 23,* 515–524.

Ebbinghaus, H. (1885). *Memory.* New York: Teacher's College.

Edgington, E. S. (1974). A new tabulation of statistical procedures used in APA journals. *American Psychologist, 29,* 25–26.

Edwards, A. L. (1962). *Experimental design in psychological research.* New York: Holt, Rinehart & Winston.

Edwards, J., Thomas, M., Rosenfeld, P., & Booth-Kewley, S. (1997). *How to conduct organizational surveys.* Thousand Oaks, CA: Sage.

Elbert, T., Ray, W., Kowalik, Z., Skinner, S., Graf, K., & Birbaumer, N. (1994). Chaos and physiology: Deterministic chaos in excitable cell assemblies. *Physiological Reviews, 74,* 1–47.

Enserink, M. (1999). Can the placebo be the cure? *Science, 284,* 238–240.

Enserink, M. (2000). Are placebo-controlled drug trials ethical? *Science, 288,* 416.

Ericsson, K. A., & Polson, P. (1988a). A cognitive analysis of exceptional memory for restaurant orders. In

M. Chi, R. Glaser, & M. Farr (Eds.), *The nature of expertise.* Hillsdale, NJ: Erlbaum.

Ericsson, K. A., & Polson, P. (1988b). An experimental analysis of the mechanisms of a memory skill. *Journal of Experimental Psychology: Learning, Memory, and Cognition, 14,* 305–316.

Ericsson, K. A., & Simon, H. A. (1980). Verbal report as data. *Psychological Review, 87,* 215–251.

Eysenck, H. J. (1976). Behavior therapy: Dogma or applied science. In M. P. Feldman & A. Broadhurst (Eds.), *Theoretical and experimental bases of the behavior therapies.* London: Wiley.

Fendrich, D., Healy, A., & Bourne, L. (1991). Long-term repetition effects for motoric and perceptual procedures. *Journal of Experimental Psychology: Learning, Memory and Cognition, 17,* 137–151.

Festinger, L., Riecken, H., & Schachter, S. (1956). *When prophecy fails.* Minneapolis: University of Minnesota Press.

Field, M., & Behrman, R. (2004). *The ethical conduct of clinical research involving children.* Washington, DC: National Academies Press.

Fink, A., & Kosecoff, J. (1998). *How to conduct surveys* (2nd ed.). Thousand Oaks, CA: Sage.

Fisher, R. (1935). *The design of experiments.* Edinburgh: Oliver & Boyd.Fisher, R., & Yates, F. (1948). *Statistical tables for biological, agricultural and medical research* (3rd ed.). Edinburgh: Oliver & Boyd.

Fisher, R., & Yates, F. (1974). *Statistical tables for biological, agricultural, and medical research* (6th ed.). London: Longman Group Ldt.

Flavell, J. (1999). Cognitive development: Children's knowledge about the mind. *Annual Review of Psychology, 50,* 21–45.

Fowler, A. (1995). The CMU Cyberporn Study: The naked truth. *Professional Ethics Report, 8,* 1–4.

Fox, E., Russo, R., Bowles, R., & Dutton, K. (2001). Do threatening stimuli draw or hold visual attention in subclinical anxiety? *Journal of Experimental Psychology: General, 130,* 681–700.

Franklin, R., Allison, D., & Gorman, B. (1997). *Design and analysis of single-case research.* Hillsdale, NJ: Erlbaum.

Franklin, R., Gorman, B., Beasley, T., & Allison, D. (1998). Graphical display and visual analysis. In R. Franklin, D. Allison, & B. Gorman (Eds.), *Design and analysis of single-case research* (pp. 119–158). Hillsdale, NJ: Erlbaum.

Freeman, W. (1991). The physiology of perception. *Scientific American, 264,* 78–85.

Freeman, W. (1999). *How brains make up their minds.* London: Weidenfeld & Nicolson.

Freeman, W. (2004). How and why brains create meaning from sensory information. *International Journal of Bifurcation and Chaos, 14,* 515–530.

Freud, S. (1966). Project for a scientific psychology. In J. Strachey (Ed. and Trans.), *The standard edition of the complete psychological works of Sigmund Freud* (Vol. 1, pp. 281–397). London: Hogarth. (Original work published 1895)

Fry, L. W., & Greenfield, S. (1980). Examination of attitudinal differences between policemen and policewomen. *Journal of Applied Psychology, 65,* 123–126.

Furumoto, L. (1992). Joining separate spheres: Christine Ladd-Franklin, woman-scientist (1847–1930). *American Psychologist, 47,* 175–182.

Furumoto, L., & Scarborough, E. (1986). Placing women in the history of psychology: The first American women psychologists. *American Psychologist, 41,* 35–42.

Gaito, J. (1980). Measurement scales and statistics: Resurgence of an old misconception. *Psychological Bulletin, 87,* 564–567.

Galen. (1827). De praenotione. In D. C. G. Kuhn (Ed.), *Opera omnia, cap. vi* (Vol. 9, pp. 630–635). Lipsiae: Officina Libraria Car. Cnoblochii.

Gallup, G. (1972). Opinion polling in a democracy. In J. Tanur (Ed.), *Statistics: A guide to the unknown.* San Francisco: Holden-Day.

Galtung, J. (1967). *Theory and methods of social research.* New York: Columbia University Press.

Gaul, D. J., Craighead, W. E., & Mahoney, M. J. (1975). Relationship between eating rates and obesity. *Journal of Consulting and Clinical Psychology, 43,* 123–125.

Geary, D. (2005). *The origin of mind: Evolution of brain, cognition, and general intelligence.* Washington DC: American Psychological Association.

Gilbert, D., Fiske, S., & Lindzey, G. (1998). *The handbook of social psychology.* New York: McGraw-Hill.

Glass, G. V., & Stanley, J. C. (1970). *Statistical methods in education and psychology.* Englewood Cliffs, NJ: Prentice Hall.

Glasser, R. J. (1976). *The body is the hero.* New York: Random House.

Gleick, J. (1987). *Chaos.* New York: Penguin.

Goldberger, A., & Rigney, D. (1991). Nonlinear dynamics at the bedside. In L. Glass, P. Hunter, & A. McCulloch (Eds.), *Theory of heart.* New York: Springer-Verlag.

Gorman, B., & Allison, D. (1998). Statistical alternatives for single-case designs. In R. Franklin, D. Allison, & B. Gorman (Eds.), *Design and analysis of single-case research* (pp. 159–214). Hillsdale, NJ: Erlbaum.

Gottman, J. M. (1973). N-of-1 and N-of-2 research in psychotherapy. *Psychological Bulletin, 80,* 93–105.

Gould, S. J. (1978). The finagle factor. *Human Nature, 1,* 80–87.

Graffin, N., Ray, W., & Lundy, R. (1995). EEG concomitants of hypnosis and hypnotic susceptibility. *Journal of Abnormal Psychology, 104,* 123–131.

Granholm, E., Asarnow, R., & Marder, S. (1996). Display visual angle and attentional scanpaths on the span of apprehension task in schizophrenia. *Journal of Abnormal Psychology, 105,* 17–24.

Gray, J. A. (1979). *Pavlov.* London: Fontana.

Gray, J. A. (1990). In defense of speciesism. *Behavioral and Brain Sciences, 13,* 22–23.

Gur, R. C., & Sackeim, H. (1979). Self-deception: A concept in search of a phenomenon. *Journal of Personality and Social Psychology, 37,* 147–169.

Hains, A., & Baer, D. (1989). Interaction effects in multi-element designs: Inevitable, desirable, and ignorable. *Journal of Applied Behavioral Analysis, 22,* 57–69.

Hamann, S. (1996). Implicit memory in the tactile modality: Evidence from Braille stem completion in the blind. *Psychological Science, 7,* 284–288.

Hanson, R., Kilpatrick, D., Freedy, J., & Saunders, B. (1995). Los Angeles County after the 1992 civil disturbances: Degree of exposure and impact on mental health. *Journal of Consulting and Clinical Psychology, 63,* 987–996.

Hass, H., Fink, H., & Hartfelder, G. (1963). The placebo problem. *Psychopharmacology Service Center Bulletin, 2,* 1–65.

Hearnshaw, L. S. (1979). *Cyril Burt, psychologist.* Ithaca, NY: Cornell University Press.

Helweg, D., Roitblat, H., Nachigall, P., & Hautus, M. (1996). Recognition of aspect-dependent three-dimensional objects by an echolocating Atlantic bottlenose dolphin. *Journal of Experimental Psychology: Animal Behavior Processes, 22,* 19–31.

Herodotus. (1942). In F. R. B. Godolphin (Ed.), *The Greek historians.* New York: Random House.

Hersen, M., & Barlow, D. (1976). *Single case experimental designs.* New York: Pergamon.

Hersen, M., & Bellack, A. (1976). A multiple baseline analysis of social skills training in chronic schizophrenics. *Journal of Applied Behavior Analysis, 9,* 239–245.

Hilton, M. (1984). The impact of recent changes in California drinking-driving laws on fatal accident levels during the first postintervention year: An interrupted time series analysis. *Law and Society Review, 18,* 605–627.

Holt, R. R. (1965). Experimental methods in clinical psychology. In B. B. Wolman (Ed.), *Handbook of clinical psychology.* New York: McGraw-Hill.

Holton, G. (1952). *Introduction to concepts and theories in physical science.* Reading, MA: Addison-Wesley.

Horner, M. S. (1972). Toward an understanding of achievement related conflicts in women. *Journal of Social Issues, 28,* 157–176.

Huth, E. J. (1987). Prose style. In *Medical style and format* (pp. 260–287). Philadelphia: ISI Press.

Irwin, J., & Whitehead, P. (1991). Toward an objective psychophysics of pain. *Psychological Science, 2,* 230–235.

Jaccard, J., & Becker, M. (1990). *Statistics for the behavioral sciences* (2nd ed.). Belmont, CA: Wadsworth.

Jenni, D., & Jenni, M. (1976). Carrying behaviour in humans: Analysis of sex differences. *Science, 194,* 859–860.

Johnson-Laird, P. (1999). Deductive reasoning. *Annual Review of Psychology, 50,* 109–135.

Jones, E. (1993). Introduction to special section: Single case research in psychotherapy. *Journal of Consulting and Clinical Psychology, 61,* 371–372.

Jones, E. E., & Nisbett, R. E. (1971). *The actor and the observer: Divergent perceptions of the causes of behavior.* Morristown, NJ: General Learning Press.

Kalat, J. (1992). *Biological psychology* (4th ed.). Belmont, CA: Wadsworth.

Kardas, E. (1999). *Psychology resources on the World Wide Web.* Pacific Grove, CA: Brooks/Cole.

Kazdin, A. E. (1973). Methodological and assessment considerations in evaluating reinforcement programs in applied settings. *Journal of Applied Behavioral Analysis, 6,* 517–531.

Kazdin, A. E. (1982). *Single-case research designs.* New York: Oxford University Press.

Kazdin, A. E. (1995). Preparing and evaluating research reports. *Psychological Assessment, 7,* 228–237.

Kazdin, A. E. (2003a). Methodology: What it is and why it is so important. In A.E. Kazdin (Ed.), *Methodological issues and strategies in clinical research* (pp. 5–22). Washington, DC: American Psychological Association.

Kazdin, A. E. (2003b). *Research design in clinical psychology.* Needham Heights, MA: Allyn & Bacon.

Kelman, H. C. (1968). *A time to speak.* San Francisco: Jossey-Bass.

Kempf, A., & Remington, P. (2007). New challenges for telephone survey research in the twenty-first century. *Annual Review of Public Health, 28,* 113–126.

Keppel, G., & Saufley, W. H. (1980). *Introduction to design and analysis: A student's handbook.* San Francisco: W. H. Freeman.

Kerlinger, F. N. (1973). *Foundations of behavioral research* (2nd ed.). New York: Holt, Rinehart & Winston.

Kerlinger, F. N. (1986). *Foundations of behavioral research* (3rd ed.). New York: Holt, Rinehart & Winston.

Kitayama, S., Snibbe, A., Markus, H., & Suzuki, T. (2004). Is there any "fee"choice? Self and dissonance in two cultures. *Psychological Science, 15,* 527–533.

Klein, K., & Boals, A. (2001). Expressive writing can increase working memory capacity. *Journal of Experimental Psychology: General, 130,* 520–533.

Knatterud, M. E. (1991). Writing with the patient in mind: Don't add insult to injury. *American Medical Writers Association Journal, 6,* 10–17.

Kodak, T., Northup, J., & Kelley, M. (2007). An evaluation of the types of attention that maintain problem behavior. *Journal of Applied Behavior Analysis, 40,* 167–171.

Koestler, A. (1964). *The act of creation.* New York: Macmillan.

Kolb, B., & Whishaw, I. (1998). Brain plasticity and behavior. *Annual Review of Psychology, 49,* 43–64.

Kolb, F., & Braum, J. (1995). Blindsight in normal observers. *Nature, 377,* 336–338.

Kourany, J. (1987). *Scientific knowledge.* Belmont, CA: Wadsworth.

Kraft, C. L. (1978). A psychophysical contribution to air safety: Simulator studies of visual illusions in night visual approaches. In H. L. Pick, H. W. Leibowitz, J. E. Singer, A. Steinschneider, & H. W. Stevenson (Eds.), *Psychology: From research to practice.* New York: Plenum.

Krantz, D. H., Luce, R. D., Suppes, P., & Tversky, A. (1971). *Foundations of measurement* (Vol. 1). New York: Academic Press.

Krantz, D. S. (1979). Naturalistic study of social influences on meal size among moderately obese and nonobese subjects. *Psychosomatic Medicine, 41,* 19–27.

Kratochwill, T. (Ed.). (1978). *Single subject research.* New York: Academic Press.

Kraut, R., Olson, J., Banaji, M., Bruckman, A., Cohen, J., & Couper, M. (2004). Psychological research online: Report of Board of Scientific Affairs' Advisory Group on the Conduct of Research on the Internet. *American Psycholgist, 59,* 105–117.

Krosnick, J. (1999). Survey research. *Annual Review of Psychology, 50,* 537–567.

Kuhn, T. (1970). *The structure of scientific revolutions* (2nd ed.). Chicago: University of Chicago Press.

Lakatos, I. (1978). *The methodology of scientific research programs.* Cambridge, UK: Cambridge University Press.

Landau, B., Gleitman, H., & Spelke, E. (1981). Spatial knowledge and geometric representation in a child blind from birth. *Science, 213,* 1275–1278.

Landers, D. M., Obermier, G. E., & Patterson, A. H. (1976). Iris pigmentation and reactive motor performance. *Journal of Motor Behavior, 8,* 171–179.

Lauerman, J. (1999). Animal research. *Harvard Magazine, 101,* 49–57.

Lehner, P. N. (1979). *Handbook of ethological methods.* New York: Garland STPM Press.

Leong, F., & Austin, J. (Eds.). (1996). *The psychology research handbook: A guide for graduate students and research assistants.* Newbury Park, CA: Sage.

Levitt, L., & Leventhal, G. (1986). Litter reduction: How effective is the New York State bill? *Environment and Behavior, 18,* 467–479.

Likert, R. (1932). A technique for the measurement of attitudes. *Archives of Psychology, 19,* 44–53.

Linton, M. (1982). Transformations of memory in everyday life. In U. Neisser (Ed.), *Memory observed.* San Francisco: Freeman.

Linton, M., & Gallo, P. S. (1975). *The practical statistician.* Pacific Grove, CA: Brooks/Cole.

Loftus, E. F., & Fries, J. F. (1979). Informed consent may be hazardous to your health. *Science, 204,* 11.

Longo, D., & Bisconer, S. (2003). Threatmat of aggression for an adult diagnosed with schizophrenia at a public psychiatric hospital. *Professional Psychology, Research and Practice, 34,* 177–179.

Lord, F. M. (1953). On the statistical treatment of football numbers. *American Psychologist, 8,* 750–751.

Lorenz, K. (1952). *King Solomon's ring.* New York: Crowell.

Lorenz, K. (1973). The fashionable fallacy of dispensing with description. *Naturwissenschaften, 60,* 1–9.

Luce, D., & Narens, L. (1987). Measurement of scales on the continuum. *Science, 236,* 1527–1532.

Luo, S., & Klohnen, E. (2005). Assortative mating and marital quality in newlyweds: A couple-centered approach. *Journal of Personality and Social Psychology, 88,* 304–326.

Luria, A. R. (1972). *The man with a shattered world.* New York: Basic Books.

Lyons, E., & Chryssochoou, X. (2000). Cross-cultural research methods. In B. Breakwell & S. Hammond (Eds.), *Research methods in psychology* (2nd ed., pp. 134–146). London: Sage.

Mace, C., & Kratochwill, T. (1986). The individual subject in behavioral analysis research. In J. Valsiner (Ed.), *The individual subject and scientific psychology.* New York: Plenum.

MacLeod, C., Mathews, A., & Tata, P. (1986). Perceptual bias with emotional stimuli in normal and abnormal populations. *Journal of Abnormal Psychology, 95,* 15–20.

Maggio, R. (1991). *The bias-free word finder: A dictionary of nondiscriminatory language.* Boston: Beacon Press.

Maher, B. A. (1978a). A reader's, writer's and reviewer's guide to assessing research reports in clinical psychology. *Journal of Consulting and Clinical Psychology, 46,* 835–838.

Maher, B. A. (1978b). Stimulus sampling in clinical research: Representative design reviewed. *Journal of Consulting and Clinical Psychology, 46,* 643–647.

Mahoney, M. J. (1976). *Scientist as subject.* Cambridge, MA: Ballinger.

Manning, C., Hall, J., & Gold, P. (1990). Glucose effects on memory and other neuropsychological tests in elderly humans. *Psychological Science, 1,* 307–311.

March, L., Cienfuegos, A., Goldbloom, L., Ritter, W., Cowan, N., & Javitt, D. (1999). Normal time course of auditory recognition in schizophrenia, despite impaired precision of the auditory sensory ("echoic") memory code. *Journal of Abnormal Psychology, 108,* 69–75.

Mark, M., Cook, T. D., & Cook, F. (1984). Randomized and quasi-experimental designs in evaluation research. In L. Rutman (Ed.), *Evaluation research methods: A basic guide* (2nd ed.). Beverly Hills, CA: Sage.

Martin, G. (2004). Encoder: A connectionist model of how learning to visually encode fixated text images improves reading fluency. *Psychological Review, 111,* 617–639.

Martin, M., Sadlom, G., & Stew, G. (2006). The phenomenon of boredom. *Qualitative Research in Psychology, 3,* 193–211.

Maslow, A. H. (1966). *The psychology of science.* New York: Harper & Row.

Maslow, A. H. (1970). *Motivation and personality* (2nd ed.). New York: Harper & Row.

Maslow, A. H. (1971). *The farthest reaches of human nature.* New York: Viking.

Masuda, T., & Kitayama, S. (2003). Perceiver-induced constraint and attitude attribution in Japan and the US: A case for the cultural dependence of the correspondence bias. *Journal of Experimental Social Psychology, 40,* 409–416.

Masuda, T., & Nisbett, R. (2006). Culture and change blindness. *Cognitive Science, 30,* 381–399.

McCall, R. B. (1980). *Fundamental statistics for psychology* (2nd ed.). New York: Harcourt Brace Jovanovich.

McGuffin, P., Riley, B., & Plomin, R. (2001). Genomics and behavior. Toward behavioral genomics. *Science, 291,* 1232–1249.

McKenna, F., & Sharma, D. (1995). Intrusive cognitions: An investigation of the emotional Stroop task. *Journal of Experimental Psychology: Learning, Memory, and Cognition, 21,* 1595–1607.

Mead, M. (1928). *Coming of age in Samoa.* New York: Morrow.

Meehl, P. (1978). Theoretical risks and tabular asterisks: Sir Karl, Sir Ronald, and the slow progress of soft psychology. *Journal of Consulting and Clinical Psychology, 46,* 806–834.

Merrington, M., & Thompson, C. (1943). Tables of percentage points of the inverted beta (*F*) distribution. *Biometrika, 33,* 73–88.

Mesulam, M., & Perry, J. (1972). The diagnosis of lovesickness: Experimental psychophysiology without the polygraph. *Psychophysiology, 9,* 546–551.

Milgram, S. (1963). Behavioral study of obedience. *Journal of Abnormal and Social Psychology, 67,* 371–378.

Milgram, S. (1977). *The individual in a social world: Essays and experiments.* Reading, MA: Addison-Wesley.

Miller, G. T. (1988). *Living in the environment: An introduction to environmental science* (5th ed.). Belmont, CA: Wadsworth.

Milner, B. (1966). Amnesia following operation on the temporal lobes. In C. W. M. Whitty & O. L. Zangwill (Eds.), *Amnesia.* London: Butterworths.

Mitchell, J. (1986). Measurement scales and statistics: A clash of paradigms. *Psychological Bulletin, 100,* 398–407.

Mitroff, I. I. (1974). Norms and counter-norms in a select group of the Apollo moon scientists: A case study of the ambivalence of scientists. *American Sociological Review, 39,* 579–595.

Mitroff, I. I., & Fitzgerald, I. (1977). On the psychology of the Apollo moon scientists: A chapter in the psychology of science. *Human Relations, 30,* 657–674.

Moras, K., Telfer, L., & Barlow, D. (1993). Efficacy and specific effects data on new treatments: A case study strategy with mixed anxiety–depression. *Journal of Clinical and Consulting Psychology, 61,* 412–420.

Morell, V. (1996). Life at the top: Animals pay the high price of dominance. *Science, 271,* 292.

Mukerjee, M. (1997). Trends in animal research. *Scientific American, 276,* 86–93.

Murphy, K., & Myors, B. (1998). *Statistical power analysis.* Mahwah, NJ: Erlbaum.

Nelson, R., Badura, L., & Goldman, B. (1990). Mechanisms of seasonal cycles of behavior. *Annual Review of Psychology, 41,* 81–108.

Newcombe, N., & Arnkoff, D. (1979). Effects of speech style and sex of speaker on person perception. *Journal of Personality and Social Psychology, 37,* 1293–1303.

Newton, I. (1969). *Mathematical principles* (F. Cajori, Trans.). New York: Greenwood. (Translation first published 1729)

Nisbett, R. E., & Wilson, T. D. (1977). Telling more than we can know: Verbal reports on mental processes. *Psychological Review, 84,* 231–259.

Nosek, B., & Banaji, M. (2002). E-research: Ethics, security, design, and control in psychological research on the Internet. *Journal of Social Issues, 58,* 161–176.

Nosek, B., Banaji, M., & Greenwald, A. (2002). Harvesting implicit group attitudes and beliefs from a demonstration web site. *Group Dynamics, 6,* 101–115.

Öhman, A., Fluykt, A., & Esteves, F. (2001). Emotion drives attention: Detecting the snake in the grass. *Journal of Experimental Psychology: General, 130,* 466–478.

Okazaki, S. (1997). Sources of ethnic differences between Asian American and White American college students on measures of depression and social anxiety. *Journal of Abnormal Psychology, 106,* 52–60.

Olfson, M., Marcus, S., Druss, B., Elinson, L., Tanielian, T., & Pincus, H. (2002). National trends in the outpatient treatment of depression. *Journal of the American Medical Association, 287,* 203–209.

Orne, M. (1969). Demand characteristics and the concept of quasi-controls. In R. Rosenthal & R. L. Rosnow (Eds.), *Artifact in behavioral research.* New York: Academic Press.

Orne, M. T., & Evans, F. J. (1966). Inadvertent termination of hypnosis on hypnotized and simulating subjects. *International Journal of Clinical and Experimental Hypnosis, 14,* 61–78.

Orne, M. T., & Scheibe, K. (1964). The contribution of non-deprivation factors in the production of sensory deprivation effects: The psychology of the "panic button." *Journal of Abnormal and Social Psychology, 68,* 3–12.

Osborne, K., Rudrud, E., & Zezoney, F. (1990). Improved curveball hitting through the enhancement of visual cues. *Journal of Applied Behavioral Analysis, 23,* 371–377.

Osgood, C., Suci, G., & Tannenbaum, P. (1957). *The measurement of meaning.* Urbana: University of Illinois Press.

Pantev, C., Engelien, A., Candia, V., & Elbert, T. (2001). Representational cortex in musicians. Plastic alternations in response to musical practice. *Annals of the New York Academy of Science, 930,* 300–314.

Parsonson, B., & Baer, D. (1978). The analysis and presentation of graphic data. In T. Kratochwill (Ed.), *Single subject research.* New York: Academic Press.

Pennebaker, J. (1991). Personal communication.

Pennebaker, J., & Lay, T. (2002). Language use and personality during crises: Analyses of Mayor Rudoph Giuliani's press conferences. *Journal of Research in Personality, 36,* 271–282.

Persaud, N., McLeod, P., & Cowey, A. (2007). Post-decision wagering objectively measures awareness. *Nature Neuroscience, 10,* 257–261.

Petrinovich, L. (1979). Probabilistic functionalism: A conception of research methods. *American Psychologist, 34,* 373–390.

Petty, R., Fabrigar, L., Wegener, D., & Priester, J. (1996). Understanding data when interactions are present or hypothesized. *Psychological Science, 7,* 247–252.

Phillips, M., & Sechzer, J. (1989). *Animal research and ethical conflict.* New York: Springer-Verlag.

Piattelli-Palmarini, M. (1994). *Inevitable illusions.* New York: Wiley.

Platt, J. R. (1964). Strong inference. *Science, 146,* 347–353.

Plomin, R., Corley, R., DeFries, J., & Fulker, D. (1990). Individual differences in television viewing in early childhood. *Psychological Science, 1,* 371–377.

Popper, K. R. (1959). *The logic of scientific discovery.* New York: Basic Books.

Popper, K. R. (1972). *Objective knowledge.* Oxford, UK: Oxford University Press.

Press, W., Teukolsky, S., Vetterling, W., & Flannery, B. (1992). *Numerical recipes.* New York: Cambridge University Press.

Prince, M. (1913). *The dissociation of a personality.* New York: Longmans, Green.

Raebhausen, O. M., & Brim, O. G. (1967). Privacy and behavioral research. *American Psychologist, 22,* 423–437.

Ragnarsson, R., & Björgvinsson, T. (1991). Effects of public posting on driving speed on Icelandic traffic. *Journal of Applied Behavior Analysis, 24,* 53–58.

Ramachandran, V. (1998). *Phantoms in the brain.* New York: Morrow.

Rammsayer, T., & Rammstedt, B. (2000). Sex-related differences in time estimation: The role of personality. *Personality and Individual Differences, 29,* 301–312.

Ramsey, F., & Schafer, D. (2002). *The statistical sleuth* (2nd ed.). Pacific Grove, CA: Duxbury.

Raspberry, W. (1989, January 4). When "Black" becomes "African American." *Washington Post,* p. A19.

Ravizza, K. (1977). Peak experiences in sports. *Journal of Humanistic Psychology, 17,* 35–40.

Ray, W. J. (1989). Research designs in behavioral cardiovascular research. In N. Schneiderman, S. Weiss, & P. Kaufmann (Eds.), *Handbook of research methods in cardiovascular medicine.* New York: Plenum.

Ray, W. J., Katahn, M., & Snyder, C. R. (1971). Effects of test anxiety on acquisition, retention, and generalization of a complex verbal task in a classroom situation. *Journal of Personality and Social Psychology, 20,* 147–154.

Ray, W. J., Newcombe, N., Semon, J., & Cole, P. (1981). Spatial abilities, sex differences and EEG functioning. *Neuropsychologia, 19,* 719–722.

Ray, W., Odenwald, M., Neuner, F., Schauer, M., Ruf, M., Rockstroh, B., & Elbert, T. (2006). Decoupling neural networks from reality: Dissociative experiences in torture victims are reflected in abnormal brain waves in left frontal cortex. *Psychological Science, 17,* 825–829.

Ray, W. J., Wells, R., Elbert, T., Lutzenberger, W., & Birbaumer, N. (1991). EEG and chaos: Dimensional estimation of sensory and hypnotic processes. In D. Duke & W. Pritchard (Eds.), *Measuring chaos in the human brain.* New York: World Scientific.

Resnick, J. H., & Schwartz, T. (1973). Ethical standards as an independent variable in psychological research. *American Psychologist, 28,* 134–139.

Ristau, C. (Ed.). (1991). *Cognitive ethology: The minds of other animals.* Hillsdale, NJ: Erlbaum.

Roberts, F. S. (1979). *Measurement theory with applications to decision making utility and the social sciences.* Reading, MA: Addison-Wesley.

Roechelein, J. E. (1972). Sex differences in time estimation. *Perceptual and Motor Skills, 35,* 859–862.

Rogoff, B. (1990). *Apprenticeship in thinking: Cognitive development in social context.* New York: Oxford University Press.

Rosenhan, D. L. (1973). On being sane in insane places. *Science, 179,* 250–258.

Rosenthal, R. (1979). How often are our numbers wrong? *American Psychologist, 33,* 1005–1008.

Rosenthal, R. (1990). How are we doing in soft psychology? *American Psychologist, 45,* 775–777.

Rosenthal, R., & Fode, K. L. (1963). The effects of experimenter bias on the performance of the albino rat. *Behavioral Science, 8,* 183–189.

Rosenthal, R., & Jacobson, L. (1966). Teachers' expectancies: Determinants of pupils' IQ gains. *Psychological Report, 19,* 115–118.

Rosenthal, R., & Lawson, R. (1964). A longitudinal study of the effects of experimenter bias on the operant learning of rats. *Journal of Psychiatric Research, 2,* 61–72.

Rosenthal, R., & Rubin, D. B. (1978). Interpersonal expectancy effects: The first 345 studies. *Behavioral and Brain Sciences, 1,* 377–386.

Rosnow, R., & Rosenthal, R. (1995). "So things you learned aren't so." *Psychological Science, 6,* 3–9.

Rosnow, R., & Rosenthal, R. (1996). Contrasts and interactions redux: Five easy pieces. *Psychological Science, 7,* 253–257.

Rosnow, R., & Rosnow, M. (2005). *Writing papers in psychology.* Belmont, CA: Wadsworth.

Ross, A., & White, S. (1987). Shoplifting, impaired driving, and refusing the Breathalyzer: On seeing one's name in public places. *Evaluation Review, 11,* 254–260.

Rowsemitt, C. (1986). Seasonal variations in activity rhythms of male voles: Mediation by gonadal hormones. *Physiology and Behavior, 37,* 797–803.

Rubin, Z. (1974). Lovers and other strangers: The development of intimacy in encounters and relationships. *American Scientist, 62,* 182–190.

Ruelle, D. (1991). *Chance and chaos.* Princeton, NJ: Princeton University Press.

Rumelhart, D., & McClelland, J. (1986). *Parallel distributed processing* (Vols. 1 & 2). Cambridge, MA: MIT Press.

Runco, M. (2004). Creativity. *Annual Review of Psychology, 55,* 657–687.

Rush, C., Higgins, S., Hughes, J., & Bickel, W. (1994). Acute behavioral effects of triazolam and caffeine, alone and in combination, in humans. *Experimental and Clinical Psychopharmacology, 2,* 211–222.

Russell, B. (1984). *A history of Western philosophy.* New York: Simon & Schuster.

Sacks, O. (1973). *Awakenings.* Garden City, NY: Doubleday.

Sacks, O. (1985). *The man who mistook his wife for a hat and other clinical tales.* New York: Summit Books.

Salk, J. (1973). *The survival of the wisest.* New York: Harper & Row.

Sanderson, W., & Barlow, D. (1991). Research strategies in clinical psychology. In E. Walker (Ed.), *Clinical psychology: Historical and research foundations.* New York: Plenum.

Scarborough, E., & Furumoto, L. (1987). *Untold lives: The first generation of American women psychologists.* New York: Columbia University Press.

Schaie, K. W. (1993). Ageist language in psychological research. *American Psychologist, 48,* 49–51.

Scheaffer, R. L., Mendenhall, W., & Ott, L. (1979). *Elementary survey sampling* (2nd ed.). North Scituate, MA: Duxbury.

Schnelle, J. F., & Lee, J. F. (1974). Quasi-experimental retrospective evaluation of a prison policy change. *Journal of Applied Behavior Analysis, 7,* 483–496.

Schumacher, E. F. (1977). *A guide for the perplexed.* New York: Harper & Row.

Schuman, H., & Presser, S. (1981). *Questions and answers in attitude surveys.* New York: Academic Press.

Scoville, W. B. (1968). Amnesia after bilateral medial temporal-lobe excision: Introduction to case H. M. *Neuropsychologia, 6,* 211–213.

Scoville, W. B., & Milner, B. (1957). Loss of recent memory after bilateral hippocampal lesions. *Journal of Neurology, Neurosurgery, and Psychiatry, 20,* 11–21.

Seligman, M., & Csikszentmihalyi, M. (2000). Positive psychology. An introduction. *American Psychologist, 55,* 5–14.

Shapiro, A. (1997). *The powerful placebo: From ancient priest to modern physician.* Baltimore: Johns Hopkins University Press.

Shepard, R. N. (1983). Perceptual and analogical bases of cognition. In D. Genter & A. L. Stevens (Eds.), *Mental models.* Hillsdale, NJ: Erlbaum.

Sherif, M., Harvey, O. J., White, B., Hood, W., & Sherif, C. W. (1961). *Intergroup conflict and cooperation: The robber's cave experiment.* Norman, OK: University Book Exchange.

Shotland, R. L. (1992). *Sexual precedence, compliant sexual behavior, and token resistance to sex.* Paper presented at the 6th International Conference on Personal Relationships. Orono, ME.

Shotland, R. L., & Goodstein, L. (1983). Just because she doesn't want to doesn't mean it's rape: An experimentally based causal model of the perception of rape in a dating situation. *Social Psychology Quarterly, 46,* 220–232.

Shotland, R. L., & Stebbins, C. (1980). Bystander response to rape: Can a victim attract help? *Journal of Applied Social Psychology, 10,* 510–527.

Shotland, R. L., & Straw, M. K. (1976). Bystander response to an assault: When a man attacks a woman. *Journal of Personality and Social Psychology, 34,* 990–999.

Shotland, R. L., & Yankowski, L. (1982). The random response method: A valid and ethical indicator of the "truth" in reactive situations. *Personality and Social Psychology Bulletin, 8,* 174–179.

Sidman, M. (1960). *Tactics of scientific research.* New York: Basic Books.

Silverstein, A., & Klee, G. (1958). Effects of lysergic acid diethylamide (LSD-25) on intellectual functions. *American Medical Association Archives of Neurology and Psychiatry, 80,* 477–480.

Simon, J. L. (1978). *Basic research methods in social sciences* (2nd ed.). New York: Random House.

Skinner, H. (1984). Correlational methods in clinical research. In A. Bellack & M. Hersen (Eds.), *Research methods in clinical psychology.* New York: Pergamon.

Snyder, C. R., & Lopez, H. (Eds.). (2002). *Handbook of positive psychology.* New York: Oxford University Press.

Solomon, R. L. (1949). An extension of control group design. *Psychological Bulletin, 46,* 137–150.

Spencer-Brown, G. (1979). *Laws of form.* New York: Dutton.

Sperry, R. (1983). *Science and moral priority.* New York: Columbia University Press.

Spiegel, D., Bloom, J., Kraemer, H., & Gotthel, E. (1989). Effect of psychosocial treatment on survival of patients with metastatic breast cancer. *Lancet, 2,* 901.

Squire, L., & Zola-Morgan, S. (1991). The medial temporal lobe memory system. *Science, 253,* 1380–1386.

Stadler, M. (1995). Role of attention in implicit learning. *Journal of Experimental Psychology: Learning, Memory, and Cognition, 21,* 674–685.

Sternberg, R. (2003). *The psychologist's companion: A guide to scientific writing for students and researchers.* New York: Cambridge University Press.

Stevens, S. S. (1946). On the theory of scales of measurement. *Science, 103,* 677–680.

Stevens, S. S. (1951). Mathematics, measurement, and psychophysics. In S. S. Stevens (Ed.), *Handbook of experimental psychology.* New York: Wiley.

Stevens, S. S. (1957). On the psychophysical law. *Psychological Review, 64,* 153–181.

Stewart, H., & McAllister, H. (2001). One-at-a-time versus grouped presentation of mug book pictures: Some surprising results. *Journal of Applied Psychology, 86,* 1300–1305.

Strupp, H. H., & Hadley, S. W. (1979). Specific vs. nonspecific factors in psychotherapy. *Archives of General Psychiatry, 36,* 1125–1136.

Student [W. S. Gossett]. (1908). The probable error of a mean. *Biometrika, 6,* 1–25.

Sue, S., Fujino, D., Hu, L., Takeuchi, D., & Zane, N. (1991). Community mental health services for ethnic minority groups: A test of the cultural responsiveness hypothesis. *Journal of Consulting and Clinical Psychology, 59,* 533–540.

Suppe, F. (1977). *The structure of scientific theories* (2nd ed.). Urbana: University of Illinois Press.

Tart, C. T. (1972). States of consciousness and state specific sciences. *Science, 176,* 1203–1210.

Taylor, S., & Bogdan, R. (1998). *Introduction to qualitative research methods.* New York: Wiley.

Thomas, L. (1979). *The Medusa and the snail.* New York: Viking.

Thorndike, E. (1898). *Animal intelligence.* New York: Macmillan.

Tinbergen, E. A., & Tinbergen, N. (1972). *Early childhood autism: An ethological approach.* Berlin: Paul Parey.

Tinbergen, N. (1972). *The animal in its world.* Cambridge, MA: Harvard University Press.

Tourangeau, R. (2004). Survey research and societal change. *Annual Review of Psychology, 55,* 775–801.

Tukey, J. (1962). The future of data analysis. *Annals of Mathematical Statistics, 33,* 1–67.

Usher, M., & McClelland, J. (2004). Loss aversion and inhibition in dynamical models of multialternative choice. *Psychological Review, 111,* 757–769.

Valach, L., Michel, K., Dey, P., & Young, R. (2002). Self-confrontation interview with suicide attempters. *Counselling Psychology Quarterly, 15,* 1–22.

Valach, L., Michel, K., Young, R., & Dey, P. (2006). Suicide attempts as social goal-directed systems of joint careers, projects, and actions. *Suicide and Life-Threatening Behavior, 36,* 651–660.

Valsiner, J. (1986). *The individual subject and scientific psychology.* New York: Plenum.

Varnhagen, C. (2002). *Making sense of psychology on the web: A guide for research and critical thinking.* New York: Worth.

Veroff, J., Douvan, E., & Kulka, R. A. (1981). *The inner American.* New York: Basic Books.

Visser, P. S., Krosnick, J. A., Marquette, J., Curtain, M. (1996). Mail surveys for electron forecasting? An evaluation of the Columbus Dispatch poll. *Public Opinion Quarterly, 60,* 181–227.

Voevodsky, J. (1974). Evaluation of deceleration warning light for reducing rear-end automobile collisions. *Journal of Applied Psychology, 59,* 270–273.

Wallas, G. (1926). *The art of thought.* New York: Harcourt, Brace.

Warner, S. (1965). Randomized response: A survey technique for eliminating evasive answer bias. *Journal of the American Statistical Association, 60,* 63–69.

Warren, J. M., Zerweck, C., & Anthony, A. (1982). Effects of environmental enrichment on old mice. *Developmental Psychobiology, 15,* 13–18.

Wason, P. C. (1977). Self-contradictions. In P. N. Johnson-Laird & P. C. Wason (Eds.), *Thinking.* Cambridge, UK: Cambridge University Press.

Watkins, E., & Teasdale, J. (2001). Rumination and overgeneral memory in depression: Effects of self-focus and analytic thinking. *Journal of Abnormal Psychology, 110,* 353–357.

Watson, J. D. (1968). *The double helix.* New York: Atheneum.

Webb, E. J., Campbell, D. T., Schwartz, R. D., & Sechrest, L. (1966). *Unobtrusive measures.* Chicago: Rand McNally.

Webster-Stratton, C., & Spitzer, A. (1996). Parenting of a young child with conduct problems: New insights using qualitative methods. In T. Ollendick & R. Prinz (Eds.), *Advances in clinical child psychology* (Vol. 18, pp. 1–62). New York: Plenum.

Weiner, J. (1994). *The beak of the finch.* New York: Knopf.

West, S., Hepworth, J., McCall, M., & Reich, J. (1989). An evaluation of Arizona's July 1982 drunk driving law: Effects on the city of Phoenix. *Journal of Applied Social Psychology, 19,* 1212–1237.

West, S. G., Gunn, S. P., & Chernicky, P. (1975). Ubiquitous Watergate: An attributional analysis. *Journal of Personality and Social Psychology, 32,* 55–65.

White, L., Tursky, B., & Schwartz, G. (Eds.). (1985). *Placebo: Theory, research, and mechanism.* New York: Guilford.

Whitehead, A. N. (1925). *Science and the modern world.* New York: Macmillan.

Wilkinson, L., & Task Force on Statistical Inference (1999). Statistical methods in psychology journals: Guidelines and explanations. *American Psychologist, 54,* 594–604.

Winer, B. J. (1971). *Statistical principles in experimental design.* New York: McGraw-Hill.

Wolf, S., & Wolff, H. G. (1943). *Human gastric functioning.* New York: Oxford University Press.

Wood, N., & Cowan, N. (1995). The cocktail party phenomenon revisited: Attention and memory in the classic selective listening procedure of Cherry (1953). *Journal of Experimental Psychology: General, 124,* 243–262.

Yamane, T. (1967). *Elementary sampling theory.* Englewood Cliffs, NJ: Prentice Hall.

Young, R. A., Valach, L., & Domene, J. (2005). The action-project method in counseling psychology. *Journal of Counseling Psychology, 52,* 215–223.

Zimbardo, P. G., Haney, C., Banks, W. C., & Jaffe, D. (1975). The psychology of imprisonment: Privation, power and pathology. In D. Rosenhan & P. London (Eds.), *Theory and research in abnormal psychology* (2nd ed.). New York: Holt, Rinehart & Winston.

INDEX

Terms in **bold** can be found in the glossary.

Abscissa, 119
Abstract, 351–353
Affirming the consequent, 44
Alpha level, 170
Alternative dependent variables, 290
Analysis of factorial design, 206–224
Analysis of variance, 157–158, 200, 210–216
ANOVA. *See* Analysis of variance
Antecedent, 43
APA guidelines to ethics, 91–94
A priori tests, 205
Archival research, 273
Aristotelian approach to science, 349
Aristotle, 60, 349
Assessment of articles, guidelines for, 370–371
Authority
defined, 4
empiricism and, 5
problems with, 4

Barber, T., 257
Baseline, in single subject designs, 309–316
Behavior
experience and, 16–18
method of studying subjective reality, 18–22
objective, 22
Beta level, 170
Between-subjects design, 200–225
completely randomized, 201
multilevel completely randomized, 201–206
versus within-subjects design, 229–243
Bias, 251–258, 265–266. *See also* Experimenter effects; Personal equation; Self-fulfilling prophecies
Biased data collection, 251–254
personal equation, 251
Biased interactions with participants, 255–256
self-fulfilling prophecies, 256
ways to avoid, 256–258
Bimodal distribution, 119
Blind controls, 262. *See also* Double blind
Blind experimenters, 261
Blocking, 243. *See also* Leveling; Stratifying
Bransford, J., and Johnson, M., 164–165, 202–204
Bridgman, P., 7

Campbell, D., 381
and Stanley, J., 40, 192
Cassidy, J., 63–65
Categorical measurement, 114–115
Causation, 38
Central Limit Theorem, 150–151
Chamberlin, T., 290, 383–384
Chance variation, 138–139
Cicero, 144
Cohen's Kappa, 251
Common sense, 6
problems with, 6
Communicating results, 349–350
Completely randomized design, 201–202
Confidence interval, 343–344
Confidentiality and ethics, 90
Confirmatory reasoning, 43–44
Confound, 163, 167–168
counterbalancing, 187, 235–236
elimination, 186
equating, 186
matching, 186, 239–243
randomization, 188–190
Confounding variable, 37
Consequent, 43
Constant, 137
Construct, 56–57
Construct validity, 57
Context of experimentation, 229
Control, 182–195
counterbalancing, 187
differential order effects, 235
elimination, 187
equating, 187
examples of, 182–188, 190–193
experimental design, 190–193
experimental logic, 190–193
internal validity, 40
matching, 239–243
practice effects, 235
quasi-, 263
randomization, 188–190
through participant assignment, 182–188
Control group, 35
Cook, T., and Campbell, D., 172
Correlation, 31, 33–34, 132–138, 290–292
Correlational design, 33–34, 290–292
Counterbalancing, 187, 235–236
Craniometry, 252
Croesus, 11–13
Cultural biases, 265–266

Darwin, C., 31
Debriefing, 99, 102–103
Deception research, 97–102
debriefing and, 99, 102–103
ethics, 97–103
obedience-to-authority research, example of, 98–99
Deduction, 41
hypothesis and, 61
Degrees of freedom, 154–155
defined, 155
Demand characteristics, 262–263
Denying the antecedent, 44
Dependent variable, 37
Descriptive statistics, 112–138
Design
between-subjects, 200–225
counterbalancing, 187
ex post facto, 289–290
factorial, 200. *See also* Factorial design
interrupted time series, 282–286
Latin square, 236
matched-subjects, 239–243
mixed, 237–238
multiple time series, 284–286
naturalistic observation, 292–298
data collection and, 294–295
reactive behavior, 294
selective perception, 294–296
strengths and weaknesses, 297–298
unobtrusive measures, 294
posttest-only control group, 191
quasi-experimental, 270–298
randomized block, 241–243
blocking, 243
leveling and, 243
stratifying and, 243
single-group, pretest-posttest, 163
single-subject, 302–318
case study, 306–309
multiple baseline, 314–316
reversal, 310–313
Solomon four-group, 192
time series, 281–289
within-subjects, 229–243
advantages and disadvantages, 233–235
examples of, 232
repeated measures and, 236
sensitivity of, 232, 234
versus between-subjects, 233–235
Differential order effects, 234–235
Diffusion or imitation of treatments, 176

Disconfirmatory reasoning, 45
Discussion sections, 362–365
Dispersion, 123
Distributions
    bell-shaped, 119–120
    bimodal, 119
    normal, 119–120, 147–152
    skewed, 119
Double blind, 261–262

Ecology, 249–250
    validity and, 249–250. *See also* Validity,
        ecological
Effect size, 170
Einstein, A., 74
Elimination procedure, 186
Empiricism, 16, 28
Error
    term, 215
    variation, 166–168
Ethics, 85–109
    animal, 104–109
    anonymity and, 90
    APA guidelines and, 92–94
    confidentiality and, 90
    debriefing and, 99, 102–103
    deception and, 97–103
    defined, 85
    harm and, 91
    informed consent and, 89–90, 96–97
    institutional review board and, 94–97
    privacy and, 91
    psychological experiments and,
        86–87
    values and, 85
    voluntary participation and, 88
Experimental group, 35
Experimental method, 28, 34–39
    defined, 28
    definitions within, 34–39
    exploratory use, 38–39
    hypotheses, 55–63
    logic of, 34–39, 55–63, 193–195,
        210–215, 229–232
    science and, 28
    uses of, 38–39
Experimenter effects, 250–251, 255–256
    biased data collection, 251–254
    biased interactions with participants,
        255–256
Exploratory research, 38–39
Ex post facto design, 289–290
External validity, 40–41. *See also* Validity,
    external

Factorial design, 206–216
    advantages of, 224–225
    analysis of, 206–216
    interaction in, 208
    main effects in, 208
Falsificationism, 46
Field studies, 32–33, 271–273, 375–377

Fisher, R., 158, 303
F **ratio,** 158, 166–167, 168–172, 215
Frequency
    distribution, 118–121
    polygon, 120
Freud, S., 50, 302, 303
Funneling, 327

Galen, 11–13
Galileo, 5
Gallup, G., 339
Gambler's fallacy, 144
Generalizability, 40
Graphs, 118–121

Hawthorne effect, 258–259
History, 172–173
Holt, R., 367
Hypothesis, 27, 55–81
    chance, 168
    confound, 168
    deductive reasoning and, 59
    defined, 35
    inductive reasoning and, 58
    multiple working, 383–384
    null, 152–153, 168–172
    questions related to, 162

Ideas, acceptance through
    authority, 4–5
    common sense, 6
    reason, 6
    science, 7
    tenacity, 4
Illumination stage, 74
Incubation stage, 74
Independent variable, 36
Induction, 43, 58
    hypotheses, 58
    logic of, 58
Inferences, 39–40
    strong, 60
Inferential statistics, 142–158
    defined, 142
    hypothesis testing and, 152–153
Informed consent, 89–90, 96–97
Instrumentation, 174
Interaction effect, 208, 209–210,
    210–215
    examples of, 216–222
    factorial design, 210–215
Internal validity, 40. *See also* Validity,
    internal
    threats to, 172–176
Interrater reliability, 251
Interrupted time series design, 282–284
Intersubject replication, 311
Interval measurements, 116
Interviews
    face-to-face, 332, 334
    telephone, 335–336
Intragroup counterbalancing, 235

Intrasubject
    counterbalancing, 232
    replication, 310
Introduction, scientific paper, 353–357
Intuition and revelation, 72–73

Journals, 75
Jung, C., 50

Keil, A., 71–72
Kekulé, F., 73
Kuhn, T., 48

Ladd-Franklin, C., 22
Lakatos, I., 378
Leveling, 243
Likert, R., 328
Likert-type scale, 328
Limitations in psychology, 378–382
Logic
    confirmatory, 43
    deductive, 41, 59
    disconfirmatory, 43
    induction, 43, 58
    propositional, 41–47
Logical syllogism, 6, 43
Lorenz, K., 293

Mail questionnaires, 336–337
Main effects (treatment effect), 208
Marker variable, 19
Matched-subjects design, 239–243.
    See also Design, matched-subjects
Matching, 239–243
    control procedure, 240–241
    experimental procedure, 241–243
Maturation, 173–174
Mean, 121
Mean square, 215
    variance and, 215
Measurement, 113–117
    absolute zero, 114, 117
    association, 132–138. *See also*
        Correlation
    categorical, 114–115
    equal intervals and, 114, 116
    frequency, 118
    graphing, 118–121, 128–129
    interval, 116
    nominal, 114–115
    ordinal, 115
    ratio, 116
    scales of, 113–117
    transformation, 130–131
    variability of, 123–128
Median, 121–122
MedLINE, 77–78
Meehl, P., 304
Methods
    experimental, 28, 34–39. *See also*
        Experimental method
    section, in scientific article, 357–360

Milgram, S., 98–99
Mixed designs, 237–238. *See also*
    Design, mixed
Mode, 122
Modeling, 28
Modus ponens (confirmatory
    reasoning), 43–44
Modus tollens (disconfirmatory
    reasoning), 45
Moment measure, 133
Mortality, 175
Multileveled completely randomized
    design, 201–206
Multiple time series design, 284–286

Naturalistic observation, 27,
    292–298
    data analysis and, 295–296
    data collection and, 294–295
    functions of, 292
    reactive behavior, 294
    selective perception, 295
    strengths and weaknesses, 297–298
    techniques, 292–298
    unobtrusive observation, 294
Newcombe, N., 68–69
Newton, I., 8–9
    rules of reasoning, 8–9
Nisbett, R., and Wilson, T., 333–334
Nominal measurement, 114–115
Nonequivalent before-after design,
    286–289
Nonprobability sampling, 342
    convenience, 342
    quota, 342
    snowball, 342
Normal distribution, 119–120,
    147–152
Null hypothesis, 152–153, 168–172
    F ratio, 158, 166–167, 168–172, 215

Observation, naturalistic, 292–298. *See*
    Naturalistic observation
Operational definition, 36
Order effects, 235
Ordinal measurement, 115
Ordinate, 119
Orne, M., 262–264
Outlier, 138

Paradigm, 48, 265
Parker, J., 69–71
Parsimony, 8
Participant variable. *See* Subject factors
Partition, 137
Peirce, C., 4
Personal equation, 251
Philosophy of science. *See* Kuhn; Lakatos;
    Newton; Popper
Placebo, 260–262
Plagiarism, 253
Platt, J., 60

Popper, K., 46
Population, 142, 153
Post hoc tests, 205
Posttest-only control group design, 191
Power, 170
Practice effects, 235
Preparation stage, 73–74
Pretest-posttest control group
    design, 191
Probability, 143–147
Probability sampling, 340–342
    cluster, 341
    multistage, 341–342
    simple random, 340
    stratified random, 341
    systematic, 340–341
Proposal preparation, 367
Propositional logic, 41–47
Psychological Abstracts, 75
PsycINFO, 73–76
    example of, 77
Publications, 349–350
    abstract, 351–353
    discussion, 362–365
    guidelines for assessing, 370–371
    introduction, 353–357
    methods, 357–360
    proposal preparation, 367
    results, 361–362
    review of, 368, 370
    submission of, 368–369
PubMed, 77, 78. *See also* MedLINE
    example of, 79
Purification of ideas, 7

Qualitative methods, 29
Quantitative methods, 30
Quasi-control group, 235
Quasi-experimental design, 281–290.
    See also Design, quasi-experimental
    ex post facto, 289–290
    interrupted time series, 282–284
    multiple time series, 284–286
    nonequivalent before-after, 286–289
    time series design, 281–282
Questionnaires
    computer and Internet, 337–338
    mail, 336–337
Questions
    fixed-alternative, 326–328
    open-ended, 325–326

Random assignment, 189–190
Randomization, control and,
    188–190
Randomized block design, 241–243.
    See also Design, randomized block
Random number table, 184–185
Random sampling, 189
Range, 123
Ratio measurement, 116
Reactive behavior, 294

Reason, 6
    problems with, 6
References, in scientific paper,
    365–366
Regression, 137
    coefficient, 137
Relevance of research, 386–387
Reliability, 61–62
    interrater, 251
    personal equation, 251
    validity and, 61–62, 344
Repeated measures, within-subjects
    design, 236
Replication, 7, 310
Results
    communication of, 49–50, 349
    section, 361–362
Retrospective studies, 29, 289–290
Rights of participants, 87–88
    to anonymity, 90
    to confidentiality, 90
    to debriefing, 99
    to informed consent, 88–90
    to not be harmed, 91
    to privacy, 90
Rights of scientists, 87–88

Sample size, 170. *See also* Power
    formula, 170
Sampling, 340–342
    cluster, 341
    convenience, 342
    error, 343–344
    multistage, 341–342
    nonprobability, 342
    probability, 340–342
    quota, 342
    simple random, 340
    snowball, 342
    stratified random, 341
    systematic, 340–341
Scales of measurement, 114–117
Schumacher, E., 16–18
Science
    acceptance of ideas, 3–9
    approaches, 7
    Aristotelian approach, 349
    limitations of, 378–382
    meaning of, 1
    methods of, 7
    philosophy of. *See* Kuhn; Lakatos;
        Newton; Popper
Science Citation Index, 78
Scientific knowledge, 2
Scoville, N., and Milner, B., 308
Secondary variance, 167
Selection, 175
    maturation interaction, 176
Selective perception, 295
Self-fulfilling prophecies, 256
Semmelweis, I., 14–15
Shotland, L., 66–68

Simple randomized design, 340
Single-subject designs, 302–318. *See also*
    Design, single-subject
    advantages and disadvantages of,
        302–305
    case study, 306–309
    multielement, 316
    multiple baseline, 314–316
    reversal, 310–313
    types of, 305
Skinner, B. F., 50, 303
Slope, 137
Social Science Citation Index, 78
Solomon four-group design, 192
Standard deviation, 128
Standard error, 151–152
Statistical regression, 137
Statistics
    analysis of mixed designs, 237–238
    analysis of variance, 157–158, 200,
        210–216
    degrees of freedom, 154–155
    descriptive, 112–138
    error term, 215
    F ratio. *See F* ratio
    inferential, 142–158
    interactions. *See* Interaction effect
    main effects of, 208
    mean, 121
    median, 121–122
    mode, 122
    post hoc tests, 205
    range, 123
    significance, 166–168
    standard deviation, 100
    summary table, 215
    sum of squares, 125
    variability, 123–128
    variance, 123–128
Stratifying, 243
Strong inference, 60
Strupp, H., and Hadley, S., 202
Subject factors, 222–223, 258–264
Subject variable. *See* Subject factors

Sum of squares, 125
Survey research, 322–344
    administration methods, 332–338
    designing, 324–325
    developing questionnaires, 324–332
    interviews, 332–338
    pretesting, 329–330
    questions, types of, 325–328
    reactive questions, 331–332
    sample size, 343–344
    sampling and, 338–342
Systematic variation, 165–168

Tenacity
    defined, 4
    problems with, 4
Testing (threat to internal validity), 174
Test-retest reliability, 62
Thomas, L., 388
Time series design, 281–286
Tinbergen, N., 265
Transcendence, 387
Treatment
    effect, 166–167, 208
    main effects of, 208
    t test, 153–157
    t-test formula, 154–156
    variance, 154
Type I error, 169–170
Type II error, 169–170

Unobtrusive observation, 294

Validity, 40–41
    construct, 57
    cultural and social biases,
        265–266
    defined, 40–41
    ecological, 250
    experimenter effects, 250
    external, 40
    generalizability, 40
    internal, 40
    interrater reliability, 251

    personal equation, 251
    placebo factors, 260–262
    subject factors, 222–223, 258–264
    threats to, 172–176
Values in science, 2, 85, 384–386
Variability, 123–128. *See* Measurement,
    frequency
Variables
    dependent, 37
    independent, 37
    subject or participant, 222–223,
        258–264
    marker, 19
Variance
    analysis of, 157–158, 200, 210–216
    between groups, 166–167
    calculation of, 123–128
    defined, 125
    error (chance), 165–166
    formula for, 123–128
    secondary (uncontrolled),
        167–168
    treatment (between), 166–167
Variation
    chance, 165–166
    nonsystematic, 167
    systematic, 166–167
Verbal reports, 333–334
Verification stage, 74
Veroff, J., 332–333
Voluntary participation, 88

Wallas, G., 73–74
Whitehead, A., 7
Within-groups variance, 165–166
    F ratio and, 166
Within-subjects design, 229–243. *See also*
    Design, within-subjects

x **axis,** 119

y **axis,** 119

z scores, 131–132